[65] And they were saying many other
blasphemous things against Him.
[a] *Is 50:6; Mt 26:67; Mk 14:65*

Jesus Faces the Sanhedrin

[66] [a]When daylight came, the elders[a]
of the people, both the chief priests
and the scribes, convened and brought
Him before their •Sanhedrin. [67] They
said, [b]"If You are the •Messiah, tell
us."
[a] *Mt 27:1* [b] *Mt 26:63; Mk 14:61*

But He said to them, "If I do tell you,
you will not believe. [68] And if I ask you,
you will not answer. [69] [a]But from now
on, the Son of Man will be seated at
the right hand of the Power of God."
[a] *Ps 110:1; Dn 7:13-14*

[70] They all asked, "Are You, then, the
Son of God?"

And He said to them, "You say that I
am."

[71] "Why do we need any more testimony," they said, "since we've heard
it ourselves from His mouth?"

Jesus Faces Pilate

23 [a]Then their whole assembly
rose up and brought Him before
•Pilate. [2] They began to accuse Him,
saying, "We found this man subvert-
ing our nation, [b]opposing payment of
taxes to Caesar, and saying [c]that He
Himself is the •Messiah, a King."
[a] *Mt 27:2; Mk 15:1; Jn 18:28*
[b] *Mt 17:27; Mk 12:17* [c] *Mk 14:61-62; Jn 19:12*

[3] So Pilate asked Him, "Are You the
King of the Jews?"

He answered him, "You have said
it."[b]

[4] Pilate then told the •chief priests
and the crowds, [a]"I find no grounds for
charging this man."
[a] *Mt 27:19; Mk 15:14*

[5] But they kept … "He stirs up
the people, te…
Judea, from Ga…
even to here."

Jesus Faces Herod Antipas

[6] When Pilate heard this,[c] he asked
if the man was a Galilean. [7] Finding
that He was under [a]•Herod's jurisdiction, he sent Him to Herod, who was
also in Jerusalem during those days.
[8] Herod was [b]very glad to see Jesus;
for a long time he had wanted to see
Him, because [c]he had heard about
Him and was hoping to see some miracle[d] performed by Him. [9] So he kept
asking Him questions, but Jesus did
not answer him. [10] The chief priests
and the •scribes stood by, vehemently
accusing Him. [11] [d]Then Herod, with
his soldiers, treated Him with contempt, mocked Him, dressed Him in a
brilliant robe, and sent Him back to
Pilate. [12] That very day Herod and Pilate became friends.[e] Previously, they
had been hostile toward each other.
[a] *Lk 3:1* [b] *Lk 9:9*
[c] *Mt 14:1; Mk 6:14* [d] *Is 53:3*

Jesus or Barabbas

[13] [a]Pilate called together the chief
priests, the leaders, and the people,
[14] and said to them, "You have brought
me this man as one who subverts the
people. But in fact, after examining
Him in your presence, I have found no
grounds to charge this man with those
things you accuse Him of. [15] Neither
has Herod, because he sent Him back
to us. Clearly, He has done nothing to
deserve death. [16] [b]Therefore I will
have Him whipped[f] and ⌊then⌋ release
Him." [[17] [c]For according to the festival
he had to release someone to them.][g]
[a] *Mt 27:23; Jn 18:38* [b] *Mt 27:26; Mk 15:15; Jn 19:1*
[c] *Mt 27:15; Mk 15:6; Jn 18:39*

[18] Then they all cried out together,
"Take this man away! Release Barab-
…" [19] (He had been thrown into
… that had taken
… for murder.)

[a]**22:66** Or *council of* … nss read *heard*
"Galilee" [d]**23:8** Or … discipline or "teach a
lesson"; 1 Kg 12:11 … scourging; Lat
flagellatio [g]**23:17** …

20 Pilate, wanting to release Jesus, addressed them again, 21 but they kept
shouting, "Crucify! Crucify Him!"
22 A third time he said to them,
"Why? What has this man done
wrong? I have found in Him no
grounds for the death penalty. Therefore I will have Him whipped and
⌊then⌋ release Him."
23 But they kept up the pressure, demanding with loud voices that He be
crucified. And their voices[a] won out.
24 So Pilate decided to grant their demand 25 [a]and released the one they
were asking for, who had been thrown
into prison for rebellion and murder.
But he handed Jesus over to their will.

[a] Pr 17:15

The Way to the Cross

26 [a]As they led Him away, they seized
Simon, a Cyrenian, who was coming
in from the country, and laid the cross
on him to carry behind Jesus. 27 A great
multitude of the people followed Him,
including women who were mourning
and lamenting Him. 28 But turning to
them, Jesus said, "Daughters of Jerusalem, do not weep for Me, but weep for
yourselves and your children. 29 [b]Look,
the days are coming when they will
say, 'Blessed are the barren, the
wombs that never bore, and the
breasts that never nursed!' 30 [c]Then
they will begin **to say to the mountains, 'Fall on us!' and to the hills,
'Cover us!'**[b] 31 [d]For if they do these
things when the wood is green, what
will happen when it is dry?"

[a] Mt 27:32; Mk 15:21; Jn 19:17 [b] Lk 21:23 [c] Hs 10:8 [d] Ezk 20:47

Crucified between Two Criminals

32 [a]Two others—criminals—were also
led away to be executed with Him.
33 [b]When they arrived at the place called
The Skull, they crucified Him there,
along with the criminals, one on the
right and one on the left. [34 Then Jesus
said, "Father, forgive them, because
they do not know what they are doing."][c] And [c]they divided His clothes
and cast lots.

[a] Is 53:12; Mt 27:38 [b] Mt 27:33; Mk 15:22; Jn 19:17 [c] Ps 22:18; Mt 27:35; Mk 15:24; Jn 19:24

35 [a]The people stood watching, and
even the leaders kept scoffing: "He
saved others; let Him save Himself if
this is God's Messiah, the Chosen
One!" 36 The soldiers also mocked
Him. They came offering Him sour
wine 37 and said, "If You are the King
of the Jews, save Yourself!"

[a] Zch 12:10

38 [a]An inscription was above Him:[d]

[a] Jn 19:19

**THIS IS THE
KING OF THE JEWS**

39 [a]Then one of the criminals hanging there began to yell insults at[e] Him:
"Aren't You the Messiah? Save Yourself and us!"

[a] Mt 27:44; Mk 15:32

40 But the other answered, rebuking
him: "Don't you even fear God, since
you are undergoing the same punishment? 41 We are punished justly, because we're getting back what we
deserve for the things we did, but this
man has done nothing wrong." 42 Then
he said, "Jesus, remember me[f] when
You come into Your kingdom!"
43 And He said to him, "•I assure you:
Today you will be with Me in [a]para-
dise."

[a] Rv 2:7

The Death of Jesus

44 [a]It was now about noon,[g] and darkness came over the whole land[h] until
three,[i] 45 because the sun's light failed.[j]
[b]The curtain of the sanctuary was split

[a]**23:23** Other mss add *and those of the chief priests* [b]**23:30** Hs 10:8 [c]**23:34** Other mss omit bracketed text [d]**23:38** Other mss add *written in Greek, Latin, and Hebrew letters* [e]**23:39** Or *began to blaspheme* [f]**23:42** Other mss add *Lord* [g]**23:44** Lit *about the sixth hour* [h]**23:44** Or *whole earth* [i]**23:44** Lit *the ninth hour* [j]**23:45** Other mss read *three, and the sun was darkened*

own the middle. 46 And Jesus called
ut with a loud voice, [c]"Father, **into
'our hands I entrust My spirit.**"[a]
Saying this, He breathed His last. [a]*Mt 27:45; Mk 15:33*
[b]*Mt 27:51; Mk 15:38* [c]*Ps 31:5* [d]*Php 2:8*

47 [a]When the •centurion saw what
ıappened, he began to glorify God,
aying, "This man really was righ-
eous!" 48 All the crowds that had gath-
red for this spectacle, when they saw
vhat had taken place, went home,
triking their chests.[b] 49 [b]But all who
new Him, including the women who
ıad followed Him from Galilee, stood
ıt a distance, watching these things.
[a]*Mt 27:54* [b]*Ps 38:11*

The Burial of Jesus

50 [a]There was a good and righteous
nan named Joseph, a member of the
Sanhedrin, 51 who had not agreed
vith their plan and action. He was
rom Arimathea, a Judean town, [b]and
vas looking forward to the kingdom of
God. 52 He approached Pilate and
ısked for Jesus' body. 53 [c]Taking it
lown, he wrapped it in fine linen and
placed it in [d]a tomb cut into the rock,
vhere no one had ever been placed.[c]
54 It was preparation day, and the Sabbath was about to begin.[d] 55 The
vomen [e]who had come with Him
rom Galilee followed along and
observed the tomb and how His body
was placed. 56 Then they returned and
[g]prepared spices and perfumes. And
they rested on the Sabbath [h]according
to the commandment.
[a]*Mt 27:57; Mk 15:42; Jn 19:38* [b]*Mk 15:43* [c]*Mt 27:59* [d]*Is 53:9* [e]*Lk 8:2-3* [f]*Mk 15:47* [g]*Mk 16:1* [h]*Gn 2:3; Dt 5:14; Is 58:13*

Resurrection Morning

24 [a]On the first day of the week,
very early in the morning, they[e]
came to the tomb, bringing the spices
they had prepared. 2 They found the
stone rolled away from the tomb.
3 [b]They went in but did not find the
body of the Lord Jesus. 4 While they
were perplexed about this, [c]suddenly
two men stood by them in dazzling
clothes. 5 So the women were terrified
and bowed down to the ground.[f]
[a]*Mt 28:1; Mk 16:1; Jn 20:1* [b]*Mk 16:5* [c]*Gn 18:2; Mt 28:2-6; Mk 16:5-6; Jn 20:12*

"Why are you looking for the living
among the dead?" asked the men.
6 "He is not here, but He has been resurrected! [a]Remember how He spoke
to you when He was still in Galilee,
7 saying, 'The •Son of Man must be betrayed into the hands of sinful men, be
crucified, and rise on the third day'?"
8 And they remembered His words.
[a]*Mt 16:21; Mk 8:31; Lk 9:22*

9 [a]Returning from the tomb, they reported all these things to the Eleven
and to all the rest. 10 •Mary Magdalene,
[b]Joanna, Mary the mother of James,
and the other women with them were
telling the apostles these things. 11 But
these words seemed like nonsense to
them, and they did not believe the
women. 12 [c]Peter, however, got up and
ran to the tomb. When he stooped to
look in, he saw only the linen cloths.[g]
So he went home, amazed at what had
happened. [a]*Mt 28:8; Mk 16:10* [b]*Lk 8:3* [c]*Jn 20:3*

The Emmaus Disciples

13 Now that same day two of them
were on their way to a village called[h]
Emmaus, which was about seven
miles[i] from Jerusalem. 14 Together they
were discussing everything that had
taken place. 15 And while they were
discussing and arguing, Jesus Himself
came near and began to walk along

[a]**23:46** Ps 31:5 [b]**23:48** Mourning [c]**23:53** Or *interred,* or *laid* [d]**23:54** Lit *was dawning;* not in the morning but at sundown Friday [e]**24:1** Other mss add *and other women with them* [f]**24:5** Lit *and inclined their faces to the ground* [g]**24:12** Other mss add *lying there* [h]**24:13** Lit *village, which name is* [i]**24:13** Lit *about 60 stadia;* 1 *stadion* = 600 feet

with them. 16 But [a]they[a] were prevented from recognizing Him. 17 Then
He asked them, "What is this dispute
that you're having[b] with each other as
you are walking?" And they stopped
⌊walking and looked⌋ discouraged.

[a] Jn 20:14; 21:4

18 The one [a]named Cleopas answered Him, "Are You the only visitor
in Jerusalem who doesn't know the
things that happened there in these
days?"

[a] Jn 19:25

19 "What things?" He asked them.
So they said to Him, "The things
concerning Jesus the •Nazarene, who
was a Prophet powerful in action and
speech before God and all the people,
20 and how our •chief priests and leaders handed Him over to be sentenced
to death, and they crucified Him. 21 But
we were hoping that He was the One
who was about to redeem Israel. Besides all this, it's the third day since
these things happened. 22 Moreover,
some women from our group astounded us. They arrived early at the
tomb, 23 and when they didn't find His
body, they came and reported that they
had seen a vision of angels who said
He was alive. 24 Some of those who
were with us went to the tomb and
found it just as the women had said,
but they didn't see Him."
25 He said to them, "How unwise
and slow you are to believe in your
hearts all that the prophets have spoken! 26 [a]Didn't the •Messiah have to
suffer these things and enter into His
glory?" 27 Then beginning with [b]Moses
and [c]all the Prophets, He interpreted
for them the things concerning Himself in all the Scriptures.

[a] Is 53 [b] Gn 3:15; 49:10; Dt 18:15 [c] Ps 22; Is 7:14; 9:6; 42:1; 53; Jr 33:14; Mc 5:2; Mal 3:1; 4:2

28 They came near the village where
they were going, and He gave the impression that He was going farther.
29 But they urged Him: "Stay with us,
because it's almost evening, and now
the day is almost over." So He went in
to stay with them.
30 It was as He reclined at the table
with them that He took the bread,
blessed and broke it, and gave it to
them. 31 Then their eyes were opened,
and they recognized Him, but He disappeared from their sight. 32 So they
said to each other, "Weren't our hearts
ablaze within us while He was talking
with us on the road and explaining the
Scriptures to us?" 33 That very hour
they got up and returned to Jerusalem.
They found the Eleven and those with
them gathered together, 34 who said,[c]
"The Lord has certainly been raised,
and [a]has appeared to Simon!" 35 Then
they began to describe what had happened on the road and how He was
made known to them in the breaking
of the bread.

[a] 1Co 15:5

The Reality of the Risen Jesus

36 And as they were saying these
things, He Himself stood among them.
He said to them, "Peace to you!" 37 But
they were startled and terrified and
thought they were seeing a ghost.
38 "Why are you troubled?" He asked
them. "And why do doubts arise in
your hearts? 39 Look at My hands and
My feet, that it is I Myself! Touch Me
and see, because a ghost does not have
flesh and bones as you can see I have."
40 Having said this, He showed them
His hands and feet. 41 But while they
still could not believe[d] because of
⌊their⌋ joy and were amazed, He asked
them, "Do you have anything here to
eat?" 42 So they gave Him a piece of a
broiled fish,[e] 43 [a]and He took it and ate
in their presence.

[a] Ac 10:41

44 Then He told them, [a]"These are
My words that I spoke to you while I

[a]**24:16** Lit *their eyes* [b]**24:17** Lit *What are these words that you are exchanging* [c]**24:34** Gk is specific that this refers to the Eleven and those with them. [d]**24:41** Or *they still disbelieved* [e]**24:42** Other mss add *and some honeycomb*

Trusting Christ For Salvation

We must first see ourselves as sinners, recognize Christ died for us and rose again and trust in Him alone for salvation. When you come to understand God's simple plan of salvation it is often helpful to tell God in prayer that you are trusting in Him. It is important to realize though, that saying a prayer doesn't save you. It is trusting Christ that saves you. You are saved the moment you trust Christ alone as your only way to heaven. Prayer is only the means by which you tell God what you are doing.

If you want to trust Christ to save you, here's how you can express to God what you are doing in prayer:

> *"Dear God, I come to You now in the name of Your Son, Jesus Christ. I acknowledge I have sinned before You and deserve to be separated forever from You. But I now understand that Your Son, Jesus Christ, shed His blood on the cross in my place and died for my sins, and that on the third day He arose from the grave. Right now I am trusting Christ alone as my only way to heaven, believing that He paid for all of my sins by dying as my substitute. Thank You that according to Your word I have right now received Your free gift of eternal life. Help me to now live a life that expresses my gratitude to You for saving me."*

If you have trusted Christ, memorize John 5:24, "I assure you: Anyone who hears My word and believes Him who sent Me has eternal life and will not come under judgment but has passed from death to life."

You may be wondering, "What next?"

- **You will want to be baptized. Baptism has nothing to do with salvation, but it is a first step in discipleship**

and a way of publicly declaring to others you have accepted Christ's forgiveness of your sins.

- **Begin now to study the Bible daily and spend time alone with God in prayer. Starting with the Book of John on the next page is an excellent place to begin your daily reading.**

- **Ask Jesus to help you grow as a Christian and to be bold in talking to others about what He has done for you.**

- **Find a church that believes in teaching the Bible and attend regularly.**

May God help you to be a testimony to many of His love and saving power.

MY RECORD OF SALVATION

On the _______ day of ______________, 20____,

I, ____, trusted Jesus Christ as my personal Savior and gave myself to Him as Lord of my life.

Witnessed by: ____

____

was still with you—that everything
written about Me in the Law of Moses,
the Prophets, and the Psalms must be
fulfilled.” 45 Then [b]He opened their
minds to understand the Scriptures.
46 He also said to them, “This is what is
written:[a] the Messiah would suffer and
rise from the dead the third day, 47 and
repentance for[b] forgiveness of sins
would be proclaimed in His name [c]to
all the nations, beginning at Jerusalem.
48 [d]You are witnesses of these things.
49 [e]And look, I am sending you[c] what
My Father promised. As for you, stay
in the city[d] until you are empowered[e]
from on high.”

[a]Mt 16:21 [b]2Co 4:6 [c]Ps 22:27; Is 49:6; Jr 31:34; Hs 2:23; Mc 4:2; Mal 1:11 [d]Ac 1:22 [e]Ac 2:1

The Ascension of Jesus

50 Then He led them out as far as Bethany, and lifting up His hands He blessed
them. 51 And while He was blessing
them, [a]He left them and was carried up
into heaven. 52 After worshiping Him,
they returned to Jerusalem with great
joy. 53 And they were continually [b]in the
•temple complex blessing God.[f]

[a]Ac 1:9 [b]Ac 2:46

JOHN

Prologue

1 In the beginning [a]was
the Word,[g]
and the Word was with God,
and the [b]Word was God.
2 He was with God
in the beginning.
3 All things were created
through Him,
and apart from Him
not one thing was created
that has been created.
4 Life was in Him,[h]
and that life was the light
of men.
5 [c]That light shines in the darkness,
yet the darkness did not
overcome[i] it.

[a]Rv 19:13 [b]Is 9:6; Php 2:6 [c]Jn 3:19

6 [a]There was a man named John
who was sent from God.
7 He came as a witness
to testify about the light,
so that all might believe
through him.[j]
8 [b]He was not the light,
but he came to testify
about the light.
9 [c]The true light, who gives light
to everyone,
was coming into the world.[k]

[a]Mal 3:1 [b]Ac 13:25 [c]Is 49:6

10 He was in the world,
and [a]the world was created
through Him,
yet the world did not recognize
Him.
11 [b]He came to His own,[l]
and His own people[l]
did not receive Him.
12 But [c]to all
who did receive Him,

[a]**24:46** Other mss add *and thus it was necessary that* [b]**24:47** Other mss read *repentance and* [c]**24:49** Lit *upon you* [d]**24:49** Other mss add *of Jerusalem* [e]**24:49** Lit *clothed with power* [f]**24:53** Other mss read *praising and blessing God. Amen.* [g]**1:1** The *Word* (Gk *Logos*) is a title for Jesus as the communication and the revealer of God the Father; Jn 1:14,18; Rv 19:13. [h]**1:3–4** Other punctuation is possible: . . . *not one thing was created. What was created in Him was life* [i]**1:5** Or *grasp*, or *comprehend*, or *overtake*; Jn 12:35 [j]**1:7** Or *through it* (the light) [k]**1:9** Or *The true light who comes into the world gives light to everyone*, or *The true light enlightens everyone coming into the world.* [l]**1:11** The same Gk adjective is used twice in this verse: the first refers to all that Jesus owned as Creator (*to His own*); the second refers to the Jews (*His own people*).

He gave them the right to be[a]
children of God,
to those who believe in His name,
13 who were born,
not of blood,[b]
or of the will of the flesh,
or of the will of man,[c]
[d]but of God.

[a] *Ps 33:6; 1Co 8:6* [b] *Lk 19:14; 23:18* [c] *Is 56:5; Rm 8:15* [d] *Jms 1:18*

14 [a]The Word [b]became [c]flesh[d]
and took up residence[e] among us.
[d]We observed His glory,
the glory as
the •One and Only Son[f]
from the Father,
[e]full of grace and truth.
15 (John testified concerning Him
and exclaimed,
"This was the One of whom
I said,
'The One coming after me
has surpassed me,
[f]because He existed
before me.'")
16 Indeed, [g]we have all received
grace after grace
from His fullness,
17 for although [h]the law was given
through Moses,
[i]grace and [j]truth came
through Jesus Christ.
18 [k]No one has ever seen God.[g]
[l]The One and Only Son[h] —
the One who is
at [m]the Father's side[i] —
He has revealed Him.

[a] *1Tm 3:16* [b] *Rm 1:3* [c] *Heb 2:14* [d] *Mt 17:2* [e] *Col 2:3* [f] *Col 1:17* [g] *Eph 1:6* [h] *Ex 20:1* [i] *Rm 5:21* [j] *Jn 14:6* [k] *Ex 33:20* [l] *1Jn 4:9* [m] *Jn 10:30*

John the Baptist's Testimony

19 This is John's testimony when the
•Jews from Jerusalem sent priests and
Levites to ask him, "Who are you?"
20 He did not refuse to answer, but he
declared: "I am not the •Messiah."
21 "What then?" they asked him.
"Are you [a]Elijah?" [a] *Mal 4:5*
[a]"I am not," he said. [a] *Lk 1:17*
"Are you the Prophet?"[j]
"No," he answered.
22 "Who are you, then?" they asked.
"We need to give an answer to those
who sent us. What can you tell us
about yourself?"
23 He said, "I am a **voice of one crying out in the wilderness: Make
straight the way of the Lord**[k] —just as
[a]Isaiah the prophet said." [a] *Is 40:3*

24 Now they had been sent from the
•Pharisees. 25 So they asked him, "Why
then do you baptize if you aren't the
Messiah, or Elijah, or the Prophet?"
26 "I baptize with[l] water," John answered them. [a]"Someone stands among
you, but you don't know ⌊Him⌋. 27 He is
the One coming after me,[m] whose san-
dal strap I'm not worthy to untie."
[a] *Mal 3:1*

28 All this happened in Bethany[n]
across the Jordan,[o] where John was
baptizing.

The Lamb of God

29 The next day John saw Jesus coming toward him and said, "Here is [a]the
Lamb of God, [b]who takes away the sin
of the world! 30 This is the One I told
you about: 'After me comes a man who

[a]**1:12** Or *become* [b]**1:13** Lit *bloods*; the pl form of *blood* occurs only here in the NT. It may refer either to lineal descent (that is, blood from one's father and mother) or to the OT sacrificial system (that is, the various blood sacrifices). Neither is the basis for birth into the family of God. [c]**1:13** Or *not of human lineage, or of human capacity, or of human volition* [d]**1:14** The eternally existent Word (vv. 1–2) took on full humanity, but without sin; Heb 4:15. [e]**1:14** Lit *and tabernacled*, or *and dwelt in a tent*; this word occurs only here in John. A related word, referring to the Festival of Tabernacles, occurs only in 7:2; Ex 40:34–38. [f]**1:14** *Son* is implied from the reference to the Father and from Gk usage. [g]**1:18** Since God is an infinite being, no one can see Him in His absolute essential nature; Ex 33:18–23. [h]**1:18** Other mss read *God* [i]**1:18** Lit *is in the bosom of the Father* [j]**1:21** Probably = the Prophet in Dt 18:15 [k]**1:23** Is 40:3 [l]**1:26** Or *in* [m]**1:27** Other mss add *who came before me* [n]**1:28** Other mss read *in Bethabara* [o]**1:28** Another Bethany, near Jerusalem, was the home of Lazarus, Martha, and Mary; Jn 11:1.

has surpassed me, because He existed
before me.’ 31 I didn’t know Him, but I
came baptizing with[a] water so He
might be revealed to Israel.”

[a] *Is 53:7; 1Pt 1:19*
[b] *1Co 15:3; Gl 1:4; Heb 1:3; Rv 1:5*

32 And John testified, “I watched the
Spirit descending from heaven like a
dove, and He rested on Him. 33 I didn’t
know Him, but He[b] who sent me to
baptize with[a] water told me, ‘The One
you see the Spirit descending and resting on—[a]He is the One who baptizes
with[a] the Holy Spirit.’ 34 I have seen
and testified that He is the Son of
God!”[c] [a] *Jn 14:26; 20:22*

35 Again the next day, John was
standing with two of his disciples.
36 When he saw Jesus passing by, he
said, “Look! The Lamb of God!”
37 The two disciples heard him say
this and followed Jesus. 38 When Jesus
turned and noticed them following
Him, He asked them, “What are you
looking for?”

They said to Him, “•Rabbi” (which
means “Teacher”), “where are You
staying?”
39 “Come and you’ll see,” He replied.
So they went and saw where He was
staying, and they stayed with Him that
day. It was about 10 in the morning.[d]
40 Andrew, Simon Peter’s brother,
was one of the two who heard John and
followed Him. 41 He first found his
own brother [a]Simon and told him, “We
have found the Messiah!”[e] (which
means “Anointed One”), 42 and he
brought ⌊Simon⌋ to Jesus. [a] *Mt 4:18*

When Jesus saw him, He said, “You
are Simon, son of John.[f] You will be
called •Cephas” (which means “Rock”).

Philip and Nathanael

43 The next day He[g] decided to leave
for Galilee. Jesus found Philip and told
him, “Follow Me!”
44 Now [a]Philip was from Bethsaida,
the hometown of Andrew and Peter.
45 Philip found [b]Nathanael[h] and told
him, “We have found the One Moses
wrote about in the Law (and so did the
[c]prophets): Jesus the son of Joseph,
from Nazareth!” [a] *Jn 12:21* [b] *Jn 21:2*
[c] *Lk 24:27*

46 “Can anything good come out of
Nazareth?” Nathanael asked him.

“Come and see,” Philip answered.
47 Then Jesus saw Nathanael coming
toward Him and said about him, “Here
is a true Israelite; no deceit is in him.”
48 “How do you know me?” Nathanael asked.

“Before Philip called you, when you
were under the fig tree, I saw you,”
Jesus answered.
49 “Rabbi,” Nathanael replied, “You
are the Son of God! You are [a]the King
of Israel!” [a] *Mt 21:5; 27:11; Jn 19:14-19*

50 Jesus responded to him, “Do you
believe ⌊only⌋ because I told you I saw
you under the fig tree? You[i] will see
greater things than this.” 51 Then He
said, “•I assure you: You[j] will see
heaven opened and the angels of God
ascending and descending on [a]the
•Son of Man.” [a] *Dn 7:13*

The First Sign: Turning Water into Wine

2 On the third day a wedding took
place in Cana of Galilee. Jesus’
mother was there, and 2 Jesus and His
disciples were invited to the wedding
as well. 3 When the wine ran out,

[a]**1:31,33** Or *in* [b]**1:33** *He* refers to God the Father, who gave John a sign to help him identify the Messiah. Vv. 32–34 indicate that John did not know that Jesus was the Messiah until the Spirit descended upon Him at His baptism. [c]**1:34** Other mss read *is the Chosen One of God* [d]**1:39** Lit *about the tenth hour.* Various methods of reckoning time were used in the ancient world. John probably used a different method from the other 3 Gospels. If John used the same method of time reckoning as the other 3 Gospels, the translation would be: *It was about four in the afternoon.* [e]**1:41** In the NT, the word Messiah translates the Gk word *Christos* (“Anointed One”), except here and in Jn 4:25 where it translates *Messias.* [f]**1:42** Other mss read *Simon, son of Jonah* [g]**1:43** Or *he,* referring either to Peter (v. 42) or Andrew (vv. 40–41) [h]**1:45** Probably the Bartholomew of the other Gospels and Acts [i]**1:50** *You* (sg in Gk) refers to Nathanael. [j]**1:51** *You* is pl in Gk and refers to Nathanael and the other disciples.

Jesus' mother told Him, "They don't
have any wine."

4 [a]"What has this concern of yours to
do with Me,[a] [b]•woman?" Jesus asked.
[c]"My hour[b] has not yet come."
[a] Lk 2:49 [b] Jn 19:26 [c] Ec 3:1

5 "Do whatever He tells you," His
mother told the servants.

6 Now six stone water jars had been
set there [a]for Jewish purification. Each
contained 20 or 30 gallons.[c] [a] Mk 7:3

7 "Fill the jars with water," Jesus told
them. So they filled them to the brim.
8 Then He said to them, "Now draw
some out and take it to the chief servant."[d] And they did.

9 When the chief servant tasted the
water (after it had become wine), he
did not know where it came from—
though the servants who had drawn
the water knew. He called the groom
10 and told him, "Everybody sets out
the fine wine first, then, after people
have drunk freely, the inferior. But you
have kept the fine wine until now."

11 Jesus performed this first sign[e] in
Cana of Galilee. [a]He displayed His
glory, and His disciples believed in
Him. [a] Jn 1:14

12 After this, He went down to Capernaum, together with His mother,
[a]His brothers, and His disciples, and
they stayed there only a few days.
[a] Mt 12:46

Cleansing the Temple Complex

13 [a]The Jewish •Passover was near, so
Jesus went up to Jerusalem. 14 [b]In the
•temple complex He found people selling oxen, sheep, and doves, and ⌊He
also found⌋ the money changers sitting
there. 15 After making a whip out of
cords, He drove everyone out of the
temple complex with their sheep and
oxen. He also poured out the money
changers' coins and overturned the tables. 16 He told those who were selling
doves, "Get these things out of here!
Stop turning [c]My Father's house into a
marketplace!"[f] [a] Ex 12:14 [b] Mt 21:12;
Mk 11:15; Lk 19:45 [c] Ps 93:5

17 And His disciples remembered
that it is written: [a]**Zeal for Your house
will consume Me.**[g] [a] Ps 69:9

18 So the Jews replied to Him, "What
sign ⌊of authority⌋ will You show us for
doing these things?"

19 Jesus answered, [a]"Destroy this
sanctuary, and I will raise it up in three
days." [a] Mt 26:61

20 Therefore the Jews said, "This
sanctuary took 46 years to build, and
will You raise it up in three days?"

21 But He was speaking about the
sanctuary of His body. 22 So when He
was raised from the dead, [a]His disciples remembered that He had said this.
And they believed the Scripture and
the statement Jesus had made.
[a] Lk 24:8; Jn 14:26

23 While He was in Jerusalem at the
Passover Festival, many trusted in His
name when they saw the signs He was
doing. 24 Jesus, however, would not entrust Himself to them, since He knew
them all 25 and because He did not
need anyone to testify about man; for
[a]He Himself knew what was in man.
[a] Mt 9:4; Mk 2:8; Jn 6:64

Jesus and Nicodemus

3 There was a man from the •Phari-
sees named Nicodemus, a ruler of
the Jews. 2 This man came to Him at
night and said, "•Rabbi, we know that
You have come from God as a teacher,
for [a]no one could perform these signs
You do unless [b]God were with him."
[a] Jn 5:36; Ac 2:22 [b] Ac 10:38

[a]**2:4** Or *You and I see things differently*; lit *What to Me and to you*; Mt 8:29; Mk 1:24; 5:7; Lk 8:28 [b]**2:4** The time of His sacrificial death and exaltation; Jn 7:30; 8:20; 12:23,27; 13:1; 17:1 [c]**2:6** Lit *2 or 3 measures* [d]**2:8** Lit *ruler of the table*; perhaps *master of the feast*, or *headwaiter* [e]**2:11** Lit *this beginning of the signs*; Jn 4:54; 20:30. Seven miraculous signs occur in John's Gospel and are so noted in the headings. [f]**2:16** Lit *a house of business* [g]**2:17** Ps 69:9

3 Jesus replied, "•I assure you:
[a]Unless someone is born again,[a] he
cannot see the kingdom of God."
[a] Jn 1:13; 2Co 5:17; Ti 3:5

4 "But how can anyone be born
when he is old?" Nicodemus asked
Him. "Can he enter his mother's
womb a second time and be born?"
5 Jesus answered, "I assure you:
[a]Unless someone is born of water and
the Spirit,[b] he cannot enter the kingdom of God. 6 Whatever is born of the
flesh is flesh, and whatever is born of
the Spirit is spirit. 7 Do not be amazed
that I told you that you[c] must be born
again. 8 [b]The wind[d] blows where it
pleases, and you hear its sound, but
you don't know where it comes from
or where it is going. So it is with everyone born of the Spirit."
[a] Mk 16:16; Ac 2:38 [b] Ec 11:5

9 "How can these things be?" asked
Nicodemus.
10 "Are you a teacher[e] of Israel and
don't know these things?" Jesus replied. 11 "I assure you: We speak what
We know and We testify to what We
have seen, but you[f] do not accept Our
testimony.[g] 12 If I have told you about
things that happen on earth and you
don't believe, how will you believe if I
tell you about things of heaven? 13 [a]No
one has ascended into heaven except
the One who descended from heaven
—the •Son of Man.[h] 14 [b]Just as Moses
lifted up the snake in the wilderness,
so the Son of Man must be lifted up,
15 so that everyone who believes in
Him will[i] have eternal life. [a] Pr 30:4
[b] Nm 21:9; Jn 8:28

16 [a]"For God loved the world in this
way: He gave His •One and Only Son,
so that everyone who believes in Him
will not perish but have eternal life.
17 [b]For God did not send His Son into
the world that He might condemn the
world, but that the world might be
saved through Him. 18 [c]Anyone who
believes in Him is not condemned, but
anyone who does not believe is already
condemned, because he has not believed in the name of the One and
Only Son of God. [a] Lk 2:14; Rm 5:8
[b] Lk 9:56; 1Jn 4:14 [c] Rm 8:1

19 "This, then, is the judgment: [a]the
light has come into the world, and people loved darkness rather than the light
because their deeds were evil. 20 For
everyone who practices wicked things
hates the light and avoids it,[j] so that his
deeds may not be exposed. 21 But anyone who lives by[k] the truth comes to
the light, so that his works may be
shown to be accomplished by God."[l]
[a] Jn 1:4

Jesus and John the Baptist

22 After this, Jesus and His disciples
went to the Judean countryside, where
He spent time with them [a]and baptized. 23 John also was baptizing in
Aenon near [b]Salim, because there was
plenty of water there. People were
coming and being baptized, 24 since
[c]John had not yet been thrown into
prison. [a] Jn 4:2 [b] Gn 14:18 [c] Mt 14:3

25 Then a dispute arose between
John's disciples and a •Jew[m] about purification. 26 So they came to John and
told him, "Rabbi, [a]the One you testified about, and who was with you
across the Jordan, is baptizing—and
everyone is flocking to Him." [a] Jn 1:34

27 John responded, "No one can receive a single thing unless it's given to
him from heaven. 28 You yourselves

[a]**3:3** The same Gk word can mean *again* or *from above* (also in v. 7). [b]**3:5** Or *spirit*, or *wind*; the Gk word *pneuma* can mean *wind*, *spirit*, or *Spirit*, each of which occurs in this context. [c]**3:7** The pronoun is pl in Gk. [d]**3:8** The Gk word *pneuma* can mean *wind*, *spirit*, or *Spirit*, each of which occurs in this context. [e]**3:10** Or *the teacher* [f]**3:11** The word *you* in Gk is pl here and throughout v. 12. [g]**3:11** The pl forms (*We*, *Our*) refer to Jesus and His authority to speak for the Father. [h]**3:13** Other mss add *who is in heaven* [i]**3:15** Other mss add *not perish, but* [j]**3:20** Lit *and does not come to the light* [k]**3:21** Lit *who does* [l]**3:21** It is possible that Jesus' words end at v. 15. Ancient Gk did not have quotation marks. [m]**3:25** Other mss read *and the Jews*

can testify that I said, 'I am not the
•Messiah, but [a]I've been sent ahead of
Him.' 29 He who has the bride is the
groom. But the groom's friend, who
stands by and listens for him, rejoices
greatly[a] at the groom's voice. So this
joy of mine is complete. 30 [b]He must increase, [c]but I must decrease."

[a] *Mal 3:1; Mt 3* [b] *Is 9:7* [c] *Php 3:8-9*

The One from Heaven

31 [a]The One who comes from above
[b]is above all. The one who is from the
earth is earthly and speaks in earthly
terms.[b] [c]The One who comes from
heaven is above all. 32 [d]He testifies to
what He has seen and heard, yet no
one accepts His testimony. 33 The one
who has accepted His testimony [e]has
affirmed that God is true. 34 [f]For God
sent Him, and He speaks God's words,
since He[c] gives the Spirit [g]without
measure. 35 [h]The Father loves the Son
and has given all things into His hands.
36 [i]The one who believes in the Son has
eternal life, but the one who refuses to
believe in the Son will not see life; instead, [j]the wrath of God remains on
him.

[a] *Jn 8:23* [b] *Mt 28:18* [c] *Eph 1:21* [d] *Jn 15:15* [e] *2Co 1:22* [f] *Jn 7:16* [g] *Jn 1:16* [h] *Dn 7:14* [i] *Rm 1:17* [j] *Gl 3:10*

Jesus and the Samaritan Woman

4 When Jesus[d] knew that the •Phar-
isees heard He was making and
baptizing more disciples than John
2 (though Jesus Himself was not baptizing, but His disciples were), 3 He
left Judea and went again to Galilee.
4 He had to travel through Samaria,
5 so He came to a town of Samaria
called Sychar near the property[e] [a]that
Jacob had given his son Joseph.
6 Jacob's well was there, and Jesus,
worn out from His journey, sat down
at the well. It was about six in the
evening.[f]

[a] *Jos 24:32*

7 A woman of Samaria came to draw
water.

"Give Me a drink," Jesus said to her,
8 for His disciples had gone into town
to buy food.

9 "How is it that You, a Jew, ask for a
drink from me, a •Samaritan woman?"
she asked Him. For [a]Jews do not associate with[g] Samaritans.[h]

[a] *Ezr 4:3*

10 Jesus answered, "If you knew [a]the
gift of God, and who is saying to you,
'Give Me a drink,' you would ask Him,
and He would give you [b]living water."

[a] *Rm 8:32; 1Co 1:30* [b] *Zch 13:1*

11 "Sir," said the woman, "You don't
even have a bucket, and the well is
deep. So where do you get this 'living
water'? 12 You aren't greater than our
father Jacob, are you? He gave us the
well and drank from it himself, as did
his sons and livestock."

13 Jesus said, "Everyone who drinks
from this water will get thirsty again.
14 But [a]whoever drinks from the water
that I will give him will never get
thirsty again—ever! In fact, the water I
will give him [b]will become a well[i] of
water springing up within him for eternal life."

[a] *Jn 6:35* [b] *Jn 7:38*

15 "Sir," the woman said to Him,
"give me this water so I won't get
thirsty and come here to draw water."

16 "Go call your husband," He told
her, "and come back here."

17 "I don't have a husband," she answered.

"You have correctly said, 'I don't
have a husband,'" Jesus said. 18 "For
you've had five husbands, and the man
you now have is not your husband.
What you have said is true."

19 "Sir," the woman replied, [a]"I see
that You are a prophet. 20 Our fathers
worshiped [b]on this mountain,[j] yet you
⌊Jews⌋ say that the place to worship is
in [c]Jerusalem."

[a] *Lk 7:16* [b] *Jdg 9:7* [c] *2Ch 7:12*

[a]**3:29** Lit *with joy rejoices* [b]**3:31** Or *of earthly things* [c]**3:34** Other mss read *since God* [d]**4:1** Other mss read *the Lord* [e]**4:5** Lit *piece of land* [f]**4:6** Lit *the sixth hour*; see note at Jn 1:39; an alternate time reckoning would be *noon* [g]**4:9** Or *do not share vessels with* [h]**4:9** Other mss omit *For Jews do not associate with Samaritans.* [i]**4:14** Or *spring* [j]**4:20** Mount Gerizim, where there had been a Samaritan temple that rivaled Jerusalem's

21 Jesus told her, "Believe Me,
•woman, an hour is coming [a]when you
will worship the Father neither on this
mountain nor in Jerusalem. 22 You Samaritans[a] worship what [b]you do not
know. We worship what we do know,
because [c]salvation is from the Jews.
23 But an hour is coming, and is now
here, when the true worshipers will
worship the Father in [d]spirit and
[e]truth. Yes, the Father wants such people to worship Him. 24 [f]God is spirit,
and those who worship Him must worship in spirit and truth."

a Mal 1:11; 1Tm 2:8 b 2Kg 17:29 c Is 2:3; Rm 9:4-5 d 1Co 3:16; Php 3:3 e Jn 1:17 f Ac 17:24-29

25 The woman said to Him, "I know
that [a]•Messiah[b] is coming" (who is
called Christ). "When He comes, He
will explain everything to us." *a Dt 18:15*

26 [a]"I am ⌊He⌋," Jesus told her, "the
One speaking to you." *a Mt 16:20; Jn 9:37*

The Ripened Harvest

27 Just then His disciples arrived, and
they were amazed that He was talking
with a woman. Yet no one said, "What
do You want?" or "Why are You talking
with her?"
28 Then the woman left her water jar,
went into town, and told the men,
29 "Come, see a man who told me everything I ever did! Could this be the
Messiah?" 30 They left the town and
made their way to Him.
31 In the meantime the disciples kept
urging Him, "•Rabbi, eat something."
32 But He said, "I have food to eat
that you don't know about."
33 The disciples said to one another,
"Could someone have brought Him
something to eat?"
34 [a]"My food is to do the will of Him
who sent Me and to finish His work,"
Jesus told them. 35 "Don't you say,
'There are still four more months, then
comes the harvest'? Listen ⌊to what⌋
I'm telling you: Open[c] your eyes and
look at the fields, [b]for they are ready[d]
for harvest. 36 [c]The reaper is already receiving pay and gathering fruit for eternal life, so the sower and reaper can
rejoice together. 37 For in this case the
saying is true: 'One sows and another
reaps.' 38 I sent you to reap what you
didn't labor for; others have labored,
and you have benefited from[e] their labor."

a Jn 6:38 b Mt 9:37 c Dn 12:3; 1Co 3:8; Jms 5:20

The Savior of the World

39 [a]Now many Samaritans from that
town believed in Him because of what
the woman said[f] when she testified,
"He told me everything I ever did."
40 Therefore, when the Samaritans
came to Him, they asked Him to stay
with them, and He stayed there two
days. 41 [b]Many more believed because
of what He said.[g] 42 And they told the
woman, "We no longer believe because of what you said, for [c]we have
heard for ourselves and know that this
really is the [d]Savior of the world."[h]

a Gn 49:10 b Is 42:1 c 1Jn 4:14 d Is 49:6; Jn 1:29; Eph 2:13

A Galilean Welcome

43 After two days He left there for Galilee. 44 [a]Jesus Himself testified that a
prophet has no honor in his own country. 45 When they entered Galilee, the
Galileans welcomed Him [b]because
they had seen everything He did in
Jerusalem during the festival. [c]For they
also had gone to the festival.

a Mt 13:57; Mk 6:4 b Jn 2:23 c Dt 16:16

The Second Sign: Healing an Official's Son

46 Then He went again to Cana of Galilee, [a]where He had turned the water

[a]**4:22** *Samaritans* is implied since the Gk verb and pronoun are pl. [b]**4:25** In the NT, the word Messiah translates the Gk word *Christos* ("Anointed One"), except here and in Jn 1:41 where it translates *Messias.* [c]**4:35** Lit *Raise* [d]**4:35** Lit *white* [e]**4:38** Lit *you have entered into* [f]**4:39** Lit *because of the woman's word* [g]**4:41** Lit *because of His word* [h]**4:42** Other mss add *the Messiah*

into wine. There was a certain royal official whose son was ill at Capernaum.
47 When this man heard that Jesus had
come from Judea into Galilee, he went
to Him and pleaded with Him to come
down and heal his son, for he was
about to die. *[a] Jn 2:1,11*

48 Jesus told him, [a]“Unless you ⌊peo-
ple⌋ see signs and wonders, you will
not believe.” *[a] Mt 16:1; Lk 16:31*

49 “Sir,” the official said to Him,
“come down before my boy dies!”
50 [a]“Go,” Jesus told him, “your son
will live.” The man believed what[a]
Jesus said to him and departed.
[a] Mt 8:13

51 While he was still going down, his
•slaves met him saying that his boy
was alive. 52 He asked them at what
time he got better. “Yesterday at seven
in the morning[b] the fever left him,”
they answered. 53 The father realized
this was the very hour at which Jesus
had told him, “Your son will live.”
Then he himself believed, along with
his whole household.
54 This therefore was the second sign
Jesus performed after He came from
Judea to Galilee.

The Third Sign: Healing the Sick

5 After [a]this, a Jewish festival took
place, and Jesus went up to Jerusalem. 2 [b]By the Sheep Gate in Jerusalem
there is a pool, called Bethesda[c] in Hebrew, which has five colonnades.[d]
3 Within these lay a multitude of
the sick—blind, lame, and paralyzed
[—waiting for the moving of the water, 4 because an angel would go down
into the pool from time to time and
stir up the water. Then the first one
who got in after the water was stirred
up recovered from whatever ailment
he had].[e] *[a] Lv 23:2 [b] Neh 3:1*

5 One man was there who had been
sick for 38 years. 6 When Jesus saw
him lying there [a]and knew he had already been there a long time, He said
to him, [b]“Do you want to get well?”
[a] Heb 4:13 [b] Is 55:1

7 “Sir,” the sick man answered, “I
don’t have a man to put me into the
pool when the water is stirred up, but
while I’m coming, someone goes
down ahead of me.”
8 [a]“Get up,” Jesus told him, “pick up
your bedroll and walk!” 9 Instantly the
man got well, picked up his bedroll,
and started to walk. *[a] Mt 9:6*

Now that day was the Sabbath, 10 so
the •Jews said to the man who had
been healed, “This is the Sabbath! [a]It’s
illegal for you to pick up your bedroll.”
[a] Ex 20:10; Mt 12:2

11 He replied, “The man who made
me well told me, ‘Pick up your bedroll
and walk.’ ”
12 “Who is this man who told you,
‘Pick up ⌊your bedroll⌋ and walk?’ ”
they asked. 13 But the man who was
cured did not know who it was, because Jesus had slipped away into the
crowd that was there.[f]
14 After this, Jesus found him in the
•temple complex and said to him,
“See, you are well. [a]Do not sin any
more, so that something worse doesn’t
happen to you.” 15 The man went and
reported to the Jews that it was Jesus
who had made him well. *[a] Jn 8:11*

Honoring the Father and the Son

16 Therefore, the Jews began persecuting Jesus[g] because He was doing
these things on the Sabbath. 17 But
Jesus responded to them, [a]“My Father
is still working, and I am working
also.” 18 This is why the Jews [b]began
trying all the more to kill Him: not only

[a]**4:50** Lit *the word* [b]**4:52** Or *seven in the evening*; lit *at the seventh hour*; see note at Jn 1:39; an alternate time reckoning would be *at one in the afternoon* [c]**5:2** Other mss read *Bethzatha*; other mss read *Bethsaida* [d]**5:2** Rows of columns supporting a roof [e]**5:3–4** Other mss omit bracketed text [f]**5:13** Lit *slipped away, there being a crowd in that place* [g]**5:16** Other mss add *and trying to kill Him*

was He breaking the Sabbath, but He
was even calling God His own Father,
[c]making Himself equal with God.
[a]Jn 9:4 [b]Jn 7:19 [c]Jn 10:30

19 Then Jesus replied, "•I assure you:
[a]The Son is not able to do anything on
His own, but only what He sees the Father doing. For whatever the Father[a]
does, the Son also does these things in
the same way. 20 For [b]the Father loves
the Son and shows Him everything He
is doing, and He will show Him greater
works than these so that you will be
amazed. 21 And just as the Father raises
the dead and gives them life, [c]so the Son
also gives life to anyone He wants to.
22 The Father, in fact, judges no one but
[d]has given all judgment to the Son, 23 so
that all people will [e]honor the Son just
as they honor the Father. Anyone who
does not honor the Son does not honor
the Father who sent Him.
[a]Jn 8:28 [b]Mt 3:17 [c]Jn 11:25 [d]Mt 11:27 [e]1Jn 2:23

Life and Judgment

24 "I assure you: Anyone who hears
My word and believes Him who sent
Me has eternal life and will not come
under judgment [a]but has passed from
death to life.
[a]1Jn 3:14

25 "I assure you: An hour is coming,
and is now here, when [a]the dead will
hear the voice of the Son of God, and
those who hear will live. 26 For just as
the Father has [b]life in Himself, so also
He has granted to the Son to have life
in Himself. 27 And He has granted Him
the right to pass judgment, [c]because
He is the •Son of Man. 28 Do not be
amazed at this, because a time is coming when all who are in the graves will
hear His voice 29 [d]and come out—
[e]those who have done good things, to
the resurrection of life, but those who
have done wicked things, to the resurrection of judgment.
[a]Eph 2:1,5 [b]Ac 17:31 [c]Dn 7:13 [d]1Co 15:52 [e]Dn 12:2; Lk 14:14

30 "I can do nothing on My own. I
judge only as I hear, and My judgment
is righteous, because I do not seek My
own will, but the will of Him who
sent Me.

Four Witnesses to Jesus

31 [a]"If I testify about Myself, My testimony is not valid.[b] 32 There is Another who testifies about Me, and I
know that the testimony He gives
about Me is valid.[c] 33 You have sent
⌊messengers⌋ to John, [b]and he has testified to the truth. 34 I don't receive
man's testimony, but I say these things
so that you may be saved. 35 John[d] was
a burning and shining lamp, and for a
time [c]you were willing to enjoy his
light.
[a]Is 55:4 [b]Jn 1:15 [c]Lk 3:15

36 "But [a]I have a greater testimony
than John's because of [b]the works that
the Father has given Me to accomplish. These very works I am doing testify about Me that the Father has se
Me. 37 The Father who sent Me [c]h
Himself testified about Me. You have
not heard His voice at any time, [d]and
you haven't seen His form. 38 You don't
have His word living in you, because
you don't believe the One He sent.
39 [e]You pore over[e] the Scriptures because you think you have eternal life in
them, [f]yet they testify about Me.
40 And you are not willing to come to
Me that you may have life.
[a]1Jn 5:9 [b]Mt 11:4-5 [c]Mt 3:17 [d]Jn 1:18 [e]Is 8:20 [f]Dt 18:15; Lk 24:27

41 "I do not accept glory from men,
42 but I know you—that you have no
love for God within you. 43 I have come
in My Father's name, yet you don't
accept Me. If someone else comes in
his own name, you will accept him.
44 How can you believe? While accepting glory from one another, you don't
seek [a]the glory that comes from the
only God. 45 Do not think that I will accuse you to the Father. Your accuser is

[a]**5:19** Lit *whatever that One* [b]**5:31** Or *not true* [c]**5:32** Or *true* [d]**5:35** Lit *That man* [e]**5:39** In Gk this could be a command: *Pore over . . .*

Moses, on whom you have set your
hope. 46 For if you believed Moses, you
would believe Me, [b]because he wrote
about Me. 47 But if [c]you don't believe
his writings, how will you believe My
words?" *[a]Mt 25:21-23 [b]Gn 3:15; Dt 18:15*
[c]Lk 16:29,31

The Fourth Sign: Feeding 5,000

6 After [a]this, Jesus crossed the Sea
of Galilee (or Tiberias). 2 And a
huge crowd was following Him because they saw the signs that He was
performing on the sick. 3 So Jesus
went up a mountain and sat down
there with His disciples. *[a]Mt 14:15*

4 [a]Now the •Passover, a Jewish festival, was near. 5 Therefore, [b]when Jesus
looked up and noticed a huge crowd
coming toward Him, He asked Philip,
"Where will we buy bread so these
people can eat?" 6 He asked this to test
him, for He Himself knew what He
was going to do. *[a]Lv 23:5 [b]Mt 14:14*

7 Philip answered, [a]"Two hundred
•denarii worth of bread wouldn't be
enough for each of them to have a little." *[a]Mk 6:37*

8 One of His disciples, Andrew, Simon Peter's brother, said to Him,
9 "There's a boy here who has five barley loaves and two fish—but what are
they for so many?"

10 Then Jesus said, "Have the people
sit down."

There was plenty of grass in that
place, so they sat down. The men numbered about 5,000. 11 Then Jesus took
the loaves, and after [a]giving thanks He
distributed them to those who were
seated—so also with the fish, as much
as they wanted. *[a]1Tm 4:5*

12 When they were full, He told His
disciples, "Collect the leftovers so that
nothing is wasted." 13 So they collected
them and filled 12 baskets with the
pieces from the five barley loaves that
were left over by those who had eaten.

14 When the people saw the sign[a] He
had done, they said, "This really is [a]the
Prophet who was to come into the
world!" 15 Therefore, when Jesus knew
that they were about to come and take
Him by force to make Him king, He
withdrew again[b] to the mountain by
Himself. *[a]Gn 49:10; Dt 18:18*

The Fifth Sign: Walking on Water

16 [a]When evening came, His disciples went down to the sea, 17 got into a
boat, and started across the sea to Capernaum. Darkness had already set in,
but Jesus had not yet come to them.
18 Then a high wind arose, and the sea
began to churn. 19 After they had
rowed about three or four miles,[c] they
saw Jesus walking on the sea. He was
coming near the boat, and they were
afraid. *[a]Mt 14:23*

20 But He said to them, "It is I.[d] Don't
be afraid!" 21 Then they were willing to
take Him on board, and at once the
boat was at the shore where they were
heading.

The Bread of Life

22 The next day, the crowd that had
stayed on the other side of the sea
knew there had been only one boat.[e]
⌊They also knew⌋ that Jesus had not
boarded the boat with His disciples,
but that His disciples had gone off
alone. 23 Some boats from Tiberias
came near the place where they ate
the bread after the Lord gave thanks.
24 When the crowd saw that neither
Jesus nor His disciples were there,
they got into the boats and went to Capernaum looking for Jesus.

25 When they found Him on the
other side of the sea, they said to Him,
"•Rabbi, when did You get here?"

[a]**6:14** Other mss read *signs* [b]**6:15** A previous withdrawal is mentioned in Mk 6:31–32, an event that occurred just before the feeding of the 5,000. [c]**6:19** Lit *25 or 30 stadia*; 1 *stadion* = 600 feet [d]**6:20** Lit *I am* [e]**6:22** Other mss add *into which His disciples had entered*

26 Jesus answered, "•I assure you:
You are looking for Me, not because
you saw the signs, but because you ate
the loaves and were filled. 27 Don't
work for the food that perishes but [a]for
the food that lasts for eternal life,
which the •Son of Man will give you,
[b]because God the Father has set His
seal of approval on Him."

[a]*Jn 4:14* [b]*Mt 3:17; 17:5*

28 "What can we do to perform the
works of God?" they asked.
29 Jesus replied, "This is the work of
God: that you believe in the One He
has sent."
30 [a]"What sign then are You going to
do so we may see and believe You?"
they asked. "What are You going to
perform? 31 [b]Our fathers ate the manna
in the wilderness, just as it is written:
[c]**He gave them bread from heaven to**
eat."[a b]

[a]*Mt 12:38* [b]*Ex 16:15* [c]*Neh 9:15; Ps 78:24*

32 Jesus said to them, "I assure you:
Moses didn't give you the bread from
heaven, but My Father gives you the
real bread from heaven. 33 For the
bread of God is the One who comes
down from heaven and gives life to the
world."
34 Then they said, "Sir, give us this
bread always!"
35 "I am the bread of life," Jesus told
them. [a]"No one who comes to Me will
ever be hungry, and no one who believes in Me will ever be thirsty again.
36 But as I told you, you've seen Me,[c]
and yet you do not believe. 37 Everyone
the Father gives Me will come to Me,
[b]and the one who comes to Me I will
never cast out. 38 For I have come
down from heaven, [c]not to do My will,
[d]but the will of Him who sent Me.
39 This is the will of Him who sent Me:
[e]that I should lose none of those He
has given Me but should raise them up
on the last day. 40 For this is the will of
My Father: [f]that everyone who sees
the Son and believes in Him may have
eternal life, and I will raise him up on
the last day."

[a]*Jn 4:14; 7:37* [b]*Jr 31:34; Jn 10:28-29* [c]*Jn 5:30* [d]*Jn 4:34* [e]*Jn 17:12* [f]*Jn 4:14*

41 Therefore the Jews started complaining about Him, because He said,
"I am the bread that came down from
heaven." 42 They were saying, "Isn't
this Jesus the son of Joseph, whose father and mother we know? How can
He now say, 'I have come down from
heaven'?"
43 Jesus answered them, "Stop complaining among yourselves. 44 No one
can come to Me unless the Father who
sent Me draws[d] him, and I will raise
him up on the last day. 45 [a]It is written
in the Prophets: **And they will all be**
taught by God.[e] Everyone who has listened to and learned from the Father
comes to Me— 46 [b]not that anyone has
seen the Father except [c]the One who
is from God. He has seen the Father.

[a]*Is 54:13; Mc 4:2* [b]*Jn 1:18* [c]*Mt 11:27; Jn 7:29*

47 "I assure you: [a]Anyone who believes[f] has eternal life. 48 I am the bread
of life. 49 Your fathers ate the manna in
the wilderness, and they died. 50 This
is the bread that comes down from
heaven so that anyone may eat of it
and not die. 51 I am the living bread
that came down from heaven. If anyone eats of this bread he will live forever. [b]The bread that I will give for the
life of the world is My flesh."

[a]*Jn 3:16* [b]*Heb 10:10*

52 At that, the Jews argued among
themselves, "How can this man give
us His flesh to eat?"
53 So Jesus said to them, "I assure
you: Unless [a]you eat the flesh of the
Son of Man and drink His blood, you do
not have life in yourselves. 54 Anyone

[a]**6:31** Bread miraculously provided by God for the Israelites [b]**6:31** Ex 16:4; Ps 78:24 [c]**6:36** Other mss omit *Me* [d]**6:44** Or *brings*, or *leads*; see the use of this Gk verb in Jn 12:32; 21:6; Ac 16:19; Jms 2:6. [e]**6:45** Is 54:13 [f]**6:47** Other mss add *in Me*

who eats My flesh and drinks My
blood has eternal life, and I will raise
him up on the last day, 55 because My
flesh is real food and My blood is real
drink. 56 The one who eats My flesh
and drinks My blood [b]lives in Me, and
I in him. 57 Just as the living Father sent
Me and I live because of the Father, so
the one who feeds on Me will live because of Me. 58 This is the bread that
came down from heaven; it is not like
the manna[a] your fathers ate—and they
died. The one who eats this bread will
live forever."

[a] Mt 26:26 [b] Jn 14:23; Rm 8:9; Eph 3:17; 5:30

59 He said these things while teaching in the •synagogue in Capernaum.

Many Disciples Desert Jesus

60 Therefore, when [a]many of His disciples heard this, they said, "This
teaching is hard! Who can accept[b] it?"

[a] Mt 11:6

61 Jesus, knowing in Himself that His
disciples were complaining about this,
asked them, "Does this offend you?
62 [a]Then what if you were to observe
the Son of Man ascending to where He
was before? 63 [b]The Spirit is the One
who gives life. The flesh doesn't help
at all. The words that I have spoken to
you [c]are spirit and are life. 64 But there
are some among you who don't believe." (For [d]Jesus knew from the beginning those who would not[c] believe
and the one who would betray Him.)
65 He said, "This is why I told you that
no one can come to Me unless it is
granted to him by the Father."

[a] Mk 16:19; Ac 1:9 [b] Rm 8:2 [c] Eph 1:17 [d] Jn 2:24; 13:11

66 From that moment many of His
disciples [a]turned back and no longer
accompanied Him. 67 Therefore Jesus
said to the Twelve, "You don't want to
go away too, do you?"

[a] Lk 9:62; Heb 6:4-6

68 Simon Peter answered, "Lord,
who will we go to? You have the words
of eternal life. 69 We have come to believe and know that You are the Holy
One of God!"[d]

70 Jesus replied to them, "Didn't I
choose you, the Twelve? Yet one of you
is the Devil!" 71 He was referring to Judas, Simon Iscariot's son,[e f] one of the
Twelve, because he was going to betray Him.

The Unbelief of Jesus' Brothers

7 After this, Jesus traveled in Galilee, since He did not want to
travel in Judea because the •Jews were
trying to kill Him. 2 [a]The Jewish Festival of Tabernacles[g h] was near, 3 so His
[b]brothers said to Him, "Leave here
and go to Judea so Your disciples can
see Your works that You are doing.
4 For no one does anything in secret
while he's seeking public recognition.
If You do these things, show Yourself
to the world." 5 (For [c]not even His
brothers believed in Him.)

[a] Lv 23:34 [b] Mt 12:46 [c] Mk 3:21

6 Jesus told them, [a]"My time has not
yet arrived, but your time is always at
hand. 7 [b]The world cannot hate you,
but it does hate Me [c]because I testify
about it—that its deeds are evil. 8 Go
up to the festival yourselves. I'm not
going up to the festival yet,[i] [d]because
My time has not yet fully come."
9 After He had said these things, He
stayed in Galilee.

[a] Ec 3:1-2 [b] Jn 15:19 [c] Jn 3:19 [d] Jn 8:20

Jesus at the Festival of Tabernacles

10 After His brothers had gone up to
the festival, then He also went up, not
openly but secretly. 11 [a]The Jews were
looking for Him at the festival and saying, "Where is He?" 12 And [b]there was

[a]**6:58** Other mss omit *the manna* [b]**6:60** Lit *hear* [c]**6:64** Other mss omit *not* [d]**6:69** Other mss read *You are the Messiah, the Son of the Living God* [e]**6:71** Other mss read *Judas Iscariot, Simon's son* [f]**6:71** Lit *Judas, of Simon Iscariot* [g]**7:2** Or *Booths* [h]**7:2** One of 3 great Jewish religious festivals, along with Passover and Pentecost; Ex 23:14; Dt 16:16 [i]**7:8** Other mss omit *yet*

a lot of discussion about Him among the crowds. [c]Some were saying, "He's a good man." Others were saying, "No, on the contrary, He's deceiving the people." 13 Still, nobody was talking publicly about Him because they feared the Jews.

[a]Jn 11:56 [b]Jn 9:16 [c]Lk 7:16

14 When the festival was already half over, Jesus went up into the •temple complex and began to teach. 15 [a]Then the Jews were amazed and said, "How does He know the Scriptures, since He hasn't been trained?"

[a]Mt 13:54

16 Jesus answered them, [a]"My teaching isn't Mine but is from the One who sent Me. 17 [b]If anyone wants to do His will, he will understand whether the teaching is from God or if I am speaking on My own. 18 [c]The one who speaks for himself seeks his own glory. But He who seeks the glory of the One who sent Him is true, and there is no unrighteousness in Him. 19 [d]Didn't Moses give you the law? Yet none of you keeps the law! [e]Why do you want to kill Me?"

[a]Jn 3:31-34; 8:28; 12:49 [b]Lk 8:15 [c]Jn 5:41 [d]Ac 7:38 [e]Mt 12:14

20 [a]"You have a demon!" the crowd responded. "Who wants to kill You?"

[a]Jn 8:48

21 "I did one work, and you are all amazed," Jesus answered. 22 "Consider this: [a]Moses has given you circumcision—not that it comes from Moses [b]but from the fathers—and you circumcise a man on the Sabbath. 23 If a man receives circumcision on the Sabbath so that the law of Moses won't be broken, are you angry at Me because [c]I made a man entirely well on the Sabbath? 24 [d]Stop judging according to outward appearances; rather judge according to righteous judgment."

[a]Lv 12:3 [b]Gn 17:10 [c]Jn 5:8 [d]Pr 24:23; Jn 8:15

The Identity of the Messiah

25 Some of the people of Jerusalem were saying, "Isn't this the man they want to kill? 26 Yet, look! He's speaking publicly and they're saying nothing to Him. Can it be true that the authorities know He is the •Messiah? 27 But we know where this man is from. When the Messiah comes, nobody will know where He is from."

28 As He was teaching in the temple complex, Jesus cried out, [a]"You know Me and you know where I am from. Yet [b]I have not come on My own, but the One who sent Me [c]is true. You [d]don't know Him; 29 [e]I know Him because I am from Him, and He sent Me."

[a]Jn 8:14 [b]Jn 5:43 [c]Jn 5:32 [d]Jn 1:18 [e]Jn 10:15

30 Then they tried to seize Him. Yet no one laid a hand on Him because His hour[a] had not yet come. 31 However, many from the crowd believed in Him and said, "When the Messiah comes, He won't perform more signs than this man has done, will He?"

32 The •Pharisees heard the crowd muttering these things about Him, so the •chief priests and the Pharisees sent temple police to arrest Him.

33 Then Jesus said, [a]"I am only with you for a short time. Then I'm going to the One who sent Me. 34 You [b]will look for Me, but you will not find Me; and where I am, you cannot come."

[a]Jn 13:33 [b]Jn 8:21

35 Then the Jews said to one another, "Where does He intend to go so we won't find Him? He doesn't intend to go to [a]the Dispersion[b] among the Greeks and teach the Greeks, does He? 36 What is this remark He made: 'You will look for Me, and you will not find Me; and where I am, you cannot come'?"

[a]Is 11:12

[a]**7:30** The time of His sacrificial death and exaltation; Jn 2:4; 8:20; 12:23,27; 13:1; 17:1 [b]**7:35** Jewish people scattered throughout Gentile lands who spoke Gk and were influenced by Gk culture

The Promise of the Spirit

37 On the last and most important
day of the festival, Jesus stood up and
cried out, [a]"If anyone is thirsty, he
should come to Me[a] and drink! 38 [b]The
one who believes in Me, as the Scripture has said,[b] [c]will have streams of living water flow from deep within him."
39 [d]He said this about the Spirit, whom
those who believed in Him were going
to receive, for the Spirit[c] had not yet
been received,[d] [e] because Jesus had
not yet been [e]glorified.

[a]Is 55:1 [b]Dt 18:15 [c]Is 12:3 [d]Is 44:3; Jn 16:7 [e]Jn 12:16

The People Are Divided over Jesus

40 When some from the crowd heard
these words, they said, "This really is
[a]the Prophet!"[f] 41 Others said, [b]"This is
the Messiah!" But some said, "Surely
the Messiah doesn't come from Galilee, does He? 42 [c]Doesn't the Scripture
say that the Messiah comes from
David's offspring[g] and from the town
of Bethlehem, [d]where David once
lived?" 43 So a division occurred among
the crowd because of Him. 44 Some of
them wanted to seize Him, but no one
laid hands on Him.

[a]Dt 18:15 [b]Jn 4:42 [c]Mc 5:2 [d]1Sm 16:1

Debate over Jesus' Claims

45 Then the temple police came to
the chief priests and Pharisees, who
asked them, "Why haven't you brought
Him?"

46 The police answered, "No man
ever spoke like this!"[h]

47 Then the Pharisees responded to
them: "Are you fooled too? 48 Have any
of the rulers believed in Him? Or any
of the Pharisees? 49 But this crowd,
which doesn't know the law, is accursed!"

50 Nicodemus—[a]the one who came
to Him previously, being one of them
—said to them, 51 [b]"Our law doesn't
judge a man before it hears from him
and knows what he's doing, does it?"

[a]Jn 3:2 [b]Dt 1:17; 17:8

52 "You aren't from Galilee too, are
you?" they replied. "Investigate and
you will see that [a]no prophet arises
from Galilee."[i]

[a]Is 9:1-2; Jn 1:46

[53 So each one went to his house.
8 1 But Jesus went to the •Mount of
Olives.

An Adulteress Forgiven

2 At dawn He went to the •temple
complex again, and all the people were
coming to Him. He sat down and began to teach them.

3 Then the •scribes and the •Phari-
sees brought a woman caught in adultery, making her stand in the center.
4 "Teacher," they said to Him, "this
woman was caught in the act of committing adultery. 5 [a]In the law Moses
commanded us to stone such women.
So what do You say?" 6 They asked this
to trap Him, in order that they might
have evidence to accuse Him.

[a]Lv 20:10; Dt 5:18

Jesus stooped down and started writing on the ground with His finger.
7 When they persisted in questioning
Him, He stood up and said to them,
[a]"The one without sin among you
should be the first to throw a stone at
her."

[a]Dt 17:7; Jb 5:12; Mt 7:1-5

8 Then He stooped down again and
continued writing on the ground.
9 [a]When they heard this, they left one
by one, starting with the older men.
Only He was left, with the woman in
the center. 10 When Jesus stood up, He

[a]**7:37** Other mss omit *to Me* [b]**7:38** Jesus may have had several OT passages in mind; Is 58:11; Ezk 47:1–12; Zch 14:8 [c]**7:39** Other mss read *Holy Spirit* [d]**7:39** Other mss read *had not yet been given* [e]**7:39** Lit *the Spirit was not yet*; the word *received* is implied from the previous clause. [f]**7:40** Probably = the Prophet in Dt 18:15 [g]**7:42** Lit *seed* [h]**7:46** Other mss read *like this man* [i]**7:52** Jonah and probably other prophets did come from Galilee; 2 Kgs 14:25

said to her, "•Woman, where are they?
Has no one condemned you?"
[a] Ec 7:22; Rm 2:22

11 "No one, Lord,"[a] she answered.
[a]"Neither do I condemn you," said
Jesus. "Go, and from now on do not sin
any more."][b]
[a] Lk 9:56

The Light of the World

12 Then Jesus spoke to them again: "I
am the light of the world. Anyone who
follows Me will never walk in the darkness but will have the light of life."
13 So the Pharisees said to Him,
[a]"You are testifying about Yourself.
Your testimony is not valid."[c]
[a] Jn 5:31

14 "Even if I testify about Myself,"
Jesus replied, "My testimony is valid,[d]
because I know where I came from
and where I'm going. But [a]you don't
know where I come from or where
I'm going. 15 [b]You judge by human
standards.[e] [c]I judge no one. 16 And if I
do judge, My judgment is true, because [d]I am not alone, but I and the Father who sent Me ⌊judge together⌋.
17 [e]Even in your law it is written that
the witness of two men is valid. 18 I am
the One who testifies about Myself,
and [f]the Father who sent Me testifies
about Me."
[a] Jn 7:28 [b] Jn 7:24 [c] Jn 3:17 [d] Jn 14:10-11; 16:32 [e] Dt 17:6 [f] Jn 5:37

19 Then they asked Him, "Where is
Your Father?"
[a]"You know neither Me nor My Father," Jesus answered. [b]"If you knew
Me, you would also know My Father."
20 He spoke these words by [c]the treasury,[f] while teaching in the temple
complex. But [d]no one seized Him, because His hour[g] had not come.
[a] Jn 16:3 [b] Jn 14:7 [c] Mk 12:41 [d] Jn 7:8,30

Jesus Predicts His Departure

21 Then He said to them again, "I'm
going away; [a]you will look for Me, and
you will die in your sin. Where I'm going, you cannot come."
[a] Jn 13:33

22 So the Jews said again, "He won't
kill Himself, will He, since He
says, 'Where I'm going, you cannot
come'?"
23 [a]"You are from below," He told
them, "I am from above. You are of
this world; I am not of this world.
24 Therefore I told you that you will
die in your sins. [b]For if you do not believe that I am ⌊He⌋,[h] you will die in
your sins."
[a] Jn 3:31 [b] Mk 16:16

25 "Who are You?" they questioned.
"Precisely what I've been telling you
from the very beginning," Jesus told
them. 26 "I have many things to say and
to judge about you, but [a]the One who
sent Me is true, and what I have heard
from Him—[b]these things I tell the
world."
[a] Jn 7:28 [b] Jn 3:32

27 They did not know He was speaking to them about the Father. 28 So
Jesus said to them, "When you [a]lift up
the •Son of Man, then you will know
that I am ⌊He⌋, and [b]that I do nothing
on My own. But [c]just as the Father
taught Me, I say these things. 29 [d]The
One who sent Me is with Me. He has
not left Me alone, [e]because I always do
what pleases Him."
[a] Jn 3:14 [b] Jn 5:19,30 [c] Jn 3:11 [d] Jn 14:10 [e] Jn 4:34

Truth and Freedom

30 As He was saying these things,
many believed in Him. 31 So Jesus said
to the Jews who had believed Him, "If
you continue in My word,[i] you really
are My disciples. 32 You will know the
truth, and [a]the truth will set you
free."
[a] Is 61:1; Rm 6:14

[a]**8:11** Or *Sir*; Jn 4:15,49; 5:7; 6:34; 9:36 [b]**8:11** Other mss omit bracketed text [c]**8:13** The law of Moses required at least 2 witnesses to make a claim legally valid (v. 17). [d]**8:14** Or *true* [e]**8:15** Lit *You judge according to the flesh* [f]**8:20** A place for offerings to be given, perhaps in the court of women [g]**8:20** The time of His sacrificial death and exaltation; Jn 2:4; 7:30; 12:23,27; 13:1; 17:1 [h]**8:24** Jesus claimed to be deity, but the Pharisees didn't understand His meaning. [i]**8:31** Or *My teaching*, or *My message*

33 [a]"We are descendants[a] of Abraham," they answered Him, "and we
have never been enslaved to anyone.
How can You say, 'You will become
free'?" *a Lv 25:42*

34 Jesus responded, "•I assure you:
[a]Everyone who commits sin is a slave
of sin. 35 [b]A slave does not remain in
the household forever, but a son does
remain forever. 36 Therefore [c]if the Son
sets you free, you really will be free. 37 I
know you are descendants[a] of Abraham, but [d]you are trying to kill Me because My word[b] is not welcome among
you. 38 I speak what I have seen in the
presence of the Father,[c] and therefore
you do what you have heard from your
father." *a Pr 5:22; Rm 6 b Gl 4:30 c Rm 8:2; 2Co 3:17 d Jn 7:19*

39 "Our father is [a]Abraham!" they replied. *a Mt 3:9*

"If you were Abraham's children,"
Jesus told them, "you would do what
Abraham did. 40 But now you are trying
to kill Me, a man who has told you the
truth that I heard from God. Abraham
did not do this! 41 You're doing what
your father does."

"We weren't born of sexual immorality," they said. [a]"We have one
Father—God." *a Is 63:16*

42 Jesus said to them, "If God were
your Father, you would love Me,
[a]because I came from God and I am
here. [b]For I didn't come on My own,
but He sent Me. 43 [c]Why don't you understand what I say? Because you cannot listen to[d] My word. 44 You are of
your father the Devil, and you want to
carry out your father's desires. He was
a murderer from the beginning and
has not stood in the truth, because
there is no truth in him. When he tells
a lie, he speaks from his own nature,[e]
because he is a liar and the father of liars.[f] 45 Yet because I tell the truth, you
do not believe Me. 46 Who among you
can convict Me of sin? If I tell the
truth, why don't you believe Me?
47 The one who is from God listens to
God's words. This is why you don't listen, because you are not from God."
a Jn 1:14; 3:16 b Jn 5:43 c Jn 7:17

Jesus and Abraham

48 The Jews responded to Him,
"Aren't we right in saying that You're
a •Samaritan and have a demon?"

49 "I do not have a demon," Jesus answered. "On the contrary, I honor My
Father and you dishonor Me. 50 [a]I do
not seek My glory; the One who seeks
it also judges. 51 I assure you: [b]If anyone keeps My word, he will never see
death—ever!" *a Jn 5:41 b Jn 5:24*

52 Then the Jews said, "Now we
know You have a demon. [a]Abraham
died and so did the prophets. You say,
'If anyone keeps My word, he will
never taste death—ever!' 53 Are You
greater than our father Abraham who
died? Even the prophets died. Who do
You pretend to be?"[g] *a Zch 1:5*

54 "If I glorify Myself," Jesus answered, "My glory is nothing. My Father—you say about Him, 'He is our
God'—[a]He is the One who glorifies
Me. 55 [b]You've never known Him, but
I know Him. If I were to say I don't
know Him, I would be a liar like you.
But I do know Him, and I keep His
word. 56 Your father Abraham was
overjoyed that he would see My day;
[c]he saw it and rejoiced." *a Jn 16:14 b Jn 7:28 c Heb 11:13*

57 The Jews replied, "You aren't 50
years old yet, and You've seen
Abraham?"[h]

58 Jesus said to them, "I assure you:
Before Abraham was, [a]I am."[i]
a Ex 3:14; Col 1:17

[a]**8:33,37** Or *offspring*; lit *seed*; Jn 7:42 [b]**8:37** Or *My teaching*, or *My message* [c]**8:38** Other mss read *of My Father* [d]**8:43** Or *cannot hear* [e]**8:44** Lit *from his own things* [f]**8:44** Lit *of it* [g]**8:53** Lit *Who do You make Yourself?* [h]**8:57** Other mss read *and Abraham has seen You?* [i]**8:58** *I AM* is the name God gave Himself at the burning bush; Ex 3:13–14; see note at Jn 8:24.

59 At that, they picked up stones to
throw at Him. But Jesus was hidden[a]
and went out of the temple complex.[b]

The Sixth Sign: Healing a Man Born Blind

9 As He was passing by, He saw a
man blind from birth. 2 His disciples questioned Him: "•Rabbi, who
sinned, this man or his parents, that
he was born blind?"
3 "Neither this man nor his parents
sinned," Jesus answered. "⌊This came
about⌋ [a]so that God's works might be
displayed in him. 4 [b]We[c] must do the
works of Him who sent Me[d] while it is
day. Night is coming when no one can
work. 5 As long as I am in the world, [c]I
am the light of the world."

[a] Mt 11:5; Jn 11:4 [b] Jn 4:34; 5:36; 12:35 [c] Is 49:6; Lk 2:32; Jn 1:5,9; 8:12

6 After He said these things [a]He spit
on the ground, made some mud from
the saliva, and spread the mud on his
eyes. 7 "Go," He told him, "wash in the
pool of Siloam" (which means "Sent").
[b]So he left, washed, and came back seeing. *[a] Mk 7:33 [b] Is 42:7*

8 His neighbors and those who formerly had seen him as a beggar said,
"Isn't this the man who sat begging?"
9 Some said, "He's the one." "No," others were saying, "but he looks like him."
He kept saying, "I'm the one!"
10 Therefore they asked him, "Then
how were your eyes opened?"
11 He answered, "The man called
Jesus made mud, spread it on my eyes,
and told me, 'Go to Siloam and wash.'
So when I went and washed I received
my sight."
12 "Where is He?" they asked.
"I don't know," he said.

The Healed Man's Testimony

13 They brought the man who used
to be blind to the •Pharisees. 14 The day
that Jesus made the mud and opened
his eyes was a Sabbath. 15 So again the
Pharisees asked him how he received
his sight.
"He put mud on my eyes," he told
them. "I washed and I can see."
16 Therefore some of the Pharisees
said, "This man is not from God, for He
doesn't keep the Sabbath!" But others
were saying, [a]"How can a sinful man
perform such signs?" And [b]there was a
division among them. *[a] Jn 3:2 [b] Jn 7:12,43*

17 Again they asked the blind man,[e]
"What do you say about Him, since He
opened your eyes?"
[a]"He's a prophet," he said. *[a] Dt 18:15*

18 The Jews did not believe this
about him—that he was blind and received sight—until they summoned
the parents of the one who had received his sight.
19 They asked them, "Is this your
son, ⌊the one⌋ you say was born blind?
How then does he now see?"
20 "We know this is our son and that
he was born blind," his parents answered. 21 "But we don't know how he
now sees, and we don't know who
opened his eyes. Ask him; he's of age.
He will speak for himself." 22 His parents said these things because they
[a]were afraid of the Jews, since the Jews
had already agreed that if anyone con-
fessed Him as •Messiah, he [b]would be
banned from the •synagogue. 23 This is
why his parents said, "He's of age; ask
him." *[a] Jn 7:13 [b] Jn 12:42*

24 So a second time they summoned
the man who had been blind and told
him, [a]"Give glory to God.[f] We know
that this man is a sinner!" *[a] Jos 7:19*

25 He answered, "Whether or not
He's a sinner, I don't know. One thing
I do know: I was blind, and now I can
see!"

[a]**8:59** Or *Jesus hid Himself* [b]**8:59** Other mss add *and having gone through their midst, He passed by* [c]**9:4** Other mss read *I* [d]**9:4** Other mss read *sent us* [e]**9:17** = the man who had been blind [f]**9:24** *Give glory to God* was a solemn charge to tell the truth; Jos 7:19.

26 Then they asked him, "What did He do to you? How did He open your eyes?"

27 "I already told you," he said, "and you didn't listen. Why do you want to hear it again? You don't want to become His disciples too, do you?"

28 They ridiculed him: "You're that man's disciple, but we're Moses' disciples. 29 We know that God has spoken to Moses. But this man—[a]we don't know where He's from!" *[a]Jn 1:10*

30 [a]"This is an amazing thing," the man told them. "You don't know where He is from, yet He opened my eyes! 31 We know that [b]God doesn't listen to sinners, but if anyone is God-fearing and does His will, He listens to him. 32 Throughout history[a] no one has ever heard of someone opening the eyes of a person born blind. 33 If this man were not from God, He wouldn't be able to do anything." *[a]Jn 3:10 [b]Pr 15:29; Is 1:15; Mc 3:4*

34 "You were born entirely in sin," they replied, "and are you trying to teach us?" Then they threw him out.[b]

The Blind Man's Sight and the Pharisees' Blindness

35 When Jesus heard that they had thrown the man out, He found him and asked, "Do you believe in [a]the •Son of Man?"[c] *[a]Mk 1:1; Jn 10:36*

36 "Who is He, Sir, that I may believe in Him?" he asked.

37 Jesus answered, "You have seen Him; in fact, [a]He is the One speaking with you." *[a]Jn 4:26*

38 "I believe, Lord!" he said, and he worshiped Him.

39 Jesus said, [a]"I came into this world for judgment, [b]in order that those who do not see will see and those who do see will become blind." *[a]Jn 5:22 [b]Mt 13:13*

40 Some of the Pharisees who were with Him heard these things and asked Him, "We aren't blind too, are we?"

41 [a]"If you were blind," Jesus told them, "you wouldn't have sin.[d] But now that you say, 'We see'—your sin remains. *[a]Jn 15:22*

The Ideal Shepherd

10 "•I assure you: Anyone who doesn't enter the sheep pen by the door but climbs in some other way, is a thief and a robber. 2 The one who enters by the door is the shepherd of the sheep. 3 The doorkeeper opens it for him, and the sheep hear his voice. He calls his own sheep by name and leads them out. 4 When he has brought all his own outside, he goes ahead of them. The sheep follow him because they recognize his voice. 5 They will never follow a stranger; instead they will run away from him, because they don't recognize the voice of strangers."

6 Jesus gave them this illustration, but they did not understand what He was telling them.

The Good Shepherd

7 So Jesus said again, "I assure you: I am [a]the door of the sheep. 8 [b]All who came before Me[e] are thieves and robbers, but the sheep didn't listen to them. 9 I am the door. If anyone enters by Me, he will be saved and will come in and go out and find pasture. 10 [c]A thief comes only to steal and to kill and to destroy. I have come that they may have life and have it in abundance. *[a]Eph 2:18; Heb 10:19 [b]Jr 23:1; Ezk 22:25 [c]Mt 7:15*

11 [a]"I am the good shepherd. The good shepherd lays down his life for the sheep. 12 The hired man, since he is not the shepherd and doesn't own the sheep, [b]leaves them[f] and runs

[a]**9:32** Lit *From the age* [b]**9:34** = they banned him from the synagogue; v. 22 [c]**9:35** Other mss read *the Son of God* [d]**9:41** To *have sin* is an idiom that refers to guilt caused by sin. [e]**10:8** Other mss omit *before Me* [f]**10:12** Lit *leaves the sheep*

away when he sees a wolf coming. The wolf then snatches and scatters them. 13 ⌊This happens⌋ because he is a hired man and doesn't care about the sheep.

[a] Is 40:11; 1Pt 2:25 [b] Zch 11:16

14 "I am the good shepherd. [a]I know My own sheep, and [b]they know Me, 15 as the Father knows Me, and I know the Father. I lay down My life for the sheep. 16 But I have [c]other sheep that are not of this fold; I must bring them also, and they will listen to My voice. [d]Then there will be one flock, one shepherd. 17 This is why the Father loves Me, [e]because I am laying down My life so I may take it up again. 18 No one takes it from Me, but I lay it down on My own. I have the right to lay it down, and I have the right to take it up again. [f]I have received this command from My Father."

[a] 2Tm 2:19 [b] Is 53:6-7 [c] Is 56:8 [d] Eph 2:14 [e] 2Co 5:15; Heb 2:9 [f] Ac 2:24

19 Again a division took place among the Jews because of these words. 20 Many of them were saying, "He has a demon and He's crazy! Why do you listen to Him?" 21 Others were saying, "These aren't the words of someone demon-possessed. [a]Can a demon open the eyes of the blind?"

[a] Ps 94:9; Is 35:4-5

Jesus at the Festival of Dedication

22 Then the Festival of Dedication[a] took place in Jerusalem, and it was winter. 23 Jesus was walking in the •temple complex in Solomon's Colonnade.[b] 24 Then the Jews surrounded Him and asked, "How long are You going to keep us in suspense?[c] If You are the •Messiah, tell us plainly."[d]

25 "I did tell you and you don't believe," Jesus answered them. "The works that I do in My Father's name testify about Me. 26 But [a]you don't believe because you are not My sheep.[e] 27 My sheep hear My voice, I know them, and they follow Me. 28 I give them eternal life, and they will never perish—ever! No one will snatch them out of My hand. 29 [b]My Father, who has given them to Me, is greater than all. No one is able to snatch them out of the Father's hand. 30 [c]The Father and I are one."[f]

[a] Jn 8:47 [b] Jn 14:28; 17:2,6 [c] Jn 1:1,14

Renewed Efforts to Stone Jesus

31 Again the Jews picked up rocks to stone Him.

32 Jesus replied, "I have shown you many good works from the Father. Which of these works are you stoning Me for?"

33 "We aren't stoning You for a good work," the Jews answered, "but for blasphemy, because You—being a man—[a]make Yourself God."

[a] Jn 5:18; Php 2:6

34 Jesus answered them, [a]"Isn't it written in your law,[g] **I said, you are gods?**[h] 35 If He called those whom the word of God came to 'gods'—and the Scripture cannot be broken— 36 do you say, 'You are blaspheming' to the One [b]the Father set apart and [c]sent into the world, because I said: I am [d]the Son of God? 37 [e]If I am not doing My Father's works, don't believe Me. 38 But if I am doing them and you don't believe Me, believe the works. This way you will know and understand[i] [f]that the Father is in Me and I in the Father." 39 Then they were trying again to seize Him, yet He eluded their grasp.

[a] Ps 82:6 [b] Jn 6:27 [c] Jn 3:17 [d] Jn 9:35 [e] Jn 15:24 [f] Jn 14:10

Many beyond the Jordan Believe in Jesus

40 So He departed again across the Jordan to the place [a]where John had

[a]**10:22** Or *Hanukkah*, also called *the Feast of Lights*; this festival commemorated the rededication of the temple in 164 B.C. [b]**10:23** Rows of columns supporting a roof [c]**10:24** Lit *How long are you taking away our life?* [d]**10:24** Or *openly*, or *publicly* [e]**10:26** Other mss add *just as I told you* [f]**10:30** Lit *I and the Father—We are one.* [g]**10:34** Other mss read *in the law* [h]**10:34** Ps 82:6 [i]**10:38** Other mss read *know and believe*

been baptizing earlier, and He remained there. 41 Many came to Him
and said, "John never did a sign, [b]but
everything John said about this man
was true." 42 And many believed in
Him there. [a] Jn 1:28 [b] Jn 1:15

Lazarus Dies at Bethany

11 Now a man was sick, Lazarus,
from Bethany, the village of
[a]Mary and her sister Martha. 2 [b]Mary
was the one who anointed the Lord
with fragrant oil and wiped His feet
with her hair, and it was her brother
Lazarus who was sick. 3 So the sisters
sent a message to Him: "Lord, the one
You love is sick." [a] Lk 10:38 [b] Mt 26:7

4 When Jesus heard it, He said, "This
sickness will not end in death but is
[a]for the glory of God, so that the Son of
God may be glorified through it."
5 (Jesus loved Martha, her sister, and
Lazarus.) 6 So when He heard that he
was sick, [b]He stayed two more days in
the place where He was. 7 Then after
that, He said to the disciples, "Let's go
to Judea again." [a] Jn 9:3 [b] Jn 10:40

8 "•Rabbi," the disciples told Him,
"just now [a]the Jews tried to stone You,
and You're going there again?" [a] Jn 10:31

9 "Aren't there 12 hours in a day?"
Jesus answered. [a]"If anyone walks during the day, he doesn't stumble, because he sees the light of this world.
10 [b]If anyone walks during the night,
he does stumble, because the light is
not in him." 11 He said this, and then
He told them, "Our friend Lazarus
[c]has fallen •asleep, but I'm on My way
to wake him up." [a] Pr 4:18; Jn 9:4
[b] Pr 4:18-19; Jn 12:35 [c] Mt 9:24

12 Then the disciples said to Him,
"Lord, if he has fallen asleep, he will
get well."

13 Jesus, however, was speaking
about his death, but they thought He
was speaking about natural sleep. 14 So
Jesus then told them plainly, "Lazarus
has died. 15 I'm glad for you that I
wasn't there so that you may believe.
But let's go to him."

16 Then Thomas (called "Twin") said
to his fellow disciples, "Let's go so that
we may die with Him."

The Resurrection and the Life

17 When Jesus arrived, He found that
Lazarus had already been in the tomb
four days. 18 Bethany was near Jerusalem (about two miles[a] away). 19 Many
of the Jews had come to Martha and
Mary to comfort them about their
brother. 20 As soon as Martha heard
that Jesus was coming, she went to
meet Him. But Mary remained seated
in the house.

21 Then Martha said to Jesus, "Lord,
if You had been here, my brother
wouldn't have died. 22 Yet even now I
know that [a]whatever You ask from
God, God will give You." [a] Mk 9:23-24

23 "Your brother will [a]rise again,"
Jesus told her. [a] Dn 12:2

24 Martha said, [a]"I know that he will
rise again in the resurrection at the last
day." [a] Jn 5:29

25 Jesus said to her, "I am [a]the resurrection and the [b]life. [c]The one who believes in Me, even if he dies, will live.
26 Everyone who lives and believes in
Me will never die—ever. Do you be-
lieve this?" [a] Jn 5:21 [b] Jn 1:4; 6:35 [c] Jn 3:36

27 "Yes, Lord," she told Him, [a]"I believe You are the •Messiah, the Son of
God, who was to come into the
world." [a] Mt 11:3; Jn 4:42

Jesus Shares the Sorrow of Death

28 Having said this, she went back
and called her sister Mary, saying in
private, "The Teacher is here and is
calling for you."

29 As soon as she heard this, she got
up quickly and went to Him. 30 Jesus

[a]**11:18** Lit *15 stadia*; 1 *stadion* = 600 feet

had not yet come into the village but was still in the place where Martha had met Him. 31 The Jews who were with her in the house consoling her saw that Mary got up quickly and went out. So they followed her, supposing that she was going to the tomb to cry there.

32 When Mary came to where Jesus was and saw Him, she fell at His feet and told Him, "Lord, if You had been here, my brother would not have died!"

33 When Jesus saw her crying, and the Jews who had come with her crying, He was angry[a] in His spirit and deeply moved. 34 "Where have you put him?" He asked.

"Lord," they told Him, "come and see."

35 Jesus wept.

36 So the Jews said, "See how He loved him!" 37 But some of them said, "Couldn't He [a]who opened the blind man's eyes also have kept this man from dying?"

[a] Jn 9:6

The Seventh Sign: Raising Lazarus from the Dead

38 Then Jesus, angry in Himself again, came to the tomb. It was a cave, and a stone was lying against it. 39 "Remove the stone," Jesus said.

Martha, the dead man's sister, told Him, "Lord, he already stinks. It's been four days."

40 Jesus said to her, "Didn't I tell you that if you believed you would see the glory of God?"

41 So they removed the stone. Then Jesus raised His eyes and said, "Father, I thank You that You heard Me. 42 I know that You always hear Me, but [a]because of the crowd standing here I said this, so they may believe You sent Me." 43 After He said this, He shouted with a loud voice, "Lazarus, come out!" 44 The dead man came out bound hand and foot with linen strips and with his face wrapped in a cloth. Jesus said to them, "Loose him and let him go."

[a] Jn 12:30

The Plot to Kill Jesus

45 Therefore many of the Jews who came to Mary and saw what He did believed in Him. 46 But some of them went to the •Pharisees and told them what Jesus had done.

47 [a]So the •chief priests and the Pharisees convened the •Sanhedrin and said, [b]"What are we going to do since this man does many signs? 48 If we let Him continue in this way, everybody will believe in Him! Then [c]the Romans will come and remove both our place[b] and our nation."

[a] Mt 26:3 [b] Jn 12:19 [c] Dn 9:26; Zch 13:7-8

49 One of them, [a]Caiaphas, who was high priest that year, said to them, "You know nothing at all! 50 [b]You're not considering that it is to your[c] advantage that one man should die for the people rather than the whole nation perish." 51 He did not say this on his own, but being high priest that year he prophesied that Jesus was going to die for the nation, 52 and [c]not for the nation only, [d]but also to unite the scattered children of God. 53 So from that day on they plotted to kill Him. 54 Therefore Jesus no longer walked openly among the Jews but departed from there to the countryside near the wilderness, to a town called [e]Ephraim. And He stayed there with the disciples.

[a] Lk 3:2 [b] Jn 18:14 [c] Is 49:6 [d] Jn 10:16 [e] 2Ch 13:19

55 The Jewish •Passover was near, and many went up to Jerusalem from the country [a]to purify[d] themselves before the Passover. 56 [b]They were looking for

[a]**11:33** The Gk word is very strong and probably indicates Jesus' anger against sin's tyranny and death.
[b]**11:48** The temple or possibly all of Jerusalem [c]**11:50** Other mss read *to our* [d]**11:55** The law of Moses required God's people to purify or cleanse themselves so they could celebrate the Passover. Jews often came to Jerusalem a week early to do this; Nm 9:4–11.

Jesus and asking one another as they stood in the •temple complex: [c]"What do you think? He won't come to the festival, will He?" 57 The chief priests and the Pharisees had given orders that if anyone knew where He was, he should report it so they could arrest Him. *[a]Ex 19:10 [b]Jn 7:11 [c]Ps 2*

The Anointing at Bethany

12 Six days before the •Passover, Jesus came to Bethany [a]where Lazarus[a] was, the one Jesus had raised from the dead. 2 [b]So they gave a dinner for Him there; Martha was serving them, and Lazarus was one of those reclining at the table with Him. 3 Then [c]Mary took a pound of fragrant oil—pure and expensive nard—anointed Jesus' feet, and wiped His feet with her hair. So the house was filled with the fragrance of the oil. *[a]Jn 11 [b]Mt 26:6 [c]Lk 10:38-39; Jn 11:2*

4 Then one of His disciples, Judas Iscariot (who was about to betray Him), said, 5 "Why wasn't this fragrant oil sold for 300 •denarii[b] and given to the poor?" 6 He didn't say this because he cared about the poor but because [a]he was a thief. He was in charge of the money-bag and would steal part of what was put in it. *[a]Pr 26:25; Jn 13:29*

7 Jesus answered, "Leave her alone; she has kept it for the day of My burial. 8 For you always have [a]the poor with you, but you do not always have Me." *[a]Mt 26:11; Mk 14:7*

The Decision to Kill Lazarus

9 Then a large crowd of the Jews learned He was there. They came not only because of Jesus, but also to see Lazarus the one He had raised from the dead. 10 Therefore the •chief priests decided to also kill Lazarus, 11 [a]because he was the reason many of the Jews were deserting them[c] and believing in Jesus. *[a]Mk 15:10; Jn 11:45*

The Triumphal Entry

12 [a]The next day, when the large crowd that had come to the festival heard that Jesus was coming to Jerusalem, 13 they took palm branches and went out to meet Him. They kept shouting: [b]"•***Hosanna!*** **Blessed is He who comes in the name of the Lord**[d] —the King of Israel!" *[a]Lk 19:35 [b]Ps 72:17-19; 118:25-26*

14 Jesus found a young donkey and sat on it, just as it is written: 15 [a]**Fear no more, Daughter Zion; look! your King is coming, sitting on a donkey's colt.**[e] *[a]Is 62:11; Zch 9:9*

16 His disciples [a]did not understand these things at first. [b]However, when Jesus was glorified, [c]then they remembered that these things had been written about Him and that they had done these things to Him. 17 Meanwhile the crowd, which had been with Him when He called Lazarus out of the tomb and raised him from the dead, continued to testify.[f] 18 This is also why the crowd met Him, because they heard He had done this sign. *[a]Lk 18:34 [b]Jn 7:39 [c]Jn 14:26*

19 Then the •Pharisees said to one another, "You see? You've accomplished nothing. Look—the world has gone after Him!"

Jesus Predicts His Crucifixion

20 Now some Greeks were among those [a]who went up to worship at the festival. 21 So they came to Philip, who was from Bethsaida in Galilee, and requested of him, "Sir, we want to see Jesus." *[a]1Kg 8:41; Is 2:3*

22 Philip went and told Andrew; then Andrew and Philip went and told

[a]**12:1** Other mss read *Lazarus who died* [b]**12:5** This amount was about a year's wages for a common worker. [c]**12:11** Lit *going away* [d]**12:13** Ps 118:25–26 [e]**12:15** Zch 9:9 [f]**12:17** Other mss read *Meanwhile the crowd, which had been with Him, continued to testify that He had called Lazarus out of the tomb and raised him from the dead.*

Jesus. 23 Jesus replied to them, [a]"The
hour has come for the •Son of Man to
be glorified. *[a] Jn 13:32*

24 "•I assure you: [a]Unless a grain of
wheat falls into the ground and dies, it
remains by itself. But if it dies, it produces a large crop.[a] 25 [b]The one who
loves his life will lose it, and the one
who hates his life in this world will
keep it for eternal life. 26 If anyone
serves Me, he must follow Me.
[c]Where I am, there My servant also
will be. If anyone serves Me, the Fa-
ther will honor him. *[a] 1Co 15:36 [b] Lk 9:24 [c] 1Th 4:17*

27 [a]"Now My soul is troubled. What
should I say—Father, save Me from this
hour? [b]But that is why I came to this
hour. 28 Father, glorify Your name!"[b] *[a] Lk 12:50 [b] Lk 22:53*

Then a voice came from heaven: "I
have glorified it, and I will glorify it
again!"
29 The crowd standing there heard it
and said it was thunder. Others said,
"An angel has spoken to Him!"
30 Jesus responded, [a]"This voice
came, not for Me, but for you. 31 Now
is the judgment of this world. Now
[b]the ruler of this world will be cast out.
32 As for Me, if I am lifted up[c] from the
earth I will draw [c]all ⌊people⌋ to Myself." 33 He said this to signify what
kind of death He was about to die. *[a] Jn 11:42 [b] Lk 10:18; Jn 14:30 [c] Rm 5:18*

34 Then the crowd replied to Him,
[a]"We have heard from the law that the
•Messiah will remain forever. So how
can You say, 'The Son of Man must be
lifted up'?[c] Who is this Son of Man?" *[a] Is 9:7*

35 Jesus answered, [a]"The light will
be with you only a little longer. Walk
while you have the light so that darkness doesn't overtake you. [b]The one
who walks in darkness doesn't know
where he's going. 36 While you have
the light, believe in the light so that
you may become [c]sons of light." Jesus
said this, then went away and hid from
them. *[a] Jn 1:5-9 [b] Jn 11:10 [c] Lk 16:8*

Isaiah's Prophecies Fulfilled

37 Even though He had performed so
many signs in their presence, they did
not believe in Him. 38 But this was to
fulfill the word of Isaiah the prophet,
who said:[d]

> [a]**Lord, who has believed**
> **our message?**
> **And who has the arm**
> **of the Lord been**
> **revealed to?**[e] *[a] Is 53:1*

39 This is why they were unable to
believe, because Isaiah also said:

> 40 [a]**He has blinded their eyes**
> **and hardened their hearts,**
> **so that they would not see**
> **with their eyes**
> **or understand**
> **with their hearts,**
> **and be converted,**
> **and I would heal them.**[f]

41 [b]Isaiah said these things because[g] he
saw His glory and spoke about Him. *[a] Is 6:9-10; Mt 13:14 [b] Is 6:1*

42 Nevertheless, many did believe in
Him even among the rulers, but because of the Pharisees they did not
confess Him, so they would not be
banned from the •synagogue. 43 [a]For
they loved praise from men more than
praise from God.[h] *[a] Lk 16:15*

A Summary of Jesus' Mission

44 Then Jesus cried out, [a]"The one
who believes in Me believes not in
Me, but in Him who sent Me. 45 And
[b]the one who sees Me sees Him who
sent Me. 46 [c]I have come as a light into

[a]**12:24** Lit *produces much fruit* [b]**12:28** Other mss read *Your Son* [c]**12:32,34** Or *exalted* [d]**12:38** Lit *which he said* [e]**12:38** Is 53:1 [f]**12:40** Is 6:10 [g]**12:41** Other mss read *when* [h]**12:43** Lit *loved glory of men more than glory of God*; v. 41; Jn 5:41

the world, so that everyone who believes in Me would not remain in darkness. 47 If anyone hears My words and
doesn't keep them, [d]I do not judge
him; for [e]I did not come to judge the
world but to save the world. 48 [f]The
one who rejects Me and doesn't accept
My sayings has this as his judge:[a] [g]the
word I have spoken will judge him on
the last day. 49 For [h]I have not spoken
on My own, but the Father Himself
who sent Me has given Me a command
as to what I should say and what I
should speak. 50 I know that His command is eternal life. So the things that
I speak, I speak just as the Father has
told Me." *[a] Mt 10:40; Jn 13:20*
[b] Jn 14:9 [c] Jn 3:19 [d] Jn 5:45 [e] Jn 3:17
[f] Lk 10:16 [g] Mk 16:16 [h] Jn 8:38

Jesus Washes His Disciples' Feet

13 Before the •Passover Festival,
Jesus knew that His hour had
come to depart from this world to the
Father. Having loved His own who
were in the world, He loved them to
the end.[b]

2 Now by the time of supper, [a]the
Devil had already put it into the heart
of Judas, Simon Iscariot's son, to betray
Him. 3 Jesus knew [b]that the Father had
given everything into His hands, that
He had come from God, and that He
was going back to God. 4 [c]So He got up
from supper, laid aside His robe, took a
towel, and tied it around Himself.
5 Next, He poured water into a basin
and began to wash His disciples' feet
and to dry them with the towel tied
around Him. *[a] Lk 22:3 [b] Jn 3:35*
[c] Lk 22:27

6 He came to Simon Peter, who asked
Him, "Lord, [a]are You going to wash my
feet?" *[a] Mt 3:14*

7 Jesus answered him, "What I'm doing you don't understand now, but afterwards you will know."

8 "You will never wash my feet—
ever!" Peter said.

Jesus replied, [a]"If I don't wash you,
you have no part with Me."
[a] Is 52:15; 1Co 6:11

9 Simon Peter said to Him, "Lord, not
only my feet, but also my hands and
my head."

10 "One who has bathed," Jesus told
him, "doesn't need to wash anything
except his feet, but he is completely
clean. [a]You are clean, but not all of
you." 11 For He knew who would betray Him. This is why He said, "You are
not all clean." *[a] Jn 15:3*

The Meaning of Footwashing

12 When Jesus had washed their feet
and put on His robe, He reclined[c] again
and said to them, "Do you know what
I have done for you? 13 [a]You call Me
Teacher and Lord. This is well said, for
I am. 14 [b]So if I, your Lord and Teacher,
have washed your feet, [c]you also ought
to wash one another's feet. 15 For [d]I
have given you an example that you
also should do just as I have done for
you. *[a] 1Co 8:6 [b] Lk 22:27 [c] Php 2:2-5 [d] 1Pt 2:21*

16 [a]"•I assure you: A slave is not
greater than his master,[d] and a messenger is not greater than the one who
sent him. 17 If you know these things,
you are blessed [b]if you do them. 18 I'm
not speaking about all of you; [c]I know
those I have chosen. But the Scripture
must be fulfilled: [d]**The one who eats
My bread[e] has raised his heel against
Me.**[f] *[a] Lk 6:40 [b] Jms 1:25*
[c] Jn 17:12 [d] Ps 41:9

19 "I am telling you now before it
happens, so that when it does happen
you will believe that I am ⌊He⌋. 20 [a]I assure you: The one who receives
whomever I send receives Me, and the
one who receives Me receives Him
who sent Me." *[a] Lk 10:16*

[a]**12:48** Lit *has the one judging him* [b]**13:1** *to the end* = *completely* or *always* [c]**13:12** At important meals the custom was to recline on a mat at a low table and lean on the left elbow. [d]**13:16** Or *lord* [e]**13:18** Other mss read *eats bread with Me* [f]**13:18** Ps 41:9

Judas' Betrayal Predicted

21 [a]When Jesus had said this, He was
troubled in His spirit and testified, "I
assure you: [b]One of you will betray
Me!" [a]*Lk 22:21* [b]*Ac 1:17*

22 The disciples started looking at
one another—uncertain which one He
was speaking about. 23 One of His disciples, the [a]one Jesus loved, was reclining close beside Jesus.[a] 24 Simon Peter
motioned to him to find out who it was
He was talking about. 25 So he leaned
back against Jesus and asked Him,
"Lord, who is it?" [a]*Jn 19:26*

26 Jesus replied, "He's the one I give
the piece of bread to after I have
dipped it." When He had dipped the
bread, He gave it to Judas, Simon Iscariot's son.[b] 27 [a]After ⌊Judas ate⌋ the piece
of bread, Satan entered him. Therefore
Jesus told him, "What you're doing, do
quickly." [a]*Lk 22:3; Jn 6:70*

28 None of those reclining at the table knew why He told him this.
29 Since [a]Judas kept the money-bag,
some thought that Jesus was telling
him, "Buy what we need for the festival," or that he should give something
to the poor. 30 After receiving the piece
of bread, he went out immediately.
And it was night. [a]*Jn 12:6*

The New Commandment

31 When he had gone out, Jesus said,
"Now the •Son of Man is glorified, and
[a]God is glorified in Him. 32 [b]If God is
glorified in Him,[c] God will also glorify
Him in Himself and will glorify Him at
once. [a]*Jn 14:13* [b]*Jn 17:1*

33 "Children, I am with you a little
while longer. You will look for Me, and
just as I told the Jews, 'Where I am going you cannot come,' so now I tell
you.

34 [a]"I give you a new commandment:
love one another. Just as I have loved
you, you must also love one another.
35 By this all people will know that you
are My disciples, if you have love for
one another." [a]*Lv 19:18; Eph 5:2*

Peter's Denials Predicted

36 "Lord," Simon Peter said to Him,
"where are You going?"

Jesus answered, "Where I am going
you cannot follow Me now, [a]but you
will follow later." [a]*Jn 21:18; 2Pt 1:14*

37 "Lord," Peter asked, "why can't I
follow You now? I will [a]lay down my
life for You!" [a]*Lk 22:33*

38 Jesus replied, "Will you lay down
your life for Me? I assure you: A
rooster will not crow until you have
denied Me three times.

The Way to the Father

14 "Your heart must not be troubled. Believe[d] in God; believe
also in Me. 2 [a]In My Father's house are
many dwelling places;[e] if not, I would
have told you. [b]I am going away to prepare a place for you. 3 If I go away and
prepare a place for you, [c]I will come
back and receive you to Myself, so that
[d]where I am you may be also. 4 You
know the way where I am going."[f]
[a]*2Co 5:1* [b]*Jn 13:33* [c]*Mt 25:32-34* [d]*Jn 12:26; 17:24*

5 "Lord," Thomas said, "we don't
know where You're going. How can
we know the way?"

6 Jesus told him, "I am [a]the way, [b]the
truth, and [c]the life. [d]No one comes to
the Father except through Me.
[a]*Mt 11:27* [b]*Jn 1:17* [c]*Jn 1:4* [d]*Jn 10:9*

Jesus Reveals the Father

7 "If you know Me, you will also
know[g] My Father. From now on you do
know Him and have seen Him."

[a]**13:23** Lit *reclining at Jesus' breast*; that is, on His right; Jn 1:18 [b]**13:26** Other mss read *Judas Iscariot, Simon's son* [c]**13:32** Other mss omit *If God is glorified in Him* [d]**14:1** Or *You believe* [e]**14:2** The Vg used the Lat term *mansio*, a traveler's resting place. The Gk word is related to the verb *meno*, meaning *remain* or *stay*, which occurs 40 times in John. [f]**14:4** Other mss read this verse: *And you know where I am going, and you know the way* [g]**14:7** Other mss read *If you had known Me, you would have known*

8 "Lord," said Philip, "show us the
Father, and that's enough for us."
9 Jesus said to him, "Have I been
among you all this time without your
knowing Me, Philip? [a]The one who
has seen Me has seen the Father. How
can you say, 'Show us the Father'?
10 Don't you believe that [b]I am in the
Father and the Father is in Me? [c]The
words I speak to you I do not speak on
My own. The Father who lives in Me
does His works. 11 Believe Me that I am
in the Father and the Father is in Me.
Otherwise, believe[a] because of the
works themselves.

a Col 1:15; Heb 1:3 b Jn 10:38 c Jn 5:19

Praying in Jesus' Name

12 "•I assure you: The one who believes in Me will also do the works that
I do. And he will do even greater works
than these, because I am going to the
Father. 13 [a]Whatever you ask in My
name, I will do it so that the Father may
be glorified in the Son. 14 If you ask Me[b]
anything in My name, I will do it.[c]

a Mt 7:7-8; Jn 15:7,16

Another Counselor Promised

15 [a]"If you love Me, you will keep[d]
My commandments. 16 And I will ask
the Father, and [b]He will give you another •Counselor to be with you forever. 17 He is the Spirit of truth. [c]The
world is unable to receive Him because it doesn't see Him or know Him.
But you do know Him, because He remains with you [d]and will be[e] in you.
18 I will not leave you as orphans; I am
coming to you.

a Mt 10:37 b Rm 8:15 c Rm 8:7 d 1Jn 2:27

The Father, the Son, and the Holy Spirit

19 "In a little while the world will see
Me no longer, but [a]you will see Me.
[b]Because I live, you will live too. 20 In
that day you will know that [c]I am in My
Father, you are in Me, and I am in you.
21 The one who has My commands and
keeps them is the one who loves Me.
And the one who loves Me will be
loved by My Father. I also will love him
and will reveal Myself to him."

a Jn 16:16 b 1Co 15:20 c Jn 10:38

22 Judas (not Iscariot) said to Him,
"Lord, how is it You're going to reveal
Yourself to us and not to the world?"
23 Jesus answered, "If anyone loves
Me, he will keep My word. My Father
will love him, and [a]We will come to
him and make Our home with him.
24 The one who doesn't love Me will
not keep My words. [b]The word that
you hear is not Mine but is from the
Father who sent Me.

a 1Jn 2:24 b Jn 7:16

25 "I have spoken these things to you
while I remain with you. 26 But [a]the
Counselor, the Holy Spirit—the Father
will send Him in My name—[b]will
teach you all things and remind you of
everything I have told you.

a Lk 24:49 b 1Jn 2:27

Jesus' Gift of Peace

27 [a]"Peace I leave with you. My peace
I give to you. I do not give to you as the
world gives. Your heart must not be
troubled or fearful. 28 You have heard
Me tell you, 'I am going away and I am
coming to you.' If you loved Me, you
would have rejoiced that I am going to
the Father, because [b]the Father is
greater than I. 29 I have told you now before it happens so that when it does
happen you may believe. 30 I will not
talk with you much longer, [c]because the
ruler of the world is coming. [d]He has no
power over Me.[f] 31 On the contrary, ⌊I
am going away⌋[g] so that the world may
know that I love the Father. [e]Just as the
Father commanded Me, so I do.

a Php 4:7 b 1Co 11:3 c Jn 12:31 d 1Jn 3:5 e Php 2:8

"Get up; let's leave this place.

[a]**14:11** Other mss read *believe Me* [b]**14:14** Other mss omit *Me* [c]**14:14** Other mss omit all of v. 14 [d]**14:15** Other mss read *If you love Me, keep* (as a command) [e]**14:17** Other mss read *and is* [f]**14:30** Lit *He has nothing in Me* [g]**14:31** Probably refers to the cross

The Vine and the Branches

15 “I am the true vine, and My Father is the vineyard keeper.
2 [a]Every branch in Me that does not
produce fruit He removes, and He
prunes every branch that produces
fruit so that it will produce more fruit.
3 [b]You are already clean because of the
word I have spoken to you. 4 [c]Remain
in Me, and I in you. Just as a branch is
unable to produce fruit by itself unless
it remains on the vine, so neither can
you unless you remain in Me. *[a]Mt 15:13*
[b]Jn 13:10 [c]Eph 2:21-22

5 “I am the vine; you are the
branches. The one who remains in Me
and I in him produces much [a]fruit, because you can do nothing without Me.
6 [b]If anyone does not remain in Me, he
is thrown aside like a branch and he
withers. They gather them, throw
them into the fire, and they are
burned. 7 If you remain in Me and My
words remain in you, ask whatever
you want and it will be done for you.
8 [c]My Father is glorified by this: that
you produce much fruit and prove to
be[a] My disciples. *[a]Pr 11:30; Lk 13:6-9*
[b]Heb 6:4-6 [c]Mt 5:16

Christlike Love

9 “As the Father has loved Me, I have
also loved you. Remain in My love. 10 If
you keep My commands you will remain in My love, just as I have kept My
Father’s commands and remain in His
love.

11 “I have spoken these things to you
so that My joy may be in you and your
joy may be complete. 12 [a]This is My
command: love one another as I have
loved you. 13 [b]No one has greater love
than this, that someone would lay
down his life for his friends. 14 You are
My friends if you do what I command
you. 15 I do not call you slaves anymore,
because a slave doesn’t know what his
master[b] is doing. I have called you
friends, [c]because I have made known
to you everything I have heard from
My Father. 16 [d]You did not choose Me,
but I chose you. I [e]appointed you that
you should go out and produce fruit
and that your fruit should remain, so
that whatever you ask the Father in My
name, He will give you. 17 This is what
I command you: love one another.
[a]1Th 4:9 [b]Rm 5:7; Eph 5:2 [c]Mt 13:11
[d]1Jn 4:10 [e]Mk 16:15

Persecutions Predicted

18 [a]“If the world hates you, understand that it hated Me before it hated
you. 19 [b]If you were of the world, the
world would love ⌊you as⌋ its own.
However, [c]because you are not of the
world, but I have chosen you out of it,
the world hates you. 20 Remember the
word I spoke to you: ‘A slave is not
greater than his master.’ If they persecuted Me, they will also persecute you.
If they kept My word, they will also
keep yours. 21 But they will do all these
things to you on account of My name,
because they don’t know the One who
sent Me. 22 [d]If I had not come and spoken to them, they would not have sin.[c]
[e]Now they have no excuse for their
sin. 23 [f]The one who hates Me also
hates My Father. 24 If I had not done
the works among them that no one
else has done, they would not have sin.
Now they have seen and hated both
Me and My Father. 25 But ⌊this hap-
pened⌋ so that the statement written in
their law might be fulfilled: [g]**They
hated Me for no reason.**[d]
[a]1Jn 3:1 [b]1Jn 4:5 [c]Jn 17:14 [d]Jn 9:41
[e]Rm 1:20 [f]1Jn 2:23 [g]Ps 69:4

Coming Testimony and Rejection

26 [a]“When the •Counselor comes,
the One I will send to you from the Father—the Spirit of truth who proceeds
from the Father—[b]He will testify

[a]**15:8** Or *and become* [b]**15:15** Or *lord* [c]**15:22** To *have sin* is an idiom that refers to guilt caused by sin.
[d]**15:25** Ps 69:4

about Me. 27 [c]You also will testify, because [d]you have been with Me from the beginning.

[a] Jn 14:26 [b] 1Jn 5:6 [c] Ac 1:8 [d] Lk 1:2

16 "I have told you these things to keep you from stumbling. 2 They will ban you from the •synagogues. In fact, a time is coming when anyone who kills you will think he is offering service to God. 3 They will do [a]these things because they haven't known the Father or Me. 4 But I have told you these things so that when their time[a] comes you may remember I told them to you. I didn't tell you these things from the beginning, because I was with you.

[a] Rm 10:2

The Counselor's Ministry

5 "But now I am going away to Him who sent Me, and not one of you asks Me, 'Where are You going?' 6 Yet, because I have spoken these things to you, sorrow has filled your heart. 7 Nevertheless, I am telling you the truth. It is for your benefit that I go away, because if I don't go away the •Counselor will not come to you. [a]If I go, I will send Him to you. 8 When He comes, He will convict the world about sin, righteousness, and judgment: 9 [b]about sin, because they do not believe in Me; 10 [c]about righteousness, because I am going to the Father and you will no longer see Me; 11 and [d]about judgment, because [e]the ruler of this world has been judged.

[a] Ac 2:33 [b] Ac 2:22 [c] Ac 2:32; 1Co 1:30 [d] Mt 12:18,36 [e] Jn 12:31

12 "I still have many things to tell you, but you can't bear them now. 13 When the Spirit of truth comes, [a]He will guide you into all the truth. For He will not speak on His own, but He will speak whatever He hears. He will also [b]declare to you what is to come. 14 He will glorify Me, because He will take from what is Mine and declare it to you. 15 [c]Everything the Father has is Mine. This is why I told you that He takes from what is Mine and will declare it to you.

[a] Jn 14:26 [b] 1Tm 4:1 [c] Mt 11:27; Jn 17:10

Sorrow Turned to Joy

16 "A little while and you will no longer see Me; again a little while and you will see Me."[b]

17 Therefore some of His disciples said to one another, "What is this He tells us: 'A little while and you will not see Me; again a little while and you will see Me'; and, 'because I am going to the Father'?" 18 They said, "What is this He is saying,[c] 'A little while'? We don't know what He's talking about!"

19 Jesus knew they wanted to question Him, so He said to them, "Are you asking one another about what I said, 'A little while and you will not see Me; again a little while and you will see Me'?

20 "•I assure you: You will weep and wail, but the world will rejoice. You will become sorrowful, but your sorrow will turn to joy. 21 When a woman is in labor she has pain because her time has come. But when she has given birth to a child, she no longer remembers the suffering because of the joy that a person has been born into the world. 22 So you also have sorrow[d] now. But I will see you again. [a]Your hearts will rejoice, and no one will rob you of your joy. 23 In that day you will not ask Me anything.

[a] Lk 24:41; Jn 20:20

[a]"I assure you: Anything you ask the Father in My name, He will give you. 24 Until now you have asked for nothing in My name. Ask and you will receive, that your joy may be complete.

[a] Jn 14:13

Jesus the Victor

25 "I have spoken these things to you in figures of speech. A time is coming

[a]**16:4** Other mss read *when the time* [b]**16:16** Other mss add *because I am going to the Father* [c]**16:18** Other mss omit *He is saying* [d]**16:22** Other mss read *will have sorrow*

when I will no longer speak to you in
figures, but I will tell you plainly about
the Father. 26 In that day you will ask in
My name. I am not telling you that I will
make requests to the Father on your behalf. 27 [a]For the Father Himself loves
you, because you have loved Me [b]and
have believed that I came from God.[a]
28 [c]I came from the Father and have
come into the world. Again, I am leaving the world and going to the Father."

[a] Jd 20-21 [b] Jn 3:13 [c] Jn 13:3

29 "Ah!" His disciples said. "Now
You're speaking plainly and not using
any figurative language. 30 Now we
know that [a]You know everything and
don't need anyone to question You. By
this [b]we believe that You came from
God."

[a] Jn 21:17 [b] Jn 17:8

31 Jesus responded to them, "Do you
now believe? 32 Look: An hour is coming, and has come, when each of you
will be scattered to his own home, and
you will leave Me alone. Yet I am not
alone, because the Father is with Me.
33 I have told you these things so that
[a]in Me you may have peace. [b]You will
have suffering in this world. Be coura-
geous! [c]I have conquered the world."

[a] Jn 14:27 [b] Mt 10:38 [c] Rm 8:37; 1Co 15:27

Jesus Prays for Himself

17 Jesus spoke these things, looked
up to heaven, and said:

Father,
the hour has come.
Glorify Your Son
so that the Son may glorify You,
2 [a]for You gave Him authority
over all flesh;[b]
so He may give eternal life
[b]to all You have given Him.
3 [c]This is eternal life:
that they may know You,
the only true God,
and the One
You have sent—Jesus Christ.
4 I have glorified You on the earth
by completing the work
You gave Me to do.
5 Now, Father, glorify Me
in Your presence
with that glory [d]I had with You
before the world existed.

[a] Mt 11:27; Php 2:10 [b] Jn 6:37 [c] Is 53:11 [d] Jn 1:1

Jesus Prays for His Disciples

6 [a]I have revealed Your name
to the men You gave Me
from the world.
They were Yours, You gave them
to Me,
and they have kept Your word.
7 Now they know that all things
You have given to Me are
from You,
8 because the words that You
gave Me,
I have given them.
They have received them
and have known for certain
that I came from You.
They have believed
that You sent Me.
9 [b]I pray[c] for them.
I am not praying for the world
but for those You have given Me,
because they are Yours.
10 [c]All My things are Yours,
and Yours are Mine,
and I have been glorified
in them.

[a] Ps 22:22 [b] 1Jn 5:19 [c] Rm 8:30

11 I am no longer in the world,
but they are in the world,
and I am coming to You.
Holy Father,
protect[d] them by Your name
that You have given Me,
so that they may be one
as [a]We are one.
12 While I was with them,
[b]I was protecting them
by Your name

[a]**16:27** Other mss read *from the Father* [b]**17:2** Or *people* [c]**17:9** Lit *ask* (throughout this passage)
[d]**17:11** Lit *keep* (throughout this passage)

that You have given Me.
I guarded them and [c]not one
of them is lost,
[d]except the son of destruction,[a]
[e]so that the Scripture may be
fulfilled. *[a] Jn 10:30 [b] Jn 10:28 [c] Jn 18:9 [d] Jn 13:18 [e] Ac 1:20*

13 Now I am coming to You,
and I speak these things
in the world
so that they may have My joy
completed in them.
14 I have given them Your word.
The world hated them
because they are not
of the world,
as I am not of the world.
15 I am not praying
[a]that You take them
out of the world
but that You protect them
from the evil one.
16 They are not of the world,
as I am not of the world.
17 Sanctify[b] them by the truth;
Your word is truth.
18 As You sent Me into the world,
I also have sent them
into the world.
19 [b]I sanctify Myself for them,
so they also may be sanctified
by the truth. *[a] Gl 1:4 [b] Heb 10:10*

Jesus Prays for All Believers

20 I pray not only for these,
but also for those who believe
in Me
through their message.
21 May they all be one,
as [a]You, Father, are in Me
and I am in You.
May they also be one[c] in Us,
so the world may believe
You sent Me.
22 I have given them the glory
You have given Me.
[b]May they be one as We are one.
23 I am in them and You are in Me.
[c]May they be made
completely one,
so the world may know You have
sent Me
and have loved them as
You have loved Me. *[a] Jn 10:38 [b] 1Jn 1:3 [c] Rm 12:5; Gl 3:28*

24 [a]Father,
I desire those You have given Me
to be with Me where I am.
Then they will [b]see My glory,
which You have given Me
because You loved Me
before the world's foundation.
25 Righteous Father!
The world has not known You.
However, I have known You,
and these have known
that You sent Me.
26 I made Your name known
to them
and will make it known,
so the love
You have loved Me with
may be in them and [c]I may be
in them. *[a] 1Th 4:17 [b] 1Jn 3:2 [c] Eph 3:17*

Jesus Betrayed

18 After Jesus had said these
things, He [a]went out with His
disciples across the Kidron Valley,
where there was a garden, and He and
His disciples went into it. 2 Judas, who
betrayed Him, also knew the place,
[b]because Jesus often met there with
His disciples. 3 [c]So Judas took a •com-
pany of soldiers and some temple police from the •chief priests and the
•Pharisees and came there with lan-
terns, torches, and weapons.
[a] Lk 22:39 [b] Lk 21:37 [c] Mt 26:47

4 Then Jesus, knowing everything
that was about to happen to Him, went
out and said to them, "Who is it you're
looking for?"

[a]**17:12** The one destined for destruction, loss, or perdition [b]**17:17** Set apart for special use [c]**17:21** Other mss omit *one*

5 “Jesus the •Nazarene,” they answered.
“I am He,”[a] Jesus told them.
Judas, who betrayed Him, was also
standing with them. 6 When He told
them, “I am He,” they stepped back
and fell to the ground.
7 Then He asked them again, “Who
is it you’re looking for?”
“Jesus the Nazarene,” they said.
8 “I told you I am ⌊He⌋,” Jesus replied.
“So if you’re looking for Me, let these
men go.” 9 This was to fulfill the words
He had said: [a]“I have not lost one of
those You have given Me.” *[a] Jn 6:39*

10 [a]Then Simon Peter, who had a
sword, drew it, struck the high priest’s
slave, and cut off his right ear. (The
slave’s name was Malchus.) *[a] Lk 22:49*

11 At that, Jesus said to Peter,
“Sheathe your sword! Am I not to
drink [a]the cup the Father has given
Me?” *[a] Mt 20:22*

Jesus Arrested and Taken to Annas

12 Then the company of soldiers, the
commander, and the Jewish temple
police arrested Jesus and tied Him up.
13 [a]First they led Him to [b]Annas, for he
was the father-in-law of Caiaphas, who
was high priest that year. 14 [c]Caia-
phas was the one who had advised the
Jews that it was advantageous that one
man should die for the people. *[a] Mt 26:57 [b] Lk 3:2 [c] Jn 11:50*

Peter Denies Jesus

15 Meanwhile Simon Peter was following Jesus, as was another disciple.
That disciple was an acquaintance of
the high priest; so he went with Jesus
into the high priest’s courtyard. 16 But
Peter remained standing outside by
the door. So the other disciple, the one
known to the high priest, went out and
spoke to the girl who was the doorkeeper and brought Peter in.
17 Then the slave girl who was the
doorkeeper said to Peter, “You aren’t
one of this man’s disciples too, are
you?”
“I am not!” he said. 18 Now the
slaves and the temple police had made
a charcoal fire, because it was cold.
They were standing there warming
themselves, and Peter was standing
with them, warming himself.

Jesus before Annas

19 The high priest questioned Jesus
about His disciples and about His
teaching.

20 [a]“I have spoken openly to the
world,” Jesus answered him. “I have
always taught in the •synagogue and in
the •temple complex, where all the
Jews congregate, and I haven’t spoken
anything in secret. 21 Why do you question Me? Question those who heard
what I told them. Look, they know
what I said.” *[a] Mt 26:55*

22 When He had said these things,
one of the temple police standing by
[a]slapped Jesus, saying, “Is this the way
you answer the high priest?” *[a] Is 50:6*

23 [a]“If I have spoken wrongly,” Jesus
answered him, “give evidence[b] about
the wrong; but if rightly, why do you
hit Me?” *[a] Heb 12:3*

24 Then Annas sent Him bound to
Caiaphas the high priest.

Peter Denies Jesus Twice More

25 Now Simon Peter was standing
and warming himself. [a]They said to
him, “You aren’t one of His disciples
too, are you?” *[a] Mk 14:69*

He denied it and said, “I am not!”
26 One of the high priest’s slaves, a
relative of the man whose ear Peter
had cut off, said, “Didn’t I see you with
Him in the garden?”
27 Peter then denied it again. [a]Im-
mediately a rooster crowed.
[a] Mt 26:74; Jn 13:38

[a]**18:5** Lit *I am*; see note at Jn 8:58 [b]**18:23** Or *him, testify*

Jesus before Pilate

28 [a]Then they took Jesus from Caiaphas to the governor's •headquarters. It was early morning. They did not enter the headquarters themselves; otherwise they would be defiled and unable to eat the •Passover. *[a] Mt 27:2*

29 Then •Pilate came out to them and said, "What charge do you bring against this man?"

30 They answered him, "If this man weren't a criminal,[a] we wouldn't have handed Him over to you."

31 So Pilate told them, "Take Him yourselves and judge Him according to your law."

"It's not legal[b] for us to put anyone to death," the Jews declared. 32 They said this [a]so that Jesus' words might be fulfilled signifying what sort of death He was going to die. *[a] Mt 20:19*

33 Then Pilate went back into the headquarters, summoned Jesus, and said to Him, "Are You the King of the Jews?"

34 Jesus answered, "Are you asking this on your own, or have others told you about Me?"

35 "I'm not a Jew, am I?" Pilate replied. "Your own nation and the chief priests handed You over to me. What have You done?"

36 [a]"My kingdom is not of this world," said [b]Jesus. "If My kingdom were of this world, My servants[c] would fight, so that I wouldn't be handed over to the Jews. As it is, My kingdom does not have its origin here."[d] *[a] Is 9:6 [b] 1Tm 6:13*

37 "You are a king then?" Pilate asked.

"You say that I'm a king," Jesus replied. "I was born for this, and I have come into the world for this: [a]to testify to the truth. Everyone who [b]is of the truth listens to My voice." *[a] Is 55:4; Rv 1:5 [b] Jn 8:47*

38 "What is truth?" said Pilate.

Jesus or Barabbas

After he had said this, he went out to the Jews again and told them, [a]"I find no grounds for charging Him. 39 You have a custom that I release one ⌊prisoner⌋ to you at the Passover. So, do you want me to release to you the King of the Jews?" *[a] Mt 27; Mk 15; Lk 23; Jn 19:4,6*

40 They shouted back, "Not this man, but Barabbas!" [a]Now Barabbas was a revolutionary.[e] *[a] Lk 23:19*

Jesus Flogged and Mocked

19 Then [a]•Pilate took Jesus and had Him flogged. 2 The soldiers also twisted together a crown of thorns, put it on His head, and threw a purple robe around Him. 3 And they repeatedly came up to Him and said, "Hail, King of the Jews!" and were slapping His face. *[a] Mt 20:19; Mk 15:15; Lk 18:33*

4 Pilate went outside again and said to them, "Look, I'm bringing Him outside to you [a]to let you know I find no grounds for charging Him." *[a] Jn 18:38*

Pilate Sentences Jesus to Death

5 Then Jesus came out wearing the crown of thorns and the purple robe. Pilate said to them, "Here is the man!"

6 [a]When the •chief priests and the temple police saw Him, they shouted, "Crucify! Crucify!" *[a] Ac 3:13*

Pilate responded, "Take Him and crucify Him yourselves, for I find no grounds for charging Him."

7 [a]"We have a law," the Jews replied to him, "and according to that law He must die, because [b]He made Himself[f] the Son of God." *[a] Lv 24:16 [b] Mt 26:65*

8 When Pilate heard this statement, he was more afraid than ever. 9 He went back into the •headquarters and asked Jesus, "Where are You from?"

[a]**18:30** Lit *an evil doer* [b]**18:31** According to Roman law [c]**18:36** Or *attendants*, or *helpers* [d]**18:36** Lit *My kingdom is not from here* [e]**18:40** Or *robber*; see Jn 10:1,8 for the same Gk word used here [f]**19:7** He claimed to be

[a]But Jesus did not give him an answer.
10 So Pilate said to Him, "You're not
talking to me? Don't You know that I
have the authority to release You and
the authority to crucify You?"
[a] *Is 53:7; Mt 27:12,14*

11 [a]"You would have no authority
over Me at all," Jesus answered him,
"if it hadn't been given you from
above. This is why the one who
handed Me over to you has the greater
sin."[a]
[a] *Ac 2:23*

12 From that moment Pilate made
every effort[b] to release Him. But the
Jews shouted, [a]"If you release this
man, you are not Caesar's friend. Anyone who makes himself a king op-
poses Caesar!"
[a] *Lk 23:2*

13 When Pilate heard these words,
he brought Jesus outside. He sat down
on the judge's bench in a place called
the Stone Pavement (but in Hebrew
Gabbatha). 14 [a]It was the preparation
day for the •Passover, and it was about
six in the morning.[c] Then he told the
Jews, "Here is your king!"
[a] *Mt 27:62*

15 But they shouted, "Take Him
away! Take Him away! Crucify Him!"

Pilate said to them, "Should I crucify
your king?"

"We have no king but Caesar!" the
chief priests answered.

16 [a]So then, because of them, he
handed Him over to be crucified.
[a] *Mt 27:26,31; Mk 15:15; Lk 23:24*

The Crucifixion

Therefore they took Jesus away.[d]
17 Carrying His own cross, [a]He went
out to what is called Skull Place, which
in Hebrew is called *Golgotha*. 18 [b]There
they crucified Him and two others with
Him, one on either side, with Jesus in
the middle. 19 Pilate also had a sign let-
tered and put on the cross. The inscription was:
[a] *1Kg 21:13; Lk 23:33; Heb 13:12* [b] *Is 53:12; Gl 3:13*

JESUS THE NAZARENE
THE KING OF THE JEWS

20 Many of the Jews read this sign,
because the place where Jesus was crucified was near the city, and it was
written in Hebrew,[e] Latin, and Greek.
21 So the chief priests of the Jews said
to Pilate, "Don't write, 'The King of
the Jews,' but that He said, 'I am the
King of the Jews.'"

22 Pilate replied, "What I have written, I have written."

23 When the soldiers crucified Jesus,
they took His clothes and divided them
into four parts, a part for each soldier.
They also took the tunic, which was
seamless, woven in one piece from the
top. 24 So they said to one another,
"Let's not tear it, but toss for it, to see
who gets it." ⌊They did this⌋ to fulfill
the Scripture that says: [a]**They divided
My clothes among themselves, and
they cast lots for My clothing.**[f] And
this is what the soldiers did.
[a] *Ps 22:18; Mt 27:35*

Jesus' Provision for His Mother

25 Standing by the cross of Jesus were
His mother, His mother's sister, Mary
the wife of Clopas, and •Mary
Magdalene. 26 When Jesus saw His
mother and [a]the disciple He loved
standing there, He said to His mother,
"•Woman, here is your son." 27 Then
He said to the disciple, "Here is your
mother." And from that hour the disciple took her into his home.
[a] *Jn 13:23*

The Finished Work of Jesus

28 After this, when Jesus knew that
everything was now accomplished

[a]**19:11** To *have sin* is an idiom that refers to guilt caused by sin. [b]**19:12** Lit *Pilate was trying* [c]**19:14** Lit *the sixth hour*, see note at Jn 1:39; an alternate time reckoning would be *about noon* [d]**19:16** Other mss add *and led Him out* [e]**19:20** Or *Aramaic* [f]**19:24** Ps 22:18

[a]that the Scripture might be fulfilled,
He said, "I'm thirsty!" 29 A jar full of
sour wine was sitting there; so they
fixed a sponge full of sour wine on hyssop[a] and held it up to His mouth.

a Ps 69:21

30 When Jesus had received the sour
wine, He said, [a]"It is finished!" Then
bowing His head, He [b]gave up His
spirit.

a Jn 17:4 b Php 2:8

Jesus' Side Pierced

31 [a]Since it was the preparation day,
the Jews [b]did not want the bodies to
remain on the cross on the Sabbath
(for that Sabbath was [c]a special[b] day).
They requested that Pilate have the
men's legs broken and that ⌊their bod-
ies⌋ be taken away. 32 So the soldiers
came and broke the legs of the first
man and of the other one who had
been crucified with Him. 33 When they
came to Jesus, they did not break His
legs since they saw that He was already
dead. 34 But one of the soldiers pierced
His side with a spear, and at once
[d]blood and water came out. 35 [e]He who
saw this has testified so that you also
may believe. His testimony is true, and
he knows he is telling the truth. 36 For
these things happened [f]so that the
Scripture would be fulfilled: **Not one
of His bones will be broken.**[c] 37 Also,
another Scripture says: [g]**They will
look at the One they pierced.**[d]

*a Mk 15:42 b Dt 21:23 c Ex 12:18
d Zch 13:1 e Jn 20:31; 1Jn 1:1
f Ex 12:46; Ps 34:20 g Zch 12:10*

Jesus' Burial

38 [a]After this, Joseph of Arimathea,
who was a disciple of Jesus—but secretly [b]because of his fear of the
Jews—asked Pilate that he might remove Jesus' body. Pilate gave him permission, so he came and took His body
away. 39 [c]Nicodemus (who had previously come to Him at night) also came,
bringing a mixture of about 75 pounds[e]
of myrrh and aloes. 40 Then they took
Jesus' body and wrapped it in linen
cloths with the aromatic spices, according to the burial custom of the
Jews. 41 There was a garden in the
place where He was crucified. A [d]new
tomb was in the garden; no one had
yet been placed in it. 42 [e]They placed
Jesus there because of the Jewish preparation and since the tomb was nearby.

*a Mt 27:57 b Pr 29:25 c Jn 3:1-2
d Mt 27:60; Lk 23:53 e Is 53:9*

The Empty Tomb

20 On the [a]first day of the week
•Mary Magdalene came to the
tomb early, while it was still dark. She
saw that the stone had been removed[f]
from the tomb. 2 So she ran to Simon
Peter and to the [b]other disciple, the
one Jesus loved, and said to them,
"They have taken the Lord out of the
tomb, and we don't know where they
have put Him!"

a Mt 28:1 b Jn 13:23

3 At that, [a]Peter and the other disciple went out, heading for the tomb.
4 The two were running together, but
the other disciple outran Peter and got
to the tomb first. 5 Stooping down, he
saw [b]the linen cloths lying there, yet
he did not go in. 6 Then, following
him, Simon Peter came also. He entered the tomb and saw the linen
cloths lying there. 7 The wrapping that
had been on His head was not lying
with the linen cloths but was folded
up in a separate place by itself. 8 The
other disciple, who had reached the
tomb first, then entered the tomb,
saw, and believed. 9 For they still did
not understand the [c]Scripture that He
must rise from the dead. 10 Then the
disciples went home again.

*a Lk 24:12 b Jn 19:40
c Ps 16:10; Mt 16:21*

[a]**19:29** Or *with hyssop* [b]**19:31** Lit *great* [c]**19:36** Ex 12:46; Nm 9:12; Ps 34:20 [d]**19:37** Zch 12:10
[e]**19:39** Lit *100 litrai*; a Roman *litrai* = 12 ounces [f]**20:1** Lit *She saw the stone removed*

Mary Magdalene Sees the Risen Lord

11 [a]But Mary stood outside facing the tomb, crying. As she was crying, she stooped to look into the tomb. 12 She saw two angels in white sitting there, one at the head and one at the feet, where Jesus' body had been lying. 13 They said to her, "•Woman, why are you crying?" *[a]Mk 16:5*

"Because they've taken away my Lord," she told them, "and I don't know where they've put Him." 14 [a]Having said this, she turned around and saw Jesus standing there, [b]though she did not know it was Jesus.
[a]Mt 28:9 [b]Lk 24:16,31; Jn 21:4

15 "Woman," Jesus said to her, "why are you crying? Who is it you are looking for?"

Supposing He was the gardener, she replied, "Sir, if you've removed Him, tell me where you've put Him, and I will take Him away."

16 Jesus said, "Mary."

Turning around, she said to Him in Hebrew, *"Rabbouni!"*[a] —which means "Teacher."

17 "Don't cling to Me," Jesus told her, "for I have not yet ascended to the Father. But go to [a]My brothers and tell them that [b]I am ascending to My Father and your Father—to My God and your God." *[a]Mt 28:10 [b]Jn 16:28*

18 [a]Mary Magdalene went and announced to the disciples, "I have seen the Lord!" And she told them what[b] He had said to her. *[a]Mt 28:10; Lk 24:10*

The Disciples Commissioned

19 [a]In the evening of that first day of the week, the disciples were ⌊gathered together⌋ with the doors locked because of their fear of the Jews. Then Jesus came, stood among them, and said to them, "Peace to you!"
[a]Mk 16:14; Lk 24:36

20 Having said this, He [a]showed them His hands and His side. [b]So the disciples rejoiced when they saw the Lord. *[a]1Jn 1:1 [b]Jn 16:22*

21 Jesus said to them again, "Peace to you! [a]As the Father has sent Me, I also send you." 22 After saying this, He breathed on them and said,[c] "Receive the Holy Spirit. 23 [b]If you forgive the sins of any, they are forgiven them; if you retain ⌊the sins of⌋ any, they are retained." *[a]Mt 28:18-19; Jn 17:18-19 [b]Mt 16:19*

Thomas Sees and Believes

24 But one of the Twelve, Thomas ([a]called "Twin"), was not with them when Jesus came. 25 So the other disciples kept telling him, "We have seen the Lord!" *[a]Jn 11:16*

But he said to them, "If I don't see the mark of the nails in His hands, put my finger into the mark of the nails, and put my hand into His side, I will never believe!"

26 After eight days His disciples were indoors again, and Thomas was with them. Even though the doors were locked, Jesus came and stood among them. He said, [a]"Peace to you!"
[a]Is 9:6-7; Col 1:20

27 Then He said to Thomas, "Put your finger here and observe My hands. [a]Reach out your hand and put it into My side. Don't be an unbeliever, but a believer." *[a]1Jn 1:1*

28 Thomas responded to Him, [a]"My Lord and my God!" *[a]Ps 73:25-26; 1Tm 1:17*

29 Jesus said, "Because you have seen Me, you have believed.[d] [a]Those who believe without seeing are blessed." *[a]1Pt 1:8*

The Purpose of This Gospel

30 [a]Jesus performed many other signs in the presence of His disciples that are not written in this book. 31 [b]But these

[a]**20:16** *Rabbouni* is also used in Mk 10:51 [b]**20:18** Lit *these things* [c]**20:22** Lit *He breathed and said to them* [d]**20:29** Or *have you believed?* (as a question)

are written so that you may believe
Jesus is the •Messiah, the Son of God,[a]
[c]and by believing you may have life in
His name. *[a] Jn 21:25*
[b] Lk 1:4 [c] Jn 3:15-16

Jesus' Third Appearance to the Disciples

21 After this, Jesus revealed Himself again to His disciples by the
Sea of Tiberias.[b] He revealed Himself
in this way:
2 Simon Peter, Thomas (called
"Twin"), [a]Nathanael from Cana of Galilee, [b]Zebedee's sons, and two others
of His disciples were together.
[a] Jn 1:45 [b] Mt 4:21

3 "I'm going fishing," Simon Peter
said to them.
"We're coming with you," they told
him. They went out and got into the
boat, but that night they caught nothing.
4 When daybreak came, Jesus stood
on the shore. However, the disciples
[a]did not know it was Jesus. *[a] Jn 20:14*

5 [a]"Men,"[c] Jesus called to them, "you
don't have any fish, do you?"
[a] Lk 24:41

"No," they answered.
6 [a]"Cast the net on the right side of
the boat," He told them, "and you'll
find some." So they did,[d] and they
were unable to haul it in because of the
large number of fish. 7 Therefore the
disciple, the one Jesus loved, said to
Peter, "It is the Lord!" *[a] Lk 5:4*

When Simon Peter heard that it was
the Lord, he tied his outer garment
around him[e] (for he was stripped) and
plunged into the sea. 8 But since they
were not far from land (about 100
yards[f] away), the other disciples came
in the boat, dragging the net full of fish.
9 When they got out on land, they saw
a charcoal fire there, with fish lying on
it, and bread.
10 "Bring some of the fish you've just
caught," Jesus told them. 11 So Simon
Peter got up and hauled the net ashore,
full of large fish—153 of them. Even
though there were so many, the net
was not torn.
12 [a]"Come and have breakfast," Jesus
told them. None of the disciples dared
ask Him, "Who are You?" because they
knew it was the Lord. 13 Jesus came,
took the bread, and gave it to them. He
did the same with the fish. *[a] Ac 10:41*

14 This was now [a]the third time[g]
Jesus appeared[h] to the disciples after
He was raised from the dead.
[a] Jn 20:19,26

Jesus' Threefold Restoration of Peter

15 When they had eaten breakfast,
Jesus asked Simon Peter, "Simon, son
of John,[i] do you [a]love[j] Me more than
these?" *[a] Mt 26:33*

"Yes, Lord," he said to Him, "You
know that I love You."
"Feed My lambs," He told him.
16 A second time He asked him, "Simon, son of John, do you love Me?"
"Yes, Lord," he said to Him, "You
know that I love You."
"Shepherd My sheep," He told him.
17 He asked him [a]the third time, "Simon, son of John, do you love Me?"
[a] Jn 13:38

Peter was grieved that He asked him
the third time, "Do you love Me?" He
said, "Lord, [a]You know everything!
You know that I love You."
[a] Jn 2:24-25; 6:64

[a]**20:31** Or *that the Messiah, the Son of God, is Jesus* [b]**21:1** The Sea of Galilee; *Sea of Tiberias* is used only in John; Jn 6:1,23 [c]**21:5** Lit *Children* [d]**21:6** Lit *they cast* [e]**21:7** Lit *he girded his garment* [f]**21:8** Lit *about 200 cubits* [g]**21:14** The other two are in Jn 20:19–29. [h]**21:14** Lit *was revealed* (see v. 1) [i]**21:15–17** Other mss read *Simon, son of Jonah*; Jn 1:42; Mt 16:17 [j]**21:15–17** Two synonyms are translated *love* in this conversation: *agapao*, the first 2 times by Jesus (vv. 15–16); and *phileo*, the last time by Jesus (v. 17) and all 3 times by Peter (vv. 15–17). Peter's threefold confession of love for Jesus corresponds to his earlier threefold denial of Jesus; Jn 18:15–18,25–27.

"Feed My sheep," Jesus said. 18 [a]"•I
assure you: When you were young,
you would tie your belt and walk wherever you wanted. But when you grow
old, you will stretch out your hands
and someone else will tie you and
carry you where you don't want to go."
19 He said this to signify [b]by what kind
of death he would glorify God.[a] After
saying this, He told him, "Follow Me!"

[a]Jn 13:36 [b]Php 1:20; 2Pt 1:14

Correcting a False Report

20 So Peter turned around and saw the
disciple [a]Jesus loved following them.
⌊That disciple⌋ was the one who had
leaned back against Jesus at the supper
and asked, "Lord, who is the one that's
going to betray You?" 21 When Peter
saw him, he said to Jesus, "Lord—what
about him?"

[a]Jn 13:23,25

22 "If I want him to remain [a]until I
come," Jesus answered, "what is [b]that
to you? As for you, follow Me."

[a]Mt 16:27 [b]Dt 29:29

23 So this report[b] spread to the brothers[c] that this disciple would not die.
Yet Jesus did not tell him that he would
not die, but, "If I want him to remain
until I come, what is that to you?"

Epilogue

24 This is the disciple who testifies to
these things and who wrote them
down. We know that his testimony is
true.
25 And there are also many other
things that Jesus did, which, if they
were written one by one, I suppose not
even the world itself could contain the
books[d] that would be written.

ACTS

Prologue

1 I wrote the first narrative, [a]The-
ophilus, about all that Jesus began
to do and teach 2 [b]until the day He
was taken up, after He had given orders through the Holy Spirit to the
apostles whom He had chosen. 3 After
He had suffered, [c]He also presented
Himself alive to them by many con-
vincing proofs, appearing to them during 40 days and speaking about the
kingdom of God.

[a]Lk 1:3 [b]1Tm 3:16; Heb 1:3 [c]1Co 15:5

The Holy Spirit Promised

4 While He was together with them,[e]
He commanded them not to leave
Jerusalem, but to wait for the Father's
promise. "This," ⌊He said, [a]"is what⌋
you heard from Me; 5 [b]for John baptized with water, [c]but you will be baptized with the Holy Spirit not many
days from now."

[a]Jn 14:16 [b]Ac 11:16 [c]Jl 2:28-29; Mt 3:11; Ac 2:4

6 So when they had come together,
they asked Him, "Lord, at this time
are You [a]restoring the kingdom to Israel?"

[a]Is 1:26; Dn 7:27

7 He said to them, "It is not for you to
know times or periods that the Father
has set by His own authority. 8 But you
will receive power when the Holy Spirit
has come upon you, and you will be My
witnesses in Jerusalem, in all Judea and
Samaria, and to the ends[f] of the earth."

[a]**21:19** Jesus predicts that Peter would be martyred. Church tradition says that Peter was crucified upside down. [b]**21:23** Lit *this word* [c]**21:23** The word *brothers* refers to the whole Christian community. [d]**21:25** Lit *scroll* [e]**1:4** Or *He was eating with them*, or *He was lodging with them* [f]**1:8** Lit *the end*

The Ascension

9 [a]After He had said this, He was
taken up as they were watching, and a
cloud received Him out of their sight.
10 While He was going, they were gaz-
ing into heaven, and suddenly two
men in white clothes stood by them.
11 They said, "Men of Galilee, why do
you stand looking up into heaven? This
Jesus, who has been taken from you
into heaven, [b]will come in the same
way that you have seen Him going into
heaven." *[a] Jn 6:62 [b] Jn 14:3; 1Th 1:10; Rv 1:7*

United in Prayer

12 Then they returned to Jerusalem
from the mount called Olive Grove,
which is near Jerusalem—a Sabbath
day's journey away. 13 When they arrived, they went to the room upstairs
where they were staying:

> Peter, John,
> James, Andrew,
> Philip, Thomas,
> Bartholomew, Matthew,
> James the son of Alphaeus,
> [a]Simon the Zealot, and [b]Judas
> the son of James.

14 All these were continually united in
prayer,[a] along with [c]the women, including Mary[b] the mother of Jesus,
and [d]His brothers. *[a] Lk 6:15 [b] Jd 1 [c] Lk 23:49 [d] Mt 13:55*

Matthias Chosen

15 During these days Peter stood up
among the brothers[c]—the number of
people who were together was about
120—and said: 16 "Brothers, the Scripture had to be fulfilled [a]that the Holy
Spirit through the mouth of David
spoke in advance about Judas, [b]who
became a guide to those who arrested
Jesus. 17 For [c]he was one of our number and was allotted a share in this
ministry." 18 [d]Now this man acquired a
field with his unrighteous wages; and
falling headfirst, he burst open in the
middle, and all his insides spilled out.
19 This became known to all the residents of Jerusalem, so that in their own
language that field is called *Hakel-
dama*, that is, Field of Blood. 20 "For it
is written in the Book of Psalms:

> **[e]Let his dwelling become**
> **desolate;**
> **let no one live in it;**[d] and
> **Let someone else take**
> **his position.**[e]

[a] Ps 41:9 [b] Jn 18:3 [c] Lk 6:16 [d] Mt 27:5 [e] Ps 69:25

21 "Therefore, from among the men
who have accompanied us during the
whole time the Lord Jesus went in and
out among us— 22 beginning from the
baptism of John until the day He was
taken up from us—from among these,
it is necessary that one become [a]a witness with us of His resurrection."
[a] Heb 2:3

23 So they proposed two: Joseph,
called Barsabbas, who was also known
as Justus, and Matthias. 24 Then they
prayed, "You, Lord, [a]know the hearts
of all; show which of these two You
have chosen 25 to take the place[f] in this
apostolic service that Judas left to go to
his own place." 26 Then they cast lots
for them, and the lot fell to Matthias.
So he was numbered with the 11 apostles. *[a] Jn 2:24; Heb 4:13*

Pentecost

2 When [a]the day of Pentecost had
arrived, [b]they were all together in
one place. 2 Suddenly a sound like
that of a violent rushing wind came
from heaven, and [c]it filled the whole
house where they were staying. 3 And
tongues, like flames of fire that were
divided, appeared to them and rested
on each one of them. 4 Then [d]they
were all filled with the Holy Spirit and

[a]**1:14** Other mss add *and petition* [b]**1:14** Or *prayer, with their wives and Mary* [c]**1:15** Other mss read *disciples* [d]**1:20** Ps 69:25 [e]**1:20** Ps 109:8 [f]**1:25** Other mss read *to share*

began [e]to speak in different languages, as the Spirit gave them ability
for speech. *[a]Lv 23:15 [b]Ac 1:14 [c]Ac 4:31 [d]Jn 14:26; Ac 1:5 [e]Mk 16:17; 1Co 12:10*

5 There were Jews [a]living in Jerusalem, devout men from every nation
under heaven. 6 When this sound occurred, the multitude came together
and was confused because each one
heard them speaking in his own language. 7 And they were astounded and
amazed, saying,[a] "Look, aren't all these
who are speaking Galileans? 8 How is it
that we hear, each of us, in our own
native language? 9 Parthians, Medes,
Elamites; those who live in Mesopotamia, in Judea and [b]Cappadocia, Pontus
and Asia, 10 Phrygia and Pamphylia,
Egypt and the parts of Libya near
Cyrene; visitors from Rome, both Jews
and [c]•proselytes, 11 Cretans and Ar-
abs—we hear them speaking in our
own languages the magnificent acts of
God." 12 And they were all astounded
and perplexed, saying to one another,
"What could this be?" 13 But some
sneered and said, "They're full of new
wine!"

[a]Ex 23:17 [b]1Pt 1:1 [c]Ex 12:48; Is 56:6

Peter's Sermon

14 But Peter stood up with the
Eleven, raised his voice, and proclaimed to them: "Jewish men and all
you residents of Jerusalem, let this be
known to you and pay attention to my
words. 15 For these people are not
drunk, as you suppose, since it's only
nine in the morning.[b] 16 On the contrary, this is what was spoken through
the prophet Joel:

17 [a]**And it will be** in the last days,
says God,
that [b]**I will pour out My Spirit
on all humanity;
then your sons
and** [c]**your daughters
will prophesy,
your young men will see
visions,
and your old men will dream
dreams.**
18 **I will even pour out My Spirit
on My male and female slaves
in those days,**
and they will prophesy.
19 [d]**I will display wonders
in the heaven** above
and signs on the earth below:
**blood and fire and a cloud
of smoke.**
20 [e]**The sun will be turned
to darkness,
and the moon to blood,
before the great and
remarkable day of the Lord
comes;**
21 **then** [f]**whoever calls
on the name of the Lord
will be saved.**[c]

[a]Is 44:3; Jl 2:28 [b]Ac 10:45 [c]Ac 21:9 [d]Jl 2:30 [e]Mt 24:29 [f]Rm 10:13

22 "Men of Israel, listen to these
words: This Jesus the •Nazarene was a
man pointed out to you by God [a]with
miracles, wonders, and signs that God
did among you through Him, just as
you yourselves know. 23 Though He
[b]was delivered up according to God's
determined plan and foreknowledge,
you used[d] lawless people[e] to nail Him
to a cross and kill Him. 24 [c]God raised
Him up, ending the pains of death, because it was not possible for Him to be
held by it. 25 For David says of Him:

[d]**I saw the Lord ever before me;
because He is at my right hand,
I will not be shaken.**
26 **Therefore my heart was glad,
and my tongue rejoiced.
Moreover my flesh will rest
in hope,**
27 **because You will not leave
my soul in •Hades,**

[a]**2:7** Other mss add *to one another* [b]**2:15** Lit *it's the third hour of the day* [c]**2:17–21** Jl 2:28–32
[d]**2:23** Other mss read *you have taken* [e]**2:23** Or *used the hand of lawless ones*

or allow Your [e]Holy One
to see decay.
28 **You have revealed**
the paths of life to me;
You will fill me with gladness
in Your presence.[a]

[a]Heb 2:4 [b]Lk 24:44 [c]Ac 3:15; 4:10 [d]Ps 16:8-11 [e]Ps 16:10

29 "Brothers, I can confidently speak
to you about the patriarch David: he is
both dead and buried, and his tomb is
with us to this day. 30 Since he was a
prophet, he knew that God had sworn
an oath to him to seat [a]one of his
descendants[b] [c] on his throne. 31 Seeing
this in advance, he spoke concerning
the resurrection of the •Messiah:

[b]**He**[d] **was not left in Hades,**
and His **flesh**
did not experience decay.[e]

[a]Ps 132:11; Lk 1:32 [b]Ps 16:10

32 "God has resurrected this Jesus.
[a]We are all witnesses of this. 33 Therefore, [b]since He has been exalted to the
right hand of God and [c]has received
from the Father the promised Holy
Spirit, He has poured out what you
both see and hear. 34 For it was not
David who ascended into the heavens,
but he himself says:

[d]**The Lord said to my Lord,**
'Sit at My right hand
35 **until I make Your enemies**
Your footstool.'[f]

[a]Lk 24:46-48 [b]Ac 5:31; Php 2:9 [c]Ac 1:4 [d]Ps 110:1

36 "Therefore let all the house of Israel know with certainty that God [a]has
made this Jesus, whom you crucified,
both Lord and Messiah!"

[a]Ac 5:31

Forgiveness through the Messiah

37 When they heard this, [a]they were
pierced to the heart and said to Peter
and the rest of the apostles: "Brothers,
what must we do?"

[a]Zch 12:10

38 [a]"Repent," Peter said to them,
"and be baptized, each of you, in the
name of Jesus the Messiah for the forgiveness of your sins, and you will receive the gift of the Holy Spirit. 39 For
the promise is for you and [b]for your
children, and [c]for all who are far off,[g]
as many as the Lord our God will call."
40 And with many other words he testified and strongly urged them, saying,
"Be saved from this corrupt[h] generation!"

[a]Lk 24:47; Ac 3:19 [b]Jl 2:28 [c]Eph 2:13

A Generous and Growing Church

41 So those who accepted his message were baptized, and that day about
3,000 people were added to them.
42 And they devoted themselves to the
apostles' teaching, to fellowship, to the
breaking of bread, and to prayers.
43 Then fear came over everyone,
and [a]many wonders and signs were being performed through the apostles.
44 Now all the believers were together
and [b]had everything in common. 45 So
they sold their possessions and property and [c]distributed the proceeds to
all, as anyone had a need.[i] 46 And every
day they devoted themselves ⌊to meet-
ing⌋ together [d]in the •temple complex,
and broke bread from house to house.
They ate their food with gladness and
simplicity of heart, 47 praising God and
[e]having favor with all the people. And
every day [f]the Lord added to them[j]
those who were being saved.

[a]Mk 16:17 [b]Ac 4:32 [c]Is 58:7 [d]Lk 24:53 [e]Rm 14:18 [f]Rm 8:30

Healing of a Lame Man

3 Now Peter and John were going
up together to the •temple complex at the hour of prayer at three in
the afternoon.[k] 2 And a man who was

[a]**2:25–28** Ps 16:8–11 [b]**2:30** Other mss add *according to the flesh to raise up the Messiah* [c]**2:30** Lit *one from the fruit of his loin* [d]**2:31** Other mss read *His soul* [e]**2:31** Ps 16:10 [f]**2:34–35** Ps 110:1 [g]**2:39** Remote in time or space [h]**2:40** Or *crooked*, or *twisted* [i]**2:45** Or *to all, according to one's needs* [j]**2:47** Other mss read *to the church* [k]**3:1** Lit *at the ninth hour*

lame from his mother's womb was carried there and placed every day at the temple gate called Beautiful, so he could beg from those entering the temple complex. 3 When he saw Peter and John about to enter the temple complex, he asked for help. 4 Peter, along with John, looked at him intently and said, "Look at us." 5 So he turned to them,[a] expecting to get something from them. 6 But Peter said, "I have neither [a]silver nor gold, but what I have, I give to you: [b]In the name of Jesus Christ the •Nazarene, get up and walk!" 7 Then, taking him by the right hand he raised him up, and at once his feet and ankles became strong. 8 So he [c]jumped up, stood, and started to walk, and he entered the temple complex with them—walking, leaping, and praising God. 9 All the people saw him walking and praising God, 10 and they recognized that he was the one who used to sit and beg at the Beautiful Gate of the temple complex. So they were filled with awe and astonishment at what had happened to him. *[a] 1Pt 4:10 [b] Ac 4:10 [c] Is 35:6*

Preaching in Solomon's Colonnade

11 While he[b] was holding on to Peter and John, all the people, greatly amazed, ran toward them in [a]what is called Solomon's Colonnade. 12 When Peter saw this, he addressed the people: "Men of Israel, why are you amazed at this? Or why do you stare at us, [b]as though by our own power or godliness we had made him walk? 13 [c]The God of Abraham, Isaac, and Jacob, the God of our fathers, [d]has glorified His Servant Jesus, whom you handed over and denied in the presence of •Pilate, when he had decided to release Him. 14 But you denied the [e]Holy and [f]Righteous One, and asked to have a murderer given to you. 15 And you killed the source[c] of life, whom God raised from the dead; we are witnesses of this. 16 [g]By faith in His name, His name has made this man strong, whom you see and know. So the faith that comes through Him has given him this perfect health in front of all of you. *[a] Jn 10:23 [b] 2Co 3:5 [c] Ac 5:30 [d] Php 2:9 [e] Mk 1:24; Lk 1:35 [f] Ac 7:52 [g] 1Pt 1:21*

17 "And now, brothers, I know that you did it [a]in ignorance, just as your leaders also did. 18 But what God predicted [b]through the mouth of all the prophets—that His •Messiah would suffer—He has fulfilled in this way. 19 Therefore repent and turn back, that your sins may be wiped out so that seasons of refreshing may come from the presence of the Lord, 20 and He may send Jesus, who has been appointed Messiah for you. 21 [c]Heaven must welcome[d] Him until the times of the [d]restoration of all things, which God spoke about by the mouth of His holy prophets from the beginning. 22 Moses said:[e]

> **The Lord your God will raise up for you [e]a Prophet like me from among your brothers. You must listen to Him in everything He will say to you. 23 And it will be that [f]everyone who will not listen to that Prophet will be completely cut off from the people.**[f]

[a] Lk 23:34; 1Co 2:8 [b] Ps 22 [c] Ac 1:11; Heb 8:1 [d] Mt 17:11 [e] Dt 18:15,19 [f] Mk 16:16; Heb 2:2-3

24 "In addition, all the prophets who have spoken, from Samuel and those after him, have also announced these days. 25 [a]You are the sons of the prophets and of the covenant that God made with your forefathers, saying to Abraham, [b]**And in your seed all the**

[a]**3:5** Or *he paid attention to them* [b]**3:11** Other mss read *the lame man who was healed* [c]**3:15** Or *the Prince,* or *the Ruler* [d]**3:21** Or *receive,* or *retain* [e]**3:22** Other mss add *to the fathers* [f]**3:22–23** Dt 18:15–19

families of the earth will be blessed.[a]
26 God raised up His Servant[b] and sent
Him first to you to bless you by turning
each of you from your evil ways."

[a] Rm 9:4,8 [b] Gn 12:3

Peter and John Arrested

4 Now as they were speaking to the
people, the priests, the commander of the temple guard, and the
•Sadducees confronted them, 2 because
they were provoked that they were
teaching the people and proclaiming in
the person of Jesus[c] the resurrection
from the dead. 3 So they seized them
and put them in custody until the next
day, since it was already evening. 4 But
many of those who heard the message
believed, and the number of the men
came to about 5,000.

Peter and John Face the Jewish Leadership

5 The next day, their rulers, elders,
and •scribes assembled in Jerusalem
6 with [a]Annas the high priest, Caiaphas, John and Alexander, and all the
members of the high-priestly family.[d]
7 After they had Peter and John stand[e]
before them, they asked the question:
[b]"By what power or in what name
have you done this?"

[a] Lk 3:2 [b] Mt 21:23

8 [a]Then Peter was filled with the Holy
Spirit and said to them, "Rulers of the
people and elders:[f] 9 If we are being examined today about a good deed done
to a disabled man—by what means he
was healed— 10 let it be known to all of
you and to all the people of Israel, [b]that
by the name of Jesus Christ the •Naza-
rene—whom you crucified and whom
God raised from the dead—by Him this
man is standing here before you
healthy. 11 [c]This ⌊Jesus⌋ is

The stone despised by you
builders,
who has become
the cornerstone.[g]

12 [d]There is salvation in no one else,
for there is no other name under
heaven given to people by which we
must be saved."

[a] Lk 12:11 [b] Ac 3:6
[c] Ps 118:22; Is 28:16; Mt 21:42 [d] Mt 1:21

The Name Forbidden

13 When they observed the boldness
of Peter and John [a]and realized that
they were uneducated and untrained
men, they were amazed and knew that
they had been with Jesus. 14 And since
they saw the man who had been
healed standing with them, they had
nothing to say in response. 15 After
they had ordered them to leave the
•Sanhedrin, they conferred among
themselves, 16 saying, [b]"What should
we do with these men? For an obvious
sign, [c]evident to all who live in Jerusalem, has been done through them, and
we cannot deny it! 17 But so this does
not spread any further among the people, let's threaten them against speaking to anyone in this name again." 18 So
they called for them and ordered them
not to preach or teach at all in the
name of Jesus.

[a] Mt 11:25; 1Co 1:27
[b] Jn 11:47 [c] Ac 3:9

19 But Peter and John answered
them, [a]"Whether it's right in the sight
of God ⌊for us⌋ to listen to you rather
than to God, you decide; 20 [b]for we are
unable to stop speaking about what
[c]we have seen and heard."

[a] Ac 5:29; Gl 1:10 [b] Ac 1:8 [c] 1Jn 1:1

21 After threatening them further,
they released them. They found no way
to punish them, [a]because the people
were all giving glory to God [b]over what
had been done; 22 for the man was over
40 years old on whom this sign of healing had been performed.

[a] Ac 5:26 [b] Ac 3:7-8

[a]**3:25** Gn 12:3; 18:18; 22:18; 26:4 [b]**3:26** Other mss add *Jesus* [c]**4:2** Lit *proclaiming in Jesus* [d]**4:6** Or *high-priestly class*, or *high-priestly clan* [e]**4:7** Lit *had placed them* [f]**4:8** Other mss add *of Israel* [g]**4:11** Ps 118:22

Commissioning the Twelve

[a]Now He was going around the villages in a circuit, teaching. 7 [b]He summoned the Twelve and began to send
them out in pairs and gave them authority over unclean spirits. 8 He instructed them to take nothing for the
road except a walking stick: no bread,
no traveling bag, no money in their
belts. 9 They were to wear sandals, but
not put on an extra shirt. 10 Then [c]He
said to them, "Whenever you enter a
house, stay there until you leave that
place. 11 [d]If any place does not welcome you and people refuse to listen to
you, when you leave there, shake the
dust off your feet as a testimony against
them."[a]

a Mt 9:35 b Mt 10:1; Lk 9:1 c Mt 10:11 d Mt 10:14

12 So they went out and preached
that people should repent. 13 And they
were driving out many demons,
[a]anointing many sick people with oil,
and healing.

a Jms 5:14

John the Baptist Beheaded

14 [a]King •Herod heard of this, because Jesus' name had become well
known. Some[b] said, "John the Baptist
has been raised from the dead, and
that's why supernatural powers are at
work in him." 15 But others [b]said,
"He's Elijah." Still others said, "He's a
prophet[c] —like one of the prophets."

a Mt 14:1 b Mt 16:14

16 When Herod heard of it, he said,
"John, the one I beheaded, has been
raised!" 17 For Herod himself had given
orders to arrest John and to chain him
in prison on account of Herodias, his
brother Philip's wife, whom he had
married. 18 John had been telling
Herod, "It [a]is not lawful for you to have
your brother's wife!" 19 So Herodias
held a grudge against him and wanted
to kill him. But she could not,
20 because Herod was in awe of[d] John
and was protecting him, knowing he
was a righteous and holy man. When
Herod heard him he would be very disturbed,[e] yet would hear him gladly.

a Lv 18:16

21 [a]Now an opportune time came on
his birthday, when Herod gave a banquet for his nobles, military commanders, and the leading men of Galilee.
22 When Herodias' own daughter[f]
came in and danced, she pleased
Herod and his guests. The king said to
the girl, "Ask me whatever you want,
and I'll give it to you." 23 So he swore
oaths to her: "Whatever [b]you ask me I
will give you, up to half my kingdom."

a Mt 14:6 b Ec 5:2; Rm 1:28-31

24 Then she went out and said to her
mother, "What should I ask for?"
[a]"John the Baptist's head!" she said.

a Mt 14:8

25 Immediately she hurried to the
king and said, "I want you to give me
John the Baptist's head on a platter—right now!"
26 Though the king was deeply distressed, because of his oaths and the
guests[g] he did not want to refuse her.
27 The king immediately sent for an ex-
ecutioner and commanded him to
bring John's head. So he went and beheaded him in prison, 28 brought his
head on a platter, and gave it to the girl.
Then the girl gave it to her mother.
29 When his disciples[h] heard about it,
they came and [a]removed his corpse
and placed it in a tomb.

a Mt 14:12

Feeding 5,000

30 [a]The apostles gathered around
Jesus and reported to Him all that they
had done and taught. 31 [b]He said to
them, "Come away by yourselves to a

[a]**6:11** Other mss add *I assure you, it will be more tolerable for Sodom or Gomorrah on judgment day than for that town.* [b]**6:14** Other mss read *He* [c]**6:15** Lit *Others said, "A prophet* [d]**6:20** Or *Herod feared* [e]**6:20** Other mss read *When he heard him, he did many things* [f]**6:22** Other mss read *When his daughter Herodias* [g]**6:26** Lit *and those reclining at the table* [h]**6:29** John's disciples

remote place and rest a while." For
many people were coming and going,
and they did not even have time to eat.
32 So they went away in the boat by
themselves to a remote place, 33 but
many saw them leaving and recognized them. People ran there by land
from all the towns and arrived ahead of
them.[a] 34 So as He stepped ashore, He
saw a huge crowd and [c]had compassion on them, because they were like
sheep without a shepherd. Then [d]He
began to teach them many things.

[a]Lk 9:10 [b]Mt 14:13 [c]Mt 9:36; Mt 14:14 [d]Is 61:1; Lk 9:11

35 [a]When it was already late, His disciples approached Him and said, "This
place is a wilderness, and it is already
late! 36 Send them away, so they can go
into the surrounding countryside and
villages to buy themselves something
to eat."

[a]Mt 14:15; Lk 9:12

37 "You give them something to eat,"
He responded.

They said to Him, [a]"Should we go
and buy 200 •denarii worth of bread
and give them something to eat?"

[a]Mt 15:33; Jn 6:7

38 And He asked them, "How many
loaves do you have? Go look."

When they found out they said,
[a]"Five, and two fish."

[a]Mt 14:17; Lk 9:13; Jn 6:9

39 Then He instructed them to have
all the people sit down[b] in groups on
the green grass. 40 So they sat down in
ranks of hundreds and fifties. 41 Then
He took the five loaves and the two
fish, and looking up to heaven, He
[a]blessed and broke the loaves. He kept
giving them to His disciples to set before the people. He also divided the
two fish among them all. 42 Everyone
ate and was filled. 43 Then they picked
up 12 baskets full of pieces of bread
and fish. 44 Now those who ate the
loaves were 5,000 men.

[a]Mt 14:19

Walking on the Water

45 [a]Immediately He made His disciples get into the boat and go ahead of
Him to the other side, to Bethsaida,
while He dismissed the crowd. 46 After
He said good-bye to them, He went
away to the mountain to pray.
47 [b]When evening came, the boat was
in the middle of the sea, and He was
alone on the land. 48 He saw them being battered as they rowed,[c] because
the wind was against them. Around
three in the morning[d] He came toward
them walking on the sea and wanted
to pass by them. 49 When they saw
Him walking on the sea, they thought
it was a ghost and cried out; 50 for they
all saw Him and were terrified. Immediately He spoke with them and said,
"Have courage! It is I. Don't be afraid."
51 Then He got into the boat with
them, and the wind ceased. They were
completely astounded,[e] 52 because
[c]they had not understood about the
loaves. Instead, their hearts were hardened.

[a]Mt 14:22; Jn 6:17 [b]Mt 14:23; Jn 6:16-17 [c]Mt 16:9-11

Miraculous Healings

53 [a]When they had crossed over, they
came to land at Gennesaret and
beached the boat. 54 As they got out of
the boat, people immediately recognized Him. 55 They hurried throughout
that vicinity and began to carry the
sick on stretchers to wherever they
heard He was. 56 Wherever He would
go, into villages, towns, or the country,
they laid the sick in the marketplaces
and begged Him that they might touch
just the •tassel of His robe. And everyone who touched it was made well.

[a]Mt 14:34

The Traditions of the Elders

7 [a]The •Pharisees and some of the
•scribes who had come from Jerus-

[a]**6:33** Other mss add *and gathered around Him* [b]**6:39** Lit *people recline* [c]**6:48** Or *them struggling as they rowed* [d]**6:48** Lit *Around the fourth watch of the night* = 3 to 6 a.m. [e]**6:51** Lit *were astounded in themselves*

lem gathered around Him. [2] They ob-
erved that some of His disciples were
ating their bread with unclean—that
s, unwashed—hands. [3] (For the Phari-
ees, in fact all the Jews, will not eat
nless they wash their hands ritually,
eeping the tradition of the elders.
When they come from the market-
lace, they do not eat unless they have
washed. And there are many other
customs they have received and keep,
ike the washing of cups, jugs, copper
tensils, and dining couches.[a]) [5] [b]Then
he Pharisees and the scribes asked
Him, "Why don't Your disciples live
according to the tradition of the elders,
nstead of eating bread with ritually
unclean[b] hands?" *[a]Mt 15:1 [b]Mt 15:2*

[6] He answered them, "Isaiah prophesied correctly about you hypocrites, as
t is written:

> **[a]These people honor Me**
> **with their lips,**
> **but their heart is far from Me.**
> 7 **They worship Me in vain,**
> **teaching as doctrines**
> **the commands of men.**[c]
>
> *[a]Is 29:13; Mt 15:8*

[8] Disregarding the command of God,
you keep the tradition of men."[d] [9] He
also said to them, "You [a]completely in-
validate God's command in order to
maintain[e] your tradition! [10] For Moses
said:

> **[b]Honor your father**
> **and your mother;**[f] and,
> **[c]Whoever speaks evil of father**
> **or mother**
> **must be put to death.**[g] *[a]Is 24:5*
> *[b]Ex 20:12; Mt 15:4 [c]Lv 20:9*

[11] But you say, 'If a man tells his father
or mother: Whatever benefit you
might have received from me is [a]Cor-
ban'" (that is, a gift ⌊committed to the
temple⌋), [12] "you no longer let him do
anything for his father or mother.
[13] You revoke God's word by your tradition that you have handed down.
And you do many other similar
things." [14] Summoning the crowd
again, He told them, "Listen to Me, all
of you, and understand: [15] Nothing
that goes into a person from outside
can defile him, but the things that
come out of a person are what defile
him. [16] If anyone has ears to hear, he
should listen!"[h] *[a]Mt 15:5*

[17] [a]When He went into the house
away from the crowd, the disciples
asked Him about the parable. [18] And
He said to them, "Are you also as lacking in understanding? Don't you realize that nothing going into a man from
the outside can defile him? [19] For it
doesn't go into his heart but into the
stomach and is eliminated."[i] (As a result, He made all foods clean.[j]) [20] Then
He said, "What comes out of a person—that defiles him. [21] [b]For from
within, out of people's hearts, come
evil thoughts, sexual immoralities,
thefts, murders, [22] adulteries, greed,
evil actions, deceit, lewdness, stingi-
ness,[k] blasphemy, pride, and foolishness. [23] All these evil things come from
within and defile a person."
[a]Mt 15:15 [b]Mt 15:19

A Gentile Mother's Faith

[24] [a]He got up and departed from there
to the region of Tyre and Sidon.[l] He entered a house and did not want anyone
to know it, but He could not escape notice. [25] Instead, immediately after hearing about Him, a woman whose little
daughter had an unclean spirit came
and fell at His feet. [26] Now the woman
was Greek, a Syrophoenician by birth,

[a]**7:4** Other mss omit *and dining couches* [b]**7:5** Other mss read *with unwashed* [c]**7:6–7** Is 29:13
[d]**7:8** Other mss add *The washing of jugs, and cups, and many other similar things you practice.* [e]**7:9** Other
mss read *to establish* [f]**7:10** Ex 20:12; Dt 5:16 [g]**7:10** Ex 21:17; Lv 20:9 [h]**7:16** Other mss omit this verse
7:19 Lit *goes out into the toilet* [j]**7:19** Other mss read *is eliminated, making all foods clean."* [k]**7:22** Lit *evil*
eye [l]**7:24** Other mss omit *and Sidon*

and she kept asking Him to drive the demon out of her daughter. 27 He said to her, [b]"Allow the children to be satisfied first, because it isn't right to take the children's bread and throw it to the dogs."

[a]*Mt 15:21* [b]*Mt 7:6; 10:5-6; 15:23-28*

28 But she replied to Him, "Lord, even the dogs under the table eat the children's crumbs."

29 Then He told her, "Because of this reply, you may go. The demon has gone out of your daughter." 30 When she went back to her home, she found her child lying on the bed, and the demon was gone.

Jesus Does Everything Well

31 [a]Again, leaving the region of Tyre, He went by way of Sidon to the Sea of Galilee, through[a] the region of the •Decapolis. 32 [b]They brought to Him a deaf man who also had a speech difficulty, and begged Jesus to lay His hand on him. 33 So He took him away from the crowd privately. After putting His fingers in the man's ears and spitting, He touched his tongue. 34 Then, looking up to heaven, He sighed deeply and said to him, *"Ephphatha!"*[b] (that is, "Be opened!"). 35 [c]Immediately his ears were opened, his speech difficulty was removed,[c] and he began to speak clearly. 36 Then He ordered them to tell no one, but the more He would order them, the more they would proclaim it.

[a]*Mt 15:29* [b]*Mt 9:32; Lk 11:14* [c]*Is 35:5-6; Mt 11:5*

37 They were extremely astonished and said, "He has done everything well! He even makes deaf people hear, and people unable to speak, talk!"

Feeding 4,000

8 In those days there was again [a]a large crowd, and they had nothing to eat. He summoned the disciples and said to them, 2 "I have compassion on the crowd, because they've already stayed with Me three days and have nothing to eat. 3 If I send them home famished,[d] they will collapse on the way, and some of them have come a long distance."

[a]*Mt 15:3*

4 His disciples answered Him, "Where [a]can anyone get enough bread here in this desolate place to fill these people?"

[a]*Nm 11:21-22; Mt 15:3*

5 [a]"How many loaves do you have?" He asked them.

[a]*Mt 15:3*

"Seven," they said. 6 Then He commanded the crowd to sit down on the ground. Taking the seven loaves, He [a]gave thanks, broke the ⌊loaves⌋, and kept on giving ⌊them⌋ to His disciples to set before ⌊the people⌋. So they served the ⌊loaves⌋ to the crowd. 7 They also had a few small fish, and when [b]He had blessed them, He said these were to be served as well. 8 They ate and were filled. Then they collected seven large baskets of leftover pieces. 9 About 4,000 ⌊men⌋ were there. He dismissed them 10 and [c]immediately got into the boat with His disciples and went to the district of Dalmanutha.[e]

[a]*Mt 15:36; Mk 6:41-44* [b]*Mt 14:19* [c]*Mt 15:39*

The Yeast of the Pharisees and Herod

11 [a]The •Pharisees came out and began to argue with Him, demanding of Him a sign from heaven to test Him. 12 But sighing deeply in His spirit, He said, "Why does this generation demand a sign? •I assure you: No sign will be given to this generation!" 13 Then He left them, got on board ⌊the boat⌋ again, and went to the other side.

[a]*Mt 12:38; 16:1; Jn 6:30*

14 [a]They had forgotten to take bread and had only one loaf with them in the boat. 15 [b]Then He commanded them:

[a]**7:31** Or *into* [b]**7:34** An Aram expression [c]**7:35** Lit *opened, the bond of his tongue was untied* [d]**8:3** Or *fasting* [e]**8:10** Probably on the western shore of the Sea of Galilee

'Watch out! Beware of the yeast of the
Pharisees and the yeast of •Herod."
[a]Mt 16:5 [b]Mt 16:6; Lk 12:1

16 They were discussing among
themselves [a]that they did not have any
bread. 17 Aware of this, He said to
them, "Why are you discussing that
you do not have any bread? [b]Do you
not yet understand or comprehend? Is
your heart hardened? 18 [c]**Do you have
eyes, and not see, and do you have
ears, and not hear?**[a] And do you not
remember? 19 [d]When I broke the five
loaves for the 5,000, how many baskets full of pieces of bread did you collect?"
[a]Mt 16:7 [b]Mt 16:8 [c]Jr 5:21; Ezk 12:2
[d]Mt 14:20; Mk 6:43; Lk 9:17; Jn 6:13

"Twelve," they told Him.
20 [a]"When I broke the seven loaves
for the 4,000, how many large baskets
full of pieces of bread did you collect?"
[a]Mt 15:37

"Seven," they said.
21 And He said to them, [a]"Don't you
understand yet?"
[a]Mk 6:52

Healing a Blind Man

22 Then they came to Bethsaida.
They brought a blind man to Him and
begged Him to touch him. 23 He took
the blind man by the hand and brought
him out of the village. Spitting on his
eyes and laying His hands on him, He
asked him, "Do you see anything?"
24 He looked up and said, "I see people—they look to me like trees walking."
25 Again Jesus placed His hands on
the man's eyes, and he saw distinctly.
He was cured and could see everything
clearly. 26 Then He sent him home, saying, "Don't even go into the village."[b]

Peter's Confession of the Messiah

27 [a]Jesus went out with His disciples
to the villages of Caesarea Philippi.
And on the road He asked His disciples, "Who do people say that I am?"
[a]Mt 16:13; Lk 9:18

28 They answered Him, "John the
Baptist; others, Elijah; still others, one
of the prophets."
29 "But you," He asked them again,
"who do you say that I am?"
Peter answered Him, [a]"You are the
•Messiah!"
[a]Mt 16:16; Jn 6:69

30 And He [a]strictly warned them to
tell no one about Him.
[a]Mt 16:20

His Death and Resurrection Predicted

31 Then [a]He began to teach them
that the •Son of Man must suffer many
things, and be rejected by the elders,
the •chief priests, and the •scribes, be
killed, and rise after three days. 32 He
was openly talking about this. So Peter
took Him aside and began to rebuke
Him.
[a]Mt 16:21; Lk 9:22

33 But turning around and looking at
His disciples, He rebuked Peter and
said, "Get behind Me, Satan, because
you're not thinking about God's concerns,[c] but man's!"

Take Up Your Cross

34 Summoning the crowd along with
His disciples, He said to them, [a]"If anyone wants to be My follower, he must
deny himself, take up his cross, and follow Me. 35 For [b]whoever wants to save
his •life will lose it, but whoever loses
his life because of Me and the gospel
will save it. 36 For what does it benefit
a man to gain the whole world yet lose
his life? 37 What can a man give in exchange for his life? 38 [c]For whoever is
ashamed of Me and of My words in
this adulterous and sinful generation,
the Son of Man will also be ashamed of
him when He comes in the glory of His
Father with the holy angels."
[a]Mt 10:38; 16:24; Lk 9:23; 14:27
[b]Mt 10:39; 16:25; Jn 12:25
[c]Mt 10:33; Lk 9:26; 12:9

9 Then He said to them, [a]"•I assure
you: There are some standing

[a]**8:18** Jr 5:21; Ezk 12:2 [b]**8:26** Other mss add *or tell anyone in the village* [c]**8:33** Lit *about the things of God*

here who will not taste death until they see [b]the kingdom of God come in power." [a]*Mt 16:28; Lk 9:27* [b]*Mt 24:30; 25:31*

The Transfiguration

2 [a]After six days Jesus took Peter, James, and John and led them up on a high mountain by themselves to be alone. He was transformed[a] in front of them, 3 and His clothes became dazzling—extremely [b]white as no launderer on earth could whiten them. 4 Elijah appeared to them with Moses, and they were talking with Jesus. [a]*Mt 17:1; Lk 9:28* [b]*Dn 7:9*

5 Then Peter said to Jesus, "•Rabbi, it is good for us to be here! Let us make three •tabernacles: one for You, one for Moses, and one for Elijah"— 6 because he did not know what he should say, since they were terrified.

7 [a]A cloud appeared, overshadowing them, and a voice came from the cloud:

> This is My beloved Son;
> [b]listen to Him! [a]*2Pt 1:17* [b]*Heb 1:1-2*

8 Then suddenly, looking around, they no longer saw anyone with them except Jesus alone.

9 [a]As they were coming down from the mountain, He ordered them to tell no one what they had seen until the •Son of Man had risen from the dead. 10 They kept this word to themselves, discussing what "rising from the dead" meant. [a]*Mt 17:9*

11 Then they began to question Him, "Why do the •scribes say [a]that Elijah must come first?" [a]*Mal 4:5; Mt 17:10*

12 "Elijah does come first and restores everything," He replied. [a]"How then is it written about the Son of Man that He must suffer many things and [b]be treated with contempt? 13 But I tell you that [c]Elijah really has come, and they did to him whatever they wanted, just as it is written about him." [a]*Is 50:6; 53:2; Zch 13:7* [b]*Lk 23:11* [c]*Mt 11:14; 17:12*

The Power of Faith over a Demon

14 [a]When they came to the disciples, they saw a large crowd around them and scribes disputing with them. 15 All of a sudden, when the whole crowd saw Him, they were amazed[b] and ran to greet Him. 16 Then He asked them, "What are you arguing with them about?" [a]*Mt 17:14; Lk 9:37*

17 [a]Out of the crowd, one man answered Him, "Teacher, I brought my son to You. He has a spirit that makes him unable to speak. 18 Wherever it seizes him, it throws him down, and he foams at the mouth, grinds his teeth, and becomes rigid. So I asked Your disciples to drive it out, but they couldn't." [a]*Mt 17:14; Lk 9:38*

19 He replied to them, "You unbelieving generation! How long will I be with you? How long must I put up with you? Bring him to Me." 20 So they brought him to Him. [a]When the spirit saw Him, it immediately convulsed the boy. He fell to the ground and rolled around, foaming at the mouth. 21 "How long has this been happening to him?" Jesus asked his father. [a]*Lk 9:42*

"From childhood," he said. 22 "And many times it has thrown him into fire or water to destroy him. But if You can do anything, have compassion on us and help us."

23 Then Jesus said to him, [a]"'If You can?'[c] [d] Everything is possible to the one who believes." [a]*Mt 17:20; Mk 11:23; Lk 17:6*

24 Immediately the father of the boy cried out, "I do believe! Help my unbelief."

25 When Jesus saw that a crowd was rapidly coming together, He [a]rebuked the unclean spirit, saying to it, "You mute and deaf spirit,[e] I command you: come out of him and never enter him again!" [a]*Mt 17:18*

[a]**9:2** Or *transfigured* [b]**9:15** Or *surprised* [c]**9:23** Other mss add *believe* [d]**9:23** Jesus appears to quote the father's words in v. 22 and then comment on them. [e]**9:25** A spirit that caused the boy to be deaf and unable to speak

26 Then it came out, shrieking and
convulsing him[a] violently. The boy became like a corpse, so that many said,
"He's dead." 27 But Jesus, taking him by
the hand, raised him, and he stood up.
28 [a]After He went into a house, His
disciples asked Him privately, "Why
couldn't we drive it out?"

[a]*Mt 17:19*

29 And He told them, "This kind can
come out by nothing but prayer [and
fasting]."[b]

The Second Prediction of His Death

30 Then they left that place and made
their way through Galilee, but He did
not want anyone to know it. 31 [a]For He
was teaching His disciples and telling
them, "The Son of Man is being betrayed[c] into the hands of men. They
will kill Him, and after He is killed, He
will rise three days later." 32 But they
did not understand this statement, and
they were afraid to ask Him.

[a]*Mt 16:21; 17:22; Lk 9:44*

Who is the Greatest?

33 [a]Then they came to Capernaum.
When He was in the house, He asked
them, "What were you arguing about
on the way?" 34 But they were silent,
[b]because on the way they had been arguing with one another about who was
the greatest. 35 Sitting down, He called
the Twelve and said to them, [c]"If anyone wants to be first, he must be last of
all and servant of all." 36 Then [d]He took
a child, had him stand among them,
and taking him in His arms, He said to
them, 37 "Whoever welcomes[d] one little child such as this in My name welcomes Me. And [e]whoever welcomes
Me does not welcome Me, but Him
who sent Me."

[a]*Mt 18:1; Lk 9:46* [b]*Pr 13:10* [c]*Mt 20:26-27* [d]*Mt 18:2* [e]*Mt 10:40; Lk 9:48; Jn 13:20*

In His Name

38 John said to Him, "Teacher, we
saw someone[e] driving out demons in
Your name, and we tried to stop him
because he wasn't following us."
39 "Don't stop him," said Jesus, "because there is no one who will perform
a miracle in My name who can soon afterwards speak evil of Me. 40 For [a]who-
ever is not against us is for us. 41 [b]And
whoever gives you a cup of water to
drink because of My name,[f] since you
belong to the •Messiah—I assure you:
He will never lose his reward.

[a]*Mt 12:30* [b]*Mt 10:42*

Warnings from Jesus

42 [a]"But whoever •causes the downfall of one of these little ones who believe in Me—it would be better for him
if a heavy millstone[g] were hung around
his neck and he were thrown into the
sea. 43 [b]And if your hand causes your
downfall, cut it off. It is better for you to
enter life maimed than to have two
hands and go to •hell—the unquench-
able fire, [44 where

> [c]**Their worm does not die,**
> **and the fire**
> **is not quenched.**][b h]

[a]*Mt 18:6* [b]*Mt 18:8* [c]*Is 66:24*

45 And if your foot causes your downfall, cut it off. It is better for you to enter life lame than to have two feet and
be thrown into hell— [the unquench-
able fire, 46 where

> **Their worm does not die,**
> **and the fire**
> **is not quenched.**][b h]

47 And if your eye causes your downfall, [a]gouge it out. It is better for you to
enter the kingdom of God with one
eye than to have two eyes and be
thrown into hell, 48 where

[a]**9:26** Other mss omit *him* [b]**9:29,44,46** Other mss omit bracketed text [c]**9:31** Or *handed over*
[d]**9:37** Or *Whoever receives* [e]**9:38** Other mss add *who didn't go along with us* [f]**9:41** Lit *drink in the name*;
= Messiah [g]**9:42** A millstone turned by a donkey [h]**9:44,46** Is 66:24

Their worm does not die,
and the fire is not quenched.[a]

[a] Mt 5:29

49 For everyone will be salted with
fire.[b c] 50 [a]Salt is good, but if the salt
should lose its flavor, how can you
make it salty? [b]Have salt among yourselves and [c]be at peace with one an-
other." [a] Mt 5:13; Lk 14:34 [b] Col 4:6 [c] Rm 14:19

The Question of Divorce

10 [a]He set out from there and went
to the region of Judea and across
the Jordan. Then crowds converged
on Him again and, as He usually did,
He began teaching them once more.
2 [b]Some •Pharisees approached Him to
test Him. They asked, "Is it lawful for
a man to divorce ⌊his⌋ wife?"

[a] Mt 19:1; Jn 10:40 [b] Mt 19:3

3 He replied to them, "What did
Moses command you?"
4 They said, [a]"Moses permitted us to
write divorce papers and send her
away." [a] Dt 24:1; Mt 19:7

5 But Jesus told them, [a]"He wrote
this commandment for you because of
the hardness of your hearts. 6 But from
the beginning of creation [b]God[d] **made**
them male and female.[e] [a] Dt 9:6

[b] Gn 1:27; Mt 19:4

7 [a]**For this reason a man**
will leave
his father and mother
[and be joined to his wife,][f]
8 **and the two will become**
one flesh.[g]

So they are no longer two, but one
flesh. 9 Therefore what God has joined
together, man must not separate."

[a] Gn 2:24

10 Now in the house the disciples
questioned Him again about this matter. 11 And He said to them, [a]"Whoever
divorces his wife and marries another
commits adultery against her. 12 Also, if
she divorces her husband and marries
another, she commits adultery."

[a] Mt 5:32; 19:9; Lk 16:18

Blessing the Children

13 [a]Some people were bringing little
children to Him so He might touch
them, but His disciples rebuked them.
14 When Jesus saw it, He was indignant
and said to them, "Let the little children come to Me. Don't stop them, for
[b]the kingdom of God belongs to such
as these. 15 •I assure you: [c]Whoever
does not welcome[h] the kingdom of
God like a little child will never enter
it." 16 [d]After taking them in His arms,
He laid His hands on them and blessed
them. [a] Mt 19:13; Lk 18:15

[b] Mt 19:14; Lk 18:16 [c] Mt 18:3 [d] Is 40:11

The Rich Young Ruler

17 [a]As He was setting out on a journey, a man ran up, knelt down before
Him, and asked Him, "Good Teacher,
what must I do to inherit eternal
life?" [a] Mt 19:16; Lk 18:18

18 "Why do you call Me good?" Jesus
asked him. "No one is good but One
—God. 19 You know the commandments:

[a]**Do not murder;**
do not commit adultery;
do not steal;
do not bear false witness;
do not defraud;
honor your father
and mother."[i] [a] Ex 20:12-16

20 He said to Him, "Teacher, I have
kept all these from my youth."
21 Then, looking at him, Jesus loved
him and said to him, "You lack one
thing: Go, sell all you have and give to
the poor, and you will have [a]treasure
in heaven. Then come,[j] follow Me."

[a]**9:48** Is 66:24 [b]**9:49** Other mss add *and every sacrifice will be salted with salt* [c]**9:49** Lv 2:16; Ezk 43:24 [d]**10:6** Other mss omit *God* [e]**10:6** Gn 1:27; 5:2 [f]**10:7** Other mss omit bracketed text [g]**10:7–8** Gn 2:24 [h]**10:15** Or *not receive* [i]**10:19** Ex 20:12–16; Dt 5:16–20 [j]**10:21** Other mss add *taking up the cross, and*

22 But he was stunned[a] at this demand, and he went away grieving, because he had many possessions. *a Mt 19:21*

Possessions and the Kingdom

23 [a]Jesus looked around and said to His disciples, "How hard it is for those who have wealth to enter the kingdom of God!" 24 But the disciples were astonished at His words. Again Jesus said to them, "Children, how hard it is[b] to enter the kingdom of God! 25 It is easier for a camel to go through the eye of a needle than for a rich person to enter the kingdom of God." *a Mt 19:23; Lk 18:24*

26 So they were even more astonished, saying to one another, "Then who can be saved?"

27 Looking at them, Jesus said, "With men it is impossible, but not with God, because [a]all things are possible with God." *a Jr 32:17; Mt 19:26*

28 [a]Peter began to tell Him, "Look, we have left everything and followed You." *a Mt 19:27; Lk 18:28*

29 "I assure you," Jesus said, "there is no one who has left house, brothers or sisters, mother or father,[c] children, or fields because of Me and the gospel, 30 [a]who will not receive 100 times more, now at this time—houses, brothers and sisters, mothers and children, and fields, with persecutions—and eternal life in the age to come. 31 [b]But many who are first will be last, and the last first." *a Mt 5:11-12; Lk 18:30; Jn 16:22-23 b Mt 19:30; Lk 13:30*

The Third Prediction of His Death

32 [a]They were on the road, going up to Jerusalem, and Jesus was walking ahead of them. They were astonished, but those who followed Him were afraid. [b]Taking the Twelve aside again, He began to tell them the things that would happen to Him. *a Mt 20:17; Lk 18:31 b Mk 8:31; 9:31; Lk 18:31*

33 "Listen! We are going up to Jerusalem. The •Son of Man will be handed over to the •chief priests and the •scribes, and they will condemn Him to death. Then they will hand Him over to the Gentiles, 34 and they will mock Him, spit on Him, flog[d] Him, and kill Him, and He will rise after three days."

Suffering and Service

35 [a]Then James and John, the sons of Zebedee, approached Him and said, "Teacher, we want You to do something for us if we ask You." *a Mt 20:20*

36 "What do you want Me to do for you?" He asked them.

37 They answered Him, "Allow us to sit at Your right and at Your left in Your glory."

38 But Jesus said to them, "You don't know what you're asking. Are you able to drink the cup I drink or to be baptized with the baptism I am baptized with?"

39 "We are able," they told Him.

Jesus said to them, "You will drink the cup I drink, and you will be baptized with the baptism I am baptized with. 40 But to sit at My right or left is not Mine to give; instead, it is for those it has been prepared for." 41 [a]When the ⌊other⌋ 10 ⌊disciples⌋ heard this, they began to be indignant with James and John. *a Mt 20:24*

42 Jesus called them over and said to them, [a]"You know that those who are regarded as rulers of the Gentiles dominate them, and their men of high positions exercise power over them. 43 [b]But it must not be like that among you. On the contrary, whoever wants to become great among you must be your servant, 44 and whoever wants to be first among you must be a •slave to all. 45 For even [c]the Son of Man did not come to be served, but to serve, and [d]to give His life—a ransom for many."[e] *a Lk 22:25 b Mt 20:26 c Mt 20:28; Lk 22:27 d Is 53:10; 2Co 5:21*

[a]**10:22** Or *he became gloomy* [b]**10:24** Other mss add *for those trusting in wealth* [c]**10:29** Other mss add *or wife* [d]**10:34** Or *scourge* [e]**10:45** Or *in the place of many*; Is 53:10–12

A Blind Man Healed

46 [a]They came to Jericho. And as He was leaving Jericho with His disciples and a large crowd, Bartimaeus (the son of Timaeus), a blind beggar, was sitting by the road. 47 When he heard that it was Jesus the •Nazarene, he began to cry out, "Son of David, Jesus, have mercy on me!" 48 Many people told him to keep quiet, but he was crying out all the more, "Have mercy on me, Son of David!" *[a] Mt 20:29; Lk 18:35*

49 Jesus stopped and said, "Call him."

So they called the blind man and said to him, "Have courage! Get up; He's calling for you." 50 He threw off his coat, jumped up, and came to Jesus.

51 Then Jesus answered him, "What do you want Me to do for you?"

"*Rabbouni,*"[a] the blind man told Him, "I want to see!"

52 "Go your way," Jesus told him. "Your faith has healed you." Immediately [a]he could see and began to follow Him on the road. *[a] Is 35:5; 42:6-7; Mk 8:22-26*

The Triumphal Entry

11 [a]When they approached Jerusalem, at Bethphage and Bethany near the •Mount of [b]Olives, He sent two of His disciples 2 and told them, "Go into the village ahead of you. As soon as you enter it, you will [c]find a young donkey tied there, on which no one has ever sat. Untie it and bring it here. 3 If anyone says to you, 'Why are you doing this?' say, [d]'The Lord needs it and will send it back here right away.'" *[a] Mt 21:1; Lk 19:29 [b] Ac 1:12 [c] Jn 12:14 [d] Heb 2:7-9*

4 So they went and found a young donkey outside in the street, tied by a door. They untied it, 5 and some of those standing there said to them, "What are you doing, untying the donkey?" 6 They answered them just as Jesus had said, so they let them go. 7 Then they brought the donkey to Jesus and threw their robes on it, [a]and He sat on it. *[a] Zch 9:9*

8 [a]Many people spread their robes on the road, and others spread leafy branches cut from the fields.[b] 9 Then those who went ahead and those who followed [b]kept shouting:

> •*Hosanna!*
> [c]**Blessed is He who comes**
> **in the name of the Lord!**[c]
> 10 Blessed is the coming kingdom
> of our father David!
> ***Hosanna*** in the highest heaven!

[a] Mt 21:8 [b] Is 62:11; Mt 21:9, Lk 19:37-38; Jn 12:13 [c] Ps 118:26

11 [a]And He went into Jerusalem and into the •temple complex. After looking around at everything, since it was already late, He went out to Bethany with the Twelve. *[a] Mal 3:1; Mt 21:12*

The Barren Fig Tree Is Cursed

12 [a]The next day when they came out from Bethany, He was hungry. 13 [b]After seeing in the distance a fig tree with leaves, He went to find out if there was anything on it. When He came to it, He found nothing but leaves, because it was not the season for figs. 14 He said to it, "May no one ever eat fruit from you again!" And His disciples heard it. *[a] Mt 21:18 [b] Mt 21:19*

Cleansing the Temple Complex

15 [a]They came to Jerusalem, and He went into the temple complex and began to throw out those buying and selling in the temple. He overturned the money changers' tables and the chairs of those selling doves, 16 and would not permit anyone to carry goods through the temple complex. *[a] Mt 21:12; Lk 19:45; Jn 2:14*

17 Then He began to teach them: "Is it not written, [a]**My house will be**

[a]**10:51** Hb for *my teacher*; Jn 20:16 [b]**11:8** Other mss read *others were cutting leafy branches from the trees and spreading them on the road* [c]**11:9** Ps 118:26

called a house of prayer for all na-
:ions?[a] But [b]you have made it a den of
:hieves!"[b] 18 Then the •chief priests
ind [c]the •scribes heard it and started
ooking for a way to destroy Him. For
:hey were afraid of Him, because the
vhole crowd was astonished by His
:eaching. [a] Is 56:7 [b] Jr 7:11 [c] Mt 21:45-46; Lk 19:47

19 And whenever evening came,
:hey would go out of the city.

The Barren Fig Tree Is Withered

20 [a]Early in the morning, as they
vere passing by, they saw the fig tree
vithered from the roots up. 21 Then
Peter remembered and said to Him,
"•Rabbi, look! The fig tree that You
:ursed is withered." [a] Mt 21:19

22 Jesus replied to them, "Have faith
n God. 23 [a]•I assure you: If anyone says
o this mountain, 'Be lifted up and
hrown into the sea,' and does not
loubt in his heart, but believes that
vhat he says will happen, it will be
lone for him. 24 Therefore, I tell you,
all the things you pray and ask
or—believe that you have received[c]
hem, and you will have them. 25 And
vhenever you stand praying, if you
iave anything against anyone, [c]forgive
iim, so that your Father in heaven will
ilso forgive you your wrongdoing.[d]
26 But [d]if you don't forgive, neither will
our Father in heaven forgive your
vrongdoing."][e] [a] Mt 21:21; Lk 17:6 [b] Mt 7:7; 18:19; 21:22; Jn 14:13; 16:24 [c] Mt 6:14 [d] Mt 18:35

Messiah's Authority Challenged

27 They came again to Jerusalem. [a]As
He was walking in the temple complex, the chief priests, the scribes, and
he elders came and asked Him, 28 "By
vhat authority are You doing these
hings? Who gave You this authority to
lo these things?" [a] Mt 21:23; Lk 20:1

29 Jesus said to them, "I will ask you
one question; then answer Me, and I
will tell you by what authority I am doing these things. 30 Was John's baptism
from heaven or from men? Answer
Me."

31 They began to argue among themselves: "If we say, 'From heaven,' He
will say, 'Then why didn't you believe
him?' 32 But if we say, 'From men' "—
they were afraid of the crowd, because
everyone thought that John was a genuine prophet. 33 So they answered
Jesus, "We don't know."

And Jesus said to them, [a]"Neither will I tell you by what authority I do these things." [a] Jb 5:13

The Parable of the Vineyard Owner

12 Then He began to speak to them
in parables: "A man planted [a]a
vineyard, put a fence around it, dug
out a pit for a winepress, and built a
watchtower. Then he leased it to tenant farmers and went away. 2 At harvest time he sent a •slave to the
farmers to collect some of the fruit of
the vineyard from the farmers. 3 But
they took him, beat him, and sent him
away empty-handed. 4 Again he sent
another slave to them, and they[f] hit
him on the head and treated him
shamefully.[g] 5 Then he sent another,
and they killed that one. ⌊He⌋ also
⌊sent⌋ many others; they beat some
and they [b]killed some. [a] Mt 21:33; Lk 20:9 [b] 2Ch 36:16; Mt 23:34,37

6 "He still had one to send, a [a]be-
loved son. Finally he sent him to them,
saying, 'They will respect my son.' [a] Ps 2:7; Mt 1:23

7 "But those tenant farmers said
among themselves, 'This is [a]the heir.
Come, let's kill him, and the inheritance will be ours!' 8 So they seized

[a]11:17 Is 56:7 [b]11:17 Jr 7:11 [c]11:24 Other mss read *you receive*; other mss read *you will receive* [d]11:25 These are the only uses of this word in Mk. It means "the violation of the Law" or "stepping over a boundary" or "departing from the path" or "trespass." [e]11:26 Other mss omit bracketed text [f]12:4 Other mss add *threw stones and* [g]12:4 Other mss add *and sent him off*

him, [b]killed him, and threw him out of
the vineyard. [a]Ps 2:8; Heb 1:2 [b]Ac 2:23

9 "Therefore, what will the owner[a] of
the vineyard do? He will come and destroy the farmers and [a]give the vineyard to others. 10 Haven't you read this
Scripture:

> [b]**The stone that**
> **the builders rejected**
> **has become the cornerstone.**[b]
> 11 **This came from the Lord**
> **and [c]is wonderful in**
> **our eyes?"**[c]

[a]Ac 28:23-28 [b]Ps 118:22-23; Mt 21:42; Lk 20:17-18 [c]1Tm 3:16

12 [a]Because they knew He had said
this parable against them, they were
looking for a way to arrest Him, but
they were afraid of the crowd. So they
left Him and went away. [a]Mt 21:45-46

God and Caesar

13 [a]Then they sent some of the •Phar-
isees and the •Herodians to Him to
trap Him by what He said.[d] 14 When
they came, they said to Him, "Teacher,
we know You are truthful and defer to
no one, for You don't show partiality[e]
but teach truthfully the way of God. Is
it lawful to pay taxes to Caesar or not?
15 Should we pay, or should we not
pay?" [a]Mt 22:15; Lk 20:20

But knowing their hypocrisy, He
said to them, "Why are you testing
Me? Bring Me a •denarius to look at."
16 So they brought one. "Whose image
and inscription is this?" He asked
them.

"Caesar's," they said.

17 Then Jesus told them, "Give
back to Caesar the things that are
Caesar's, and to God the things that
are God's." And they were amazed at
Him.

The Sadducees and the Resurrection

18 [a]Some •Sadducees, [b]who say there
is no resurrection, came to Him and
questioned Him: 19 "Teacher, [c]Moses
wrote for us that **if a man's brother**
dies, leaves his wife behind, and
leaves no child, his brother should
take the wife and produce •offspring
for his brother.[f] 20 There were seven
brothers. The first took a wife, and dying, left no offspring. 21 The second
also took her, and he died, leaving no
offspring. And the third likewise.
22 The seven also[g] left no offspring. Last
of all, the woman died too. 23 In the
resurrection, when they rise,[h] whose
wife will she be, since the seven had
married her?"[i]

[a]Mt 22:23; Lk 20:27 [b]Ac 23:8 [c]Dt 25:5

24 Jesus told them, "Are you not deceived [a]because you don't know the
Scriptures or [b]the power of God? 25 For
when they rise from the dead, they
neither marry nor are given in marriage but [c]are like angels in heaven.
26 Now concerning the dead being
raised—haven't you read in the book
of Moses, in the passage about the
burning bush, how God spoke to him:
[d]**I am the God of Abraham and the**
God of Isaac and the God of Jacob?
27 He is not God of the dead but of the
living. You are badly deceived."

[a]Dn 12:2; 1Tm 1:7 [b]Jr 32:17 [c]Mt 22:30; Lk 20:35-36 [d]Ex 3:6

The Primary Commandments

28 [a]One of the •scribes approached.
When he heard them debating and
saw that Jesus answered them well, he
asked Him, "Which commandment is
the most important of all?"[k] [a]Mt 22:34

29 "This is the most important,"
Jesus answered:

[a]**12:9** Or *lord* [b]**12:10** Lit *the head of the corner* [c]**12:10–11** Ps 118:22–23 [d]**12:13** Lit *trap Him in (a) word* [e]**12:14** Lit *don't look on the face of men*; that is, on the outward appearance [f]**12:19** Gn 38:8; Dt 25:5 [g]**12:22** Other mss add *had taken her and* [h]**12:23** Other mss omit *when they rise* [i]**12:23** Lit *the seven had her as a wife* [j]**12:26** Ex 3:6,15–16 [k]**12:28** Lit *Which commandment is first of all?* [l]**12:29** Other mss add *of all the commandments*

[a]**Listen, Israel! The Lord our
God, the Lord is One.**[a] 30 **Love
the Lord your God with all your
heart, with all your soul, with
all your mind, and with all your
strength.**[b] [c]
[a] Dt 6:4

31 "The second is: [a]**Love your neighbor as yourself.**[d] There is no other
commandment greater than these." *[a] Lv 19:18*

32 Then the scribe said to Him, "You
are right, Teacher! You have correctly
said that He is One, [a]and there is no
one else except Him. 33 And to love
Him with all your heart, with all your
understanding,[e] and with all your
strength, and to love your neighbor as
yourself, [b]is far more ⌊important⌋ than
all the burnt offerings and sacrifices."
[a] Dt 4:39; Is 45:6 [b] Hs 6:6; Mc 6:8

34 When Jesus saw that he answered
intelligently, He said to him, "You are
not far from the kingdom of God."
[a]And no one dared to question Him
any longer.
[a] Mt 22:46

The Question about the Messiah

35 [a]So Jesus asked this question as He
taught in the •temple complex, "How
can the scribes say that the •Messiah is
the Son of David? 36 David himself says
[b]by the Holy Spirit:

> [c]**The Lord declared to my Lord,**
> **'Sit at My right hand**
> **until I put Your enemies**
> **under Your feet.'**[f]

37 David himself calls Him 'Lord';
[d]how then can the Messiah be his
Son?" And the large crowd was listening to Him with delight.
[a] Lk 20:41 [b] 2Sm 23:2 [c] Ps 110:1 [d] Rm 1:3; 9:5

Warning against the Scribes

38 He also said in His teaching,
[a]"Beware of the scribes, who want to
go around in long robes, and who
[b]want greetings in the marketplaces,
39 the front seats in the •synagogues,
and the places of honor at banquets.
40 [c]They devour widows' houses and
say long prayers just for show. These
will receive harsher punishment."
[a] Mt 23:1; Lk 20:46 [b] Lk 11:43 [c] Mt 23:14

The Widow's Gift

41 [a]Sitting across from the temple
treasury, He watched how the crowd
dropped money [b]into the treasury.
Many rich people were putting in large
sums. 42 And a poor widow came and
dropped in two tiny coins worth very
little.[g] 43 Summoning His disciples, He
said to them, "•I assure you: [c]This poor
widow has put in more than all those
giving to the temple treasury. 44 For
they all gave out of their surplus, but
she out of her poverty has put in everything she possessed—all she had to
live on."
[a] Lk 21:1 [b] 2Kg 12:9 [c] 2Co 8:12

Destruction of the Temple Predicted

13 [a]As He was going out of the
•temple complex, one of His disciples said to Him, "Teacher, look!
What massive stones! What impres-
sive buildings!"
[a] Mt 24:1

2 Jesus said to him, "Do you see
these great buildings? [a]Not one stone
will be left here on another that will
not be thrown down!"
[a] Lk 19:44

Signs of the End of the Age

3 While He was sitting on the
•Mount of Olives across from the temple complex, Peter, James, John, and
Andrew asked Him privately, 4 [a]"Tell
us, when will these things happen?
And what will be the sign when all
these things are about to take place?"
[a] Lk 21:7

12:29 Or *The Lord our God is one Lord.* [b]**12:30** Dt 6:4–5; Jos 22:5 [c]**12:30** Other mss add *This is the first commandment.* [d]**12:31** Lv 19:18 [e]**12:33** Other mss add *with all your soul* [f]**12:36** Ps 110:1 [g]**12:42** Lit *dropped in two lepta, which is a quadrans*; the *lepton* was the smallest and least valuable Gk coin in use. The *quadrans*, 1/64 of a daily wage, was the smallest Roman coin.

5 Then Jesus began by telling them:
[a]“Watch out that no one deceives you.
6 Many will come in My name, saying,
‘I am He,’ and they will deceive many.
7 When you hear of wars and rumors of
wars, don’t be alarmed; these things
must take place, but the end is not yet.
8 For nation will rise up against nation,
and kingdom against kingdom. There
will be earthquakes in various places,
and famines.[a] These are the beginning
of birth pains.

[a] Jr 29:8

Persecutions Predicted

9 “But you, [a]be on your guard! They
will hand you over to sanhedrins,[b] and
you will be flogged in the •synagogues.
You will stand before governors and
kings because of Me, as a witness to
them. 10 And [b]the good news[c] must
first be proclaimed to all nations. 11 [c]So
when they arrest you and hand you
over, don’t worry beforehand what you
will say. On the contrary, whatever is
given to you in that hour—say it. For it
isn’t you speaking, [d]but the Holy Spirit.
12 Then [e]brother will betray brother to
death, and a father his child. Children
will rise up against parents and put
them to death. 13 And you will be hated
by everyone because of My name. But
[f]the one who endures to the end will
be delivered.[d]

[a] Mt 10:17 [b] Mt 24:14 [c] Lk 12:11; 21:14 [d] Ac 2:4 [e] Mc 7:6; Mt 24:10; Lk 21:16 [f] Rv 2:7,10; 3:10

The Great Tribulation

14 [a]“When you see the [b]**abomination
that causes desolation**[e] standing
where it should not” (let the reader
understand),[f] “then [c]those in Judea
must flee to the mountains! 15 A man
on the housetop must not come down
or go in to get anything out of his
house. 16 And a man in the field must
not go back to get his clothes. 17 [d]Woe
to pregnant women and nursing mothers in those days! 18 Pray it[g] won’t happen in winter. 19 [e]For those will be
days of tribulation, the kind that hasn’t
been from the beginning of the world,[h]
which God created, until now and
never will be again! 20 Unless the Lord
limited those days, no one would survive.[i] But He limited those days because of the elect, whom He chose.

[a] Mt 24:15 [b] Dn 9:27 [c] Lk 21:2 [d] Lk 23:29 [e] Dt 28:15; Jl 2:2

21 [a]“Then if anyone tells you, ‘Look,
here is the •Messiah! Look—there!’ do
not believe it! 22 For false messiahs[j] and
false prophets will rise up and will perform signs and wonders to lead astray,
[b]if possible, the elect. 23 And [c]you must
watch! I have told you everything in
advance.

[a] Mt 24:5,23-25; Lk 21: [b] Mt 24:24 [c] Lk 21:8; 2Pt 3:1

The Coming of the Son of Man

24 [a]“But in those days, after that tribulation:

> The sun will be darkened,
> and the moon will not shed
> its light;
> 25 the stars will be falling
> from the sky,
> and the celestial powers
> will be shaken.

26 [b]Then they will see the •Son of Man
coming in clouds with great power and
glory. 27 He will send out the angels
and gather His elect from the four
winds, from the end of the earth to the
end of the sky.

[a] Zph 1:15; Lk 21:25 [b] Dn 7:13; Mt 16:27; 24:3

The Parable of the Fig Tree

28 “Learn this parable from the fig
tree: As soon as its branch becomes
tender and sprouts leaves, you know
that summer is near. 29 In the same

[a]**13:8** Other mss add *and disturbances* [b]**13:9** Local Jewish courts or local councils [c]**13:10** Or *the gospel* [d]**13:13** Or *saved* [e]**13:14** Dn 9:27 [f]**13:14** These are, most likely, Mark’s words to his readers. [g]**13:18** Other mss read *pray that your escape* [h]**13:19** Lit *creation* [i]**13:20** Lit *days, all flesh would not survive* [j]**13:22** Or *false christs*

way, when you see these things happening, know[a] that He[b] is near—at the
door! 30 •I assure you: This generation
will certainly not pass away until all
these things take place. 31 Heaven and
earth will pass away, but [a]My words
will never pass away. *[a] Nm 23:19; Is 40:8*

No One Knows the Day or Hour

32 "Now concerning that day or hour
no one knows—neither the angels in
heaven nor the Son—except the Father. 33 Watch! Be alert![c] For you don't
know when the time is ⌊coming⌋. 34 [a]It
is like a man on a journey, who left his
house, gave authority to his •slaves,
gave each one his work, and commanded the doorkeeper to be alert.
35 [b]Therefore be alert, since you don't
know when the master of the house
is coming—whether in the evening
or at midnight or at the crowing of
the rooster or early in the morning.
36 Otherwise, he might come suddenly
and find you sleeping. 37 And what I
say to you, I say to everyone: Be alert!"
[a] Mt 25:14 [b] 2Pt 3

The Plot to Kill Jesus

14 After [a]two days it was the •Pass-
over and the Festival of •Unleav-
ened Bread. The •chief priests and the
•scribes were looking for a treacherous
way to arrest and kill Him. 2 "Not during the festival," they said, "or there
may be rioting among the people."
[a] Ex 12:6-20; Mt 26:2

The Anointing at Bethany

3 [a]While He was in Bethany at the
house of Simon who had a serious skin
disease, as He was reclining at the table, a woman came with an alabaster
jar of pure and expensive fragrant oil of
nard. She broke the jar and poured it
on His head. 4 But some were express-
ing indignation to one another: "Why
has this fragrant oil been wasted? 5 For
this oil might have been sold for more
than 300 •denarii and given to the
poor." And they began to scold her.
[a] Mt 26:6

6 Then Jesus said, "Leave her alone.
Why are you bothering her? She has
done a noble thing for Me. 7 [a]You always have the poor with you, and you
can do good for them whenever you
want, but you do not always have Me.
8 She has done what she could; she has
anointed My body in advance for
burial. 9 •I assure you: Wherever the
gospel is proclaimed in the whole
world, what this woman has done will
also be told in memory of her."
[a] Dt 15:11; Jn 12:8

10 [a]Then Judas Iscariot, one of the
Twelve, went to the chief priests to
hand Him over to them. 11 And when
they heard this, they were glad and
promised to give him [b]silver.[d] So he
started looking for a good opportunity
to betray Him. *[a] Mt 10:4; Jn 18:2-3*
[b] Zch 11:12

Preparation for Passover

12 [a]On the first day of Unleavened
Bread, when they sacrifice the Passover lamb, His disciples asked Him,
"Where do You want us to go and prepare the Passover so You may eat it?"
[a] Mt 26:17; Lk 22:7

13 So He sent two of His disciples and
told them, "Go into the city, and a man
carrying a water jug will meet you. Follow him. 14 Wherever he enters, tell
the owner of the house, 'The Teacher
says, "Where is the guest room for Me
[a]to eat the Passover with My disciples?"' 15 He will show you a large
room upstairs, furnished and ready.
Make the preparations for us there."
16 So the disciples went out, entered
the city, and found it just as He had told
them, and they prepared the Passover.
[a] Ex 12:6

[a]**13:29** Or *you know* [b]**13:29** Or *it*; = summer [c]**13:33** Other mss add *and pray* [d]**14:11** Or *money*; in Mt 26:15 it is specified as 30 pieces of silver; see Zch 11:12–13

Betrayal at the Passover

[17] [a]When evening came, He arrived with the Twelve. [18] While they were reclining and eating, Jesus said, [b]"I assure you: One of you will betray Me—one who is eating with Me!"

[a] Mt 26:20; Lk 22:14 [b] Jn 13:21

[19] They began to be distressed and to say to Him one by one, "Surely not I?"

[20] He said to them, "⌊It is⌋ one of the Twelve—the one who is dipping ⌊bread⌋ with Me in the bowl. [21] For [a]the •Son of Man will go just as it is written about Him, but woe to that man by whom the Son of Man is betrayed! It would have been better for that man if he had not been born."

[a] Is 53:1,12

The First Lord's Supper

[22] [a]As they were eating, He took bread, blessed and broke it, gave it to them, and said, "Take ⌊it⌋;[a] this is My body."

[a] Mt 26:26; Lk 22:19; 1Co 11:23

[23] Then He took a cup, and after giving thanks, He gave it to them, and so they all drank from it. [24] He said to them, "This is [a]My blood ⌊that establishes⌋ the covenant;[b] it is shed for many. [25] I assure you: I will no longer drink of the fruit of the vine until that day when I drink it in a new way[c] in the kingdom of God." [26] [b]After singing psalms,[d] they went out to the •Mount of Olives.

[a] Ex 24:8; 1Co 11:25 [b] Mt 26:30

Peter's Denial Predicted

[27] [a]Then Jesus said to them, "All of you will run away,[e] [f] because it is written:

> [b]**I will strike the shepherd,**
> **and the sheep**
> **will be scattered.**[g]

[28] But [c]after I have been resurrected, I will go ahead of you to Galilee."

[a] Mt 26:31; Jn 16:32
[b] Is 53:2-10; Zch 13:7 [c] Mk 16:7

[29] [a]Peter told Him, "Even if everyone runs away, I will certainly not!"

[a] Jr 9:23-24

[30] "I assure you," Jesus said to him, "today, this very night, before the rooster crows twice, you will deny Me three times!"

[31] But he kept insisting, "If I have to die with You, I will never deny You!" And they all said the same thing.

The Prayer in the Garden

[32] [a]Then they came to a place named Gethsemane, and He told His disciples, "Sit here while [b]I pray." [33] He took Peter, James, and John with Him, and He began to be deeply distressed and horrified. [34] Then He said to them, [c]"My soul is swallowed up in sorrow[h]—to the point of death. Remain here and stay awake." [35] Then He went a little farther, fell to the ground, and began to pray that if it were possible the hour might pass from Him. [36] And He said, "•*Abba*, Father! All things are possible for You. Take this cup away from Me. [d]Nevertheless, not what I will, but what You will."

[a] Mt 26:36; Lk 22:39; Jn 18:1 [b] Mt 26:38-44
[c] Is 53:3-4,12; Jn 12:27 [d] Jn 5:30

[37] Then He came and found them sleeping. "Simon, are you sleeping?" He asked Peter. "Couldn't you stay awake one hour? [38] Stay awake and pray so that you won't enter into temptation. The spirit is willing, but the flesh is weak."

[39] Once again He went away and prayed, saying the same thing. [40] And He came again and found them sleeping, because they could not keep their eyes open.[i] They did not know what to say to Him. [41] Then He came a third time and said to them, "Are you still sleeping and resting? Enough! [a]The time has come. Look, the Son of Man

[a]**14:22** Other mss add *eat;* [b]**14:24** Other mss read *the new covenant* [c]**14:25** Or *drink new wine*; lit *drink it new* [d]**14:26** Pss 113–118 were sung during and after the Passover meal. [e]**14:27** Other mss add *because of Me this night* [f]**14:27** Or •*stumble* [g]**14:27** Zch 13:7 [h]**14:34** Or *I am deeply grieved* [i]**14:40** Lit *because their eyes were weighed down*

is being betrayed into the hands of sinners. 42 [b]Get up; let's go! See—My betrayer is near." [a]*Jn 13:1* [b]*Mt 26:46; Jn 18:1-2*

The Judas Kiss

43 [a]While He was still speaking, Judas, one of the Twelve, suddenly arrived. With him was a mob, with swords and clubs, from the chief priests, the scribes, and the elders. 44 His betrayer had given them a signal. "The One I kiss," he said, "He's the One; arrest Him and take Him away under guard." 45 So when he came, he went right up to Him and said, "•Rabbi!"—and kissed Him. 46 Then they took hold of Him and arrested Him. 47 And one of those who stood by drew his sword, struck the high priest's •slave, and cut off his ear.

[a]*Mt 26:47; Lk 22:47; Jn 18:3*

48 [a]But Jesus said to them, "Have you come out with swords and clubs, as though I were a criminal,[a] to capture Me? 49 Every day I was among you, teaching in the •temple complex, and you didn't arrest Me. But the [b]Scriptures must be fulfilled." 50 [c]Then they all deserted Him and ran away.

[a]*Mt 26:55; Lk 22:52* [b]*Ps 22:6; Is 53:7; Lk 22:37* [c]*Jn 16:32*

51 Now a certain young man,[b] having a linen cloth wrapped around his naked body, was following Him. They caught hold of him, 52 but he left the linen cloth behind and ran away naked.

Jesus Faces the Sanhedrin

53 [a]They led Jesus away to the high priest, and all the chief priests, the elders, and the scribes convened. 54 Peter followed Him at a distance, right into the high priest's courtyard. He was sitting with the temple police,[c] warming himself by the fire.[d]

[a]*Mt 26:57; Lk 22:54; Jn 18:13*

55 [a]The chief priests and the whole •Sanhedrin were looking for testimony against Jesus to put Him to death, but they could find none. 56 For many were giving [b]false testimony against Him, but the testimonies did not agree. 57 Some stood up and were giving false testimony against Him, stating, 58 "We heard Him say, [c]'I will demolish this sanctuary made by ⌊human⌋ hands, and in three days I will build another not made by hands.'" 59 Yet their testimony did not agree even on this.

[a]*Mt 26:59* [b]*Pr 6:19; 19:5* [c]*Mk 15:29; Jn 2:19*

60 [a]Then the high priest stood up before them all and questioned Jesus, "Don't You have an answer to what these men are testifying against You?" 61 But [b]He kept silent and did not answer anything. [c]Again the high priest questioned Him, "Are You the •Messiah, the Son of the Blessed One?"

[a]*Mt 26:62* [b]*Is 53:7; 1Pt 2:23* [c]*Mt 26:63*

62 "I am," said Jesus, [a]"and all of you[e] will see **the [b]Son of Man seated at the right hand** of the Power and **coming with the clouds of heaven.**"[f] [a]*Mt 16:27; Mk 8:38; Lk 22:69* [b]*Ps 110:1; Dn 7:13*

63 Then the high priest tore his robes and said, "Why do we still need witnesses? 64 You have heard the [a]blasphemy! What is your decision?"[g]

[a]*Lv 24:16*

And they all condemned Him to be deserving of death. 65 Then some began to [a]spit on Him, to blindfold Him, and to beat Him, saying, "Prophesy!" Even the temple police took Him and slapped Him. [a]*Is 50:6; 53:3*

Peter Denies His Lord

66 [a]While Peter was in the courtyard below, one of the high priest's servants came. 67 When she saw Peter warming himself, she looked at him and said,

[a]**14:48** Lit *as against a criminal* [b]**14:51** Perhaps John Mark who later wrote this Gospel [c]**14:54** Or *the officers*; lit *the servants* [d]**14:54** Lit *light* [e]**14:62** Lit *and you* (pl in Gk) [f]**14:62** Ps 110:1; Dn 7:13 [g]**14:64** Lit *How does it appear to you?*

"You also were with that •Nazarene, Jesus." [a] *Mt 26:58*

68 But he denied it: "I don't know or understand what you're talking about!" Then he went out to the entryway, and a rooster crowed.[a]

69 [a]When the servant saw him again she began to tell those standing nearby, "This man is one of them!" [a] *Mt 26:71; Lk 22:58; Jn 18:25*

70 But again he denied it. [a]After a little while those standing there said to Peter again, "You certainly are one of them, since you're also a Galilean!"[b] [a] *Mt 26:73; Lk 22:59; Jn 18:26*

71 Then he started to curse[c] and to swear with an oath, "I don't know this man you're talking about!"

72 Immediately a rooster crowed a second time, and Peter remembered when Jesus had spoken the word to him, "Before the rooster crows twice, you will deny Me three times." [a]When he thought about it, he began to weep.[d] [a] *Zch 12:10*

Jesus Faces Pilate

15 [a]As soon as it was morning, the •chief priests had a meeting with the elders, •scribes, and the whole •Sanhedrin. After tying Jesus up, they led Him away and handed Him over to •Pilate. [a] *Jn 18:28*

2 [a]So Pilate asked Him, "Are You the King of the Jews?" [a] *Mt 2:2; Jn 18:33-37*

He answered him, [a]"You have said it."[e] [a] *1Tm 6:13*

3 And the chief priests began to accuse Him of many things. 4 [a]Then Pilate questioned Him again, "Are You not answering anything? Look how many things they are accusing You of!" 5 [b]But Jesus still did not answer anything, so Pilate was amazed. [a] *Jn 19:10* [b] *Is 53:7; Jn 19:9*

Jesus or Barabbas

6 [a]At the festival it was Pilate's custom to release for the people a prisoner they requested. 7 There was one named Barabbas, who was in prison with rebels who had committed murder during the rebellion. 8 The crowd came up and began to ask ⌊Pilate⌋ to do for them as was his custom. 9 So Pilate answered them, "Do you want me to release the King of the Jews for you?" 10 For he knew it was because of envy that the chief priests had handed Him over. 11 But [b]the chief priests stirred up the crowd so that he would release Barabbas to them instead. [a] *Mt 27:15; Lk 23:17; Jn 18:39* [b] *Mt 27:20*

12 Pilate asked them again, "Then what do you want me to do with the One you call [a]the King of the Jews?" 13 Again they shouted, "Crucify Him!" [a] *Ps 2:6-7; Is 9:6-7; Jr 23:5-6; Mc 5:2; Zch 9:9*

14 Then Pilate said to them, "Why? What has He done wrong?"

But they shouted, "Crucify Him!" all the more.

15 [a]Then, willing to gratify the crowd, Pilate released Barabbas to them. And after having Jesus flogged,[f] he handed Him over to be crucified. [a] *Jn 19:1,16*

Mocked by the Military

16 Then the soldiers led Him away into the courtyard (that is, •headquarters) and called the whole •company together. 17 They dressed Him in a purple robe, twisted together a crown of thorns, and put it on Him. 18 And they began to salute Him, "Hail, King of the Jews!" 19 They kept hitting Him on the head with a reed and spitting on Him. Getting down on their knees, they were paying Him homage. 20 When they had mocked Him, they stripped Him of the

[a]**14:68** Other mss omit *and a rooster crowed* [b]**14:70** Other mss add *and your speech shows it* [c]**14:71** To call down curses on himself if what he said weren't true [d]**14:72** Or *he burst into tears*, or *he broke down* [e]**15:2** Or *That is true*, an affirmative oath; Mt 26:64; 27:11 [f]**15:15** Roman flogging was done with a whip made of leather strips embedded with pieces of bone or metal that brutally tore the flesh.

purple robe, put His clothes on Him,
and led Him out to crucify Him.

Crucified between Two Criminals

21 [a]They forced a man coming in
from the country, who was passing by,
to carry Jesus' cross. He was Simon, a
Cyrenian, the father of Alexander and
[b]Rufus. 22 [c]And they brought Jesus to
the place called *Golgotha* (which
means Skull Place). 23 [d]They tried to
give Him wine mixed with myrrh, but
He did not take it. 24 Then they crucified Him [e]and divided His clothes, casting lots for them to decide what each
would get. 25 Now [f]it was nine in the
morning[a] when they crucified Him.
26 The inscription of the charge written
against Him was

[a] *Mt 27:32; Lk 23:26* [b] *Rm 16:13* [c] *Jn 19:17*
[d] *Ps 69:21* [e] *Ps 22:18; Jn 19:23* [f] *Mt 27:45; Lk 23:44*

THE KING OF THE JEWS

27 They crucified two criminals[b] with
Him, one on His right and one on His
left. [28 So the Scripture was fulfilled
that says: [a]**And He was counted
among outlaws.**][c d] 29 [b]Those who
passed by were yelling insults at[e] Him,
shaking their heads, and saying, "Ha!
The One [c]who would demolish the
sanctuary and build it in three days,
30 save Yourself by coming down from
the cross!" 31 In the same way, the
chief priests with the scribes were
mocking Him to one another and saying, "He saved others; He cannot save
Himself! 32 Let the •Messiah, the King
of Israel, come down now from the
cross, so that we may see and believe."
[d]Even those who were crucified with
Him were taunting Him.

[a] *Is 53:12; Lk 22:37* [b] *Ps 22:7*
[c] *Mk 14:58; Jn 2:19* [d] *1Pt 2:23*

The Death of Jesus

33 [a]When it was noon,[f] darkness
came over the whole land[g] until three
in the afternoon.[h] 34 And at three[h] Jesus
cried out with a loud voice, [b]***"Eloi,
Eloi, lemá***[i] ***sabachtháni?"*** which is
translated, **"My God, My God, why
have You forsaken Me?"**[j]

[a] *Lk 23:44*
[b] *Ps 22:1*

35 When some of those standing
there heard this, they said, "Look, He's
calling for Elijah!" 36 [a]Someone ran and
filled a sponge with sour wine, fixed it
on a reed, offered Him a drink, and
said, "Let's see if Elijah comes to take
Him down!"

[a] *Mt 27:48; Jn 19:29*

37 [a]But Jesus let out a loud cry and
breathed His last. 38 Then [b]the curtain
of the sanctuary[k] was split in two from
top to bottom. 39 When the •centurion,
who was standing opposite Him, saw
the way He[l] breathed His last, he said,
"This man really was God's Son!"[m]

[a] *Mt 27:50; Lk 23:46; Jn 19:30* [b] *Ex 26:31*

40 [a]There were also women looking
on from a distance. Among them were
•Mary Magdalene, Mary the mother of
James the younger and of Joses, and
Salome. 41 When He was in Galilee,
they would [b]follow Him and help Him.
Many other women had come up with
Him to Jerusalem.

[a] *Lk 23:49* [b] *Lk 8:2*

The Burial of Jesus

42 [a]When it was already evening, because it was preparation day (that is,
the day before the Sabbath), 43 Joseph
of Arimathea, a prominent member
of the Sanhedrin who was himself
[b]looking forward to the kingdom of
God, came and boldly went in to Pilate
and asked for Jesus' body. 44 Pilate was
surprised that He was already dead.
Summoning the centurion, he asked

[a]**15:25** Lit *was the third hour* [b]**15:27** Or *revolutionaries* [c]**15:28** Other mss omit bracketed text [d]**15:28** Is 53:12 [e]**15:29** Lit *passed by blasphemed* [f]**15:33** Lit *the sixth hour* [g]**15:33** Or *whole earth* [h]**15:33,34** Lit *the ninth hour* [i]**15:34** Other mss read *lama*; other mss read *lima* [j]**15:34** Ps 22:1 [k]**15:38** A heavy curtain separated the inner room of the temple from the outer. [l]**15:39** Other mss read *saw that He cried out like this and* [m]**15:39** Or *the Son of God*; Mk 1:1

him whether He had already died.
45 When he found out from the centurion, he gave the corpse to Joseph.
46 [c]After he bought some fine linen, he
took Him down and wrapped Him in
the linen. Then he placed Him in a
tomb cut out of the rock, and rolled a
stone against the entrance to the tomb.
47 Now Mary Magdalene and Mary the
mother of Joses were watching where
He was placed.

[a]Mt 27:57; Lk 23:50; Jn 19:38 [b]Is 30:18; 64:4 [c]Is 53:9

Resurrection Morning

16 [a]When the Sabbath was over,
•Mary Magdalene, Mary the
mother of James, and Salome [b]bought
spices, so they could go and anoint
Him. 2 [c]Very early in the morning, on
the first day of the week, they went to
the tomb at sunrise. 3 They were saying
to one another, "Who will roll away the
stone from the entrance to the tomb
for us?" 4 Looking up, they observed
that the stone—which was very large
—had been rolled away. 5 [d]When they
entered the tomb, they saw a young
man[a] dressed in a long white robe sitting on the right side; they were
amazed and alarmed.[b]

[a]Mt 28:1 [b]Lk 23:56 [c]Jn 20:1 [d]Lk 24:3

6 [a]"Don't be alarmed," he told them.
"You are looking for Jesus the •Naza-
rene, who was crucified. He has [b]been
resurrected! He is not here! See the
place where they put Him. 7 But go, tell
His disciples and Peter, 'He is going
ahead of you to Galilee; you will see
Him there [c]just as He told you.'"

[a]Mt 28:5 [b]Jn 2:19 [c]Mt 26:32

8 So they went out and started running from the tomb, because trembling
and astonishment overwhelmed them.
[a]And they said nothing to anyone,
since they were afraid.

[a]Mt 28:8

Appearances of the Risen Lord

[9 Early on the first day of the week,
after He had risen, [a]He appeared first to
Mary Magdalene, [b]out of whom He had
driven seven demons. 10 She went and
reported to those who had been with
Him, as they were mourning and weeping. 11 [c]Yet, when they heard that He
was alive and had been seen by her,
they did not believe it. 12 Then after this,
He appeared in a different form to two
of them walking on their way into the
country. 13 And they went and reported
it to the rest, who did not believe them
either.

[a]Jn 20:14 [b]Lk 8:2 [c]Lk 24:11

The Great Commission

14 [a]Later, He appeared to the Eleven
themselves as they were reclining at
the table. He rebuked their unbelief
and hardness of heart, because they did
not believe those who saw Him after
He had been resurrected. 15 [b]Then He
said to them, "Go into all the world and
preach the gospel to the whole creation. 16 [c]Whoever believes and is baptized will be saved, but whoever does
not believe will be condemned. 17 And
these signs will accompany those who
believe: [d]In My name [e]they will drive
out demons; they will speak in new languages; 18 [f]they will pick up snakes;[c] if
they should drink anything deadly, it
will never harm them; [g]they will lay
hands on the sick, and they will get
well."

[a]Lk 24:36; 1Co 15:5 [b]Mt 28:19; Jn 15:16 [c]Jn 3:18,36 [d]Ac 5:16 [e]Ac 2:4 [f]Ac 28:5 [g]Ac 9:17

The Ascension

19 Then after speaking to them, the
Lord Jesus was taken up into heaven
and [a]sat down at the right hand of God.
20 And they went out and preached everywhere, the Lord working with them
and confirming the word by the accom-
panying signs.][d]

[a]Heb 1:3

[a]**16:5** In Mt 28:2, the young man = an angel [b]**16:5** *Amazed and alarmed* translate the idea of one Gk word. [c]**16:18** Other mss add *with their hands* [d]**16:9–20** Other mss omit bracketed text

LUKE

The Dedication to Theophilus

1 Many have undertaken to compile
a narrative about [a]the events that
have been fulfilled[a] among us, 2 [b]just
as the original eyewitnesses and servants of the word handed them down
to us. 3 It also seemed good to me,
since I have carefully investigated everything from the very first, to write
to you in orderly sequence, most honorable Theophilus, 4 so that you may
know the certainty of the things about
which you have been instructed.[b]

[a] Jn 20:31; Ac 1:1-3 [b] 1Pt 5:1; 2Pt 1:16; 1Jn 1:1

Gabriel Predicts John's Birth

5 [a]In the days of King •Herod of Judea,
there was a priest [b]of Abijah's division[c]
named Zechariah. His wife was from
the daughters of Aaron, and her name
was Elizabeth. 6 Both were righteous
in God's sight, living without blame according to all the commandments and
requirements of the Lord. 7 But they
had no children[d] because Elizabeth
could not conceive,[e] and both of them
were well along in years.[f]

[a] Mt 2:1 [b] 1Ch 24:10,19

8 [a]When his division was on duty and
he was serving as priest before God, 9 it
happened that he was chosen by lot, according to the custom of the priesthood,
to enter the sanctuary of the Lord and
[b]burn incense. 10 At the hour of incense
the whole assembly of the people was
praying outside. 11 An angel of the Lord
appeared to him, standing to the right of
the altar of incense. 12 When Zechariah
saw him, he was startled and overcome
with fear.[g] 13 But the angel said to him:

Do not be afraid, Zechariah,
because your prayer
has been heard.
Your wife Elizabeth will bear you
a son,
and you will name him John.
14 There will be joy and delight
for you,
and many will rejoice
at his birth.
15 For he will be great in the sight
of the Lord
and [c]will never drink wine
or beer.
He will be filled
with the Holy Spirit
[d]while still
in his mother's womb.
16 [e]He will turn many
of the sons of Israel
to the Lord their God.
17 [f]And he will go before Him
in the spirit and power of Elijah,
to turn the hearts of fathers
to their children,
and the disobedient
to the understanding
of the righteous,
to make ready for the [g]Lord
a prepared people.

[a] 2Ch 8:14 [b] Ex 30:7-8 [c] Nm 6:3 [d] Jr 1:5 [e] Dn 12:3 [f] Mt 11:14 [g] Is 40:3

18 "How can I know this?" Zechariah
asked the angel. "For I am an old man,
and my wife is well along in years."[h]
19 The angel answered him, "I am
[a]Gabriel, who stands in the presence
of God, and I was sent to speak to you
and tell you this good news. 20 Now listen! [b]You will become silent and unable to speak until the day these things

[a]**1:1** Or *events that have been accomplished,* or *events most surely believed* [b]**1:4** Or *informed* [c]**1:5** One of the 24 divisions of priests appointed by David for temple service; 1 Ch 24:10 [d]**1:7** Lit *child* [e]**1:7** Lit *Elizabeth was sterile* or *barren* [f]**1:7** Lit *in their days* [g]**1:12** Lit *and fear fell on him* [h]**1:18** Lit *in her days*

take place, because you did not believe
my words, which will be fulfilled in
their proper time." [a]Dn 8:16 [b]Ezk 24:27

21 Meanwhile, the people were waiting for Zechariah, amazed that he
stayed so long in the sanctuary. 22 When
he did come out, he could not speak to
them. Then they realized that he had
seen a vision in the sanctuary. He kept
making signs to them and remained
speechless. 23 When [a]the days of his
ministry were completed, he went back
home. [a]2Kg 11:5; 1Ch 9:33

24 After these days his wife Elizabeth
conceived and kept herself in seclu-
sion for five months. She said, 25 "The
Lord has done this for me. He has
looked with favor in these days to take
away my disgrace among the people."

Gabriel Predicts Jesus' Birth

26 In the sixth month, the angel Gab-
riel was sent by God to a town in Galilee called Nazareth, 27 to a [a]virgin
•engaged to a man named Joseph, of
the house of David. The virgin's name
was Mary. 28 And ⌊the angel⌋ came to
her and said, "Rejoice, favored woman! The Lord is with you."[a] 29 But she
was deeply troubled by this statement,
wondering what kind of greeting this
could be. 30 Then the angel told her:

Do not be afraid, Mary,
for you have found favor
with God.
31 [b]Now listen:
You will conceive and give birth
to a son,
and you will call
His name JESUS.
32 He will be [c]great
and will be called
the Son of the Most High,
and the [d]Lord God will give Him
the throne of His father David.
33 [e]He will reign over the house
of Jacob forever,
and His kingdom will have
no end.

[a]Is 7:14 [b]Gl 4:4 [c]Php 2:10 [d]Is 9:6-7; Jr 33:15-17 [e]Dn 7:14

34 Mary asked the angel, "How can
this be, since I have not been intimate
with a man?"[b]
35 The angel replied to her:

"The Holy Spirit will come
upon you,
and the power of the Most High
will overshadow you.
Therefore the holy One
to be born
will be called [a]the Son of God.

36 And consider your relative Elizabeth—even she has conceived a son in
her old age, and this is the sixth month
for her who was called barren. 37 For
[b]nothing will be impossible with God."
[a]Jn 20:31 [b]Jr 32:17

38 "I am the Lord's •slave,"[c] said
Mary. "May it be done to me according
to your word." Then the angel left her.

Mary's Visit to Elizabeth

39 In those days Mary set out and
hurried to a town in the hill country
of Judah 40 where she entered Zechariah's house and greeted Elizabeth.
41 When Elizabeth heard Mary's greeting, the baby leaped inside her,[d] and
Elizabeth was filled with the Holy
Spirit. 42 Then she exclaimed with a
loud cry:

You are the most blessed
of women,
and your child will be blessed![e]

43 How could this happen to me, that
the mother of my Lord should come to
me? 44 For you see, when the sound of
your greeting reached my ears, the

[a]**1:28** Other mss add *blessed are you among women* [b]**1:34** Lit *since I do not know a man* [c]**1:38** Lit *Look, the Lord's slave* [d]**1:41** Lit *leaped in her abdomen* or *womb* [e]**1:42** Lit *and the fruit of your abdomen* (or *womb*) *is blessed*

baby leaped for joy inside me![a] 45 She
who has believed is blessed because
what was spoken to her by the Lord
will be fulfilled!"

Mary's Praise

46 And Mary said:

*a*My soul proclaims the greatness
of[b] the Lord,
47 and my spirit has rejoiced in God
my Savior,
48 because *b*He has looked
with favor
on the humble condition
of His •slave.
Surely, from now on
*c*all generations
will call me blessed,
49 because the Mighty One
has done great things for me,
and His name is holy.
50 *d*His mercy is from generation
to generation
on those who fear Him.
51 *e*He has done a mighty deed
with His arm;
*f*He has scattered the proud
because of the thoughts
of their hearts;
52 *g*He has toppled the mighty
from their thrones
and exalted the lowly.
53 *h*He has satisfied the hungry
with good things
and sent the rich away empty.
54 He has helped His servant Israel,
*i*mindful of His mercy,[c]
55 just as He spoke to our ancestors,
to Abraham and his
descendants[d] forever.

a 1Sm 2:1 b Ps 138:6 c Lk 11:27 d Ex 34:6-7 e Ps 98:1 f Ps 33:10 g 1Sm 2:6 h 1Sm 2:5 i Ps 98:3

56 And Mary stayed with her about
three months; then she returned to
her home.

The Birth and Naming of John

57 Now the time had come for Elizabeth to give birth, and she had a son.
58 Then her neighbors and relatives
heard that the Lord had shown her His
great mercy,[e] and they rejoiced with
her.

59 When they came to circumcise the
child *a*on the eighth day, they were going to name him Zechariah, after his father. 60 But his mother responded,
"No! He will be called John." *a Lv 12:3*

61 Then they said to her, "None of
your relatives has that name." 62 So
they motioned to his father to find out
what he wanted him to be called. 63 He
asked for a writing tablet and wrote:

HIS NAME IS JOHN

And they were all amazed. 64 Immediately his mouth was opened and his
tongue ⌊set free⌋, and he began to
speak, praising God. 65 Fear came on
all those who lived around them, and
all these things were being talked
about throughout the hill country of
Judea. 66 All who heard about ⌊him⌋
took ⌊it⌋ to heart, saying, "What then
will this child become?" For, indeed,
the Lord's hand was with him.

Zechariah's Prophecy

67 Then his father Zechariah *a*was
filled with the Holy Spirit and prophesied:

68 Praise the Lord, the God
of Israel,
because He has visited
and provided redemption
for His people.
69 He has raised up a •horn
of salvation[f] for us
in the house of His servant
David,

[a]**1:44** Lit *in my abdomen* or *womb* [b]**1:46** Or *soul magnifies* [c]**1:54** Because He remembered His mercy; see Ps 98:3 [d]**1:55** Or *offspring*; lit *seed* [e]**1:58** Lit *the Lord magnified His mercy with her* [f]**1:69** A strong Savior

70 [b]just as He spoke by the mouth
of His holy prophets
in ancient times;
71 salvation from our enemies
and from the clutches[a] of those
who hate us.
72 [c]He has dealt mercifully
with our fathers
and remembered
His holy covenant—
73 [d]the oath that He swore
to our father Abraham.
He has given us the privilege,
74 since we have been rescued
from our enemies' clutches,[b]
to serve Him without fear
75 [e]in holiness and righteousness
in His presence all our days.
76 And child, you will be called
a prophet of the Most High,
for [f]you will go before the Lord
to prepare His ways,
77 to give His people knowledge
of salvation
through the forgiveness
of their sins.
78 Because of our God's merciful
compassion,
[g]the Dawn from on high
will visit us
79 [h]to shine on those who live
in darkness
and the shadow of death,
to guide our feet into the way
of peace.

a Jl 2:28 b Jr 23:5 c Lv 26:42 d Gn 12:3 e Jr 32:39 f Is 40:3 g Nm 24:17; Is 11:1 h Is 9:2

80 The child grew up and became
spiritually strong, and he was in the
wilderness until the day of his public
appearance to Israel.

The Birth of Jesus

2 In those days a decree went out
from Caesar Augustus[c] that the
whole empire[d] should be registered.
2 This first registration took place
while[e] Quirinius was governing Syria.
3 So everyone went to be registered,
each to his own town.
4 And Joseph also went up from the
town of Nazareth in Galilee, to Judea,
to [a]the city of David, which is called
Bethlehem, [b]because he was of the
house and family line of David, 5 to be
registered along with Mary, who was
•engaged to him[f] and was pregnant.
6 While they were there, the time
came for her to give birth. 7 Then [c]she
gave birth to her firstborn Son, and she
wrapped Him snugly in cloth and [d]laid
Him in a feeding trough—because
there was no room for them at the inn.

a Mc 5:2 b Mt 1:16; Lk 1:27 c Mt 1:25 d Is 53:2

The Shepherds and the Angels

8 In the same region, shepherds
were staying out in the fields and keeping watch at night over their flock.
9 Then an angel of the Lord stood before[g] them, and the glory of the Lord
shone around them, and they were terrified.[h] 10 But the angel said to them,
"Don't be afraid, for look, I proclaim to
you good news of great joy [a]that will be
for all the people: 11 [b]today a Savior,
[c]who is •Messiah the Lord, was born
for you in the city of David. 12 This will
be the sign for you: you will find a baby
wrapped snugly in cloth and lying in a
feeding trough."

a Is 2:2; 60:3 b Is 7:14; 9:6 c Php 2:11

13 [a]Suddenly there was a multitude
of the heavenly host with the angel,
praising God and saying:

14 Glory to God
in the highest heaven,
and [b]peace on earth to people
[c]He favors![i] [j]

a Ps 103:20 b Is 57:19 c Eph 2:4,7

[a]**1:71** Lit *the hand* [b]**1:74** Lit *from the hand of enemies* [c]**2:1** Emperor who ruled the Roman Empire 27 B.C.–A.D. 14; also known as Octavian, he established the peaceful era known as the *Pax Romana*; Caesar was a title of Roman emperors. [d]**2:1** Or *the whole inhabited world* [e]**2:2** Or *This registration was the first while*, or *This registration was before* [f]**2:5** Other mss read *was his engaged wife* [g]**2:9** Or *Lord appeared to* [h]**2:9** Lit *they feared a great fear* [i]**2:14** Other mss read *earth good will to people* [j]**2:14** Or *earth to men of good will*

15 When the angels had left them and
returned to heaven, the shepherds said
to one another, "Let's go straight to Bethlehem and see what has happened,
which the Lord has made known to
us."

16 They hurried off and found both
Mary and Joseph, and the baby who
was lying in the feeding trough. 17 After seeing ⌊them⌋, they reported the
message they were told about this
child, 18 and all who heard it were
amazed at what the shepherds said to
them. 19 But Mary was treasuring up all
these things[a] in her heart and meditat-
ing on them. 20 The shepherds returned, glorifying and praising God for
all they had seen and heard, just as
they had been told.

The Circumcision and Presentation of Jesus

21 [a]When the eight days were completed for His circumcision, He was
named [b]JESUS—the name given by
the angel before He was conceived.[b]
22 And when [c]the days of their purification according to the law of Moses
were finished, they brought Him up
to Jerusalem to present Him to the
Lord 23 (just as it is written in the law
of the Lord: [d]**Every firstborn male**[c]
will be dedicated[d] **to the Lord**[e])
24 and to offer a sacrifice (according to
what is stated in the law of the Lord:
a pair of turtledoves or two young
pigeons[f]).

[a]Lv 12:3 [b]Mt 1:21 [c]Lv 12:2 [d]Ex 13:2

Simeon's Prophetic Praise

25 There was a man in Jerusalem
whose name was Simeon. This man
was righteous and devout, [a]looking forward to Israel's consolation,[g] and the
Holy Spirit was on him. 26 It had been
revealed to him by the Holy Spirit that
he would not see death before he saw
the Lord's Messiah. 27 Guided by the
Spirit, he entered[h] the •temple complex. When the parents brought in the
child Jesus to perform for Him what
was customary under the law,
28 Simeon took Him up in his arms,
praised God, and said:

29 Now, Master,
You can dismiss Your •slave
in peace,
according to Your word.
30 For my eyes have seen
Your salvation.
31 You have prepared ⌊it⌋
in the presence of all peoples—
32 [b]a light for revelation
to the Gentiles[i]
and glory to Your people Israel.

[a]Is 40:1 [b]Is 9:2

33 His father and mother[j] were
amazed at what was being said about
Him. 34 Then Simeon blessed them and
told His mother Mary: "Indeed, this
child is destined to cause the [a]fall and
rise of many in Israel and to be [b]a sign
that will be opposed[k]— 35 and [c]a
sword will pierce your own soul—that
the thoughts[l] of many hearts may be
revealed."

[a]Is 8:14 [b]Mt 26:65-67 [c]Jn 19:25

Anna's Testimony

36 There was also a prophetess,
Anna, a daughter of Phanuel, of the
tribe of Asher. She was well along in
years,[m] having lived with her husband
seven years after her marriage,[n] 37 and
was a widow for 84 years.[o] She did not
leave the temple complex, serving God
night and day with fastings and
prayers. 38 At that very moment,[p] she
came up and began to thank God and
to speak about Him to all who were

[a]**2:19** Lit *these words* [b]**2:21** Or *conceived in the womb* [c]**2:23** Lit *"Every male that opens a womb* [d]**2:23** Lit *be called holy* [e]**2:23** Ex 13:2,12 [f]**2:24** Lv 5:11; 12:8 [g]**2:25** The coming of the Messiah with His salvation for the nation; Lk 2:26,30; Is 40:1; 61:2 [h]**2:27** Lit *And in the Spirit, he came into the* [i]**2:32** Or *the nations* [j]**2:33** Other mss read *But Joseph and His mother* [k]**2:34** Or *spoken against* [l]**2:35** Or *schemes* [m]**2:36** Lit *in many days* [n]**2:36** Lit *years from her virginity* [o]**2:37** Or *she was a widow until the age of 84* [p]**2:38** Lit *very hour*

[a]looking forward to the redemption of
Jerusalem.[a] *[a]Lm 3:25-26*

The Family's Return to Nazareth

39 When they had completed everything according to the law of the Lord,
they returned to Galilee, to their own
town of Nazareth. 40 The boy grew up
and became strong, filled with wisdom, and God's grace was on Him.

In His Father's House

41 [a]Every year His parents traveled to
Jerusalem for the •Passover Festival.
42 When He was 12 years old, they
went up according to the custom of the
festival. 43 After those days were over,
as they were returning, the boy Jesus
stayed behind in Jerusalem, but His
parents[b] did not know it. 44 Assuming
He was in the traveling party, they
went a day's journey. Then they began
looking for Him among their relatives
and friends. 45 When they did not find
Him, they returned to Jerusalem to
search for Him. 46 After three days,
they found Him in the temple complex
sitting among the teachers, [b]listening
to them and asking them questions.
47 And all those who heard Him were
astounded at His understanding and
His answers. 48 When His parents saw
Him, they were astonished, and His
mother said to Him, "Son, why have
You treated us like this? Your father
and I have been anxiously searching
for You." *[a]Ex 23:14-17 [b]Is 11:1-4*

49 "Why were you searching for
Me?" He asked them. "Didn't you
know that I had to be in [a]My Father's
house?"[c] 50 But they did not understand what He said to them.
[a]Mal 3:1-2; Jn 4:34

In Favor with God and with People

51 Then He went down with them
and came to Nazareth and was obedient to them. His mother kept all these
things in her heart. 52 And Jesus increased in wisdom and stature, and in
favor with God and with people.

The Messiah's Herald

3 In the fifteenth year of the reign of
Tiberius Caesar,[d] while Pontius
•Pilate was governor of Judea, •Herod
was tetrarch[e] of Galilee, his brother
Philip tetrarch of the region of Iturea[f]
and Trachonitis,[f] and Lysanias tetrarch
of Abilene,[g] 2 during the high priesthood of [a]Annas and Caiaphas, God's
word came to John the son of Zechariah in the wilderness. 3 [b]He went into
all the vicinity of the Jordan, preaching a baptism of repentance[h] [c]for the
forgiveness of sins, 4 as it is written in
the book of the words of the prophet
Isaiah:

[d]A voice of one crying out
in the wilderness:
"Prepare the way for the Lord;
make His paths straight!
5 **Every valley will be filled,**
and every mountain and hill
will be made low;[i]
the crooked
will become straight,
the rough ways smooth,
6 **and [e]everyone[j] will see**
the salvation of God."[k]

[a]Jn 18:13 [b]Mal 4:6; Mt 3:1; Mk 1:4 [c]Lk 1:77 [d]Is 40:3; Mt 3:3 [e]Is 52:10

7 He then said to the crowds who
came out to be baptized by him,
[a]"Brood of vipers! Who warned you to
flee from the coming wrath? 8 Therefore produce fruit consistent with re-

[a]**2:38** Other mss read *in Jerusalem* [b]**2:43** Other mss read *but Joseph and His mother* [c]**2:49** Or *be involved in My Father's interests* (or *things*), or *be among My Father's people* [d]**3:1** Emperor who ruled the Roman Empire A.D. 14–37 [e]**3:1** Or *ruler* [f]**3:1** A small province northeast of Galilee [g]**3:1** A small Syrian province [h]**3:3** Or *baptism based on repentance* [i]**3:5** Lit *be humbled* [j]**3:6** Lit *all flesh* [k]**3:4–6** Is 40:3–5

pentance. And don't start saying to
yourselves, 'We have Abraham as our
father,' for I tell you that God is able to
raise up children for Abraham from
these stones! 9 Even now the ax is
ready to strike[a] the root of the trees!
Therefore [b]every tree that doesn't produce good fruit will be cut down and
thrown into the fire." [a]*Mt 3:7* [b]*Mt 3:10*

10 "What then should we do?" the
crowds were asking him.

11 He replied to them, [a]"The one
who has two shirts[b] must share with
someone who has none, and the one
who has food must do the same."
[a]*2Co 8:14*

12 [a]Tax collectors also came to be
baptized, and they asked him, "Teacher, what should we do?" [a]*Mt 21:32*

13 He told them, [a]"Don't collect any
more than what you have been autho-
rized." [a]*Mc 6:8*

14 Some soldiers also questioned
him: "What should we do?"

He said to them, "Don't take money
from anyone by force [a]or false accusation; be satisfied with your wages."
[a]*Ex 23:1*

15 Now the people were waiting ex-
pectantly, and all of them were debating in their minds[c] whether John
might be the •Messiah. 16 John answered them all, [a]"I baptize you with[d]
water, but One is coming who is more
powerful than I. I am not worthy to untie the strap of His sandals. He will baptize you with[d] [b]the Holy Spirit and fire.
17 His winnowing shovel[e] is in His
hand to clear His threshing floor and
[c]gather the wheat into His barn, but
the chaff He will burn up with a fire
that never goes out." 18 Then, along
with many other exhortations, he proclaimed good news to the people.
19 But [d]Herod the tetrarch, being rebuked by him about Herodias, his
brother's wife, and about all the evil
things Herod had done, 20 added this to
everything else—he locked John up in
prison. [a]*Mt 3:11* [b]*Jn 7:39* [c]*Mc 4:12*
[d]*Mt 11:2; Mk 6:17*

The Baptism of Jesus

21 When all the people were baptized, [a]Jesus also was baptized. As He
was praying, heaven opened, 22 and
the Holy Spirit descended on Him in a
physical appearance like a dove. And a
voice [b]came from heaven:

You are My beloved Son.
I take delight in You!
[a]*Mt 3:13; Jn 1:32* [b]*Mt 3:17*

The Genealogy of Jesus Christ

23 As He began ⌊His ministry⌋, Jesus
was about 30 years old and was
thought to be[f] the

[a]son of Joseph, ⌊son⌋[g] of Heli,
24 ⌊son⌋ of Matthat, ⌊son⌋ of Levi,
⌊son⌋ of Melchi, ⌊son⌋ of Jannai,
⌊son⌋ of Joseph,
25 ⌊son⌋ of Mattathias,
⌊son⌋ of Amos, ⌊son⌋ of Nahum,
⌊son⌋ of Esli, ⌊son⌋ of Naggai,
26 ⌊son⌋ of Maath,
⌊son⌋ of Mattathias,
⌊son⌋ of Semein, ⌊son⌋ of Josech,
⌊son⌋ of Joda, 27 ⌊son⌋ of Joanan,
⌊son⌋ of Rhesa,
⌊son⌋ of Zerubbabel,
⌊son⌋ of Shealtiel, ⌊son⌋ of Neri,
28 ⌊son⌋ of Melchi, ⌊son⌋ of Addi,
⌊son⌋ of Cosam,
⌊son⌋ of Elmadam,
⌊son⌋ of Er, 29 ⌊son⌋ of Joshua,
⌊son⌋ of Eliezer, ⌊son⌋ of Jorim,
⌊son⌋ of Matthat, ⌊son⌋ of Levi,
30 ⌊son⌋ of Simeon, ⌊son⌋ of Judah,
⌊son⌋ of Joseph, ⌊son⌋ of Jonam,

[a]**3:9** Lit *the ax lies at* [b]**3:11** Lit *tunics* [c]**3:15** Or *hearts* [d]**3:16** Or *in* [e]**3:17** A wooden farm implement used to toss threshed grain into the wind so the lighter chaff would blow away and separate from the heavier grain [f]**3:23** People did not know about His virgin birth; Lk 1:26–38; Mt 1:18–25 [g]**3:23** The relationship in some cases may be more distant than a son.

⌊son⌋ of Eliakim, 31 ⌊son⌋ of Melea,
⌊son⌋ of Menna, ⌊son⌋ of Mattatha,
⌊son⌋ of [b]Nathan, [c]⌊son⌋ of David,
32 [d]⌊son⌋ of Jesse, ⌊son⌋ of Obed,
⌊son⌋ of Boaz, ⌊son⌋ of Salmon,[a]
⌊son⌋ of Nahshon,
33 ⌊son⌋ of Amminadab,
⌊son⌋ of Ram,[b] ⌊son⌋ of Hezron,
⌊son⌋ of Perez, ⌊son⌋ of Judah,
34 ⌊son⌋ of Jacob, ⌊son⌋ of Isaac,
⌊son⌋ of Abraham, [e]⌊son⌋ of Terah,
⌊son⌋ of Nahor, 35 ⌊son⌋ of Serug,
⌊son⌋ of Reu, ⌊son⌋ of Peleg,
⌊son⌋ of Eber, ⌊son⌋ of Shelah,
36 [f]⌊son⌋ of Cainan,
⌊son⌋ of Arphaxad,
[g]⌊son⌋ of Shem, ⌊son⌋ of Noah,
⌊son⌋ of Lamech,
37 ⌊son⌋ of Methuselah,
⌊son⌋ of Enoch, ⌊son⌋ of Jared,
⌊son⌋ of Mahalaleel,
⌊son⌋ of Cainan,
38 ⌊son⌋ of Enos, ⌊son⌋ of Seth,
⌊son⌋ of Adam, [h]⌊son⌋ of God.

[a]Mt 13:55; Jn 6:42 [b]Zch 12:12
[c]2Sm 5:14 [d]Ru 4:18-22 [e]Gn 11:24,26
[f]Gn 11:12 [g]Gn 11:10 [h]Gn 1:26-27

The Temptation of Jesus

4 Then [a]Jesus returned from the
Jordan, full of the Holy Spirit, and
was led by the Spirit in the wilderness
2 for 40 days to be [b]tempted by the
Devil. He ate nothing during those
days, and when they were over,[c] He
was hungry. 3 The Devil said to Him,
"If You are the Son of God, tell this
stone to become bread.".

[a]Is 61:1; Mt 4:1; Mk 1:12 [b]Heb 2:18

4 But Jesus answered him, [a]"It is
written: **Man must not live on bread
alone."**[d] [e] .

[a]Dt 8:3; Mt 4:4

5 So he took Him up[f] and showed
Him all the kingdoms of the world in a
moment of time. 6 The Devil said to
Him, "I will give You their splendor
and all this authority, [a]because it has
been given over to me, and I can give
it to anyone I want. 7 If You, then, will
worship me,[g] all will be Yours.".

[a]Jn 12:31; 14:30

8 And Jesus answered him,[h] [a]"It is
written:

> **Worship the Lord your God,**
> **and serve Him only."**[i]

[a]Dt 10:20

9 [a]So he took Him to Jerusalem, had
Him stand on the pinnacle of the temple, and said to Him, "If You are the
Son of God, throw Yourself down from
here. 10 For [b]it is written:

> **He will give His angels orders**
> **concerning you,**
> **to protect you,**[j] 11 and
> **they will support you**
> **with their hands,**
> **so that you will not strike**
> **your foot against a stone."**[k]

[a]Mt 4:5 [b]Ps 91:11

12 And Jesus answered him, [a]"It is
said: **Do not test the Lord your God."**[l]

[a]Dt 6:16

13 After the Devil had finished every
temptation, he departed from Him [a]for
a time.

[a]Heb 4:15

Ministry in Galilee

14 [a]Then Jesus returned to [b]Galilee
in the power of the Spirit, and news
about Him spread throughout the entire vicinity. 15 He was teaching in their
•synagogues, being [c]acclaimed[m] by everyone.

[a]Mt 4:12 [b]Ac 10:37 [c]Is 52:13

Rejection at Nazareth

16 He came to [a]Nazareth, where He
had been brought up. As usual, He entered the synagogue on the Sabbath

[a]**3:32** Other mss read *Sala* [b]**3:33** Other mss read *Amminadab, son of Aram, son of Joram*; other mss read *Amminadab, son of Admin, son of Arni* [c]**4:2** Lit *were completed* [d]**4:4** Other mss add *but on every word of God* [e]**4:4** Dt 8:3 [f]**4:5** Other mss read *So the Devil took Him up on a high mountain* [g]**4:7** Lit *will fall down before me* [h]**4:8** Other mss add *"Get behind Me, Satan!* [i]**4:8** Dt 6:13 [j]**4:10** Ps 91:11 [k]**4:11** Ps 91:12 [l]**4:12** Dt 6:16 [m]**4:15** Or *glorified*

day and stood up to read. 17 The scroll
of the prophet Isaiah was given to Him,
and unrolling the scroll, He found the
place where it was written:

18 [b]**The Spirit of the Lord is**
on Me,
because He has anointed Me
to preach good news
to the poor.
He has sent Me[a]
to proclaim freedom[b]
to the captives
and recovery of sight
to the blind,
to set free the oppressed,
19 **to proclaim the** [c]**year**
of the Lord's favor.[c d]

[a]Mt 2:23 [b]Is 61:1-2 [c]2Co 6:2

20 He then rolled up the scroll, gave
it back to the attendant, and sat down.
And the eyes of everyone in the synagogue were fixed on Him. 21 He began
by saying to them, "Today as you listen, this Scripture has been fulfilled."
22 They were all speaking well of
Him[e] and were amazed by the gracious
words that came from His mouth, yet
they said, [a]"Isn't this Joseph's son?"

[a]Jn 6:42

23 Then He said to them, "No doubt
you will quote this proverb[f] to Me:
'Doctor, heal yourself.' 'All we've
heard that took place in [a]Capernaum,
do here in [b]Your hometown also.'"

[a]Mt 4:13 [b]Mt 13:54

24 He also said, "•I assure you: [a]No
prophet is accepted in his hometown.
25 But I say to you, there were certainly
[b]many widows in Israel in Elijah's
days, when the sky was shut up for
three years and six months while a
great famine came over all the land.
26 Yet Elijah was not sent to any of
them—but to a widow at Zarephath in
Sidon. 27 [c]And in the prophet Elisha's
time, there were many in Israel who
had serious skin diseases, yet not one
of them was healed[g]—only Naaman
the Syrian."

[a]Mt 13:57; Mk 6:4; Jn 4:44 [b]1Kg 17:9; 18:1 [c]2Kg 5:14

28 When they heard this, everyone in
the synagogue was enraged. 29 They
got up, drove Him out of town, and
brought Him to the edge[h] of the hill
their town was built on, intending to
hurl Him over the cliff. 30 But He
[a]passed right through the crowd and
went on His way.

[a]Jn 8:59

Driving Out an Unclean Spirit

31 Then [a]He went down to Capernaum, a town in Galilee, and was
teaching them on the Sabbath. 32 They
were astonished at His teaching
[b]because His message had authority.
33 [c]In the synagogue there was a man
with an unclean demonic spirit who
cried out with a loud voice, 34 "Leave
us alone![i] What do You have to do with
us,[j] Jesus—•Nazarene? Have You come
to destroy us? I know who You
are—[d]the Holy One of God!"

[a]Mt 4:13; Mk 1:21 [b]Mt 7:28-29 [c]Mk 1:23 [d]Is 49:7; Lk 1:35

35 But Jesus rebuked him and said,
"Be quiet and come out of him!"
And throwing him down before
them, the demon came out of him
without hurting him at all. 36 They
were all struck with amazement and
kept saying to one another, "What is
this message? For He commands the
unclean spirits with authority and
power, and they come out!" 37 [a]And
news about Him began to go out to every place in the vicinity.

[a]Mc 5:4

Healings at Capernaum

38 [a]After He left the synagogue, He
entered Simon's house. Simon's
mother-in-law was suffering from a

[a]**4:18** Other mss add *to heal the brokenhearted,* [b]**4:18** Or *release,* or *forgiveness* [c]**4:19** The time of messianic grace [d]**4:18–19** Is 61:1–2 [e]**4:22** Or *They were testifying against Him* [f]**4:23** Or *parable* [g]**4:27** Lit *cleansed* [h]**4:29** Lit *brow* [i]**4:34** Or *Ha!,* or *Ah!* [j]**4:34** Lit *What to us and to You*

high fever, and they asked Him about
her. 39 So He stood over her and rebuked the fever, and it left her. She got
up immediately and began to serve
them. [a]Mt 8:14; Mk 1:29

40 [a]When the sun was setting, all
those who had anyone sick with various diseases brought them to Him. As
He laid His hands on each one of them,
He would heal them. 41 [b]Also, demons
were coming out of many, shouting
and saying, "You are the Son of God!"
But He rebuked them and would not
allow them to speak, because they
knew He was the •Messiah.
[a]Mt 8:16; Mk 1:32 [b]Mk 1:25,34

Preaching in Galilee

42 [a]When it was day, He went out
and made His way to a deserted place.
But the crowds were searching for
Him. They came to Him and tried to
keep Him from leaving them. 43 But He
said to them, [b]"I must proclaim the
good news about the kingdom of God
to the other towns also, because I was
sent for this purpose." 44 [c]And He was
preaching in the synagogues of Galilee.[a] [a]Mt 14:13; Mk 1:35
[b]Mk 1:14-15; Jn 9:4 [c]Mt 4:23

The First Disciples

5 [a]As the crowd was pressing in on
Jesus to hear God's word, He was
standing by Lake Gennesaret.[b] 2 He
saw two boats at the edge of the lake;[c]
the fishermen had left them and were
washing their nets. 3 He got into one of
the boats, which belonged to Simon,
and asked him to put out a little from
the land. Then He sat down and was
teaching the crowds from the boat.
[a]Mt 4:18; Mk 1:16

4 When He had finished speaking,
He said to Simon, [a]"Put out into deep
water and let down[d] your nets for a
catch." [a]Jn 21:6

5 "Master," Simon replied, "we've
worked hard all night long and caught
nothing! But at Your word, I'll let down
the nets."[e]

6 When they did this, they caught a
great number of fish, and their nets[e] began to tear. 7 So they signaled to their
partners in the other boat to come and
help them; they came and filled both
boats so full that they began to sink.

8 When Simon Peter saw this, he fell
at Jesus' knees and said, "Go away
from me, because I'm a sinful man,
Lord!" 9 For he and all those with him
were amazed[f] at the catch of fish they
took, 10 and so were James and John,
Zebedee's sons, who were Simon's
partners.

"Don't be afraid," Jesus told Simon.
[a]"From now on you will be catching
people!" 11 Then they brought the
boats to land, [b]left everything, and followed Him. [a]Mt 4:19; Mk 1:17
[b]Mt 4:20; Mk 1:18

Cleansing a Leper

12 [a]While He was in one of the
towns, a man was there who had a serious skin disease all over him. He saw
Jesus, fell facedown, and begged Him:
"Lord, if You are willing, [b]You can
make me clean."[g] [a]Mt 8:2; Mk 1:40
[b]Mk 1:40-41

13 Reaching out His hand, He
touched him, saying, "I am willing; be
made clean," and immediately the disease left him. 14 [a]Then He ordered him
to tell no one: "But go and show yourself to the priest, and offer [b]what
Moses prescribed for your cleansing as
a testimony to them." [a]Mt 8:4 [b]Lv 14

15 But the news[h] about Him spread
even more, [a]and large crowds would

[a]**4:44** Other mss read *Judea* [b]**5:1** = Sea of Galilee [c]**5:2** Lit *boats standing by the lake* [d]**5:4** Lit *and you* (Gk pl) *let down* [e]**5:5,6** Other mss read *net* (Gk sg) [f]**5:9** Or *For amazement had seized him and all those with him* [g]**5:12** In these verses, *clean* includes healing, ceremonial purification, return to fellowship with people, and worship in the temple; Lv 14:1–32. [h]**5:15** Lit *the word*

come together to hear Him and to be
healed of their sicknesses. 16 Yet He often withdrew to deserted places and
prayed. [a]*Mt 4:25*

The Son of Man Forgives and Heals

17 On one of those days while He was
teaching, •Pharisees and teachers of
the law were sitting there who had
come from every village of Galilee and
Judea, and also from Jerusalem. And
the Lord's power to heal was in Him.
18 [a]Just then some men came, carrying
on a stretcher a man who was paralyzed. They tried to bring him in and
set him down before Him. 19 Since
they could not find a way to bring him
in because of the crowd, they went up
on the roof and lowered him on the
stretcher through the roof tiles into the
middle of the crowd before Jesus.
[a]*Mt 9:2; Mk 2:3*

20 Seeing their faith He said, "Friend,[a]
[a]your sins are forgiven you." [a]*Mt 9:2*

21 [a]Then the •scribes and the Pharisees began to reason: "Who is this man
who speaks blasphemies? [b]Who can
forgive sins but God alone?"
[a]*Mt 9:3; Mk 2:6-7* [b]*Ex 34:7; Is 1:18; 43:25*

22 But perceiving their thoughts,
Jesus replied to them, "Why are you
reasoning this in your hearts?[b]
23 Which is easier: to say, 'Your sins are
forgiven you,' or to say, 'Get up and
walk'? 24 But so you may know that the
[a]•Son of Man has authority on earth to
forgive sins"—He told the paralyzed
man, "I tell you: get up, pick up your
stretcher, and go home." [a]*Ac 5:31*

25 Immediately he got up before
them, picked up what he had been lying on, and went home [a]glorifying
God. 26 Then everyone was astounded,
and they were giving glory to God. And
they were filled with awe and said,
"We have seen incredible things today!" [a]*Ps 103:1*

The Call of Levi

27 [a]After this, Jesus went out and saw
a tax collector named Levi sitting at the
tax office, and He said to him, "Follow
Me!" 28 So, leaving everything behind,
he got up and began to follow Him. [a]*Mt
9:9; Mk 2:13-14*

Dining with Sinners

29 [a]Then Levi hosted a grand banquet for Him at his house. Now there
was a large crowd of tax collectors and
others who were guests[c] with them.
30 But the Pharisees and their scribes
were complaining to His disciples,
"Why do you eat and drink with tax
collectors and sinners?" [a]*Mt 9:10; Mk 2:15*

31 Jesus replied to them, "The
healthy don't need a doctor, but the
sick do. 32 [a]I have not come to call the
righteous, but sinners to repentance."
[a]*Mt 9:13; 1Tm 1:15*

A Question about Fasting

33 Then they said to Him, [a]"John's
disciples fast often and say prayers, and
those of the Pharisees do the same, but
Yours eat and drink."[d] [a]*Mt 9:14; Mk 2:18*

34 Jesus said to them, "You can't
make the wedding guests[e] fast while
the groom is with them, can you?
35 But the days will come when the
groom [a]will be taken away from
them—then they will fast in those
days." [a]*Zch 13:7; Jn 7:33*

36 [a]He also told them a parable: "No
one tears a patch from a new garment
and puts it on an old garment. Otherwise, not only will he tear the new, but
also the piece from the new garment
will not match the old. 37 And no one
puts new wine into old wineskins.
Otherwise, the new wine will burst

[a]**5:20** Lit *Man* [b]**5:22** Or *minds* [c]**5:29** Lit *were reclining* (at the table); at important meals the custom was to recline on a mat at a low table and lean on the left elbow. [d]**5:33** Other mss read *"Why do John's . . . drink?"* (as a question) [e]**5:34** Or *the friends of the groom*; lit *sons of the bridal chamber*

the skins, it will spill, and the skins
will be ruined. 38 But new wine should
be put into fresh wineskins.[a] 39 And no
one, after drinking old wine, wants
new, because he says, 'The old is
better.' "[b] *[a] Mt 9:16-17; Mk 2:21-22*

Lord of the Sabbath

6 [a]On a Sabbath,[c] He passed
through the grainfields. His disciples were picking heads of grain, rub-
bing them in their hands, and eating
them. 2 But some of the •Pharisees
said, [b]"Why are you doing what is not
lawful on the Sabbath?" *[a] Mt 12:1; Mk 2:23*
[b] Ex 20:10; Mt 12:2; Mk 2:24

3 Jesus answered them, "Haven't you
read [a]what David and those who were
with him did when he was hungry—
4 how he entered the house of God,
and took and ate the •sacred bread,
[b]which is not lawful for any but the
priests to eat? He even gave some to
those who were with him." 5 Then He
told them, "The •Son of Man is Lord of
the Sabbath." *[a] 1Sm 21:6 [b] Ex 29:33*

The Man with the Paralyzed Hand

6 [a]On another Sabbath He entered
the •synagogue and was teaching. A
man was there whose right hand was
paralyzed. 7 The •scribes and Pharisees were watching Him closely, to
see if He would heal on the Sabbath,
so that they could find a charge against
Him. 8 But He [b]knew their thoughts
and told the man with the paralyzed
hand, "Get up and stand here."[d] So he
got up and stood there. 9 Then Jesus
said to them, "I ask you: [c]is it lawful
on the Sabbath to do good or to do
evil, to save life or to destroy it?"
10 After looking around at them all, He
told him, "Stretch out your hand." He
did so, and his hand was restored.[e]
11 They, however, were filled with rage
and started discussing with one another what they might do to Jesus.
[a] Mt 12:9; Mk 3:1 [b] Lk 5:22
[c] Mt 12:12-13; Mk 3:4

The 12 Apostles

12 [a]During those days He went out to
the mountain to pray and spent all
night in prayer to God. 13 When daylight came, He summoned His disciples, [b]and He chose 12 of them—He
also named them apostles:

14 Simon, [c]whom He also
named Peter,
and Andrew his brother;
James and John;
Philip and Bartholomew;
15 Matthew and Thomas;
James the son of Alphaeus,
and Simon called the Zealot;
16 Judas [d]the son of James,
and Judas Iscariot, who became
a traitor. *[a] Mt 14:23 [b] Mt 10:1*
[c] Jn 1:42 [d] Ac 1:13; Jd 1

Teaching and Healing

17 After coming down with them, He
stood on a level place with a large
crowd of His disciples and a great multitude of people from all Judea and
Jerusalem and from the seacoast of
Tyre and Sidon. 18 They came to hear
Him and to be healed of their diseases;
and those tormented by unclean spirits
were made well. 19 The whole crowd
[a]was trying to touch Him, because
[b]power was coming out from Him and
healing them all. *[a] Mt 14:36 [b] Mk 5:30*

The Beatitudes

20 Then looking up at[f] His disciples,
He said:

[a]Blessed are you who are poor,
because the kingdom of God
is yours.

[a]**5:38** Other mss add *And so both are preserved.* [b]**5:39** Other mss read *is good* [c]**6:1** Other mss read *a second-first Sabbath*; perhaps a special Sabbath [d]**6:8** Lit *stand in the middle* [e]**6:10** Other mss add *as sound as the other* [f]**6:20** Lit *Then lifting up His eyes to*

21 [b]Blessed are you
who are hungry now,
because you will be filled.
[c]Blessed are you who weep now,
because you will laugh.
22 [d]Blessed are you when people
hate you,
when they exclude you,
insult you,
and slander your name as evil,
because of the Son of Man.

[a]Mt 5:3 [b]Is 55:1 [c]Is 61:3 [d]Mt 5:11

23 [a]"Rejoice in that day and leap for
joy! Take note—your reward is great in
heaven, because [b]this is the way their
ancestors used to treat the prophets.

[a]Mt 5:12 [b]2Ch 36:16

Woe to the Self-Satisfied

24 [a]But woe to you who are rich,
because [b]you have received
your comfort.
25 [c]Woe to you who are full now,
because you will be hungry.
[d]Woe to you[a]
who are laughing now,
because you will mourn
and weep.
26 Woe to you[a]
when all people speak well
of you,
because this is the way
their ancestors
used to treat the false prophets.

[a]Am 6:1; Lk 12:21 [b]Mt 6:2 [c]Is 65:13 [d]Pr 14:13

Love Your Enemies

27 [a]"But I say to you who listen: Love
your enemies, do good to those who
hate you, 28 bless those who curse you,
[b]pray for those who mistreat you. 29 [c]If
anyone hits you on the cheek, offer the
other also. And if anyone takes away
your coat, don't hold back your shirt either. 30 [d]Give to everyone who asks
from you, and from one who takes
away your things, don't ask for them
back. 31 Just as you want others to do
for you, do the same for them. 32 [e]If you
love those who love you, what credit is
that to you? Even sinners love those
who love them. 33 If you do what is
good to those who are good to you,
what credit is that to you? Even sinners do that. 34 [f]And if you lend to
those from whom you expect to receive, what credit is that to you? Even
sinners lend to sinners to be repaid in
full. 35 But love your enemies, do what
is good, and [g]lend, expecting nothing
in return. Then your reward will be
great, and [h]you will be sons of the
Most High. For He is gracious to the
ungrateful and evil. 36 [i]Be merciful, just
as your Father also is merciful.

[a]Pr 25:21 [b]Lk 23:34 [c]Mt 5:39 [d]Dt 15:7 [e]Mt 5:46 [f]Mt 5:42 [g]Dt 15:7-8 [h]Mt 5:45 [i]Mt 5:48

Do Not Judge

37 [a]"Do not judge, and you will not
be judged. Do not condemn, and you
will not be condemned. Forgive, and
you will be forgiven. 38 [b]Give, and it
will be given to you; a good measure—pressed down, shaken together,
and running over—will be poured into
your lap. For [c]with the measure you
use,[b] it will be measured back to you."

[a]Mt 7:1 [b]Pr 19:17 [c]Mt 7:2; Mk 4:24

39 He also told them a parable: [a]"Can
the blind guide the blind? Won't they
both fall into a pit? 40 A [b]disciple is not
above his teacher, but everyone who is
fully trained will be like his teacher.

[a]Mt 15:14 [b]Mt 10:24; Jn 13:16

41 [a]"Why do you look at the speck in
your brother's eye, but don't notice the
log in your own eye? 42 Or how can you
say to your brother, 'Brother, let me
take out the speck that is in your eye,'
when you yourself don't see the log in
your eye? Hypocrite! First take the log
out of your eye, and then you will see
clearly to take out the speck in your
brother's eye.

[a]Mt 7:3

[a]**6:25,26** Other mss omit *to you* [b]**6:38** Lit *you measure*

A Tree and Its Fruit

43 [a]"A good tree doesn't produce bad fruit; on the other hand, a bad tree doesn't produce good fruit. 44 For [b]each tree is known by its own fruit. Figs aren't gathered from thornbushes, or grapes picked from a bramble bush. 45 [c]A good man produces good out of the good storeroom of his heart. An evil man produces evil out of the evil storeroom, for his mouth speaks from the overflow of the heart. *[a]Ps 92:12-14 [b]Mt 12:33 [c]Rm 8:5-8*

The Two Foundations

46 "Why do you call Me 'Lord, Lord,' and don't do the things I say? 47 [a]I will show you what someone is like who comes to Me, hears My words, and acts on them: 48 He is like a man building a house, who dug deep[a] and laid the foundation on the rock. When the flood came, [b]the river crashed against that house and couldn't shake it, because it was well built. 49 But the one who hears and does not act is like a man who built a house on the ground without a foundation. The river crashed against it, and immediately it collapsed. And the [c]destruction of that house was great!" *[a]Mt 7:24 [b]Ps 125:1 [c]Jb 8:13; Heb 10:28-31*

A Centurion's Faith

7 When He had concluded all His sayings in the hearing of the people, He entered Capernaum. 2 [a]A •centurion's •slave, who was highly valued by him, was sick and about to die. 3 When the centurion heard about Jesus, he sent some Jewish elders to Him, requesting Him to come and save the life of his slave. 4 When they reached Jesus, they pleaded with Him earnestly, saying, "He is worthy for You to grant this, 5 because he loves our nation and has built us a •synagogue." 6 Jesus went with them, and when He was not far from[b] the house, the centurion sent friends to tell Him, "Lord, don't trouble Yourself, since I am not worthy to have You come under my roof. 7 That is why I didn't even consider myself worthy to come to You. But say the word, and my servant will be cured.[c] 8 For I too am a man placed under authority, having soldiers under my command.[d] I say to this one, 'Go!' and he goes; and to another, 'Come!' and he comes; and to my slave, 'Do this!' and he does it." *[a]Mt 8:5*

9 Jesus heard this and was amazed at him, and turning to the crowd following Him, He said, "I tell you, I have not found so great a faith even [a]in Israel!" 10 When those who had been sent returned to the house, they found the •slave in good health. *[a]Rm 9:4*

A Widow's Son Raised to Life

11 Soon afterwards He was on His way to a town called Nain. His disciples and a large crowd were traveling with Him. 12 Just as He neared the gate of the town, a dead man was being carried out. He was his mother's only son, and she was a widow. A large crowd from the city was also with her. 13 When the Lord saw her, [a]He had compassion on her and said, "Don't cry." 14 Then He came up and touched the open coffin,[e] and the pallbearers stopped. And He said, "Young man, I tell you, [b]get up!" *[a]Heb 4:15 [b]Lk 8:54; Jn 11:43*

15 The dead man sat up and began to speak, and Jesus gave him to his mother. 16 Then fear[f] came over everyone, and they glorified God, saying, [a]"A great prophet has risen among us," and [b]"God has visited[g] His people." 17 This report about Him went throughout Judea and all the vicinity. *[a]Lk 24:19; Jn 4:19; 6:14; 7:40-41; 9:17 [b]Lk 1:68*

[a]**6:48** Lit *dug and went deep* [b]**7:6** Lit *and He already was not far from* [c]**7:7** Other mss read *and let my servant be cured* [d]**7:8** Lit *under me* [e]**7:14** Or *the bier* [f]**7:16** Or *awe* [g]**7:16** Or *come to help*

In Praise of John the Baptist

18 [a]Then John's disciples told him
about all these things. So John summoned two of his disciples 19 and sent
them to the Lord, asking, "Are You
[b]the One who is to come, or should we
look for someone else?" *[a] Mt 11:2*
[b] Ezk 34:23; Mc 5:2; Hg 2:7; Zch 9:9; Mal 3:1-3

20 When the men reached Him, they
said, "John the Baptist sent us to ask
You, 'Are You the One who is to come,
or should we look for someone else?'"
21 At that time Jesus healed many
people of diseases, plagues, and evil
spirits, and He granted sight to many
blind people. 22 [a]He replied to them,
"Go and report to John the things you
have seen and heard: [b]The blind receive their sight, the lame walk, those
with skin diseases are healed,[a] the deaf
hear, the dead are raised, and [c]the poor
have the good news preached to them.
23 And anyone who is not offended because of Me is blessed." 24 [d]After John's
messengers left, He began to speak to
the crowds about John: "What did you
go out into the wilderness to see? A
reed swaying in the wind? 25 What then
did you go out to see? A man dressed in
soft robes? Look, those who are splen-
didly dressed[b] and live in luxury are in
royal palaces. 26 What then did you go
out to see? A prophet? Yes, I tell you,
and far more than a prophet. 27 This is
the one it is written about:

> [e]**Look, I am sending**
> **My messenger**
> **ahead of You;**[c]
> **he will prepare Your way**
> **before You.**[d]

28 I tell you, among those born of
women no one is greater than John,[e]
but the least in the kingdom of God is
greater than he." *[a] Mt 11:4 [b] Is 42:6-7*
[c] Is 61:1 [d] Mt 11:7 [e] Is 40:3; Mal 3:1

29 (And when all the people, including the tax collectors, heard this, they
acknowledged God's way of righteousness,[f] [a]because they had been baptized
with John's baptism. 30 But since the
•Pharisees and experts in the law had
not been baptized by him, they rejected the plan of God for themselves.)
[a] Mt 3:5-7; Lk 3:12

An Unresponsive Generation

31 [a]"To what then should I compare
the people of this generation, and what
are they like? 32 They are like children
sitting in the marketplace and calling
to each other:

> We played the flute for you,
> but you didn't dance;
> we sang a lament,
> but you didn't weep!

33 For [b]John the Baptist did not come
eating bread or drinking wine, and you
say, 'He has a demon!' 34 The •Son of
Man has come eating and drinking,
and you say, 'Look, a glutton and a
drunkard, a friend of tax collectors and
sinners!' 35 [c]Yet wisdom is vindicated[g]
by all her children." *[a] Mt 11:16*
[b] Mt 3:4; Lk 1:15 [c] Mt 11:19

Much Forgiveness, Much Love

36 Then one of the Pharisees invited
Him to eat with him. He entered the
Pharisee's house and reclined at the table. 37 And a [a]woman in the town who
was a sinner found out that Jesus was
reclining at the table in the Pharisee's
house. She brought an alabaster flask
of fragrant oil 38 and stood behind Him
at His feet, weeping, and began to
wash His feet with her tears. She
wiped His feet with the hair of her
head, kissing them and anointing them
with the fragrant oil.
[a] Mt 26:6-13; Lk 8:2; Jn 11:2; 12:1-8

[a]**7:22** Lit *cleansed* [b]**7:25** Or *who have glorious robes* [c]**7:27** Lit *messenger before Your face*
[d]**7:27** Mal 3:1 [e]**7:28** Other mss read *women is not a greater prophet than John the Baptist* [f]**7:29** Lit *they justified God* [g]**7:35** Or *wisdom is declared right*

39 When the Pharisee who had invited Him saw this, he said to himself,
[a]"This man, if He were a prophet,
would know who and what kind of
woman this is who is touching
Him—she's a sinner!"
[a] Lk 15:2

40 Jesus replied to him, "Simon, I
have something to say to you."
"Teacher," he said, "say it."
41 "A creditor had two debtors. One
owed 500 •denarii, and the other 50.
42 Since they could not pay it back, he
graciously forgave them both. So,
which of them will love him more?"
43 Simon answered, "I suppose the
one he forgave more."
"You have judged correctly," He told
him. 44 Turning to the woman, He said
to Simon, "Do you see this woman? I
entered your house; you gave Me no
water for My feet, but she, with her
tears, has washed My feet and wiped
them with her hair. 45 You gave Me no
kiss, but she hasn't stopped kissing My
feet since I came in. 46 You didn't
anoint My head with oil, but she has
anointed My feet with fragrant oil.
47 [a]Therefore I tell you, her many sins
have been forgiven; that's why[a] she
loved much. But the one who is forgiven little, loves little." 48 Then He
said to her, [b]"Your sins are forgiven."
[a] 1Tm 1:14 [b] Mt 9:2; Mk 2:5

49 Those [a]who were at the table with
Him began to say among themselves,
"Who is this man who even forgives
sins?"
[a] Is 53:3

50 And He said to the woman, [a]"Your
faith has saved you. Go in peace."
[a] Mt 9:22; Mk 5:34; Lk 8:48; 17:19

Many Women Support Christ's Work

8 Soon afterwards He was traveling
from one town and village to another, preaching and telling the good
news of the kingdom of God. The
Twelve were with Him, 2 and also
[a]some women who had been healed of
evil spirits and sicknesses: Mary, called
•Magdalene ([b]seven demons had come
out of her); 3 Joanna the wife of Chuza,
•Herod's steward; Susanna; and many
others who were supporting them
from their possessions.
[a] Mt 27:55-56
[b] Mk 16:9

The Parable of the Sower

4 [a]As a large crowd was gathering,
and people were flocking to Him from
every town, He said in a parable: 5 "A
sower went out to sow his seed. As he
was sowing, some fell along the path;
it was trampled on, and the birds of the
sky ate it up. 6 Other seed fell on the
rock; when it sprang up, it withered,
since it lacked moisture. 7 Other seed
fell among thorns; the thorns sprang
up with it and choked it. 8 Still other
seed fell on good ground; when it
sprang up, it produced a crop: 100
times ⌊what was sown⌋." As He said
this, He called out, "Anyone who has
ears to hear should listen!"
[a] Mt 13:2; Mk 4:1

Why Jesus Used Parables

9 [a]Then His disciples asked Him,
"What does this parable mean?" 10 So
He said, "The secrets[b] of the kingdom
of God have been given for you to
know, but to the rest it is in parables,
so that

> [b]**Looking they may not see,**
> **and hearing they may**
> **not understand.**[c]

[a] Mt 13:10; Mk 4:10
[b] Is 6:9; Mk 4:12

The Parable of the Sower Explained

11 [a]"This is the meaning of the parable:[d] The seed is the word of God.
12 The seeds [b]along the path are those
who have heard. Then [c]the Devil

[a]**7:47** Her love shows that she has been forgiven [b]**8:10** The Gk word *mysteria* does not mean "mysteries" in the Eng sense; it means what we can know only by divine revelation. [c]**8:10** Is 6:9 [d]**8:11** Lit *But this is the parable:*

comes and takes away the word from their hearts, so that they may not believe and be saved. 13 And the seeds on the rock are those who, when they hear, welcome the word with joy. Having no root, these believe for a while and depart in a time of testing. 14 As for the seed that fell among thorns, these are the ones who, when they have heard, go on their way and are choked with worries, [d]riches, and pleasures of life, and produce no mature fruit. 15 But the seed in the good ground—these are the ones who,[a] having heard the word with an honest and good heart, hold on to it and by enduring, [e]bear fruit.

[a]Mt 13:18; Mk 4:14
[b]Jms 1:23-24 [c]2Co 2:11
[d]Mt 19:23 [e]2Pt 1:5-10

Using Your Light

16 [a]"No one, after lighting a lamp, covers it with a basket or puts it under a bed, but puts it on a lampstand so that those who come in may see the light. 17 [b]For nothing is concealed that won't be revealed, and nothing hidden that won't be made known and come to light. 18 Therefore, take care how you listen. [c]For whoever has, more will be given to him; and whoever does not have, even what he thinks he has will be taken away from him."

[a]Mt 5:15; Mk 4:21
[b]Ec 12:14; Mk 4:22
[c]Mt 25:29; Mk 4:25

True Relationships

19 [a]Then His mother and brothers came to Him, but they could not meet with Him because of the crowd. 20 He was told, "Your mother and Your brothers are standing outside, wanting to see You."

[a]Mt 12:46; Mk 3:31

21 But He replied to them, "My mother and My brothers are those who hear and do the word of God."

Wind and Wave Obey the Master

22 [a]One day He and His disciples got into a boat, and He told them, "Let's cross over to the other side of the lake." So they set out, 23 and as they were sailing He fell asleep. Then a fierce windstorm came down on the lake; they were being swamped and were in danger. 24 They came and woke Him up, saying, "Master, Master, we're going to die!" [b]Then He got up and rebuked the wind and the raging waves. So they ceased, and there was a calm. 25 He said to them, "Where is your faith?"

[a]Mt 8:23; Mk 4:35
[b]Jb 28:11; 38:11

They were [a]fearful and amazed, asking one another, "Who can this be?[b] He commands even the winds and the waves, and they obey Him!"

[a]Mt 8:27; Mk 4:41

Demons Driven Out by the Master

26 [a]Then they sailed to the region of the Gerasenes,[c] which is opposite Galilee. 27 When He got out on land, a demon-possessed man from the town met Him. For a long time he had worn no clothes and did not stay in a house but in the tombs. 28 When he saw Jesus, he cried out, fell down before Him, and said in a loud voice, "What do You have to do with me,[d] Jesus, You Son of the Most High God? I beg You, don't torment me!" 29 For He had commanded the unclean spirit to come out of the man. Many times it had seized him, and although he was guarded, bound by chains and shackles, he would snap the restraints and be driven by the demon into deserted places.

[a]Mt 8:28; Mk 5:1

30 "What is your name?" Jesus asked him.

"Legion," he said—because many demons had entered him. 31 And they

[a]**8:15** Or *these are the kind who* [b]**8:25** Lit *Who then is this?* [c]**8:26** Other mss read *the Gadarenes*
[d]**8:28** Lit *What to me and to You*

begged Him not to banish them to the
•abyss.
32 A large herd of pigs was there,
feeding on the hillside. The demons
begged Him to permit them to enter
the pigs, and He gave them permission. 33 The demons came out of the
man and entered the pigs, and the
herd rushed down the steep bank into
the lake and drowned. 34 When the
men who tended them saw what had
happened, they ran off and reported it
in the town and in the countryside.
35 Then people went out to see what
had happened. They came to Jesus and
found the man the demons had departed from, sitting at Jesus' feet,
dressed and in his right mind. And
they were afraid. 36 Meanwhile the
eyewitnesses reported to them how
the demon-possessed man was delivered. 37 [a]Then all the people of the
Gerasene region[a] asked Him to leave
them, because they were gripped by
great fear. So getting into the boat, He
returned. *a Mt 8:34*

38 [a]The man from whom the demons
had departed kept begging Him to be
with Him. But He sent him away and
said, 39 "Go back to your home, and tell
all that God has done for you." And off
he went, proclaiming throughout the
town all that Jesus had done for him.
a Mk 5:18

A Girl Restored and a Woman Healed

40 When Jesus returned, the crowd
welcomed Him, for they were all
expecting Him. 41 [a]Just then, a man
named Jairus came. He was a leader of
the •synagogue. He fell down at Jesus'
feet and pleaded with Him to come to
his house, 42 because he had an only
daughter about 12 years old, and she
was at death's door.[b] *a Mt 9:18; Mk 5:22*

While He was going, the crowds
were nearly crushing Him. 43 [a]A
woman suffering from bleeding for 12
years, who had spent all she had on
doctors[c] yet could not be healed by
any, 44 approached from behind and
[b]touched the •tassel of His robe. Instantly her bleeding stopped.
a Lv 15:25; Mt 9:20 b Mk 5:27-28

45 "Who touched Me?" Jesus asked.
When they all denied it, Peter[d] said,
"Master, the crowds are hemming You
in and pressing against You."[e]
46 "Somebody did touch Me," said
Jesus. "I know that [a]power has gone
out from Me." 47 When the woman
saw that she was discovered,[f] she
came trembling and fell down before
Him. In the presence of all the people,
she declared the reason she had
touched Him and how she was instantly cured. 48 "Daughter," He said to
her, "your faith has made you well.[g] Go
in peace." *a Mk 5:30*

49 [a]While He was still speaking,
someone came from the synagogue
leader's ⌊house⌋, saying, "Your daughter is dead. Don't bother the Teacher
anymore." *a Mk 5:35*

50 When Jesus heard it, He answered
him, "Don't be afraid. [a]Only believe,
and she will be made well." 51 After He
came to the house, He let no one enter
with Him except Peter, John, James,
and the child's father and mother.
52 Everyone was crying and mourning
for her. But He said, "Stop crying, for
she is not dead but asleep." *a Mk 5:36*

53 They started laughing at Him, because they knew she was dead. 54 So
He[h] took her by the hand and called
out, "Child, [a]get up!" 55 Her spirit returned, and she got up at once. Then
He gave orders that she be given something to eat. 56 Her parents were as-

[a]**8:37** Other mss read *the Gadarenes* [b]**8:42** Lit *she was dying* [c]**8:43** Other mss omit *who had spent all she had on doctors* [d]**8:45** Other mss add *and those with him* [e]**8:45** Other mss add *and You say, 'Who touched Me?'* [f]**8:47** Lit *she had not escaped notice* [g]**8:48** Or *has saved you* [h]**8:54** Other mss add *having put them all outside*

tounded, but He [b]instructed them to
tell no one what had happened.
[a]Lk 7:14; Jn 11:43 [b]Mk 5:43

Commissioning the Twelve

9 [a]Summoning the Twelve, He gave
them power and authority over all
the demons, and ⌊power⌋ to heal[a] diseases. 2 Then [b]He sent them to proclaim the kingdom of God and to heal
the sick. [a]Mt 10:1; Mk 3:13 [b]Mt 10:7-8; Mk 6:12

3 [a]"Take nothing for the road," He
told them, "no walking stick, no traveling bag, no bread, no money; and don't
take an extra shirt. 4 [b]Whatever house
you enter, stay there and leave from
there. 5 [c]If they do not welcome you,
when you leave that town, shake off
the dust from your feet as a testimony
against them." 6 So they went out and
traveled from village to village, proclaiming the good news and healing
everywhere. [a]Mt 10:9; Mk 6:8
[b]Mt 10:11; Mk 6:10 [c]Mt 10:14

Herod's Desire to See Jesus

7 [a]•Herod the tetrarch heard about everything that was going on. He was perplexed, because some said that John had
been raised from the dead, 8 some that
Elijah had appeared, and others that one
of the ancient prophets had risen. 9 "I
beheaded John," Herod said, "but who
is this I hear such things about?" [b]And
he wanted to see Him. [a]Mk 6:14 [b]Lk 23:8

Feeding 5,000

10 [a]When the apostles returned, they
reported to Jesus all that they had
done. [b]He took them along and withdrew privately to a[b] town called Bethsaida. 11 When the crowds found out,
they followed Him. He welcomed
them, spoke to them about the kingdom of God, and cured[c] those who
needed healing. [a]Mk 6:30 [b]Mt 14:13

12 [a]Late in the day,[d] the Twelve approached and said to Him, "Send the
crowd away, so they can go into the
surrounding villages and countryside
to find food and lodging, because we
are in a deserted place here." [a]Jn 6:1-6

13 "You give them something to eat,"
He told them.

"We have no more than five loaves
and two fish," they said, "unless we go
and buy food for all these people."
14 (For about 5,000 men were there.)

Then He told His disciples, "Have
them sit down[e] in groups of about 50
each." 15 They did so, and had them all
sit down. 16 Then He took the five
loaves and the two fish, and looking up
to heaven, He blessed and broke them.
He kept giving them to the disciples to
set before the crowd. 17 Everyone [a]ate
and was filled. Then they picked up[f] 12
baskets of leftover pieces. [a]Ps 145:15-16

Peter's Confession of the Messiah

18 [a]While He was praying in private
and His disciples were with Him, He
asked them, "Who do the crowds say
that I am?" [a]Mt 16:13

19 They answered, [a]"John the Baptist; others, Elijah; still others, that one
of the ancient prophets has come
back."[g] [a]Mt 14:2

20 "But you," He asked them, "who
do you say that I am?"

[a]Peter answered, "God's •Messiah!"
[a]Mk 8:29; Jn 6:69

His Death and Resurrection Predicted

21 [a]But He strictly warned and instructed them to tell this to no one,

[a]**9:1** In this passage, different Gk words are translated as *heal.* In Eng, "to heal" or "to cure" are synonyms with little distinction in meaning. Technically, we do not heal or cure diseases. People are healed or cured from diseases. [b]**9:10** Other mss add *deserted place near a* [c]**9:11** Or *healed*; in this passage, different Gk words are translated as *heal.* In Eng, "to heal" or "to cure" are synonyms with little distinction in meaning. Technically, we do not heal or cure diseases. People are healed or cured from diseases. [d]**9:12** Lit *When the day began to decline* [e]**9:14** Lit *them recline* [f]**9:17** Lit *Then were picked up by them* [g]**9:19** Lit *has risen*

22 saying, [b]"The •Son of Man must suffer many things and be rejected by the
elders, •chief priests, and •scribes, be
killed, and be raised the third day."
[a]Mt 16:20 [b]Mt 16:21; Mk 8:31; Lk 18:31

Take Up Your Cross

23 [a]Then He said to ⌊them⌋ all, "If
anyone wants to come with[a] Me, he
must deny himself, take up his cross
daily,[b] and follow Me. 24 For whoever
wants to save his •life will lose it, but
whoever loses his life because of Me
will save it. 25 [b]What is a man benefited
if he gains the whole world, yet loses
or forfeits himself? 26 [c]For whoever is
ashamed of Me and My words, the Son
of Man will be ashamed of him when
He comes in His glory and that of the
Father and the holy angels. 27 [d]I tell
you the truth: there are some standing
here who will not taste death until
they see the kingdom of God."
[a]Mt 10:38; Mk 8:34; Lk 14:27
[b]Mt 16:26; Mk 8:36 [c]Mk 8:38 [d]Mt 16:28

The Transfiguration

28 [a]About eight days after these
words, He took along Peter, John, and
James, and went up on the mountain
to pray. 29 As He was praying, the appearance of His face changed, and His
clothes became dazzling white. 30 Suddenly, two men were talking with
Him—Moses and [b]Elijah. 31 They appeared in [c]glory and were speaking of
His death,[c] which He was about to accomplish in Jerusalem. *[a]Mt 17:1*
[b]2Kg 2:11 [c]Php 3:21; Col 3:4

32 Peter and those with him were in
a deep sleep,[d] and when they became
fully awake, they saw His glory and the
two men who were standing with
Him. 33 As the two men were departing from Him, Peter said to Jesus,
"Master, it's good for us to be here! Let
us make three •tabernacles: one for
You, one for Moses, and one for Elijah"—not knowing what he said.
34 While he was saying this, a cloud
appeared and overshadowed them.
They became afraid as they entered
the cloud. 35 Then [a]a voice came from
the cloud, saying:

> This is My Son,
> the Chosen One;[e]
> listen to Him!

[a]Mt 3:17; Jn 12:28; 2Pt 1:16-17

36 After the voice had spoken, only
Jesus was found. [a]They kept silent, and
in those days told no one what they
had seen. *[a]Mt 17:9*

The Power of Faith over a Demon

37 [a]The next day, when they came
down from the mountain, a large
crowd met Him. 38 Just then a man
from the crowd cried out, "Teacher, I
beg You to look at my son, because he's
my only ⌊child⌋. 39 Often a spirit seizes
him; suddenly he shrieks, and it throws
him into convulsions until he foams at
the mouth;[f] wounding[g] him, it hardly
ever leaves him. 40 I begged Your disciples to drive it out, but they couldn't."
[a]Mt 17:14

41 Jesus replied, "You unbelieving
and rebellious[h] generation! How long
will I be with you and put up with you?
Bring your son here."
42 As the boy was still approaching,
the demon knocked him down and
threw him into severe convulsions.
But Jesus rebuked the unclean spirit,
cured the boy, and gave him back to
his father. 43 And they were all astonished at the greatness of God.

The Second Prediction of His Death

While everyone was amazed at all
the things He was doing, He told His

[a]**9:23** Lit *come after* [b]**9:23** Other mss omit *daily* [c]**9:31** Or *departure*; Gk *exodus* [d]**9:32** Lit *were weighed down with sleep* [e]**9:35** Other mss read *the Beloved* [f]**9:39** Lit *convulsions with foam* [g]**9:39** Or *bruising*, or *mauling* [h]**9:41** Or *corrupt*, or *perverted*, or *twisted*; Dt 32:5

disciples, 44 [a]"Let these words sink in:[a]
the Son of Man is about to be betrayed
into the hands of men." [a] Mt 17:22

45 [a]But they did not understand this
statement; it was concealed from them
so that they could not grasp it, and they
were afraid to ask Him about it.[b]
[a] Mk 9:32

Who Is the Greatest?

46 [a]Then an argument started among
them about who would be the greatest
of them. 47 But Jesus, knowing the
thoughts of their hearts, took a little
child and had him stand next to Him.
48 He told them, [b]"Whoever welcomes[c]
this little child in My name welcomes
Me. And whoever welcomes Me welcomes Him who sent Me. [c]For whoever is least among you—this one is
great." [a] Mt 18:1 [b] Mk 9:37; Jn 12:44
[c] Mt 23:11-12

In His Name

49 [a]John responded, "Master, we saw
someone driving out demons in Your
name, and we tried to stop him because he does not follow us." [a] Mk 9:38

50 "Don't stop him," Jesus told him,
"because [a]whoever is not against you
is for you."[d] [a] Mt 12:30; Lk 11:23

The Journey to Jerusalem

51 When the days were coming to a
close for [a]Him to be taken up,[e] He determined[f] to journey to Jerusalem.
52 He sent messengers ahead of Him,
and on the way they entered a village
of the •Samaritans to make preparations for Him. 53 But they did not welcome Him, because He determined to
journey to Jerusalem. 54 When the disciples James and John saw this, they
said, "Lord, do You want us to [b]call
down fire from heaven to consume
them?"[g] [a] Mk 16:19; Ac 1:2
[b] 1Kg 18:22-38; 2Kg 1:10,12

55 But He turned and rebuked them,[h]
56 and they went to another village.

Following Jesus

57 [a]As they were traveling on the
road someone said to Him, "I will follow You wherever You go!" [a] Mt 8:19

58 Jesus told him, "Foxes have dens,
and birds of the sky[i] have nests, but
the Son of Man has no place to lay His
head." 59 [a]Then He said to another,
"Follow Me." [a] Mt 8:21

"Lord," he said, "first let me go bury
my father."[j]

60 But He told him, "Let the dead
bury their own dead, but you go and
spread the news of the kingdom of
God."

61 Another also said, "I will follow
You, Lord, but first let me go and say
good-bye to those at my house."

62 But Jesus said to him, [a]"No one
who puts his hand to the plow and
looks back is fit for the kingdom of
God." [a] Heb 6:4

Sending Out the Seventy

10 After this, the Lord appointed
70[k] others, and He [a]sent them
ahead of Him in pairs to every town
and place where He Himself was
about to go. 2 He told them: "The harvest is abundant, but the workers are
few. Therefore, pray to the Lord of the
harvest to send out workers into His
harvest. 3 Now go; [b]I'm sending you
out like lambs among wolves. 4 [c]Don't
carry a money-bag, traveling bag, or
sandals; don't greet anyone along the
road. 5 [d]Whatever house you enter,
first say, 'Peace to this household.' 6 If

[a]**9:44** Lit *Put these words in your ears* [b]**9:45** Lit *about this statement* [c]**9:48** Or *receives* throughout the verse [d]**9:50** Other mss read *against us is for us* [e]**9:51** His ascension [f]**9:51** Lit *He stiffened His face to go*; Is 50:7 [g]**9:54** Other mss add *as Elijah also did* [h]**9:55–56** Other mss add *and said, "You don't know what kind of spirit you belong to. 56 For the Son of Man did not come to destroy people's lives but to save them."* [i]**9:58** Wild birds, as opposed to domestic birds [j]**9:59** Not necessarily meaning his father was already dead [k]**10:1** Other mss read *72*

a son of peace[a] is there, your peace
will rest on him; but if not, it will return to you. 7 [e]Remain in the same
house, eating and drinking what they
offer, for [f]the worker is worthy of his
wages. Don't be moving from house to
house. 8 When you enter any town,
and they welcome you, eat the things
set before you. 9 [g]Heal the sick who
are there, and tell them, [h]'The kingdom of God has come near you.'
10 When you enter any town, and they
don't welcome you, go out into its
streets and say, 11 [i]'We are wiping off
⌊as a witness⌋ against you even the
dust of your town that clings to our
feet. Know this for certain: the kingdom of God has come near.' 12 I tell
you, [j]on that day it will be more tolerable for Sodom than for that town.

[a]Mt 10:1 [b]Mt 10:16 [c]Mt 10:9; Lk 9:3 [d]Mt 10:12 [e]Mt 10:11 [f]Mt 10:10 [g]Lk 9:2 [h]Dn 2:44; Mt 3:2 [i]Mt 10:14 [j]Ezk 16:48-50

Unrepentant Towns

13 [a]"Woe to you, Chorazin! Woe to
you, Bethsaida! [b]For if the miracles that
were done in you had been done in
Tyre and Sidon, they would have [c]re-
pented long ago, sitting in sackcloth and
ashes! 14 But it will be more tolerable for
Tyre and Sidon at the judgment than for
you. 15 [d]And you, Capernaum, will you
be exalted to heaven? No, you will go
down to •Hades! 16 [e]Whoever listens to
you listens to Me. Whoever rejects you
rejects Me. [f]And whoever rejects Me rejects the One who sent Me."

[a]Mt 11:21 [b]Ezk 3:6 [c]Jnh 3:5 [d]Mt 11:23 [e]Jn 13:20 [f]Jn 5:23

The Return of the Seventy

17 The Seventy[b] returned with joy,
saying, "Lord, even the demons submit to us in Your name."
18 He said to them, [a]"I watched Satan fall from heaven like a lightning
flash. 19 Look, I have given you the authority to trample on snakes and scorpions and over all the power of the
enemy; nothing will ever harm you.
20 However, don't rejoice that[c] the spirits submit to you, but rejoice that your
names are written in heaven."

[a]Jn 12:31; 16:11

The Son Reveals the Father

21 [a]In that same hour He[d] rejoiced in
the Holy[e] Spirit and said, "I praise[f] You,
Father, Lord of heaven and earth, because You have hidden these things
from [b]the wise and the learned and
have revealed them to infants. Yes, Father, because this was Your good pleasure.[g] 22 [c]All things have[h] been entrusted to Me by My Father. [d]No one
knows who the Son is except the Father, and who the Father is except the
Son, and anyone to whom the Son desires[i] to reveal Him."

[a]Mt 11:25 [b]1Co 1:19 [c]Mt 28:18 [d]Jn 1:18

23 Then turning to His disciples He
said privately, [a]"The eyes that see the
things you see are blessed! 24 For I tell
you that many prophets and kings
wanted to see the things you see yet
didn't see them; to hear the things you
hear yet didn't hear them."

[a]Mt 13:16

The Parable of the Good Samaritan

25 Just then an expert in the law stood
up to test Him, saying, [a]"Teacher, what
must I do to inherit eternal life?"

[a]Mt 22:35

26 "What is written in the law?" He
asked him. "How do you read it?"
27 He answered:

[a]Love the Lord your God with all your heart, with all your soul,

[a]**10:6** A peaceful person; one open to the message of the kingdom [b]**10:17** Other mss read *The Seventy-two* [c]**10:20** Lit *don't rejoice in this, that* [d]**10:21** Other mss read *Jesus* [e]**10:21** Other mss omit *Holy* [f]**10:21** Or *thank*, or *confess* [g]**10:21** Lit *was well-pleasing in Your sight* [h]**10:22** Other mss read *And turning to the disciples, He said, "Everything has* [i]**10:22** Or *wills*, or *chooses*

**with all your strength, and with
all your mind; and [b]your neighbor as yourself.**[a]

[a]Dt 6:5; Mk 12:30-31 [b]Lv 19:18

28 "You've answered correctly," He
told him. "Do this and [a]you will live."

[a]Lv 18:5

29 But wanting to [a]justify himself, he
asked Jesus, "And who is my neighbor?"

[a]Lk 16:15

30 Jesus took up ⌊the question⌋ and
said: "A man was going down from
Jerusalem to Jericho and fell into the
hands of robbers. They stripped him,
beat him up, and fled, leaving him half
dead. 31 A priest happened to be going
down that road. When he saw him, he
passed by on the other side. 32 In the
same way, a Levite, when he arrived at
the place and saw him, passed by on
the other side. 33 But a •Samaritan on
his journey came up to him, and when
he saw ⌊the man⌋, he had compassion.
34 He went over to him and bandaged
his wounds, pouring on oil and wine.
Then he put him on his own animal,
brought him to an inn, and took care of
him. 35 The next day[b] he took out two
•denarii, gave them to the innkeeper,
and said, 'Take care of him. When I
come back I'll reimburse you for whatever extra you spend.'

36 "Which of these three do you
think proved to be a neighbor to the
man who fell into the hands of the robbers?"

37 "The one who showed mercy to
him," he said.

Then Jesus told him, "Go and do the
same."

Martha and Mary

38 While they were traveling, He entered a village, and a woman named
Martha welcomed Him into her home.[c]
39 She had a sister named Mary, who
also sat at the Lord's[d] feet and was listening to what He said.[e] 40 But Martha
was distracted by her many tasks, and
she came up and asked, "Lord, don't
You care that my sister has left me to
serve alone? So tell her to give me a
hand."[f]

41 The Lord[g] answered her, "Martha,
Martha, you are worried and upset
about many things, 42 but one thing is
necessary. Mary has made the right
choice,[h] and it will not be taken away
from her."

The Model Prayer

11 He was praying in a certain
place, and when He finished,
one of His disciples said to Him,
"Lord, [a]teach us to pray, just as John
also taught his disciples."

[a]Ps 19:14; Rm 8:26-27

2 He said to them, "Whenever you
pray, say:

[a]Father,[i]
Your name be honored as holy.
[b]Your kingdom come.[j]
3 Give us each day
our daily bread.[k]
4 And forgive us our sins,
for [c]we ourselves also
forgive everyone
in debt[l] to us.
[d]And do not bring us
into temptation."[m]

[a]Is 63:16; Mt 5:16
[b]Is 11:9; Dn 7:14
[c]Mt 6:12,14 [d]Mt 6:13

Keep Asking, Searching, Knocking

5 He also said to them: "Suppose one
of you[n] has a friend and goes to him at
midnight and says to him, 'Friend,
lend me three loaves of bread, 6 because a friend of mine on a journey has

[a]**10:27** Dt 6:5; Lv 19:18 [b]**10:35** Other mss add *as he was leaving* [c]**10:38** Other mss omit *into her home* [d]**10:39** Other mss read *at Jesus'* [e]**10:39** Lit *to His word* or *message* [f]**10:40** Or *tell her to help me* [g]**10:41** Other mss read *Jesus* [h]**10:42** Lit *has chosen the good part* [i]**11:2** Other mss read *Our Father in heaven* [j]**11:2** Other mss add *Your will be done on earth as it is in heaven* [k]**11:3** Or *our bread for tomorrow* [l]**11:4** Or *everyone who wrongs us* [m]**11:4** Other mss add *But deliver us from the evil one* [n]**11:5** Lit *Who of you*

come to me, and I don't have anything
to offer him.'[a] 7 Then he will answer
from inside and say, 'Don't bother me!
The door is already locked, and my
children and I have gone to bed. I can't
get up to give you anything.' 8 I tell
you, even though he won't get up and
give him anything because he is his
friend, yet because of his persistence,[b]
he will get up and give him as much as
he needs.

9 [a]"So I say to you, keep asking,[c] and
it will be given to you. Keep searching,[d] and you will find. Keep knocking,[e] and the door will be opened to
you. 10 For everyone who asks receives, and the one who searches
finds, and to the one who knocks, the
door will be opened. 11 [b]What father
among you, if his son[f] asks for a fish,
will give him a snake instead of a fish?
12 Or if he asks for an egg, will give
him a scorpion? 13 If you then, who are
evil, know how to give good gifts to
your children, how much more will
the heavenly Father give[g] the Holy
Spirit to those who ask Him?"

a Mt 7:7; Mk 11:24; Jn 15:7 b Mt 7:9

A House Divided

14 [a]Now He was driving out a demon
that was mute.[h] When the demon
came out, the man who had been
mute, spoke, and the crowds were
amazed. 15 But some of them said,
[b]"He drives out demons by •Beelzebul,
the ruler of the demons!" 16 And others, as a test, [c]were demanding of Him
a sign from heaven.

a Mt 9:32 b Mt 9:34 c Mt 12:38

17 [a]Knowing their thoughts, He told
them: "Every kingdom divided against
itself is headed for destruction, and a
house divided against itself falls. 18 If
Satan also is divided against himself,
how will his kingdom stand? For you
say I drive out demons by Beelzebul.
19 And if I drive out demons by Beelzebul, who is it [b]your sons[i] drive them
out by? For this reason they will be
your judges. 20 If I drive out demons by
the finger of God, then the kingdom of
God has come to you. 21 [c]When a
strong man, fully armed, guards his estate, his possessions are secure.[j] 22 But
when one stronger than he attacks and
overpowers him, he takes from him all
his weapons[k] he trusted in, and divides
up his plunder. 23 [d]Anyone who is not
with Me is against Me, and anyone
who does not gather with Me scatters.

a Mk 3:24 b Mk 9:38; Lk 9:49 c Mt 12:29; Mk 3:27 d Mt 12:30

An Unclean Spirit's Return

24 [a]"When an unclean spirit comes
out of a man, it roams through water-
less places looking for rest, and not
finding rest, it then[l] says, 'I'll go back
to my house where I came from.'
25 And returning, it finds ⌊the house⌋
swept and put in order. 26 Then it goes
and brings seven other spirits more
evil than itself, and they enter and settle down there. As a result, [b]that man's
last condition is worse than the first."

a Mt 12:43 b Heb 6:4

True Blessedness

27 As He was saying these things, a
woman from the crowd raised her
voice and said to Him, "The womb that
bore You and the one who nursed You
are blessed!"

28 He said, "Even more, [a]those who
hear the word of God and keep it are
blessed!"

a Ps 112:1; Is 48:17-18

The Sign of Jonah

29 [a]As the crowds were increasing,
He began saying: "This generation is

[a]**11:6** Lit *I have nothing to set before him* [b]**11:8** Or *annoying persistence*, or *shamelessness* [c]**11:9** Or *you, ask* [d]**11:9** Or *Search* [e]**11:9** Or *Knock* [f]**11:11** Other mss read *son asks for bread, would give him a stone? Or if he* [g]**11:13** Lit *the Father from heaven will give* [h]**11:14** A demon that caused the man to be mute [i]**11:19** Your exorcists [j]**11:21** Lit *his possessions are in peace* [k]**11:22** Gk *panoplia*, the armor and weapons of a foot soldier; Eph 6:11,13 [l]**11:24** Other mss omit *then*

an evil generation. It demands a sign,
but no sign will be given to it except
the sign of Jonah.[a] 30 For just as [b]Jonah
became a sign to the people of Nineveh, so also the •Son of Man will be to
this generation. 31 [c]The queen of the
south will rise up at the judgment with
the men of this generation and condemn them, because she came from
the ends of the earth to hear the wisdom of Solomon, and look—[d]some-
thing greater than Solomon is here!
32 The men of Nineveh will rise up at
the judgment with this generation and
condemn it, because [e]they repented
at Jonah's proclamation, and look—
something greater than Jonah is here!

[a] Mt 12:38-39 [b] Jnh 1:17 [c] 1Kg 10:1 [d] Is 9:6 [e] Jnh 3:5

The Lamp of the Body

33 [a]"No one lights a lamp and puts it
in the cellar or under a basket,[b] but on
a lampstand, so that those who come
in may see its light. 34 [b]Your eye is the
lamp of the body. When your eye is
good, your whole body is also full of
light. But when it is bad, your body is
also full of darkness. 35 Take care then,
that the light in you is not darkness.
36 If therefore your whole body is full of
light, with no part of it in darkness, the
whole body will be full of light, as
when a lamp shines its light on you."[c]

[a] Mt 5:15; Mk 4:21; Lk 8:16 [b] Mt 6:22

Religious Hypocrisy Denounced

37 As He was speaking, a •Pharisee
asked Him to dine with him. So He
went in and reclined at the table.
38 When the Pharisee saw this, he was
amazed that He did not first perform
the ritual washing[d] before dinner.
39 [a]But the Lord said to him: "Now you
Pharisees clean the outside of the cup
and dish, but [b]inside you are full of
greed and evil. 40 Fools! Didn't He who
made the outside make the inside too?
41 [c]But give to charity what is within,[e]
and then everything is clean for you.

[a] Mt 23:25 [b] Pr 26:24; Jr 4:14 [c] Is 58:7

42 [a]"But woe to you Pharisees! [b]You
give a tenth[f] of mint, rue, and every
kind of herb, and you bypass[g] justice
and love for God.[h] These things you
should have done without neglecting
the others.

[a] Mt 23:23 [b] 1Sm 15:22

43 [a]"Woe to you Pharisees! You love
the front seat in the •synagogues and
greetings in the marketplaces.

[a] Mt 23:6

44 [a]"Woe to you![i] You are like un-
marked graves; the people who walk
over them don't know it."

[a] Mt 23:27

45 One of the experts in the law answered Him, "Teacher, when You say
these things You insult us too."
46 Then He said: "Woe also to [a]you
experts in the law! You load people
with burdens that are hard to carry, yet
you yourselves don't touch these burdens with one of your fingers.

[a] Mt 23:4

47 [a]"Woe to you! You build monuments[j] to the prophets, and your fathers killed them. 48 Therefore you are
witnesses that you approve[k] the deeds
of your fathers, for they killed them,
and you build their monuments.[l]
49 Because of this, the wisdom of God
said, [b]'I will send them prophets and
apostles, and some of them they will
kill and persecute,' 50 so that this generation may be held responsible for the
blood of all the prophets shed since the
foundation of the world[m] — 51 [c]from
the blood of Abel to the blood of Zechariah, who perished between the altar
and the sanctuary.

[a] Mt 23:29 [b] Mt 23:34 [c] Gn 4:8

[a]**11:29** Other mss add *the prophet* [b]**11:33** Other mss omit *or under a basket* [c]**11:36** Or *shines on you with its rays* [d]**11:38** Lit *He did not first wash* [e]**11:41** Or *But donate from the heart as charity* [f]**11:42** Or *a tithe* [g]**11:42** Or *neglect* [h]**11:42** Lit *the justice and the love of God* [i]**11:44** Other mss read *you scribes and Pharisees, hypocrites!* [j]**11:47** Or *graves* [k]**11:48** Lit *witnesses and approve* [l]**11:48** Other mss omit *their monuments* [m]**11:50** Lit *so that the blood of all . . . world may be required of this generation,*

"Yes, I tell you, this generation will
be held responsible.[a]
52 [a]"Woe to you experts in the law!
You have taken away the key of knowledge! You didn't go in yourselves, and
you hindered those who were going
in." *[a] Mt 23:13*

53 When He left there,[b] the •scribes
and the Pharisees began to oppose
Him fiercely and to cross-examine Him
about many things; 54 they were lying
in wait for Him [a]to trap Him in something He said.[c] *[a] Mk 12:13*

Beware of Religious Hypocrisy

12 In [a]these circumstances,[d] a
crowd of many thousands came
together, so that they were trampling
on one another. He began to say to His
disciples first: [b]"Be on your guard
against the yeast[e] of the •Pharisees,
which is hypocrisy. 2 [c]There is nothing
covered that won't be uncovered,
nothing hidden that won't be made
known. 3 Therefore whatever you
have said in the dark will be heard in
the light, and what you have whis-
pered in an ear in private rooms will
be proclaimed on the housetops.
[a] Mt 16:6; Mk 8:15 [b] Mt 16:12 [c] Mk 4:22; Lk 8:17

Fear God

4 [a]"And I say to you, My friends,
don't fear those who kill the body, and
after that can do nothing more. 5 But I
will show you the One to fear: Fear
Him who has authority to throw ⌊peo-
ple⌋ into •hell after death. Yes, I say to
you, this is the One to fear! 6 Aren't
five sparrows sold for two [b]pennies?[f]
Yet not one of them is forgotten in
God's sight. 7 Indeed, the hairs of your
head are all counted. Don't be afraid;
you are worth more than many sparrows! *[a] Is 8:12-13; 51:7-13 [b] Mt 10:29*

Acknowledging Christ

8 [a]"And I say to you, anyone who acknowledges Me before men, the •Son
of Man will also acknowledge him before the angels of God, 9 but whoever
denies Me before men will be denied
before the angels of God. 10 [b]Anyone
who speaks a word against the Son of
Man will be forgiven, but the one who
blasphemes against the Holy Spirit will
not be forgiven. 11 [c]Whenever they
bring you before •synagogues and rulers and authorities, don't worry about
how you should defend yourselves or
what you should say. 12 For the Holy
Spirit will teach you at that very hour
what must be said." *[a] Mt 10:32; Mk 8:38*
[b] Mt 12:31-32; Mk 3:28
[c] Mt 10:19; Mk 13:11

The Parable of the Rich Fool

13 Someone from the crowd said to
Him, "Teacher, tell my brother to divide the inheritance with me."
14 "Friend,"[g] He said to him, "who
appointed Me a judge or arbitrator over
you?" 15 He then told them, "Watch out
and be on guard against all greed because one's life is not in the abundance
of his possessions."
16 Then He told them a parable: "A
rich man's land was very productive.
17 He thought to himself, 'What should
I do, since I don't have anywhere to
store my crops? 18 I will do this,' he
said. 'I'll tear down my barns and build
bigger ones and store all my grain and
my goods there. 19 Then I'll say to myself, [a]"You[h] have many goods stored up
for many years. Take it easy; eat, drink,
and enjoy yourself."' *[a] Pr 27:1; Ec 11:9*

20 "But God said to him, 'You fool!
This very night your •life is demanded
of you. [a]And the things you have prepared—whose will they be?' *[a] Ps 39:6*

[a]**11:51** Lit *you, it will be required of this generation* [b]**11:53** Other mss read *And as He was saying these things to them* [c]**11:54** Other mss add *so that they might bring charges against Him* [d]**12:1** Or *Meanwhile,* or *At this time,* or *During this period* [e]**12:1** Or *leaven* [f]**12:6** Lit *two assaria;* the *assarion* (sg) was a small copper coin [g]**12:14** Lit *Man* [h]**12:19** Lit *say to my soul, "Soul, you*

21 “That’s how it is with the one who
stores up treasure for himself [a]and is
not rich toward God.” [a] Mt 6:20

The Cure for Anxiety

22 Then He said to His disciples:
“Therefore I tell you, [a]don’t worry
about your life, what you will eat; or
about the body, what you will wear.
23 For life is more than food and the
body more than clothing. 24 Consider
the ravens: they don’t sow or reap;
they don’t have a storeroom or a barn;
yet [b]God feeds them. Aren’t you worth
much more than the birds? 25 Can any
of you add a •cubit to his height[a] by
worrying? 26 If then you’re not able to
do even a little thing, why worry about
the rest? [a] Mt 6:20 [b] Ps 147:9

27 “Consider how the wildflowers
grow: they don’t labor or spin thread.
Yet I tell you, not even Solomon in all
his splendor was adorned like one of
these! 28 If that’s how God clothes the
grass, which is in the field today and is
thrown into the furnace tomorrow,
how much more will He do for
you—you of little faith? 29 Don’t keep
striving for what you should eat and
what you should drink, and don’t be
anxious. 30 For the Gentile world eagerly seeks all these things, and your
Father [a]knows that you need them.
[a] Mt 6:31-32

31 [a]“But seek His kingdom, and these
things will be provided for you.
32 Don’t be afraid, little flock, because
[b]your Father delights to give you the
kingdom. 33 [c]Sell your possessions and
give to the poor. [d]Make money-bags for
yourselves that won’t grow old, an in-
exhaustible treasure in heaven, where
no thief comes near and no moth de-
stroys. 34 For where your treasure is,
there your heart will be also. [a] Mt 6:33
[b] Mt 11:25 [c] Mt 19:21 [d] Mt 6:20

Ready for the Master’s Return

35 “Be ready for service[b] and have
[a]your lamps lit. 36 You must be like people waiting for their master to return[c]
from the wedding banquet so that
when he comes and knocks, they can
open ⌊the door⌋ for him at once.
37 [b]Those •slaves the master will find
alert when he comes will be blessed. •I
assure you: He will get ready,[d] have
them recline at the table, then come
and serve them. 38 If he comes in the
middle of the night, or even near
dawn,[e] and finds them alert, those
slaves are blessed. 39 But know this: if
the homeowner had known at what
hour the thief was coming, he would
not have let his house be broken into.
40 [c]You also be ready, because the Son
of Man is coming at an hour that you
do not expect.” [a] Mt 5:16 [b] Mt 24:46;
2Pt 1:10-11 [c] Mt 25:13; Mk 13:33

Rewards and Punishment

41 “Lord,” Peter asked, “are You telling this parable to us or to everyone?”
42 The Lord said: [a]“Who then is the
faithful and sensible manager his master will put in charge of his household
servants to give them their allotted
food at the proper time? 43 That •slave
whose master finds him working when
he comes will be rewarded. 44 I tell you
the truth: [b]he will put him in charge of
all his possessions. 45 But if that slave
says in his heart, ‘My master is delay-
ing his coming,’ and starts to beat the
male and female slaves, and to eat and
drink and get drunk, 46 that slave’s
master will come on a day he does not
expect him and at an hour he does not
know. He will cut him to pieces[f] and
assign him a place with the unbelievers.[g] 47 And [c]that slave who knew his
master’s will and didn’t prepare himself or do it[h] will be severely beaten.

[a]**12:25** Or *add one moment to his life-span* [b]**12:35** Lit *Let your loins be girded*; an idiom for tying up loose outer clothing in preparation for action; Ex 12:11 [c]**12:36** Lit *master, when he should return* [d]**12:37** Lit *will gird himself* [e]**12:38** Lit *even in the second or third watch* [f]**12:46** Lit *him in two* [g]**12:46** Or *unfaithful*, or *untrustworthy* [h]**12:47** Lit *or do toward his will*

48 But the one who did not know and
did things deserving of blows will be
beaten lightly. Much will be required
of everyone who has been given much.
And even more will be expected of the
one who has been entrusted with
more.[a]

[a] Mt 24:45-46 [b] Lk 19:15-19 [c] Jms 4:17

Not Peace but Division

49 "I came to bring fire on the earth,
and how I wish it were already set
ablaze! 50 But [a]I have a baptism to be
baptized with, and how it consumes
Me until it is finished! 51 [b]Do you think
that I came here to give peace to the
earth? No, I tell you, but rather division! 52 [c]From now on, five in one
household will be divided: three
against two, and two against three.

[a] Mt 20:22 [b] Mt 10:34 [c] Mt 10:35

53 **They will be divided,**
father against son,
son against father,
mother against daughter,
daughter against mother,
mother-in-law against
her daughter-in-law,
and daughter-in-law
against mother-in-law."[b]

Interpreting the Time

54 He also said to the crowds:
[a]"When you see a cloud rising in the
west, right away you say, 'A storm is
coming,' and so it does. 55 And when
the south wind is blowing, you say, 'It's
going to be a scorcher!' and it is.
56 [b]Hypocrites! You know how to interpret the appearance of the earth and
the sky, but why don't you know how
to interpret [c]this time?

[a] Mt 16:2 [b] 1Co 1:19-27 [c] Lk 19:42-44

Settling Accounts

57 "Why don't you judge for yourselves what is right? 58 [a]As you are going with your adversary to the ruler,
make an effort to settle with him on
the way. Then he won't drag you before the judge, the judge hand you over
to the bailiff, and the bailiff throw you
into prison. 59 I tell you, [b]you will
never get out of there until you have
paid the last cent."[c]

[a] Pr 25:8 [b] Mt 5:26

Repent or Perish

13 At that time, some people came
and reported to Him [a]about the
Galileans whose blood •Pilate had
mixed with their sacrifices. 2 And He[d]
responded to them, "Do you think
that these Galileans were more sinful
than all Galileans because they suffered these things? 3 No, I tell you; but
unless you repent, you will all perish
as well! 4 Or those 18 that the tower
in Siloam fell on and killed—do you
think they were more sinful than all
the people who live in Jerusalem?
5 No, I tell you; but [b]unless you repent, you will all perish as well!"

[a] Ac 5:37 [b] Ezk 18:30

The Parable of the Barren Fig Tree

6 And He told this parable: [a]"A man
had a fig tree that was planted in his
vineyard. He came looking for fruit on
it and found none. 7 He told the vineyard worker, 'Listen, for three years I
have come looking for fruit on this fig
tree and haven't found any. Cut it
down! Why should it even waste the
soil?'

[a] Is 5:2

8 "But he replied to him, 'Sir,[e] leave
it this year also, until I dig around it
and fertilize it. 9 Perhaps it will bear
fruit next year, but if not, you can cut
it down.'"

Healing a Daughter of Abraham

10 As He was teaching in one of the
•synagogues on the Sabbath, 11 a
woman was there who had been dis-

[a]**12:48** Or *much* [b]**12:53** Mc 7:6 [c]**12:59** Gk *lepton*, the smallest and least valuable copper coin in use
[d]**13:2** Other mss read *Jesus* [e]**13:8** Or *Lord*

abled by a spirit[a] for over 18 years. She
was bent over and could not straighten
up at all.[b] 12 When Jesus saw her, He
called out to her,[c] "Woman, you are
free of your disability." 13 Then He laid
His hands on her, and instantly she
was restored and began to glorify God.
14 But the leader of the synagogue,
[a]indignant because Jesus had healed
on the Sabbath, responded by telling
the crowd, [b]"There are six days when
work should be done; therefore come
on those days and be healed and [c]not
on the Sabbath day." [a] *Jn 5:15-16*
[b] *Ex 20:9*
[c] *Lk 14:3*

15 But the Lord answered him and
said, "Hypocrites! [a]Doesn't each one of
you untie his ox or donkey from the
feeding trough on the Sabbath and lead
it to water? 16 Satan has bound this
woman, a daughter of Abraham, for 18
years—shouldn't she be untied from
this bondage on the Sabbath day?"
[a] *Lk 14:5*

17 When He had said these things,
all His adversaries were humiliated,
but the whole crowd was rejoicing
over all the glorious things He was doing.

The Parables of the Mustard Seed and of the Yeast

18 [a]He said therefore, "What is the
kingdom of God like, and what can I
compare it to? 19 It's like a mustard
seed that a man took and sowed in his
garden. It grew and became a tree, and
the birds of the sky nested in its
branches." [a] *Mk 4:30*

20 Again He said, "What can I compare the kingdom of God to? 21 It's like
yeast that a woman took and mixed
into 50 [a]pounds[d] of flour until it spread
through the entire mixture."[e]
[a] *Mt 13:33*

The Narrow Way

22 [a]He went through one town and
village after another, teaching and making His way to Jerusalem. 23 "Lord,"
someone asked Him, "are there few being saved?"[f] [a] *Mt 9:35; Mk 6:6*

He said to them, 24 "Make every effort to enter through the narrow door,
because I tell you, many will try to enter and won't be able 25 once the homeowner gets up and shuts the door.
Then you will stand[g] outside and
knock on the door, saying, [a]'Lord,
open up for us!' He will answer you, [b]'I
don't know you or where you're from.'
26 Then you will say,[h] [c]'We ate and
drank in Your presence, and You
taught in our streets!' 27 [d]But He will
say, 'I tell you, I don't know you or
where you're from. Get away from Me,
all you workers of unrighteousness!'
28 [e]There will be weeping and gnash-
ing of teeth in that place, when you see
Abraham, Isaac, Jacob, and all the
prophets in the kingdom of God but
yourselves thrown out. 29 [f]They will
come from east and west, from north
and south, and recline at the table in
the kingdom of God. 30 [g]Note this:
some are last who will be first, and
some are first who will be last." [a] *Lk 6:46* [b] *Mt 7:23* [c] *Ti 1:16* [d] *Mt 7:23*
[e] *Mt 8:11-12* [f] *Is 49:6-12* [g] *Mt 19:30; Mk 10:31*

Jesus and Herod Antipas

31 At that time some •Pharisees came
and told Him, "Go, get out of here!
•Herod wants to kill You!"
32 He said to them, "Go tell that fox,
'Look! I'm driving out demons and performing healings today and tomorrow,
and on the third day[i] [a]I will complete
My work.'[j] 33 Yet I must travel today, tomorrow, and the next day, because it is
not possible for a prophet to perish outside of Jerusalem! [a] *Heb 2:10*

[a]**13:11** Lit *had a spirit of disability* [b]**13:11** Or *straighten up completely* [c]**13:12** Or *He summoned her* [d]**13:21** Lit *3 sata*; about 40 quarts [e]**13:21** Or *until all of it was leavened* [f]**13:23** Or *are the saved few?* (in number); lit *are those being saved few?* [g]**13:25** Lit *you will begin to stand* [h]**13:26** Lit *you will begin to say* [i]**13:32** Very shortly [j]**13:32** Lit *I will be finished*

Jesus' Lamentation over Jerusalem

34 [a]"Jerusalem, Jerusalem! The city who kills the prophets and stones those who are sent to her. How often I wanted to gather your children together, as a hen gathers her chicks under her wings, but you were not willing! 35 See, [b]your house[a] is abandoned to you. And I tell you, [c]you will not see Me until the time comes when you say, [d]**Blessed is He who comes in the name of the Lord!**"[b]

[a] Neh 9:26-27 [b] Is 1:7; Lk 21:24 [c] Pr 1:24-30 [d] Is 62:11; Mt 21:9; Mk 11:10; Lk 19:38; Jn 12:13

A Sabbath Controversy

14 One Sabbath, when He went to eat[c] at the house of one of the leading •Pharisees, they were watching Him closely. 2 There in front of Him was a man whose body was swollen with fluid.[d] 3 In response, Jesus asked the law experts and the Pharisees, [a]"Is it lawful to heal on the Sabbath or not?" 4 But they kept silent. He took the man, healed him, and sent him away. 5 And to them, He said, [b]"Which of you whose son or ox falls into a well, will not immediately pull him out on the Sabbath day?" 6 To this they could find no answer.

[a] Mt 12:10 [b] Dt 22:4; Lk 13:15

Teachings on Humility

7 He told a parable to those who were invited, when He noticed how they would choose the best places for themselves: 8 "When you are invited by someone to a wedding banquet, don't recline at the best place, because a more distinguished person than you may have been invited by your host.[e] 9 The one who invited both of you may come and say to you, 'Give your place to this man,' and then in humiliation, you will proceed to take the lowest place.

10 [a]"But when you are invited, go and recline in the lowest place, so that when the one who invited you comes, he will say to you, 'Friend, move up higher.' You will then be honored in the presence of all the other guests. 11 [b]For everyone who exalts himself will be humbled, and the one who humbles himself will be exalted."

[a] Pr 15:33 [b] Jb 22:29; Mt 23:12

12 He also said to the one who had invited Him, "When you give a lunch or a dinner, don't invite your friends, your brothers, your relatives, or your rich neighbors, because they might invite you back, and you would be repaid. 13 On the contrary, when you host a banquet, invite those who are poor, maimed, lame, or blind. 14 And you will be blessed, because they cannot repay you; for you will be [a]repaid at the resurrection of the righteous."

[a] Dn 12:2; Mt 25:46

The Parable of the Large Banquet

15 When one of those who reclined at the table with Him heard these things, he said to Him, "The one who will eat bread in the kingdom of God is blessed!"

16 [a]Then He told him: "A man was giving a large banquet and invited many. 17 At the time of the banquet, he sent his slave to tell those who were invited, 'Come, because everything is now ready.'

[a] Mt 22:2

18 "But without exception[f] they all began to make excuses. The first one said to him, [a]'I have bought a field, and I must go out and see it. I ask you to excuse me.'

[a] Mt 6:24; Lk 8:14

19 "Another said, 'I have bought five yoke of oxen, and I'm going to try them out. I ask you to excuse me.'

20 "And another said, 'I just got married,[g] and therefore I'm unable to come.'

[a]**13:35** Probably the temple; Jr 12:7; 22:5 [b]**13:35** Ps 118:26 [c]**14:1** Lit *eat bread*; = eat a meal [d]**14:2** Afflicted with dropsy or edema [e]**14:8** Lit *by him* [f]**14:18** Lit *And from one* (voice) [g]**14:20** Lit *I have married a woman*

21 "So the slave came back and reported these things to his master. Then
in anger, the master of the house told
his slave, [a]'Go out quickly into the
streets and alleys of the city, and bring
in here the poor, maimed, blind, and
lame!' [a]*Mt 28:18-19*

22 " 'Master,' the slave said, 'what
you ordered has been done, and
there's still room.'

23 "Then the master told the slave,
'Go out into the highways and lanes
and [a]make them come in, so that my
house may be filled. 24 For I tell you,
[b]not one of those men who were invited will enjoy my banquet!' "
[a]*2Co 5:20* [b]*Mt 8:11-12*

The Cost of Following Jesus

25 Now great crowds were traveling
with Him. So He turned and said to
them: 26 [a]"If anyone comes to Me and
does not hate his own father and
mother, wife and children, brothers
and sisters—[b]yes, and even his own
life—he cannot be My disciple.
27 [c]Whoever does not bear his own
cross and come after Me cannot be My
disciple. [a]*Mt 10:37* [b]*Rv 12:11*
[c]*Mt 16:24; Mk 8:34; Lk 9:23*

28 "For which of you, wanting to
build a tower, doesn't first sit down
and calculate the cost to see if he has
enough to complete it? 29 Otherwise,
after he has laid the foundation and
cannot finish it, all the onlookers will
begin to make fun of him, 30 saying,
'This man started to build and wasn't
able to finish.'

31 "Or what king, going to war
against another king, will not first sit
down and decide if he is able with
10,000 to oppose the one who comes
against him with 20,000? 32 If not,
while the other is still far off, he sends
a delegation and asks for terms of
peace. 33 In the same way, therefore,
every one of you who does not say
good-bye to[a] all his possessions cannot
be My disciple.

34 "Now, [a]salt is good, but if salt
should lose its taste, how will it be
made salty? 35 It isn't fit for the soil or
for the manure pile; they throw it out.
Anyone who has ears to hear should
listen!" [a]*Mt 5:13*

The Parable of the Lost Sheep

15 All the tax collectors and [a]sinners
[b]were approaching to listen to
Him. 2 And the •Pharisees and •scribes
were complaining, "This man welcomes sinners and eats with them!"
[a]*Ezk 18:23* [b]*Mt 9:10;*
Mk 2:15-16; Lk 5:29

3 So He told them this parable:
4 [a]"What man among you, who has
100 sheep and [b]loses one of them,
does not leave the 99 in the open field[b]
and go after the lost one until he finds
it? 5 When he has found it, he joyfully
puts it on his shoulders, 6 and coming
home, he calls his friends and neighbors together, saying to them, 'Rejoice
with me, because I have found my lost
sheep!' 7 I tell you, in the same way,
there will be more joy in heaven over
one sinner who repents [c]than over 99
righteous people who don't need repentance. [a]*Mt 18:12* [b]*1Pt 2:25*
[c]*Lk 5:32*

The Parable of the Lost Coin

8 "Or what woman who has 10 silver
coins,[c] if she loses one coin, does not
light a lamp, sweep the house, and
search carefully until she finds it?
9 When she finds it, she calls her
women friends and neighbors together, saying, 'Rejoice with me, because I have found the silver coin I
lost!' 10 I tell you, in the same way,
there is joy in the presence of God's angels over one sinner who repents."

[a]**14:33** Or *does not renounce* or *leave* [b]**15:4** Or *the wilderness* [c]**15:8** Gk *10 drachmas*; a *drachma* was a silver coin = a •denarius.

The Parable of the Lost Son

11 He also said: "A man had two
sons. 12 The younger of them said to
his father, 'Father, give me the share of
the estate I have coming to me.' So he
distributed the assets[a] to them. 13 Not
many days later, the younger son gathered together all he had and traveled
to a distant country, where he squan-
dered his estate in foolish living.
14 After he had spent everything, a severe famine struck that country, and
he had nothing.[b] 15 Then he went to
work for[c] one of the citizens of that
country, who sent him into his fields
to feed pigs. 16 He longed to eat his fill
from[d] the carob pods[e] the pigs were
eating, but no one would give him any.
17 When he came to his senses,[f] he
said, 'How many of my father's hired
hands have more than enough food,
and here I am dying[g] of hunger![h] 18 I'll
[a]get up, go to my father, and say to
him, Father, [b]I have sinned against
heaven and in your sight. 19 I'm no
longer worthy to be called your son.
Make me like one of your hired
hands.' 20 So he got up and went to his
father. But [c]while the son was still a
long way off, his father saw him and
was filled with compassion. He ran,
threw his arms around his neck,[i] and
kissed him. 21 The son said to him, 'Father, I have sinned against heaven
[d]and in your sight. I'm no longer worthy to be called your son.'

[a] Jr 50:4,6 [b] Jb 33:27-28 [c] Is 49:15 [d] Ps 51:4

22 "But the father told his •slaves,
'Quick! Bring out [a]the best robe and
put it on him; put a ring on his finger[j]
and sandals on his feet. 23 Then bring
the fattened calf and slaughter it, and
let's celebrate with a feast, 24 [b]because
this son of mine was dead and is alive
again; he was lost and is found!' S
they began to celebrate.

[a] Is 61: [b] Rm 6:

25 "Now his older son was in th
field; as he came near the house, h
heard music and dancing. 26 So he sun
moned one of the servants and aske
what these things meant. 27 'You
brother is here,' he told him, 'and you
father has slaughtered the fattened ca
because he has him back safe an
sound.'[k]
28 "Then he became angry and didn
want to go in. So his father came ou
and pleaded with him. 29 But he re
plied to his father, 'Look, I have bee
slaving many years for you, and I hav
never disobeyed your orders, [a]yet yo
never gave me a young goat so I coul
celebrate with my friends. 30 But whe
this son of yours came, who has de
voured your assets[a] with prostitute
you slaughtered the fattened calf fo
him.'

[a] Mt 20:11-

31 " 'Son,'[l] he said to him, 'you are a
ways with me, and everything I have i
yours. 32 But we had to celebrate an
rejoice, because this brother of your
was dead and is alive again; he was los
and is found.' "

The Parable of the Dishonest Manager

16 He also said to the disciple
"There was a rich man who re
ceived an accusation that his manage
was squandering his possessions. 2 S
he called the manager in and aske
'What is this I hear about you? Giv
an [a]account of your management, be
cause you can no longer be ⌊my⌋ man
ager.'

[a] Rm 14:12; 2Co 5:

3 "Then the manager said to himsel
'What should I do, since my master i

[a]**15:12,30** Lit *livelihood*, or *living* [b]**15:14** Lit *and he began to be in need* [c]**15:15** Lit *went and joined with* [d]**15:16** Other mss read *to fill his stomach with* [e]**15:16** Seed casings of a tree used as food for cattle, pigs and sometimes the poor [f]**15:17** Lit *to himself* [g]**15:17** The word *dying* is translated *lost* in vv. 4–9 and vv. 24,32. [h]**15:17** Or *dying in the famine*; v. 14 [i]**15:20** Lit *He ran, fell on his neck* [j]**15:22** Lit *hand* [k]**15:27** L *him back healthy* [l]**15:31** Or *Child*

taking the management away from me? I'm not strong enough to dig; I'm ashamed to beg. 4 I know what I'll do so that when I'm removed from management, people will welcome me into their homes.'

5 "So he summoned each one of his master's debtors. 'How much do you owe my master?' he asked the first one.

6 "'A hundred measures of oil,' he said.

"'Take your invoice,' he told him, 'sit down quickly, and write 50.'

7 "Next he asked another, 'How much do you owe?'

"'A hundred measures of wheat,' he said.

"'Take your invoice,' he told him, 'and write 80.'

8 "The master praised the unrighteous manager because he had acted astutely. For the sons of this age are more astute than [a]the sons of light ⌊in dealing⌋ with their own people.[a] 9 And I tell you, [b]make friends for yourselves by means of the unrighteous money so that when it fails,[b] they may welcome you into eternal dwellings. 10 [c]Whoever is faithful in very little is also faithful in much, and whoever is unrighteous in very little is also unrighteous in much. 11 So if you have not been faithful with the unrighteous money, who will trust you with what is genuine? 12 And if you have not been faithful with what belongs to someone else, who will give you what is your own? 13 No [d]household slave can be the •slave of two masters, since either he will hate one and love the other, or he will be devoted to one and despise the other. You can't be slaves to both God and money."

[a] Jn 12:36; Eph 5:8 [b] Mt 6:19; Lk 11:41 [c] Mt 25:21; Lk 19:17 [d] Mt 6:24

Kingdom Values

14 The •Pharisees, [a]who were lovers of money, were listening to all these things and scoffing at Him. 15 And He told them: "You are the ones who [b]justify yourselves in the sight of others, but [c]God knows your hearts. For [d]what is highly admired by people is revolting in God's sight.

[a] Mt 23:14 [b] Mt 6:2,5,16 [c] Ps 7:9 [d] 1Sm 16:7

16 [a]"The Law and the Prophets were[c] until John; since then, the good news of the kingdom of God has been proclaimed, and everyone is strongly urged to enter it.[d] 17 But it is easier for heaven and earth to pass away than for one stroke of a letter in the law to drop out.

[a] Mt 11:12-13

18 "Everyone who divorces his wife and marries another woman commits adultery, and everyone who marries a woman divorced from her husband commits adultery.

The Rich Man and Lazarus

19 "There was a rich man who would dress in purple and fine linen, feasting lavishly every day. 20 But a poor man named Lazarus, covered with sores, was left at his gate. 21 He longed to be filled with what fell from the rich man's table, but instead the dogs would come and lick his sores. 22 One day the poor man died and [a]was carried away by the angels to [b]Abraham's side.[e] The rich man also died and was buried. 23 And being in torment in •Hades, he looked up and saw Abraham a long way off, with Lazarus at his side. 24 'Father Abraham!' he called out, 'Have mercy on me and send Lazarus to dip the tip of his finger in water and cool my tongue, because I am [c]in agony in this flame!'

[a] Heb 1:14 [b] Mt 8:11 [c] Is 66:24; Mk 9:44

[a]**16:8** Lit *own generation* [b]**16:9** Other mss read *when you fail* or *pass away* [c]**16:16** Perhaps *were proclaimed*, or *were in effect* [d]**16:16** Or *everyone is forcing his way into it* [e]**16:22** Lit *to the fold of Abraham's robe*, or *to Abraham's bosom*; see Jn 13:23

25 "'Son,'[a] Abraham said, [a]'remember that during your life you received
your good things, just as Lazarus received bad things, but now he is comforted here, while you are in agony.
26 Besides all this, a [b]great chasm has
been fixed between us and you, so that
those who want to pass over from here
to you cannot; neither can those from
there cross over to us.' *[a]Jb 21:13; Lk 6:24*
[b]2Th 1:9

27 "'Father,' he said, 'then I beg you
to send him to my father's house—
28 because I have five brothers—to
warn them, so they won't also come to
this place of torment.'
29 "But Abraham said, [a]'They have
Moses and the prophets; they should
listen to them.' *[a]Jn 5:46-47; Ac 15:21*

30 "'No, father Abraham,' he said.
'But if someone from the dead goes to
them, they will repent.'
31 "But he told him, 'If they don't listen to Moses and the prophets, [a]they
will not be persuaded if someone rises
from the dead.'" *[a]Jn 12:10*

Warnings from Jesus

17 He said to His disciples, [a]"Offenses[b] will certainly come,[c] but
[b]woe to the one they come through!
2 It would be better for him if a millstone[d] were hung around his neck
and he were thrown into the sea than
for him to cause one of these little
ones to •stumble. 3 Be on your guard.
[c]If your brother sins,[e] [d]rebuke him,
and if he repents, [e]forgive him. 4 And
if he sins against you seven times in a
day, and comes back to you seven
times, saying, 'I repent,' you must
forgive him." *[a]Mt 18:6-7; Mk 9:42*
[b]Mt 13:41-42 [c]Mt 18:15 [d]Lv 19:17 [e]Mt 18:15; 1Co 13:5

Faith and Duty

5 The apostles said to the Lord, "Increase our faith."
6 [a]"If you have faith the size of[f] a
mustard seed," the Lord said, "you can
say to this mulberry tree, 'Be uprooted
and planted in the sea,' and it will obey
you." *[a]Mt 17:20*

7 "Which one of you having a slave
plowing or tending sheep, will say to
him when he comes in from the field,
'Come at once and sit down to eat'?
8 Instead, will he not tell him, 'Prepare something for me to eat, get
ready,[g] and serve me while I eat and
drink; later you can eat and drink'?
9 Does he thank that slave because he
did what was commanded?[h] 10 In the
same way, when you have done all
that you were commanded, you
should say, 'We are [a]good-for-nothing
slaves; we've only done our duty.'"
[a]Mt 25:37-40

The 10 Lepers

11 [a]While traveling to Jerusalem, He
passed between[i] Samaria and Galilee.
12 As He entered a village, 10 men
with serious skin diseases met Him.
[b]They stood at a distance 13 and raised
their voices, saying, "Jesus, Master,
have mercy on us!" *[a]Lk 9:51; Jn 4:4*
[b]Lv 13:46

14 When He saw them, He told them,
[a]"Go and show yourselves to the
priests." And while they were going,
they were healed.[j] *[a]Lv 13:2; Mt 8:4*

15 But one of them, seeing that he
was healed, returned and, with a loud
voice, [a]gave glory to God. 16 He fell
facedown at His feet, thanking Him.
And he was [b]a •Samaritan.
[a]Ps 103:1 [b]2Kg 17:24

17 Then Jesus said, "Were not 10
cleansed? Where are the nine?
18 Didn't any return[k] to give glory to
God except this foreigner?" 19 And He
told him, "Get up and go on your way.
Your faith has made you well."[l]

[a]**16:25** Lit *Child* [b]**17:1** Or *Traps*, or *Bait-sticks*, or *Causes of stumbling*, or *Causes of sin* [c]**17:1** Lit *It is impossible for offenses not to come* [d]**17:2** Large stone used for grinding grains into flour [e]**17:3** Other mss add *against you* [f]**17:6** Lit *faith like* [g]**17:8** Lit *eat, tuck in your robe*, or *eat, gird yourself* [h]**17:9** Other mss add *I don't think so* [i]**17:11** Or *through the middle of* [j]**17:14** Lit *cleansed* [k]**17:18** Lit *Were they not found returning* [l]**17:19** Or *faith has saved you*

The Coming of the Kingdom

20 Being asked by the •Pharisees
when the kingdom of God will come,
He answered them, "The kingdom of
God is not coming with something ob-
servable; 21 no one will say,[a] 'Look
here!' or 'There!' For you see, [a]the
kingdom of God is among you."

[a] Rm 14:17

22 Then He told the disciples: [a]"The
days are coming when you will long to
see one of the days of the •Son of Man,
but you won't see it. 23 [b]They will say
to you, 'Look there!' or 'Look here!'
[c]Don't follow or run after them. 24 For
as the lightning flashes from horizon to
horizon and lights up the sky, so [d]the
Son of Man will be in His day. 25 [e]But
first He must suffer many things and be
rejected by this generation.

[a] Mt 9:15 [b] Mt 24:23; Lk 21:8 [c] 1Jn 4:1 [d] 1Tm 6:15-16 [e] Lk 9:22

26 [a]"Just as it was in the days of
Noah, so it will be in the days of the
Son of Man: 27 people went on eating,
drinking, marrying and giving in marriage until the day Noah boarded the
ark, and the flood came and destroyed
them all. 28 [b]It will be the same as it
was in the days of Lot: people went on
eating, drinking, buying, selling, plant-
ing, building. 29 But on the day Lot left
Sodom, fire and sulfur rained from
heaven and destroyed them all. 30 It
will be like that on the day the Son of
Man [c]is revealed. 31 On that day, [d]a
man on the housetop, whose belong-
ings are in the house, must not come
down to get them. Likewise the man
who is in the field must not turn back.
32 [e]Remember Lot's wife! 33 [f]Whoever
tries to make his •life secure[b] [c] will lose
it, and whoever loses his life will pre-
serve it. 34 I tell you, on that night two
will be in one bed: one will be taken
and the other will be left. 35 Two
women will be grinding grain together: one will be taken and the other
left. [36 Two will be in a field: one will
be taken, and the other will be left."][d]

[a] Gn 7 [b] Gn 19 [c] Mt 24:3,27-30 [d] Mk 13:15 [e] Gn 19:26 [f] Mt 16:25

37 "Where, Lord?" they asked Him.
He said to them, "Where the corpse
is, there also the vultures will be gathered."

The Parable of the Persistent Widow

18 He then told them a parable on
the need for them [a]to pray always and not become discouraged:
2 "There was a judge in one town who
didn't fear God or respect man. 3 And
a widow in that town kept coming to
him, saying, 'Give me justice against
my adversary.'

[a] Ps 55:16-17; Eph 6:18; Php 4:6

4 "For a while he was unwilling, but
later he said to himself, 'Even though I
don't fear God or respect man, 5 yet because this widow keeps pestering me,[e]
I will give her justice, so she doesn't
wear me out[f] by her persistent coming.'"

6 Then the Lord said, "Listen to what
the unjust judge says. 7 [a]Will not God
grant justice to His elect who cry out to
Him day and night? Will He delay ⌊to
help⌋ them?[g] 8 I tell you [b]that He will
swiftly grant them justice. Nevertheless, when the •Son of Man comes, will
He find that faith[h] on earth?"

[a] Jr 20:12 [b] 2Pt 3:8-9

The Parable of the Pharisee and the Tax Collector

9 He also told this parable to some
[a]who trusted in themselves that they
were righteous and looked down on
everyone else: 10 "Two men went up to
the •temple complex to pray, one a
•Pharisee and the other a tax collector.

[a]**17:21** Lit *they will not say* [b]**17:33** Other mss read *to save his life* [c]**17:33** Or *tries to retain his life* [d]**17:36** Other mss omit bracketed text [e]**18:5** Lit *widow causes me trouble* [f]**18:5** Or *doesn't give me a black eye*, or *doesn't ruin my reputation* [g]**18:7** Or *Will He put up with them?* [h]**18:8** Or *faith*, or *that kind of faith*, or *any faith*, or *the faith*, or *faithfulness*; the faith that persists in prayer for God's vindication

11 The Pharisee took his stand[a] and was
praying like this: [b]'God, I thank You
that I'm not like other people[b]—
greedy, unrighteous, adulterers, or
even like this tax collector. 12 I fast
twice a week; I give a tenth[c] of everything I get.' [a]Pr 30:12 [b]Is 1:15

13 "But the tax collector, [a]standing
far off, would not even raise his eyes to
heaven but kept striking his chest[d] and
saying, 'God, turn Your wrath from
me[e]—a sinner!' 14 I tell you, this one
went down to his house justified
rather than the other; [b]because everyone who exalts himself will be humbled, but the one who humbles himself
will be exalted." [a]Ps 40:12
[b]Jb 22:29; Jms 4:6

Blessing the Children

15 [a]Some people were even bringing
infants to Him so He might touch
them, but when the disciples saw it,
they rebuked them. 16 Jesus, however,
invited them: [b]"Let the little children
come to Me, and don't stop them, because the kingdom of God belongs to
such as these. 17 •I assure you: Whoever does not welcome the kingdom of
God like a little child will never enter
it." [a]Mt 19:13 [b]Pr 8:17

The Rich Young Ruler

18 [a]A ruler asked Him, "Good
Teacher, what must I do to inherit eternal life?" [a]Mt 19:16

19 "Why do you call Me good?" Jesus
asked him. "No one is good but
One—God. 20 You know the commandments:

> **[a]Do not commit adultery;**
> **do not murder;**
> **do not steal;**
> **do not bear false witness;**
> **honor your father**
> **and mother."**[f] [a]Ex 20:12

21 "I have kept all these from my
youth," he said.

22 When Jesus heard this, He told
him, "You still lack one thing: [a]sell all
that you have and distribute it to the
poor, and you will have treasure in
heaven. Then come, follow Me."
[a]Mt 6:19

23 After he heard this, he became
extremely sad, because he was very
rich.

Possessions and the Kingdom

24 Seeing that he became sad,[g] Jesus
said, [a]"How hard it is for those who
have wealth to enter the kingdom of
God! 25 For it is easier for a camel to go
through the eye of a needle than for a
rich person to enter the kingdom of
God." [a]Pr 11:28; 1Tm 6:9; Jms 2:5

26 Those who heard this asked,
"Then who can be saved?"

27 He replied, [a]"What is impossible
with men is possible with God."
[a]Jr 32:17

28 [a]Then Peter said, "Look, we have
left what we had and followed You."
[a]Mt 19:27

29 So He said to them, "I assure you:
There is no one who has left a house,
wife or brothers, parents or children
because of the kingdom of God, 30 who
will not receive many times more at
this time, and eternal life [a]in the age to
come." [a]Rv 2:17

The Third Prediction of His Death

31 [a]Then He took the Twelve aside
and told them, "Listen! We are going
up to Jerusalem. Everything [b]that is
written through the prophets about
the Son of Man will be accomplished.
32 For [c]He will be handed over to the
Gentiles, and He will be mocked, insulted, spit on; 33 and after they flog

[a]**18:11** Or *Pharisee stood by himself* [b]**18:11** Or *like the rest of men* [c]**18:12** Or *give tithes*
[d]**18:13** Mourning [e]**18:13** Lit *God, be propitious*; = May Your wrath be turned aside by the sacrifice
[f]**18:20** Ex 20:12–16; Dt 5:16–20 [g]**18:24** Other mss omit *he became sad*

Him, they will kill Him, and He will
rise on the third day." *[a]Mt 16:21*
[b]Ps 22; Is 53 [c]Mt 27:2; Lk 23:1; Jn 18:28

34 [a]They understood none of these
things. This saying[a] was hidden from
them, and they did not grasp what was
said. *[a]Mk 9:32*

A Blind Man Receives His Sight

35 [a]As He drew near Jericho, a blind
man was sitting by the road begging.
36 Hearing a crowd passing by, he inquired what this meant. 37 "Jesus the
•Nazarene is passing by," they told
him. *[a]Mt 20:29*

38 So he called out, "Jesus, Son of
David, have mercy on me!" 39 Then
those in front told him to keep quiet,[b]
but he kept crying out all the more,
"Son of David, have mercy on me!"
40 Jesus [a]stopped and commanded
that he be brought to Him. When he
drew near, He asked him, 41 "What do
you want Me to do for you?" *[a]Heb 2:17*
"Lord," he said, "I want to see!"
42 "Receive your sight!" Jesus told
him. [a]"Your faith has healed you."[c]
43 Instantly [b]he could see, and he began to follow Him, [c]glorifying God. All
the people, when they saw it, gave
praise to God. *[a]Lk 17:19 [b]Is 35:5 [c]Ps 103:1*

Jesus Visits Zacchaeus

19 He entered [a]Jericho and was
passing through. 2 There was a
man named Zacchaeus who was a
chief tax collector, and he was rich.
3 He was trying to see who Jesus was,
but he was not able because of the
crowd, since he was a short man. 4 So
running ahead, he climbed up a sy-
camore tree to see Jesus, since He was
about to pass that way. 5 When Jesus
came to the place, He looked up and
said to him, "Zacchaeus, hurry and
come down, because today I must stay
at your house." *[a]Jos 6:26; 1Kg 16:34*

6 So he quickly came down and welcomed Him joyfully. 7 All who saw it
began to complain, [a]"He's gone to
lodge with a sinful man!" *[a]Mt 9:11*

8 But Zacchaeus stood there and said
to the Lord, "Look, I'll give[d] half of my
possessions to the poor, Lord! And if I
have extorted anything from anyone,
[a]I'll pay[e] back four times as much!"
[a]Ex 22:1; Lv 6:1-5

9 "Today salvation has come to this
house," Jesus told him, "because he
too is a son of Abraham. 10 [a]For the
•Son of Man has come to seek and to
save the lost."[f] *[a]Mt 9:13; Mk 2:17; Lk 5:32*

The Parable of the 10 Minas

11 As they were listening to this, He
went on to tell a parable because He
was near Jerusalem, and [a]they thought
the kingdom of God was going to appear right away. *[a]Lk 17:20; 2Th 2:1-3*

12 [a]Therefore He said: "A nobleman
traveled to a far country to receive for
himself authority to be king[g] and then
return. 13 He called 10 of his •slaves,
gave them 10 minas,[h] and told them,
'Engage in business until I come back.'
[a]Mt 25:14

14 [a]"But his subjects hated him and
sent a delegation after him, saying,
'We don't want this man to rule over
us!' *[a]Jn 1:11*

15 "At his return, having received the
authority to be king,[g] he summoned
those •slaves he had given the money
to so he could find out how much they
had made in business. 16 The first came
forward and said, 'Master, your mina
has earned 10 more minas.'
17 "'Well done, good[i] •slave!' he told
him. 'Because you have been [a]faithful

[a]**18:34** The meaning of the saying [b]**18:39** Or *those in front rebuked him* [c]**18:42** Or *has saved you* [d]**19:8** Or *I give* [e]**19:8** Or *I pay* [f]**19:10** Or *save what was lost* [g]**19:12,15** Lit *to receive for himself a kingdom* or *sovereignty* [h]**19:13** = Gk coin worth 100 drachmas or about 100 days' wages [i]**19:17** Or *capable*

in a very small matter, have authority
over 10 towns.' [a]*Lk 16:10*

18 "The second came and said, 'Master, your mina has made five minas.'
19 "So he said to him, 'You will be
over five towns.'
20 "And another came and said,
'Master, here is your mina. I have kept
it hidden away in a cloth 21 because I
was afraid of you, for you're a tough
man: you collect what you didn't deposit and reap what you didn't sow.'
22 "He told him, [a]'I will judge you by
what you have said,[a] you evil •slave! ⌊If⌋
[b]you knew I was a tough man, collect-
ing what I didn't deposit and reaping
what I didn't sow, 23 why didn't you
put my money in the bank? And when
I returned, I would have collected it
with interest!' 24 So he said to those
standing there, 'Take the mina away
from him and give it to the one who
has 10 minas.' [a]*Jb 15:6* [b]*Mt 25:26*

25 "But they said to him, 'Master, he
has 10 minas.'
26 " 'I tell you, [a]that to everyone who
has, more will be given; and from the
one who does not have, even what he
does have will be taken away. 27 But
bring here these enemies of mine,
who did not want me to rule over
them, and slaughter[b] them in my
presence.' " [a]*Mt 13:12; Lk 8:18*

The Triumphal Entry

28 When He had said these things,
[a]He went on ahead, going up to Jerusalem. 29 [b]As He approached Bethphage
and Bethany, at the place called the
•Mount of Olives, He sent two of the
disciples 30 and said, "Go into the village ahead of you. As you enter it, you
will find a young donkey tied there, on
which no one has ever sat. Untie it and
bring it here. 31 If anyone asks you,
'Why are you untying it?' say this: 'The
Lord needs it.' " [a]*Mk 10:32; Lk 9:51*
[b]*Zch 14:4; Mt 21:1; Mk 11:1*

32 So those who were sent left and
found it just as He had told them. 33 As
they were untying the young donkey,
its owners said to them, "Why are you
untying the donkey?"
34 "The Lord needs it," they said.
35 Then they brought it to Jesus, [a]and
after throwing their robes on the donkey, they helped Jesus get on it. 36 [b]As
He was going along, they were spreading their robes on the road. 37 Now He
came near the path down the Mount of
Olives, and the whole crowd of the disciples began to praise God joyfully with
a loud voice for all the miracles they
had seen:

38 [c]**Blessed is the King**
who comes in the name
of the Lord.[c] [d]
[d]Peace in heaven
and glory in the highest heaven!

[a]*Mk 11:7; Jn 12:14* [b]*Mt 21:8*
[c]*Mt 21:9; Mk 11:9* [d]*Lk 2:14*

39 Some of the •Pharisees from the
crowd told Him, "Teacher, rebuke Your
disciples."
40 He answered, "I tell you, if they
were to keep silent, [a]the stones would
cry out!" [a]*Hab 2:11*

Jesus' Love for Jerusalem

41 As He approached and saw the
city, He wept over it, 42 saying, "If you
knew this day what ⌊would bring⌋
peace—but now it is hidden from
your eyes. 43 For the days will come
on you when your enemies will [a]build
an embankment against you, sur-
round you, and hem you in on every
side. 44 They will crush you and your
children within you to the ground,
and [b]they will not leave one stone on
another in you, because [c]you did not
recognize the time of your visitation."
[a]*Jr 6:3,6; Lk 21:20* [b]*Mk 13:2; Lk 21:6* [c]*Lk 1:68*

Cleansing the Temple Complex

45 [a]He went into the •temple complex and began to throw out those

[a]**19:22** Lit *you out of your mouth* [b]**19:27** Or *execute* [c]**19:38** The words *the King* are substituted for *He* in Ps 118:26. [d]**19:38** Ps 118:26

who were selling,[a] 46 and He said, [b]"It
is written, **My house will be a house
of prayer,** but [c]you have made it **a den
of thieves!**"[b] *[a]Mt 21:12 [b]Is 56:7 [c]Jr 7:11*

47 Every day He was teaching in the
temple complex. [a]The •chief priests,
the •scribes, and the leaders of the people were looking for a way to destroy
Him, 48 but they could not find a way to
do it, because all the people were cap-
tivated by what they heard.[c]
[a]Mk 11:18; Jn 7:19

The Authority of Jesus Challenged

20 [a]One day[d] as He was teaching
the people in the •temple complex and proclaiming the good news,
the •chief priests and the •scribes,
with the elders, came up 2 and said to
Him: "Tell us, by what authority are
You doing these things? Who is it who
gave You this authority?" *[a]Mt 21:23*

3 He answered them, "I will also ask
you a question. Tell Me, 4 was the baptism of John from heaven or from
men?"

5 They discussed it among themselves: "If we say, 'From heaven,' He
will say, 'Why didn't you believe him?'
6 But if we say, 'From men,' all the people will stone us, [a]because they are
convinced that John was a prophet."
[a]Mt 14:5

7 So they answered that they did not
know its origin.[e]

8 And Jesus said to them, [a]"Neither
will I tell you by what authority I do
these things." *[a]Jb 5:12-13*

The Parable of the Vineyard Owner

9 Then He began to tell the people
this parable: [a]"A man planted a vineyard, leased it to tenant farmers, and
went away for a long time. 10 At harvest time [b]he sent a •slave to the farmers so that they might give him some
fruit from the vineyard. But the farmers beat him and sent him away
empty-handed. 11 He sent yet another
slave, but they beat that one too,
treated him shamefully, and sent him
away empty-handed. 12 [c]And he sent
yet a third, but they wounded this one
too and threw him out. *[a]Is 5:1; Jr 2:21*
[b]2Ch 36:15-16 [c]Neh 9:29-30

13 "Then the owner of the vineyard
said, 'What should I do? I will send
[a]my beloved son. Perhaps[f] they will respect him.' *[a]Is 7:14; Jn 3:16*

14 "But when the tenant farmers saw
him, they discussed it among themselves and said, 'This is [a]the heir. Let's
kill him, so the inheritance will be
ours!' 15 So they threw him out of the
vineyard and [b]killed him.
[a]Is 9:6; Php 2:9-11; Heb 1:2 [b]Jn 19

"Therefore, what will the owner of
the vineyard do to them? 16 He will
come and destroy those farmers and
give the vineyard to others."

But when they heard this they said,
"No—never!"

17 But He looked at them and said,
"Then what is the meaning of this
Scripture:[g]

> [a]**The stone that**
> **the builders rejected—**
> **this has become**
> **the cornerstone?**[h] [i]

18 Everyone who falls on that stone
will be broken to pieces, and if it falls
on anyone, it will grind him to pow-
der!" *[a]Ps 118:22*

19 Then the scribes and the chief
priests looked for a way to get their
hands on Him that very hour, because
they knew He had told this parable
against them, but they feared the people.

[a]**19:45** Other mss add *and buying in it* [b]**19:46** Is 56:7; Jr 7:11 [c]**19:48** Lit *people hung on what they heard* [d]**20:1** Lit *It happened on one of the days* [e]**20:7** Or *know where it was from* [f]**20:13** Other mss add *when they see him* [g]**20:17** Lit *What then is this that is written* [h]**20:17** Lit *the head of the corner* [i]**20:17** Ps 118:22

God and Caesar

20 [a]They[a] watched closely and sent
spies who pretended to be righteous,[b]
so they could catch Him in what He
said,[c] to hand Him over to the governor's rule and authority. 21 They questioned Him, [b]"Teacher, we know that
You speak and teach correctly, and You
don't show partiality,[d] but teach truthfully the way of God. 22 Is it lawful for
us to pay taxes to Caesar or not?"

[a]Mt 22:15 [b]Mk 12:14

23 But detecting their craftiness, He
said to them,[e] 24 "Show Me a •denar-
ius. Whose image and inscription does
it have?"

"Caesar's," they said.

25 "Well then," He told them, "give
back to Caesar the things that are Caesar's and to God the things that are
God's."

26 They were not able to catch Him
in what He said[c] in public,[f] and being
amazed at His answer, they became silent.

The Sadducees and the Resurrection

27 [a]Some of the •Sadducees, who say
there is no resurrection, came up and
questioned Him: 28 "Teacher, [b]Moses
wrote for us that **if a man's brother** has
a wife, and **dies childless, his brother
should take the wife and produce
•offspring for his brother.**[g] 29 Now
there were seven brothers. The first
took a wife and died without children.
30 Also the second[h] 31 and the third took
her. In the same way, all seven died and
left no children. 32 Finally, the woman
died too. 33 Therefore, in the resurrection, whose wife will the woman be?
For all seven had married her."[i]

[a]Mt 22:23; Mk 12:18
[b]Dt 25:5

34 Jesus told them, "The sons of this
age marry and are given in marriage.
35 But those who are [a]counted worthy
to take part in that age and in the resurrection from the dead neither marry
nor are given in marriage. 36 For they
cannot die anymore, because [b]they are
like angels and are sons of God, since
they are sons of the resurrection.
37 [c]Moses even indicated ⌊in the pas-
sage⌋ about the burning bush that the
dead are raised, where he calls the Lord
**the God of Abraham and the God of
Isaac and the God of Jacob.**[j] 38 [d]He is
not God of the dead but of the living, because [e]all are living to[k] Him."

[a]2Th 1:5 [b]Mt 22:30; Mk 12:25 [c]Ex 3:6
[d]Ps 16:5-11; Rm 4:17 [e]Rm 6:10-11

39 Some of the scribes answered,
"Teacher, You have spoken well."
40 And they no longer dared to ask Him
anything.

The Question about the Messiah

41 Then He said to them, [a]"How can
they say that the •Messiah is the Son of
David? 42 For David himself says in the
Book of Psalms:

> [b]**The Lord declared to my Lord,**
> **'Sit at My right hand**
> 43 **until I make Your enemies**
> **Your footstool.'**[l]

44 David calls Him 'Lord'; how then
can the Messiah be his Son?"

[a]Mk 12:35 [b]Ps 110:1

Warning against the Scribes

45 [a]While all the people were listening, He said to His disciples, 46 [b]"Beware of the scribes, who want to go
around in long robes and who love
greetings in the marketplaces, the
front seats in the •synagogues, and the
places of honor at banquets. 47 [c]They

[a]**20:20** The scribes and chief priests of v. 19 [b]**20:20** Or *upright*; that is, loyal to God's law [c]**20:20,26** Lit *catch Him in [a] word* [d]**20:21** Lit *You don't receive a face* [e]**20:23** Other mss add *"Why are you testing Me?* [f]**20:26** Lit *in front of the people* [g]**20:28** Dt 25:5 [h]**20:30** Other mss add *took her as wife, and he died without children* [i]**20:33** Lit *had her as wife* [j]**20:37** Ex 3:6,15 [k]**20:38** Or *with* [l]**20:42–43** Ps 110:1

devour widows' houses and say long
prayers just for show. These [d]will receive greater punishment."[a]

[a]Mt 23:1; Mk 12:38 [b]Mt 23:5 [c]Mt 23:14 [d]Lk 12:47

The Widow's Gift

21 He looked up [a]and saw the rich
dropping their offerings into the
temple treasury. 2 He also saw a poor
widow dropping in two tiny coins.[b]
3 "I tell you the truth," He said. [b]"This
poor widow has put in more than all
of them. 4 For all these people have
put in gifts out of their surplus, but
she out of her poverty has put in all
she had to live on."

[a]Mk 12:41 [b]2Co 8:12

Destruction of the Temple Predicted

5 [a]As some were talking about the
•temple complex, how it was adorned
with beautiful stones and gifts dedicated to God,[c] He said, 6 "These things
that you see—the days will come
when [b]not one stone will be left on another that will not be thrown down!"

[a]Mt 24:1; Mk 13:1 [b]Mt 24:2; Mk 13:2; Lk 19:44

Signs of the End of the Age

7 "Teacher," they asked Him, "so
when will these things be? And what
will be the sign when these things are
about to take place?"
8 Then He said, [a]"Watch out that you
are not deceived. For many will come
in My name, saying, 'I am He,' and,
'The time is near.' Don't follow them.
9 When you hear of wars and rebel-
lions,[d] don't be alarmed. Indeed, these
things must take place first, but the
end won't come right away."

[a]Mt 24:4; Mk 13:5

10 [a]Then He told them: "Nation will
be raised up against nation, and kingdom against kingdom. 11 There will be
violent earthquakes, and famines and
plagues in various places, and there
will be terrifying sights and great signs
from heaven. 12 But before all these
things, they will lay their hands on you
and persecute you. They will hand you
over to the •synagogues [b]and prisons,
and you will be brought before kings
and governors because of My name.
13 [c]It will lead to an opportunity for you
to witness.[e] 14 [d]Therefore make up
your minds[f] not to prepare your defense ahead of time, 15 for I will give
you such words[g] and a wisdom [e]that
none of your adversaries will be able to
resist or contradict. 16 [f]You will even be
betrayed by parents, brothers, relatives, and friends. [g]They will kill some
of you. 17 [h]You will be hated by everyone because of My name, 18 but not a
hair of your head will be lost. 19 By your
endurance gain[h] your •lives.

[a]Mt 24:7 [b]Ac 4:3; 5:18; 25:23 [c]Php 1:28 [d]Mt 10:19 [e]Ac 6:10 [f]Mc 7:6 [g]Ac 7:59 [h]Mt 10:22

The Destruction of Jerusalem

20 [a]"When you see Jerusalem surrounded by armies, then recognize
that its desolation has come near.
21 Then those in Judea must flee to the
mountains! Those inside the city[i] must
leave it, and those who are in the
country must not enter it, 22 because
these are days of vengeance to fulfill
[b]all the things that are written. 23 Woe
to pregnant women and nursing mothers in those days, for there will be
great distress in the land[j] and wrath
against this people. 24 They will fall by
the edge of the sword and be led captive into all the nations, and Jerusalem
will be trampled by the Gentiles[k] [c]until
the times of the Gentiles are fulfilled.

[a]Mt 24:15 [b]Dn 9:26-27; Zch 11 [c]Dn 9:27

[a]**20:47** Or *judgment* [b]**21:2** Lit *two lepta*; the *lepton* was the smallest and least valuable Gk coin in use.
[c]**21:5** Gifts given to the temple in fulfillment of vows to God [d]**21:9** Or *insurrections*, or *revolutions*
[e]**21:13** Lit *lead to a testimony for you* [f]**21:14** Lit *Therefore place* (determine) *in your hearts* [g]**21:15** Lit *you a mouth* [h]**21:19** Other mss read *endurance you will gain* [i]**21:21** Lit *inside her* [j]**21:23** Or *the earth*
[k]**21:24** Or *nations*

The Coming of the Son of Man

25 [a]"Then there will be signs in the sun, moon, and stars; and there will be anguish on the earth among nations bewildered by the roaring sea and waves. 26 People will faint from fear and expectation of the things that are coming on the world, [b]because the celestial powers will be shaken. 27 Then they will see the •Son of Man [c]coming in a cloud with power and great glory. 28 But when these things begin to take place, stand up and lift your heads, because your redemption is near!"

[a] *Is 13:10,13; Dn 7:13; Jl 2:30-31; Mk 13:24-26* [b] *Mt 24:29* [c] *Rv 1:7*

The Parable of the Fig Tree

29 [a]Then He told them a parable: "Look at the fig tree, and all the trees. 30 As soon as they put out ⌊leaves⌋ you can see for yourselves and recognize that summer is already near. 31 In the same way, when you see these things happening, recognize[a] that the kingdom of God is near. 32 •I assure you: This generation will certainly not pass away until all things take place. 33 Heaven and earth will pass away, but My words will never pass away.

[a] *Mk 13:28*

The Need for Watchfulness

34 [a]"Be on your guard, so that your minds are not dulled[b] from carousing,[c] drunkenness, and worries of life, or that day will come on you unexpectedly 35 like a trap. For it will come on all who live on the face of the whole earth. 36 [b]But be alert at all times, praying that you may have strength[d] to escape all these things that are going to take place and [c]to stand before the Son of Man."

[a] *Rm 13:13* [b] *Mt 24:42; Mk 13:33* [c] *Eph 6:13*

37 [a]During the day, He was teaching [b]in the temple complex, but in the evening He would go out and spend the night on what is called the •Mount of Olives. 38 Then all the people would come early in the morning [c]to hear Him in the temple complex.

[a] *Jn 8:2* [b] *Lk 22:39* [c] *Hg 2:7; Mal 3:1*

The Plot to Kill Jesus

22 [a]The Festival of •Unleavened Bread, which is called •Passover, was drawing near. 2 [b]The •chief priests and the •scribes were looking for a way to put Him to death, because they were afraid of the people.

[a] *Ex 12:3-28; Mt 26:2; Mk 14:1* [b] *Ps 2:2*

3 [a]Then Satan entered Judas, called Iscariot, who was numbered among the Twelve. 4 He went away and discussed with the chief priests and temple police how he could hand Him over to them. 5 They were glad and [b]agreed to give him silver.[e] 6 So he accepted ⌊the offer⌋ and started looking for a good opportunity to betray Him to them when the crowd was not present.

[a] *Mt 26:14; Mk 14:10* [b] *Zch 11:12*

Preparation for Passover

7 [a]Then the Day of Unleavened Bread came when the Passover lamb had to be sacrificed. 8 Jesus sent Peter and John, saying, "Go and prepare the Passover meal for us, so we can eat it."

[a] *Mt 26:17; Mk 14:12*

9 "Where do You want us to prepare it?" they asked Him.

10 "Listen," He said to them, "when you've entered the city, a man carrying a water jug will meet you. Follow him into the house he enters. 11 Tell the owner of the house, 'The Teacher asks you, "Where is the guest room where I can eat the Passover with My disciples?"' 12 Then he will show you a large, furnished room upstairs. Make the preparations there."

[a]**21:31** Or *you know* [b]**21:34** Lit *your hearts are not weighed down* [c]**21:34** Or *hangovers* [d]**21:36** Other mss read *you may be counted worthy* [e]**22:5** Or *money*; Mt 26:15 specifies 30 pieces of silver; Zch 11:12–13

13 So they went and found it just as
He had told them, and they prepared
the Passover.

The First Lord's Supper

14 When the hour came, He reclined
at the table, and the apostles with Him.
15 Then He said to them, "I have fervently desired to eat this Passover with
you before I suffer. 16 For I tell you, I
will not eat it again[a] [a]until it is fulfilled
in the kingdom of God." 17 Then He
took a cup, and after giving thanks, He
said, "Take this and share it among
yourselves. 18 For [b]I tell you, from now
on I will not drink of the fruit of the
vine until the kingdom of God comes."

[a] *Ac 10:41; Rv 19:9*
[b] *Mt 26:29; Mk 14:25*

19 And He took bread, gave thanks,
broke it, gave it to them, and said,
"This is My body, which is given for
you. [a]Do this in remembrance of Me."

[a] *1Co 11:24*

20 In the same way He also took the
cup after supper and said, [a]"This cup is
the new covenant ⌊established by⌋ My
blood; it is shed for you.[b] 21 [b]But look,
the hand of the one betraying Me is at
the table with Me! 22 For the •Son of
Man will go away [c]as it has been determined, but woe to that man by whom
He is betrayed!"

[a] *1Co 10:16*
[b] *Ps 41:9; Mk 14:18; Jn 13:21,26* [c] *Is 53*

23 So they began to argue among
themselves which of them it could be
who was going to do this thing.

The Dispute over Greatness

24 [a]Then a dispute also arose among
them about who should be considered
the greatest. 25 [b]But He said to them,
"The kings of the Gentiles dominate
them, and those who have authority
over them are called[c] 'Benefactors.'[d]
26 But it must not be like that among
you. On the contrary, [c]whoever is
greatest among you must become
like the youngest, and whoever leads,
like the one serving. 27 For who is
greater, the one at the table or the one
serving? Isn't it the one at the table?
But [d]I am among you as the One who
serves. 28 You are the ones who stood
by Me in [e]My trials. 29 [f]I bestow on you
a kingdom, just as My Father bestowed
one on Me, 30 so that [g]you may eat and
drink at My table in My kingdom. And
[h]you will sit on thrones judging the 12
tribes of Israel.

[a] *Mk 9:34; Lk 9:46*
[b] *Mt 20:25* [c] *Lk 9:48* [d] *Mt 20:28; Php 2:7*
[e] *Heb 4:15* [f] *Lk 12:32* [g] *Lk 12:37* [h] *Mt 19:28*

Peter's Denial Predicted

31 "Simon, Simon,[e] look out! Satan
has asked to sift you[f] like wheat. 32 [a]But
I have prayed for you[g] that your faith
may not fail. [b]And you, when you have
turned back, strengthen your brothers."

[a] *Jn 17:9* [b] *Jn 21:15*

33 "Lord," he told Him, "I'm ready to
go with You both to prison and to
death!"

34 [a]"I tell you, Peter," He said, "the
rooster will not crow today until[h] you
deny three times that you know Me!"

[a] *Mt 26:34*

Money-Bag, Backpack, and Sword

35 [a]He also said to them, "When I
sent you out without money-bag, traveling bag, or sandals, did you lack anything?"

[a] *Mt 10:9; Lk 9:3*

"Not a thing," they said.

36 Then He said to them, "But now,
whoever has a money-bag should
take it, and also a traveling bag. And
whoever doesn't have a sword should
sell his robe and buy one. 37 For I tell
you, what is written must be fulfilled
in Me: [a]**And He was counted among
the outlaws.**[i] Yes, what is written

[a]**22:16** Other mss omit *again* [b]**22:19–20** Other mss omit *which is given for you* (v. 19) through the end of v. 20 [c]**22:25** Or *them call themselves* [d]**22:25** Title of honor given to those who benefited the public good [e]**22:31** Other mss read *Then the Lord said, "Simon, Simon* [f]**22:31** *you* (pl in Gk) [g]**22:32** *you* (sg in Gk) [h]**22:34** Other mss read *before* [i]**22:37** Is 53:12

about Me is coming to its fulfillment." [a]Is 53:12; Mk 15:28

38 "Lord," they said, "look, here are
two swords."

"Enough of that!"[a] He told them.

The Prayer in the Garden

39 He went out and made His way as
usual to the •Mount of Olives, and the
disciples followed Him. 40 [a]When He
reached the place, He told them, "Pray
that you may not enter into temptation." 41 Then He withdrew from them
about a stone's throw, knelt down, and
began to pray, 42 "Father, if You are
willing, take this cup away from
Me—nevertheless, [b]not My will, but
Yours, be done." [a]Mt 26:36; Mk 14:38 [b]Jn 6:38

[43 Then [a]an angel from heaven appeared to Him, strengthening Him.
44 Being in anguish, He prayed more
fervently, and His sweat became like
drops of blood falling to the ground.][b]
45 When He got up from prayer and
came to the disciples, He found them
sleeping, exhausted from their grief.[c]
46 "Why are you sleeping?" He asked
them. "Get up and pray, so that you
won't enter into temptation." [a]Mt 4:11

The Judas Kiss

47 While He was still speaking, suddenly a mob was there, and one of the
Twelve named Judas was leading
them. He came near Jesus to kiss Him,
48 but Jesus said to him, "Judas, are you
betraying the Son of Man with a kiss?"

49 When those around Him saw what
was going to happen, they asked,
"Lord, should we strike with the
sword?" 50 Then [a]one of them struck
the high priest's slave and cut off his
right ear. [a]Mt 26:51; Mk 14:47

51 But Jesus responded, "No more of
this!"[d] And touching his ear, He healed
him. 52 Then Jesus said to the chief
priests, temple police, and the elders
who had come for Him, "Have you
come out with swords and clubs as if I
were a criminal?[e] 53 Every day while I
was with you in the •temple complex,
you never laid a hand on Me. But this
is your hour—and the dominion of
darkness."

Peter Denies His Lord

54 [a]They seized Him, led Him away,
and brought Him into the high priest's
house. [b]Meanwhile Peter was following at a distance. 55 [c]They lit a fire in
the middle of the courtyard and sat
down together, and Peter sat among
them. 56 When a servant saw him sitting in the firelight, and looked closely
at him, she said, "This man was with
Him too." [a]Mt 26:57 [b]Jn 18:15 [c]Mt 26:69; Mk 14:66

57 But he denied it: "Woman, I don't
know Him!"

58 [a]After a little while, someone else
saw him and said, "You're one of them
too!" [a]Mt 26:71; Mk 14:69; Jn 18:25

"Man, I am not!" Peter said.

59 About an hour later, another kept
insisting, "This man was certainly
with Him, since he's also a Galilean."

60 But Peter said, "Man, I don't know
what you're talking about!" Immediately, while he was still speaking, a
rooster crowed. 61 Then the Lord
turned and looked at Peter. [a]So Peter
remembered the word of the Lord,
how He had said to him, [b]"Before the
rooster crows today, you will deny Me
three times." 62 And he went outside
and wept bitterly. [a]Mt 26:75; Mk 14:72 [b]Jn 13:38

Jesus Mocked and Beaten

63 [a]The men who were holding Jesus
started mocking and beating Him.
64 After blindfolding Him, they kept[f]
asking, "Prophesy! Who hit You?"

[a]**22:38** Or *It is enough!* [b]**22:43–44** Other mss omit bracketed text [c]**22:45** Lit *sleeping from grief* [d]**22:51** Lit *Permit as far as this* [e]**22:52** Lit *as against a criminal* [f]**22:64** Other mss add *striking Him on the face and*

65 And they were saying many other
blasphemous things against Him.
a Is 50:6; Mt 26:67; Mk 14:65

Jesus Faces the Sanhedrin

66 aWhen daylight came, the elders[a]
of the people, both the chief priests
and the scribes, convened and brought
Him before their •Sanhedrin. 67 They
said, b"If You are the •Messiah, tell
us."
a Mt 27:1 b Mt 26:63; Mk 14:61

But He said to them, "If I do tell you,
you will not believe. 68 And if I ask you,
you will not answer. 69 aBut from now
on, the Son of Man will be seated at
the right hand of the Power of God."
a Ps 110:1; Dn 7:13-14

70 They all asked, "Are You, then, the
Son of God?"

And He said to them, "You say that I
am."

71 "Why do we need any more testimony," they said, "since we've heard
it ourselves from His mouth?"

Jesus Faces Pilate

23 aThen their whole assembly
rose up and brought Him before
•Pilate. 2 They began to accuse Him,
saying, "We found this man subvert-
ing our nation, bopposing payment of
taxes to Caesar, and saying cthat He
Himself is the •Messiah, a King."
a Mt 27:2; Mk 15:1; Jn 18:28
b Mt 17:27; Mk 12:17 c Mk 14:61-62; Jn 19:12

3 So Pilate asked Him, "Are You the
King of the Jews?"

He answered him, "You have said
it."[b]

4 Pilate then told the •chief priests
and the crowds, a"I find no grounds for
charging this man." a Mt 27:19; Mk 15:14

5 But they kept insisting, "He stirs up
the people, teaching throughout all
Judea, from Galilee where He started
even to here."

Jesus Faces Herod Antipas

6 When Pilate heard this,[c] he asked
if the man was a Galilean. 7 Finding
that He was under a•Herod's jurisdiction, he sent Him to Herod, who was
also in Jerusalem during those days.
8 Herod was bvery glad to see Jesus;
for a long time he had wanted to see
Him, because che had heard about
Him and was hoping to see some miracle[d] performed by Him. 9 So he kept
asking Him questions, but Jesus did
not answer him. 10 The chief priests
and the •scribes stood by, vehemently
accusing Him. 11 dThen Herod, with
his soldiers, treated Him with contempt, mocked Him, dressed Him in a
brilliant robe, and sent Him back to
Pilate. 12 That very day Herod and Pilate became friends.[e] Previously, they
had been hostile toward each other.
a Lk 3:1 b Lk 9:9
c Mt 14:1; Mk 6:14 d Is 53:3

Jesus or Barabbas

13 aPilate called together the chief
priests, the leaders, and the people,
14 and said to them, "You have brought
me this man as one who subverts the
people. But in fact, after examining
Him in your presence, I have found no
grounds to charge this man with those
things you accuse Him of. 15 Neither
has Herod, because he sent Him back
to us. Clearly, He has done nothing to
deserve death. 16 bTherefore I will
have Him whipped[f] and ⌊then⌋ release
Him." [17 cFor according to the festival
he had to release someone to them.][g]
a Mt 27:23; Jn 18:38 b Mt 27:26; Mk 15:15; Jn 19:1
c Mt 27:15; Mk 15:6; Jn 18:39

18 Then they all cried out together,
"Take this man away! Release Barabbas to us!" 19 (He had been thrown into
prison for a rebellion that had taken
place in the city, and for murder.)

[a]**22:66** Or *council of elders* [b]**23:3** Or *That is true*; an affirmative oath [c]**23:6** Other mss read *heard "Galilee"* [d]**23:8** Or *sign* [e]**23:12** Lit *friends with one another* [f]**23:16** Gk *paideuo;* to discipline or "teach a lesson"; 1 Kg 12:11,14 LXX; 2 Ch 10:11,14; perhaps a way of referring to the Roman scourging; Lat *flagellatio* [g]**23:17** Other mss omit bracketed text

20 Pilate, wanting to release Jesus, addressed them again, 21 but they kept
shouting, "Crucify! Crucify Him!"
22 A third time he said to them,
"Why? What has this man done
wrong? I have found in Him no
grounds for the death penalty. Therefore I will have Him whipped and
⌊then⌋ release Him."
23 But they kept up the pressure, demanding with loud voices that He be
crucified. And their voices[a] won out.
24 So Pilate decided to grant their demand 25 [a]and released the one they
were asking for, who had been thrown
into prison for rebellion and murder.
But he handed Jesus over to their will.

[a] *Pr 17:15*

The Way to the Cross

26 [a]As they led Him away, they seized
Simon, a Cyrenian, who was coming
in from the country, and laid the cross
on him to carry behind Jesus. 27 A great
multitude of the people followed Him,
including women who were mourning
and lamenting Him. 28 But turning to
them, Jesus said, "Daughters of Jerusalem, do not weep for Me, but weep for
yourselves and your children. 29 [b]Look,
the days are coming when they will
say, 'Blessed are the barren, the
wombs that never bore, and the
breasts that never nursed!' 30 [c]Then
they will begin **to say to the mountains, 'Fall on us!' and to the hills,
'Cover us!'**[b] 31 [d]For if they do these
things when the wood is green, what
will happen when it is dry?"

[a] *Mt 27:32; Mk 15:21; Jn 19:17* [b] *Lk 21:23* [c] *Hs 10:8* [d] *Ezk 20:47*

Crucified between Two Criminals

32 [a]Two others—criminals—were also
led away to be executed with Him.
33 [b]When they arrived at the place called
The Skull, they crucified Him there
along with the criminals, one on th
right and one on the left. [34 Then Jesu
said, "Father, forgive them, becaus
they do not know what they are do
ing."][c] And [c]they divided His clothe
and cast lots.

[a] *Is 53:12; Mt 27:3* [b] *Mt 27:33; Mk 15:22; Jn 19:17* [c] *Ps 22:18; Mt 27:35; Mk 15:24; Jn 19:2*

35 [a]The people stood watching, an
even the leaders kept scoffing: "H
saved others; let Him save Himself
this is God's Messiah, the Chose
One!" 36 The soldiers also mocke
Him. They came offering Him sou
wine 37 and said, "If You are the Kin
of the Jews, save Yourself!"

[a] *Zch 12:1*

38 [a]An inscription was above Him:

[a] *Jn 19:1*

THIS IS THE
KING OF THE JEWS

39 [a]Then one of the criminals hang
ing there began to yell insults at[e] Him
"Aren't You the Messiah? Save Your
self and us!"

[a] *Mt 27:44; Mk 15:3*

40 But the other answered, rebuking
him: "Don't you even fear God, since
you are undergoing the same punishment? 41 We are punished justly, because we're getting back what we
deserve for the things we did, but this
man has done nothing wrong." 42 Then
he said, "Jesus, remember me[f] when
You come into Your kingdom!"
43 And He said to him, "•I assure you:
Today you will be with Me in [a]para-
dise."

[a] *Rv 2:7*

The Death of Jesus

44 [a]It was now about noon,[g] and darkness came over the whole land[h] until
three,[i] 45 because the sun's light failed.[j]
[b]The curtain of the sanctuary was split

[a]**23:23** Other mss add *and those of the chief priests* [b]**23:30** Hs 10:8 [c]**23:34** Other mss omit bracketed text [d]**23:38** Other mss add *written in Greek, Latin, and Hebrew letters* [e]**23:39** Or *began to blaspheme* [f]**23:42** Other mss add *Lord* [g]**23:44** Lit *about the sixth hour* [h]**23:44** Or *whole earth* [i]**23:44** Lit *the ninth hour* [j]**23:45** Other mss read *three, and the sun was darkened*

down the middle. 46 And Jesus called out with a loud voice, [c]"Father, **into Your hands I entrust My spirit.**"[a] [d]Saying this, He breathed His last. [a]*Mt 27:45; Mk 15:33* [b]*Mt 27:51; Mk 15:38* [c]*Ps 31:5* [d]*Php 2:8*

47 [a]When the •centurion saw what happened, he began to glorify God, saying, "This man really was righteous!" 48 All the crowds that had gathered for this spectacle, when they saw what had taken place, went home, striking their chests.[b] 49 [b]But all who knew Him, including the women who had followed Him from Galilee, stood at a distance, watching these things. [a]*Mt 27:54* [b]*Ps 38:11*

The Burial of Jesus

50 [a]There was a good and righteous man named Joseph, a member of the •Sanhedrin, 51 who had not agreed with their plan and action. He was from Arimathea, a Judean town, [b]and was looking forward to the kingdom of God. 52 He approached Pilate and asked for Jesus' body. 53 [c]Taking it down, he wrapped it in fine linen and placed it in [d]a tomb cut into the rock, where no one had ever been placed.[c] 54 It was preparation day, and the Sabbath was about to begin.[d] 55 The women [e]who had come with Him from Galilee followed along and [f]observed the tomb and how His body was placed. 56 Then they returned and [g]prepared spices and perfumes. And they rested on the Sabbath [h]according to the commandment.

[a]*Mt 27:57; Mk 15:42; Jn 19:38* [b]*Mk 15:43* [c]*Mt 27:59* [d]*Is 53:9* [e]*Lk 8:2-3* [f]*Mk 15:47* [g]*Mk 16:1* [h]*Gn 2:3; Dt 5:14; Is 58:13*

Resurrection Morning

24 [a]On the first day of the week, very early in the morning, they[e] came to the tomb, bringing the spices they had prepared. 2 They found the stone rolled away from the tomb. 3 [b]They went in but did not find the body of the Lord Jesus. 4 While they were perplexed about this, [c]suddenly two men stood by them in dazzling clothes. 5 So the women were terrified and bowed down to the ground.[f]

[a]*Mt 28:1; Mk 16:1; Jn 20:1* [b]*Mk 16:5* [c]*Gn 18:2; Mt 28:2-6; Mk 16:5-6; Jn 20:12*

"Why are you looking for the living among the dead?" asked the men. 6 "He is not here, but He has been resurrected! [a]Remember how He spoke to you when He was still in Galilee, 7 saying, 'The •Son of Man must be betrayed into the hands of sinful men, be crucified, and rise on the third day'?" 8 And they remembered His words.

[a]*Mt 16:21; Mk 8:31; Lk 9:22*

9 [a]Returning from the tomb, they reported all these things to the Eleven and to all the rest. 10 •Mary Magdalene, [b]Joanna, Mary the mother of James, and the other women with them were telling the apostles these things. 11 But these words seemed like nonsense to them, and they did not believe the women. 12 [c]Peter, however, got up and ran to the tomb. When he stooped to look in, he saw only the linen cloths.[g] So he went home, amazed at what had happened. [a]*Mt 28:8; Mk 16:10* [b]*Lk 8:3* [c]*Jn 20:3*

The Emmaus Disciples

13 Now that same day two of them were on their way to a village called[h] Emmaus, which was about seven miles[i] from Jerusalem. 14 Together they were discussing everything that had taken place. 15 And while they were discussing and arguing, Jesus Himself came near and began to walk along

[a]**23:46** Ps 31:5 [b]**23:48** Mourning [c]**23:53** Or *interred*, or *laid* [d]**23:54** Lit *was dawning*; not in the morning but at sundown Friday [e]**24:1** Other mss add *and other women with them* [f]**24:5** Lit *and inclined their faces to the ground* [g]**24:12** Other mss add *lying there* [h]**24:13** Lit *village, which name is* [i]**24:13** Lit *about 60 stadia*; 1 *stadion* = 600 feet

with them. 16 But [a]they[a] were prevented from recognizing Him. 17 Then He asked them, "What is this dispute that you're having[b] with each other as you are walking?" And they stopped ⌊walking and looked⌋ discouraged.

[a] Jn 20:14; 21:4

18 The one [a]named Cleopas answered Him, "Are You the only visitor in Jerusalem who doesn't know the things that happened there in these days?"

[a] Jn 19:25

19 "What things?" He asked them.

So they said to Him, "The things concerning Jesus the •Nazarene, who was a Prophet powerful in action and speech before God and all the people, 20 and how our •chief priests and leaders handed Him over to be sentenced to death, and they crucified Him. 21 But we were hoping that He was the One who was about to redeem Israel. Besides all this, it's the third day since these things happened. 22 Moreover, some women from our group astounded us. They arrived early at the tomb, 23 and when they didn't find His body, they came and reported that they had seen a vision of angels who said He was alive. 24 Some of those who were with us went to the tomb and found it just as the women had said, but they didn't see Him."

25 He said to them, "How unwise and slow you are to believe in your hearts all that the prophets have spoken! 26 [a]Didn't the •Messiah have to suffer these things and enter into His glory?" 27 Then beginning with [b]Moses and [c]all the Prophets, He interpreted for them the things concerning Himself in all the Scriptures.

[a] Is 53 [b] Gn 3:15; 49:10; Dt 18:15 [c] Ps 22; Is 7:14; 9:6; 42:1; 53; Jr 33:14; Mc 5:2; Mal 3:1; 4:2

28 They came near the village where they were going, and He gave the impression that He was going farther. 29 But they urged Him: "Stay with us, because it's almost evening, and now the day is almost over." So He went in to stay with them.

30 It was as He reclined at the table with them that He took the bread, blessed and broke it, and gave it to them. 31 Then their eyes were opened, and they recognized Him, but He disappeared from their sight. 32 So they said to each other, "Weren't our hearts ablaze within us while He was talking with us on the road and explaining the Scriptures to us?" 33 That very hour they got up and returned to Jerusalem. They found the Eleven and those with them gathered together, 34 who said,[c] "The Lord has certainly been raised, and [a]has appeared to Simon!" 35 Then they began to describe what had happened on the road and how He was made known to them in the breaking of the bread.

[a] 1Co 15:5

The Reality of the Risen Jesus

36 And as they were saying these things, He Himself stood among them. He said to them, "Peace to you!" 37 But they were startled and terrified and thought they were seeing a ghost. 38 "Why are you troubled?" He asked them. "And why do doubts arise in your hearts? 39 Look at My hands and My feet, that it is I Myself! Touch Me and see, because a ghost does not have flesh and bones as you can see I have." 40 Having said this, He showed them His hands and feet. 41 But while they still could not believe[d] because of ⌊their⌋ joy and were amazed, He asked them, "Do you have anything here to eat?" 42 So they gave Him a piece of a broiled fish,[e] 43 [a]and He took it and ate in their presence.

[a] Ac 10:41

44 Then He told them, [a]"These are My words that I spoke to you while I

[a] **24:16** Lit *their eyes* [b] **24:17** Lit *What are these words that you are exchanging* [c] **24:34** Gk is specific that this refers to the Eleven and those with them. [d] **24:41** Or *they still disbelieved* [e] **24:42** Other mss add *and some honeycomb*

Trusting Christ For Salvation

We must first see ourselves as sinners, recognize Christ died for us and rose again and trust in Him alone for salvation. When you come to understand God's simple plan of salvation it is often helpful to tell God in prayer that you are trusting in Him. It is important to realize though, that saying a prayer doesn't save you. It is trusting Christ that saves you. You are saved the moment you trust Christ alone as your only way to heaven. Prayer is only the means by which you tell God what you are doing.

If you want to trust Christ to save you, here's how you can express to God what you are doing in prayer:

> *"Dear God, I come to You now in the name of Your Son, Jesus Christ. I acknowledge I have sinned before You and deserve to be separated forever from You. But I now understand that Your Son, Jesus Christ, shed His blood on the cross in my place and died for my sins, and that on the third day He arose from the grave. Right now I am trusting Christ alone as my only way to heaven, believing that He paid for all of my sins by dying as my substitute. Thank You that according to Your word I have right now received Your free gift of eternal life. Help me to now live a life that expresses my gratitude to You for saving me."*

If you have trusted Christ, memorize John 5:24, "I assure you: Anyone who hears My word and believes Him who sent Me has eternal life and will not come under judgment but has passed from death to life."

You may be wondering, "What next?"

- **You will want to be baptized. Baptism has nothing to do with salvation, but it is a first step in discipleship**

and a way of publicly declaring to others you have accepted Christ's forgiveness of your sins.

- **Begin now to study the Bible daily and spend time alone with God in prayer. Starting with the Book of John on the next page is an excellent place to begin your daily reading.**

- **Ask Jesus to help you grow as a Christian and to be bold in talking to others about what He has done for you.**

- **Find a church that believes in teaching the Bible and attend regularly.**

May God help you to be a testimony to many of His love and saving power.

MY RECORD OF SALVATION

On the _______ day of _______________, 20____,

I, ____, trusted Jesus Christ as my personal Savior and gave myself to Him as Lord of my life.

Witnessed by: ___________________________________

____

was still with you—that everything
written about Me in the Law of Moses,
the Prophets, and the Psalms must be
fulfilled." 45 Then [b]He opened their
minds to understand the Scriptures.
46 He also said to them, "This is what is
written:[a] the Messiah would suffer and
rise from the dead the third day, 47 and
repentance for[b] forgiveness of sins
would be proclaimed in His name [c]to
all the nations, beginning at Jerusalem.
48 [d]You are witnesses of these things.
49 [e]And look, I am sending you[c] what
My Father promised. As for you, stay
in the city[d] until you are empowered[e]
from on high."

[a]Mt 16:21 [b]2Co 4:6 [c]Ps 22:27; Is 49:6; Jr 31:34; Hs 2:23; Mc 4:2; Mal 1:11 [d]Ac 1:22 [e]Ac 2:1

The Ascension of Jesus

50 Then He led them out as far as Bethany, and lifting up His hands He blessed
them. 51 And while He was blessing
them, [a]He left them and was carried up
into heaven. 52 After worshiping Him,
they returned to Jerusalem with great
joy. 53 And they were continually [b]in the
•temple complex blessing God.[f]

[a]Ac 1:9 [b]Ac 2:46

JOHN

Prologue

1 In the beginning [a]was
the Word,[g]
and the Word was with God,
and the [b]Word was God.
2 He was with God
in the beginning.
3 All things were created
through Him,
and apart from Him
not one thing was created
that has been created.
4 Life was in Him,[h]
and that life was the light
of men.
5 [c]That light shines in the darkness,
yet the darkness did not
overcome[i] it.

[a]Rv 19:13 [b]Is 9:6; Php 2:6 [c]Jn 3:19

6 [a]There was a man named John
who was sent from God.
7 He came as a witness
to testify about the light,
so that all might believe
through him.[j]
8 [b]He was not the light,
but he came to testify
about the light.
9 [c]The true light, who gives light
to everyone,
was coming into the world.[k]

[a]Mal 3:1 [b]Ac 13:25 [c]Is 49:6

10 He was in the world,
and [a]the world was created
through Him,
yet the world did not recognize
Him.
11 [b]He came to His own,[l]
and His own people[l]
did not receive Him.
12 But [c]to all
who did receive Him,

[a]**24:46** Other mss add *and thus it was necessary that* [b]**24:47** Other mss read *repentance and* [c]**24:49** Lit *upon you* [d]**24:49** Other mss add *of Jerusalem* [e]**24:49** Lit *clothed with power* [f]**24:53** Other mss read *praising and blessing God. Amen.* [g]**1:1** The *Word* (Gk *Logos*) is a title for Jesus as the communication and the revealer of God the Father; Jn 1:14,18; Rv 19:13. [h]**1:3–4** Other punctuation is possible: . . . *not one thing was created. What was created in Him was life* [i]**1:5** Or *grasp*, or *comprehend*, or *overtake*; Jn 12:35 [j]**1:7** Or *through it* (the light) [k]**1:9** Or *The true light who comes into the world gives light to everyone*, or *The true light enlightens everyone coming into the world.* [l]**1:11** The same Gk adjective is used twice in this verse: the first refers to all that Jesus owned as Creator (*to His own*); the second refers to the Jews (*His own people*).

He gave them the right to be[a]
children of God,
to those who believe in His name,
13 who were born,
not of blood,[b]
or of the will of the flesh,
or of the will of man,[c]
[d]but of God.

a Ps 33:6; 1Co 8:6 b Lk 19:14; 23:18 c Is 56:5; Rm 8:15 d Jms 1:18

14 [a]The Word [b]became [c]flesh[d]
and took up residence[e] among us.
[d]We observed His glory,
the glory as
the •One and Only Son[f]
from the Father,
[e]full of grace and truth.
15 (John testified concerning Him
and exclaimed,
"This was the One of whom
I said,
'The One coming after me
has surpassed me,
[f]because He existed
before me.'")
16 Indeed, [g]we have all received
grace after grace
from His fullness,
17 for although [h]the law was given
through Moses,
[i]grace and [j]truth came
through Jesus Christ.
18 [k]No one has ever seen God.[g]
[l]The One and Only Son[h] —
the One who is
at [m]the Father's side[i] —
He has revealed Him.

a 1Tm 3:16 b Rm 1:3 c Heb 2:14 d Mt 17:2 e Col 2:3 f Col 1:17 g Eph 1:6 h Ex 20:1 i Rm 5:21 j Jn 14:6 k Ex 33:20 l 1Jn 4:9 m Jn 10:30

John the Baptist's Testimony

19 This is John's testimony when the
•Jews from Jerusalem sent priests and
Levites to ask him, "Who are you?"
20 He did not refuse to answer, but he
declared: "I am not the •Messiah."
21 "What then?" they asked him.
"Are you [a]Elijah?"

a Mal 4:5

[a]"I am not," he said.

a Lk 1:17

"Are you the Prophet?"[j]
"No," he answered.
22 "Who are you, then?" they asked.
"We need to give an answer to those
who sent us. What can you tell us
about yourself?"
23 He said, "I am a **voice of one crying out in the wilderness: Make
straight the way of the Lord**[k] —just as
[a]Isaiah the prophet said."

a Is 40:3

24 Now they had been sent from the
•Pharisees. 25 So they asked him, "Why
then do you baptize if you aren't the
Messiah, or Elijah, or the Prophet?"
26 "I baptize with[l] water," John answered them. [a]"Someone stands among
you, but you don't know ⌊Him⌋. 27 He is
the One coming after me,[m] whose san-
dal strap I'm not worthy to untie."

a Mal 3:1

28 All this happened in Bethany[n]
across the Jordan,[o] where John was
baptizing.

The Lamb of God

29 The next day John saw Jesus coming toward him and said, "Here is [a]the
Lamb of God, [b]who takes away the sin
of the world! 30 This is the One I told
you about: 'After me comes a man who

[a]**1:12** Or *become* [b]**1:13** Lit *bloods*; the pl form of *blood* occurs only here in the NT. It may refer either to lineal descent (that is, blood from one's father and mother) or to the OT sacrificial system (that is, the various blood sacrifices). Neither is the basis for birth into the family of God. [c]**1:13** Or *not of human lineage, or of human capacity, or of human volition* [d]**1:14** The eternally existent Word (vv. 1–2) took on full humanity, but without sin; Heb 4:15. [e]**1:14** Lit *and tabernacled*, or *and dwelt in a tent*; this word occurs only here in John. A related word, referring to the Festival of Tabernacles, occurs only in 7:2; Ex 40:34–38. [f]**1:14** *Son* is implied from the reference to the Father and from Gk usage. [g]**1:18** Since God is an infinite being, no one can see Him in His absolute essential nature; Ex 33:18–23. [h]**1:18** Other mss read *God* [i]**1:18** Lit *is in the bosom of the Father* [j]**1:21** Probably = the Prophet in Dt 18:15 [k]**1:23** Is 40:3 [l]**1:26** Or *in* [m]**1:27** Other mss add *who came before me* [n]**1:28** Other mss read *in Bethabara* [o]**1:28** Another Bethany, near Jerusalem, was the home of Lazarus, Martha, and Mary; Jn 11:1.

has surpassed me, because He existed
before me.' 31 I didn't know Him, but I
came baptizing with[a] water so He
might be revealed to Israel."

[a] Is 53:7; 1Pt 1:19
[b] 1Co 15:3; Gl 1:4; Heb 1:3; Rv 1:5

32 And John testified, "I watched the
Spirit descending from heaven like a
dove, and He rested on Him. 33 I didn't
know Him, but He[b] who sent me to
baptize with[a] water told me, 'The One
you see the Spirit descending and resting on—[a]He is the One who baptizes
with[a] the Holy Spirit.' 34 I have seen
and testified that He is the Son of
God!"[c]

[a] Jn 14:26; 20:22

35 Again the next day, John was
standing with two of his disciples.
36 When he saw Jesus passing by, he
said, "Look! The Lamb of God!"
37 The two disciples heard him say
this and followed Jesus. 38 When Jesus
turned and noticed them following
Him, He asked them, "What are you
looking for?"
They said to Him, "•Rabbi" (which
means "Teacher"), "where are You
staying?"
39 "Come and you'll see," He replied.
So they went and saw where He was
staying, and they stayed with Him that
day. It was about 10 in the morning.[d]
40 Andrew, Simon Peter's brother,
was one of the two who heard John and
followed Him. 41 He first found his
own brother [a]Simon and told him, "We
have found the Messiah!"[e] (which
means "Anointed One"), 42 and he
brought ⌊Simon⌋ to Jesus.

[a] Mt 4:18

When Jesus saw him, He said, "You
are Simon, son of John.[f] You will be
called •Cephas" (which means "Rock").

Philip and Nathanael

43 The next day He[g] decided to leave
for Galilee. Jesus found Philip and told
him, "Follow Me!"
44 Now [a]Philip was from Bethsaida,
the hometown of Andrew and Peter.
45 Philip found [b]Nathanael[h] and told
him, "We have found the One Moses
wrote about in the Law (and so did the
[c]prophets): Jesus the son of Joseph,
from Nazareth!"

[a] Jn 12:21 [b] Jn 21:2
[c] Lk 24:27

46 "Can anything good come out of
Nazareth?" Nathanael asked him.
"Come and see," Philip answered.
47 Then Jesus saw Nathanael coming
toward Him and said about him, "Here
is a true Israelite; no deceit is in him."
48 "How do you know me?" Nathanael asked.
"Before Philip called you, when you
were under the fig tree, I saw you,"
Jesus answered.
49 "Rabbi," Nathanael replied, "You
are the Son of God! You are [a]the King
of Israel!"

[a] Mt 21:5; 27:11; Jn 19:14-19

50 Jesus responded to him, "Do you
believe ⌊only⌋ because I told you I saw
you under the fig tree? You[i] will see
greater things than this." 51 Then He
said, "•I assure you: You[j] will see
heaven opened and the angels of God
ascending and descending on [a]the
•Son of Man."

[a] Dn 7:13

The First Sign: Turning Water into Wine

2 On the third day a wedding took
place in Cana of Galilee. Jesus'
mother was there, and 2 Jesus and His
disciples were invited to the wedding
as well. 3 When the wine ran out,

[a]**1:31,33** Or *in* [b]**1:33** *He* refers to God the Father, who gave John a sign to help him identify the Messiah. Vv. 32–34 indicate that John did not know that Jesus was the Messiah until the Spirit descended upon Him at His baptism. [c]**1:34** Other mss read *is the Chosen One of God* [d]**1:39** Lit *about the tenth hour.* Various methods of reckoning time were used in the ancient world. John probably used a different method from the other 3 Gospels. If John used the same method of time reckoning as the other 3 Gospels, the translation would be: *It was about four in the afternoon.* [e]**1:41** In the NT, the word Messiah translates the Gk word *Christos* ("Anointed One"), except here and in Jn 4:25 where it translates *Messias.* [f]**1:42** Other mss read *Simon, son of Jonah* [g]**1:43** Or *he,* referring either to Peter (v. 42) or Andrew (vv. 40–41) [h]**1:45** Probably the Bartholomew of the other Gospels and Acts [i]**1:50** *You* (sg in Gk) refers to Nathanael. [j]**1:51** *You* is pl in Gk and refers to Nathanael and the other disciples.

Jesus' mother told Him, "They don't
have any wine."
4 [a]"What has this concern of yours to
do with Me,[a] [b]•woman?" Jesus asked.
[c]"My hour[b] has not yet come."
[a]Lk 2:49 [b]Jn 19:26 [c]Ec 3:1

5 "Do whatever He tells you," His
mother told the servants.
6 Now six stone water jars had been
set there [a]for Jewish purification. Each
contained 20 or 30 gallons.[c] *[a]Mk 7:3*

7 "Fill the jars with water," Jesus told
them. So they filled them to the brim.
8 Then He said to them, "Now draw
some out and take it to the chief servant."[d] And they did.
9 When the chief servant tasted the
water (after it had become wine), he
did not know where it came from—
though the servants who had drawn
the water knew. He called the groom
10 and told him, "Everybody sets out
the fine wine first, then, after people
have drunk freely, the inferior. But you
have kept the fine wine until now."
11 Jesus performed this first sign[e] in
Cana of Galilee. [a]He displayed His
glory, and His disciples believed in
Him. *[a]Jn 1:14*

12 After this, He went down to Capernaum, together with His mother,
[a]His brothers, and His disciples, and
they stayed there only a few days.
[a]Mt 12:46

Cleansing the Temple Complex

13 [a]The Jewish •Passover was near, so
Jesus went up to Jerusalem. 14 [b]In the
•temple complex He found people selling oxen, sheep, and doves, and ⌊He
also found⌋ the money changers sitting
there. 15 After making a whip out of
cords, He drove everyone out of the
temple complex with their sheep and
oxen. He also poured out the money
changers' coins and overturned the tables. 16 He told those who were selling
doves, "Get these things out of here!
Stop turning [c]My Father's house into a
marketplace!"[f] *[a]Ex 12:14 [b]Mt 21:12; Mk 11:15; Lk 19:45 [c]Ps 93:5*

17 And His disciples remembered
that it is written: [a]**Zeal for Your house
will consume Me.**[g] *[a]Ps 69:9*

18 So the Jews replied to Him, "What
sign ⌊of authority⌋ will You show us for
doing these things?"
19 Jesus answered, [a]"Destroy this
sanctuary, and I will raise it up in three
days." *[a]Mt 26:61*

20 Therefore the Jews said, "This
sanctuary took 46 years to build, and
will You raise it up in three days?"
21 But He was speaking about the
sanctuary of His body. 22 So when He
was raised from the dead, [a]His disciples remembered that He had said this.
And they believed the Scripture and
the statement Jesus had made.
[a]Lk 24:8; Jn 14:26

23 While He was in Jerusalem at the
Passover Festival, many trusted in His
name when they saw the signs He was
doing. 24 Jesus, however, would not entrust Himself to them, since He knew
them all 25 and because He did not
need anyone to testify about man; for
[a]He Himself knew what was in man.
[a]Mt 9:4; Mk 2:8; Jn 6:64

Jesus and Nicodemus

3 There was a man from the •Phari-
sees named Nicodemus, a ruler of
the Jews. 2 This man came to Him at
night and said, "•Rabbi, we know that
You have come from God as a teacher,
for [a]no one could perform these signs
You do unless [b]God were with him."
[a]Jn 5:36; Ac 2:22 [b]Ac 10:38

[a]**2:4** Or *You and I see things differently*; lit *What to Me and to you*; Mt 8:29; Mk 1:24; 5:7; Lk 8:28 [b]**2:4** The time of His sacrificial death and exaltation; Jn 7:30; 8:20; 12:23,27; 13:1; 17:1 [c]**2:6** Lit *2 or 3 measures* [d]**2:8** Lit *ruler of the table*; perhaps *master of the feast*, or *headwaiter* [e]**2:11** Lit *this beginning of the signs*; Jn 4:54; 20:30. Seven miraculous signs occur in John's Gospel and are so noted in the headings. [f]**2:16** Lit *a house of business* [g]**2:17** Ps 69:9

3 Jesus replied, "•I assure you:
[a]Unless someone is born again,[a] he
cannot see the kingdom of God."

[a] Jn 1:13; 2Co 5:17; Ti 3:5

4 "But how can anyone be born
when he is old?" Nicodemus asked
Him. "Can he enter his mother's
womb a second time and be born?"
5 Jesus answered, "I assure you:
[a]Unless someone is born of water and
the Spirit,[b] he cannot enter the kingdom of God. 6 Whatever is born of the
flesh is flesh, and whatever is born of
the Spirit is spirit. 7 Do not be amazed
that I told you that you[c] must be born
again. 8 [b]The wind[d] blows where it
pleases, and you hear its sound, but
you don't know where it comes from
or where it is going. So it is with everyone born of the Spirit."

[a] Mk 16:16; Ac 2:38 [b] Ec 11:5

9 "How can these things be?" asked
Nicodemus.
10 "Are you a teacher[e] of Israel and
don't know these things?" Jesus replied. 11 "I assure you: We speak what
We know and We testify to what We
have seen, but you[f] do not accept Our
testimony.[g] 12 If I have told you about
things that happen on earth and you
don't believe, how will you believe if I
tell you about things of heaven? 13 [a]No
one has ascended into heaven except
the One who descended from heaven
—the •Son of Man.[h] 14 [b]Just as Moses
lifted up the snake in the wilderness,
so the Son of Man must be lifted up,
15 so that everyone who believes in
Him will[i] have eternal life.

[a] Pr 30:4 [b] Nm 21:9; Jn 8:28

16 [a]"For God loved the world in this
way: He gave His •One and Only Son,
so that everyone who believes in Him
will not perish but have eternal life.
17 [b]For God did not send His Son into
the world that He might condemn the
world, but that the world might be
saved through Him. 18 [c]Anyone who
believes in Him is not condemned, but
anyone who does not believe is already
condemned, because he has not believed in the name of the One and
Only Son of God.

[a] Lk 2:14; Rm 5:8 [b] Lk 9:56; 1Jn 4:14 [c] Rm 8:1

19 "This, then, is the judgment: [a]the
light has come into the world, and people loved darkness rather than the light
because their deeds were evil. 20 For
everyone who practices wicked things
hates the light and avoids it,[j] so that his
deeds may not be exposed. 21 But anyone who lives by[k] the truth comes to
the light, so that his works may be
shown to be accomplished by God."[l]

[a] Jn 1:4

Jesus and John the Baptist

22 After this, Jesus and His disciples
went to the Judean countryside, where
He spent time with them [a]and baptized. 23 John also was baptizing in
Aenon near [b]Salim, because there was
plenty of water there. People were
coming and being baptized, 24 since
[c]John had not yet been thrown into
prison.

[a] Jn 4:2 [b] Gn 14:18 [c] Mt 14:3

25 Then a dispute arose between
John's disciples and a •Jew[m] about purification. 26 So they came to John and
told him, "Rabbi, [a]the One you testified about, and who was with you
across the Jordan, is baptizing—and
everyone is flocking to Him."

[a] Jn 1:34

27 John responded, "No one can receive a single thing unless it's given to
him from heaven. 28 You yourselves

---

[a] **3:3** The same Gk word can mean *again* or *from above* (also in v. 7). [b] **3:5** Or *spirit*, or *wind*; the Gk word *pneuma* can mean *wind*, *spirit*, or *Spirit*, each of which occurs in this context. [c] **3:7** The pronoun is pl in Gk. [d] **3:8** The Gk word *pneuma* can mean *wind*, *spirit*, or *Spirit*, each of which occurs in this context. [e] **3:10** Or *the teacher* [f] **3:11** The word *you* in Gk is pl here and throughout v. 12. [g] **3:11** The pl forms (*We*, *Our*) refer to Jesus and His authority to speak for the Father. [h] **3:13** Other mss add *who is in heaven* [i] **3:15** Other mss add *not perish, but* [j] **3:20** Lit *and does not come to the light* [k] **3:21** Lit *who does* [l] **3:21** It is possible that Jesus' words end at v. 15. Ancient Gk did not have quotation marks. [m] **3:25** Other mss read *and the Jews*

can testify that I said, 'I am not the
•Messiah, but [a]I've been sent ahead of
Him.' 29 He who has the bride is the
groom. But the groom's friend, who
stands by and listens for him, rejoices
greatly[a] at the groom's voice. So this
joy of mine is complete. 30 [b]He must increase, [c]but I must decrease."

[a]Mal 3:1; Mt 3 [b]Is 9:7 [c]Php 3:8-9

The One from Heaven

31 [a]The One who comes from above
[b]is above all. The one who is from the
earth is earthly and speaks in earthly
terms.[b] [c]The One who comes from
heaven is above all. 32 [d]He testifies to
what He has seen and heard, yet no
one accepts His testimony. 33 The one
who has accepted His testimony [e]has
affirmed that God is true. 34 [f]For God
sent Him, and He speaks God's words,
since He[c] gives the Spirit [g]without
measure. 35 [h]The Father loves the Son
and has given all things into His hands.
36 [i]The one who believes in the Son has
eternal life, but the one who refuses to
believe in the Son will not see life; instead, [j]the wrath of God remains on
him.

[a]Jn 8:23 [b]Mt 28:18 [c]Eph 1:21 [d]Jn 15:15 [e]2Co 1:22 [f]Jn 7:16 [g]Jn 1:16 [h]Dn 7:14 [i]Rm 1:17 [j]Gl 3:10

Jesus and the Samaritan Woman

4 When Jesus[d] knew that the •Phar-
isees heard He was making and
baptizing more disciples than John
2 (though Jesus Himself was not baptizing, but His disciples were), 3 He
left Judea and went again to Galilee.
4 He had to travel through Samaria,
5 so He came to a town of Samaria
called Sychar near the property[e] [a]that
Jacob had given his son Joseph.
6 Jacob's well was there, and Jesus,
worn out from His journey, sat down
at the well. It was about six in the
evening.[f]

[a]Jos 24:32

7 A woman of Samaria came to draw
water.
"Give Me a drink," Jesus said to her,
8 for His disciples had gone into town
to buy food.
9 "How is it that You, a Jew, ask for a
drink from me, a •Samaritan woman?"
she asked Him. For [a]Jews do not associate with[g] Samaritans.[h]

[a]Ezr 4:3

10 Jesus answered, "If you knew [a]the
gift of God, and who is saying to you,
'Give Me a drink,' you would ask Him,
and He would give you [b]living water."

[a]Rm 8:32; 1Co 1:30 [b]Zch 13:1

11 "Sir," said the woman, "You don't
even have a bucket, and the well is
deep. So where do you get this 'living
water'? 12 You aren't greater than our
father Jacob, are you? He gave us the
well and drank from it himself, as did
his sons and livestock."
13 Jesus said, "Everyone who drinks
from this water will get thirsty again.
14 But [a]whoever drinks from the water
that I will give him will never get
thirsty again—ever! In fact, the water I
will give him [b]will become a well[i] of
water springing up within him for eternal life."

[a]Jn 6:35 [b]Jn 7:38

15 "Sir," the woman said to Him,
"give me this water so I won't get
thirsty and come here to draw water."
16 "Go call your husband," He told
her, "and come back here."
17 "I don't have a husband," she answered.
"You have correctly said, 'I don't
have a husband,'" Jesus said. 18 "For
you've had five husbands, and the man
you now have is not your husband.
What you have said is true."
19 "Sir," the woman replied, [a]"I see
that You are a prophet. 20 Our fathers
worshiped [b]on this mountain,[j] yet you
⌊Jews⌋ say that the place to worship is
in [c]Jerusalem."

[a]Lk 7:16 [b]Jdg 9:7 [c]2Ch 7:12

[a]**3:29** Lit *with joy rejoices* [b]**3:31** Or *of earthly things* [c]**3:34** Other mss read *since God* [d]**4:1** Other mss read *the Lord* [e]**4:5** Lit *piece of land* [f]**4:6** Lit *the sixth hour*; see note at Jn 1:39; an alternate time reckoning would be *noon* [g]**4:9** Or *do not share vessels with* [h]**4:9** Other mss omit *For Jews do not associate with Samaritans.* [i]**4:14** Or *spring* [j]**4:20** Mount Gerizim, where there had been a Samaritan temple that rivaled Jerusalem's

21 Jesus told her, "Believe Me,
•woman, an hour is coming [a]when you
will worship the Father neither on this
mountain nor in Jerusalem. 22 You Samaritans[a] worship what [b]you do not
know. We worship what we do know,
because [c]salvation is from the Jews.
23 But an hour is coming, and is now
here, when the true worshipers will
worship the Father in [d]spirit and
[e]truth. Yes, the Father wants such people to worship Him. 24 [f]God is spirit,
and those who worship Him must worship in spirit and truth."

[a] *Mal 1:11; 1Tm 2:8* [b] *2Kg 17:29*
[c] *Is 2:3; Rm 9:4-5* [d] *1Co 3:16; Php 3:3*
[e] *Jn 1:17* [f] *Ac 17:24-29*

25 The woman said to Him, "I know
that [a]•Messiah[b] is coming" (who is
called Christ). "When He comes, He
will explain everything to us." [a] *Dt 18:15*

26 [a]"I am ⌊He⌋," Jesus told her, "the
One speaking to you." [a] *Mt 16:20; Jn 9:37*

The Ripened Harvest

27 Just then His disciples arrived, and
they were amazed that He was talking
with a woman. Yet no one said, "What
do You want?" or "Why are You talking
with her?"

28 Then the woman left her water jar,
went into town, and told the men,
29 "Come, see a man who told me everything I ever did! Could this be the
Messiah?" 30 They left the town and
made their way to Him.

31 In the meantime the disciples kept
urging Him, "•Rabbi, eat something."

32 But He said, "I have food to eat
that you don't know about."

33 The disciples said to one another,
"Could someone have brought Him
something to eat?"

34 [a]"My food is to do the will of Him
who sent Me and to finish His work,"
Jesus told them. 35 "Don't you say,
'There are still four more months, then
comes the harvest'? Listen ⌊to what⌋
I'm telling you: Open[c] your eyes and
look at the fields, [b]for they are ready[d]
for harvest. 36 [c]The reaper is already receiving pay and gathering fruit for eternal life, so the sower and reaper can
rejoice together. 37 For in this case the
saying is true: 'One sows and another
reaps.' 38 I sent you to reap what you
didn't labor for; others have labored,
and you have benefited from[e] their labor."

[a] *Jn 6:38* [b] *Mt 9:37*
[c] *Dn 12:3; 1Co 3:8; Jms 5:20*

The Savior of the World

39 [a]Now many Samaritans from that
town believed in Him because of what
the woman said[f] when she testified,
"He told me everything I ever did."
40 Therefore, when the Samaritans
came to Him, they asked Him to stay
with them, and He stayed there two
days. 41 [b]Many more believed because
of what He said.[g] 42 And they told the
woman, "We no longer believe because of what you said, for [c]we have
heard for ourselves and know that this
really is the [d]Savior of the world."[h]

[a] *Gn 49:10* [b] *Is 42:1* [c] *1Jn 4:14*
[d] *Is 49:6; Jn 1:29; Eph 2:13*

A Galilean Welcome

43 After two days He left there for Galilee. 44 [a]Jesus Himself testified that a
prophet has no honor in his own country. 45 When they entered Galilee, the
Galileans welcomed Him [b]because
they had seen everything He did in
Jerusalem during the festival. [c]For they
also had gone to the festival.

[a] *Mt 13:57; Mk 6:4* [b] *Jn 2:23* [c] *Dt 16:16*

The Second Sign: Healing an Official's Son

46 Then He went again to Cana of Galilee, [a]where He had turned the water

[a]**4:22** *Samaritans* is implied since the Gk verb and pronoun are pl. [b]**4:25** In the NT, the word Messiah translates the Gk word *Christos* ("Anointed One"), except here and in Jn 1:41 where it translates *Messias*. [c]**4:35** Lit *Raise* [d]**4:35** Lit *white* [e]**4:38** Lit *you have entered into* [f]**4:39** Lit *because of the woman's word* [g]**4:41** Lit *because of His word* [h]**4:42** Other mss add *the Messiah*

into wine. There was a certain royal official whose son was ill at Capernaum.
47 When this man heard that Jesus had
come from Judea into Galilee, he went
to Him and pleaded with Him to come
down and heal his son, for he was
about to die. *[a] Jn 2:1,11*

48 Jesus told him, [a]"Unless you ⌊peo-
ple⌋ see signs and wonders, you will
not believe." *[a] Mt 16:1; Lk 16:31*

49 "Sir," the official said to Him,
"come down before my boy dies!"
50 [a]"Go," Jesus told him, "your son
will live." The man believed what[a]
Jesus said to him and departed.
[a] Mt 8:13

51 While he was still going down, his
•slaves met him saying that his boy
was alive. 52 He asked them at what
time he got better. "Yesterday at seven
in the morning[b] the fever left him,"
they answered. 53 The father realized
this was the very hour at which Jesus
had told him, "Your son will live."
Then he himself believed, along with
his whole household.
54 This therefore was the second sign
Jesus performed after He came from
Judea to Galilee.

The Third Sign: Healing the Sick

5 After [a]this, a Jewish festival took
place, and Jesus went up to Jerusalem. 2 [b]By the Sheep Gate in Jerusalem
there is a pool, called Bethesda[c] in Hebrew, which has five colonnades.[d]
3 Within these lay a multitude of
the sick—blind, lame, and paralyzed
[—waiting for the moving of the water, 4 because an angel would go down
into the pool from time to time and
stir up the water. Then the first one
who got in after the water was stirred
up recovered from whatever ailment
he had].[e] *[a] Lv 23:2 [b] Neh 3:1*

5 One man was there who had been
sick for 38 years. 6 When Jesus saw
him lying there [a]and knew he had already been there a long time, He said
to him, [b]"Do you want to get well?"
[a] Heb 4:13 [b] Is 55:1

7 "Sir," the sick man answered, "I
don't have a man to put me into the
pool when the water is stirred up, but
while I'm coming, someone goes
down ahead of me."
8 [a]"Get up," Jesus told him, "pick up
your bedroll and walk!" 9 Instantly the
man got well, picked up his bedroll,
and started to walk. *[a] Mt 9:6*

Now that day was the Sabbath, 10 so
the •Jews said to the man who had
been healed, "This is the Sabbath! [a]It's
illegal for you to pick up your bedroll."
[a] Ex 20:10; Mt 12:2

11 He replied, "The man who made
me well told me, 'Pick up your bedroll
and walk.'"
12 "Who is this man who told you,
'Pick up ⌊your bedroll⌋ and walk?'"
they asked. 13 But the man who was
cured did not know who it was, because Jesus had slipped away into the
crowd that was there.[f]
14 After this, Jesus found him in the
•temple complex and said to him,
"See, you are well. [a]Do not sin any
more, so that something worse doesn't
happen to you." 15 The man went and
reported to the Jews that it was Jesus
who had made him well. *[a] Jn 8:11*

Honoring the Father and the Son

16 Therefore, the Jews began persecuting Jesus[g] because He was doing
these things on the Sabbath. 17 But
Jesus responded to them, [a]"My Father
is still working, and I am working
also." 18 This is why the Jews [b]began
trying all the more to kill Him: not only

[a]**4:50** Lit *the word* [b]**4:52** Or *seven in the evening*; lit *at the seventh hour*; see note at Jn 1:39; an alternate time reckoning would be *at one in the afternoon* [c]**5:2** Other mss read *Bethzatha*; other mss read *Bethsaida* [d]**5:2** Rows of columns supporting a roof [e]**5:3–4** Other mss omit bracketed text [f]**5:13** Lit *slipped away, there being a crowd in that place* [g]**5:16** Other mss add *and trying to kill Him*

was He breaking the Sabbath, but He
was even calling God His own Father,
[c]making Himself equal with God.

[a] Jn 9:4 [b] Jn 7:19 [c] Jn 10:30

19 Then Jesus replied, "•I assure you:
[a]The Son is not able to do anything on
His own, but only what He sees the Father doing. For whatever the Father[a]
does, the Son also does these things in
the same way. 20 For [b]the Father loves
the Son and shows Him everything He
is doing, and He will show Him greater
works than these so that you will be
amazed. 21 And just as the Father raises
the dead and gives them life, [c]so the Son
also gives life to anyone He wants to.
22 The Father, in fact, judges no one but
[d]has given all judgment to the Son, 23 so
that all people will [e]honor the Son just
as they honor the Father. Anyone who
does not honor the Son does not honor
the Father who sent Him.

[a] Jn 8:28 [b] Mt 3:17 [c] Jn 11:25 [d] Mt 11:27 [e] 1Jn 2:23

Life and Judgment

24 "I assure you: Anyone who hears
My word and believes Him who sent
Me has eternal life and will not come
under judgment [a]but has passed from
death to life.

[a] 1Jn 3:14

25 "I assure you: An hour is coming,
and is now here, when [a]the dead will
hear the voice of the Son of God, and
those who hear will live. 26 For just as
the Father has [b]life in Himself, so also
He has granted to the Son to have life
in Himself. 27 And He has granted Him
the right to pass judgment, [c]because
He is the •Son of Man. 28 Do not be
amazed at this, because a time is coming when all who are in the graves will
hear His voice 29 [d]and come out—
[e]those who have done good things, to
the resurrection of life, but those who
have done wicked things, to the resurrection of judgment.

[a] Eph 2:1,5 [b] Ac 17:31 [c] Dn 7:13 [d] 1Co 15:52 [e] Dn 12:2; Lk 14:14

30 "I can do nothing on My own. I
judge only as I hear, and My judgment
is righteous, because I do not seek My
own will, but the will of Him who
sent Me.

Four Witnesses to Jesus

31 [a]"If I testify about Myself, My testimony is not valid.[b] 32 There is Another who testifies about Me, and I
know that the testimony He gives
about Me is valid.[c] 33 You have sent
⌊messengers⌋ to John, [b]and he has testified to the truth. 34 I don't receive
man's testimony, but I say these things
so that you may be saved. 35 John[d] was
a burning and shining lamp, and for a
time [c]you were willing to enjoy his
light.

[a] Is 55:4 [b] Jn 1:15 [c] Lk 3:15

36 "But [a]I have a greater testimony
than John's because of [b]the works that
the Father has given Me to accomplish. These very works I am doing testify about Me that the Father has sent
Me. 37 The Father who sent Me [c]has
Himself testified about Me. You have
not heard His voice at any time, [d]and
you haven't seen His form. 38 You don't
have His word living in you, because
you don't believe the One He sent.
39 [e]You pore over[e] the Scriptures because you think you have eternal life in
them, [f]yet they testify about Me.
40 And you are not willing to come to
Me that you may have life.

[a] 1Jn 5:9 [b] Mt 11:4-5 [c] Mt 3:17 [d] Jn 1:18 [e] Is 8:20 [f] Dt 18:15; Lk 24:27

41 "I do not accept glory from men,
42 but I know you—that you have no
love for God within you. 43 I have come
in My Father's name, yet you don't
accept Me. If someone else comes in
his own name, you will accept him.
44 How can you believe? While accepting glory from one another, you don't
seek [a]the glory that comes from the
only God. 45 Do not think that I will accuse you to the Father. Your accuser is

[a]**5:19** Lit *whatever that One* [b]**5:31** Or *not true* [c]**5:32** Or *true* [d]**5:35** Lit *That man* [e]**5:39** In Gk this could be a command: *Pore over . . .*

Moses, on whom you have set your
hope. 46 For if you believed Moses, you
would believe Me, [b]because he wrote
about Me. 47 But if [c]you don't believe
his writings, how will you believe My
words?" *[a]Mt 25:21-23 [b]Gn 3:15; Dt 18:15*
[c]Lk 16:29,31

The Fourth Sign: Feeding 5,000

6 After [a]this, Jesus crossed the Sea
of Galilee (or Tiberias). 2 And a
huge crowd was following Him because they saw the signs that He was
performing on the sick. 3 So Jesus
went up a mountain and sat down
there with His disciples. *[a]Mt 14:15*

4 [a]Now the •Passover, a Jewish festival, was near. 5 Therefore, [b]when Jesus
looked up and noticed a huge crowd
coming toward Him, He asked Philip,
"Where will we buy bread so these
people can eat?" 6 He asked this to test
him, for He Himself knew what He
was going to do. *[a]Lv 23:5 [b]Mt 14:14*

7 Philip answered, [a]"Two hundred
•denarii worth of bread wouldn't be
enough for each of them to have a little." *[a]Mk 6:37*

8 One of His disciples, Andrew, Simon Peter's brother, said to Him,
9 "There's a boy here who has five barley loaves and two fish—but what are
they for so many?"
10 Then Jesus said, "Have the people
sit down."

There was plenty of grass in that
place, so they sat down. The men numbered about 5,000. 11 Then Jesus took
the loaves, and after [a]giving thanks He
distributed them to those who were
seated—so also with the fish, as much
as they wanted. *[a]1Tm 4:5*

12 When they were full, He told His
disciples, "Collect the leftovers so that
nothing is wasted." 13 So they collected
them and filled 12 baskets with the
pieces from the five barley loaves that
were left over by those who had eaten.
14 When the people saw the sign[a] He
had done, they said, "This really is [a]the
Prophet who was to come into the
world!" 15 Therefore, when Jesus knew
that they were about to come and take
Him by force to make Him king, He
withdrew again[b] to the mountain by
Himself. *[a]Gn 49:10; Dt 18:18*

The Fifth Sign: Walking on Water

16 [a]When evening came, His disciples went down to the sea, 17 got into a
boat, and started across the sea to Capernaum. Darkness had already set in,
but Jesus had not yet come to them.
18 Then a high wind arose, and the sea
began to churn. 19 After they had
rowed about three or four miles,[c] they
saw Jesus walking on the sea. He was
coming near the boat, and they were
afraid. *[a]Mt 14:23*

20 But He said to them, "It is I.[d] Don't
be afraid!" 21 Then they were willing to
take Him on board, and at once the
boat was at the shore where they were
heading.

The Bread of Life

22 The next day, the crowd that had
stayed on the other side of the sea
knew there had been only one boat.[e]
⌊They also knew⌋ that Jesus had not
boarded the boat with His disciples,
but that His disciples had gone off
alone. 23 Some boats from Tiberias
came near the place where they ate
the bread after the Lord gave thanks.
24 When the crowd saw that neither
Jesus nor His disciples were there,
they got into the boats and went to Capernaum looking for Jesus.

25 When they found Him on the
other side of the sea, they said to Him,
"•Rabbi, when did You get here?"

[a]**6:14** Other mss read *signs* [b]**6:15** A previous withdrawal is mentioned in Mk 6:31–32, an event that occurred just before the feeding of the 5,000. [c]**6:19** Lit *25 or 30 stadia*; 1 *stadion* = 600 feet [d]**6:20** Lit *I am*
[e]**6:22** Other mss add *into which His disciples had entered*

26 Jesus answered, "•I assure you:
You are looking for Me, not because
you saw the signs, but because you ate
the loaves and were filled. 27 Don't
work for the food that perishes but [a]for
the food that lasts for eternal life,
which the •Son of Man will give you,
[b]because God the Father has set His
seal of approval on Him."

[a] *Jn 4:14* [b] *Mt 3:17; 17:5*

28 "What can we do to perform the
works of God?" they asked.
29 Jesus replied, "This is the work of
God: that you believe in the One He
has sent."
30 [a]"What sign then are You going to
do so we may see and believe You?"
they asked. "What are You going to
perform? 31 [b]Our fathers ate the manna
in the wilderness, just as it is written:
[c]**He gave them bread from heaven to
eat.**"[a b]

[a] *Mt 12:38* [b] *Ex 16:15* [c] *Neh 9:15; Ps 78:24*

32 Jesus said to them, "I assure you:
Moses didn't give you the bread from
heaven, but My Father gives you the
real bread from heaven. 33 For the
bread of God is the One who comes
down from heaven and gives life to the
world."
34 Then they said, "Sir, give us this
bread always!"
35 "I am the bread of life," Jesus told
them. [a]"No one who comes to Me will
ever be hungry, and no one who believes in Me will ever be thirsty again.
36 But as I told you, you've seen Me,[c]
and yet you do not believe. 37 Everyone
the Father gives Me will come to Me,
[b]and the one who comes to Me I will
never cast out. 38 For I have come
down from heaven, [c]not to do My will,
[d]but the will of Him who sent Me.
39 This is the will of Him who sent Me:
[e]that I should lose none of those He
has given Me but should raise them up
on the last day. 40 For this is the will of
My Father: [f]that everyone who sees
the Son and believes in Him may have
eternal life, and I will raise him up on
the last day."

[a] *Jn 4:14; 7:37* [b] *Jr 31:34; Jn 10:28-29* [c] *Jn 5:30* [d] *Jn 4:34* [e] *Jn 17:12* [f] *Jn 4:14*

41 Therefore the Jews started complaining about Him, because He said,
"I am the bread that came down from
heaven." 42 They were saying, "Isn't
this Jesus the son of Joseph, whose father and mother we know? How can
He now say, 'I have come down from
heaven'?"
43 Jesus answered them, "Stop complaining among yourselves. 44 No one
can come to Me unless the Father who
sent Me draws[d] him, and I will raise
him up on the last day. 45 [a]It is written
in the Prophets: **And they will all be
taught by God.**[e] Everyone who has listened to and learned from the Father
comes to Me— 46 [b]not that anyone has
seen the Father except [c]the One who
is from God. He has seen the Father.

[a] *Is 54:13; Mc 4:2* [b] *Jn 1:18* [c] *Mt 11:27; Jn 7:29*

47 "I assure you: [a]Anyone who believes[f] has eternal life. 48 I am the bread
of life. 49 Your fathers ate the manna in
the wilderness, and they died. 50 This
is the bread that comes down from
heaven so that anyone may eat of it
and not die. 51 I am the living bread
that came down from heaven. If anyone eats of this bread he will live forever. [b]The bread that I will give for the
life of the world is My flesh."

[a] *Jn 3:16* [b] *Heb 10:10*

52 At that, the Jews argued among
themselves, "How can this man give
us His flesh to eat?"
53 So Jesus said to them, "I assure
you: Unless [a]you eat the flesh of the
Son of Man and drink His blood, you do
not have life in yourselves. 54 Anyone

[a]**6:31** Bread miraculously provided by God for the Israelites [b]**6:31** Ex 16:4; Ps 78:24 [c]**6:36** Other mss omit *Me* [d]**6:44** Or *brings*, or *leads*; see the use of this Gk verb in Jn 12:32; 21:6; Ac 16:19; Jms 2:6. [e]**6:45** Is 54:13 [f]**6:47** Other mss add *in Me*

who eats My flesh and drinks My
blood has eternal life, and I will raise
him up on the last day, 55 because My
flesh is real food and My blood is real
drink. 56 The one who eats My flesh
and drinks My blood [b]lives in Me, and
I in him. 57 Just as the living Father sent
Me and I live because of the Father, so
the one who feeds on Me will live because of Me. 58 This is the bread that
came down from heaven; it is not like
the manna[a] your fathers ate—and they
died. The one who eats this bread will
live forever." *a Mt 26:26 b Jn 14:23; Rm 8:9; Eph 3:17; 5:30*

59 He said these things while teaching in the •synagogue in Capernaum.

Many Disciples Desert Jesus

60 Therefore, when [a]many of His disciples heard this, they said, "This
teaching is hard! Who can accept[b] it?"
a Mt 11:6

61 Jesus, knowing in Himself that His
disciples were complaining about this,
asked them, "Does this offend you?
62 [a]Then what if you were to observe
the Son of Man ascending to where He
was before? 63 [b]The Spirit is the One
who gives life. The flesh doesn't help
at all. The words that I have spoken to
you [c]are spirit and are life. 64 But there
are some among you who don't believe." (For [d]Jesus knew from the beginning those who would not[c] believe
and the one who would betray Him.)
65 He said, "This is why I told you that
no one can come to Me unless it is
granted to him by the Father."
a Mk 16:19; Ac 1:9 b Rm 8:2 c Eph 1:17 d Jn 2:24; 13:11

66 From that moment many of His
disciples [a]turned back and no longer
accompanied Him. 67 Therefore Jesus
said to the Twelve, "You don't want to
go away too, do you?" *a Lk 9:62; Heb 6:4-6*

68 Simon Peter answered, "Lord,
who will we go to? You have the words
of eternal life. 69 We have come to believe and know that You are the Holy
One of God!"[d]

70 Jesus replied to them, "Didn't I
choose you, the Twelve? Yet one of you
is the Devil!" 71 He was referring to Judas, Simon Iscariot's son,[e] [f] one of the
Twelve, because he was going to betray Him.

The Unbelief of Jesus' Brothers

7 After this, Jesus traveled in Galilee, since He did not want to
travel in Judea because the •Jews were
trying to kill Him. 2 [a]The Jewish Festival of Tabernacles[g] [h] was near, 3 so His
[b]brothers said to Him, "Leave here
and go to Judea so Your disciples can
see Your works that You are doing.
4 For no one does anything in secret
while he's seeking public recognition.
If You do these things, show Yourself
to the world." 5 (For [c]not even His
brothers believed in Him.) *a Lv 23:34 b Mt 12:46 c Mk 3:21*

6 Jesus told them, [a]"My time has not
yet arrived, but your time is always at
hand. 7 [b]The world cannot hate you,
but it does hate Me [c]because I testify
about it—that its deeds are evil. 8 Go
up to the festival yourselves. I'm not
going up to the festival yet,[i] [d]because
My time has not yet fully come."
9 After He had said these things, He
stayed in Galilee. *a Ec 3:1-2 b Jn 15:19 c Jn 3:19 d Jn 8:20*

Jesus at the Festival of Tabernacles

10 After His brothers had gone up to
the festival, then He also went up, not
openly but secretly. 11 [a]The Jews were
looking for Him at the festival and saying, "Where is He?" 12 And [b]there was

[a]**6:58** Other mss omit *the manna* [b]**6:60** Lit *hear* [c]**6:64** Other mss omit *not* [d]**6:69** Other mss read *You are the Messiah, the Son of the Living God* [e]**6:71** Other mss read *Judas Iscariot, Simon's son* [f]**6:71** Lit *Judas, of Simon Iscariot* [g]**7:2** Or *Booths* [h]**7:2** One of 3 great Jewish religious festivals, along with Passover and Pentecost; Ex 23:14; Dt 16:16 [i]**7:8** Other mss omit *yet*

a lot of discussion about Him among the crowds. [c]Some were saying, "He's a good man." Others were saying, "No, on the contrary, He's deceiving the people." 13 Still, nobody was talking publicly about Him because they feared the Jews. [a]Jn 11:56 [b]Jn 9:16 [c]Lk 7:16

14 When the festival was already half over, Jesus went up into the •temple complex and began to teach. 15 [a]Then the Jews were amazed and said, "How does He know the Scriptures, since He hasn't been trained?" [a]Mt 13:54

16 Jesus answered them, [a]"My teaching isn't Mine but is from the One who sent Me. 17 [b]If anyone wants to do His will, he will understand whether the teaching is from God or if I am speaking on My own. 18 [c]The one who speaks for himself seeks his own glory. But He who seeks the glory of the One who sent Him is true, and there is no unrighteousness in Him. 19 [d]Didn't Moses give you the law? Yet none of you keeps the law! [e]Why do you want to kill Me?" [a]Jn 3:31-34; 8:28; 12:49 [b]Lk 8:15 [c]Jn 5:41 [d]Ac 7:38 [e]Mt 12:14

20 [a]"You have a demon!" the crowd responded. "Who wants to kill You?" [a]Jn 8:48

21 "I did one work, and you are all amazed," Jesus answered. 22 "Consider this: [a]Moses has given you circumcision—not that it comes from Moses [b]but from the fathers—and you circumcise a man on the Sabbath. 23 If a man receives circumcision on the Sabbath so that the law of Moses won't be broken, are you angry at Me because [c]I made a man entirely well on the Sabbath? 24 [d]Stop judging according to outward appearances; rather judge according to righteous judgment." [a]Lv 12:3 [b]Gn 17:10 [c]Jn 5:8 [d]Pr 24:23; Jn 8:15

The Identity of the Messiah

25 Some of the people of Jerusalem were saying, "Isn't this the man they want to kill? 26 Yet, look! He's speaking publicly and they're saying nothing to Him. Can it be true that the authorities know He is the •Messiah? 27 But we know where this man is from. When the Messiah comes, nobody will know where He is from."

28 As He was teaching in the temple complex, Jesus cried out, [a]"You know Me and you know where I am from. Yet [b]I have not come on My own, but the One who sent Me [c]is true. You [d]don't know Him; 29 [e]I know Him because I am from Him, and He sent Me." [a]Jn 8:14 [b]Jn 5:43 [c]Jn 5:32 [d]Jn 1:18 [e]Jn 10:15

30 Then they tried to seize Him. Yet no one laid a hand on Him because His hour[a] had not yet come. 31 However, many from the crowd believed in Him and said, "When the Messiah comes, He won't perform more signs than this man has done, will He?"

32 The •Pharisees heard the crowd muttering these things about Him, so the •chief priests and the Pharisees sent temple police to arrest Him.

33 Then Jesus said, [a]"I am only with you for a short time. Then I'm going to the One who sent Me. 34 You [b]will look for Me, but you will not find Me; and where I am, you cannot come." [a]Jn 13:33 [b]Jn 8:21

35 Then the Jews said to one another, "Where does He intend to go so we won't find Him? He doesn't intend to go to [a]the Dispersion[b] among the Greeks and teach the Greeks, does He? 36 What is this remark He made: 'You will look for Me, and you will not find Me; and where I am, you cannot come'?" [a]Is 11:12

[a]**7:30** The time of His sacrificial death and exaltation; Jn 2:4; 8:20; 12:23,27; 13:1; 17:1 [b]**7:35** Jewish people scattered throughout Gentile lands who spoke Gk and were influenced by Gk culture

The Promise of the Spirit

37 On the last and most important
day of the festival, Jesus stood up and
cried out, [a]"If anyone is thirsty, he
should come to Me[a] and drink! 38 [b]The
one who believes in Me, as the Scripture has said,[b] [c]will have streams of living water flow from deep within him."
39 [d]He said this about the Spirit, whom
those who believed in Him were going
to receive, for the Spirit[c] had not yet
been received,[d] [e] because Jesus had
not yet been [e]glorified. *[a] Is 55:1 [b] Dt 18:15*
[c] Is 12:3 [d] Is 44:3; Jn 16:7 [e] Jn 12:16

The People Are Divided over Jesus

40 When some from the crowd heard
these words, they said, "This really is
[a]the Prophet!"[f] 41 Others said, [b]"This is
the Messiah!" But some said, "Surely
the Messiah doesn't come from Galilee, does He? 42 [c]Doesn't the Scripture
say that the Messiah comes from
David's offspring[g] and from the town
of Bethlehem, [d]where David once
lived?" 43 So a division occurred among
the crowd because of Him. 44 Some of
them wanted to seize Him, but no one
laid hands on Him.
[a] Dt 18:15 [b] Jn 4:42 [c] Mc 5:2 [d] 1Sm 16:1

Debate over Jesus' Claims

45 Then the temple police came to
the chief priests and Pharisees, who
asked them, "Why haven't you brought
Him?"

46 The police answered, "No man
ever spoke like this!"[h]

47 Then the Pharisees responded to
them: "Are you fooled too? 48 Have any
of the rulers believed in Him? Or any
of the Pharisees? 49 But this crowd,
which doesn't know the law, is accursed!"

50 Nicodemus—[a]the one who came
to Him previously, being one of them
—said to them, 51 [b]"Our law doesn't
judge a man before it hears from him
and knows what he's doing, does it?"
[a] Jn 3:2
[b] Dt 1:17; 17:8

52 "You aren't from Galilee too, are
you?" they replied. "Investigate and
you will see that [a]no prophet arises
from Galilee."[i] *[a] Is 9:1-2; Jn 1:46*

[53 So each one went to his house.
8 1 But Jesus went to the •Mount of
Olives.

An Adulteress Forgiven

2 At dawn He went to the •temple
complex again, and all the people were
coming to Him. He sat down and began to teach them.

3 Then the •scribes and the •Phari-
sees brought a woman caught in adultery, making her stand in the center.
4 "Teacher," they said to Him, "this
woman was caught in the act of committing adultery. 5 [a]In the law Moses
commanded us to stone such women.
So what do You say?" 6 They asked this
to trap Him, in order that they might
have evidence to accuse Him.
[a] Lv 20:10; Dt 5:18

Jesus stooped down and started writing on the ground with His finger.
7 When they persisted in questioning
Him, He stood up and said to them,
[a]"The one without sin among you
should be the first to throw a stone at
her." *[a] Dt 17:7; Jb 5:12; Mt 7:1-5*

8 Then He stooped down again and
continued writing on the ground.
9 [a]When they heard this, they left one
by one, starting with the older men.
Only He was left, with the woman in
the center. 10 When Jesus stood up, He

[a]**7:37** Other mss omit *to Me* [b]**7:38** Jesus may have had several OT passages in mind; Is 58:11; Ezk 47:1–12; Zch 14:8 [c]**7:39** Other mss read *Holy Spirit* [d]**7:39** Other mss read *had not yet been given* [e]**7:39** Lit *the Spirit was not yet*; the word *received* is implied from the previous clause. [f]**7:40** Probably = the Prophet in Dt 18:15 [g]**7:42** Lit *seed* [h]**7:46** Other mss read *like this man* [i]**7:52** Jonah and probably other prophets did come from Galilee; 2 Kgs 14:25

said to her, "•Woman, where are they?
Has no one condemned you?"
[a] Ec 7:22; Rm 2:22

11 "No one, Lord,"[a] she answered.
[a]"Neither do I condemn you," said
Jesus. "Go, and from now on do not sin
any more."][b]
[a] Lk 9:56

The Light of the World

12 Then Jesus spoke to them again: "I
am the light of the world. Anyone who
follows Me will never walk in the darkness but will have the light of life."
13 So the Pharisees said to Him,
[a]"You are testifying about Yourself.
Your testimony is not valid."[c]
[a] Jn 5:31

14 "Even if I testify about Myself,"
Jesus replied, "My testimony is valid,[d]
because I know where I came from
and where I'm going. But [a]you don't
know where I come from or where
I'm going. 15 [b]You judge by human
standards.[e] [c]I judge no one. 16 And if I
do judge, My judgment is true, because [d]I am not alone, but I and the Father who sent Me ⌊judge together⌋.
17 [e]Even in your law it is written that
the witness of two men is valid. 18 I am
the One who testifies about Myself,
and [f]the Father who sent Me testifies
about Me."
[a] Jn 7:28 [b] Jn 7:24 [c] Jn 3:17 [d] Jn 14:10-11; 16:32 [e] Dt 17:6 [f] Jn 5:37

19 Then they asked Him, "Where is
Your Father?"
[a]"You know neither Me nor My Father," Jesus answered. [b]"If you knew
Me, you would also know My Father."
20 He spoke these words by [c]the treasury,[f] while teaching in the temple
complex. But [d]no one seized Him, because His hour[g] had not come.
[a] Jn 16:3 [b] Jn 14:7 [c] Mk 12:41 [d] Jn 7:8,30

Jesus Predicts His Departure

21 Then He said to them again, "I'm
going away; [a]you will look for Me, and
you will die in your sin. Where I'm going, you cannot come."
[a] Jn 13:33

22 So the Jews said again, "He won't
kill Himself, will He, since He
says, 'Where I'm going, you cannot
come'?"
23 [a]"You are from below," He told
them, "I am from above. You are of
this world; I am not of this world.
24 Therefore I told you that you will
die in your sins. [b]For if you do not believe that I am ⌊He⌋,[h] you will die in
your sins."
[a] Jn 3:31 [b] Mk 16:16

25 "Who are You?" they questioned.
"Precisely what I've been telling you
from the very beginning," Jesus told
them. 26 "I have many things to say and
to judge about you, but [a]the One who
sent Me is true, and what I have heard
from Him—[b]these things I tell the
world."
[a] Jn 7:28 [b] Jn 3:32

27 They did not know He was speaking to them about the Father. 28 So
Jesus said to them, "When you [a]lift up
the •Son of Man, then you will know
that I am ⌊He⌋, and [b]that I do nothing
on My own. But [c]just as the Father
taught Me, I say these things. 29 [d]The
One who sent Me is with Me. He has
not left Me alone, [e]because I always do
what pleases Him."
[a] Jn 3:14 [b] Jn 5:19,30 [c] Jn 3:11 [d] Jn 14:10 [e] Jn 4:34

Truth and Freedom

30 As He was saying these things,
many believed in Him. 31 So Jesus said
to the Jews who had believed Him, "If
you continue in My word,[i] you really
are My disciples. 32 You will know the
truth, and [a]the truth will set you
free."
[a] Is 61:1; Rm 6:14

[a]**8:11** Or *Sir*; Jn 4:15,49; 5:7; 6:34; 9:36 [b]**8:11** Other mss omit bracketed text [c]**8:13** The law of Moses required at least 2 witnesses to make a claim legally valid (v. 17). [d]**8:14** Or *true* [e]**8:15** Lit *You judge according to the flesh* [f]**8:20** A place for offerings to be given, perhaps in the court of women [g]**8:20** The time of His sacrificial death and exaltation; Jn 2:4; 7:30; 12:23,27; 13:1; 17:1 [h]**8:24** Jesus claimed to be deity, but the Pharisees didn't understand His meaning. [i]**8:31** Or *My teaching*, or *My message*

33 [a]"We are descendants[a] of Abraham," they answered Him, "and we
have never been enslaved to anyone.
How can You say, 'You will become
free'?"
[a] *Lv 25:42*

34 Jesus responded, "•I assure you:
[a]Everyone who commits sin is a slave
of sin. 35 [b]A slave does not remain in
the household forever, but a son does
remain forever. 36 Therefore [c]if the Son
sets you free, you really will be free. 37 I
know you are descendants[a] of Abraham, but [d]you are trying to kill Me because My word[b] is not welcome among
you. 38 I speak what I have seen in the
presence of the Father,[c] and therefore
you do what you have heard from your
father."
[a] *Pr 5:22; Rm 6* [b] *Gl 4:30* [c] *Rm 8:2; 2Co 3:17* [d] *Jn 7:19*

39 "Our father is [a]Abraham!" they replied.
[a] *Mt 3:9*

"If you were Abraham's children,"
Jesus told them, "you would do what
Abraham did. 40 But now you are trying
to kill Me, a man who has told you the
truth that I heard from God. Abraham
did not do this! 41 You're doing what
your father does."

"We weren't born of sexual immorality," they said. [a]"We have one
Father—God."
[a] *Is 63:16*

42 Jesus said to them, "If God were
your Father, you would love Me,
[a]because I came from God and I am
here. [b]For I didn't come on My own,
but He sent Me. 43 [c]Why don't you understand what I say? Because you cannot listen to[d] My word. 44 You are of
your father the Devil, and you want to
carry out your father's desires. He was
a murderer from the beginning and
has not stood in the truth, because
there is no truth in him. When he tells
a lie, he speaks from his own nature,[e]
because he is a liar and the father of liars.[f] 45 Yet because I tell the truth, you
do not believe Me. 46 Who among you
can convict Me of sin? If I tell the
truth, why don't you believe Me?
47 The one who is from God listens to
God's words. This is why you don't listen, because you are not from God."
[a] *Jn 1:14; 3:16* [b] *Jn 5:43* [c] *Jn 7:17*

Jesus and Abraham

48 The Jews responded to Him,
"Aren't we right in saying that You're
a •Samaritan and have a demon?"

49 "I do not have a demon," Jesus answered. "On the contrary, I honor My
Father and you dishonor Me. 50 [a]I do
not seek My glory; the One who seeks
it also judges. 51 I assure you: [b]If anyone keeps My word, he will never see
death—ever!"
[a] *Jn 5:41* [b] *Jn 5:24*

52 Then the Jews said, "Now we
know You have a demon. [a]Abraham
died and so did the prophets. You say,
'If anyone keeps My word, he will
never taste death—ever!' 53 Are You
greater than our father Abraham who
died? Even the prophets died. Who do
You pretend to be?"[g]
[a] *Zch 1:5*

54 "If I glorify Myself," Jesus answered, "My glory is nothing. My Father—you say about Him, 'He is our
God'—[a]He is the One who glorifies
Me. 55 [b]You've never known Him, but
I know Him. If I were to say I don't
know Him, I would be a liar like you.
But I do know Him, and I keep His
word. 56 Your father Abraham was
overjoyed that he would see My day;
[c]he saw it and rejoiced."
[a] *Jn 16:14* [b] *Jn 7:28* [c] *Heb 11:13*

57 The Jews replied, "You aren't 50
years old yet, and You've seen
Abraham?"[h]

58 Jesus said to them, "I assure you:
Before Abraham was, [a]I am."[i]
[a] *Ex 3:14; Col 1:17*

[a]**8:33,37** Or *offspring*; lit *seed*; Jn 7:42 [b]**8:37** Or *My teaching*, or *My message* [c]**8:38** Other mss read *of My Father* [d]**8:43** Or *cannot hear* [e]**8:44** Lit *from his own things* [f]**8:44** Lit *of it* [g]**8:53** Lit *Who do You make Yourself?* [h]**8:57** Other mss read *and Abraham has seen You?* [i]**8:58** *I AM* is the name God gave Himself at the burning bush; Ex 3:13–14; see note at Jn 8:24.

59 At that, they picked up stones to
throw at Him. But Jesus was hidden[a]
and went out of the temple complex.[b]

The Sixth Sign: Healing a Man Born Blind

9 As He was passing by, He saw a
man blind from birth. 2 His disciples questioned Him: "•Rabbi, who
sinned, this man or his parents, that
he was born blind?"
3 "Neither this man nor his parents
sinned," Jesus answered. "⌊This came
about⌋ [a]so that God's works might be
displayed in him. 4 [b]We[c] must do the
works of Him who sent Me[d] while it is
day. Night is coming when no one can
work. 5 As long as I am in the world, [c]I
am the light of the world."

[a] Mt 11:5; Jn 11:4 [b] Jn 4:34; 5:36; 12:35
[c] Is 49:6; Lk 2:32; Jn 1:5,9; 8:12

6 After He said these things [a]He spit
on the ground, made some mud from
the saliva, and spread the mud on his
eyes. 7 "Go," He told him, "wash in the
pool of Siloam" (which means "Sent").
[b]So he left, washed, and came back seeing.

[a] Mk 7:33 [b] Is 42:7

8 His neighbors and those who formerly had seen him as a beggar said,
"Isn't this the man who sat begging?"
9 Some said, "He's the one." "No," others were saying, "but he looks like him."
He kept saying, "I'm the one!"
10 Therefore they asked him, "Then
how were your eyes opened?"
11 He answered, "The man called
Jesus made mud, spread it on my eyes,
and told me, 'Go to Siloam and wash.'
So when I went and washed I received
my sight."
12 "Where is He?" they asked.
"I don't know," he said.

The Healed Man's Testimony

13 They brought the man who used
to be blind to the •Pharisees. 14 The day
that Jesus made the mud and opened
his eyes was a Sabbath. 15 So again the
Pharisees asked him how he received
his sight.
"He put mud on my eyes," he told
them. "I washed and I can see."
16 Therefore some of the Pharisees
said, "This man is not from God, for He
doesn't keep the Sabbath!" But others
were saying, [a]"How can a sinful man
perform such signs?" And [b]there was a
division among them.

[a] Jn 3:2
[b] Jn 7:12,43

17 Again they asked the blind man,[e]
"What do you say about Him, since He
opened your eyes?"
[a]"He's a prophet," he said. [a] Dt 18:15
18 The Jews did not believe this
about him—that he was blind and received sight—until they summoned
the parents of the one who had received his sight.
19 They asked them, "Is this your
son, ⌊the one⌋ you say was born blind?
How then does he now see?"
20 "We know this is our son and that
he was born blind," his parents answered. 21 "But we don't know how he
now sees, and we don't know who
opened his eyes. Ask him; he's of age.
He will speak for himself." 22 His parents said these things because they
[a]were afraid of the Jews, since the Jews
had already agreed that if anyone con-
fessed Him as •Messiah, he [b]would be
banned from the •synagogue. 23 This is
why his parents said, "He's of age; ask
him."

[a] Jn 7:13 [b] Jn 12:42

24 So a second time they summoned
the man who had been blind and told
him, [a]"Give glory to God.[f] We know
that this man is a sinner!"

[a] Jos 7:19

25 He answered, "Whether or not
He's a sinner, I don't know. One thing
I do know: I was blind, and now I can
see!"

[a]**8:59** Or *Jesus hid Himself* [b]**8:59** Other mss add *and having gone through their midst, He passed by* [c]**9:4** Other mss read *I* [d]**9:4** Other mss read *sent us* [e]**9:17** = the man who had been blind [f]**9:24** *Give glory to God* was a solemn charge to tell the truth; Jos 7:19.

26 Then they asked him, "What did
He do to you? How did He open your
eyes?"
27 "I already told you," he said, "and
you didn't listen. Why do you want to
hear it again? You don't want to become His disciples too, do you?"
28 They ridiculed him: "You're that
man's disciple, but we're Moses' disciples. 29 We know that God has spoken
to Moses. But this man—[a]we don't
know where He's from!"

[a] *Jn 1:10*

30 [a]"This is an amazing thing," the
man told them. "You don't know
where He is from, yet He opened my
eyes! 31 We know that [b]God doesn't
listen to sinners, but if anyone is
God-fearing and does His will, He listens to him. 32 Throughout history[a] no
one has ever heard of someone opening the eyes of a person born blind. 33 If
this man were not from God, He
wouldn't be able to do anything."

[a] *Jn 3:10* [b] *Pr 15:29; Is 1:15; Mc 3:4*

34 "You were born entirely in sin,"
they replied, "and are you trying to
teach us?" Then they threw him out.[b]

The Blind Man's Sight and the Pharisees' Blindness

35 When Jesus heard that they had
thrown the man out, He found him
and asked, "Do you believe in [a]the
•Son of Man?"[c]

[a] *Mk 1:1; Jn 10:36*

36 "Who is He, Sir, that I may believe
in Him?" he asked.
37 Jesus answered, "You have seen
Him; in fact, [a]He is the One speaking
with you."

[a] *Jn 4:26*

38 "I believe, Lord!" he said, and he
worshiped Him.
39 Jesus said, [a]"I came into this world
for judgment, [b]in order that those who
do not see will see and those who do
see will become blind."

[a] *Jn 5:22* [b] *Mt 13:13*

40 Some of the Pharisees who were
with Him heard these things and asked
Him, "We aren't blind too, are we?"
41 [a]"If you were blind," Jesus told
them, "you wouldn't have sin.[d] But
now that you say, 'We see'—your sin
remains.

[a] *Jn 15:22*

The Ideal Shepherd

10 "•I assure you: Anyone who
doesn't enter the sheep pen by
the door but climbs in some other
way, is a thief and a robber. 2 The one
who enters by the door is the shepherd of the sheep. 3 The doorkeeper
opens it for him, and the sheep hear
his voice. He calls his own sheep by
name and leads them out. 4 When he
has brought all his own outside, he
goes ahead of them. The sheep follow
him because they recognize his voice.
5 They will never follow a stranger; instead they will run away from him, because they don't recognize the voice
of strangers."
6 Jesus gave them this illustration,
but they did not understand what He
was telling them.

The Good Shepherd

7 So Jesus said again, "I assure you: I
am [a]the door of the sheep. 8 [b]All who
came before Me[e] are thieves and robbers, but the sheep didn't listen to
them. 9 I am the door. If anyone enters
by Me, he will be saved and will come
in and go out and find pasture. 10 [c]A
thief comes only to steal and to kill and
to destroy. I have come that they may
have life and have it in abundance.

[a] *Eph 2:18; Heb 10:19*
[b] *Jr 23:1; Ezk 22:25* [c] *Mt 7:15*

11 [a]"I am the good shepherd. The
good shepherd lays down his life for
the sheep. 12 The hired man, since he
is not the shepherd and doesn't own
the sheep, [b]leaves them[f] and runs

[a]**9:32** Lit *From the age* [b]**9:34** = they banned him from the synagogue; v. 22 [c]**9:35** Other mss read *the Son of God* [d]**9:41** To *have sin* is an idiom that refers to guilt caused by sin. [e]**10:8** Other mss omit *before Me* [f]**10:12** Lit *leaves the sheep*

away when he sees a wolf coming. The wolf then snatches and scatters them. 13 ⌊This happens⌋ because he is a hired man and doesn't care about the sheep.

[a] Is 40:11; 1Pt 2:25 [b] Zch 11:16

14 "I am the good shepherd. [a]I know My own sheep, and [b]they know Me, 15 as the Father knows Me, and I know the Father. I lay down My life for the sheep. 16 But I have [c]other sheep that are not of this fold; I must bring them also, and they will listen to My voice. [d]Then there will be one flock, one shepherd. 17 This is why the Father loves Me, [e]because I am laying down My life so I may take it up again. 18 No one takes it from Me, but I lay it down on My own. I have the right to lay it down, and I have the right to take it up again. [f]I have received this command from My Father."

[a] 2Tm 2:19 [b] Is 53:6-7 [c] Is 56:8 [d] Eph 2:14 [e] 2Co 5:15; Heb 2:9 [f] Ac 2:24

19 Again a division took place among the Jews because of these words. 20 Many of them were saying, "He has a demon and He's crazy! Why do you listen to Him?" 21 Others were saying, "These aren't the words of someone demon-possessed. [a]Can a demon open the eyes of the blind?"

[a] Ps 94:9; Is 35:4-5

Jesus at the Festival of Dedication

22 Then the Festival of Dedication[a] took place in Jerusalem, and it was winter. 23 Jesus was walking in the •temple complex in Solomon's Colonnade.[b] 24 Then the Jews surrounded Him and asked, "How long are You going to keep us in suspense?[c] If You are the •Messiah, tell us plainly."[d]

25 "I did tell you and you don't believe," Jesus answered them. "The works that I do in My Father's name testify about Me. 26 But [a]you don't believe because you are not My sheep.[e] 27 My sheep hear My voice, I know them, and they follow Me. 28 I give them eternal life, and they will never perish—ever! No one will snatch them out of My hand. 29 [b]My Father, who has given them to Me, is greater than all. No one is able to snatch them out of the Father's hand. 30 [c]The Father and I are one."[f]

[a] Jn 8:47 [b] Jn 14:28; 17:2,6 [c] Jn 1:1,14

Renewed Efforts to Stone Jesus

31 Again the Jews picked up rocks to stone Him.

32 Jesus replied, "I have shown you many good works from the Father. Which of these works are you stoning Me for?"

33 "We aren't stoning You for a good work," the Jews answered, "but for blasphemy, because You—being a man—[a]make Yourself God."

[a] Jn 5:18; Php 2:6

34 Jesus answered them, [a]"Isn't it written in your law,[g] **I said, you are gods?**[h] 35 If He called those whom the word of God came to 'gods'—and the Scripture cannot be broken— 36 do you say, 'You are blaspheming' to the One [b]the Father set apart and [c]sent into the world, because I said: I am [d]the Son of God? 37 [e]If I am not doing My Father's works, don't believe Me. 38 But if I am doing them and you don't believe Me, believe the works. This way you will know and understand[i] [f]that the Father is in Me and I in the Father." 39 Then they were trying again to seize Him, yet He eluded their grasp.

[a] Ps 82:6 [b] Jn 6:27 [c] Jn 3:17 [d] Jn 9:35 [e] Jn 15:24 [f] Jn 14:10

Many beyond the Jordan Believe in Jesus

40 So He departed again across the Jordan to the place [a]where John had

[a]**10:22** Or *Hanukkah*, also called *the Feast of Lights*; this festival commemorated the rededication of the temple in 164 B.C. [b]**10:23** Rows of columns supporting a roof [c]**10:24** Lit *How long are you taking away our life?* [d]**10:24** Or *openly*, or *publicly* [e]**10:26** Other mss add *just as I told you* [f]**10:30** Lit *I and the Father—We are one.* [g]**10:34** Other mss read *in the law* [h]**10:34** Ps 82:6 [i]**10:38** Other mss read *know and believe*

been baptizing earlier, and He remained there. 41 Many came to Him
and said, "John never did a sign, [b]but
everything John said about this man
was true." 42 And many believed in
Him there. [a]Jn 1:28 [b]Jn 1:15

Lazarus Dies at Bethany

11 Now a man was sick, Lazarus,
from Bethany, the village of
[a]Mary and her sister Martha. 2 [b]Mary
was the one who anointed the Lord
with fragrant oil and wiped His feet
with her hair, and it was her brother
Lazarus who was sick. 3 So the sisters
sent a message to Him: "Lord, the one
You love is sick." [a]Lk 10:38 [b]Mt 26:7

4 When Jesus heard it, He said, "This
sickness will not end in death but is
[a]for the glory of God, so that the Son of
God may be glorified through it."
5 (Jesus loved Martha, her sister, and
Lazarus.) 6 So when He heard that he
was sick, [b]He stayed two more days in
the place where He was. 7 Then after
that, He said to the disciples, "Let's go
to Judea again." [a]Jn 9:3 [b]Jn 10:40

8 "•Rabbi," the disciples told Him,
"just now [a]the Jews tried to stone You,
and You're going there again?" [a]Jn 10:31

9 "Aren't there 12 hours in a day?"
Jesus answered. [a]"If anyone walks during the day, he doesn't stumble, because he sees the light of this world.
10 [b]If anyone walks during the night,
he does stumble, because the light is
not in him." 11 He said this, and then
He told them, "Our friend Lazarus
[c]has fallen •asleep, but I'm on My way
to wake him up." [a]Pr 4:18; Jn 9:4
[b]Pr 4:18-19; Jn 12:35 [c]Mt 9:24

12 Then the disciples said to Him,
"Lord, if he has fallen asleep, he will
get well."

13 Jesus, however, was speaking
about his death, but they thought He
was speaking about natural sleep. 14 So
Jesus then told them plainly, "Lazarus
has died. 15 I'm glad for you that I
wasn't there so that you may believe.
But let's go to him."

16 Then Thomas (called "Twin") said
to his fellow disciples, "Let's go so that
we may die with Him."

The Resurrection and the Life

17 When Jesus arrived, He found that
Lazarus had already been in the tomb
four days. 18 Bethany was near Jerusalem (about two miles[a] away). 19 Many
of the Jews had come to Martha and
Mary to comfort them about their
brother. 20 As soon as Martha heard
that Jesus was coming, she went to
meet Him. But Mary remained seated
in the house.

21 Then Martha said to Jesus, "Lord,
if You had been here, my brother
wouldn't have died. 22 Yet even now I
know that [a]whatever You ask from
God, God will give You." [a]Mk 9:23-24

23 "Your brother will [a]rise again,"
Jesus told her. [a]Dn 12:2

24 Martha said, [a]"I know that he will
rise again in the resurrection at the last
day." [a]Jn 5:29

25 Jesus said to her, "I am [a]the resurrection and the [b]life. [c]The one who believes in Me, even if he dies, will live.
26 Everyone who lives and believes in
Me will never die—ever. Do you be-
lieve this?" [a]Jn 5:21 [b]Jn 1:4; 6:35 [c]Jn 3:36

27 "Yes, Lord," she told Him, [a]"I believe You are the •Messiah, the Son of
God, who was to come into the
world." [a]Mt 11:3; Jn 4:42

Jesus Shares the Sorrow of Death

28 Having said this, she went back
and called her sister Mary, saying in
private, "The Teacher is here and is
calling for you."

29 As soon as she heard this, she got
up quickly and went to Him. 30 Jesus

[a]**11:18** Lit *15 stadia*; 1 *stadion* = 600 feet

had not yet come into the village but
was still in the place where Martha
had met Him. 31 The Jews who were
with her in the house consoling her
saw that Mary got up quickly and went
out. So they followed her, supposing
that she was going to the tomb to cry
there.
32 When Mary came to where Jesus
was and saw Him, she fell at His feet
and told Him, "Lord, if You had been
here, my brother would not have
died!"
33 When Jesus saw her crying, and
the Jews who had come with her crying, He was angry[a] in His spirit and
deeply moved. 34 "Where have you put
him?" He asked.
"Lord," they told Him, "come and
see."
35 Jesus wept.
36 So the Jews said, "See how He
loved him!" 37 But some of them said,
"Couldn't He [a]who opened the blind
man's eyes also have kept this man
from dying?"

[a] *Jn 9:6*

The Seventh Sign: Raising Lazarus from the Dead

38 Then Jesus, angry in Himself
again, came to the tomb. It was a cave,
and a stone was lying against it.
39 "Remove the stone," Jesus said.
Martha, the dead man's sister, told
Him, "Lord, he already stinks. It's been
four days."
40 Jesus said to her, "Didn't I tell you
that if you believed you would see the
glory of God?"
41 So they removed the stone. Then
Jesus raised His eyes and said, "Father,
I thank You that You heard Me. 42 I
know that You always hear Me, but
[a]because of the crowd standing here I
said this, so they may believe You sent
Me." 43 After He said this, He shouted
with a loud voice, "Lazarus, come
out!" 44 The dead man came out bound
hand and foot with linen strips and
with his face wrapped in a cloth. Jesus
said to them, "Loose him and let him
go."

[a] *Jn 12:30*

The Plot to Kill Jesus

45 Therefore many of the Jews who
came to Mary and saw what He did believed in Him. 46 But some of them
went to the •Pharisees and told them
what Jesus had done.
47 [a]So the •chief priests and the Pharisees convened the •Sanhedrin and
said, [b]"What are we going to do since
this man does many signs? 48 If we let
Him continue in this way, everybody
will believe in Him! Then [c]the Romans
will come and remove both our place[b]
and our nation."

[a] *Mt 26:3* [b] *Jn 12:19* [c] *Dn 9:26; Zch 13:7-8*

49 One of them, [a]Caiaphas, who was
high priest that year, said to them,
"You know nothing at all! 50 [b]You're
not considering that it is to your[c] advantage that one man should die for
the people rather than the whole nation perish." 51 He did not say this on
his own, but being high priest that
year he prophesied that Jesus was going to die for the nation, 52 and [c]not for
the nation only, [d]but also to unite the
scattered children of God. 53 So from
that day on they plotted to kill Him.
54 Therefore Jesus no longer walked
openly among the Jews but departed
from there to the countryside near the
wilderness, to a town called [e]Ephraim.
And He stayed there with the disciples.

[a] *Lk 3:2* [b] *Jn 18:14* [c] *Is 49:6* [d] *Jn 10:16* [e] *2Ch 13:19*

55 The Jewish •Passover was near, and
many went up to Jerusalem from the
country [a]to purify[d] themselves before
the Passover. 56 [b]They were looking for

[a]**11:33** The Gk word is very strong and probably indicates Jesus' anger against sin's tyranny and death.
[b]**11:48** The temple or possibly all of Jerusalem [c]**11:50** Other mss read *to our* [d]**11:55** The law of Moses required God's people to purify or cleanse themselves so they could celebrate the Passover. Jews often came to Jerusalem a week early to do this; Nm 9:4–11.

Jesus and asking one another as they
stood in the •temple complex: [c]"What
do you think? He won't come to the
festival, will He?" 57 The chief priests
and the Pharisees had given orders
that if anyone knew where He was, he
should report it so they could arrest
Him.

[a] Ex 19:10 [b] Jn 7:11 [c] Ps 2

The Anointing at Bethany

12 Six days before the •Passover,
Jesus came to Bethany [a]where
Lazarus[a] was, the one Jesus had raised
from the dead. 2 [b]So they gave a dinner for Him there; Martha was serving
them, and Lazarus was one of those
reclining at the table with Him. 3 Then
[c]Mary took a pound of fragrant oil—
pure and expensive nard—anointed
Jesus' feet, and wiped His feet with
her hair. So the house was filled with
the fragrance of the oil.

[a] Jn 11 [b] Mt 26:6 [c] Lk 10:38-39; Jn 11:2

4 Then one of His disciples, Judas Iscariot (who was about to betray Him),
said, 5 "Why wasn't this fragrant oil
sold for 300 •denarii[b] and given to the
poor?" 6 He didn't say this because he
cared about the poor but because [a]he
was a thief. He was in charge of the
money-bag and would steal part of
what was put in it.

[a] Pr 26:25; Jn 13:29

7 Jesus answered, "Leave her alone;
she has kept it for the day of My burial.
8 For you always have [a]the poor with
you, but you do not always have Me."

[a] Mt 26:11; Mk 14:7

The Decision to Kill Lazarus

9 Then a large crowd of the Jews
learned He was there. They came not
only because of Jesus, but also to see
Lazarus the one He had raised from the
dead. 10 Therefore the •chief priests decided to also kill Lazarus, 11 [a]because
he was the reason many of the Jews
were deserting them[c] and believing in
Jesus.

[a] Mk 15:10; Jn 11:45

The Triumphal Entry

12 [a]The next day, when the large
crowd that had come to the festival
heard that Jesus was coming to Jerusalem, 13 they took palm branches and
went out to meet Him. They kept
shouting: [b]"•***Hosanna!*** **Blessed is He
who comes in the name of the
Lord**[d] —the King of Israel!"

[a] Lk 19:35 [b] Ps 72:17-19; 118:25-26

14 Jesus found a young donkey and
sat on it, just as it is written: 15 [a]**Fear
no more, Daughter Zion; look! your
King is coming, sitting on a donkey's
colt.**[e]

[a] Is 62:11; Zch 9:9

16 His disciples [a]did not understand
these things at first. [b]However, when
Jesus was glorified, [c]then they remembered that these things had been written about Him and that they had done
these things to Him. 17 Meanwhile the
crowd, which had been with Him
when He called Lazarus out of the
tomb and raised him from the dead,
continued to testify.[f] 18 This is also why
the crowd met Him, because they
heard He had done this sign.

[a] Lk 18:34 [b] Jn 7:39 [c] Jn 14:26

19 Then the •Pharisees said to one another, "You see? You've accomplished
nothing. Look—the world has gone after Him!"

Jesus Predicts His Crucifixion

20 Now some Greeks were among
those [a]who went up to worship at the
festival. 21 So they came to Philip, who
was from Bethsaida in Galilee, and requested of him, "Sir, we want to see
Jesus."

[a] 1Kg 8:41; Is 2:3

22 Philip went and told Andrew; then
Andrew and Philip went and told

[a]**12:1** Other mss read *Lazarus who died* [b]**12:5** This amount was about a year's wages for a common worker. [c]**12:11** Lit *going away* [d]**12:13** Ps 118:25–26 [e]**12:15** Zch 9:9 [f]**12:17** Other mss read *Meanwhile the crowd, which had been with Him, continued to testify that He had called Lazarus out of the tomb and raised him from the dead.*

Jesus. 23 Jesus replied to them, [a]"The
hour has come for the •Son of Man to
be glorified.

[a] Jn 13:32

24 "•I assure you: [a]Unless a grain of
wheat falls into the ground and dies, it
remains by itself. But if it dies, it produces a large crop.[a] 25 [b]The one who
loves his life will lose it, and the one
who hates his life in this world will
keep it for eternal life. 26 If anyone
serves Me, he must follow Me.
[c]Where I am, there My servant also
will be. If anyone serves Me, the Father will honor him.

[a] 1Co 15:36 [b] Lk 9:24 [c] 1Th 4:17

27 [a]"Now My soul is troubled. What
should I say—Father, save Me from this
hour? [b]But that is why I came to this
hour. 28 Father, glorify Your name!"[b]

[a] Lk 12:50 [b] Lk 22:53

Then a voice came from heaven: "I
have glorified it, and I will glorify it
again!"
29 The crowd standing there heard it
and said it was thunder. Others said,
"An angel has spoken to Him!"
30 Jesus responded, [a]"This voice
came, not for Me, but for you. 31 Now
is the judgment of this world. Now
[b]the ruler of this world will be cast out.
32 As for Me, if I am lifted up[c] from the
earth I will draw [c]all ⌊people⌋ to Myself." 33 He said this to signify what
kind of death He was about to die.

[a] Jn 11:42 [b] Lk 10:18; Jn 14:30 [c] Rm 5:18

34 Then the crowd replied to Him,
[a]"We have heard from the law that the
•Messiah will remain forever. So how
can You say, 'The Son of Man must be
lifted up'?[c] Who is this Son of Man?"

[a] Is 9:7

35 Jesus answered, [a]"The light will
be with you only a little longer. Walk
while you have the light so that darkness doesn't overtake you. [b]The one
who walks in darkness doesn't know
where he's going. 36 While you have
the light, believe in the light so that
you may become [c]sons of light." Jesus
said this, then went away and hid from
them.

[a] Jn 1:5-9 [b] Jn 11:10 [c] Lk 16:8

Isaiah's Prophecies Fulfilled

37 Even though He had performed so
many signs in their presence, they did
not believe in Him. 38 But this was to
fulfill the word of Isaiah the prophet,
who said:[d]

> **[a]Lord, who has believed**
> **our message?**
> **And who has the arm**
> **of the Lord been**
> **revealed to?**[e]

[a] Is 53:1

39 This is why they were unable to
believe, because Isaiah also said:

> 40 **[a]He has blinded their eyes**
> **and hardened their hearts,**
> **so that they would not see**
> **with their eyes**
> **or understand**
> **with their hearts,**
> **and be converted,**
> **and I would heal them.**[f]

41 [b]Isaiah said these things because[g] he
saw His glory and spoke about Him.

[a] Is 6:9-10; Mt 13:14 [b] Is 6:1

42 Nevertheless, many did believe in
Him even among the rulers, but because of the Pharisees they did not
confess Him, so they would not be
banned from the •synagogue. 43 [a]For
they loved praise from men more than
praise from God.[h]

[a] Lk 16:1

A Summary of Jesus' Mission

44 Then Jesus cried out, [a]"The one
who believes in Me believes not in
Me, but in Him who sent Me. 45 And
[b]the one who sees Me sees Him who
sent Me. 46 [c]I have come as a light into

[a]**12:24** Lit *produces much fruit* [b]**12:28** Other mss read *Your Son* [c]**12:32,34** Or *exalted* [d]**12:38** Lit *which he said* [e]**12:38** Is 53:1 [f]**12:40** Is 6:10 [g]**12:41** Other mss read *when* [h]**12:43** Lit *loved glory of men more than glory of God*; v. 41; Jn 5:41

the world, so that everyone who believes in Me would not remain in darkness. 47 If anyone hears My words and
doesn't keep them, [d]I do not judge
him; for [e]I did not come to judge the
world but to save the world. 48 [f]The
one who rejects Me and doesn't accept
My sayings has this as his judge:[a] [g]the
word I have spoken will judge him on
the last day. 49 For [h]I have not spoken
on My own, but the Father Himself
who sent Me has given Me a command
as to what I should say and what I
should speak. 50 I know that His command is eternal life. So the things that
I speak, I speak just as the Father has
told Me."

[a] Mt 10:40; Jn 13:20 [b] Jn 14:9 [c] Jn 3:19 [d] Jn 5:45 [e] Jn 3:17 [f] Lk 10:16 [g] Mk 16:16 [h] Jn 8:38

Jesus Washes His Disciples' Feet

13 Before the •Passover Festival,
Jesus knew that His hour had
come to depart from this world to the
Father. Having loved His own who
were in the world, He loved them to
the end.[b]

2 Now by the time of supper, [a]the
Devil had already put it into the heart
of Judas, Simon Iscariot's son, to betray
Him. 3 Jesus knew [b]that the Father had
given everything into His hands, that
He had come from God, and that He
was going back to God. 4 [c]So He got up
from supper, laid aside His robe, took a
towel, and tied it around Himself.
5 Next, He poured water into a basin
and began to wash His disciples' feet
and to dry them with the towel tied
around Him.

[a] Lk 22:3 [b] Jn 3:35 [c] Lk 22:27

6 He came to Simon Peter, who asked
Him, "Lord, [a]are You going to wash my
feet?"

[a] Mt 3:14

7 Jesus answered him, "What I'm doing you don't understand now, but afterwards you will know."

8 "You will never wash my feet—
ever!" Peter said.

Jesus replied, [a]"If I don't wash you,
you have no part with Me."

[a] Is 52:15; 1Co 6:11

9 Simon Peter said to Him, "Lord, not
only my feet, but also my hands and
my head."

10 "One who has bathed," Jesus told
him, "doesn't need to wash anything
except his feet, but he is completely
clean. [a]You are clean, but not all of
you." 11 For He knew who would betray Him. This is why He said, "You are
not all clean."

[a] Jn 15:3

The Meaning of Footwashing

12 When Jesus had washed their feet
and put on His robe, He reclined[c] again
and said to them, "Do you know what
I have done for you? 13 [a]You call Me
Teacher and Lord. This is well said, for
I am. 14 [b]So if I, your Lord and Teacher,
have washed your feet, [c]you also ought
to wash one another's feet. 15 For [d]I
have given you an example that you
also should do just as I have done for
you.

[a] 1Co 8:6 [b] Lk 22:27 [c] Php 2:2-5 [d] 1Pt 2:21

16 [a]"•I assure you: A slave is not
greater than his master,[d] and a messenger is not greater than the one who
sent him. 17 If you know these things,
you are blessed [b]if you do them. 18 I'm
not speaking about all of you; [c]I know
those I have chosen. But the Scripture
must be fulfilled: [d]**The one who eats
My bread**[e] **has raised his heel against
Me.**[f]

[a] Lk 6:40 [b] Jms 1:25 [c] Jn 17:12 [d] Ps 41:9

19 "I am telling you now before it
happens, so that when it does happen
you will believe that I am ⌊He⌋. 20 [a]I assure you: The one who receives
whomever I send receives Me, and the
one who receives Me receives Him
who sent Me."

[a] Lk 10:16

[a]**12:48** Lit *has the one judging him* [b]**13:1** *to the end* = *completely* or *always* [c]**13:12** At important meals the custom was to recline on a mat at a low table and lean on the left elbow. [d]**13:16** Or *lord* [e]**13:18** Other mss read *eats bread with Me* [f]**13:18** Ps 41:9

Judas' Betrayal Predicted

21 [a]When Jesus had said this, He was
troubled in His spirit and testified, "I
assure you: [b]One of you will betray
Me!" [a]Lk 22:21 [b]Ac 1:17

22 The disciples started looking at
one another—uncertain which one He
was speaking about. 23 One of His disciples, the [a]one Jesus loved, was reclining close beside Jesus.[a] 24 Simon Peter
motioned to him to find out who it was
He was talking about. 25 So he leaned
back against Jesus and asked Him,
"Lord, who is it?" [a]Jn 19:26

26 Jesus replied, "He's the one I give
the piece of bread to after I have
dipped it." When He had dipped the
bread, He gave it to Judas, Simon Iscariot's son.[b] 27 [a]After ⌊Judas ate⌋ the piece
of bread, Satan entered him. Therefore
Jesus told him, "What you're doing, do
quickly." [a]Lk 22:3; Jn 6:70

28 None of those reclining at the table knew why He told him this.
29 Since [a]Judas kept the money-bag,
some thought that Jesus was telling
him, "Buy what we need for the festival," or that he should give something
to the poor. 30 After receiving the piece
of bread, he went out immediately.
And it was night. [a]Jn 12:6

The New Commandment

31 When he had gone out, Jesus said,
"Now the •Son of Man is glorified, and
[a]God is glorified in Him. 32 [b]If God is
glorified in Him,[c] God will also glorify
Him in Himself and will glorify Him at
once. [a]Jn 14:13 [b]Jn 17:1

33 "Children, I am with you a little
while longer. You will look for Me, and
just as I told the Jews, 'Where I am going you cannot come,' so now I tell
you.

34 [a]"I give you a new commandment:
love one another. Just as I have loved
you, you must also love one another.
35 By this all people will know that you
are My disciples, if you have love for
one another." [a]Lv 19:18; Eph 5:2

Peter's Denials Predicted

36 "Lord," Simon Peter said to Him,
"where are You going?"

Jesus answered, "Where I am going
you cannot follow Me now, [a]but you
will follow later." [a]Jn 21:18; 2Pt 1:14

37 "Lord," Peter asked, "why can't I
follow You now? I will [a]lay down my
life for You!" [a]Lk 22:33

38 Jesus replied, "Will you lay down
your life for Me? I assure you: A
rooster will not crow until you have
denied Me three times.

The Way to the Father

14 "Your heart must not be troubled. Believe[d] in God; believe
also in Me. 2 [a]In My Father's house are
many dwelling places;[e] if not, I would
have told you. [b]I am going away to prepare a place for you. 3 If I go away and
prepare a place for you, [c]I will come
back and receive you to Myself, so that
[d]where I am you may be also. 4 You
know the way where I am going."[f]
[a]2Co 5:1 [b]Jn 13:33 [c]Mt 25:32-34 [d]Jn 12:26; 17:24

5 "Lord," Thomas said, "we don't
know where You're going. How can
we know the way?"

6 Jesus told him, "I am [a]the way, [b]the
truth, and [c]the life. [d]No one comes to
the Father except through Me.
[a]Mt 11:27 [b]Jn 1:17 [c]Jn 1:4 [d]Jn 10:9

Jesus Reveals the Father

7 "If you know Me, you will also
know[g] My Father. From now on you do
know Him and have seen Him."

[a]**13:23** Lit *reclining at Jesus' breast*; that is, on His right; Jn 1:18 [b]**13:26** Other mss read *Judas Iscariot, Simon's son* [c]**13:32** Other mss omit *If God is glorified in Him* [d]**14:1** Or *You believe* [e]**14:2** The Vg used the Lat term *mansio*, a traveler's resting place. The Gk word is related to the verb *meno*, meaning *remain* or *stay*, which occurs 40 times in John. [f]**14:4** Other mss read this verse: *And you know where I am going, and you know the way* [g]**14:7** Other mss read *If you had known Me, you would have known*

8 "Lord," said Philip, "show us the
Father, and that's enough for us."
9 Jesus said to him, "Have I been
among you all this time without your
knowing Me, Philip? [a]The one who
has seen Me has seen the Father. How
can you say, 'Show us the Father'?
10 Don't you believe that [b]I am in the
Father and the Father is in Me? [c]The
words I speak to you I do not speak on
My own. The Father who lives in Me
does His works. 11 Believe Me that I am
in the Father and the Father is in Me.
Otherwise, believe[a] because of the
works themselves. *[a]Col 1:15; Heb 1:3*
[b]Jn 10:38 [c]Jn 5:19

Praying in Jesus' Name

12 "•I assure you: The one who believes in Me will also do the works that
I do. And he will do even greater works
than these, because I am going to the
Father. 13 [a]Whatever you ask in My
name, I will do it so that the Father may
be glorified in the Son. 14 If you ask Me[b]
anything in My name, I will do it.[c]
[a]Mt 7:7-8; Jn 15:7,16

Another Counselor Promised

15 [a]"If you love Me, you will keep[d]
My commandments. 16 And I will ask
the Father, and [b]He will give you another •Counselor to be with you forever. 17 He is the Spirit of truth. [c]The
world is unable to receive Him because it doesn't see Him or know Him.
But you do know Him, because He remains with you [d]and will be[e] in you.
18 I will not leave you as orphans; I am
coming to you. *[a]Mt 10:37 [b]Rm 8:15*
[c]Rm 8:7 [d]1Jn 2:27

The Father, the Son, and the Holy Spirit

19 "In a little while the world will see
Me no longer, but [a]you will see Me.
[b]Because I live, you will live too. 20 In
that day you will know that [c]I am in My
Father, you are in Me, and I am in you.
21 The one who has My commands and
keeps them is the one who loves Me.
And the one who loves Me will be
loved by My Father. I also will love him
and will reveal Myself to him."
[a]Jn 16:16 [b]1Co 15:20 [c]Jn 10:38

22 Judas (not Iscariot) said to Him,
"Lord, how is it You're going to reveal
Yourself to us and not to the world?"
23 Jesus answered, "If anyone loves
Me, he will keep My word. My Father
will love him, and [a]We will come to
him and make Our home with him.
24 The one who doesn't love Me will
not keep My words. [b]The word that
you hear is not Mine but is from the
Father who sent Me. *[a]1Jn 2:24 [b]Jn 7:16*

25 "I have spoken these things to you
while I remain with you. 26 But [a]the
Counselor, the Holy Spirit—the Father
will send Him in My name—[b]will
teach you all things and remind you of
everything I have told you.
[a]Lk 24:49 [b]1Jn 2:27

Jesus' Gift of Peace

27 [a]"Peace I leave with you. My peace
I give to you. I do not give to you as the
world gives. Your heart must not be
troubled or fearful. 28 You have heard
Me tell you, 'I am going away and I am
coming to you.' If you loved Me, you
would have rejoiced that I am going to
the Father, because [b]the Father is
greater than I. 29 I have told you now before it happens so that when it does
happen you may believe. 30 I will not
talk with you much longer, [c]because the
ruler of the world is coming. [d]He has no
power over Me.[f] 31 On the contrary, ⌊I
am going away⌋[g] so that the world may
know that I love the Father. [e]Just as the
Father commanded Me, so I do. *[a]Php 4:7*
[b]1Co 11:3 [c]Jn 12:31 [d]1Jn 3:5 [e]Php 2:8

"Get up; let's leave this place.

[a]**14:11** Other mss read *believe Me* [b]**14:14** Other mss omit *Me* [c]**14:14** Other mss omit all of v. 14
[d]**14:15** Other mss read *If you love Me, keep* (as a command) [e]**14:17** Other mss read *and is* [f]**14:30** Lit *He has nothing in Me* [g]**14:31** Probably refers to the cross

The Vine and the Branches

15 “I am the true vine, and My Father is the vineyard keeper.
2 [a]Every branch in Me that does not
produce fruit He removes, and He
prunes every branch that produces
fruit so that it will produce more fruit.
3 [b]You are already clean because of the
word I have spoken to you. 4 [c]Remain
in Me, and I in you. Just as a branch is
unable to produce fruit by itself unless
it remains on the vine, so neither can
you unless you remain in Me.

[a] Mt 15:13 [b] Jn 13:10 [c] Eph 2:21-22

5 “I am the vine; you are the
branches. The one who remains in Me
and I in him produces much [a]fruit, because you can do nothing without Me.
6 [b]If anyone does not remain in Me, he
is thrown aside like a branch and he
withers. They gather them, throw
them into the fire, and they are
burned. 7 If you remain in Me and My
words remain in you, ask whatever
you want and it will be done for you.
8 [c]My Father is glorified by this: that
you produce much fruit and prove to
be[a] My disciples.

[a] Pr 11:30; Lk 13:6-9 [b] Heb 6:4-6 [c] Mt 5:16

Christlike Love

9 “As the Father has loved Me, I have
also loved you. Remain in My love. 10 If
you keep My commands you will remain in My love, just as I have kept My
Father’s commands and remain in His
love.

11 “I have spoken these things to you
so that My joy may be in you and your
joy may be complete. 12 [a]This is My
command: love one another as I have
loved you. 13 [b]No one has greater love
than this, that someone would lay
down his life for his friends. 14 You are
My friends if you do what I command
you. 15 I do not call you slaves anymore,
because a slave doesn’t know what his
master[b] is doing. I have called you
friends, [c]because I have made known
to you everything I have heard from
My Father. 16 [d]You did not choose Me,
but I chose you. I [e]appointed you that
you should go out and produce fruit
and that your fruit should remain, so
that whatever you ask the Father in My
name, He will give you. 17 This is what
I command you: love one another.

[a] 1Th 4:9 [b] Rm 5:7; Eph 5:2 [c] Mt 13:11 [d] 1Jn 4:10 [e] Mk 16:15

Persecutions Predicted

18 [a]“If the world hates you, understand that it hated Me before it hated
you. 19 [b]If you were of the world, the
world would love ⌊you as⌋ its own.
However, [c]because you are not of the
world, but I have chosen you out of it,
the world hates you. 20 Remember the
word I spoke to you: ‘A slave is not
greater than his master.’ If they persecuted Me, they will also persecute you.
If they kept My word, they will also
keep yours. 21 But they will do all these
things to you on account of My name,
because they don’t know the One who
sent Me. 22 [d]If I had not come and spoken to them, they would not have sin.[c]
[e]Now they have no excuse for their
sin. 23 [f]The one who hates Me also
hates My Father. 24 If I had not done
the works among them that no one
else has done, they would not have sin.
Now they have seen and hated both
Me and My Father. 25 But ⌊this hap-
pened⌋ so that the statement written in
their law might be fulfilled: [g]**They
hated Me for no reason.**[d]

[a] 1Jn 3:1 [b] 1Jn 4:5 [c] Jn 17:14 [d] Jn 9:41 [e] Rm 1:20 [f] 1Jn 2:23 [g] Ps 69:4

Coming Testimony and Rejection

26 [a]“When the •Counselor comes,
the One I will send to you from the Father—the Spirit of truth who proceeds
from the Father—[b]He will testify

[a]**15:8** Or *and become* [b]**15:15** Or *lord* [c]**15:22** To *have sin* is an idiom that refers to guilt caused by sin.
[d]**15:25** Ps 69:4

about Me. 27 [c]You also will testify, because [d]you have been with Me from
the beginning. [a]Jn 14:26 [b]1Jn 5:6
[c]Ac 1:8 [d]Lk 1:2

16 "I have told you these things to
keep you from stumbling. 2 They
will ban you from the •synagogues. In
fact, a time is coming when anyone
who kills you will think he is offering
service to God. 3 They will do [a]these
things because they haven't known
the Father or Me. 4 But I have told you
these things so that when their time[a]
comes you may remember I told them
to you. I didn't tell you these things
from the beginning, because I was
with you. [a]Rm 10:2

The Counselor's Ministry

5 "But now I am going away to Him
who sent Me, and not one of you asks
Me, 'Where are You going?' 6 Yet, because I have spoken these things to
you, sorrow has filled your heart.
7 Nevertheless, I am telling you the
truth. It is for your benefit that I go
away, because if I don't go away the
•Counselor will not come to you. [a]If I
go, I will send Him to you. 8 When He
comes, He will convict the world about
sin, righteousness, and judgment:
9 [b]about sin, because they do not believe in Me; 10 [c]about righteousness,
because I am going to the Father and
you will no longer see Me; 11 and
[d]about judgment, because [e]the ruler of
this world has been judged. [a]Ac 2:33
[b]Ac 2:22 [c]Ac 2:32; 1Co 1:30
[d]Mt 12:18,36 [e]Jn 12:31

12 "I still have many things to tell
you, but you can't bear them now.
13 When the Spirit of truth comes, [a]He
will guide you into all the truth. For He
will not speak on His own, but He will
speak whatever He hears. He will also
[b]declare to you what is to come. 14 He
will glorify Me, because He will take
from what is Mine and declare it to
you. 15 [c]Everything the Father has is
Mine. This is why I told you that He
takes from what is Mine and will declare it to you. [a]Jn 14:26 [b]1Tm 4:1
[c]Mt 11:27; Jn 17:10

Sorrow Turned to Joy

16 "A little while and you will no
longer see Me; again a little while and
you will see Me."[b]
17 Therefore some of His disciples
said to one another, "What is this He
tells us: 'A little while and you will not
see Me; again a little while and you
will see Me'; and, 'because I am going
to the Father'?" 18 They said, "What is
this He is saying,[c] 'A little while'? We
don't know what He's talking about!"
19 Jesus knew they wanted to question Him, so He said to them, "Are you
asking one another about what I said,
'A little while and you will not see Me;
again a little while and you will see
Me'?
20 "•I assure you: You will weep and
wail, but the world will rejoice. You
will become sorrowful, but your sorrow will turn to joy. 21 When a woman
is in labor she has pain because her
time has come. But when she has
given birth to a child, she no longer remembers the suffering because of the
joy that a person has been born into
the world. 22 So you also have sorrow[d]
now. But I will see you again. [a]Your
hearts will rejoice, and no one will rob
you of your joy. 23 In that day you will
not ask Me anything. [a]Lk 24:41; Jn 20:20

[a]"I assure you: Anything you ask the
Father in My name, He will give you.
24 Until now you have asked for nothing in My name. Ask and you will receive, that your joy may be complete.
[a]Jn 14:13

Jesus the Victor

25 "I have spoken these things to you
in figures of speech. A time is coming

[a]**16:4** Other mss read *when the time* [b]**16:16** Other mss add *because I am going to the Father* [c]**16:18** Other mss omit *He is saying* [d]**16:22** Other mss read *will have sorrow*

when I will no longer speak to you in
figures, but I will tell you plainly about
the Father. 26 In that day you will ask in
My name. I am not telling you that I will
make requests to the Father on your behalf. 27 [a]For the Father Himself loves
you, because you have loved Me [b]and
have believed that I came from God.[a]
28 [c]I came from the Father and have
come into the world. Again, I am leaving the world and going to the Father."

a Jd 20-21 b Jn 3:13 c Jn 13:3

29 "Ah!" His disciples said. "Now
You're speaking plainly and not using
any figurative language. 30 Now we
know that [a]You know everything and
don't need anyone to question You. By
this [b]we believe that You came from
God."

a Jn 21:17 b Jn 17:8

31 Jesus responded to them, "Do you
now believe? 32 Look: An hour is coming, and has come, when each of you
will be scattered to his own home, and
you will leave Me alone. Yet I am not
alone, because the Father is with Me.
33 I have told you these things so that
[a]in Me you may have peace. [b]You will
have suffering in this world. Be coura-
geous! [c]I have conquered the world."

a Jn 14:27 b Mt 10:38 c Rm 8:37; 1Co 15:27

Jesus Prays for Himself

17 Jesus spoke these things, looked up to heaven, and said:

Father,
the hour has come.
Glorify Your Son
so that the Son may glorify You,
2 [a]for You gave Him authority
over all flesh;[b]
so He may give eternal life
[b]to all You have given Him.
3 [c]This is eternal life:
that they may know You,
the only true God,
and the One
You have sent—Jesus Christ.
4 I have glorified You on the earth
by completing the work
You gave Me to do.
5 Now, Father, glorify Me
in Your presence
with that glory [d]I had with You
before the world existed.

a Mt 11:27; Php 2:10 b Jn 6:37 c Is 53:11 d Jn 1:1

Jesus Prays for His Disciples

6 [a]I have revealed Your name
to the men You gave Me
from the world.
They were Yours, You gave them
to Me,
and they have kept Your word.
7 Now they know that all things
You have given to Me are
from You,
8 because the words that You
gave Me,
I have given them.
They have received them
and have known for certain
that I came from You.
They have believed
that You sent Me.
9 [b]I pray[c] for them.
I am not praying for the world
but for those You have given Me,
because they are Yours.
10 [c]All My things are Yours,
and Yours are Mine,
and I have been glorified
in them.

a Ps 22:22 b 1Jn 5:19 c Rm 8:30

11 I am no longer in the world,
but they are in the world,
and I am coming to You.
Holy Father,
protect[d] them by Your name
that You have given Me,
so that they may be one
as [a]We are one.
12 While I was with them,
[b]I was protecting them
by Your name

[a]**16:27** Other mss read *from the Father* [b]**17:2** Or *people* [c]**17:9** Lit *ask* (throughout this passage)
[d]**17:11** Lit *keep* (throughout this passage)

that You have given Me.
I guarded them and [c]not one
of them is lost,
[d]except the son of destruction,[a]
[e]so that the Scripture may be
fulfilled. [a]Jn 10:30 [b]Jn 10:28
[c]Jn 18:9 [d]Jn 13:18 [e]Ac 1:20

13 Now I am coming to You,
and I speak these things
in the world
so that they may have My joy
completed in them.
14 I have given them Your word.
The world hated them
because they are not
of the world,
as I am not of the world.
15 I am not praying
[a]that You take them
out of the world
but that You protect them
from the evil one.
16 They are not of the world,
as I am not of the world.
17 Sanctify[b] them by the truth;
Your word is truth.
18 As You sent Me into the world,
I also have sent them
into the world.
19 [b]I sanctify Myself for them,
so they also may be sanctified
by the truth. [a]Gl 1:4 [b]Heb 10:10

Jesus Prays for All Believers

20 I pray not only for these,
but also for those who believe
in Me
through their message.
21 May they all be one,
as [a]You, Father, are in Me
and I am in You.
May they also be one[c] in Us,
so the world may believe
You sent Me.
22 I have given them the glory
You have given Me.
[b]May they be one as We are one.
23 I am in them and You are in Me.
[c]May they be made
completely one,
so the world may know You have
sent Me
and have loved them as
You have loved Me. [a]Jn 10:38
[b]1Jn 1:3 [c]Rm 12:5; Gl 3:28

24 [a]Father,
I desire those You have given Me
to be with Me where I am.
Then they will [b]see My glory,
which You have given Me
because You loved Me
before the world's foundation.
25 Righteous Father!
The world has not known You.
However, I have known You,
and these have known
that You sent Me.
26 I made Your name known
to them
and will make it known,
so the love
You have loved Me with
may be in them and [c]I may be
in them. [a]1Th 4:17
[b]1Jn 3:2 [c]Eph 3:17

Jesus Betrayed

18 After Jesus had said these
things, He [a]went out with His
disciples across the Kidron Valley,
where there was a garden, and He and
His disciples went into it. 2 Judas, who
betrayed Him, also knew the place,
[b]because Jesus often met there with
His disciples. 3 [c]So Judas took a •com-
pany of soldiers and some temple police from the •chief priests and the
•Pharisees and came there with lan-
terns, torches, and weapons.
[a]Lk 22:39 [b]Lk 21:37 [c]Mt 26:47

4 Then Jesus, knowing everything
that was about to happen to Him, went
out and said to them, "Who is it you're
looking for?"

[a]**17:12** The one destined for destruction, loss, or perdition [b]**17:17** Set apart for special use [c]**17:21** Other mss omit *one*

5 "Jesus the •Nazarene," they answered.
"I am He,"[a] Jesus told them.
Judas, who betrayed Him, was also
standing with them. 6 When He told
them, "I am He," they stepped back
and fell to the ground.
7 Then He asked them again, "Who
is it you're looking for?"
"Jesus the Nazarene," they said.
8 "I told you I am ⌊He⌋," Jesus replied.
"So if you're looking for Me, let these
men go." 9 This was to fulfill the words
He had said: [a]"I have not lost one of
those You have given Me." *[a] Jn 6:39*

10 [a]Then Simon Peter, who had a
sword, drew it, struck the high priest's
slave, and cut off his right ear. (The
slave's name was Malchus.) *[a] Lk 22:49*

11 At that, Jesus said to Peter,
"Sheathe your sword! Am I not to
drink [a]the cup the Father has given
Me?" *[a] Mt 20:22*

Jesus Arrested and Taken to Annas

12 Then the company of soldiers, the
commander, and the Jewish temple
police arrested Jesus and tied Him up.
13 [a]First they led Him to [b]Annas, for he
was the father-in-law of Caiaphas, who
was high priest that year. 14 [c]Caia-
phas was the one who had advised the
Jews that it was advantageous that one
man should die for the people. *[a] Mt 26:57 [b] Lk 3:2 [c] Jn 11:50*

Peter Denies Jesus

15 Meanwhile Simon Peter was following Jesus, as was another disciple.
That disciple was an acquaintance of
the high priest; so he went with Jesus
into the high priest's courtyard. 16 But
Peter remained standing outside by
the door. So the other disciple, the one
known to the high priest, went out and
spoke to the girl who was the doorkeeper and brought Peter in.
17 Then the slave girl who was the
doorkeeper said to Peter, "You aren't
one of this man's disciples too, are
you?"
"I am not!" he said. 18 Now the
slaves and the temple police had made
a charcoal fire, because it was cold.
They were standing there warming
themselves, and Peter was standing
with them, warming himself.

Jesus before Annas

19 The high priest questioned Jesus
about His disciples and about His
teaching.
20 [a]"I have spoken openly to the
world," Jesus answered him. "I have
always taught in the •synagogue and in
the •temple complex, where all the
Jews congregate, and I haven't spoken
anything in secret. 21 Why do you question Me? Question those who heard
what I told them. Look, they know
what I said." *[a] Mt 26:55*

22 When He had said these things,
one of the temple police standing by
[a]slapped Jesus, saying, "Is this the way
you answer the high priest?" *[a] Is 50:6*

23 [a]"If I have spoken wrongly," Jesus
answered him, "give evidence[b] about
the wrong; but if rightly, why do you
hit Me?" *[a] Heb 12:3*

24 Then Annas sent Him bound to
Caiaphas the high priest.

Peter Denies Jesus Twice More

25 Now Simon Peter was standing
and warming himself. [a]They said to
him, "You aren't one of His disciples
too, are you?" *[a] Mk 14:69*

He denied it and said, "I am not!"
26 One of the high priest's slaves, a
relative of the man whose ear Peter
had cut off, said, "Didn't I see you with
Him in the garden?"
27 Peter then denied it again. [a]Im-
mediately a rooster crowed.
[a] Mt 26:74; Jn 13:38

[a]**18:5** Lit *I am*; see note at Jn 8:58 [b]**18:23** Or *him, testify*

Jesus before Pilate

28 [a]Then they took Jesus from Caiaphas to the governor's •headquarters.
It was early morning. They did not enter the headquarters themselves; otherwise they would be defiled and
unable to eat the •Passover. [a] *Mt 27:2*

29 Then •Pilate came out to them and
said, "What charge do you bring
against this man?"
30 They answered him, "If this man
weren't a criminal,[a] we wouldn't have
handed Him over to you."
31 So Pilate told them, "Take Him
yourselves and judge Him according to
your law."
"It's not legal[b] for us to put anyone to
death," the Jews declared. 32 They said
this [a]so that Jesus' words might be fulfilled signifying what sort of death He
was going to die. [a] *Mt 20:19*

33 Then Pilate went back into the
headquarters, summoned Jesus, and
said to Him, "Are You the King of the
Jews?"
34 Jesus answered, "Are you asking
this on your own, or have others told
you about Me?"
35 "I'm not a Jew, am I?" Pilate replied. "Your own nation and the chief
priests handed You over to me. What
have You done?"
36 [a]"My kingdom is not of this world,"
said [b]Jesus. "If My kingdom were of this
world, My servants[c] would fight, so that
I wouldn't be handed over to the Jews.
As it is, My kingdom does not have its
origin here."[d] [a] *Is 9:6* [b] *1Tm 6:13*

37 "You are a king then?" Pilate asked.
"You say that I'm a king," Jesus replied. "I was born for this, and I have
come into the world for this: [a]to testify
to the truth. Everyone who [b]is of the
truth listens to My voice."
[a] *Is 55:4; Rv 1:5* [b] *Jn 8:47*

38 "What is truth?" said Pilate.

Jesus or Barabbas

After he had said this, he went out to
the Jews again and told them, [a]"I find
no grounds for charging Him. 39 You
have a custom that I release one ⌊pris-
oner⌋ to you at the Passover. So, do you
want me to release to you the King of
the Jews?" [a] *Mt 27; Mk 15; Lk 23; Jn 19:4,6*

40 They shouted back, "Not this man,
but Barabbas!" [a]Now Barabbas was a
revolutionary.[e] [a] *Lk 23:19*

Jesus Flogged and Mocked

19 Then [a]•Pilate took Jesus and had
Him flogged. 2 The soldiers also
twisted together a crown of thorns,
put it on His head, and threw a purple
robe around Him. 3 And they repeatedly came up to Him and said, "Hail,
King of the Jews!" and were slapping
His face. [a] *Mt 20:19; Mk 15:15; Lk 18:33*

4 Pilate went outside again and said
to them, "Look, I'm bringing Him outside to you [a]to let you know I find no
grounds for charging Him." [a] *Jn 18:38*

Pilate Sentences Jesus to Death

5 Then Jesus came out wearing the
crown of thorns and the purple robe.
Pilate said to them, "Here is the man!"
6 [a]When the •chief priests and the
temple police saw Him, they shouted,
"Crucify! Crucify!" [a] *Ac 3:13*

Pilate responded, "Take Him and
crucify Him yourselves, for I find no
grounds for charging Him."
7 [a]"We have a law," the Jews replied
to him, "and according to that law He
must die, because [b]He made Himself[f]
the Son of God." [a] *Lv 24:16* [b] *Mt 26:65*

8 When Pilate heard this statement,
he was more afraid than ever. 9 He
went back into the •headquarters and
asked Jesus, "Where are You from?"

[a]**18:30** Lit *an evil doer* [b]**18:31** According to Roman law [c]**18:36** Or *attendants,* or *helpers* [d]**18:36** Lit *My kingdom is not from here* [e]**18:40** Or *robber*; see Jn 10:1,8 for the same Gk word used here [f]**19:7** He claimed to be

[a]But Jesus did not give him an answer.
10 So Pilate said to Him, “You’re not
talking to me? Don’t You know that I
have the authority to release You and
the authority to crucify You?”
[a] Is 53:7; Mt 27:12,14

11 [a]“You would have no authority
over Me at all,” Jesus answered him,
“if it hadn’t been given you from
above. This is why the one who
handed Me over to you has the greater
sin.”[a] *[a] Ac 2:23*

12 From that moment Pilate made
every effort[b] to release Him. But the
Jews shouted, [a]“If you release this
man, you are not Caesar’s friend. Anyone who makes himself a king op-
poses Caesar!” *[a] Lk 23:2*

13 When Pilate heard these words,
he brought Jesus outside. He sat down
on the judge’s bench in a place called
the Stone Pavement (but in Hebrew
Gabbatha). 14 [a]It was the preparation
day for the •Passover, and it was about
six in the morning.[c] Then he told the
Jews, “Here is your king!” *[a] Mt 27:62*

15 But they shouted, “Take Him
away! Take Him away! Crucify Him!”
Pilate said to them, “Should I crucify
your king?”
“We have no king but Caesar!” the
chief priests answered.
16 [a]So then, because of them, he
handed Him over to be crucified.
[a] Mt 27:26,31; Mk 15:15; Lk 23:24

The Crucifixion

Therefore they took Jesus away.[d]
17 Carrying His own cross, [a]He went
out to what is called Skull Place, which
in Hebrew is called *Golgotha*. 18 [b]There
they crucified Him and two others with
Him, one on either side, with Jesus in
the middle. 19 Pilate also had a sign let-
tered and put on the cross. The inscription was: *[a] 1Kg 21:13; Lk 23:33; Heb 13:12*
[b] Is 53:12; Gl 3:13

JESUS THE NAZARENE
THE KING OF THE JEWS

20 Many of the Jews read this sign,
because the place where Jesus was crucified was near the city, and it was
written in Hebrew,[e] Latin, and Greek.
21 So the chief priests of the Jews said
to Pilate, “Don’t write, ‘The King of
the Jews,’ but that He said, ‘I am the
King of the Jews.’ ”
22 Pilate replied, “What I have written, I have written.”
23 When the soldiers crucified Jesus,
they took His clothes and divided them
into four parts, a part for each soldier.
They also took the tunic, which was
seamless, woven in one piece from the
top. 24 So they said to one another,
“Let’s not tear it, but toss for it, to see
who gets it.” ⌊They did this⌋ to fulfill
the Scripture that says: [a]**They divided
My clothes among themselves, and
they cast lots for My clothing.**[f] And
this is what the soldiers did.
[a] Ps 22:18; Mt 27:35

Jesus’ Provision for His Mother

25 Standing by the cross of Jesus were
His mother, His mother’s sister, Mary
the wife of Clopas, and •Mary
Magdalene. 26 When Jesus saw His
mother and [a]the disciple He loved
standing there, He said to His mother,
“•Woman, here is your son.” 27 Then
He said to the disciple, “Here is your
mother.” And from that hour the disciple took her into his home. *[a] Jn 13:23*

The Finished Work of Jesus

28 After this, when Jesus knew that
everything was now accomplished

[a]**19:11** To *have sin* is an idiom that refers to guilt caused by sin. [b]**19:12** Lit *Pilate was trying* [c]**19:14** Lit *the sixth hour*, see note at Jn 1:39; an alternate time reckoning would be *about noon* [d]**19:16** Other mss add *and led Him out* [e]**19:20** Or *Aramaic* [f]**19:24** Ps 22:18

[a]that the Scripture might be fulfilled,
He said, "I'm thirsty!" 29 A jar full of
sour wine was sitting there; so they
fixed a sponge full of sour wine on hyssop[a] and held it up to His mouth.
[a]*Ps 69:21*

30 When Jesus had received the sour
wine, He said, [a]"It is finished!" Then
bowing His head, He [b]gave up His
spirit. [a]*Jn 17:4* [b]*Php 2:8*

Jesus' Side Pierced

31 [a]Since it was the preparation day,
the Jews [b]did not want the bodies to
remain on the cross on the Sabbath
(for that Sabbath was [c]a special[b] day).
They requested that Pilate have the
men's legs broken and that ⌊their bod-
ies⌋ be taken away. 32 So the soldiers
came and broke the legs of the first
man and of the other one who had
been crucified with Him. 33 When they
came to Jesus, they did not break His
legs since they saw that He was already
dead. 34 But one of the soldiers pierced
His side with a spear, and at once
[d]blood and water came out. 35 [e]He who
saw this has testified so that you also
may believe. His testimony is true, and
he knows he is telling the truth. 36 For
these things happened [f]so that the
Scripture would be fulfilled: **Not one
of His bones will be broken.**[c] 37 Also,
another Scripture says: [g]**They will
look at the One they pierced.**[d]
[a]*Mk 15:42* [b]*Dt 21:23* [c]*Ex 12:18*
[d]*Zch 13:1* [e]*Jn 20:31; 1Jn 1:1*
[f]*Ex 12:46; Ps 34:20* [g]*Zch 12:10*

Jesus' Burial

38 [a]After this, Joseph of Arimathea,
who was a disciple of Jesus—but secretly [b]because of his fear of the
Jews—asked Pilate that he might remove Jesus' body. Pilate gave him permission, so he came and took His body
away. 39 [c]Nicodemus (who had previously come to Him at night) also came,
bringing a mixture of about 75 pounds[e]
of myrrh and aloes. 40 Then they took
Jesus' body and wrapped it in linen
cloths with the aromatic spices, according to the burial custom of the
Jews. 41 There was a garden in the
place where He was crucified. A [d]new
tomb was in the garden; no one had
yet been placed in it. 42 [e]They placed
Jesus there because of the Jewish preparation and since the tomb was nearby.
[a]*Mt 27:57* [b]*Pr 29:25* [c]*Jn 3:1-2*
[d]*Mt 27:60; Lk 23:53* [e]*Is 53:9*

The Empty Tomb

20 On the [a]first day of the week
•Mary Magdalene came to the
tomb early, while it was still dark. She
saw that the stone had been removed[f]
from the tomb. 2 So she ran to Simon
Peter and to the [b]other disciple, the
one Jesus loved, and said to them,
"They have taken the Lord out of the
tomb, and we don't know where they
have put Him!" [a]*Mt 28:1* [b]*Jn 13:23*

3 At that, [a]Peter and the other disciple went out, heading for the tomb.
4 The two were running together, but
the other disciple outran Peter and got
to the tomb first. 5 Stooping down, he
saw [b]the linen cloths lying there, yet
he did not go in. 6 Then, following
him, Simon Peter came also. He entered the tomb and saw the linen
cloths lying there. 7 The wrapping that
had been on His head was not lying
with the linen cloths but was folded
up in a separate place by itself. 8 The
other disciple, who had reached the
tomb first, then entered the tomb,
saw, and believed. 9 For they still did
not understand the [c]Scripture that He
must rise from the dead. 10 Then the
disciples went home again.
[a]*Lk 24:12* [b]*Jn 19:40*
[c]*Ps 16:10; Mt 16:21*

[a]**19:29** Or *with hyssop* [b]**19:31** Lit *great* [c]**19:36** Ex 12:46; Nm 9:12; Ps 34:20 [d]**19:37** Zch 12:10
[e]**19:39** Lit *100 litrai*; a Roman *litrai* = 12 ounces [f]**20:1** Lit *She saw the stone removed*

Mary Magdalene Sees the Risen Lord

11 [a]But Mary stood outside facing the tomb, crying. As she was crying, she stooped to look into the tomb. 12 She saw two angels in white sitting there, one at the head and one at the feet, where Jesus' body had been lying. 13 They said to her, "•Woman, why are you crying?"

[a] Mk 16:5

"Because they've taken away my Lord," she told them, "and I don't know where they've put Him." 14 [a]Having said this, she turned around and saw Jesus standing there, [b]though she did not know it was Jesus.

[a] Mt 28:9 [b] Lk 24:16,31; Jn 21:4

15 "Woman," Jesus said to her, "why are you crying? Who is it you are looking for?"

Supposing He was the gardener, she replied, "Sir, if you've removed Him, tell me where you've put Him, and I will take Him away."

16 Jesus said, "Mary."

Turning around, she said to Him in Hebrew, *"Rabbouni!"*[a] —which means "Teacher."

17 "Don't cling to Me," Jesus told her, "for I have not yet ascended to the Father. But go to [a]My brothers and tell them that [b]I am ascending to My Father and your Father—to My God and your God."

[a] Mt 28:10 [b] Jn 16:28

18 [a]Mary Magdalene went and announced to the disciples, "I have seen the Lord!" And she told them what[b] He had said to her.

[a] Mt 28:10; Lk 24:10

The Disciples Commissioned

19 [a]In the evening of that first day of the week, the disciples were ⌊gathered together⌋ with the doors locked because of their fear of the Jews. Then Jesus came, stood among them, and said to them, "Peace to you!"

[a] Mk 16:14; Lk 24:36

20 Having said this, He [a]showed them His hands and His side. [b]So the disciples rejoiced when they saw the Lord.

[a] 1Jn 1:1 [b] Jn 16:22

21 Jesus said to them again, "Peace to you! [a]As the Father has sent Me, I also send you." 22 After saying this, He breathed on them and said,[c] "Receive the Holy Spirit. 23 [b]If you forgive the sins of any, they are forgiven them; if you retain ⌊the sins of⌋ any, they are retained."

[a] Mt 28:18-19; Jn 17:18-19 [b] Mt 16:19

Thomas Sees and Believes

24 But one of the Twelve, Thomas ([a]called "Twin"), was not with them when Jesus came. 25 So the other disciples kept telling him, "We have seen the Lord!"

[a] Jn 11:16

But he said to them, "If I don't see the mark of the nails in His hands, put my finger into the mark of the nails, and put my hand into His side, I will never believe!"

26 After eight days His disciples were indoors again, and Thomas was with them. Even though the doors were locked, Jesus came and stood among them. He said, [a]"Peace to you!"

[a] Is 9:6-7; Col 1:20

27 Then He said to Thomas, "Put your finger here and observe My hands. [a]Reach out your hand and put it into My side. Don't be an unbeliever, but a believer."

[a] 1Jn 1:1

28 Thomas responded to Him, [a]"My Lord and my God!" *[a] Ps 73:25-26; 1Tm 1:17*

29 Jesus said, "Because you have seen Me, you have believed.[d] [a]Those who believe without seeing are blessed."

[a] 1Pt 1:8

The Purpose of This Gospel

30 [a]Jesus performed many other signs in the presence of His disciples that are not written in this book. 31 [b]But these

[a]**20:16** *Rabbouni* is also used in Mk 10:51 [b]**20:18** Lit *these things* [c]**20:22** Lit *He breathed and said to them* [d]**20:29** Or *have you believed?* (as a question)

are written so that you may believe
Jesus is the •Messiah, the Son of God,[a]
[c]and by believing you may have life in
His name.

[a]Jn 21:25 [b]Lk 1:4 [c]Jn 3:15-16

Jesus' Third Appearance to the Disciples

21 After this, Jesus revealed Himself again to His disciples by the
Sea of Tiberias.[b] He revealed Himself
in this way:
2 Simon Peter, Thomas (called
"Twin"), [a]Nathanael from Cana of Galilee, [b]Zebedee's sons, and two others
of His disciples were together.

[a]Jn 1:45 [b]Mt 4:21

3 "I'm going fishing," Simon Peter
said to them.
"We're coming with you," they told
him. They went out and got into the
boat, but that night they caught nothing.
4 When daybreak came, Jesus stood
on the shore. However, the disciples
[a]did not know it was Jesus.

[a]Jn 20:14

5 [a]"Men,"[c] Jesus called to them, "you
don't have any fish, do you?"

[a]Lk 24:41

"No," they answered.
6 [a]"Cast the net on the right side of
the boat," He told them, "and you'll
find some." So they did,[d] and they
were unable to haul it in because of the
large number of fish. 7 Therefore the
disciple, the one Jesus loved, said to
Peter, "It is the Lord!"

[a]Lk 5:4

When Simon Peter heard that it was
the Lord, he tied his outer garment
around him[e] (for he was stripped) and
plunged into the sea. 8 But since they
were not far from land (about 100
yards[f] away), the other disciples came
in the boat, dragging the net full of fish.
9 When they got out on land, they saw
a charcoal fire there, with fish lying on
it, and bread.
10 "Bring some of the fish you've just
caught," Jesus told them. 11 So Simon
Peter got up and hauled the net ashore,
full of large fish—153 of them. Even
though there were so many, the net
was not torn.
12 [a]"Come and have breakfast," Jesus
told them. None of the disciples dared
ask Him, "Who are You?" because they
knew it was the Lord. 13 Jesus came,
took the bread, and gave it to them. He
did the same with the fish.

[a]Ac 10:41

14 This was now [a]the third time[g]
Jesus appeared[h] to the disciples after
He was raised from the dead.

[a]Jn 20:19,26

Jesus' Threefold Restoration of Peter

15 When they had eaten breakfast,
Jesus asked Simon Peter, "Simon, son
of John,[i] do you [a]love[j] Me more than
these?"

[a]Mt 26:33

"Yes, Lord," he said to Him, "You
know that I love You."
"Feed My lambs," He told him.
16 A second time He asked him, "Simon, son of John, do you love Me?"
"Yes, Lord," he said to Him, "You
know that I love You."
"Shepherd My sheep," He told him.
17 He asked him [a]the third time, "Simon, son of John, do you love Me?"

[a]Jn 13:38

Peter was grieved that He asked him
the third time, "Do you love Me?" He
said, "Lord, [a]You know everything!
You know that I love You."

[a]Jn 2:24-25; 6:64

[a]**20:31** Or *that the Messiah, the Son of God, is Jesus* [b]**21:1** The Sea of Galilee; *Sea of Tiberias* is used only in John; Jn 6:1,23 [c]**21:5** Lit *Children* [d]**21:6** Lit *they cast* [e]**21:7** Lit *he girded his garment* [f]**21:8** Lit *about 200 cubits* [g]**21:14** The other two are in Jn 20:19–29. [h]**21:14** Lit *was revealed* (see v. 1) [i]**21:15–17** Other mss read *Simon, son of Jonah*; Jn 1:42; Mt 16:17 [j]**21:15–17** Two synonyms are translated *love* in this conversation: *agapao*, the first 2 times by Jesus (vv. 15–16); and *phileo*, the last time by Jesus (v. 17) and all 3 times by Peter (vv. 15–17). Peter's threefold confession of love for Jesus corresponds to his earlier threefold denial of Jesus; Jn 18:15–18,25–27.

"Feed My sheep," Jesus said. 18 [a]"•I
assure you: When you were young,
you would tie your belt and walk wherever you wanted. But when you grow
old, you will stretch out your hands
and someone else will tie you and
carry you where you don't want to go."
19 He said this to signify [b]by what kind
of death he would glorify God.[a] After
saying this, He told him, "Follow Me!"

[a] Jn 13:36 [b] Php 1:20; 2Pt 1:14

Correcting a False Report

20 So Peter turned around and saw the
disciple [a]Jesus loved following them.
⌊That disciple⌋ was the one who had
leaned back against Jesus at the supper
and asked, "Lord, who is the one that's
going to betray You?" 21 When Peter
saw him, he said to Jesus, "Lord—what
about him?"

[a] Jn 13:23,25

22 "If I want him to remain [a]until I
come," Jesus answered, "what is [b]that
to you? As for you, follow Me."

[a] Mt 16:27 [b] Dt 29:29

23 So this report[b] spread to the brothers[c] that this disciple would not die.
Yet Jesus did not tell him that he would
not die, but, "If I want him to remain
until I come, what is that to you?"

Epilogue

24 This is the disciple who testifies to
these things and who wrote them
down. We know that his testimony is
true.

25 And there are also many other
things that Jesus did, which, if they
were written one by one, I suppose not
even the world itself could contain the
books[d] that would be written.

ACTS

Prologue

1 I wrote the first narrative, [a]The-
ophilus, about all that Jesus began
to do and teach 2 [b]until the day He
was taken up, after He had given orders through the Holy Spirit to the
apostles whom He had chosen. 3 After
He had suffered, [c]He also presented
Himself alive to them by many con-
vincing proofs, appearing to them during 40 days and speaking about the
kingdom of God.

[a] Lk 1:3 [b] 1Tm 3:16; Heb 1:3 [c] 1Co 15:5

The Holy Spirit Promised

4 While He was together with them,[e]
He commanded them not to leave
Jerusalem, but to wait for the Father's
promise. "This," ⌊He said, [a]"is what⌋
you heard from Me; 5 [b]for John baptized with water, [c]but you will be baptized with the Holy Spirit not many
days from now."

[a] Jn 14:16 [b] Ac 11:16 [c] Jl 2:28-29; Mt 3:11; Ac 2:4

6 So when they had come together,
they asked Him, "Lord, at this time
are You [a]restoring the kingdom to Israel?"

[a] Is 1:26; Dn 7:27

7 He said to them, "It is not for you to
know times or periods that the Father
has set by His own authority. 8 But you
will receive power when the Holy Spirit
has come upon you, and you will be My
witnesses in Jerusalem, in all Judea and
Samaria, and to the ends[f] of the earth."

[a]**21:19** Jesus predicts that Peter would be martyred. Church tradition says that Peter was crucified upside down. [b]**21:23** Lit *this word* [c]**21:23** The word *brothers* refers to the whole Christian community. [d]**21:25** Lit *scroll* [e]**1:4** Or *He was eating with them*, or *He was lodging with them* [f]**1:8** Lit *the end*

The Ascension

9 [a]After He had said this, He was
taken up as they were watching, and a
cloud received Him out of their sight.
10 While He was going, they were gaz-
ing into heaven, and suddenly two
men in white clothes stood by them.
11 They said, "Men of Galilee, why do
you stand looking up into heaven? This
Jesus, who has been taken from you
into heaven, [b]will come in the same
way that you have seen Him going into
heaven." *[a]Jn 6:62 [b]Jn 14:3; 1Th 1:10; Rv 1:7*

United in Prayer

12 Then they returned to Jerusalem
from the mount called Olive Grove,
which is near Jerusalem—a Sabbath
day's journey away. 13 When they arrived, they went to the room upstairs
where they were staying:

Peter, John,
James, Andrew,
Philip, Thomas,
Bartholomew, Matthew,
James the son of Alphaeus,
[a]Simon the Zealot, and [b]Judas
the son of James.

14 All these were continually united in
prayer,[a] along with [c]the women, including Mary[b] the mother of Jesus,
and [d]His brothers. *[a]Lk 6:15 [b]Jd 1*
[c]Lk 23:49 [d]Mt 13:55

Matthias Chosen

15 During these days Peter stood up
among the brothers[c]—the number of
people who were together was about
120—and said: 16 "Brothers, the Scripture had to be fulfilled [a]that the Holy
Spirit through the mouth of David
spoke in advance about Judas, [b]who
became a guide to those who arrested
Jesus. 17 For [c]he was one of our number and was allotted a share in this
ministry." 18 [d]Now this man acquired a
field with his unrighteous wages; and
falling headfirst, he burst open in the
middle, and all his insides spilled out.
19 This became known to all the residents of Jerusalem, so that in their own
language that field is called *Hakel-
dama*, that is, Field of Blood. 20 "For it
is written in the Book of Psalms:

[e]Let his dwelling become
desolate;
let no one live in it;[d] and
Let someone else take
his position.[e] *[a]Ps 41:9 [b]Jn 18:3*
[c]Lk 6:16 [d]Mt 27:5 [e]Ps 69:25

21 "Therefore, from among the men
who have accompanied us during the
whole time the Lord Jesus went in and
out among us— 22 beginning from the
baptism of John until the day He was
taken up from us—from among these,
it is necessary that one become [a]a witness with us of His resurrection."
[a]Heb 2:3

23 So they proposed two: Joseph,
called Barsabbas, who was also known
as Justus, and Matthias. 24 Then they
prayed, "You, Lord, [a]know the hearts
of all; show which of these two You
have chosen 25 to take the place[f] in this
apostolic service that Judas left to go to
his own place." 26 Then they cast lots
for them, and the lot fell to Matthias.
So he was numbered with the 11 apostles. *[a]Jn 2:24; Heb 4:13*

Pentecost

2 When [a]the day of Pentecost had
arrived, [b]they were all together in
one place. 2 Suddenly a sound like
that of a violent rushing wind came
from heaven, and [c]it filled the whole
house where they were staying. 3 And
tongues, like flames of fire that were
divided, appeared to them and rested
on each one of them. 4 Then [d]they
were all filled with the Holy Spirit and

[a]**1:14** Other mss add *and petition* [b]**1:14** Or *prayer, with their wives and Mary* [c]**1:15** Other mss read *disciples* [d]**1:20** Ps 69:25 [e]**1:20** Ps 109:8 [f]**1:25** Other mss read *to share*

began [e]to speak in different languages, as the Spirit gave them ability
for speech. [a]Lv 23:15 [b]Ac 1:14 [c]Ac 4:31 [d]Jn 14:26; Ac 1:5 [e]Mk 16:17; 1Co 12:10

5 There were Jews [a]living in Jerusalem, devout men from every nation
under heaven. 6 When this sound occurred, the multitude came together
and was confused because each one
heard them speaking in his own language. 7 And they were astounded and
amazed, saying,[a] "Look, aren't all these
who are speaking Galileans? 8 How is it
that we hear, each of us, in our own
native language? 9 Parthians, Medes,
Elamites; those who live in Mesopotamia, in Judea and [b]Cappadocia, Pontus
and Asia, 10 Phrygia and Pamphylia,
Egypt and the parts of Libya near
Cyrene; visitors from Rome, both Jews
and [c]•proselytes, 11 Cretans and Ar-
abs—we hear them speaking in our
own languages the magnificent acts of
God." 12 And they were all astounded
and perplexed, saying to one another,
"What could this be?" 13 But some
sneered and said, "They're full of new
wine!"

[a]Ex 23:17 [b]1Pt 1:1 [c]Ex 12:48; Is 56:6

Peter's Sermon

14 But Peter stood up with the
Eleven, raised his voice, and proclaimed to them: "Jewish men and all
you residents of Jerusalem, let this be
known to you and pay attention to my
words. 15 For these people are not
drunk, as you suppose, since it's only
nine in the morning.[b] 16 On the contrary, this is what was spoken through
the prophet Joel:

17 [a]**And it will be in the last days,**
says God,
that [b]I will pour out My Spirit
on all humanity;
then your sons
and [c]your daughters
will prophesy,
your young men will see
visions,
and your old men will dream
dreams.
18 **I will even pour out My Spirit**
on My male and female slaves
in those days,
and they will prophesy.
19 [d]**I will display wonders**
in the heaven above
and signs on the earth below:
blood and fire and a cloud
of smoke.
20 [e]**The sun will be turned**
to darkness,
and the moon to blood,
before the great and
remarkable day of the Lord
comes;
21 **then [f]whoever calls**
on the name of the Lord
will be saved.[c]

[a]Is 44:3; Jl 2:28 [b]Ac 10:45 [c]Ac 21:9 [d]Jl 2:30 [e]Mt 24:29 [f]Rm 10:13

22 "Men of Israel, listen to these
words: This Jesus the •Nazarene was a
man pointed out to you by God [a]with
miracles, wonders, and signs that God
did among you through Him, just as
you yourselves know. 23 Though He
[b]was delivered up according to God's
determined plan and foreknowledge,
you used[d] lawless people[e] to nail Him
to a cross and kill Him. 24 [c]God raised
Him up, ending the pains of death, because it was not possible for Him to be
held by it. 25 For David says of Him:

[d]**I saw the Lord ever before me;**
because He is at my right hand,
I will not be shaken.
26 **Therefore my heart was glad,**
and my tongue rejoiced.
Moreover my flesh will rest
in hope,
27 **because You will not leave**
my soul in •Hades,

[a]**2:7** Other mss add *to one another* [b]**2:15** Lit *it's the third hour of the day* [c]**2:17–21** Jl 2:28–32
[d]**2:23** Other mss read *you have taken* [e]**2:23** Or *used the hand of lawless ones*

or allow Your [e]Holy One
to see decay.
28 **You have revealed**
the paths of life to me;
You will fill me with gladness
in Your presence.[a]

[a]Heb 2:4 [b]Lk 24:44 [c]Ac 3:15; 4:10 [d]Ps 16:8-11 [e]Ps 16:10

29 "Brothers, I can confidently speak
to you about the patriarch David: he is
both dead and buried, and his tomb is
with us to this day. 30 Since he was a
prophet, he knew that God had sworn
an oath to him to seat [a]one of his
descendants[b] [c] on his throne. 31 Seeing
this in advance, he spoke concerning
the resurrection of the •Messiah:

[b]**He**[d] **was not left in Hades,**
and His **flesh**
did not experience decay.[e]

[a]Ps 132:11; Lk 1:32 [b]Ps 16:10

32 "God has resurrected this Jesus.
[a]We are all witnesses of this. 33 Therefore, [b]since He has been exalted to the
right hand of God and [c]has received
from the Father the promised Holy
Spirit, He has poured out what you
both see and hear. 34 For it was not
David who ascended into the heavens,
but he himself says:

[d]**The Lord said to my Lord,**
'Sit at My right hand
35 **until I make Your enemies**
Your footstool.'[f]

[a]Lk 24:46-48 [b]Ac 5:31; Php 2:9 [c]Ac 1:4 [d]Ps 110:1

36 "Therefore let all the house of Israel know with certainty that God [a]has
made this Jesus, whom you crucified,
both Lord and Messiah!"

[a]Ac 5:31

Forgiveness through the Messiah

37 When they heard this, [a]they were
pierced to the heart and said to Peter
and the rest of the apostles: "Brothers,
what must we do?"

[a]Zch 12:10

38 [a]"Repent," Peter said to them,
"and be baptized, each of you, in the
name of Jesus the Messiah for the forgiveness of your sins, and you will receive the gift of the Holy Spirit. 39 For
the promise is for you and [b]for your
children, and [c]for all who are far off,[g]
as many as the Lord our God will call."
40 And with many other words he testified and strongly urged them, saying,
"Be saved from this corrupt[h] generation!"

[a]Lk 24:47; Ac 3:19 [b]Jl 2:28 [c]Eph 2:13

A Generous and Growing Church

41 So those who accepted his message were baptized, and that day about
3,000 people were added to them.
42 And they devoted themselves to the
apostles' teaching, to fellowship, to the
breaking of bread, and to prayers.
43 Then fear came over everyone,
and [a]many wonders and signs were being performed through the apostles.
44 Now all the believers were together
and [b]had everything in common. 45 So
they sold their possessions and property and [c]distributed the proceeds to
all, as anyone had a need.[i] 46 And every
day they devoted themselves ⌊to meet-
ing⌋ together [d]in the •temple complex,
and broke bread from house to house.
They ate their food with gladness and
simplicity of heart, 47 praising God and
[e]having favor with all the people. And
every day [f]the Lord added to them[j]
those who were being saved.

[a]Mk 16:17 [b]Ac 4:32 [c]Is 58:7 [d]Lk 24:53 [e]Rm 14:18 [f]Rm 8:30

Healing of a Lame Man

3 Now Peter and John were going
up together to the •temple complex at the hour of prayer at three in
the afternoon.[k] 2 And a man who was

[a]**2:25–28** Ps 16:8–11 [b]**2:30** Other mss add *according to the flesh to raise up the Messiah* [c]**2:30** Lit *one from the fruit of his loin* [d]**2:31** Other mss read *His soul* [e]**2:31** Ps 16:10 [f]**2:34–35** Ps 110:1
[g]**2:39** Remote in time or space [h]**2:40** Or *crooked*, or *twisted* [i]**2:45** Or *to all, according to one's needs*
[j]**2:47** Other mss read *to the church* [k]**3:1** Lit *at the ninth hour*

lame from his mother's womb was
carried there and placed every day at
the temple gate called Beautiful, so he
could beg from those entering the
temple complex. 3 When he saw Peter
and John about to enter the temple
complex, he asked for help. 4 Peter,
along with John, looked at him intently and said, "Look at us." 5 So he
turned to them,[a] expecting to get
something from them. 6 But Peter
said, "I have neither [a]silver nor gold,
but what I have, I give to you: [b]In the
name of Jesus Christ the •Nazarene,
get up and walk!" 7 Then, taking him
by the right hand he raised him up,
and at once his feet and ankles became strong. 8 So he [c]jumped up,
stood, and started to walk, and he entered the temple complex with
them—walking, leaping, and praising
God. 9 All the people saw him walking
and praising God, 10 and they recognized that he was the one who used to
sit and beg at the Beautiful Gate of the
temple complex. So they were filled
with awe and astonishment at what
had happened to him.

a 1Pt 4:10 b Ac 4:10 c Is 35:6

Preaching in Solomon's Colonnade

11 While he[b] was holding on to Peter
and John, all the people, greatly
amazed, ran toward them in [a]what is
called Solomon's Colonnade. 12 When
Peter saw this, he addressed the people: "Men of Israel, why are you
amazed at this? Or why do you stare at
us, [b]as though by our own power or
godliness we had made him walk?
13 [c]The God of Abraham, Isaac, and Jacob, the God of our fathers, [d]has glorified His Servant Jesus, whom you
handed over and denied in the presence of •Pilate, when he had decided
to release Him. 14 But you denied the
[e]Holy and [f]Righteous One, and asked
to have a murderer given to you.
15 And you killed the source[c] of life,
whom God raised from the dead; we
are witnesses of this. 16 [g]By faith in His
name, His name has made this man
strong, whom you see and know. So
the faith that comes through Him has
given him this perfect health in front of
all of you.

a Jn 10:23 b 2Co 3:5 c Ac 5:30 d Php 2:9 e Mk 1:24; Lk 1:35 f Ac 7:52 g 1Pt 1:21

17 "And now, brothers, I know that
you did it [a]in ignorance, just as your
leaders also did. 18 But what God predicted [b]through the mouth of all the
prophets—that His •Messiah would
suffer—He has fulfilled in this way.
19 Therefore repent and turn back, that
your sins may be wiped out so that seasons of refreshing may come from the
presence of the Lord, 20 and He may
send Jesus, who has been appointed
Messiah for you. 21 [c]Heaven must welcome[d] Him until the times of the
[d]restoration of all things, which God
spoke about by the mouth of His holy
prophets from the beginning. 22 Moses
said:[e]

The Lord your God will raise up
for you [e]a Prophet like me from
among your brothers. You must
listen to Him in everything He
will say to you. 23 And it will be
that [f]everyone who will not lis-
ten to that Prophet will be com-
pletely cut off from the people.[f]

a Lk 23:34; 1Co 2:8 b Ps 22 c Ac 1:11; Heb 8:1 d Mt 17:11 e Dt 18:15,19 f Mk 16:16; Heb 2:2-3

24 "In addition, all the prophets who
have spoken, from Samuel and those
after him, have also announced these
days. 25 [a]You are the sons of the prophets and of the covenant that God made
with your forefathers, saying to Abraham, [b]**And in your seed all the**

[a]**3:5** Or *he paid attention to them* [b]**3:11** Other mss read *the lame man who was healed* [c]**3:15** Or *the Prince, or the Ruler* [d]**3:21** Or *receive, or retain* [e]**3:22** Other mss add *to the fathers* [f]**3:22–23** Dt 18:15–19

families of the earth will be blessed.[a]
26 God raised up His Servant[b] and sent
Him first to you to bless you by turning
each of you from your evil ways."

[a] Rm 9:4,8 [b] Gn 12:3

Peter and John Arrested

4 Now as they were speaking to the
people, the priests, the commander of the temple guard, and the
•Sadducees confronted them, 2 because
they were provoked that they were
teaching the people and proclaiming in
the person of Jesus[c] the resurrection
from the dead. 3 So they seized them
and put them in custody until the next
day, since it was already evening. 4 But
many of those who heard the message
believed, and the number of the men
came to about 5,000.

Peter and John Face the Jewish Leadership

5 The next day, their rulers, elders,
and •scribes assembled in Jerusalem
6 with [a]Annas the high priest, Caiaphas, John and Alexander, and all the
members of the high-priestly family.[d]
7 After they had Peter and John stand[e]
before them, they asked the question:
[b]"By what power or in what name
have you done this?"

[a] Lk 3:2 [b] Mt 21:23

8 [a]Then Peter was filled with the Holy
Spirit and said to them, "Rulers of the
people and elders:[f] 9 If we are being examined today about a good deed done
to a disabled man—by what means he
was healed— 10 let it be known to all of
you and to all the people of Israel, [b]that
by the name of Jesus Christ the •Naza-
rene—whom you crucified and whom
God raised from the dead—by Him this
man is standing here before you
healthy. 11 [c]This ⌊Jesus⌋ is

The stone despised by you
builders,
who has become
the cornerstone.[g]

12 [d]There is salvation in no one else
for there is no other name unde
heaven given to people by which w
must be saved."

[a] Lk 12:11 [b] Ac 3
[c] Ps 118:22; Is 28:16; Mt 21:42 [d] Mt 1:2

The Name Forbidden

13 When they observed the boldnes
of Peter and John [a]and realized tha
they were uneducated and untraine
men, they were amazed and knew tha
they had been with Jesus. 14 And sinc
they saw the man who had bee
healed standing with them, they ha
nothing to say in response. 15 Afte
they had ordered them to leave th
•Sanhedrin, they conferred amon
themselves, 16 saying, [b]"What shoul
we do with these men? For an obviou
sign, [c]evident to all who live in Jerusa
lem, has been done through them, an
we cannot deny it! 17 But so this doe
not spread any further among the peo
ple, let's threaten them against speak
ing to anyone in this name again." 18 S
they called for them and ordered then
not to preach or teach at all in th
name of Jesus.

[a] Mt 11:25; 1Co 1:2
[b] Jn 11:47 [c] Ac 3:

19 But Peter and John answere
them, [a]"Whether it's right in the sigh
of God ⌊for us⌋ to listen to you rathe
than to God, you decide; 20 [b]for we are
unable to stop speaking about wha
[c]we have seen and heard."

[a] Ac 5:29; Gl 1:10 [b] Ac 1:8 [c] 1Jn 1:

21 After threatening them further
they released them. They found no way
to punish them, [a]because the people
were all giving glory to God [b]over wha
had been done; 22 for the man was over
40 years old on whom this sign of heal
ing had been performed.

[a] Ac 5:26 [b] Ac 3:7-

---

[a] **3:25** Gn 12:3; 18:18; 22:18; 26:4 [b] **3:26** Other mss add *Jesus* [c] **4:2** Lit *proclaiming in Jesus* [d] **4:6** Or *high-priestly class*, or *high-priestly clan* [e] **4:7** Lit *had placed them* [f] **4:8** Other mss add *of Israel* [g] **4:11** Ps 118:22

Prayer for Boldness

23 After they were released, they
went to their own fellowship[a] and reported all that the •chief priests and
the elders had said to them. 24 When
they heard this, they [a]raised their
voices to God unanimously and said,
"Master, [b]You are the One who made
the heaven, the earth, and the sea,
and everything in them. 25 You said
through the Holy Spirit, by the mouth
of our father David Your servant:[b]

> **[c]Why did the Gentiles rage,**
> **and the peoples plot**
> **futile things?**
> 26 **The kings of the earth**
> **took their stand,**
> **and the rulers assembled**
> **together**
> **against the Lord and**
> **against His •Messiah.**[c]

a Jr 20:13 b Jr 32:17 c Ps 2:1-2

27 "For, in fact, in this city both
•Herod and Pontius •Pilate, with the
Gentiles and the peoples of Israel, assembled together against [a]Your holy
Servant Jesus, [b]whom You anointed,
28 [c]to do whatever Your hand and Your
plan had predestined to take place.
29 And now, Lord, consider their
threats, and grant that Your slaves
[d]may speak Your message with complete boldness, 30 while You stretch out
Your hand for healing, [e]signs, and
wonders to be performed [f]through the
name of Your holy Servant Jesus."
31 When they had prayed, [g]the place
where they were assembled was
shaken, and they were all filled with
the Holy Spirit and began to speak
God's message with boldness.

a Heb 7:26 b Is 61:1; Jn 10:36 c Ac 2:23 d Ezk 2:6 e Ac 5:12 f Ac 3:6 g Ac 2:2,4

Believers Sharing

32 Now the multitude of those who
believed [a]were of one heart and soul,
and [b]no one said that any of his possessions was his own, but instead they
held everything in common. 33 And
with [c]great power the apostles were
giving testimony to the resurrection of
the Lord Jesus, and [d]great grace was on
all of them. 34 For [e]there was not a
needy person among them, [f]because
all those who owned lands or houses
sold them, brought the proceeds of the
things that were sold, 35 and laid them
at the apostles' feet. [g]This was then
distributed to each person as anyone
had a need.

a Rm 15:5; Php 1:27 b Ac 2:44 c Mk 16:20 d Ac 2:47 e 1Jn 3:17 f Ac 2:45 g Ac 6:1

36 Joseph, a Levite and a Cypriot by
birth, whom the apostles named Barnabas, which is translated Son of Encouragement, 37 [a]sold a field he owned,
brought the money, and laid it at the
apostles' feet.

a Mt 19:29; Lk 12:33

Lying to the Holy Spirit

5 But a man named Ananias, with
Sapphira his wife, sold a piece of
property. 2 However, [a]he kept back part
of the proceeds with his wife's knowledge, and brought a portion of it and
laid it at the apostles' feet.

a 1Tm 6:10

3 [a]Then Peter said, "Ananias, why
has [b]Satan filled your heart to lie to the
Holy Spirit and keep back part of the
proceeds from the field? 4 Wasn't it
yours while you possessed it? And after
it was sold, wasn't it at your disposal?
Why is it that you planned this thing in
your heart? You have not lied to men
but to God!" 5 When he heard these
words, Ananias dropped dead, and a
great fear came on all who heard. 6 The
young men got up, wrapped ⌊his body⌋,
carried him out, and buried him.

a Dt 23:21 b Lk 22:3; Jms 4:7

7 There was an interval of about
three hours; then his wife came in, not
knowing what had happened. 8 "Tell

[a]**4:23** Or *friends,* or *companions* [b]**4:25** Other mss read *through the mouth of David Your servant*
[c]**4:25–26** Ps 2:1–2

me," Peter asked her, "did you sell the
field for this price?"
"Yes," she said, "for that price."
9 Then Peter said to her, "Why did
you agree [a]to test the Spirit of the
Lord? Look! The feet of those who
have buried your husband are at the
door, and they will carry you out!"
[a]Mt 4:7

10 Instantly she dropped dead at his
feet. When the young men came in,
they found her dead, carried her out,
and buried her beside her husband.
11 Then great fear came on the whole
church and on all who heard these
things.

Apostolic Signs and Wonders

12 [a]Many signs and wonders were
being done among the people through
the hands of the apostles. By common
consent they would all meet in Solomon's Colonnade. 13 [b]None of the
rest dared to join them, [c]but the people praised them highly. 14 Believers
were added to the Lord in increasing
num- bers—crowds of both men and
women. 15 As a result, they would
carry the sick out into the streets and
lay them on beds and pallets so that
when Peter came by, at least his
shadow might fall on some of them.
16 In addition, a multitude came together from the towns surrounding
Jerusalem, bringing [d]sick people and
those who were tormented by unclean
spirits, and they were all healed.
[a]Mk 16:15-20; Ac 14:3 [b]Jn 9:22 [c]Ac 2:47 [d]Mk 16:17

In and Out of Prison

17 [a]Then the high priest took action.
He and all his colleagues, those who
belonged to the party of the •Saddu-
cees, were filled with jealousy. 18 [b]So
they arrested[a] the apostles and put
them in the city jail. 19 But [c]an angel of
the Lord opened the doors of the jail
during the night, brought them out,
and said, 20 "Go and stand in the •tem-
ple complex, and tell the people [d]all
about this life." 21 In obedience to this,
they entered the temple complex at
daybreak and began to teach.
[a]Ac 4:1-2 [b]Lk 21:12 [c]Ps 34:7; Heb 1:14 [d]Jn 6:68

The Apostles on Trial Again

When the high priest and those who
were with him arrived, they convened
the •Sanhedrin—the full Senate of the
sons of Israel—and sent ⌊orders⌋ to the
jail to have them brought. 22 But when
the temple police got there, they did
not find them in the jail, so they returned and reported, 23 "We found the
jail securely locked, with the guards
standing in front of the doors; but
when we opened them, we found no
one inside!" 24 As[b] [a]the captain of the
temple police and the •chief priests
heard these things, they were baffled
about them, as to what could come of
this.
[a]Ac 4:1

25 Someone came and reported to
them, "Look! The men you put in jail
are standing in the temple complex
and teaching the people." 26 Then the
captain went with the temple police
and brought them in without force, because they were afraid the people
might stone them. 27 When they had
brought them in, they had them stand
before the Sanhedrin, and the high
priest asked, 28 [a]"Didn't we strictly order you not to teach in this name? And
look, you have filled Jerusalem with
your teaching and are [b]determined to
bring this man's [c]blood on us!"
[a]Ac 4:18 [b]Ac 2:23; 3:15 [c]Mt 27:25

29 But Peter and the apostles replied,
[a]"We must obey God rather than men.
30 The God of our fathers raised up
Jesus, whom you had murdered by
[b]hanging Him on a tree. 31 [c]God exalted this man to His right hand as
[d]ruler and [e]Savior, [f]to grant repentance

[a]**5:18** Lit *laid hands on* [b]**5:24** Other mss add *the high priest and*

to Israel, and forgiveness of sins.
32 [g]We are witnesses of these things,
and so is the Holy Spirit whom God has
given to those who obey Him."

[a]Gl 1:10 [b]Gl 3:13 [c]Php 2:9; Heb 2:10 [d]Ac 3:15 [e]Mt 1:21 [f]Eph 1:7 [g]Jn 15:26-27

Gamaliel's Advice

33 When they heard this, they were
enraged and wanted to kill them. 34 A
•Pharisee named [a]Gamaliel, a teacher
of the law who was respected by all the
people, stood up in the Sanhedrin and
ordered the men[a] to be taken outside
for a little while. 35 He said to them,
"Men of Israel, be careful about what
you're going to do to these men. 36 Not
long ago Theudas rose up, claiming to
be somebody, and a group of about 400
men rallied to him. He was killed, and
all his partisans were dispersed and
came to nothing. 37 After this man, Judas the Galilean rose up in the [b]days of
the census and attracted a following.[b]
That man also perished, and all his partisans were scattered. 38 And now, I tell
you, stay away from these men and
leave them alone. For [c]if this plan or
this work is of men, it will be over-
thrown; 39 [d]but if it is of God, you will
not be able to overthrow them. You
may even be found fighting against
God." So they were persuaded by him.
40 After they called in the apostles [e]and
had them flogged, they ordered them
not to speak in the name of Jesus and
released them. 41 Then they went out
from the presence of the Sanhedrin,
[f]rejoicing that they were counted worthy to be dishonored on behalf of the
name.[c] 42 Every day in the temple complex, and in various homes, they continued teaching and proclaiming the
good news that the •Messiah is Jesus.[d]

[a]Ac 22:3 [b]Lk 2:1 [c]Pr 21:30 [d]1Co 1:25 [e]Mk 13:9 [f]Mt 5:12; 2Co 12:10; Php 1:29

Seven Chosen to Serve

6 In those days, [a]as the number of
the disciples was multiplying,
there arose a complaint by the Hel-
lenistic Jews[e] against the Hebraic
Jews[f] that their widows were being
overlooked [b]in the daily distribution.
2 Then the Twelve summoned the
whole company of the disciples and
said, [c]"It would not be right for us to
give up preaching about God to wait
on tables. 3 Therefore, brothers, select
from among you seven men of good
reputation, full of the Spirit and wisdom, whom we can appoint to this
duty. 4 But we will devote ourselves to
prayer and to the preaching ministry."
5 The proposal pleased the whole company. So they chose Stephen, a man
full of faith and the Holy Spirit, and
[d]Philip, Prochorus, Nicanor, Timon,
Parmenas, and Nicolaus, a •proselyte
from Antioch. 6 They had them stand
before the apostles, [e]who prayed and
[f]laid their hands on them.[g]

[a]Ps 72:16 [b]Ac 4:35 [c]2Tm 2:4 [d]Ac 8:5 [e]Pr 16:3 [f]Ac 8:17; 1Tm 4:14

7 So [a]the preaching about God flourished, the number of the disciples in
Jerusalem multiplied greatly, and a
large group of priests became obedient
to the faith.

[a]Col 1:6

Stephen Accused of Blasphemy

8 Stephen, full of grace and power,
was performing great wonders and
signs among the people. 9 Then some
from what is called the Freedmen's
•Synagogue, composed of both Cyre-
nians and Alexandrians, and some
from Cilicia and Asia, came forward
and disputed with Stephen. 10 But
[a]they were unable to stand up against
the wisdom and the Spirit by whom
he spoke.

[a]Is 54:17; Lk 21:15

[a]**5:34** Other mss read *apostles* [b]**5:37** Lit *and drew people after him* [c]**5:41** Other mss add *of Jesus*, or *of Christ* [d]**5:42** Or *that Jesus is the Messiah* [e]**6:1** Jews of Gk language and culture [f]**6:1** Jews of Aram or Hb language and culture [g]**6:6** The laying on of hands signified the prayer of blessing for the beginning of a new ministry.

11 Then they induced men to say,
"We heard him speaking blasphemous
words against Moses and God!"
12 They stirred up the people, the elders, and the •scribes; so they came
up, dragged him off, and took him to
the •Sanhedrin. 13 They also presented
false witnesses who said, "This man
does not stop speaking blasphemous
words against this holy place and the
law. 14 For we heard him say that Jesus,
this •Nazarene, will [a]destroy this place
and change the customs that Moses
handed down to us." 15 And all who
were sitting in the Sanhedrin looked
intently at him and saw that his face
was like the face of an angel. *[a]Mt 24:2*

Stephen's Address

7 "Is this true?"[a] the high priest
asked.
2 "Brothers and fathers," he said,
"listen: The God of glory appeared to
our father Abraham when he was in
Mesopotamia, before he settled in Haran, 3 and said to him:

> **Get out of your country**
> **and away from**
> **your relatives,**
> **and come to the land**
> **[a]that I will show you.**[b]

[a]Gn 12:1

4 "Then [a]he came out of the land of
the Chaldeans and settled in Haran.
And from there, after his father died,
God had him move to this land in
which you now live. 5 He didn't give
him an inheritance in it, not even a
foot of ground, [b]but He promised to
give it to him as a possession, and to
his descendants after him, even
though he was childless. 6 God spoke
in this way:

> **[c]His descendants would be**
> **strangers in a foreign country,**
> **and they would enslave**
> **and oppress them**
> **for [d]400 years.**
>
> 7 **I will judge the nation**
> **that they will serve as slaves,**
> **God said.**
> **After this, they will come out**
> **and [e]worship Me**
> **in this place.**[c]

8 [f]Then He gave him the covenant of
circumcision. [g]This being so, he fathered Isaac and circumcised him on
the eighth day; [h]Isaac did the same
with Jacob, and [i]Jacob with the 12 patriarchs. *[a]Gn 11:31 [b]Gn 12:7*
[c]Gn 15:13-14 [d]Ex 12:40 [e]Ex 3:12
[f]Gn 17:9 [g]Gn 21:2 [h]Gn 25:26 [i]Ex 1:1

The Patriarchs in Egypt

9 [a]"The patriarchs became jealous of
Joseph and sold him into Egypt, [b]but
God was with him 10 and rescued him
out of all his troubles. [c]He gave him favor and wisdom in the sight of Pharaoh, king of Egypt, who appointed
him governor over Egypt and over his
whole household. 11 Then a famine
came over all of Egypt and Canaan,
with great suffering, and our forefathers could find no food. 12 When Jacob heard there was grain in Egypt, he
sent our forefathers the first time.
13 The second time, Joseph was revealed to his brothers, and Joseph's
family became known to Pharaoh.
14 [d]Joseph then invited his father Jacob
and all his relatives, [e]75 people in
all, 15 and Jacob went down to Egypt.
[f]He and our forefathers died there,
16 [g]were carried back to Shechem, and
were placed in [h]the tomb that Abraham had bought for a sum of silver
from the sons of Hamor in Shechem.
[a]Gn 37:4 [b]Gn 39:2
[c]Gn 42:6 [d]Gn 45:9 [e]Gn 46:27
[f]Gn 49:33 [g]Ex 13:19 [h]Gn 23:16

Moses, a Rejected Savior

17 "As [a]the time was drawing near to
fulfill the promise that God had made
to Abraham, the people flourished and
multiplied in Egypt 18 until a different

[a]**7:1** Lit *"Are these things so?"* [b]**7:3** Gn 12:1 [c]**7:6–7** Gn 15:13–14

king ruled over Egypt[a] who did not
know Joseph. 19 He dealt deceitfully
with our race and oppressed our forefathers by making them leave their
infants outside so they wouldn't survive.[b] 20 [b]At this time Moses was born,
and he [c]was beautiful before God. He
was nursed in his father's home three
months, 21 and when he was left outside, Pharaoh's daughter adopted and
raised him as her own son. 22 So Moses
was educated in all the wisdom of the
Egyptians, and was powerful in his
speech and actions. *[a]Gn 15:13 [b]Ex 2:2 [c]Heb 11:23*

23 [a]"As he was approaching the age
of 40, he decided[c] to visit his brothers,
the sons of Israel. 24 When he saw one
of them being mistreated, he came to
his rescue and avenged the oppressed
man by striking down the Egyptian.
25 He assumed his brothers would understand that God would give them deliverance through him, but they did
not understand. 26 The next day he
showed up while they were fighting
and tried to reconcile them peacefully,
saying, 'Men, you are brothers. Why
are you mistreating each other?'
[a]Ex 2:11

27 "But the one [a]who was mistreating his neighbor pushed him[d] away,
saying:

**Who appointed you a ruler and a
judge over us? 28 Do you want to
kill me, the same way you killed
the Egyptian yesterday?**[e] *[a]Ex 2:14*

29 [a]"At this disclosure, Moses fled
and became an exile in the land of Mid-
ian, where he fathered two sons.
30 After 40 years had passed, [b]an angel[f]
appeared to him in the desert of Mount
Sinai, in the flame of a burning bush.
31 When Moses saw it, he was amazed
at the sight. As he was approaching to
look at it, the voice of the Lord came:
32 [c]**I am the God of your forefathers—the God of Abraham, of Isaac,
and of Jacob.**[g] So Moses began to tremble and did not dare to look.
[a]Ex 2:15 [b]Ex 3:2 [c]Ex 3:6,15

33 [a]"Then the Lord said to him:

**Take the sandals off your feet,
because the place where you are
standing is holy ground. 34 I have
certainly seen the oppression of
My people in Egypt; I have heard
their groaning and have come
down to rescue them. And now,
come, I will send you to Egypt.**[h]
[a]Ex 3:5,7-8,10

35 "This Moses, whom they rejected
when they said, **Who appointed you a
ruler and a judge?**[e] —this one God
sent as a ruler and a redeemer [a]by
means of the angel who appeared to
him in the bush. 36 [b]This man led them
out and performed wonders and signs
in the land of Egypt, at the Red Sea,
[c]and in the desert for 40 years.
[a]Ex 14:19; Nm 20:16 [b]Ex 12:41 [c]Ex 16:1

Israel's Rebellion against God

37 "This is the Moses who said to the
sons of Israel, **God**[i] **will raise up for
you [a]a Prophet like me from among
your brothers.**[j] 38 [b]He is the one who
was in the congregation in the desert
together with the angel who spoke to
him on Mount Sinai, and with our forefathers. [c]He received living oracles to
give to us. 39 Our forefathers were unwilling to obey him, but pushed him
away, and in their hearts turned back
to Egypt. 40 [d]They told Aaron:

**Make us gods who will go be-
fore us. As for this Moses who
brought us out of the land of**

[a]**7:18** Other mss omit *over Egypt* [b]**7:19** A common pagan practice of population control by leaving infants outside to die [c]**7:23** Lit *40, it came into his heart* [d]**7:27** Moses [e]**7:27–28,35** Ex 2:14 [f]**7:30** Other mss add *of the Lord* [g]**7:32** Ex 3:6,15 [h]**7:33–34** Ex 3:5,7–8,10 [i]**7:37** Other mss read *'The Lord your God* [j]**7:37** Dt 18:15

**Egypt, we don't know what's be-
come of him.**[a]

41 They even made a calf in those days,
offered sacrifice to the idol, and were
celebrating what their hands had
made. 42 Then [e]God turned away and
gave them up to worship the host of
heaven, as it is written in the book of
the prophets:

Did you bring Me offerings
and sacrifices
for 40 years in the desert,
[f]O house of Israel?
43 **No, you took up**
the tent of Moloch[b]
and the star of
your god Rephan,[c]
the images that you made
to worship.
So I will deport you
beyond Babylon![d]

[a] Dt 18:15 [b] Ex 19:3 [c] Ex 21:1 [d] Ex 32:1 [e] Ezk 20:25; Dt 17:3 [f] Am 5:25-27

God's Real Tabernacle

44 "Our forefathers had the tabernacle of the testimony in the desert, just
as He who spoke to Moses commanded
him [a]to make it according to the pattern he had seen. 45 [b]Our forefathers in
turn received it and with Joshua
brought it in when they dispossessed
the nations that God drove out before
our fathers, until the days of David.
46 [c]He found favor in God's sight and
[d]asked that he might provide a dwelling place for the God[e] of Jacob. 47 But it
was Solomon who built Him a house.
48 However, [e]the Most High does not
dwell in sanctuaries made with hands,
as the prophet says:

49 **[f]Heaven is My throne,**
and earth My footstool.
What sort of house
will you build for Me?
says the Lord,
or what is My resting place?
50 **Did not My hand make all**
these things?[f]

[a] Ex 25:40 [b] Jos 3:14 [c] 1Sm 15:28 [d] 1Kg 8:17 [e] 2Ch 2:6 [f] Is 66:1-2

Resisting the Holy Spirit

51 "You [a]stiff-necked people with
[b]uncircumcised hearts and ears! You
are always resisting the Holy Spirit;
as your forefathers did, so do you.
52 [c]Which of the prophets did your fathers not persecute? They even killed
those who announced beforehand the
coming of [d]the Righteous One, whose
betrayers and murderers you have
now become. 53 [e]You received the law
under the direction of angels and yet
have not kept it."

[a] Is 48:4 [b] Ezk 44:9 [c] 2Ch 36:16 [d] Ac 3:14 [e] Ex 20:1

The First Christian Martyr

54 When they heard these things,
they were enraged in their hearts[g] and
gnashed their teeth at him. 55 But
Stephen, filled by the Holy Spirit,
gazed into heaven. He saw God's glory,
with[h] Jesus standing at the right hand
of God, and he said, 56 "Look! [a]I see the
heavens opened and the [b]•Son of Man
standing at the right hand of God!"

[a] Mt 3:16 [b] Dn 7:13

57 Then they screamed at the top of
their voices, stopped their ears, and
rushed together against him. 58 They
threw him out of the city [a]and began to
stone him. And [b]the witnesses laid
their robes at the feet of a young man
named Saul. 59 They were stoning
Stephen as he called out: "Lord Jesus,
[c]receive my spirit!" 60 Then he knelt
down and cried out with a loud voice,
[d]"Lord, do not charge them with this
sin!" And saying this, he [e]fell •asleep.[i]

[a] Lv 24:16 [b] Dt 13:9 [c] Ps 31:5 [d] Mt 5:44 [e] 1Th 4:13

[a]**7:40** Ex 32:1,23 [b]**7:43** Canaanite or Phoenician sky or sun god [c]**7:43** Perhaps an Assyrian star god—the planet Saturn [d]**7:42–43** Am 5:25–27 [e]**7:46** Other mss read *house* [f]**7:49–50** Is 66:1–2 [g]**7:54** Or *were cut to the quick* [h]**7:55** Lit *and* [i]**7:60** He died; see Jn 11:11; 1 Co 11:30; 1 Th 4:13–15

Saul the Persecutor

8 [a]Saul agreed with putting him to death. *[a]Ac 7:58*

On that day a severe persecution broke out against the church in Jerusalem, and [a]all except the apostles were scattered throughout the land of Judea and Samaria. 2 But devout men buried Stephen and mourned deeply over him. 3 Saul, however, [b]was ravaging the church, and he would enter house after house, drag off men and women, and put them in prison. *[a]Ac 11:19 [b]1Co 15:9; Gl 1:13*

Philip in Samaria

4 So [a]those who were scattered went on their way proclaiming the message of good news. 5 [b]Philip went down to a[a] city in Samaria and preached the •Messiah to them. 6 The crowds paid attention with one mind to what Philip said, as they heard and saw the signs he was performing. 7 For unclean spirits, crying out with a loud voice, came out of many who were possessed, and many who were paralyzed and lame were healed. 8 So there was great joy in that city. *[a]Mt 10:23; Ac 11:19 [b]Ac 6:5*

The Response of Simon

9 A man named Simon had previously [a]practiced sorcery in that city and astounded the •Samaritan people, while claiming to be somebody great. 10 They all paid attention to him, from the least of them to the greatest, and they said, "This man is called the Great Power of God!"[b] 11 They were attentive to him because he had astounded them with his sorceries for a long time. 12 But when they believed Philip, as he proclaimed the good news [b]about the kingdom of God and the name of Jesus Christ, both men and women were baptized. 13 Then even Simon himself [c]believed. And after he was baptized, he went around constantly with[c] Philip and was astounded as he observed the signs and great miracles that were being performed. *[a]Ac 13:6 [b]Ac 1:3 [c]Lk 8:13*

Simon's Sin

14 When the apostles who were at Jerusalem heard that Samaria had welcomed God's message, they sent Peter and John to them. 15 After they went down there, they prayed for them, [a]that they might receive the Holy Spirit. 16 For He had not yet come down on[d] any of them; [b]they had only been baptized in the name of the Lord Jesus. 17 Then Peter and John [c]laid their hands on them, and they received the Holy Spirit. *[a]Mt 18:19; Jn 14:13-14 [b]Mt 28:19 [c]Ac 6:6*

18 When Simon saw that the Holy[e] Spirit was given through the laying on of the apostles' hands, he offered them money, 19 saying, "Give me this power too, so that anyone I lay hands on may receive the Holy Spirit."

20 But Peter told him, "May your silver be destroyed with you, because [a]you thought [b]the gift of God could be obtained with money! 21 You have no part or share in this matter, because your [c]heart is not right before God. 22 Therefore repent of this wickedness of yours, and pray to the Lord [d]that the intent of your heart may be forgiven you. 23 For I see you [e]are poisoned by bitterness and bound by iniquity." *[a]Mt 10:8 [b]Ac 2:38 [c]Pr 11:20; Jr 17:9 [d]Is 55:7 [e]Heb 12:15*

24 "Please [a]pray[f] to the Lord for me," Simon replied, "so that nothing you[f] have said may happen to me." *[a]Jms 5:16*

25 Then, after they had testified and spoken the message of the Lord, they traveled back to Jerusalem, evangelizing many villages of the Samaritans.

[a]**8:5** Other mss read *the* [b]**8:10** Or *This is the power of God called Great* [c]**8:13** Or *he kept close company with* [d]**8:16** Or *yet fallen on* [e]**8:18** Other mss omit *Holy* [f]**8:24** Gk words *you* and *pray* are plural

The Conversion of the Ethiopian Official

26 [a]An angel of the Lord spoke to
Philip: "Get up and go south to the
road that goes down from Jerusalem to
desert Gaza."[a] 27 So he got up and
went. There was an [b]Ethiopian man, a
eunuch and high official of Candace,
queen of the Ethiopians, who was in
charge of her entire treasury. [c]He had
come to worship in Jerusalem 28 and
was sitting in his chariot on his way
home, reading the prophet Isaiah
aloud.

[a]*Heb 1:14* [b]*Ps 68:31; Zph 3:10* [c]*Is 56:3-8*

29 The Spirit told Philip, "Go and join
that chariot."
30 When Philip ran up to it, he heard
him reading the prophet Isaiah, and
said, "Do you understand what you're
reading?"
31 "How can I," he said, "unless someone guides me?" So he invited Philip to
come up and sit with him. 32 Now the
Scripture passage he was reading was
this:

[a]He was led like a sheep
to the slaughter,
and as a lamb is silent
before its shearer,
so He does not open
His mouth.
33 **In His humiliation justice**
was denied Him.
Who will describe
His generation?
For His life is taken
from the earth.[b]

[a]*Is 53:7*

34 The eunuch replied to Philip, "I
ask you, who is the prophet saying this
about—himself or another person?"
35 So Philip proceeded[c] to tell him the
good news about Jesus, [a]beginning
from that Scripture.

[a]*Lk 24:27*

36 As they were traveling down the
road, they came to some water. The
eunuch said, "Look, there's water!
What would keep me from being baptized?" [37 And Philip said, [a]"If you believe with all your heart you may." And
he replied, [b]"I believe that Jesus Christ
is the Son of God."][d] 38 Then he ordered the chariot to stop, and both
Philip and the eunuch went down into
the water, and he baptized him.
39 When they came up out of the water,
the Spirit of the Lord carried Philip
away, and the eunuch did not see him
any longer. But he went on his way rejoicing. 40 Philip appeared in[e] Azotus,[f]
and passing through, he was evangelizing all the towns until he came to Caesarea.

[a]*Mt 28:19; Mk 16:16* [b]*Jn 6:69*

The Damascus Road

9 Meanwhile [a]Saul, still breathing
threats and murder against the
disciples of the Lord, went to the high
priest 2 and requested letters from him
to the •synagogues in Damascus, so
that if he found any who belonged to
the Way, either men or women, he
might bring them as prisoners to
Jerusalem. 3 [b]As he traveled and was
nearing Damascus, a light from
heaven suddenly flashed around him.
4 Falling to the ground, he heard a
voice saying to him, "Saul, Saul, [c]why
are you persecuting Me?"

[a]*Ac 8:3; Gl 1:13* [b]*Ac 22:6* [c]*Mt 25:40; 1Co 12:12*

5 "Who are You, Lord?" he said.
"I am Jesus, whom you are [a]perse-
cuting," He replied. 6 "But get up and
go into the city, and you will be told
what you [b]must do."

[a]*Ac 5:39* [b]*Ac 2:37*

7 [a]The men who were traveling with
him stood speechless, hearing the
sound but seeing no one. 8 Then Saul
got up from the ground, and though his

[a]**8:26** Perhaps old Gaza or the road near the desert [b]**8:32–33** Is 53:7–8 [c]**8:35** Lit *Philip opened his mouth* [d]**8:37** Other mss omit bracketed text [e]**8:40** Or *Philip was found at,* or *Philip found himself in* [f]**8:40** Or *Ashdod*

eyes were open, he could see nothing.
So they took him by the hand and led
him into Damascus. 9 He was unable to
see for three days, and did not eat or
drink. *[a] Ac 22:9*

Saul's Baptism

10 Now in Damascus there was a disciple named Ananias. And the Lord
said to him in a vision, "Ananias!"
"Here I am, Lord!" he said.
11 "Get up and go to the street called
Straight," the Lord said to him, "to the
house of Judas, and ask for a man [a]from
Tarsus named Saul, since he is praying
there. 12 In a vision[a] he has seen a man
named Ananias coming in and placing
his hands on him so he may regain his
sight." *[a] Ac 21:39*

13 "Lord," Ananias answered, "I
have heard from many people about
this man, how much harm he has done
to Your saints in Jerusalem. 14 And he
has authority here from the •chief
priests to arrest all who call on Your
name."
15 But the Lord said to him, "Go! For
[a]this man is My chosen instrument to
carry My name before [b]Gentiles,
[c]kings, and the sons of Israel. 16 [d]I will
certainly show him how much he
must suffer for My name!"
[a] Ac 13:2; 22:21; Rm 1:1 [b] Rm 1:5
[c] Ac 25:22 [d] 2Co 11:23

17 [a]So Ananias left and entered the
house. Then he placed his hands on
him and said, "Brother Saul, the Lord
Jesus, who appeared to you on the road
you were traveling, has sent me so you
may regain your sight and [b]be filled
with the Holy Spirit." *[a] Ac 22:12 [b] Ac 2:4*

18 At once something like scales fell
from his eyes, and he regained his
sight. Then he got up and was baptized. 19 And after taking some food, he
regained his strength.

Saul Proclaiming the Messiah

[a]Saul[b] was with the disciples in
Damascus for some days.
20 Immediately he began proclaiming
Jesus in the synagogues: "He is the Son
of God."
[a] Ac 26:20

21 But all who heard him were astounded and said, "Isn't this the man
who, in Jerusalem, was destroying
those who called on this name, and
then came here for the purpose of taking them as prisoners to the chief
priests?"
22 But Saul grew more capable, [a]and
kept confounding the Jews who lived
in Damascus by proving that this One
is the •Messiah. *[a] Ac 18:28*

23 After many days had passed, [a]the
Jews conspired to kill him, 24 but their
plot became known to Saul. So they
were watching the gates day and night
intending to kill him, 25 but his disciples took him by night and lowered
him in a large basket through ⌊an opening in⌋ the wall. *[a] Ac 23:12*

Saul in Jerusalem

26 [a]When he arrived in Jerusalem, he
tried to associate with the disciples,
but they were all afraid of him, since
they did not believe he was a disciple.
27 [b]Barnabas, however, took him and
brought him to the apostles and explained to them how, on the road, Saul[c]
had seen the Lord, and that He had
talked to him, and how in Damascus
he had spoken boldly in the name of
Jesus. 28 Saul[c] was coming and going
with them in Jerusalem, speaking
boldly in the name of the Lord. 29 He
conversed and debated with the Helle-
nistic Jews,[d] but they attempted to kill
him. 30 When the brothers found out,
they took him down to Caesarea and
sent him off to Tarsus.
[a] Ac 22:17; Gl 1:17 [b] Ac 4:36

[a]**9:12** Other mss omit *In a vision* [b]**9:19** Lit *He* [c]**9:27,28** Lit *he* [d]**9:29** Lit *Hellenists*; that is, Gk-speaking Jews

[31] So the church throughout all Judea, Galilee, and Samaria had peace, being built up and walking in the fear of the Lord and in the encouragement of the Holy Spirit, and it increased in numbers.

The Healing of Aeneas

[32] As Peter was traveling [a]from place to place,[a] he also came down to the saints[b] who lived in Lydda. [33] There he found a man named Aeneas, who was paralyzed and had been bedridden for eight years. [34] Peter said to him, "Aeneas, [b]Jesus Christ heals you. Get up and make your own bed,"[c] and immediately he got up. [35] So all who lived in Lydda and Sharon saw him and turned to the Lord.

[a] Ac 8:14 [b] Ac 3:6

Dorcas Restored to Life

[36] In Joppa there was a disciple named Tabitha, which is translated Dorcas.[d] She was always doing [a]good works and acts of charity. [37] In those days she became sick and died. After washing her, they placed her in a room upstairs. [38] Since Lydda was near Joppa, the disciples heard that Peter was there and sent two men to him who begged him, "Don't delay in coming with us." [39] So Peter got up and went with them. When he arrived, they led him to the room upstairs. And all the widows approached him, weeping and showing him the robes and clothes that Dorcas had made while she was with them. [40] Then Peter sent them all out of the room. He knelt down, prayed, and turning toward the body [b]said, "Tabitha, get up!" She opened her eyes, saw Peter, and sat up. [41] He gave her his hand and helped her stand up. Then he called the saints and widows and presented her alive. [42] This became known throughout all Joppa, and many believed in the Lord. [43] And Peter[e] stayed on many days in Joppa with [c]Simon, a leather tanner.[f]

[a] Pr 31:31; Jn 15:5,8 [b] Mk 5:41 [c] Ac 10:6

Cornelius' Vision

10 There was a man in Caesarea named Cornelius, a •centurion of what was called the Italian •Regiment. [2] He was a devout man and feared God along with his whole household. [a]He did many charitable deeds for the ⌊Jewish⌋ people and always prayed to God. [3] At about three in the afternoon[g] [b]he distinctly saw in a vision [c]an angel of God who came in and said to him, "Cornelius!"

[a] Jos 24:15 [b] Ac 11:13 [c] Heb 1:14

[4] Looking intently at him, he became afraid and said, "What is it, Lord?"

And he told him, [a]"Your prayers and your acts of charity have come up as a memorial offering before God. [5] Now send men to Joppa and call for Simon, who is also named Peter. [6] He is lodging with [b]Simon, a tanner, whose house is by the sea."

[a] Pr 15:8,29; 1Pt 3:12 [b] Ac 9:43

[7] When the angel who spoke to him had gone, he called two of his household slaves and a devout soldier, who was one of those who attended him. [8] After explaining everything to them, he sent them to Joppa.

Peter's Vision

[9] The next day, as they were traveling and nearing the city, Peter went up to pray on the housetop at about [a]noon.[h] [10] Then he became hungry and wanted to eat, but while they were preparing something he went into a visionary state. [11] He saw heaven opened and an object coming down that resembled a large sheet being lowered to the earth by its four corners. [12] In it were all the four-footed animals and reptiles of the earth, and the birds of

[a]**9:32** Lit *Peter was passing through all* [b]**9:32** The believers [c]**9:34** Or *and get ready to eat* [d]**9:36** *Dorcas* = Gazelle [e]**9:43** Lit *he* [f]**9:43** Tanners were considered ritually unclean because of their occupation. [g]**10:3** Lit *about the ninth hour* [h]**10:9** Lit *about the sixth hour*

the sky. 13 Then a voice said to him, "Get up, Peter; kill and eat!" *[a]Ps 55:17*

14 "No, Lord!" Peter said. [a]"For I have never eaten anything common[a] and unclean!" *[a]Lv 11:4; Dt 14:3*

15 Again, a second time, a voice said to him, [a]"What God has made clean, you must not call common." 16 This happened three times, and then the object was taken up into heaven. *[a]Mt 15:11; 1Tm 4:4; Ti 1:15*

Peter Visits Cornelius

17 While Peter was deeply perplexed about what the vision he had seen might mean, the men who had been sent by Cornelius, having asked directions to Simon's house, stood at the gate. 18 They called out, asking if Simon, who was also named Peter, was lodging there.

19 While Peter was thinking about the vision, the Spirit told him, [a]"Three men are here looking for you. 20 [b]Get up, go downstairs, and accompany them with no doubts at all, because I have sent them." *[a]Ac 8:29* *[b]Mt 28:19; Ac 15:7*

21 Then Peter went down to the men and said, "Here I am, the one you're looking for. What is the reason you're here?"

22 They said, "Cornelius, a centurion, an upright and God-fearing man, who has a good reputation with the whole Jewish nation, was divinely directed by a holy angel to call you to his house and to hear a message from you." 23 Peter[b] then invited them in and gave them lodging.

The next day he got up and set out with them, and some of the brothers from Joppa went with him. 24 The following day he entered Caesarea. Now Cornelius was expecting them and had called together his relatives and close friends. 25 When Peter entered, Cornelius met him, fell at his feet, and worshiped him.

26 But Peter helped him up and said, "Stand up! I myself am also a man." 27 While talking with him, he went on in and found that many had come together there. 28 Peter[b] said to them, "You know [a]it's forbidden for a Jewish man to associate with or visit a foreigner. But [b]God has shown me that I must not call any person common or unclean. 29 That's why I came without any objection when I was sent for. So I ask, 'Why did you send for me?'" *[a]Jn 4:9; Gl 2:12 [b]Ac 15:8*

30 Cornelius replied, "Four days ago at this hour, at three in the afternoon,[c] I was[d] praying in my house. Just then a man in a dazzling robe stood before me 31 and said, 'Cornelius, your prayer has been heard, and your acts of charity have been remembered in God's sight. 32 Therefore send someone to Joppa and invite Simon here, who is also named Peter. He is lodging in Simon the tanner's house by the sea.'[e] 33 Therefore I immediately sent for you, and you did the right thing in coming. So we are all present before God, to hear everything you have been commanded by the Lord."

Good News for Gentiles

34 Then Peter began to speak: [a]"In truth, I understand that God doesn't show favoritism, 35 but [b]in every nation the person who fears Him and does righteousness is acceptable to Him. 36 He sent the message to the sons of Israel, [c]proclaiming the good news of peace through Jesus Christ—[d]He is Lord of all. 37 You know the events[f] that took place throughout all Judea, beginning from Galilee after the

[a]**10:14** Perhaps *profane*, or *non-sacred*; Jews ate distinctive food according to OT law and their traditions, similar to modern kosher or non-kosher foods. [b]**10:23,28** Lit *He* [c]**10:30** Lit *at the ninth hour*
[d]**10:30** Other mss add *fasting and* [e]**10:32** Other mss add *When he arrives, he will speak to you.*
[f]**10:37** Lit *thing*, or *word*

baptism that John preached: 38 how
[e]God anointed Jesus of Nazareth with
the Holy Spirit and with power, and
how He went about doing good and
curing all who were under the tyranny
of the Devil, [f]because God was with
Him. 39 We ourselves are witnesses of
everything He did in both the Judean
country and in Jerusalem; yet they
killed Him by hanging Him on a tree.
40 God raised up this man on the third
day and permitted Him to be seen,
41 [g]not by all the people, but by us, witnesses appointed beforehand by God,
[h]who ate and drank with Him after He
rose from the dead. 42 [i]He commanded
us to preach to the people, and to solemnly testify [j]that He is the One appointed by God to be the Judge [k]of the
living and the dead. 43 [l]All the prophets
testify about Him that through His
name everyone who believes in Him
will receive forgiveness of sins."

[a] Dt 10:17 [b] Ac 15:9; 1Co 12:13 [c] Is 57:19; Eph 2:17 [d] Mt 28:18; Rm 10:12 [e] Lk 4:18 [f] Jn 1:1-18 [g] Jn 14:17 [h] Jn 21:13 [i] Mt 28:19 [j] Jn 5:22 [k] Rm 14:9 [l] Is 53:11; Zch 13:1; Mal 4:2

Gentile Conversion and Baptism

44 While Peter was still speaking
these words, the Holy Spirit came
down on all those who heard the message. 45 The circumcised believers[a]
who had come with Peter were astounded, because the gift of the Holy
Spirit had been poured out on the Gentiles also. 46 For they heard them speaking in ⌊other⌋ languages and declaring
the greatness of[b] God.

Then Peter responded, 47 "Can anyone withhold water and prevent these
from being baptized, who have received the Holy Spirit just as we
have?" 48 And he commanded them to
be baptized in the name of Jesus
Christ. Then they asked him to stay for
a few days.

Gentile Salvation Defended

11 The apostles and the brothers
who were throughout Judea
heard that the [a]Gentiles had welcomed God's message also. 2 When Peter went up to Jerusalem, [b]those who
stressed circumcision[c] argued with
him, 3 saying, [c]"You visited uncircumcised men and ate with them!"

[a] Zch 2:11; Ac 14:27; 15:3 [b] Gl 2:12 [c] Ac 10:28

4 Peter began to explain to them in
an orderly sequence, saying: 5 [a]"I was
in the town of Joppa praying, and I
saw, in a visionary state, an object
coming down that resembled a large
sheet being lowered from heaven by
its four corners, and it came to me.
6 When I looked closely and considered it, I saw the four-footed animals
of the earth, the wild beasts, the reptiles, and the birds of the sky. 7 Then I
also heard a voice telling me, 'Get up,
Peter; kill and eat!' *[a] Ac 10:9*

8 [a]" 'No, Lord!' I said. 'For nothing
common or unclean has ever entered
my mouth!' 9 But a voice answered
from heaven a second time, 'What God
has made clean, you must not call common.' *[a] Ezk 4:14*

10 "Now this happened three times,
and then everything was drawn up
again into heaven. 11 At that very moment, three men who had been sent to
me from Caesarea arrived at the house
where we were. 12 Then [a]the Spirit
told me to go with them with no
doubts at all. [b]These six brothers accompanied me, and we went into the
man's house. 13 [c]He reported to us how
he had seen the angel standing in his
house and saying, 'Send[d] to Joppa, and
call for Simon, who is also named Peter. 14 He will speak words[e] to you by
which you and all your household will
be saved.' *[a] Jn 16:13; Ac 15:7*

[b] Ac 10:23 [c] Ac 10:30

[a]**10:45** Jewish Christians who stressed circumcision; Ac 11:2; 15:5; Gl 2:12; Col 4:11; Ti 1:10 [b]**10:46** Or *and magnifying* [c]**11:2** Lit *those of the circumcision* [d]**11:13** Other mss add *men* [e]**11:14** Or *speak a message*

15 "As I began to speak, the Holy
Spirit came down on them, [a]just as on
us at the beginning. 16 Then I remembered the word of the Lord, how He
said, [b]'John baptized with water, but
[c]you will be baptized with the Holy
Spirit.' 17 [d]Therefore, if God gave them
the same gift that He also gave to us
when we believed on the Lord Jesus
Christ, [e]how could I possibly hinder
God?"

[a] *Ac 2:4* [b] *Mt 3:11* [c] *Jl 2:28* [d] *Ac 15:8-9* [e] *Ac 10:47*

18 When they heard this they became silent. Then they glorified God,
saying, [a]"So God has granted repentance resulting in life[a] to even the Gentiles!"

[a] *Rm 10:12*

The Church in Antioch

19 [a]Those who had been scattered as
a result of the persecution that started
because of Stephen made their way as
far as Phoenicia, Cyprus, and Antioch,
speaking the message to no one except
Jews. 20 But there were some of them,
Cypriot and Cyrenian men, who came
to Antioch and began speaking to the
Hellenists,[b] [c] proclaiming the good
news about the Lord Jesus. 21 The
Lord's hand was with them, and a large
number who believed [b]turned to the
Lord. 22 Then the report about them
reached the ears of the church in Jerusalem, and they sent out [c]Barnabas to
travel[d] as far as Antioch. 23 When he arrived and saw the grace of God, he was
glad, and he [d]encouraged all of them
[e]to remain true to the Lord with a firm
resolve of the heart— 24 for he was a
good man, full of the Holy Spirit and of
faith—and large numbers of people
were added to the Lord. 25 Then he[e]
went [f]to Tarsus to search for Saul,
26 and when he found him he brought
him to Antioch. For a whole year they
met with the church and taught large
numbers, and the disciples were first
called Christians in Antioch.

[a] *Ac 8:1* [b] *Ac 9:35* [c] *Ac 9:27* [d] *Ac 13:43* [e] *1Co 15:58* [f] *Ac 9:30*

Famine Relief

27 In those days some [a]prophets
came down from Jerusalem to Antioch.
28 Then one of them, named [b]Agabus,
stood up and predicted by the Spirit
that there would be a severe famine
throughout the Roman world.[f] This
took place during the time of Claudius.[g] 29 So each of the disciples, according to his ability, determined to
send [c]relief to the brothers who lived
in Judea. 30 This they did, sending it to
the elders by means of Barnabas and
Saul.

[a] *1Co 12:28* [b] *Ac 21:10* [c] *Rm 15:26; 1Co 16:1*

James Martyred and Peter Jailed

12 About that time King •Herod
[a]cruelly attacked some who belonged to the church, 2 and he killed
James, [b]John's brother, with the
sword. 3 When he saw that it pleased
the Jews, he proceeded to arrest Peter
too, during [c]the days of •Unleavened
Bread. 4 [d]After the arrest, he put him
in prison and assigned four squads of
four soldiers each to guard him, intending to bring him out to the people
after the •Passover. 5 So Peter was kept
in prison, but prayer was being made
earnestly to God for him by the
church.

[a] *Jn 15:20-21* [b] *Mt 4:21* [c] *Ex 12:14-15* [d] *Jn 21:18*

Peter Rescued

6 On the night before Herod was to
bring him out ⌊for execution⌋, Peter
was sleeping between two soldiers,
bound with two chains, while the sen-
tries in front of the door guarded the
prison. 7 Suddenly [a]an angel of the
Lord appeared, and a light shone in

[a]**11:18** Or *repentance to life* [b]**11:20** Other mss read *Greeks* [c]**11:20** In this context, a non-Jewish person who spoke Gk [d]**11:22** Other mss omit *to travel* [e]**11:25** Other mss read *Barnabas* [f]**11:28** Or *the whole world* [g]**11:28** Emperor A.D. 41–54; there was a famine A.D. 47–48.

the cell. Striking Peter on the side, he
woke him up and said, "Quick, get
up!" Then the chains fell off his wrists.
8 "Get dressed," the angel told him,
"and put on your sandals." And he did
so. "Wrap your cloak around you," he
told him, "and follow me." 9 So he
went out and followed, and he did not
know that what took place through the
angel was real, but thought he was seeing a vision. 10 After they passed the
first and second guard posts, they came
to the iron gate that leads into the city,
[b]which opened to them by itself. They
went outside and passed one street,
and immediately the angel left him.

[a]Ac 5:19 [b]Ac 16:26

11 Then Peter came to himself and
said, "Now I know for certain that [a]the
Lord has sent His angel and [b]rescued
me from Herod's grasp and from all
that the Jewish people expected."
12 When he realized this, he went to
the house of Mary, the mother of [c]John
Mark,[a] where many had assembled
and were praying. 13 He knocked at the
door in the gateway, and a servant
named Rhoda came to answer. 14 She
recognized Peter's voice, and because
of her joy she did not open the gate,
but ran in and announced that Peter
was standing at the gateway.

[a]Ps 34:7 [b]2Pt 2:9 [c]Ac 13:5; 2Tm 4:11

15 "You're crazy!" they told her. But
she kept insisting that it was true.
Then they said, "It's his angel!"
16 Peter, however, kept on knocking,
and when they opened the door and
saw him, they were astounded.
17 Motioning to them with his hand
to be silent, he explained to them how
the Lord had brought him out of the
prison. "Report these things to James[b]
and the brothers," he said. Then he departed and went to a different place.
18 At daylight, there was a great com-
motion[c] among the soldiers as to what
could have become of Peter. 19 After
Herod had searched and did not find
him, he interrogated the guards and
ordered their execution. Then Herod
went down from Judea to Caesarea and
stayed there.

Herod's Death

20 He had been very angry with the
Tyrians and Sidonians.[d] Together they
presented themselves before him, and
having won over Blastus, who was in
charge of the king's bedroom, they
asked for peace, because [a]their country was supplied with food from the
king's country. 21 So on an appointed
day, dressed in royal robes and seated
on the throne, Herod delivered a public address to them. 22 The populace began to shout, [b]"It's the voice of a god
and not of a man!" 23 At once an angel
of the Lord [c]struck him because [d]he
did not give the glory to God, and he
became infected with worms and died.
24 Then [e]God's message flourished and
multiplied. 25 And Barnabas and Saul
returned to[e] Jerusalem after they had
completed their relief mission, [f]on
which they took John Mark.[a]

[a]Ezk 27:17 [b]Jd 16 [c]Dn 4:30-37 [d]Dt 28:58-59 [e]Is 55:11; Ac 6:7 [f]Ac 15:37

Preparing for the Mission Field

13 [a]In the local church at Antioch
there were prophets and teachers: [b]Barnabas, Simeon who was called
Niger, [c]Lucius the Cyrenian, Manaen,
a close friend of •Herod the tetrarch,
and Saul.

[a]Ac 14:26 [b]Ac 9:27 [c]Rm 16:21

2 As they were ministering to[f] the
Lord and fasting, the Holy Spirit said,
[a]"Set apart for Me Barnabas and Saul
for the work that [b]I have called them
to." 3 Then, after they had fasted,
prayed, and laid hands on them,[g] they
sent them off.

[a]Gl 1:15 [b]Eph 3:7-8

[a]**12:12,25** Lit *John who was called Mark* [b]**12:17** This was James, the Lord's brother; see Mk 6:3. This was not James the apostle; see Ac 12:2. [c]**12:18** Or *was no small disturbance* [d]**12:20** The people of the area of modern Lebanon [e]**12:25** Other mss read *from* [f]**13:2** Or *were worshiping* [g]**13:3** See note at Ac 6:6

The Mission to Cyprus

4 Being sent out by the Holy Spirit,
they came down to Seleucia, and from
there they sailed to [a]Cyprus. 5 Arriving
in Salamis, they proclaimed God's message in the Jewish •synagogues. They
also had [b]John as their assistant.
6 When they had gone through the
whole island as far as Paphos, they
came across a sorcerer, a Jewish false
prophet named Bar-Jesus. 7 He was
with the •proconsul, Sergius Paulus, an
intelligent man. This man summoned
Barnabas and Saul and desired to hear
God's message. 8 But [c]Elymas, the sorcerer, which is how his name is translated, opposed them and tried to turn
the proconsul away from the faith.

[a]Ac 4:36 [b]Ac 12:25 [c]2Tm 3:8

9 Then Saul—also called Paul—filled
with the Holy Spirit, stared straight at
the sorcerer[a] 10 and said, [a]"You son of
the Devil, full of all deceit and all fraud,
enemy of all righteousness! Won't you
ever stop perverting the straight paths
of the Lord? 11 Now, look! The Lord's
hand is against you: you are going to be
blind, and will not see the sun for a
time." Suddenly a mist and darkness
fell on him, and he went around seeking someone to lead him by the hand.

[a]Jn 8:44

12 Then the proconsul, seeing what
happened, believed and was astonished at the teaching about the Lord.

Paul's Sermon in Antioch of Pisidia

13 Paul and his companions set sail
from Paphos and came to Perga in
Pamphylia. [a]John, however, left them
and went back to Jerusalem. 14 They
continued their journey from Perga
and reached Antioch in Pisidia. On the
Sabbath day they went into the synagogue and sat down. 15 [b]After the reading of the Law and the Prophets, the
leaders of the synagogue sent ⌊word⌋ to
them, saying, "Brothers, if you have
any message of encouragement for the
people, you can speak."

[a]Ac 15:38
[b]Lk 4:16

16 Then standing up, Paul motioned
with his hand and spoke: "Men of Israel, and you who fear God, listen!
17 The God of this people Israel chose
our forefathers, exalted the people during their stay in the land of Egypt, and
led them out of it with a mighty[b] arm.
18 And for about 40 years [a]He put up
with them[c] in the desert; 19 then after
destroying seven nations in the land of
Canaan, He gave their land to them as
an inheritance. 20 This all took about
450 years. After this, He gave them
judges until Samuel the prophet.
21 Then they asked for a king, so God
gave them Saul the son of Kish, a man
of the tribe of Benjamin, for 40 years.
22 [b]After removing him, He raised up
David as their king, of whom He testified: [c]'**I have found David** the son of
Jesse, **a man after My heart,**[d] who will
carry out all My will.'

[a]Dt 1:31; Is 63:9 [b]Hos 13:11
[c]1Sm 13:14; Ps 89:20

23 [a]"From this man's descendants,
according [b]to the promise, God
brought [c]the Savior, Jesus,[e] to Israel.
24 Before He came to public attention,[f]
John had previously proclaimed a baptism of repentance to all the people of
Israel. 25 Then as John was completing
his life work, he said, 'Who do you
think I am? I am not the One. But look!
Someone is coming after me, and I am
not worthy to untie the sandals on His
feet.'

[a]Ps 132:11 [b]2Sm 7:12 [c]Rm 11:26

26 "Brothers, sons of Abraham's race,
and those among you who fear God,
the message of this salvation has been
sent to us. 27 For the residents of Jerusalem and their rulers, [a]since they did

[a]**13:9** Lit *at him* [b]**13:17** Lit *with an uplifted* [c]**13:18** Other mss read *He cared for them* [d]**13:22** 1 Sm 13:14; Ps 89:20 [e]**13:23** Other mss read *brought salvation* [f]**13:24** Lit *Before the face of His entrance*

not recognize Him or the voices of the
prophets that are read every Sabbath,
have fulfilled their words[a] by con-
demning Him. 28 Though they found
no grounds for the death penalty, they
asked •Pilate to have Him killed.
29 When they had fulfilled all that had
been written about Him, they took
Him down from the tree and put Him
in a tomb. 30 [b]But God raised Him from
the dead, 31 and [c]He appeared for many
days to those who came up with Him
from Galilee to Jerusalem, who are
now His witnesses to the people.
32 And we ourselves proclaim to you
the good news of [d]the promise that
was made to our forefathers. 33 God
has fulfilled this to us their children by
raising up Jesus, as it is written in the
second Psalm:

> [e]**You are My Son;**
> **today I have become**
> **Your Father.**[b c]

[a] 1Co 2:8
[b] Mt 28:6 [c] 1Co 15:5
[d] Gn 3:15; 12:3 [e] Ps 2:7

34 Since He raised Him from the dead,
never to return to decay, He has spoken in this way, [a]**I will grant you the**
faithful covenant blessings[d] **made to**
David.[e] 35 Therefore He also says in another passage, [b]**You will not allow**
Your Holy One to see decay.[f] 36 For
David, after serving his own generation
in God's plan, fell •asleep, was buried
with his fathers, and decayed. 37 But
the One whom God raised up did not
decay. 38 Therefore, let it be known to
you, brothers, that [c]through this man
forgiveness of sins is being proclaimed
to you, 39 and [d]everyone who believes
in Him is justified from everything,
which you could not be justified from
through the law of Moses. 40 So beware
that what is said in [e]the prophets does
not happen to you:

> 41 **Look, you scoffers,**
> **marvel and vanish away,**
> **because I am doing a work**
> **in your days,**
> **a work that you will**
> **never believe,**
> **even if someone were**
> **to explain it to you."**[g]

[a] Is 55:3
[b] Ps 16:10 [c] Zch 13:1; Lk 24:47
[d] Is 53:11; 1Co 6:11 [e] Hab 1:5

Paul and Barnabas in Antioch

42 As they[h] were leaving, they[i j]
begged that these matters be presented to them the following Sabbath.
43 After the synagogue had been dismissed, many of the Jews and devout
•proselytes followed Paul and Barnabas, who were speaking with them
and persuading them to continue in
[a]the grace of God.

[a] Ac 11:23

44 The following Sabbath almost the
whole town assembled to hear the message of the Lord.[k] 45 But when the Jews
saw the crowds, they were filled with
jealousy and [a]began to oppose what
Paul was saying by insulting him.

[a] Jd 10

46 Then Paul and Barnabas boldly
said: [a]"It was necessary that God's
message be spoken to you first. But
[b]since you reject it, and consider yourselves unworthy of eternal life, we
now turn to the Gentiles! 47 For this is
what the Lord has commanded us:

> [c]**I have appointed you as a light**
> **for the Gentiles,**
> **to bring salvation to the ends**[l]
> **of the earth."**[m]

48 When the Gentiles heard this, they
rejoiced and glorified the message of
the Lord, [d]and all who had been appointed to eternal life believed. 49 So
the message of the Lord spread through

[a]**13:27** Lit *fulfilled them* [b]**13:33** Or *I have begotten You* [c]**13:33** Ps 2:7 [d]**13:34** Lit *faithful holy things* [e]**13:34** Is 55:3 [f]**13:35** Ps 16:10 [g]**13:41** Hab 1:5 [h]**13:42** Paul and Barnabas [i]**13:42** Other mss read *they were leaving the synagogue of the Jews, the Gentiles* [j]**13:42** The people [k]**13:44** Other mss read *of God* [l]**13:47** Lit *the end* [m]**13:47** Is 49:6

the whole region. 50 But the Jews in-
cited the religious women of high
standing and the leading men of the
city. They [e]stirred up persecution
against Paul and Barnabas and expelled
them from their district. 51 [f]But shaking
the dust off their feet against them,
they proceeded to Iconium. 52 And the
disciples [g]were filled with joy and the
Holy Spirit. *[a]Mt 10:6; Rm 1:16 [b]Mt 21:43 [c]Is 42:6; 49:6; Lk 2:32 [d]Rm 8:30 [e]2Tm 3:11 [f]Lk 9:5 [g]Mt 5:12; Ac 2:46*

Growth and Persecution in Iconium

14 The same thing happened in
Iconium; they entered the Jewish •synagogue and spoke in such a
way that a great number of both Jews
and Greeks believed. 2 But the Jews
who refused to believe stirred up and
poisoned the minds[a] of the Gentiles
against the brothers. 3 So they stayed
there for some time and spoke boldly,
in reliance on the Lord, [a]who testified
to the message of His grace by grant-
ing that signs and wonders be performed through them. 4 But the people
of the city were divided, some siding
with the Jews and some with the
apostles. 5 When an attempt was made
by both the Gentiles and Jews, with
their rulers, [b]to assault and stone
them, 6 they found out about it and
[c]fled to the Lycaonian towns called
Lystra and Derbe, and to the surrounding countryside. 7 And there
they kept evangelizing. *[a]Mk 16:20; Rm 15:19 [b]2Tm 3:11 [c]Mt 10:23; Ac 16:1-2*

Mistaken for Gods in Lystra

8 In Lystra a man without strength in
his feet, lame from birth,[b] and who had
never walked, sat 9 and heard Paul
speaking. After observing him closely
and seeing that he had faith to be
healed, 10 ⌊Paul⌋ said in a loud voice,
[a]"Stand up straight on your feet!" And
he jumped up and started to walk
around. *[a]Is 35:6*

11 When the crowds saw what Paul
had done, they raised their voices, saying in the Lycaonian language, "The
gods have come down to us in the form
of men!" 12 And they started to call
Barnabas, Zeus, and Paul, Hermes, because he was the main speaker. 13 Then
the priest of Zeus, whose temple was
just outside the town, brought oxen
and garlands to the gates. He, with the
crowds, intended to offer sacrifice.
14 The apostles Barnabas and Paul
tore their robes when they heard this
and rushed into the crowd, shouting:
15 "Men! Why are you doing these
things? [a]We are men also, with the
same nature as you, and we are proclaiming good news to you, that you
should turn from these [b]worthless
things [c]to the living God, [d]**who made
the heaven, the earth, the sea, and
everything in them.**[c] 16 [e]In past generations He allowed all the nations to go
their own way, 17 [f]although He did not
leave Himself without a witness, since
He did good: [g]giving you rain from
heaven and fruitful seasons, and satis-
fying your[d] hearts with food and happi-
ness." 18 Even though they said these
things, they barely stopped the crowds
from sacrificing to them. *[a]Rv 19:10 [b]1Co 8:4 [c]1Th 1:9; Rv 14:7 [d]Ex 20:1; Ps 146:6 [e]1Pt 4:3 [f]Rm 1:20 [g]Mt 5:45*

19 [a]Then some Jews came from Antioch and Iconium, and when they had
won over the crowds [b]and stoned Paul,
they dragged him out of the city, thinking [c]he was dead. 20 After the disciples
surrounded him, he got up and went
into the town. The next day he left
with Barnabas for Derbe. *[a]Ac 13:45 [b]2Co 11:25 [c]2Co 1:8*

[a]**14:2** Lit *and harmed the souls* [b]**14:8** Lit *from his mother's womb* [c]**14:15** Ex 20:11; Ps 146:6
[d]**14:17** Other mss read *our*

Church Planting

21 After they had evangelized that
town and made many disciples, they
returned to Lystra, to Iconium, and to
Antioch, 22 strengthening the hearts[a] of
the disciples by encouraging them to
continue in the faith, and by telling
them, [a]"It is necessary to pass through
many troubles on our way into the
kingdom of God." *[a] Mt 10:38*

23 When they had appointed elders in
every church and prayed with fasting,
they committed them to the Lord in
whom they had believed. 24 Then they
passed through Pisidia and came to
Pamphylia. 25 After they spoke the message in Perga, they went down to Atta-
lia. 26 From there they sailed back to
Antioch [a]where they had been entrusted to the grace of God for the work
they had completed. 27 After they arrived and gathered the church together,
they reported everything God had done
with them, and that He had [b]opened
the door of faith to the Gentiles. 28 And
they spent a considerable time[b] with
the disciples. *[a] Ac 13:1-3 [b] 1Co 16:9*

Dispute in Antioch

15 [a]Some men came down from
Judea and began to teach the
brothers: "Unless you are circumcised
[b]according to the custom prescribed
by Moses, you cannot be saved!" 2 But
after [c]Paul and Barnabas had engaged
them in serious argument and debate,
they arranged for Paul and Barnabas
and some others of them to go up to
the apostles and elders in Jerusalem
concerning this controversy. 3 When
they had been sent on their way by
the church, they passed through both
Phoenicia and Samaria, [d]explaining in
detail the conversion of the Gentiles,
and they created great joy among all
the brothers. *[a] Gl 2:12 [b] Jn 7:22*
[c] Gl 2:1 [d] Ac 14:27

4 When they arrived at Jerusalem,
they were welcomed by the church,
the apostles, and the elders, and they
reported all that God had done with
them. 5 But some of the believers from
the party of the •Pharisees stood up
and said, "It is necessary to circumcise
them and to command them to keep
the law of Moses!"

The Jerusalem Council

6 Then the apostles and the elders assembled to consider this matter. 7 After
there had been much debate, Peter
stood up and said to them: "Brothers,
you are aware that in the early days
God made a choice among you,[c] that
by my mouth the Gentiles would hear
the gospel message and believe. 8 And
God, [a]who knows the heart, testified
to them [b]by giving[d] the Holy Spirit,
just as He also did to us. 9 [c]He made
no distinction between us and them,
[d]cleansing their hearts by faith. 10 Why,
then, are you now testing God [e]by putting on the disciples' necks a yoke that
neither our forefathers nor we have
been able to bear? 11 On the contrary,
[f]we believe we are saved through the
grace of the Lord Jesus, in the same
way they are." *[a] Ac 1:24 [b] Ac 10:44*
[c] Rm 10:11 [d] Ac 10:43; Rm 8:1
[e] Mt 23:4; Gl 5:1 [f] Is 53:11; Mt 20:28; Rm 3:24

12 Then the whole assembly fell silent and listened to Barnabas and Paul
describing all the signs and wonders
God had done through them among
the Gentiles. 13 After they stopped
speaking, [a]James responded: "Brothers, listen to me! 14 Simeon[e] has reported how God first intervened to
take from the Gentiles a people for His
name. 15 And the words of the prophets agree with this, as it is written:

16 [b]**After these things I will return**
and will rebuild David's tent,
which has fallen down.

[a]**14:22** Lit *souls* [b]**14:28** Or *spent no little time* [c]**15:7** Other mss read *us* [d]**15:8** Other mss add *them*
[e]**15:14** Simon (Peter)

I will rebuild its ruins
and will set it up again,
17 so that those who are left
of mankind
may seek the Lord—
even all the Gentiles
who are called by My name,
says the Lord who does
these things,
18 which have been known
from long ago.[a] [b]

19 Therefore, in my judgment, we
should not cause difficulties for those
who [c]turn to God from among the
Gentiles, 20 but instead we should
write to them to abstain [d]from things
polluted by idols, [e]from sexual immorality, from eating anything that has
been strangled, and [f]from blood. 21 For
since ancient times, Moses has had in
every city those who proclaim him,
and [g]he is read aloud in the •syna-
gogues every Sabbath day."

a Ac 12:17 b Is 54:1-5; Hos 3:5; Am 9:11; Mc 5:2 c 1Th 1:9 d Ex 20:3 e 1Co 6:9 f Lv 3:17 g Ac 13:15

The Letter to the Gentile Believers

22 Then the apostles and the elders,
with the whole church, decided to select men from among them and to
send them to Antioch with Paul and
Barnabas: Judas, called [a]Barsabbas, and
Silas, both leading men among the
brothers. 23 They wrote this letter to be
delivered by them:[c]

From the apostles and the elders,
your brothers,
To the brothers from among the
Gentiles in Antioch, Syria, and Cilicia:
Greetings.
24 Because we have heard that
[b]some to whom we gave no autho-
rization went out from us and
troubled you with their words and
unsettled your hearts,[d] 25 we have
unanimously decided to select
men and send them to you along
with our beloved Barnabas and
Paul, 26 [c]who have risked their
lives for the name of our Lord
Jesus Christ. 27 Therefore we have
sent Judas and Silas, who will personally report the same things by
word of mouth.[e] 28 For it was [d]the
Holy Spirit's decision—and ours—
to put no greater burden on you
than these necessary things:
29 [e]that you abstain from food offered to idols, [f]from blood, from
eating anything that has been
strangled, and from sexual immorality. If you keep yourselves from
these things, you will do well.
Farewell.

a Ac 1:23 b Gl 2:4; Ti 1:10 c Ac 13:50 d Jn 16:13 e Ac 21:25 f Lv 17:14

The Outcome of the Jerusalem Letter

30 Then, being sent off, they went
down to Antioch, and after gathering
the assembly, they delivered the letter.
31 When they read it, they rejoiced because of its encouragement. 32 Both Judas and Silas, who were also [a]prophets
themselves, [b]encouraged the brothers
and strengthened them with a long
message. 33 After spending some time
there, they were sent back in peace by
the brothers to those who had sent
them.[f] [g] 35 But [c]Paul and Barnabas,
along with many others, remained in
Antioch teaching and proclaiming the
message of the Lord.

a 1Co 12:2[illegible] b Ac 14:22 c Ac 13:[illegible]

Paul and Barnabas Part Company

36 After some time had passed, Paul
said to Barnabas, "Let's go back and visit
the brothers [a]in every town where we
have preached the message of the Lord,

[a] **15:17–18** Other mss read *says the Lord who does all these things. Known to God from long ago are all His works.* [b] **15:16–18** Am 9:11–12; Is 45:21 [c] **15:23** Lit *Writing by their hand:* [d] **15:24** Other mss add *by saying, "Be circumcised and keep the law,"* [e] **15:27** Lit *things through word* [f] **15:33** Other mss read *the brothers to the apostles* [g] **15:33** Other mss add v. 34: *But Silas decided to stay there.*

and see how they're doing." 37 Barnabas
wanted to take along [b]John Mark.[a]
38 But Paul did not think it appropriate
to take along this man [c]who had deserted them in Pamphylia and had not
gone on with them to the work.
39 There was such a sharp disagreement
that they parted company, and Barnabas
took Mark with him and sailed off to Cyprus. 40 Then Paul chose Silas and departed, after being commended to the
grace of the Lord by the brothers. 41 He
traveled through Syria and Cilicia,
strengthening the churches.

[a] Ac 14:1 [b] Ac 12:12; Col 4:10; 2Tm 4:11 [c] Ac 13:13

Paul Selects Timothy

16 Then he went on to [a]Derbe and
Lystra, where there was a disciple named [b]Timothy, the son of a believing Jewish woman, but his father
was a Greek. 2 The brothers at Lystra
and Iconium [c]spoke highly of him.
3 Paul wanted Timothy[b] to go with
him, so he [d]took him and circumcised
him because of the Jews who were in
those places, since they all knew that
his father was a Greek. 4 As they traveled through the towns, they delivered the decisions [e]reached by the
apostles and elders at Jerusalem for
them to observe. 5 [f]So the churches
were strengthened in the faith and
were increased in number daily.

[a] Ac 14:6 [b] Ac 19:22; Rm 16:21; 1Co 4:17 [c] 2Tm 3:15 [d] 1Co 9:20 [e] Ac 15:28 [f] Ac 15:41

Evangelization of Europe

6 They went through the region of
Phrygia and Galatia and were prevented by the Holy Spirit from speaking
the message in the province of Asia.
7 When they came to Mysia, they tried
to go into Bithynia, but the Spirit of
Jesus did not allow them. 8 So, bypass-
ing Mysia, they came down to [a]Troas.
9 During the night [b]a vision appeared to
Paul: a Macedonian man was standing
and pleading with him, "Cross over to
Macedonia and help us!" 10 After he
had seen the vision, we[c] immediately
made efforts to set out [c]for Macedonia,
concluding that God had called us to
evangelize them.

[a] 2Co 2:12 [b] Nm 12:6 [c] 2Co 2:13

Lydia's Conversion

11 Then, setting sail from Troas, we
ran a straight course to Samothrace,
the next day to Neapolis, 12 and from
there to [a]Philippi, a Roman colony,
which is a leading city of that district of
Macedonia. We stayed in that city for a
number of days. 13 On the Sabbath day
we went outside the city gate by the
river, where we thought there was a
place of prayer. We sat down and spoke
to the women gathered there. 14 A
woman named Lydia, a dealer in purple cloth from the city of [b]Thyatira,
who worshiped God, was listening.
The Lord opened her heart to pay attention to what was spoken by Paul.
15 After she and her household were
baptized, she urged us, "If you consider me [c]a believer in the Lord, come
and stay at my house." And she persuaded us.

[a] Php 1:1 [b] Rv 2:18 [c] Gl 6:10

Paul and Silas in Prison

16 Once, as we were on our way to
prayer, a slave girl met us [a]who had a
spirit of prediction[d] and made a large
profit for her owners by fortune-tell-
ing. 17 As she followed Paul and us she
cried out, "These men are the slaves of
the •Most High God, who are proclaiming to you[e] the way of salvation."
18 And she did this for many days.

[a] 1Sm 28:7

But Paul was greatly aggravated, and
turning to the spirit, said, "I command
you in the name of Jesus Christ to

[a] **15:37** Lit *John who was called Mark* [b] **16:3** Lit *wanted this one* [c] **16:10** The use of *we* in this passage probably indicates that the author Luke is joining Paul's missionary team here. [d] **16:16** Or *a spirit by which she predicted the future* [e] **16:17** Other mss read *us*

come out of her!" [a]And it came out
right away.[a] [a]Mk 16:17

19 [a]When her owners saw that their
hope of profit was gone, [b]they seized
Paul and Silas and [c]dragged them into
the marketplace to the authorities.
20 And bringing them before the chief
magistrates, they said, "These men are
[d]seriously disturbing our city. They are
Jews, 21 and are promoting customs
that are not legal for us as Romans to
adopt or practice." [a]Php 3:19 [b]2Co 6:5 [c]Mt 10:18 [d]Ac 17:6

22 Then the mob joined in the attack
against them, and the chief magistrates
stripped off their clothes [a]and ordered
them to be beaten with rods. 23 [b]After
they had inflicted many blows on
them, they threw them in jail, ordering the jailer to keep them securely
guarded. 24 Receiving such an order, he
put them into the inner prison and se-
cured their feet in the stocks.
[a]2Co 6:5 [b]Lk 21:12

A Midnight Deliverance

25 About midnight Paul and Silas
were praying and [a]singing hymns to
God, and the prisoners were listening
to them. 26 Suddenly there was such a
violent earthquake that the foundations of the jail were shaken, and immediately [b]all the doors were opened,
and everyone's chains came loose.
27 When the jailer woke up and saw
the doors of the prison open, he drew
his sword and was going to kill himself, since he thought the prisoners
had escaped. [a]Ac 5:41 [b]Ac 5:19

28 But Paul called out in a loud voice,
"Don't harm yourself, because all of us
are here!"

29 Then the jailer[b] called for lights,
rushed in, and fell down trembling before Paul and Silas. 30 Then he escorted
them out and said, [a]"Sirs, what must I
do to be saved?" [a]Ac 2:37

31 So they said, [a]"Believe on the Lord
Jesus, and you will be saved—you and
your household." 32 Then they spoke
the message of the Lord to him along
with everyone in his house. 33 He took
them the same hour of the night and
washed their wounds. Right away he
and all his family were baptized. 34 He
brought them up into his house, set a
meal before them, and [b]rejoiced because he had believed God with his entire household. [a]Jn 6:47 [b]Rm 5:2; 1Pt 1:8

An Official Apology

35 When daylight came, the chief
magistrates sent the police to say, "Release those men!"

36 The jailer reported these words to
Paul: "The magistrates have sent orders for you to be released. So come
out now and go in peace."

37 But Paul said to them, "They beat
us in public without a trial, [a]although
we are Roman citizens, and threw us
in jail. And now are they going to
smuggle us out secretly? Certainly not!
On the contrary, let them come themselves and escort us out!" [a]Ac 22:25

38 Then the police reported these
words to the magistrates. And they
were afraid when they heard that Paul
and Silas[c] were Roman citizens. 39 So
they came and apologized to them, and
escorting them out, they urged them
to leave town. 40 After leaving the jail,
they came to Lydia's house where they
saw and [a]encouraged the brothers, and
departed. [a]2Co 1:4; 1Th 3:2-3

A Short Ministry in Thessalonica

17 Then they traveled through Am-
phipolis and Apollonia and came
to Thessalonica, where there was a
Jewish •synagogue. 2 As usual, Paul
went [a]to them, and on three Sabbath
days reasoned with them from the
Scriptures, 3 explaining and showing
[b]that the •Messiah had to suffer and

[a]**16:18** Lit *out this hour* [b]**16:29** Lit *Then he* [c]**16:38** Lit *heard they*

rise from the dead, and saying: "This
is the Messiah, Jesus, whom I am proclaiming to you." 4 [c]Then some of
them were persuaded and joined Paul
and [d]Silas, including a great number
of God-fearing Greeks, as well as a
number[a] of the leading women.

[a]Ac 9:20; 14:1 [b]Ps 22; Is 53 [c]Ac 28:24 [d]Ac 15:22,27,32,40

The Assault on Jason's House

5 But the Jews became jealous, and
when they had brought together some
scoundrels from the marketplace and
formed a mob, they set the city in an
uproar. Attacking [a]Jason's house, they
searched for them to bring them out to
the public assembly. 6 When they did
not find them, they dragged Jason and
some of the brothers before the city officials, shouting, "These men who
have turned the world upside down
have come here too, 7 and Jason has received them as guests! They are all acting contrary to Caesar's decrees,
[b]saying that there is another king—
Jesus!" 8 The Jews[b] stirred up the
crowd and the city officials who heard
these things. 9 So taking a security
bond from Jason and the others, they
released them.

[a]Rm 16:21 [b]Lk 23:2

The Beroeans Search the Scriptures

10 As soon as it was night, the brothers sent Paul and Silas off to Beroea.
On arrival, they went into the synagogue of the Jews. 11 The people here
were more open-minded than those in
Thessalonica, since they welcomed the
message with eagerness and [a]ex-
amined the Scriptures daily to see if
these things were so. 12 Consequently,
many of them believed, including a
number of the prominent Greek
women as well as men. 13 But when
the Jews from Thessalonica found out
that God's message had been proclaimed by Paul at Beroea, [b]they came
there too, agitating and disturbing[c] the
crowds. 14 [c]Then the brothers immediately sent Paul away to go to the sea,
but Silas and Timothy stayed on there.
15 Those who escorted Paul brought
him as far as Athens, and after [d]receiv-
ing instructions for Silas and Timothy
to come to him as quickly as possible,
they departed.

[a]Is 34:16; Lk 16:29 [b]Lk 11:52; 1Th 2:15 [c]Mt 10:23 [d]Ac 18:5

Paul in Athens

16 While Paul was waiting for them
in Athens, [a]his spirit was troubled
within him when he saw that the city
was full of idols. 17 So he reasoned in
the synagogue with the Jews and with
those who worshiped God, and in the
marketplace every day with those who
happened to be there. 18 Then also,
some of the Epicurean and Stoic phi-
losophers argued with him. Some said,
"What is this pseudo-intellectual[d] trying to say?"

[a]Ps 119:158

Others replied, "He seems to be a
preacher of foreign deities"—because
he was telling the good news about
Jesus and the resurrection.
19 They took him and brought him to
the Areopagus,[e] and said, "May we
learn about this new teaching you're
speaking of? 20 For what you say
sounds strange to us, and we want to
know what these ideas mean." 21 Now
all the Athenians and the foreigners
residing there spent their time on
nothing else but telling or hearing
something new.

The Areopagus Address

22 Then Paul stood in the middle of
the Areopagus and said: "Men of Athens! I see that you are [a]extremely religious in every respect. 23 For as I was

[a]**17:4** Lit *as well as not a few* [b]**17:8** Lit *They* [c]**17:13** Other mss omit *and disturbing* [d]**17:18** Lit *this seed picker*; that is, one who picks up scraps [e]**17:19** Or *Mars Hill*, the oldest and most famous court in Athens with jurisdiction in moral, religious, and civil matters

passing through and observing the objects of your worship, I even found an
altar on which was inscribed:

TO AN UNKNOWN GOD

Therefore, what you worship in ignorance, this I proclaim to you. 24 [b]The
God who made the world and everything in it—He is [c]Lord of heaven and
earth and [d]does not live in shrines
made by hands. 25 Neither is He
served by human hands, as though
[e]He needed anything, since He Himself gives everyone life and breath and
all things. 26 [f]From one man[a] He has
made every nation of men to live all
over the earth and has determined
their appointed times and [g]the bound-
aries of where they live, 27 [h]so that
they might seek God, and perhaps
they might reach out and find Him,
[i]though He is not far from each one of
us. 28 For [j]in Him we live and move
and exist, as even some of your own
poets have said, 'For we are also His
offspring.'[b] 29 Being God's offspring,
then, [k]we shouldn't think that the divine nature is like gold or silver or
stone, an image fashioned by human
art and imagination. *a Jr 50:38*
b Is 40:12,28 c Mt 11:25 d Ac 7:48
e Is 42:5 f Dt 30:20 g Dt 32:8 h Rm 1:20
i Jr 23:24 j 1Sm 25:29 k Is 40:18

30 "Therefore, [a]having overlooked the
times of ignorance, God [b]now commands all people everywhere to repent,
31 because He has set a day on which
[c]He is going to judge the world in righteousness by the Man He has appointed. He has provided proof of this
to everyone by raising Him from the
dead." *a Rm 3:25 b Lk 24:47 c Rm 2:16*

32 When they heard about resurrection of the dead, some began to ridicule
him. But others said, "We will hear you
about this again." 33 So Paul went out
from their presence. 34 [a]However, some
men joined him and believed, among
whom were Dionysius the Areopagite,
a woman named Damaris, and others
with them. *a Rm 11:5*

Founding the Corinthian Church

18 After this, he[c] left from Athens
and went to Corinth, 2 where he
found a Jewish man named [a]Aquila, a
native of Pontus, who had recently
come from Italy with his wife Priscilla
because Claudius[d] had ordered all the
Jews to leave Rome. Paul[e] came to
them, 3 and being of the same occupation, stayed with them [b]and worked,
for they were tentmakers by trade.
4 He reasoned in the •synagogue every
Sabbath and tried to persuade both
Jews and Greeks. *a 1Co 16:19; 2Tm 4:19*
b 1Co 4:12; 1Th 2:9

5 [a]When Silas and Timothy came
down from Macedonia, Paul was [b]oc-
cupied with preaching the message[f]
and solemnly testified to the Jews that
the •Messiah is Jesus. 6 But when they
resisted and blasphemed, he shook out
his clothes[g] and told them, [c]"Your
blood is on your own heads! [d]I am
clean. [e]From now on I will go to the
Gentiles." 7 So he left there and went
to the house of a man named Titius Justus, a worshiper of God, whose house
was next door to the synagogue.
8 [f]Crispus, the leader of the synagogue,
believed the Lord, along with his
whole household; and many of the
Corinthians, when they heard, believed and were baptized.
a Ac 17:14 b Jb 32:18 c Ezk 33:4
d Ezk 3:18 e Ac 28:28 f 1Co 1:14

9 Then the Lord said to Paul in a
night vision, "Don't be afraid, but keep
on speaking and don't be silent. 10 [a]For
I am with you, and no one will lay a

[a]**17:26** Other mss read *one blood* [b]**17:28** This citation is from Aratus, a third-century B.C. Gk poet. [c]**18:1** Other mss read *Paul* [d]**18:2** Roman emperor A.D. 41–54; he expelled all Jews from Rome in A.D. 49. [e]**18:2** Lit *He* [f]**18:5** Other mss read *was urged by the Spirit* [g]**18:6** A symbolic display of protest; see Ac 13:51; Mt 10:14

hand on you to hurt you, because I
have many people in this city." 11 And
he stayed there a year and six months,
teaching the word of God among
them. [a] *Is 41:10; Mt 28:20*

12 While Gallio was •proconsul of
Achaia, the Jews made a united attack
against Paul and brought him to the
judge's bench. 13 "This man," they
said, "persuades people to worship
God contrary to the law!"
14 And as Paul was about to open his
mouth, Gallio said to the Jews, [a]"If it
were a matter of a crime or of moral
evil, it would be reasonable for me to
put up with you Jews. 15 But if these
are questions about words, names, and
your own law, see to it yourselves. I
don't want to be a judge of such
things." 16 So he drove them from the
judge's bench. 17 Then they all[a] seized
[b]Sosthenes, the leader of the synagogue, and beat him in front of the
judge's bench. But none of these things
concerned Gallio. [a] *Ac 23:29; 25:19* [b] *1Co 1:1*

The Return Trip to Antioch

18 So Paul, having stayed on for many
days, said good-bye to the brothers and
sailed away to Syria. Priscilla and Aquila were with him. He [a]shaved his
head at [b]Cenchreae, because he had
taken a vow. 19 When they reached
Ephesus he left them there, but he
himself entered the synagogue and engaged in discussion with[b] the Jews.
20 And though they asked him to stay
for a longer time, he declined, 21 but
said good-bye and stated,[c] "I'll come
back to you again, [c]if God wills." Then
he set sail from Ephesus.
[a] *Ac 21:24; 1Co 9:20* [b] *Rm 16:1* [c] *Heb 6:3*

22 On landing at Caesarea, he went
up and greeted the church,[d] and went
down to Antioch. 23 He set out, traveling through one place after another in
the [a]Galatian territory and Phrygia,
[b]strengthening all the disciples.
[a] *Gl 1:2* [b] *Is 35:3*

The Eloquent Apollos

24 [a]A Jew named Apollos, a native Alexandrian, an eloquent man who was
powerful in the Scriptures, arrived in
Ephesus. 25 This man had been instructed in the way of the Lord; and being [b]fervent in spirit,[e] he spoke and
taught the things about Jesus accurately, [c]although he knew only John's
baptism. 26 He began to speak boldly in
the synagogue. After Priscilla and Aquila heard him, they took him home[f]
and explained the way of God to him
more accurately. 27 When he wanted to
cross over to Achaia, the brothers
wrote to the disciples urging them to
welcome him. After he arrived, he
[d]greatly helped those who had believed through grace. 28 For he vigor-
ously refuted the Jews in public,
[e]demonstrating through the Scriptures
that Jesus [f]is the Messiah. [a] *1Co 1:12*
[b] *Rm 12:11* [c] *Ac 19:3* [d] *1Co 3:6*
[e] *Lk 24:26,46; 1Co 15:3-4* [f] *Gn 49:10; Dt 18:15;*
Ps 16:9-10; Is 7:14; Mc 5:2; Mal 3:1

Twelve Disciples of John the Baptist

19 While Apollos was in Corinth,
Paul traveled through the inte-
rior regions and came to Ephesus. He
found some disciples 2 and asked
them, "Did you receive the Holy Spirit
when you believed?"
"No," they told him, [a]"we haven't
even heard that there is a Holy Spirit."
[a] *1Co 6:19*

3 "Then with what ⌊baptism⌋ were
you baptized?" he asked them.
[a]"With John's baptism," they replied.
[a] *Ac 18:25*

4 Paul said, [a]"John baptized with a
baptism of repentance, telling the peo-

[a]**18:17** Other mss read *Then all the Greeks* [b]**18:19** Or *and addressed* [c]**18:21** Other mss add *"By all means it is necessary to keep the coming festival in Jerusalem. But* [d]**18:22** The church in Jerusalem [e]**18:25** Or *in the Spirit* [f]**18:26** Lit *they received him*

ple that they should believe in the One
who would come after him, that is, in
Jesus."

[a] Mk 1:4-12; Ac 1:5

5 On hearing this, they were baptized [a]in the name of the Lord Jesus.
6 And when Paul had [b]laid his hands
on them, the Holy Spirit came on
them, and [c]they began to speak with
⌊other⌋ languages and to prophesy.
7 Now there were about 12 men in all.

[a] Ac 8:12,16; Rm 6:3 [b] Ac 6:6 [c] Ac 2:4

In the Lecture Hall of Tyrannus

8 Then he entered the •synagogue
and spoke boldly over a period of three
months, engaging in discussion and
trying to persuade them about the
things [a]related to the kingdom of God.
9 But [b]when some became hardened
and would not believe, slandering [c]the
Way in front of the crowd, he withdrew from them and met separately
with the disciples, conducting discus-
sions every day in the lecture hall of
Tyrannus. 10 And [d]this went on for two
years, so that all the inhabitants of the
province of Asia, both Jews and
Greeks, heard the word of the Lord.

[a] Ac 1:3 [b] 2Tm 1:15; 2Pt 2:2
[c] Ac 9:2 [d] Ac 20:31

Demonism Defeated at Ephesus

11 [a]God was performing extraordinary miracles by Paul's hands, 12 so that
even facecloths or work aprons[a] that
had touched his skin were brought to
the sick, and the diseases left them,
and the evil spirits came out of them.

[a] Mk 16:20

13 Then some of the itinerant Jewish
exorcists [a]attempted to pronounce the
name of the Lord Jesus over those who
had evil spirits, saying, "I command you
by the Jesus whom Paul preaches!"
14 Seven sons of Sceva, a Jewish •chief
priest, were doing this. 15 The evil spirit
answered them, [b]"Jesus I know, and
Paul I recognize—but who are you?"
16 Then the man who had the evil spirit
leaped on them, overpowered them all
and prevailed against them, so that they
ran out of that house naked and
wounded. 17 This became known to everyone who lived in Ephesus, both Jews
and Greeks. Then [c]fear fell on all of
them, and the name of the Lord Jesus
was magnified. 18 And many who had
become believers came confessing and
disclosing their practices, 19 while many
of those who had [d]practiced magic collected their books and burned them in
front of everyone. So they calculated
their value, and found it to be 50,000
pieces of silver. 20 [e]In this way the Lord's
message flourished and prevailed.

[a] Mk 9:38 [b] Mt 8:29; Ac 16:17
[c] Ac 2:43 [d] Is 8:19; Ac 8:9-11
[e] Is 55:11; Col 1:6

The Riot in Ephesus

21 When these events were over,
Paul [a]resolved in the Spirit to pass
through Macedonia and Achaia and go
to Jerusalem. "After I've been there,"
he said, [b]"I must see Rome as well!"
22 So after sending two of those who as-
sisted him, Timothy and [c]Erastus, to
Macedonia, he himself stayed in the
province of Asia for a while.

[a] Ac 20:22 [b] Ac 23:11 [c] Rm 16:23

23 [a]During that time there was a ma-
jor[b] disturbance about [b]the Way. 24 For
a person named Demetrius, a silver-
smith who made silver shrines of Artemis,[c] provided a great deal of[d] business
for the craftsmen. 25 When he had assembled them, as well as the workers
engaged in this type of business, he
said: "Men, you know that our pros-
perity [c]is derived from this business.
26 You both see and hear that not only
in Ephesus, but in almost the whole
province of Asia, this man Paul has
persuaded and misled a considerable
number of people by saying [d]that gods
made by hand are not gods! 27 So not

[a]**19:12** Or *that also sweatbands and sweatcloths* or *handkerchiefs* [b]**19:23** Lit *was not a little* [c]**19:24** Artemis was the ancient Gk mother goddess believed to control all fertility. [d]**19:24** Lit *provided not a little*

only do we run a risk that our business
may be discredited, but also that the
temple of the great goddess Artemis
may be despised and her magnificence
come to the verge of ruin—the very
one whom the whole province of Asia
and the world adore."

[a] *2Co 1:8* [b] *Ac 9:2* [c] *Ac 17:29* [d] *1Co 8:4*

28 When they had heard this, they
were filled with rage and began to cry
out, [a]"Great is Artemis of the Ephesians!" 29 So the city was filled with
confusion; and they rushed all together
into the amphitheater, dragging along
[b]Gaius and [c]Aristarchus, Macedonians
who were Paul's traveling companions. 30 Though Paul wanted to go in
before the people, the disciples did not
let him. 31 Even some of the provincial
officials of Asia, who were his friends,
sent word to him, pleading with him
not to take a chance by going[a] into the
amphitheater. 32 Meanwhile, some
were shouting one thing and some another, because the assembly was in
confusion, and most of them did not
know why they had come together.
33 Then some of the crowd gave Alexander advice when the Jews pushed
him to the front. So motioning with his
hand, [d]Alexander wanted to make his
defense to the people. 34 But when
they recognized that he was a Jew, a
united cry went up from all of them for
about two hours: "Great is Artemis of
the Ephesians!"

[a] *Hab 2:18-19; Rv 13:4* [b] *Rm 16:23; 1Co 1:14* [c] *Ac 20:4; Col 4:10* [d] *1Tm 1:20; 2Tm 4:14*

35 However, when the city clerk had
calmed the crowd down, he said,
"Men of Ephesus! What man is there
who doesn't know that the city of the
Ephesians is the temple guardian of
the great[b] Artemis, and of the image
that fell from heaven? 36 Therefore,
since these things are undeniable, you
must keep calm and not do anything
rash. 37 For you have brought these
men here who are not temple robbers
or blasphemers of our[c] goddess. 38 So if
Demetrius and the craftsmen who are
with him have a case against anyone,
the courts are in session, and there are
•proconsuls. Let them bring charges
against one another. 39 But if you want
something else, it must be decided in a
legal assembly. 40 In fact, we run a risk
of being charged with rioting for what
happened today, since there is no justification that we can give as a reason for
this disorderly gathering." 41 [a]After saying this, he dismissed the assembly.

[a] *Pr 15:1; Ec 9:17*

Paul in Macedonia

20 After the uproar was over, Paul
sent for the disciples, encouraged them, and after saying good-bye,
[a]departed to go to Macedonia. 2 And
when he had passed through those ar-
eas and exhorted them at length, he
came to Greece 3 and stayed three
months. When he was about to set sail
for Syria, [b]a plot was devised against
him by the Jews, so a decision was
made to go back through Macedonia.
4 He was accompanied[d] by Sopater, son
of Pyrrhus,[e] from Beroea, [c]Aristarchus
and Secundus from Thessalonica, [d]Ga-
ius from Derbe, [e]Timothy, and [f]Tych-
icus and [g]Trophimus from Asia. 5 These
men went on ahead and waited for us
in Troas, 6 but we sailed away from
Philippi after [h]the days of •Unleavened
Bread. In five days we reached them at
[i]Troas, where we spent seven days.

[a] *1Co 16:5; 2Co 7:5* [b] *2Co 11:26* [c] *Ac 27:2* [d] *Ac 19:29* [e] *Ac 16:1* [f] *Eph 6:21* [g] *Ac 21:29* [h] *Ex 23:15* [i] *2Co 2:12*

Eutychus Revived at Troas

7 On [a]the first day of the week,[f] we[g]
assembled [b]to break bread. Paul spoke
to them, and since he was about to de-

[a]**19:31** Lit *not to give himself* [b]**19:35** Other mss add *goddess* [c]**19:37** Other mss read *your* [d]**20:4** Other mss add *to Asia* [e]**20:4** Other mss omit *son of Pyrrhus* [f]**20:7** Lit *On one between the Sabbaths*; that is, Sunday [g]**20:7** Other mss read *the disciples*

part the next day, he extended his
message until midnight. 8 There were
many lamps in the room upstairs
where we were assembled, 9 and a
young man named Eutychus was sitting on a window sill and sank into a
deep sleep as Paul kept on speaking.
When he was overcome by sleep he
fell down from the third story, and was
picked up dead. 10 But Paul went
down, threw himself on him, em-
braced him, and said, "Don't be
alarmed, for his •life is in him!" 11 After
going upstairs, breaking the bread, and
eating, he conversed a considerable
time until dawn. Then he left. 12 They
brought the boy home alive and were
greatly comforted. *[a] Jn 20:1; Rv 1:10*
[b] Lk 22:19; Ac 2:42

From Troas to Miletus

13 Then we went on ahead to the ship
and sailed for Assos, from there intending to take Paul on board. For these
were his instructions, since he himself
was going by land. 14 When he met us
at Assos, we took him on board and
came to Mitylene. 15 Sailing from there,
the next day we arrived off Chios. The
following day we crossed over to Sa-
mos, and[a] the day after, we came to Miletus. 16 For Paul had decided to sail
past Ephesus so he would not have to
spend time in the province of Asia, because [a]he was hurrying [b]to be in Jerusalem, if possible, for [c]the day of
Pentecost. *[a] Ac 21:4 [b] Ac 24:17 [c] Ac 2:1*

Farewell Address to the Ephesian Elders

17 Now from Miletus, he sent to
Ephesus and called for the elders of the
church. 18 And when they came to
him, he said to them: "You know,
[a]from the first day I set foot in Asia,
how I was with you the whole time—
19 serving the Lord with all humility,
with tears, and with the trials tha
came to me through the plots of th
Jews— 20 and that I did not shrink bac
from proclaiming to you anything that
was profitable, or from teaching it to
you in public and from house to house.
21 [b]I testified to both Jews and Greeks
about [c]repentance toward God and
faith in our Lord Jesus. *[a] Ac 18:19*
[b] Ac 18:5 [c] Lk 24:47

22 "And now I am on my way t
Jerusalem, [a]bound in my spirit, no
knowing what I will encounter there,
23 ex- cept that in town after town [b]the
Holy Spirit testifies to me that chains
and afflictions are waiting for me.
24 [c]But I count my life of no value to
myself, [d]so that I may finish my course[b]
[e]and the ministry I received from the
Lord Jesus, to testify to the gospel c
God's grace. *[a] Ac 19:21 [b] Ac 9:1*
[c] Rm 8:35 [d] 1Co 9:24-27; 2Tm 4:7 [e] Ti 1:3

25 "And now I know that none of
you, among whom I went about
preaching the kingdom, will ever see
my face again. 26 Therefore I testify to
you this day that I am [a]innocent[c] of everyone's blood, 27 for I did not shrink
back from declaring to you the whole
[b]plan of God. 28 [c]Be on guard for yourselves and for all the flock, among
whom the [d]Holy Spirit has appointed
you as •overseers, to shepherd the
church of God,[d] [e]which He purchased
with His own blood. 29 I know that after my departure [f]savage wolves will
come in among you, not sparing the
flock. 30 And [g]men from among yourselves will rise up with deviant doc
trines to lure the disciples into fol
lowing them. 31 Therefore be on the
alert, remembering that night and day
[h]for three years I did not stop warning
each one of you with tears. *[a] 2Co 7:2*
[b] Mt 28:20; Eph 1:11 [c] 1Tm 4:16
[d] 1Co 12:28 [e] Eph 1:7 [f] 2Pt 2:1
[g] 1Jn 2:19 [h] Ac 19:10

[a]**20:15** Other mss add *after staying at Trogyllium* [b]**20:24** Other mss add *with joy* [c]**20:26** Lit *clean* [d]**20:28** Other mss read *church of the Lord*; other mss read *church of the Lord and God*

32 "And now[a] I commit you to God
and [a]to the message of His grace, which
is able to build you up and to give you
[b]an inheritance among all who are
sanctified. 33 [c]I have not coveted anyone's silver or gold or clothing. 34 You
yourselves know [d]that these hands
have provided for my needs, and for
those who were with me. 35 In every
way I've shown you [e]that by laboring
like this, it is necessary to help the
weak and to keep in mind the words of
the Lord Jesus, for He said, [f]'It is more
blessed to give than to receive.'"

[a] Heb 13:9 [b] Ac 26:18 [c] 1Co 9:12 [d] Ac 18:3 [e] Rm 15:1 [f] Pr 19:17; Mt 10:8

36 After he said this, he knelt down
and prayed with all of them. 37 There
was a great deal of weeping by everyone. And embracing Paul, they kissed
him, 38 grieving most of all over his
statement that they would never see
his face again. Then they escorted him
to the ship.

Warnings on the Journey to Jerusalem

21 After we tore ourselves away
from them and set sail, we came
by a direct route to Cos, the next day
to Rhodes, and from there to Patara.
2 Finding a ship crossing over to Phoenicia, we boarded and set sail. 3 After
we sighted Cyprus, leaving it on the
left, we sailed on to Syria and arrived
at Tyre, because the ship was to un-
load its cargo there. 4 So we found
some disciples and stayed there seven
days. [a]They said to Paul through the
Spirit not to go to Jerusalem. 5 When
our days there were over, we left to
continue our journey, while all of
them, with their wives and children,
escorted us out of the city. After kneel-
ing down on the beach to pray, 6 we
said good-bye to one another. Then we
boarded the ship, and they returned
home.

[a] Ac 20:23

7 When we completed our voyage
from Tyre, we reached Ptolemais,
where we greeted the brothers and
stayed with them one day. 8 The next
day we left and came to Caesarea,
where we entered the house of Philip
the evangelist, [a]who was one of the
Seven, and stayed with him. 9 This
man had four virgin daughters [b]who
prophesied.

[a] Ac 6:5 [b] Jl 2:28

10 While we were staying there many
days, a prophet named [a]Agabus came
down from Judea. 11 He came to us,
took Paul's belt, tied his own feet and
hands, and said, "This is what the Holy
Spirit says: 'In this way the Jews in
Jerusalem will bind the man who owns
this belt, and deliver him into Gentile
hands.'" 12 When we heard this, both
we and the local people begged him
not to go up to Jerusalem.

[a] Ac 11:28

13 Then Paul replied, [a]"What are you
doing, weeping and breaking my
heart? [b]For I am ready not only to be
bound, but also to die in Jerusalem for
the name of the Lord Jesus."

[a] Ac 20:24 [b] 2Co 4:10; 2Tm 4:6

14 Since he would not be persuaded,
we stopped talking and simply said,
"The Lord's will be done!"

Conflict over the Gentile Mission

15 After these days we got ready and
went up to Jerusalem. 16 Some of the
disciples from Caesarea also went with
us and brought us to Mnason, a Cypriot and an early disciple, with whom
we were to stay.
17 [a]When we reached Jerusalem,
the brothers welcomed us gladly.
18 The following day Paul went in with
us to [b]James, and all the elders were
present. 19 After greeting them, [c]he
related one by one what God did
among the Gentiles [d]through his ministry.

[a] Ac 15:4 [b] Gl 1:19; Jms 1:1 [c] Rm 15:18 [d] Col 1:28-29

[a]**20:32** Other mss add *brothers,*

20 When they heard it, they glorified
God and said, "You see, brother, how
many thousands of Jews there are who
have believed, and they are all [a]zealous
for the law. 21 But they have been told
about you that you [b]teach all the Jews
who are among the Gentiles to aban-
don Moses, by telling them not to circumcise their children or to walk in our
customs. 22 So what is to be done?[a]
They will certainly hear that you've
come. 23 Therefore do what we tell you:
We have four men who have obligated
themselves with a vow. 24 Take these
men, purify yourself along with them,
and pay for them to get their heads
[c]shaved. Then everyone will know that
what they were told about you
amounts to nothing, but that you yourself are also careful about [d]observing
the law. 25 With regard to the Gentiles
who have believed, we have written a
letter containing our decision that[b]
they should keep themselves from food
sacrificed to idols, from blood, from
what is strangled, and from sexual immorality."

[a] Rm 10:2; Gl 1:14 [b] Gl 5:1 [c] Ac 18:18 [d] 1Co 9:20

The Riot in the Temple Complex

26 Then the next day, Paul took the
men, having purified himself along
with them, and [a]entered the temple,
[b]announcing the completion of the purification days when the offering for
each of them would be made. 27 As the
seven days were about to end, the
Jews from the province of Asia saw
him in the •temple complex, stirred up
the whole crowd, and [c]seized him,
28 shouting, "Men of Israel, help! This
is the man who teaches everyone everywhere against our people, our law,
and this place. What's more, he also
brought Greeks into the temple and
has profaned this holy place." 29 For
they had previously seen [d]Trophimus
the Ephesian in the city with him, and
they supposed that Paul had brought
him into the temple complex.[c]

[a] Ac 24:18 [b] Nm 6:13 [c] 2Co 4:9; 2Tm 3:12 [d] Ac 20:4

30 The whole city was stirred up, and
the people rushed together. They
seized Paul, dragged him out of the
temple complex, and at once the gates
were shut. 31 As they were trying to kill
him, word went up to the commander
of the •regiment that all Jerusalem was
in chaos. 32 [a]Taking along soldiers and
•centurions, he immediately ran down
to them. Seeing the commander and
the soldiers, they stopped beating Paul.
33 Then the commander came up, took
him into custody, and [b]ordered him to
be bound with two chains. He asked
who he was and what he had done.
34 Some in the mob were shouting one
thing and some another. Since he was
not able to get reliable information because of the uproar, he ordered him to
be taken into the barracks. 35 When
Paul[d] got to the steps, he had to be carried by the soldiers because of the
mob's violence, 36 for the mass of people were following and yelling, [c]"Kill
him!"

[a] Ac 22:25-29; 23:2 [b] Ac 20:23 [c] Ac 22:22

Paul's Defense before the Jerusalem Mob

37 As he was about to be brought into
the barracks, Paul said to the commander, "Am I allowed to say something to you?"

He replied, "Do you know Greek?
38 Aren't you the Egyptian who raised a
rebellion some time ago and led 4,000
Assassins[e] into the desert?"

39 Paul said, [a]"I am a Jewish man from
Tarsus of Cilicia, a citizen of an important city.[f] Now I ask you, [b]let me speak
to the people."

[a] Ac 9:11; Php 3:5 [b] 1Pt 3:15

[a]**21:22** Other mss add *A multitude has to come together, since* [b]**21:25** Other mss add *they should observe no such thing, except that* [c]**21:29** The inner temple court for Jewish men [d]**21:35** Lit *he* [e]**21:38** Lit *4,000 men of the Assassins*; that is, *Sicarii*, a Lat loanword from *sica*, dagger; compare "cut-throats" or daggermen. [f]**21:39** Lit *of no insignificant city*

40 After he had given permission, Paul
stood on the steps and motioned with
his hand to the people. When there was
a great hush, he addressed them in the
22 Hebrew language: 1 "Brothers and
fathers, listen now to my defense before you." 2 When they heard
that he was addressing them in the Hebrew language, they became even qui-
eter. 3 He continued, [a]"I am a Jewish
man, born in Tarsus of Cilicia, but
brought up in this city[a] at the feet of
[b]Gamaliel, and educated [c]according to
the strict view of our patriarchal law.
[d]Being zealous for God, just as all of
you are today, 4 [e]I persecuted this Way
to the death, binding and putting both
men and women in jail, 5 as both the
high priest and the whole council of elders can testify about me. [f]Having received letters from them to [g]the
brothers, I was traveling to Damascus
to bring those who were prisoners
there to be punished in Jerusalem.

[a]Php 3:5 [b]Ac 5:34 [c]Ac 26:5
[d]Gl 1:14; Php 3:6 [e]Ac 8:3 [f]Ac 9:2 [g]Ac 9:3

Paul's Testimony

6 [a]"As I was traveling and near Damascus, about noon an intense light
from heaven suddenly flashed around
me. 7 I fell to the ground and heard a
voice saying to me, 'Saul, Saul, why are
you persecuting Me?' *[a]Ac 26:12*

8 "I answered, 'Who are You, Lord?'
"He said to me, 'I am Jesus the •Naz-
arene, whom you are persecuting!'
9 Now those who were with me saw
the light,[b] but they did not hear the
voice of the One who was speaking to
me.
10 "Then I said, 'What should I do,
Lord?'
"And the Lord told me, 'Get up and
go into Damascus, and there you will
be told about everything that is assigned for you to do.'
11 "Since I couldn't see because of the
brightness of that light, I was led by the
hand by those who were with me,
and came into Damascus. 12 [a]Someone
named Ananias, a devout man according to the law, having a good reputation with all the [b]Jews residing there,
13 came to me, stood by me, and said,
'Brother Saul, regain your sight.' And
in that very hour I looked up and saw
him. 14 Then he said, 'The God of our
fathers has [c]appointed you to know His
will, [d]to see the Righteous One, and
[e]to hear the sound of His voice.[c] 15 [f]For
you will be a witness for Him to all people of [g]what you have seen and heard.
16 And now, why delay? Get up and be
baptized, [h]and wash away your sins by
[i]calling on His name.'

[a]Ac 9:17 [b]1Tm 3:7 [c]Ac 9:15; Rm 1:1
[d]Ac 3:14; 1Co 9:1 [e]Gl 1:12 [f]Ac 23:11
[g]Ac 26:16 [h]Ac 2:38 [i]Ac 2:21

17 [a]"After I came back to Jerusalem
and was praying in the •temple complex, I went into a visionary state
18 and saw Him telling me, [b]'Hurry and
get out of Jerusalem quickly, because
they will not accept your testimony
about Me!' *[a]2Co 12:2 [b]Mt 10:17*

19 "But I said, 'Lord, [a]they know that
in •synagogue after synagogue I had
those who believed in You imprisoned
and beaten. 20 [b]And when the blood of
Your witness Stephen was being shed,
I myself was standing by and [c]approv-
ing,[d] and I guarded the clothes of those
who killed him.' *[a]Ac 8:3*
[b]Ac 7:58 [c]Rm 1:32

21 "Then He said to me, 'Go, [a]be-
cause I will send you far away to the
Gentiles.'" *[a]Ac 13:2; Rm 1:5*

Paul's Roman Protection

22 They listened to him up to this
word. Then they raised their voices,

[a]**22:3** Probably Jerusalem, but others think Tarsus [b]**22:9** Other mss add *and were afraid* [c]**22:14** Lit *to hear a voice from His mouth* [d]**22:20** Other mss add *of his murder*

shouting, [a]"Wipe this person off the
earth—it's a disgrace for him [b]to live!"
[a]Ac 21:36 [b]Ac 25:24

23 As they were yelling and flinging
aside their robes and throwing dust
into the air, 24 the commander ordered
him to be brought into the barracks, di-
recting that he be examined with the
scourge, so he could discover the reason they were shouting against him
like this. 25 As they stretched him out
for the lash, Paul said to the •centurion
standing by, [a]"Is it legal for you to
scourge a man who is a Roman citizen
and is uncondemned?" [a]Ac 16:37

26 When the centurion heard this, he
went and reported to the commander,
saying, "What are you going to do? For
this man is a Roman citizen."
27 The commander came and said to
him, "Tell me—are you a Roman citizen?"
"Yes," he said.
28 The commander replied, "I bought
this citizenship for a large amount of
money."
"But I myself was born a citizen,"
Paul said.
29 Therefore, those who were about
to examine him withdrew from him at
once. The commander too was alarmed
when he realized Paul was a Roman citizen and he had bound him.

Paul before the Sanhedrin

30 The next day, since he wanted to
find out exactly why Paul was being accused by the Jews, he released him[a]
and [a]instructed the •chief priests and
all the •Sanhedrin to convene. Then he
brought Paul down and placed him
23 before them. 1 Paul looked intently at the •Sanhedrin and
said, "Brothers, [b]I have lived my life
before God in all good conscience until
this day." 2 But the high priest Ananias
ordered those who were standing next
to him to strike him on the mouth.
3 Then Paul said to him, "God is going
to strike you, you whitewashed wall!
You are sitting there judging me according to the law, and in violation of
the law [c]are you ordering me to be
struck?" [a]Lk 21:12
[b]Ac 24:16 [c]Lv 19:35

4 And those standing nearby said,
"Do you dare revile God's high priest?"
5 [a]"I did not know, brothers," Paul
said, "that it was the high priest. For it
is written, [b]**You must not speak evil of**
a ruler of your people."[b] 6 When Paul
realized that one part of them were
•Sadducees and the other part were
•Pharisees, he cried out in the Sanhedrin, "Brothers, [c]I am a Pharisee, a son
of Pharisees! I am being judged because [d]of the hope of the resurrection
of the dead!" 7 When he said this, a dispute broke out between the Pharisees
and the Sadducees, and the assembly
was divided. 8 [e]For the Sadducees say
there is no resurrection, and no angel
or spirit, but the Pharisees affirm them
all. [a]Ac 24:17 [b]Ex 22:28 [c]Php 3:5
[d]Ac 24:15,21 [e]Mt 22:23

9 The shouting grew loud, and some
of the •scribes of the Pharisees' party
got up and argued vehemently: [a]"We
find nothing evil in this man. What [b]if
a spirit or an angel has spoken to
him?"[c] 10 When the dispute became violent, the commander feared that Paul
might be torn apart by them and ordered the troops to go down, rescue
him from them, and bring him into the
barracks. [a]Pr 16:7 [b]Ac 22:7

The Plot against Paul

11 [a]The following night, the Lord
stood by him and said, "Have courage!
For as you have testified about Me in
Jerusalem, so you must also testify in
Rome." [a]Is 41:10; Ac 18:9

12 When it was day, [a]the Jews formed
a conspiracy and bound themselves

[a]**22:30** Other mss add *from his chains* [b]**23:5** Ex 22:28 [c]**23:9** Other mss add *Let us not fight God.*

under a curse: neither to eat nor to drink until they had killed Paul. 13 There were more than 40 who had formed this plot. 14 These men went to the •chief priests and elders and said, "We have bound ourselves under a solemn curse that we won't eat anything until we have killed Paul. 15 So now you, along with the Sanhedrin, make a request to the commander that he bring him down to you[a] as if you were going to investigate his case more thoroughly. However, before he gets near, we are ready to kill him." *[a] Ac 25:3; Rm 8:31*

16 [a]But the son of Paul's sister, hearing about their ambush, came and entered the barracks and reported it to Paul. 17 Then Paul called one of the •centurions and said, "Take this young man to the commander, because he has something to report to him." *[a] Jb 5:13; Pr 21:30*

18 So he took him, brought him to the commander, and said, "The prisoner Paul called me and asked me to bring this young man to you, because he has something to tell you."

19 Then the commander took him by the hand, led him aside, and inquired privately, "What is it you have to report to me?"

20 "The Jews," he said, "have agreed to ask you to bring Paul down to the Sanhedrin tomorrow, as though they are going to hold a somewhat more careful inquiry about him. 21 Don't let them persuade you, because there are more than 40 of them [a]arranging to ambush him, men who have bound themselves under a curse not to eat or drink until they kill him. Now they are ready, waiting for a commitment from you." *[a] Is 59:7; Mc 7:2*

22 So the commander dismissed the young man and instructed him, "Don't tell anyone that you have informed me about this."

To Caesarea by Night

23 He summoned two of his centurions and said, "Get 200 soldiers ready with 70 cavalry and 200 spearmen to go to Caesarea at nine tonight.[b] 24 Also provide mounts so they can put Paul on them and bring him safely to Felix the governor."

25 He wrote a letter of this kind:

26 Claudius Lysias,
To the most excellent governor Felix:
Greetings.

27 [a]When this man had been seized by the Jews and was about to be killed by them, I arrived with my troops and rescued him because I learned that he is a Roman citizen. 28 [b]Wanting to know the charge for which they were accusing him, I brought him down before their Sanhedrin. 29 I found out that the accusations were about [c]disputed matters in their law, [d]and that there was no charge that merited death or chains. 30 When I was informed that there was a plot against the man,[c] I sent him to you right away. I also [e]ordered his accusers to state their case against him in your presence.[d] *[a] Ac 21:32; 23:10 [b] Ac 22:30 [c] Ac 18:15; 24:5-6 [d] Ac 26:31 [e] Ac 24:8*

31 Therefore, during the night, the soldiers took Paul and brought him to Antipatris as they were ordered. 32 The next day, they returned to the barracks, allowing the cavalry to go on with him. 33 When these men entered Caesarea and delivered the letter to the governor, they also presented Paul to him. 34 After he[e] read it, he asked what province he was from. So when he learned he was from Cilicia, 35 he said, [a]"I will give you a hearing whenever your accusers get here too." And

[a]**23:15** Other mss add *tomorrow* [b]**23:23** Lit *at the third hour tonight* [c]**23:30** Other mss add *by the Jews* [d]**23:30** Other mss add *Farewell* [e]**23:34** Other mss read *the governor*

he ordered that he be kept under
guard in •Herod's palace.[a]

[a] Ac 24:1

The Accusation against Paul

24 After five days [a]Ananias the
high priest came down with
some elders and a lawyer[b] named Tertullus. These men presented their
case against Paul to the governor.
2 When he was called in, Tertullus began to accuse him and said: [b]"Since
we enjoy great peace because of you,
and reforms are taking place for the
benefit of this nation by your fore-
sight, 3 we gratefully receive them always and in all places, most excellent
Felix, with all thankfulness. 4 However, so that I will not burden you any
further, I beg you in your graciousness
to give us a brief hearing. 5 [c]For we
have found this man to be a plague, an
agitator among all the Jews throughout the Roman world, and a ringleader
of the sect of the •Nazarenes! 6 [d]He
even tried to desecrate the temple, so
we apprehended him [and wanted to
judge him according to our law. 7 [e]But
Lysias the commander came and took
him from our hands, [f]commanding his
accusers to come to you.][c] 8 By examining him yourself you will be able to
discern all these things of which we
accuse him." 9 The Jews also joined in
the attack, alleging that these things
were so.

[a] Ac 23:2 [b] Ps 12:2; 55:21 [c] Mt 5:11; Lk 11:49; Jn 15:20 [d] Ac 21:28 [e] Ac 21:33 [f] Ac 23:30

Paul's Defense before Felix

10 When the governor motioned to
him to speak, Paul replied: "Because I
know you have been a judge of this nation for many years, I am glad to offer
my defense in what concerns me.
11 You are able to determine that it is
no more than 12 days since I went up
[a]to worship in Jerusalem. 12 [b]And they
didn't find me disputing with anyone
or causing a disturbance among the
crowd, either in the •temple complex
or in the •synagogues, or anywhere in
the city. 13 Neither can they provide evidence to you of what they now bring
against me. 14 But I confess this to you:
that according to [c]the Way, which they
call a sect, so I worship my [d]fathers'
God, believing all the things that are
written in the Law and in the Prophets. 15 And [e]I have a hope in God,
which these men themselves also accept, [f]that there is going to be a resurrection,[d] both of the righteous and the
unrighteous. 16 [g]I always do my best to
have a clear conscience toward God
and men. 17 After many years, [h]I came
to bring charitable gifts and offerings to
my nation, 18 and [i]while I was doing
this, some Jews from the province of
Asia found me ritually purified in the
temple, without a crowd and without
any uproar. 19 [j]It is they who ought to
be here before you to bring charges, if
they have anything against me.
20 Either let these men here state what
wrongdoing they found in me when I
stood before the •Sanhedrin, 21 or
about this one statement I cried out
while standing among them, [k]'Today I
am being judged before you concerning the resurrection of the dead.'"

[a] Ac 21:26 [b] Ac 25:8 [c] Ac 9:2 [d] Ac 3:13 [e] Ac 23:6 [f] Dn 12:2; Mt 22:31; Jn 5:28 [g] Ac 23:1 [h] Rm 15:25; 2Co 8:4; Gl 2:10 [i] Ac 21:26 [j] Ac 23:30 [k] Ac 23:6

The Verdict Postponed

22 Since Felix was accurately informed about the Way, he adjourned
the hearing, saying, "When Lysias the
commander comes down, I will decide
your case." 23 He ordered that the •cen-
turion keep Paul[e] under guard, though
he could have some freedom, and [a]that

[a] **23:35** Lit *praetorium*, a Lat word that can also refer to a military headquarters, to the governor's palace, or to the emperor's imperial guard [b] **24:1** Gk *rhetor*; compare the Eng "rhetoric," "rhetorician"—an orator skilled in public speaking. In this situation, skill in the Gk language was needed. [c] **24:6–7** Other mss omit bracketed text [d] **24:15** Other mss add *of the dead* [e] **24:23** Lit *him*

he should not prevent any of his
friends from serving[a] him.
[a] Ac 27:3

24 After some days, when Felix came
with his wife Drusilla, who was Jewish, he sent for Paul and listened to
him on the subject of faith in Christ
Jesus. 25 Now as he spoke about righteousness, self-control, and the judgment to come, Felix became afraid and
replied, "Leave for now, but when I
find time I'll call for you." 26 At the
same time he was also hoping that
[a]money would be given to him by
Paul.[b] For this reason he sent for him
quite often and conversed with him.
[a] Ex 23:8; Ps 26:10

27 After two years had passed, Felix
received a successor, Porcius Festus,
and because [a]he wished to do a favor
for the Jews, Felix left Paul in prison.
[a] Ex 23:2; Pr 29:25

Appeal to Caesar

25 Three days after Festus arrived
in the province, he went up to
Jerusalem from Caesarea. 2 Then the
•chief priests and the leaders of the
Jews presented their case against Paul
to him; and they appealed, 3 asking
him to do them a favor against Paul,[c]
that he might summon him to Jerusalem. They were [a]preparing an ambush
along the road to kill him. 4 However,
Festus answered that Paul should be
kept at Caesarea, and that he himself
was about to go there shortly. 5 "Therefore," he said, "let the men of authority among you go down with me and
accuse him, [b]if there is any wrong in
this man."
[a] Ps 37:32-33; Ac 23:12 [b] Ac 18:14

6 When he had spent not more than
eight or 10 days among them, he went
down to Caesarea. The next day,
seated at the judge's bench, he commanded Paul to be brought in. 7 When
he arrived, the Jews who had come
down from Jerusalem stood around
him [a]and brought many serious
charges that they were not able to
prove, 8 while Paul made the defense
that, "Neither against the Jewish law,
nor against the temple, nor against
Caesar have I sinned at all."
[a] 1Th 2:15; 1Pt 4:14-16

9 Then Festus, [a]wanting to do a favor
for the Jews, replied to Paul, "Are you
willing to go up to Jerusalem, there to
be tried before me on these charges?"
[a] Dt 27:19; Pr 29:25

10 But Paul said: "I am standing at
Caesar's tribunal, where I ought to be
tried. I have done no wrong to the
Jews, as even you can see very well.
11 [a]If then I am doing wrong, or have
done anything deserving of death, I do
not refuse to die, but if there is nothing
to what these men accuse me of, no
one can give me up to them. [b]I appeal
to Caesar!"
[a] Ac 18:14 [b] Ac 26:32

12 After Festus conferred with his
council, he replied, "You have appealed to Caesar; to Caesar you will
go!"

King Agrippa and Bernice Visit Festus

13 After some days had passed, King
Agrippa[d] and Bernice arrived in Caesarea and paid a courtesy call on Festus. 14 Since they stayed there many
days, Festus presented Paul's case to
the king, saying, [a]"There's a man who
was left as a prisoner by Felix. 15 When
I was in Jerusalem, the chief priests
and the elders of the Jews presented
their case and asked for a judgment
against him. 16 I answered them that
it's not the Romans' custom to give any
man up[e] before the accused confronts
the accusers face to face and has an opportunity to give a defense concerning
the charge. 17 Therefore, when they
had assembled here, I did not delay.

[a]**24:23** Other mss add *or visiting* [b]**24:26** Other mss add *so that he might release him* [c]**25:3** Lit *asking a favor against him* [d]**25:13** Herod Agrippa II ruled Palestine A.D. 52–92. [e]**25:16** Other mss add *to destruction*

The next day I sat at the judge's bench and ordered the man to be brought in. 18 Concerning him, the accusers stood up and brought no charge of the sort I was expecting. 19 [b]Instead they had some disagreements with him about their own religion and about a certain Jesus, a dead man whom Paul claimed to be alive. 20 Since I was at a loss in a dispute over such things, I asked him if he wished to go to Jerusalem and be tried there concerning these matters. 21 But when Paul appealed to be held for trial by the Emperor, I ordered him to be kept in custody until I could send him to Caesar." *a Ac 24:27* *b Ac 23:29; 1Co 1:18; 2:14*

22 Then [a]Agrippa said to Festus, "I would like to hear the man myself." *a Ac 9:15; 26:1*

"Tomorrow," he said, "you will hear him."

Paul before Agrippa

23 So the next day, Agrippa and Bernice came with [a]great pomp and entered the auditorium with the commanders and prominent men of the city. When Festus gave the command, Paul was brought in. 24 Then Festus said: "King Agrippa and all men present with us, you see this man about whom the whole Jewish community has appealed to me, both in Jerusalem and here, shouting that he should [b]not live any longer. 25 Now I realized that he had not done anything deserving of death, but when he himself appealed to the Emperor, I decided to send him. 26 I have nothing definite to write to the Emperor about him. Therefore, I have brought him before all of you, and especially before you, King Agrippa, so that after this examination is over, I may have something to write. 27 For it seems unreasonable to me to send a prisoner and not to indicate the charges against him." *a Ec 1:2; Jms 1:11 b Ac 22:22*

Paul's Defense before Agrippa

26 Agrippa said to Paul, "It is permitted for you to speak for yourself."

Then Paul stretched out his hand and began his defense: 2 "I consider myself fortunate, King Agrippa, that today I am going to make a defense before you about everything I am accused of by the Jews, 3 especially since you are an [a]expert in all the Jewish customs and controversies. Therefore I beg you to listen to me patiently. *a Dt 17:14-20*

4 "All the Jews know my way of life from my youth, which was spent from the beginning among my own nation and in Jerusalem. 5 They had previously known me for quite some time, if they were willing to testify, that according to [a]the strictest party of our religion I lived as a •Pharisee. 6 And now I stand on trial for the hope of the [b]promise made by God to our fathers, 7 ⌊the promise⌋ our 12 tribes [c]hope to attain as they earnestly serve Him night and day. Because of this hope I am being accused by the Jews, O king! 8 Why is it considered incredible by any of you that God [d]raises the dead? 9 [e]In fact, I myself supposed it was necessary to do many things in opposition to the name of Jesus the •Nazarene. 10 [f]This I actually did in Jerusalem, and I locked up many of the saints in prison, since I had received authority for that [g]from the •chief priests. When they were put to death, I cast my vote against them. 11 [h]In all the •synagogues I often tried to make them blaspheme by punishing them. Being greatly enraged at them, I even pursued them to foreign cities. *a Ac 22:3; Php 3:5 b Gn 3:15; Dt 18:15; Is 4:2; Mal 3:1 c Php 3:11 d Dn 12:2 e 1Tm 1:13 f Ac 8:3 g Ac 22:5 h Ac 22:19*

Paul's Account of His Conversion and Commission

12 [a]"Under these circumstances I was traveling to Damascus with authority and a commission from the

chief priests. 13 At midday, while on
the road, O king, I saw a light from
heaven brighter than the sun, shining
around me and those traveling with
me. 14 When we had all fallen to the
ground, I heard a voice speaking to me
in the Hebrew language, 'Saul, Saul,
why are you persecuting Me? It is hard
for you to kick against the goads.'[a]

[a] Ac 9:3

15 "But I said, 'Who are You, Lord?'
"And the Lord replied: 'I am Jesus,
whom you are persecuting. 16 But get
up and stand on your feet. For I have
appeared to you for this purpose, [a]to
appoint you as a servant and a witness
of things you have seen,[b] and of things
in which I will appear to you. 17 I will
rescue you from the people and from
the Gentiles, [b]to whom I now send
you, 18 [c]to open their eyes [d]that they
may turn [e]from darkness to light and
from the power of Satan to God, that
they may receive forgiveness of sins
and [f]a share among those who are
sanctified by faith in Me.'

[a] Ac 22:15 [b] Ac 9:15; Gl 1:15-16 [c] Lk 1:79 [d] Col 1:13 [e] 1Jn 3:5 [f] Eph 1:11

19 "Therefore, King Agrippa, I was
not disobedient to the heavenly vision.
20 Instead, I [a]preached to those in Damascus first, and to those in Jerusalem
and in all the region of Judea, and to the
Gentiles, that they should repent and
turn to God, and do [b]works worthy of
repentance. 21 For this reason [c]the Jews
seized me in the •temple complex and
were trying to kill me. 22 Since I have
obtained help that comes from God, to
this day I stand and testify to both small
and great, saying nothing else than
[d]what the prophets and [e]Moses said
would take place— 23 [f]that the •Mes-
siah must suffer, and [g]that as the first to
rise from the dead, [h]He would proclaim
light to our people and to the Gentiles."

[a] Ac 9:20 [b] Is 55:7 [c] Ac 21:30 [d] Rm 3:21 [e] Jn 5:46 [f] Is 53 [g] 1Co 15:20; Rv 1:5 [h] Is 42:6

Not Quite Persuaded

24 As he was making his defense this
way, Festus exclaimed in a loud voice,
[a]"You're out of your mind, Paul! Too
much study is driving you mad!"

[a] 1Co 1:23

25 But Paul replied, "I'm not out of
my mind, most excellent Festus. On
the contrary, I'm speaking words of
truth and good judgment. 26 For the
king knows about these matters. It is to
him I am actually speaking boldly. For
I'm not convinced that any of these
things escapes his notice, since this
was not done in a corner! 27 King
Agrippa, do you believe the prophets?
I know you believe."
28 Then Agrippa said to Paul, "Are
you going to persuade me to become a
Christian so easily?"
29 [a]"I wish before God," replied Paul,
"that whether easily or with difficulty,
not only you but all who listen to me
today might become as I am—except
for these chains."

[a] 1Co 7:7

30 So the king, the governor, Bernice,
and those sitting with them got up,
31 and when they had left they talked
with each other and said, [a]"This man
is doing nothing that deserves death or
chains."

[a] Ac 23:9; 25:25

32 Then Agrippa said to Festus, "This
man could have been released [a]if he
had not appealed to Caesar."

[a] Ac 25:11

Sailing for Rome

27 When [a]it was decided that we
were to sail to Italy, they handed
over Paul and some other prisoners to
a •centurion named Julius, of the Imperial •Regiment. 2 So when we had
boarded a ship of Adramyttium, we
put to sea, intending to sail to ports
along the coast of the province of Asia.
[b]Aristarchus, a Macedonian of Thessalonica, was with us. 3 The next day we
put in at Sidon, and Julius treated Paul

[a]**26:14** Sharp sticks used to prod animals, such as oxen in plowing [b]**26:16** Other mss read *things in which you have seen Me*

[c]kindly and allowed him to go to his
friends to receive their care. 4 When
we had put out to sea from there, we
sailed along the northern coast[a] of Cyprus because the winds were against
us. 5 After sailing through the open sea
off Cilicia and Pamphylia, we reached
Myra in Lycia. 6 There the centurion
found an Alexandrian ship sailing for
Italy and put us on board. 7 Sailing
slowly for many days, we came with
difficulty as far as Cnidus. But since
the wind did not allow us to approach
it, we sailed along the south side[a] of
Crete off Salmone. 8 With yet more difficulty we sailed along the coast, and
came to a place called Fair Havens
near the city of Lasea.

[a] Ac 25:12,25 [b] Ac 19:29; Col 4:10 [c] Ac 28:16

Paul's Advice Ignored

9 By now much time had passed, and
the voyage was already dangerous.
Since the Fast[b] was already over, Paul
gave his advice 10 and told them,
"Men, I can see that this voyage is
headed toward damage and heavy loss,
not only of the cargo and the ship, but
also of our lives." 11 But the centurion
paid attention to the captain and the
owner of the ship rather than to what
Paul said. 12 Since the harbor was un-
suitable to winter in, the majority decided to set sail from there, hoping
somehow to reach [a]Phoenix, a harbor
on Crete open to the southwest and
northwest, and to winter there.

[a] Ac 11:19

Storm-Tossed Vessel

13 When a gentle south wind sprang
up, they thought they had achieved
their purpose; they weighed anchor
and sailed along the shore of Crete.
14 But not long afterwards, a fierce
wind called the "northeaster"[c] rushed
down from the island.[d] 15 Since the
ship was caught and was unable to
head into the wind, we gave way to it
and were driven along. 16 After running under the shelter of a little island
called Cauda,[e] we were barely able to
get control of the skiff. 17 After hoisting
it up, they used ropes and tackle and
girded the ship. Then, fearing they
would run aground on the Syrtis,[f] they
lowered the drift-anchor, and in this
way they were driven along. 18 Because
we were being severely battered by
the storm, they began to jettison the
cargo the next day. 19 On the third day,
they threw the ship's gear overboard
with their own hands.

20 For many days neither sun nor
stars appeared, and the severe storm
kept raging; finally all hope that we
would be saved was disappearing.
21 Since many were going without
food, Paul stood up among them and
said, "You men should have followed
my advice not to sail from Crete and
sustain this damage and loss. 22 Now I
urge you to take courage, because
there will be no loss of any of your
lives, but only of the ship. 23 [a]For this
night an angel of the God I belong to
and [b]serve stood by me, 24 saying,
[c]'Don't be afraid, Paul. You must stand
[d]before Caesar. And, look! God has graciously given you all those who are sailing with you.' 25 Therefore, take
courage, men, [e]because I believe God
that it will be just the way it was told
to me. 26 However, [f]we must run
aground on a certain island."

[a] Ac 23:11; Heb 1:13-14 [b] Jn 12:26; Rm 1:9 [c] Is 43:1 [d] Ac 23:11 [e] 2Tm 1:12; Ti 1:2 [f] Ac 28:1

27 When the fourteenth night came,
we were drifting in the Adriatic Sea,[g]
and in the middle of the night the sailors thought they were approaching
land.[h] 28 They took a sounding and

[a]**27:4,7** Lit *sailed under the lee* [b]**27:9** The Day of Atonement [c]**27:14** Lit *Euraquilo*, a violent northeast wind [d]**27:14** Lit *from her* [e]**27:16** Or *Clauda* [f]**27:17** *Syrtis* = sand banks or bars near North Africa [g]**27:27** Part of the northern Mediterranean Sea; not the modern Adriatic Sea east of Italy [h]**27:27** Lit *thought there was land approaching them*

found it to be 120 feet[a] deep; when
they had sailed a little farther and
sounded again, they found it to be 90
feet[b] deep. 29 Then, fearing we might
run aground in some rocky place, they
dropped four anchors from the stern
and prayed for daylight to come.
30 Some sailors tried to escape from
the ship; they had let down the skiff
into the sea, pretending that they were
going to put out anchors from the bow.
31 Paul said to the centurion and the
soldiers, "Unless these men stay in the
ship, you cannot be saved." 32 Then
the soldiers cut the ropes holding the
skiff and let it drop away.
33 When it was just about daylight,
Paul urged them all to take food, saying, "Today is the fourteenth day that
you have been waiting and going
without food, having eaten nothing.
34 Therefore I urge you to take some
food. For this has to do with your sur-
vival, [a]since not a hair will be lost from
the head of any of you." 35 After he said
these things and had taken some
bread, he [b]gave thanks to God in the
presence of them all, and when he had
broken it, he began to eat. 36 They all
became encouraged and took food
themselves. 37 In all there were 276 of
us on the ship. 38 And having eaten
enough food, they began to lighten the
ship by [c]throwing the grain overboard
into the sea. *[a] Mt 10:30 [b] Rm 14:6 [c] Mt 6:25*

Shipwreck

39 When daylight came, they did not
recognize the land, but sighted a bay
with a beach. They planned to run the
ship ashore if they could. 40 After casting off the anchors, they left them in
the sea, at the same time loosening the
ropes that held the rudders. Then they
hoisted the foresail to the wind and
headed for the beach. 41 But they
struck a sandbar and [a]ran the ship
aground. The bow jammed fast and remained immovable, but the stern began to break up with the pounding of
the waves. *[a] 2Co 11:25*

42 The soldiers' plan was to kill the
prisoners so that no one could swim off
and escape. 43 But the centurion kept
them from carrying out their plan [a]be-
cause he wanted to save Paul, so he ordered those who could swim to jump
overboard first and get to land. 44 The
rest were to follow, some on planks
and some on debris from the ship. In
this way, [b]all got safely to land.
[a] Ac 23:10; 2Pt 2:9 [b] Ps 107:30

Malta's Hospitality

28 Safely ashore, we then learned
that the island was called [a]Mal-
ta. 2 The [b]local people showed us extraordinary kindness, for they lit a fire
and took us all in, since rain was falling and it was cold. 3 As Paul gathered
a bundle of brushwood and put it on
the fire, a viper came out because of
the heat and fastened itself to his
hand. 4 When the local people saw the
creature hanging from his hand, they
said to one another, "This man is
probably a murderer, and though he
has escaped the sea, Justice[c] does not
allow him to live!" 5 However, he
shook the creature off into the fire and
[c]suffered no harm. 6 They expected
that he would swell up or suddenly
drop dead. But after they waited a
long time and saw nothing unusual
happen to him, they changed their
minds and said he was a god. *[a] Ac 27:26*
[b] Lv 19:18,34; Rm 1:14
[c] Ps 91:13; Mk 16:18

Ministry in Malta

7 Now in the area around that place
was an estate belonging to the leading
man of the island, named Publius, who
welcomed us and entertained us hospi-
tably for three days. 8 It happened that
Publius' father was in bed suffering

[a]**27:28** Lit *20 fathoms* [b]**27:28** Lit *15 fathoms* [c]**28:4** Gk *Dike*, a goddess of justice

from fever and dysentery. Paul went to
him, and praying and [a]laying his hands
on him, he healed him. 9 After this, the
rest of those on the island who had diseases also came and were cured. 10 So
they heaped many [b]honors on us, and
when we sailed, they gave us what we
needed.

a 1Co 12:9,28 b 1Tm 5:17

Rome at Last

11 After three months we set sail in
an Alexandrian ship that had wintered
at the island, with the Twin Brothers[a]
as its figurehead. 12 Putting in at Syra-
cuse, we stayed three days. 13 From
there, after making a circuit along the
coast,[b] we reached Rhegium. After one
day a south wind sprang up, and the
second day we came to Puteoli.
14 There we found believers[c] and were
invited to stay with them for seven
days.

And so we came to Rome. 15 Now
the believers[c] from there had heard the
news about us and had come to meet
us as far as Forum of Appius and Three
Taverns. When Paul saw them, he
thanked God and took courage. 16 And
when we entered Rome,[d] [a]Paul was
permitted to stay by himself with the
soldier who guarded him.

a Ac 24:23

Paul's First Interview with Roman Jews

17 After three days he called together
the leaders of the Jews. And when they
had gathered he said to them: "Brothers, [a]although I have done nothing
against our people or the customs of
our forefathers, I [b]was delivered as a
prisoner from Jerusalem into the hands
of the Romans 18 who, [c]after examining me, wanted to release me, since I
had not committed a capital offense.
19 Because the Jews objected, [d]I was
compelled to appeal to Caesar; it was
not as though I had any accusation
against my nation. 20 So, for this reason
I've asked to see you and speak to you.
In fact, it is [e]for the hope of Israel that
I'm wearing [f]this chain."

a Ac 24:12; 25:8 b Ac 21:33
c Ac 22:24; 24:10; 25:8
d Ac 25:11 e Ac 26:6-7
f Ac 26:29; Eph 3:1; 6:20

21 And they said to him, "We haven't
received any letters about you from
Judea; none of the brothers has come
and reported or spoken anything evil
about you. 22 But we consider it suitable to hear from you what you think.
For concerning this sect, we are aware
that [a]it is spoken against everywhere."

a Lk 2:34; Ac 24:5

The Response to Paul's Message

23 After arranging a day with him,
many came to him at his lodging. From
dawn to dusk [a]he expounded and witnessed about the kingdom of God. He
persuaded them concerning Jesus from
both the Law of Moses and the Prophets. 24 [b]Some were persuaded by what
he said, but others did not believe.

a Ac 17:2-3; 26:22-23
b Ac 13:48-50; 14:4; 18:6-8

25 Disagreeing among themselves,
they began to leave after Paul made
one statement: "The Holy Spirit correctly spoke through the prophet Isaiah to your[e] forefathers 26 when He
said,

[a]Go to this people and say:
'You will listen and listen,
yet never understand;
and you will look and look,
yet never perceive.
27 **[b]For this people's heart**
has grown callous,
their ears are hard
of hearing,

[a]**28:11** Gk *Dioscuri,* twin sons of Zeus [b]**28:13** Other mss read *From there, casting off,* [c]**28:14,15** Lit *brothers* [d]**28:16** Other mss add *the centurion turned the prisoners over to the military commander; but* [e]**28:25** Other mss read *our*

and they have shut their eyes;
otherwise they might see
with their eyes
and hear with their ears,
understand with their heart,
and be converted—
and I would heal them.'[a]

[28] Therefore, let it be known to you
that this saving work of God has been
sent [c]to the Gentiles; they will listen!"
[[29] After he said these things, the Jews
departed, while engaging in a pro-
longed debate among themselves.][b]

[a] *Is 6:9* [b] *Is 44:18* [c] *Mt 21:41; Rm 11:11*

Paul's Ministry Unhindered

[30] Then he stayed two whole years in
his own rented house. And he welcomed all who visited him, [31] [a]pro-
claiming the kingdom of God and teaching the things concerning the Lord
Jesus Christ with full boldness and
without hindrance.

[a] *Eph 6:19; Php 1:13*

ROMANS

God's Good News for Rome

1 Paul, a slave of Christ Jesus, [a]called
as an apostle[c] and singled out for
God's good news— [2] [b]which He promised long ago through His prophets in
the Holy Scriptures— [3] concerning His
Son, Jesus Christ our Lord, who was a
descendant of David[d] according to the
flesh [4] and was established as the powerful Son of God by the resurrection
from the dead according [c]to the Spirit
of holiness.[e] [5] [d]We have received grace
and apostleship through Him to bring
about[f] the obedience of faith[g] among
[e]all the nations,[h] on behalf of His
name, [6] including yourselves who are
also Jesus Christ's by calling:

[7] To all who are in Rome, loved by
God, called as saints.

Grace to you and peace from God
our Father and the Lord Jesus Christ.

[a] *Ac 9:15; 2Co 1:1* [b] *Ti 1:2* [c] *Heb 9:14* [d] *Eph 3:8* [e] *Ac 9:15-16*

The Apostle's Desire to Visit Rome

[8] First, [a]I thank my God through
Jesus Christ for all of you because the
news of [b]your faith[i] is being reported
in all the world. [9] For God, whom I
serve with my spirit in ⌊telling⌋ the
good news about His Son, is my witness that I constantly mention you,
[10] always asking in my prayers that if it
is somehow [c]in God's will, I may now
at last succeed in coming to you. [11] For
I want very much to see you, that [d]I
may impart to you some spiritual gift to
strengthen you, [12] that is, to be mutu-
ally encouraged by each other's faith,
both yours and mine.

[a] *Php 1:3* [b] *1Th 1:8* [c] *Jms 4:15* [d] *Rm 15:29*

[13] Now I want you to know,[j] brothers,
that I [a]often planned to come to you
(but [b]was prevented until now) in order that I might have a fruitful ministry[k]
among you, just as among the rest of
the Gentiles. [14] [c]I am obligated both to
Greeks and barbarians,[l] both to the
wise and the foolish. [15] So I am eager to
preach the good news to you also who
are in Rome.

[a] *Rm 15:23* [b] *Ac 16:7* [c] *Ps 40:9*

The Righteous Will Live by Faith

[16] For [a]I am not ashamed of the gospel,[m] because [b]it is God's power for salvation to everyone who believes, first

[a]**28:26–27** Is 6:9–10 [b]**28:29** Other mss omit bracketed text [c]**1:1** Or *Jesus, a called apostle* [d]**1:3** Lit *was of the seed of David* [e]**1:4** Or *the spirit of holiness*, or *the Holy Spirit* [f]**1:5** Lit *Him into*, or *Him for* [g]**1:5** Or *the obedience that is faith*, or *the faithful obedience*, or *the obedience that comes from faith* [h]**1:5** Or *Gentiles* [i]**1:8** Or *because your faith* [j]**1:13** Lit *I don't want you to be unaware* [k]**1:13** Lit *have some fruit* [l]**1:14** Or *non-Greeks* [m]**1:16** Other mss add *of Christ*

to the Jew, and also to the Greek. 17 For
[c]in it God's righteousness is revealed
from faith to faith,[a] just as it is written:
[d]**The righteous will live by faith.**[b c]

[a] 2Tm 1:8 [b] 1Co 1:18
[c] Rm 3:21 [d] Hab 2:4

The Guilt of the Gentile World

18 [a]For God's wrath is revealed from
heaven against all godlessness and unrighteousness of people [b]who by their
unrighteousness suppress the truth,
19 since [c]what can be known[d] about
God is evident among them, because
[d]God has shown it to them. 20 From the
creation of the world [e]His invisible at-
tributes, that is, His eternal power and
divine nature, have been clearly seen,
being understood through what He has
made. As a result, people[e] are without
excuse. 21 For though they knew God,
they did not glorify Him as God [f]or
show gratitude. Instead, their thinking
became nonsense, and their senseless
minds[f] were darkened. 22 [g]Claiming to
be wise, they became fools 23 and exchanged the glory of the immortal
[h]God for images resembling mortal
man, birds, four-footed animals, and
reptiles.

[a] Rm 2:5-6 [b] Jb 24:13 [c] Ac 14:17
[d] Jn 1:9 [e] Ps 19:1 [f] Ps 106:13
[g] Jr 10:14 [h] Is 40:18

24 [a]Therefore God delivered them
over in the cravings of their hearts to
sexual impurity, so that [b]their bodies
were degraded [c]among themselves.
25 They exchanged [d]the truth of God
[e]for a lie, and worshiped and served
something created instead of the Creator, who is blessed forever. •Amen.

[a] Ps 81:12 [b] 1Co 6:18 [c] Lv 18:22
[d] 1Th 1:9 [e] Is 44:20

From Idolatry to Depravity

26 This is why God delivered them
over to [a]degrading passions. For even
their females exchanged natural sexual
intercourse[g] for what is unnatural.
27 The males in the same way also left
natural sexual intercourse[g] with females and were inflamed in their lust
for one another. Males committed
shameless acts with males and received in their own persons[h] the appropriate penalty for their perversion.[i]

[a] Jd 10

28 And because they did not think it
worthwhile to have God in their
knowledge, God delivered them over
to a worthless mind to do [a]what is
morally wrong. 29 They are filled with
all unrighteousness,[j] evil, greed, and
wickedness. They are full of envy, murder, disputes, deceit, and malice. They
are gossips, 30 slanderers, God-haters,
arrogant, proud, boastful, inventors of
evil, disobedient to parents, 31 undis-
cerning, untrustworthy, unloving,[k] and
unmerciful. 32 Although they know full
well God's just sentence—that those
who practice such things deserve to
die[l]—they not only do them, but even
applaud[m] others who practice them.

[a] Rm 1:24; Gl 5:19-21; Eph 4:19

God's Righteous Judgment

2 Therefore, anyone of you[n] who
judges is without excuse. For
when you judge another, you condemn yourself, since you, the judge,
do the same things. 2 We know that
God's judgment on those who do such
things is [a]based on the truth. 3 [b]Do
you really think—anyone of you who
judges those who do such things yet
do the same—that you will escape
God's judgment? 4 Or do you despise
[c]the riches of His kindness, restraint,
and [d]patience, not recognizing[o] that
God's kindness is intended to lead you
to repentance? 5 But because of your
hardness and unrepentant heart you

[a]**1:17** Or *revealed out of faith into faith* [b]**1:17** Or *The one who is righteous by faith will live*
[c]**1:17** Hab 2:4 [d]**1:19** Or *what is known* [e]**1:20** Lit *they* [f]**1:21** Lit *hearts* [g]**1:26,27** Lit *natural use*
[h]**1:27** Or *in themselves* [i]**1:27** Or *error* [j]**1:29** Other mss add *sexual immorality* [k]**1:31** Other mss add *unforgiving* [l]**1:32** Lit *things are worthy of death* [m]**1:32** Lit *even take pleasure in* [n]**2:1** Lit *Therefore, O man, every one* [o]**2:4** Or *patience, because you do not recognize*

are [e]storing up wrath for yourself in the day of wrath, when God's righteous judgment is revealed. 6 [f]He will **repay each one according to his works:**[a] 7 [g]eternal life to those who by patiently doing good seek for glory, honor, and immortality; 8 but [h]wrath and indignation to those who are self-seeking and disobey the truth, but are obeying unrighteousness; 9 affliction and distress for every human being who does evil, [i]first to the Jew, and also to the Greek; 10 [j]but glory, honor, and peace for everyone who does good, first to the Jew, and also to the Greek. 11 There is [k]no favoritism with God.

[a] Gn 18:25; 2Th 1:6 [b] Pr 11:21 [c] Ps 86:5 [d] Ex 34:6; 2Pt 3:9 [e] Jms 5:3 [f] Ps 62:12; Is 3:10-11; Mt 16:27 [g] Jd 21 [h] 2Th 2:12 [i] 1Pt 4:17 [j] 1Pt 1:7 [k] Dt 10:17

12 All those who sinned without the law will also perish without the law, and all those who sinned under the law will be judged by the law. 13 For [a]the hearers of the law are not righteous before God, but the doers of the law will be declared righteous.[b] 14 So, when Gentiles, who do not have the law, instinctively do what the law demands, they are a law to themselves even though they do not have the law. 15 They show that the work of the law[c] is written on their hearts. Their consciences testify in support of this, and their competing thoughts either accuse or excuse them[d] 16 [b]on the day when God judges what people have kept secret, according to my gospel [c]through Christ Jesus.

[a] Dt 30:12-14 [b] Rv 20:12 [c] Jn 5:22

Jewish Violation of the Law

17 Now [a]if[e] you call yourself a Jew, and [b]rest in the law, [c]and boast in God, 18 and [d]know His will, and approve the things that are superior, being instructed from the law, 19 and are con vinced that you are a guide for th blind, a light to those in darkness, 20 ar instructor of the ignorant, a teacher c the immature, [e]having in the law th full expression[f] of knowledge an truth— 21 [f]you then, who teach an other, do you not teach yourself? Yo who preach, "You must not steal"—d you steal? 22 You who say, "You mus not commit adultery"—do you com mit adultery? You who detest idols, [g]d you rob their temples? 23 You wh boast in the law, do you dishonor Go by breaking the law? 24 For, as it i [h]written: **The name of God is blas phemed among the Gentiles becaus of you.**[g]

[a] Rm 9:6 [b] Mc 3:11 [c] Jn 8:4 [d] Dt 4:8 [e] 2Tm 3:5 [f] Mt 23:3 [g] Mal 3:8 [h] Is 52:

Circumcision of the Heart

25 [a]For circumcision benefits you i you observe the law, but if you are lawbreaker, your circumcision has be come uncircumcision. 26 Therefore [b]i an uncircumcised man keeps the law' requirements, will his uncircumcisio not be counted as circumcision? 27 A man who is physically uncircumcised but who fulfills the law, will judge yo who are a lawbreaker in spite of havin the letter ⌊of the law⌋ and circumcision 28 For [c]a person is not a Jew who is on outwardly, and ⌊true⌋ circumcision i not something visible in the flesh 29 On the contrary, a person is a Jev [d]who is one inwardly, and [e]cir- cumci sion is of the heart—[f]by the Spirit, no the letter.[h] His praise[i] is not from mer but from God.

[a] Gl 5: [b] Ac 10:34 [c] Ac 13:26; Gl 6:1 [d] 1Pt 3:4 [e] Col 2:11 [f] Rm 7:

Paul Answers an Objection

3 So what advantage does the Jev have? Or what is the benefit of ci

[a]**2:6** Ps 62:12; Pr 24:12 [b]**2:13** Or *will be justified* or *acquitted* [c]**2:15** The code of conduct required by the law [d]**2:15** Internal debate, either in a person or among the pagan moralists [e]**2:17** Other mss read *Look—* [f]**2:20** Or *the embodiment* [g]**2:24** Is 52:5 [h]**2:29** Or *heart—spiritually, not literally* [i]**2:29** In Hb, the words *Jew, Judah,* and *praise* are related.

cumcision? 2 Considerable in every
way. First, [a]they were entrusted with
the spoken words of God. 3 What then?
If [b]some did not believe, [c]will their unbelief cancel God's faithfulness? 4 Absolutely not! [d]God must be true, but
everyone is a liar, as it is written:

> [e]**That You may be justified**
> **in Your words**
> **and triumph when You judge.**[a]

5 But if our unrighteousness high-
lights[b] God's righteousness, what are
we to say? I use a human argument:[c]
Is God unrighteous to inflict wrath?
6 Absolutely not! Otherwise, [f]how will
God judge the world? 7 But if by my lie
God's truth is amplified to His glory,
why am I also still judged as a sinner?
8 And why not say, just as some people
slanderously claim we say, "Let us do
evil so that good may come"? Their
condemnation is deserved!

a Dt 4:7-8 b Heb 4:2 c Nm 23:19 d Jn 3:33 e Ps 51:4 f Ps 9:8

The Whole World Guilty before God

9 What then? Are we any better?[d]
Not at all! For we have [a]previously
charged that both Jews and Gentiles[e]
[b]are all under sin,[f] 10 as it is written:[g]

> [c]**There is no one righteous,**
> **not even one;**
> 11 **there is no one**
> **who understands,**
> **there is no one**
> **who seeks God.**
> 12 **All have turned away,**
> **together they have become**
> **useless;**
> **there is no one**
> **who does good,**
> **there is not even one.**[h]
> 13 [d]**Their throat is an open grave;**
> **they deceive**
> **with their tongues.**[i]
> [e]**Vipers' venom is**
> **under their lips.**[j]
> 14 [f]**Their mouth is full of cursing**
> **and bitterness.**[k]
> 15 [g]**Their feet are swift**
> **to shed blood;**
> 16 **ruin and wretchedness are**
> **in their paths,**
> 17 **and the path of peace**
> **they have not known.**[l]
> 18 [h]**There is no fear of God**
> **before their eyes.**[m]

a Rm 1:28 b Gl 3:22 c Ps 14:1 d Ps 5:9 e Ps 140:3 f Ps 10:7 g Pr 1:16 h Ps 36:1

19 Now we know that whatever the
law says speaks to those who are subject to the law,[n] so that [a]every mouth
may be shut and [b]the whole world may
become subject to God's judgment.[o]
20 For [c]no flesh will be justified[p] in His
sight by the works of the law, for
[d]through the law ⌊comes⌋ the knowledge of sin.

a Ezk 16:63 b Rm 2:2 c Ps 143:2; Gl 2:16 d Rm 7:7

God's Righteousness through Faith

21 But now, [a]apart from the law,
God's righteousness has been revealed
—attested by the Law [b]and the
Prophets[q] 22 —that is, God's righteousness [c]through faith in Jesus Christ,[r] to
all who believe, since [d]there is no distinction. 23 For [e]all have sinned and fall
short of the[s] glory of God. 24 They are
justified freely [f]by His grace through the
redemption that is in Christ Jesus.
25 God presented Him [g]as a propitiation[t]

[a]**3:4** Ps 51:4 [b]**3:5** Or *shows*, or *demonstrates* [c]**3:5** Lit *I speak as a man* [d]**3:9** Are we Jews any better than the Gentiles? [e]**3:9** Lit *Greeks* [f]**3:9** Under sin's power or dominion [g]**3:10** Paul constructs this charge from a chain of OT quotations, mainly from the Psalms. [h]**3:10–12** Ps 14:1–3; 53:1–3; see Ec 7:20 [i]**3:13** Ps 5:9 [j]**3:13** Ps 140:3 [k]**3:14** Ps 10:7 [l]**3:15–17** Is 59:7–8 [m]**3:18** Ps 36:1 [n]**3:19** Lit *those in the law* [o]**3:19** Or *become guilty before God*, or *may be accountable to God* [p]**3:20** Or *will be declared righteous*, or *will be acquitted* [q]**3:21** When capitalized, *the Law and the Prophets* = OT [r]**3:22** Or *through the faithfulness of Jesus Christ* [s]**3:23** Or *and lack the* [t]**3:25** Or *as a propitiatory sacrifice*, or *as an offering of atonement*, or *as a mercy seat*; see Heb 9:5. The word *propitiation* has to do with the removal of divine wrath. Jesus' death is the means that turns God's wrath from the sinner; see 2 Co 5:21.

through faith in His blood, to demonstrate His righteousness, because in His
restraint God passed over the sins previously committed. 26 He presented
Him to demonstrate His righteousness
at the present time, so that He would be
righteous and declare righteous[a] the
one who has faith in Jesus.

[a] Rm 1:17
[b] 1Pt 1:10 [c] Rm 4
[d] Col 3:11 [e] Gl 3:22 [f] Eph 1:7
[g] Is 53:11; 1Jn 4:10

Boasting Excluded

27 Where then is boasting? It is excluded. By what kind of law?[b] By one of
works? No, on the contrary, by a law[c]
of faith. 28 For we conclude [a]that a man
is justified by faith apart from works of
law. 29 Or is God for Jews only? Is He
not also for Gentiles? Yes, for Gentiles
too, 30 since there is one God who will
justify the circumcised by faith and the
uncircumcised through faith. 31 Do we
then cancel the law through faith? Absolutely not! On the contrary, we up-
hold the law.

[a] Gl 2:16

Abraham Justified by Faith

4 What then can we say that Abraham, our forefather according to
the flesh, has found? 2 If Abraham was
justified[d] by works, then he has something to brag about—but not before
God.[e] 3 For what does the Scripture
say?

> [a]**Abraham believed God,**
> **and it was credited to him**
> **for righteousness.**[f]

4 Now [b]to the one who works, pay is
not considered as a gift, but as something owed. 5 But to the one who does
not work, but believes on Him who
declares righteous[g] [c]the ungodly, his
faith is credited for righteousness.

[a] Gn 15:6 [b] Rm 11:6
[c] Ac 13:39; Gl 2:16

David Celebrating the Same Truth

6 Likewise, David also speaks of the
blessing of the man to whom God
[a]credits righteousness apart from
works:

> 7 [b]**How happy those whose**
> **lawless acts are forgiven**
> **and whose sins are covered!**
> 8 **How happy the man whom**
> **the Lord will never charge**
> **with sin!**[h]

[a] 1Co 1:30; 2Co 5:19
[b] Ps 32:1-2

Abraham Justified before Circumcision

9 Is this blessing only for the circumcised, then? Or is it also for the uncircumcised? For we say, [a]**Faith was**
credited to Abraham for righteous-
ness.[f] 10 How then was it credited—
while he was circumcised, or uncircumcised? Not while he was circumcised, but uncircumcised. 11 And [b]he
received the sign of circumcision as a
seal of the righteousness that he had
by faith[i] while still uncircumcised.
[c]This was to make him the father of all
who believe but are not circumcised,
so that righteousness may be credited
to them also. 12 And he became the father of the circumcised, not only to
those who are circumcised, but also to
those who follow in the footsteps of
the faith our father Abraham had while
still uncircumcised.

[a] Gn 15:6
[b] Gn 17:10 [c] Lk 19:9

The Promise Granted through Faith

13 For the promise to Abraham or to
his [a]descendants that he would inherit
the world was not through the law, but
through the righteousness that comes
by faith.[i] 14 [b]If those who are of the law
are heirs, faith is made empty and the
promise is canceled. 15 For the law pro-

[a]**3:26** Or *and justify*, or *and acquit* [b]**3:27** Or *what principle?* [c]**3:27** Or *a principle* [d]**4:2** Or *was declared righteous*, or *was acquitted* [e]**4:2** He has no reason for boasting in God's presence [f]**4:3,9** Gn 15:6 [g]**4:5** Or *who acquits*, or *who justifies* [h]**4:7–8** Ps 32:1–2 [i]**4:11,13** Lit *righteousness of faith*

duces wrath; but where there is no
law, there is no transgression.

[a] Gn 12:3; Gl 3:29 [b] Gl 3:18

16 This is why the promise is by faith,
so that it may be [a]according to grace, to
guarantee it to all the descendants—
not only to those [b]who are of the law,[a]
but also to those who are of Abraham's
faith. He is the father of us all 17 in
God's sight. As it is written: [c]**I have
made you the father of many na-
tions.**[b] He believed in God, who [d]gives
life to the dead and calls [e]things into existence that do not exist. 18 Against
hope, with hope he believed, so that he
became **the father of many nations,**[b]
according to what had been spoken:
[f]**So will your descendants be.**[c] 19 [g]He
considered[d] his own body to be already
dead (since he was about a hundred
years old), and the deadness of Sarah's
womb, without weakening in the faith.
20 He did not waver in unbelief at God's
promise, but was strengthened in his
faith and gave glory to God, 21 because
he was fully convinced that what He
had promised He was also able to perform. 22 Therefore, [h]**it was credited to
him for righteousness.**[e] 23 Now **it was
credited to him** was not written for
Abraham alone, 24 but also for us. It will
be credited to us who believe [i]in Him
who raised Jesus our Lord from the
dead. 25 [j]He was delivered up for[f] our
trespasses and raised for[f] our justification.[g]

[a] Rm 3:24; Col 3:11 [b] Rm 9:8 [c] Gn 17:5 [d] Rm 8:11 [e] 1Co 1:28 [f] Gn 15:5 [g] Heb 11:11 [h] Gn 15:6 [i] Ac 13:30 [j] Is 53:5

Faith Triumphs

5 Therefore, since we have been declared righteous by faith, we have
[a]peace[h] with God through our Lord
Jesus Christ. 2 Also [b]through Him, we
have obtained access by faith[i] into this
grace [c]in which we stand, [d]and we rejoice in the hope of the glory of God.
3 And not only that, but [e]we also rejoice in our afflictions, because we
know that affliction produces endurance, 4 endurance produces proven
character, and proven character produces hope. 5 [f]This hope does not dis-
appoint, [g]because God's love has been
poured out in our hearts through the
Holy Spirit who was given to us.

[a] Is 32:17; Eph 2:14 [b] Eph 3:12; Heb 10:19 [c] 1Co 15:1 [d] Rm 15:13 [e] Rm 8:35-37 [f] Php 1:20 [g] Gl 4:6; Eph 1:13

Those Declared Righteous Are Reconciled

6 For while we were still helpless, at
the appointed moment, Christ died for
the ungodly. 7 For rarely will someone
die for a just person—though for a
good person perhaps someone might
even dare to die. 8 But [a]God proves His
own love for us in that while we were
still sinners Christ died for us! 9 Much
more then, since we have now been
declared righteous [b]by His blood, we
will be saved through Him [c]from
wrath. 10 For if, while [d]we were enemies, we were reconciled to God
through the death of His Son, ⌊then
how⌋ much more, having been reconciled, will we be saved [e]by His life!
11 And not only that, but we also rejoice in God through our Lord Jesus
Christ, through whom we have now
received reconciliation.

[a] Jn 15:13; 1Pt 3:18 [b] 1Jn 1:7 [c] 1Th 1:10 [d] 2Co 5:18 [e] Jn 14:19

Death through Adam and Life through Christ

12 Therefore, [a]just as sin entered the
world through one man, and death
through sin, in this way death spread
to all men, because all sinned.[j] 13 In
fact, sin was in the world before the
law, but [b]sin is not charged to one's

[a]**4:16** Or *not to those who are of the law only* [b]**4:17,18** Gn 17:5 [c]**4:18** Gn 15:5 [d]**4:19** Other mss read *He did not consider* [e]**4:22** Gn 15:6 [f]**4:25** Or *because of* [g]**4:25** Or *acquittal* [h]**5:1** Other mss read *faith, let us have peace*, which can also be translated *faith, let us grasp the fact that we have peace* [i]**5:2** Other mss omit *by faith* [j]**5:12** Or *have sinned*

account when there is no law. [14] Nevertheless, death reigned from Adam to Moses, even over those who did not sin in the likeness of Adam's transgression. He is a prototype of the Coming One. [a] Ezk 18:4 [b] 1Jn 3:4

[15] But the gift is not like the trespass. For if by the one man's trespass the many died, how much more have the grace of God and the gift overflowed [a]to the many by the grace of the one man, Jesus Christ. [16] And the gift is not like the one man's sin, because from one sin came the judgment, resulting in condemnation, but from many trespasses came the gift, resulting in justification.[a] [17] Since by the one man's trespass, death reigned through that one man, how much more will those who receive the overflow of grace and the gift of righteousness reign in life through the one man, Jesus Christ.

[a] Mt 20:28

[18] So then, as through one trespass there is condemnation for everyone, so also through one righteous act there is [a]life-giving justification[b] for everyone. [19] For just as through one man's disobedience the many were made sinners, so also through the one man's obedience the many will be made righteous. [20] [b]The law came along to multiply the trespass. But where sin multiplied, grace multiplied [c]even more, [21] so that, just as sin reigned in death, so also grace will reign through righteousness, resulting in eternal life through Jesus Christ our Lord.

[a] Jn 12:32; Heb 2:9 [b] Rm 3:20 [c] 1Tm 1:14

The New Life in Christ

6 What should we say then? Should we continue in sin in order that grace may multiply? [2] Absolutely not! How can we who [a]died to sin still live in it? [3] Or are you unaware that [b]all of us who were baptized into Christ Jesus were baptized into His death? [4] Therefore we were [c]buried with Him by baptism into death, in order that, [d]just as Christ was raised from the dead by the glory of the Father, [e]so we too may •walk in a new way[c] of life. [5] [f]For if we have been joined with Him in the likeness of His death, we will certainly also be[d] in the likeness of His resurrection. [6] For we know that [g]our old self[e] was crucified with Him in order that [h]sin's dominion over the body[f] may be abolished, so that we may no longer be enslaved to sin, [7] since a person who has died is freed[g] from sin's claims.[h] [8] Now [i]if we died with Christ, we believe that we will also live with Him, [9] because we know that [j]Christ, having been raised from the dead, no longer dies. Death no longer rules over Him. [10] For in that He died, He died to sin once for all; but in that He lives, He lives to God. [11] So, you too consider yourselves dead to sin, but [k]alive to God in Christ Jesus.[i]

[a] Rm 3:19-20 [b] Col 3:3
[c] Col 2:12 [d] 1Co 6:14 [e] 2Co 5:17; Gl 6:15
[f] Eph 2:5-6; Php 3:10 [g] Gl 2:20
[h] Col 2:11 [i] 2Co 5:1 [j] Rv 1:18 [k] Gl 2:19

[12] [a]Therefore do not let sin reign in your mortal body, so that you obey[j] its desires. [13] And do not offer any parts[k] of it to sin as weapons for unrighteousness. But as those who are alive from the dead, offer yourselves to God, and all the parts[k] of yourselves to God as weapons for righteousness. [14] For [b]sin will not rule over you, because you are not under law but under grace.

[a] Eph 4:22 [b] Gl 5:18; Ti 2:14

From Slaves of Sin to Slaves of God

[15] What then? Should we sin [a]because we are not under law but under grace? Absolutely not! [16] Do you not know that if you offer yourselves to

[a]**5:16** Or *acquittal* [b]**5:18** Lit *is justification of life* [c]**6:4** Or *in newness* [d]**6:5** Be joined with Him [e]**6:6** Lit *man*; that is, the person that one was in Adam [f]**6:6** Lit *that the body of sin* [g]**6:7** Lit *acquitted*, or *justified* [h]**6:7** Lit *from sin* [i]**6:11** Other mss add *our Lord* [j]**6:12** Other mss add *sin* (lit *it*) *in* [k]**6:13** Or *members*

someone[a] as obedient slaves, you are slaves of that one you obey—either of sin leading to death or of obedience leading to righteousness? 17 But thank God that, although you used to be slaves of sin, you obeyed from the heart that pattern of teaching you were entrusted to, 18 and having been [b]liberated from sin, you became enslaved to righteousness. 19 I am using a human analogy[b] because of the weakness of your flesh.[c] For just as you offered the parts[d] of yourselves as slaves to moral impurity, and to greater and greater lawlessness, so now offer them as slaves to righteousness, which results in sanctification. 20 For when you were slaves of sin, you were free from allegiance to righteousness.[e] 21 And what fruit was produced[f] then from the things you are now ashamed of? For the end of those things is death. 22 But now, since you have been liberated from sin and become enslaved to God, you have your fruit, which results in sanctification[g]—and the end is eternal life! **23 For [c]the wages of sin is death, but [d]the gift of God is eternal life in Christ Jesus our Lord.**

[a] 1Co 9:21 [b] Gl 5:1 [c] Rm 5:12 [d] Jn 3:16

An Illustration from Marriage

7 Since I am speaking to those who understand law, brothers, are you unaware that the law has authority over someone as long as he lives? 2 For example, [a]a married woman is legally bound to her husband while he lives. But if her husband dies, she is released from the law regarding the husband. 3 So then, [b]if she gives herself to another man while her husband is living, she will be called an adulteress. But if her husband dies, she is free from that law. Then, if she gives herself to another man, she is not an adulteress.

[a] 1Co 7:39 [b] Mt 5:32; 1Co 6:9

4 Therefore, my brothers, you also were [a]put to death in relation to the law through the ⌊crucified⌋ body of the •Messiah, so that you may [b]belong to another—to Him who was raised from the dead—that we may bear fruit for God. 5 For when we were in the flesh,[h] the sinful passions operated through the law in every part of us[i] and [c]bore fruit for death. 6 But now we have been released from the law, since we have died to what held us, so that we may serve [d]in the new way[j] of the Spirit and not in the old letter of the law.

[a] Rm 6:14; Gl 2:19 [b] 2Co 11:2 [c] Rm 6:21; Gl 5:19-21 [d] Gl 2:19-20

Sin's Use of the Law

7 What should we say then? Is the law sin? Absolutely not! On the contrary, [a]I would not have known sin if it were not for the law. For example, I would not have known what it is to covet if the law had not said, [b]**Do not covet.**[k] 8 And [c]sin, seizing an opportunity through the commandment, produced in me coveting of every kind. For [d]apart from the law sin is dead. 9 Once I was alive apart from the law, but when the commandment came, sin sprang to life 10 and I died. The commandment [e]that was meant for life resulted in death for me. 11 For sin, seizing an opportunity through the commandment, deceived me, and through it killed me. 12 So then, [f]the law is holy, and the commandment is holy and just and good.

[a] Rm 3:20 [b] Ex 20:17 [c] Rm 4:15 [d] 1Co 15:56 [e] Lv 18:5; 2Co 3:7 [f] 1Tm 1:8

The Problem of Sin in Us

13 Therefore, did what is good cause my death?[l] Absolutely not! On the contrary, sin, in order to be recognized as sin, was producing death in me through what is good, so that through

[a]**6:16** Lit *that to whom you offer yourselves* [b]**6:19** Lit *I speak humanly*; Paul is personifying sin and righteousness as slave masters. [c]**6:19** Or *your human nature* [d]**6:19** Or *members* [e]**6:20** Lit *free to righteousness* [f]**6:21** Lit *what fruit do you have* [g]**6:22** Or *holiness* [h]**7:5** *in the flesh* = a person's life before accepting Christ [i]**7:5** Lit *of our members* [j]**7:6** Lit *in newness* [k]**7:7** Ex 20:17 [l]**7:13** Lit *good become death to me?*

the commandment sin might become sinful beyond measure. 14 For we know that the law is spiritual; but I am made out of flesh,[a] sold into sin's power. 15 For [a]I do not understand what I am doing, because I do not practice what I want to do, but I do what I hate. 16 And if I do what I do not want to do, I agree with the law that it is good. 17 So now I am no longer the one doing it, but it is sin living in me. 18 For I know that nothing good lives [b]in me, that is, in my flesh. For the desire to do what is good is with me, but there is no ability to do it. 19 For I do not do the good that I want to do, but I practice the evil that I do not want to do. 20 Now if I do what I do not want, I am no longer the one doing it, but it is the sin that lives in me. 21 So I discover this principle:[b] when I want to do good, evil is with me. 22 For in [c]my inner self[c] I [d]joyfully agree with God's law. 23 But I see a different law in the parts of my body,[d] waging war against the law of my mind and taking me prisoner to the law of sin in the parts of my body.[d] 24 What a wretched man I am! Who will rescue me from this body of death? 25 I thank God through Jesus Christ our Lord![e] So then, with my mind I myself am a slave to the law of God, but with my flesh, to the law of sin.

a Gl 5:17 b Gn 8:21 c 2Co 4:16 d Ps 1:2

The Life-Giving Spirit

8 Therefore, no condemnation now exists for those in Christ Jesus,[f] 2 because [a]the Spirit's [b]law of life in Christ Jesus has set you[g] free from the law of sin and of death. 3 [c]What the law could not do since it was limited[h] by the flesh, God did. He condemned sin in the flesh by sending His own Son in flesh like ours under sin's domain,[i] and as a sin offering, 4 in order that the law's requirement would be accomplished in us who do not •walk according to the flesh but according to the Spirit. 5 For those whose lives are[j] according to the flesh think about the things of the flesh, but those whose lives are[j] according to the Spirit, about [d]the things of the Spirit. 6 For the mind-set of the flesh is death, but the mind-set of the Spirit is life and peace. 7 For the mind-set of the flesh is hostile to God because it does not submit itself to God's law, for it is unable to do so. 8 Those whose lives are[k] in the flesh are unable to please God. 9 You, however, are not in the flesh, but in the Spirit, since[l] [e]the Spirit of God lives in you. But if anyone does not have [f]the Spirit of Christ, he does not belong to Him. 10 Now if Christ is in you, the body is dead[m] because of sin, but the Spirit[n] is life because of righteousness. 11 And if the Spirit of Him who raised Jesus from the dead lives in you, then [g]He who raised Christ from the dead will also bring your mortal bodies to life through[o] His Spirit who lives in you.

a 2Co 3:6 b Gl 2:19 c Heb 7:18 d 1Co 2:15 e 1Co 3:16 f 1Pt 1:11 g Rm 6:4-5

The Holy Spirit's Ministries

12 So then, brothers, we are not obligated to the flesh to live according to the flesh, 13 for [a]if you live according to the flesh, you are going to die. But if by the Spirit you put to death the deeds of the body, you will live. 14 All those led by God's Spirit are God's sons. 15 For [b]you did not receive a spirit of slavery to fall back [c]into fear, but you received the [d]Spirit of adoption, by whom we cry out, "•*Abba*, Father!" 16 [e]The Spirit Himself testifies together with our spirit that we are God's children, 17 and if children, also heirs—[f]heirs of God and

[a]**7:14** Other mss read *I am carnal* [b]**7:21** Or *law* [c]**7:22** Lit *inner man* [d]**7:23** Lit *my members* [e]**7:25** Or *Thanks be to God—*(it is done) *through Jesus Christ our Lord!* [f]**8:1** Other mss add *who do not walk according to the flesh but according to the Spirit* [g]**8:2** Other mss read *me* [h]**8:3** Or *weak* [i]**8:3** Lit *in the likeness of sinful flesh* [j]**8:5** Or *those who are* [k]**8:8** Or *Those who are* [l]**8:9** Or *provided that* [m]**8:10** Or *the body will die* [n]**8:10** Or *spirit* [o]**8:11** Other mss read *because of*

co-heirs with Christ—seeing that[a] we
suffer with Him so that we may also be
glorified with Him.

[a]Rm 6:21-22; Gl 6:8 [b]Heb 2:15
[c]2Tm 1:7 [d]Gl 4:5-6 [e]Eph 1:13
[f]Jn 17:24; Ac 26:18; Gl 4:7

From Groans to Glory

18 For I consider that [a]the sufferings
of this present time are not worth com-
paring with the glory that is going to be
revealed to us. 19 For the creation [b]ea-
gerly waits with anticipation for [c]God's
sons to be revealed. 20 For [d]the creation
was subjected to futility—not willingly,
but because of Him who subjected
it—in the hope 21 that the creation itself will also be set free from the bondage of corruption into the glorious
freedom of God's children. 22 For we
know that the whole creation has been
groaning together with labor pains until now. 23 And not only that, but we
ourselves who have the Spirit as [e]the
•firstfruits—we also groan within ourselves, [f]eagerly waiting for adoption,
the redemption of our bodies. 24 Now
in this hope we were saved, [g]yet hope
that is seen is not hope, because who
hopes for what he sees? 25 But if we
hope for what we do not see, we eagerly wait for it with patience.

[a]2Co 4:17 [b]2Pt 3:13
[c]1Jn 3:2 [d]Gn 3:19 [e]2Co 5:5
[f]Lk 20:36 [g]Heb 11:1

26 In the same way the Spirit also
joins to help in our weakness, because
we do not know what to pray for as we
should, but [a]the Spirit Himself intercedes for us[b] with unspoken groanings.
27 And [b]He who searches the hearts
knows the Spirit's mind-set, because
He intercedes for the saints [c]according
to the will of God.

[a]Eph 6:18 [b]1Th 2:4 [c]1Jn 5:14

28 We know that [a]all things work
together[c] for the good[d] of those who
love God: those [b]who are called according to His purpose. 29 For those
[c]He foreknew[e] [d]He also predestined
[e]to be conformed to the image of His
Son, [f]so that He would be the firstborn
among many brothers. 30 And those He
predestined, He also [g]called; and those
He called, He also justified; [h]and those
He justified, He also glorified.

[a]Pr 12:21; 2Co 4:17 [b]2Tm 1:9
[c]2Tm 2:19 [d]Eph 1:5 [e]Jn 17:22
[f]Col 1:18 [g]Eph 4:4 [h]1Co 6:11

The Believer's Triumph

31 What then are we to say
about these things?
If God is for us, who is
against us?
32 He did not even spare
His own Son,
but offered Him up for us all;
how will He not also with Him
grant us everything?
33 Who can bring an accusation
against God's elect?
[a]God is the One who justifies.
34 Who is the one who condemns?
Christ Jesus is the One who died,
but even more,
has been raised;
He also is at the right hand
of God [b]and intercedes for us.
35 Who can separate us
from the love of Christ?
Can affliction or anguish
or persecution
or famine or nakedness
or danger or sword?
36 As it is written:
[c]**Because of You we are being
put to death all day long;
we are counted as sheep
to be slaughtered.**[f]
37 [d]No, in all these things we are
more than victorious
through Him who loved us.
38 For I am persuaded that
neither death nor life,
nor angels nor [e]rulers,

[a]**8:17** Or *provided that* [b]**8:26** Some mss omit *for us* [c]**8:28** Other mss read *that God works together in all things* [d]**8:28** The ultimate good [e]**8:29** From eternity God knew His people and entered into a personal relationship with them [f]**8:36** Ps 44:22; see Is 53:7; Zch 11:4,7

nor things present,
nor things to come,
nor powers,
39 nor height, nor depth, nor
any other created thing
will [f]have the power
to separate us
from the love of God that is
in Christ Jesus our Lord!

[a]Is 50:8 [b]Is 53:12 [c]Ps 44:22 [d]1Jn 5:4 [e]Col 1:16 [f]Jn 10:28

Israel's Rejection of Christ

9 I speak the truth in Christ—I am
not lying; my conscience is testifying to me with the Holy Spirit[a] —
2 that I have intense sorrow and con-
tinual anguish in my heart. 3 For I
could wish that I myself were cursed
and cut off[b] from the •Messiah for the
benefit of my brothers, my countrymen by physical descent.[c] 4 [a]They are
Israelites, and to them belong the
adoption, [b]the glory, the covenants,
the giving of the law, the temple service, and [c]the promises. 5 The forefathers are theirs, and from them, by
physical descent,[d] came the Messiah,
[d]who is God over all, blessed forever.[e]
•Amen.

[a]Dt 7:6; Ps 50:5 [b]Ps 63:2 [c]Rm 4:13 [d]Jn 1:1; Heb 1:8; 1Jn 5:20

God's Gracious Election of Israel

6 But it is not as though the word of
God has failed. For [a]not all who are descended from Israel are Israel. 7 [b]Nei-
ther are they all children because they
are Abraham's descendants.[f] On the
contrary, **in** [c]**Isaac your seed will be**
called.[g] 8 That is, it is not the children
by physical descent[h] who are God's
children, but the children of the promise are considered seed. 9 For this is the
statement of the promise: [d]**At this**
time I will come, and Sarah will have
a son.[i] 10 And not only that, but also
when [e]Rebekah became pregnant[j] by
Isaac our forefather 11 (for though they
had [f]not been born yet or done anything good or bad, so that God's purpose according to election might stand,
12 not from works but from the One
who calls) she was told: [g]**The older**
will serve the younger.[k] 13 As it is written: [h]**Jacob I have loved, but Esau I**
have hated.[l]

[a]Gl 6:16 [b]Gl 4:23 [c]Gn 21:12 [d]Gn 18:10,14 [e]Gn 25:21 [f]Eph 1:4 [g]Gn 25:23 [h]Mal 1:2-3

God's Selection Is Just

14 What should we say then? [a]Is
there injustice with God? Absolutely
not! 15 For He tells Moses:

[b]**I will show mercy to whom**
I show mercy,
and I will have compassion
on whom
I have compassion.[m]

16 [c]So then it does not depend on human will or effort,[n] but on God who
shows mercy. 17 For the Scripture tells
Pharaoh:

[d]**For this reason**
I raised you up:
so that I may display
My power in you,
and that My name
may be proclaimed
in all the earth.[o]

18 So then, He shows mercy to whom
He wills, and He hardens whom He
wills.

[a]Dt 32:4 [b]Ex 33:19 [c]Ps 115:3 [d]Ex 9:16

19 You will say to me, therefore,
"Why then does He still find fault? For
[a]who can resist His will?" 20 But who
are you—anyone[p] who talks back to
God? [b]Will what is formed say to the
one who formed it, "Why did you

[a]**9:1** Or *testifying with me by the Holy Spirit* [b]**9:3** Lit *were anathema* [c]**9:3** Lit *countrymen according to the flesh* [d]**9:5** Lit *them, according to the flesh* [e]**9:5** Or *the Messiah, the One who is over all, the God who is blessed forever,* or *Messiah. God, who is over all, be blessed forever* [f]**9:7** Lit *seed* [g]**9:7** Gn 21:12 [h]**9:8** Lit *children of the flesh* [i]**9:9** Gn 18:10,14 [j]**9:10** Or *Rebekah conceived by the one act of sexual intercourse* [k]**9:12** Gn 25:23 [l]**9:13** Mal 1:2–3 [m]**9:15** Ex 33:19 [n]**9:16** Lit *on the one willing,* or *on the one running* [o]**9:17** Ex 9:16 [p]**9:20** Lit *you, O man*

make me like this?" 21 Or has the
[c]potter no right over His clay, to make
from the same lump one piece of pottery for honor and another for dishonor? 22 And what if God, desiring to
display His wrath and to make His
power known, endured with much patience [d]objects of wrath ready for destruction? 23 And ⌊what if⌋ He did this
to make known the riches of His glory
on objects of mercy that He prepared
beforehand for glory— 24 on us whom
He also called, not only from the Jews
but also from the Gentiles? 25 As He
also says in Hosea:

> [e]**I will call "Not-My-People,"**
> **"My-People,"**
> **and she who is "Unloved,"**
> **"Beloved."**[a]
> 26 [f]**And it will be in the place**
> **where they were told,**
> **you are not My people,**
> **there they will be called**
> **sons of the living God.**[b]

[a] Jb 9:12 [b] Is 29:16 [c] Jr 18:6 [d] 1Th 5:9 [e] Hs 2:23 [f] Hs 1:10

27 But Isaiah cries out concerning Israel:

> [a]**Though the number**
> **of Israel's sons is like**
> **the sand of the sea,**
> **only the remnant**
> **will be saved;**
> 28 **for the Lord will execute**
> **His sentence**
> [b]**completely and decisively**
> **on the earth.**[c] [d]

29 And just as Isaiah predicted:

> [c]**If the Lord of Hosts**[e] **had not left**
> **us a seed,**
> **we would have become**
> **like Sodom,**
> **and we would have been made**
> **like Gomorrah.**[f]

[a] Is 10:22-23 [b] Is 28:22 [c] Is 1:9

Israel's Present State

30 What should we say then? Gentiles, who did not pursue righteousness, have obtained righteousness—
namely the righteousness that comes
from faith. 31 But Israel, pursuing the
law for righteousness, [a]has not
achieved the law.[g] 32 Why is that? Because they did not pursue it by faith,
but as if it were by works.[h] [b]They
stumbled over the stumbling stone.
33 As it is written:

> [c]**Look! I am putting**
> **a stone in Zion**
> **to stumble over,**
> **and a rock to trip over,**
> **yet the one who believes**
> **on Him will not**
> **be put to shame.**[i]

[a] Gl 5:4 [b] 1Co 1:23 [c] Ps 118:22; Is 28:16

Righteousness by Faith Alone

10 Brothers, my heart's desire and
prayer to God concerning them[j]
is for their salvation! 2 I can testify
about them that [a]they have zeal for
God, but not according to knowledge.
3 Because they disregarded [b]the righteousness from God and attempted to
establish their own righteousness, they
have not [c]submitted to God's righteousness. 4 For [d]Christ is the end[k] of the law
for righteousness to everyone who believes. 5 For Moses writes about the
righteousness that is from the law:
[e]**The one who does these things will
live by them.**[l] 6 But the righteousness
that comes from faith speaks like this:
[f]**Do not say in your heart, "Who will
go up to heaven?"**[m] that is, to bring
[g]Christ down 7 or, [h]**"Who will go
down into the •abyss?"**[n] that is, to
[i]bring Christ up from the dead. 8 On
the contrary, what does it say? [j]**The
message is near you, in your mouth
and in your heart.**[o] This is the message

[a]**9:25** Hs 2:23 [b]**9:26** Hs 1:10 [c]**9:28** Or *land* [d]**9:27–28** Is 10:22–23; 28:22; Hs 1:10 [e]**9:29** Gk *Sabaoth*; this word is a transliteration of the Hb word for *Hosts*, or *Armies*. [f]**9:29** Is 1:9 [g]**9:31** Other mss read *the law for righteousness* [h]**9:32** Other mss add *of the law* [i]**9:33** Is 8:14; 28:16 [j]**10:1** Other mss read *God for Israel* [k]**10:4** Or *goal* [l]**10:5** Lv 18:5 [m]**10:6** Dt 9:4; 30:12 [n]**10:7** Dt 30:13 [o]**10:8** Dt 30:14

of faith that we proclaim: 9 If you confess with your mouth, "Jesus is Lord,"
and believe in your heart that God
raised Him from the dead, you will be
saved. 10 With the heart one believes,
resulting in righteousness, and with
the mouth one confesses, resulting in
salvation. 11 Now the Scripture says,
[k]**No one who believes on Him will be
put to shame,**[a] 12 for [l]there is no distinction between Jew and Greek, since
the [m]same Lord of all [n]is rich to all who
call on Him. 13 [o]For **everyone who
calls on the name of the Lord will be
saved.**[b]

a Jn 16:2 b Ps 71:15-19 c Heb 10:29 d Mt 5:17; Gl 3:24 e Lv 18:5 f Dt 30:12 g Heb 8:1 h Dt 30:13 i 1Co 15:3-4 j Dt 30:14 k Is 28:16 l Ac 15:9 m Ac 10:36 n Eph 1:7 o Jl 2:32; Ac 2:21

Israel's Rejection of the Message

14 But how can they call on Him in
whom they have not believed? And
how can they believe without hearing
about Him? And how can they hear
without [a]a preacher? 15 And how can
they preach unless they are sent? As it
is written: [b]**How welcome**[c] **are the
feet of those**[d] **who announce the gospel of good things!**[e] 16 But [c]all did not
obey the gospel. For Isaiah says, [d]**Lord,
who has believed our message?**[f] 17 So
faith comes from what is heard, and
what is heard comes through the message about Christ.[g] 18 But I ask, "Did
they not hear?" Yes, they did:

> [e]**Their voice has gone out**
> **to all the earth,**
> **and their words to the ends**
> **of the inhabited world.**[h]

a Ti 1:3 b Is 52:7 c Heb 4:2 d Is 53:1; Jn 12:38 e Ps 19:4; Mt 24:14

19 But I ask, "Did Israel not understand?" First, Moses said:

> I [a]**will make you jealous of those**
> **who are not a nation;**
> **I will make you angry**
> **by a nation that lacks**
> **understanding.**[i]

20 And Isaiah says boldly:

> [b]**I was found by those**
> **who were not looking for Me;**
> **I revealed Myself to those**
> **who were not asking for Me.**[j]

21 But to Israel he says: [c]**All day long I
have spread out My hands to a disobedient and defiant people.**[k]

a Dt 32:21 b Is 65:1 c Is 65:2

Israel's Rejection Not Total

11 I ask, then, [a]has God rejected His
people? Absolutely not! For [b]I
too am an Israelite, a descendant of
Abraham, from the tribe of Benjamin.
2 God has not rejected His people
whom [c]He foreknew. Or do you not
know what the Scripture says in the
Elijah section—how he pleads with
God against Israel?

a Ps 94:14 b Php 3:5 c Rm 8:29

> 3 [a]**Lord, they have killed**
> **Your prophets, torn down**
> **Your altars;**
> **and I am the only one left,**
> **and they are trying to take**
> **my life!**[l]

4 But what was God's reply to him? [b]**I
have left 7,000 men for Myself who
have not bowed down to Baal.**[m] 5 [c]In
the same way, then, there is also at
the present time a remnant chosen by
grace. 6 Now [d]if by grace, then it is not
by works; otherwise grace ceases to
be grace.[n]

a 1Kg 19:10 b 1Kg 19:18 c Rm 9:27 d Dt 9:4-5

7 What then? [a]Israel did not find
what it was looking for, but the [b]elect

[a]**10:11** Is 28:16 [b]**10:13** Jl 2:32 [c]**10:15** Or *timely*, or *beautiful* [d]**10:15** Other mss read *feet of those who announce the gospel of peace, of those* [e]**10:15** Is 52:7; Nah 1:15 [f]**10:16** Is 53:1 [g]**10:17** Other mss read *God* [h]**10:18** Ps 19:4 [i]**10:19** Dt 32:21 [j]**10:20** Is 65:1 [k]**10:21** Is 65:2 [l]**11:3** 1 Kg 19:10,14 [m]**11:4** 1 Kg 19:18 [n]**11:6** Other mss add *But if of works it is no longer grace; otherwise work is no longer work.*

did find it. The rest were [c]hardened,
8 as it is written:

[d]God gave them a spirit
of stupor,
[e]eyes that cannot see and ears
that cannot hear, to this day.[a]

9 And David says:

[f]Let their feasting[b] become
a snare and a trap,
a pitfall and a retribution
to them.
10 Let their eyes be darkened
so they cannot see,
and their backs be bent
continually.[c]

[a] Rm 10:3 [b] 2Tm 2:19 [c] 2Co 3:14 [d] Is 29:10 [e] Is 29:10 [f] Ps 69:22-23

Israel's Rejection Not Final

11 I ask, then, have they stumbled so
as [a]to fall? Absolutely not! On the contrary, [b]by their stumbling,[d] salvation
has come to the Gentiles to make Israel[e] jealous. 12 Now if their stumbling[d]
brings riches for the world, and their
failure riches for the Gentiles, how
much more will their [c]full number
bring!

[a] Ezk 18:23 [b] Ac 13:46; 18:6 [c] Mc 4:1-2; Rm 11:25

13 Now I am speaking to you Gentiles. In view of the fact that [a]I am an
apostle to the Gentiles, I magnify my
ministry, 14 if I can somehow make my
own people[f] jealous and save some of
them. 15 For if their being rejected is
world reconciliation, what will their
acceptance mean but life from the
dead? 16 Now if [b]the •firstfruits offered
up are holy, so is the whole batch. And
if the root is holy, so are the branches.

[a] Ac 9:15; Gl 1:16 [b] Lv 23:10

17 Now if [a]some of the branches
were broken off, [b]and you, though a
wild olive branch, were grafted in
among them, and have come to share
in the rich root[g] of the cultivated olive
tree, 18 do not brag that you are better
than those branches. But if you do
brag—you do not sustain the root, but
the root sustains you. 19 Then you will
say, "Branches were broken off so that
I might be grafted in." 20 True enough;
they were broken off by unbelief, but
you stand by faith. [c]Do not be arrogant,
but [d]be afraid. 21 For if God did not
spare the natural branches, He will not
spare you either. 22 Therefore, consider
God's kindness and severity: severity
toward those who have fallen, but
God's kindness toward you—[e]if you remain in His kindness. Otherwise [f]you
too will be cut off. 23 And even they, if
they do not remain in unbelief, will be
grafted in, because God has the power
to graft them in again. 24 For if you
were cut off from your native wild olive, and against nature were grafted
into a cultivated olive tree, how much
more will these—the natural
branches—be grafted into their own olive tree?

[a] Jr 11:16 [b] Eph 2:12 [c] Rm 12:16 [d] Php 2:12 [e] 1Co 15:2 [f] Jn 15:2

25 So that you will not be conceited,
brothers, I do not want you to be unaware of this •mystery: a partial hard-
ening has come to Israel [a]until the full
number of the Gentiles has come in.
26 And in this way [b]all[h] Israel will be
saved, as it is written:

[c]The Liberator will come
from Zion;
He will turn away godlessness
from Jacob.
27 [d]And this will be My covenant
with them,[i]
when I take away their sins.[j]

28 Regarding the gospel, they are enemies for your advantage, but regarding election, they are [e]loved because
of their forefathers, 29 since God's

[a] 11:8 Dt 29:4; Is 29:10 [b] 11:9 Lit *table* [c] 11:9–10 Ps 69:22–23 [d] 11:11,12 Or *transgression* [e] 11:11 Lit *them* [f] 11:14 Lit *flesh* [g] 11:17 Other mss read *the root and the richness* [h] 11:26 Or *And then all* [i] 11:26–27 Is 59:20–21 [j] 11:27 Jr 31:31–34

gracious gifts and calling are [f]irrevoca-
ble.[a] 30 As you once disobeyed God,
but now have received mercy through
their disobedience, 31 so they too have
now disobeyed, ⌊resulting⌋ in mercy to
you, so that they also now[b] may receive mercy. 32 For God has imprisoned all in disobedience, so that He
may have mercy on all.

[a] Lk 21:24 [b] Is 60:15 [c] Is 59:20-21 [d] Jr 31:31-34 [e] Dt 9:5 [f] Nm 23:19

A Hymn of Praise

33 Oh, the depth of the riches
both of the wisdom
and the knowledge of God!
How unsearchable
His judgments
and untraceable His ways!
34 [a]**For who has known the mind**
of the Lord?
Or who has been
His counselor?
35 **Or [b]who has ever first given**
to Him,
and has to be repaid?[c]
36 For [c]from Him and through Him
and to Him are all things.
[d]To Him be the glory forever.
•Amen.

[a] Is 40:13 [b] Jb 35:7 [c] Jn 1:3; 1Co 8:6 [d] Rv 1:6

A Living Sacrifice

12 Therefore, brothers, by the mercies of God, I urge you to [a]pre-
sent your bodies as [b]a living sacrifice,
holy and pleasing to God; this is your
spiritual worship.[d] 2 [c]Do not be conformed to this age, but [d]be transformed by the renewing of your mind,
so that you may [e]discern what is the
good, pleasing, and perfect will of
God.

[a] 1Co 6:13 [b] Heb 10:20 [c] Eph 2:2 [d] Eph 1:18 [e] Eph 5:10,17

Many Gifts but One Body

3 For by the grace given to me, I tell
everyone among you not to think of
himself more highly than he should
think. Instead, think sensibly, as God
has distributed a measure of faith [a]to
each one. 4 Now as we have many
parts in one body, and all the parts do
not have the same function, 5 in the
same way [b]we who are many are one
body in Christ and individually members of one another. 6 [c]According to
the grace given to us, we have different gifts:

If prophecy, use it according to
the standard of faith;
7 if service, in service; [d]if teaching,
in teaching;
8 [e]if exhorting, in exhortation;
giving, with generosity;
[f]leading, with diligence;
showing mercy,
with cheerfulness.

[a] Eph 4:7 [b] Eph 1:23 [c] 1Co 12:4-11 [d] Gl 6:6 [e] 1Co 14:3 [f] 1Pt 5:2

Christian Ethics

9 Love must be without hypocrisy.
[a]Detest evil; cling to what is good.
10 Show family affection to one another with brotherly love. Outdo one
another in showing honor. 11 Do not
lack diligence; [b]be fervent in spirit;
serve the Lord. 12 [c]Rejoice in hope;
[d]be patient in affliction; be persistent
in prayer. 13 [e]Share with the saints
in their needs; [f]pursue hospitality.
14 [g]Bless those who persecute you;
bless and do not curse. 15 Rejoice with
those who rejoice; weep with those
who weep. 16 Be in agreement with
one another. Do not be proud; instead,
associate with the humble. Do not be
wise in your own estimation. 17 Do not
repay anyone evil for evil. Try to do
what is honorable in everyone's eyes.
18 If possible, on your part, live at peace
with everyone. 19 Friends, do not
avenge yourselves; instead, leave room
for His[e] wrath. For it is written: [h]**Ven-**

[a]**11:29** Or *are not taken back* [b]**11:31** Other mss omit *now* [c]**11:34–35** Is 40:13; Jb 41:11; Jr 23:18
[d]**12:1** Or *your reasonable service* [e]**12:19** Lit *the*

geance belongs to Me; I will repay,[a]
says the Lord. 20 [i]But

> **If your enemy is hungry,**
> **feed him.**
> **If he is thirsty, give him**
> **something to drink.**
> **For in so doing you will be**
> **heaping fiery coals**
> **on his head.**[b]

21 [j]Do not be conquered by evil, but
conquer evil with good.

[a] Am 5:15 [b] Rv 3:15 [c] Heb 3:6 [d] Heb 10:36 [e] Heb 6:10 [f] Heb 13:2 [g] 1Pt 3:9 [h] Dt 32:35 [i] Pr 25:21-22 [j] 1Pt 2:21

A Christian's Duties to the State

13 Everyone [a]must submit to the
governing authorities, for [b]there
is no authority except from God, and
those that exist are instituted by God.
2 So then, the one who resists the authority is opposing God's command,
and those who oppose it will bring
judgment on themselves. 3 For rulers
are not a terror to good conduct, but to
bad. Do you want to be unafraid of the
authority? [c]Do good and you will have
its approval. 4 For government is God's
servant to you for good. But if you do
wrong, be afraid, because it does not
carry the sword for no reason. For government is God's servant, an avenger
that brings wrath on the one who does
wrong. 5 Therefore, [d]you must submit,
not only because of wrath, but also because of your conscience. 6 And for this
reason you pay taxes, since the ⌊au-
thorities⌋ are God's public servants,
continually attending to these tasks.[c]
7 [e]Pay your obligations to everyone:
taxes to those you owe taxes, tolls to
those you owe tolls, [f]respect to those
you owe respect, and honor to those
you owe honor.

[a] Ti 3:1 [b] Pr 8:15; Jn 19:11 [c] 1Pt 3:13 [d] Ec 8:2 [e] Lk 20:25 [f] Lv 19:3; Pr 24:21

Love Our Primary Duty

8 Do not owe anyone anything,[d] except to love one another, for [a]the one
who loves another has fulfilled the law.
9 The commandments:

> [b]**Do not commit adultery,**
> **do not murder,**
> **do not steal,**[e]
> **do not covet,**[f]

and if there is any other commandment—all are summed up by this:
[c]**Love your neighbor as yourself.**[g]

[a] Mt 7:12 [b] Ex 20:13-17 [c] Lv 19:18; Gl 5:14

10 Love does no wrong to a neighbor.
Love, therefore, is the fulfillment of
the law.

Put On Christ

11 Besides this, knowing the time, it
is already the hour for you[h] [a]to wake up
from sleep, for now our salvation is
nearer than when we first believed.
12 The night is nearly over, and the daylight is near, so [b]let us discard the deeds
of darkness and put on the armor of
light. 13 [c]Let us •walk with decency, as
in the daylight: not in carousing and
drunkenness; not in sexual impurity
and promiscuity; [d]not in quarreling and
jealousy. 14 But [e]put on the Lord Jesus
Christ, and [f]make no plans to satisfy
the fleshly desires.

[a] 1Co 15:34 [b] Eph 6:13 [c] Php 4:8 [d] Php 2:3 [e] Gl 3:27 [f] Gl 5:16

The Law of Liberty

14 Accept anyone who [a]is weak in
faith,[i] but don't argue about
doubtful issues. 2 One person believes
he may eat anything, but one who is
weak eats only vegetables. 3 One who
eats must not look down on one who
does not eat; and one who does not eat
must not criticize [b]one who does, because God has accepted him. 4 [c]Who

[a] **12:19** Dt 32:35 [b] **12:20** Pr 25:21–22 [c] **13:6** Lit *to this very thing* [d] **13:8** Or *Leave no debt outstanding to anyone* [e] **13:9** Other mss add *you shall not bear false witness* [f] **13:9** Ex 20:13–17; Dt 5:17–21 [g] **13:9** Lv 19:18 [h] **13:11** Other mss read *for us* [i] **14:1** Or *weak in the Faith*

are you to criticize another's household slave? Before his own Lord he stands or falls. And stand he will! For the Lord is able[a] to make him stand.

[a] Is 35:3-4 [b] Col 2:16 [c] 1Co 4:4-5

5 [a]One person considers one day to be above another day. Someone else considers every day to be the same. Each one must be fully convinced in his own mind. 6 Whoever observes the day, observes it to the Lord.[b] Whoever eats, eats to the Lord, since he [b]gives thanks to God; and whoever does not eat, it is to the Lord that he does not eat, yet he thanks God. 7 For [c]none of us lives to himself, and no one dies to himself. 8 If we live, we live to the Lord; and if we die, we die to the Lord. Therefore, whether we live or die, we belong to the Lord. 9 [d]Christ died and came to life for this: that He might [e]rule over both the dead and the living. 10 But you, why do you criticize your brother? Or you, why do you look down on your brother? For [f]we will all stand before the judgment seat of God.[c] 11 For it is written:

> [g]**As I live, says the Lord,**
> **every knee will bow to Me,**
> **and every tongue will give**
> **praise to God.**[d]

12 So then, [h]each of us will give an account of himself to God.

[a] Gl 4:10 [b] 1Co 10:31 [c] Gl 2:20 [d] 2Co 5:15 [e] Ac 10:36 [f] Mt 25:31 [g] Is 45:23 [h] Mt 12:36

The Law of Love

13 Therefore, let us no longer criticize one another, but instead decide not [a]to put a stumbling block or pitfall in your brother's way. 14 (I know and am persuaded by the Lord Jesus [b]that nothing is unclean in itself. Still, [c]to someone who considers a thing to be unclean, to that one it is unclean.) 15 For if your brother is hurt by what you eat, you are no longer •walking according to love. By what you eat, do not destroy that one for whom Christ died. 16 Therefore, [d]do not let your good be slandered, 17 [e]for the kingdom of God is not eating and drinking, but righteousness, peace, and joy in the Holy Spirit. 18 Whoever serves the •Messiah in this way [f]is acceptable to God and approved by men.

[a] 1Co 8:9 [b] Ti 1:15 [c] 1Co 8:7 [d] Rm 12:17 [e] 1Co 8:8 [f] 2Co 8:21

19 So then, [a]we must pursue what promotes peace and what [b]builds up one another. 20 Do not tear down God's work because of food. [c]Everything is clean, but it is wrong for a man to cause stumbling by what he eats. 21 It is a noble thing not to eat meat, or drink wine, or do anything that makes your brother stumble.[e] 22 Do you have faith? Keep it to yourself before God. Blessed is the man who does not condemn himself by what he approves. 23 But whoever doubts stands condemned if he eats, because his eating is not from faith, and [d]everything that is not from faith is sin.

[a] Ps 34:14 [b] 1Co 14:12 [c] Ac 10:15 [d] Rm 14:5

Pleasing Others, Not Ourselves

15 Now we [a]who are strong have an obligation to bear the [b]weaknesses of those without strength, and not to please ourselves. 2 [c]Each one of us must please his neighbor for his good, in order [d]to build him up. 3 For even the •Messiah did not please Himself. On the contrary, as it is written, [e]**The insults of those who insult You have fallen on Me.**[f] 4 For [f]whatever was written before was written for our instruction, so that through our endurance and through the encouragement of the Scriptures we may have hope. 5 [g]Now may the God of endurance and encouragement grant you

[a]**14:4** Other mss read *For God has the power* [b]**14:6** Other mss add *but whoever does not observe the day, it is to the Lord that he does not observe it* [c]**14:10** Other mss read *of Christ* [d]**14:11** Is 45:23; 49:18 [e]**14:21** Other mss add *or offended or weakened* [f]**15:3** Ps 69:9

agreement with one another, according to Christ Jesus, 6 so that you may
glorify the God and Father of our Lord
Jesus Christ with a united mind and
voice. [a]Gl 6:1 [b]Rm 14:1 [c]Php 2:4-5 [d]Rm 14:19
[e]Ps 69:9 [f]2Tm 3:16 [g]Ex 34:6

Glorifying God Together

7 Therefore accept one another, [a]just
as the Messiah also accepted you, to
the glory of God. 8 Now I say that
[b]Christ has become a servant of the
circumcised[a] on behalf of the truth of
God, [c]to confirm the promises to the
fathers, 9 and so [d]that Gentiles may glorify God for His mercy. As it is written:

[e]Therefore I will praise You
among the Gentiles,
and I will sing psalms
to Your name.[b] [a]Rm 5:8; 14:1 [b]Mt 15:24 [c]Rm 3:3; 2Co 1:20
[d]Jn 10:16 [e]Ps 18:49

10 Again it says: [a]**Rejoice, you Gen-**
tiles, with His people![c] 11 And again:

[b]Praise the Lord, all
you Gentiles;
all the peoples should praise
Him![d]

12 And again, Isaiah says:

[c]The root of Jesse will appear,
the One who rises to rule
the Gentiles;
in Him the Gentiles will hope.[e]
[a]Dt 32:43 [b]Ps 117:1 [c]Is 11:10

13 Now may the God of hope fill you
with all joy and peace in believing, so
that you may overflow with hope by
the power of the Holy Spirit.

From Jerusalem to Illyricum

14 Now, my brothers, [a]I myself am
convinced about you that you also are
full of goodness, [b]filled with all knowledge, and able to instruct one another.
15 Nevertheless, to remind you, I have
written to you more boldly on some
points[f] [c]because of the grace given me
by God 16 [d]to be a minister of Christ
Jesus to the Gentiles, serving as a
priest of God's good news. My purpose
is that the offering of the Gentiles may
be acceptable, sanctified by the Holy
Spirit. 17 Therefore I have reason to
boast in Christ Jesus regarding what
pertains to God. 18 For I would not dare
say anything [e]except what Christ has
accomplished through me [f]to make the
Gentiles obedient by word and deed,
19 [g]by the power of miraculous signs
and wonders, and by the power of
God's Spirit. As a result, I have fully
proclaimed the good news about the
Messiah from Jerusalem all the way
around to Illyricum.[g] 20 So my aim is to
evangelize where Christ has not been
named, [h]in order that I will not be
building on someone else's foundation,
21 but, as it is written:

[i]Those who had no report
of Him will see,
and those who have not heard
will understand.[h] [a]2Pt 1:12
[b]1Co 8:1 [c]Rm 1:5; 12:3 [d]Gl 2:7,9
[e]Ac 14:27; 1Co 3:6-9 [f]Rm 1:5
[g]1Co 12:10-11 [h]2Co 10:13 [i]Is 52:15

Paul's Travel Plans

22 That is why [a]I have been prevented many times from coming to
you. 23 But now I no longer have any
work to do in these provinces,[i] and [b]I
have strongly desired for many years to
come to you 24 whenever I travel to
Spain.[j] For I do hope to see you when I
pass through, and to be sent on my
way there by you, once I have first enjoyed your company for a while.
25 Now, however, [c]I am traveling to
Jerusalem to serve the saints; 26 [d]for
Macedonia and Achaia[k] were pleased

[a]**15:8** The Jews [b]**15:9** 2 Sm 22:50; Ps 18:49 [c]**15:10** Dt 32:43 [d]**15:11** Ps 117:1 [e]**15:12** Is 11:10
[f]**15:15** Other mss add *brothers* [g]**15:19** A Roman province northwest of Greece on the eastern shore of the Adriatic Sea [h]**15:21** Is 52:15 [i]**15:23** Lit *now, having no longer a place in these parts* [j]**15:24** Other mss add *I will come to you.* [k]**15:26** The churches of these provinces

to make a contribution to the poor
among the saints in Jerusalem. 27 Yes,
they were pleased, and they are in-
debted to them. For if the Gentiles
have shared in their spiritual benefits,
then [e]they are obligated to minister to
Jews[a] in material needs. 28 So when I
have finished this and safely delivered
[f]the funds[b] to them, I will go by way of
you to Spain. 29 [g]But I know that when
I come to you, I will come in the
[h]fullness of the blessing[c] of Christ.

[a]Rm 1:13 [b]Ac 19:21 [c]Ac 24:17 [d]1Co 16:1 [e]1Co 9:11 [f]Php 4:17 [g]Rm 1:11 [h]Eph 3:8

30 Now I implore you, brothers,
through the Lord Jesus Christ and
[a]through the love of the Spirit, [b]to ago-
nize together with me in your prayers
to God on my behalf: 31 [c]that I may be
rescued from the unbelievers in Judea,
that my service for Jerusalem may be
acceptable to the saints, 32 and that,
[d]by God's will, I may come to you with
joy and be [e]refreshed together with
you.

[a]Php 2:1 [b]2Co 1:11 [c]2Th 3:2 [d]Jms 4:15 [e]2Co 7:13

33 The God of peace be with all of
you. •Amen.

Paul's Commendation of Phoebe

16 I commend to you our sister
Phoebe, who is a servant[d] of
the church in [a]Cenchreae. 2 [b]So you
should welcome her in the Lord in a
manner worthy of the saints, and as-
sist her in whatever matter she may
require your help. For indeed she has
been a benefactor of many—and of
me also.

[a]Ac 18:18 [b]Mt 25:40; Php 2:29

Greeting to Roman Christians

3 Give my greetings to [a]Prisca[e] and
Aquila, my co-workers in
Christ Jesus, 4 who risked their
own necks for my life. Not only
do I thank them, but so do all
the Gentile churches.
5 Greet also [b]the church that
meets in their home.
Greet my dear friend Epaenetus,
who is [c]the first convert[f] to
Christ from Asia.[g]
6 Greet Mary,[h] who [d]has worked
very hard for you.[i]
7 Greet Andronicus and Junia,[j]
my fellow countrymen and
fellow prisoners. They are
outstanding among the
apostles, and they were also in
Christ before me.
8 Greet Ampliatus, my dear friend
in the Lord.
9 Greet Urbanus, our co-worker in
Christ, and my dear friend
Stachys.
10 Greet Apelles, who is approved
in Christ.
Greet those who belong to the
household of Aristobulus.
11 Greet Herodion, my fellow
countryman.
Greet those who belong to the
household of Narcissus who are
in the Lord.
12 Greet Tryphaena and Tryphosa,
who have worked hard in the
Lord.
Greet my dear friend Persis, who
has worked very hard in the
Lord.
13 Greet Rufus, [e]chosen in the Lord;
also his mother—and mine.
14 Greet Asyncritus, Phlegon,
Hermes, Patrobas, Hermas, and
the brothers who are with
them.
15 Greet Philologus and Julia,
Nereus and his sister, and
Olympas, and all the saints who
are with them.

[a]**15:27** Lit *to them* [b]**15:28** Lit *delivered this fruit* [c]**15:29** Other mss add *of the gospel* [d]**16:1** Others interpret this term in a technical sense: *deacon*, or *deaconess*, or *minister* [e]**16:3** Traditionally, *Priscilla*, as in Ac 18:2,18,26 [f]**16:5** Lit *the firstfruits* [g]**16:5** Other mss read *Achaia* [h]**16:6** Or *Maria* [i]**16:6** Other mss read *us* [j]**16:7** Either a feminine name or *Junias*, a masculine name

16 Greet one another with a holy
kiss.
All the churches of Christ send
you greetings. [a]Ac 18:2
[b]1Co 16:19 [c]1Co 16:15
[d]1Tm 5:10 [e]Eph 1:4

Warning against Divisive People

17 Now I implore you, brothers,
watch out for those [a]who cause dissen-
sions and pitfalls contrary to the doctrine you have learned. [b]Avoid them;
18 for such people do not serve our
Lord Christ but [c]their own appetites,[a]
and [d]by smooth talk and flattering
words they deceive the hearts of the
unsuspecting. [a]Php 3:2; Col 2:8
[b]1Co 5:9; 2Th 3:6
[c]Php 3:19; 1Tm 6:5 [d]Col 2:4

Paul's Gracious Conclusion

19 The report of your obedience has
reached everyone. Therefore I rejoice
over you. But I want you to be [a]wise
about what is good, yet innocent about
what is evil. 20 The God of peace will
soon crush Satan under your feet. The
grace of our Lord Jesus be with you.
[a]Mt 10:16

21 [a]Timothy, my co-worker, and
[b]Lucius, [c]Jason, and [d]Sosipater, my fellow countrymen, greet you. [a]Ac 16:1
[b]Ac 13:1 [c]Ac 17:5 [d]Ac 20:4

22 I Tertius, who penned this epistle
in the Lord, greet you.
23 Gaius, [a]who is host to me and to
the whole church, greets you. [b]Eras-
tus, the city treasurer, and our brother
Quartus greet you. [a]1Co 1:14 [b]Ac 19:22

[24 [a]The grace of our Lord Jesus
Christ be with you all.][b] [a]1Th 5:28

Glory to God

25 Now to Him who has power to
strengthen you [a]according to my gospel and the proclamation of Jesus
Christ, [b]according to the revelation of
the sacred secret [c]kept silent for long
ages, 26 but [d]now revealed and made
known through the prophetic Scriptures, according to the command of
the eternal God, to advance the obedience of faith among all nations— 27 to
the only wise God, through Jesus
Christ—to Him be the glory forever![c]
•Amen. [a]Rm 2:16 [b]Eph 3:3,5
[c]1Co 2:7 [d]2Tm 1:10

[a]**16:18** Lit *belly* [b]**16:24** Other mss omit bracketed text; see v. 20 [c]**16:25–27** Other mss have these vv. at the end of chap 14 or 15.

1 CORINTHIANS

Greeting

1 Paul, called as an apostle of Christ
Jesus by God's will, and our
brother [a]Sosthenes:
2 To God's church at Corinth, to
those who [b]are sanctified in Christ
Jesus and [c]called as saints, with all
those in every place who call on the
name of Jesus Christ [d]our Lord—
[e]theirs and ours.
3 Grace to you and peace from God
our Father and the Lord Jesus Christ.

[a] *Ac 18:17* [b] *1Co 6:9-11* [c] *Rm 1:7* [d] *1Co 8:6* [e] *Rm 3:22*

Thanksgiving

4 I always thank my God for you because of God's grace given to you in
Christ Jesus, 5 that by Him you were
made rich in everything—[a]in all
speaking and all knowledge— 6 as [b]the
testimony about Christ was confirmed
among you, 7 so that you do not lack
any spiritual gift as you eagerly wait for
the revelation of our Lord Jesus Christ.
8 [c]He will also confirm you to the end,
[d]blameless in the day of our Lord Jesus
Christ. 9 [e]God is faithful; by Him you
were called into [f]fellowship with His
Son, Jesus Christ our Lord.

[a] *2Co 8:7* [b] *Ac 18:5* [c] *2Th 3:3* [d] *1Th 5:23* [e] *Nm 23:19; Is 49:7* [f] *Jn 15:4*

Divisions at Corinth

10 Now I urge you, brothers, in the
name of our Lord Jesus Christ, that you
all say the same thing, that there be no
divisions among you, and that you be
united with the same understanding
and the same conviction. 11 For it has
been reported to me about you, my
brothers, by members of Chloe's
household, that there are quarrels
among you. 12 What I am saying is this:
[a]each of you says, "I'm with Paul," or
"I'm with [b]Apollos," or "I'm with
[c]•Cephas," or "I'm with Christ." 13 [d]Is
Christ divided? Was it Paul who was
crucified for you? Or were you baptized in Paul's name? 14 I thank God[a] [b]
that I baptized none of you except
[e]Crispus and [f]Gaius, 15 so that no one
can say you had been baptized in my
name. 16 I did, in fact, baptize the
household of [g]Stephanas; beyond that,
I don't know if I baptized anyone else.
17 [h]For Christ did not send me to baptize, but to preach the gospel—not
with clever words, so that the cross of
Christ will not be emptied ⌊of its ef-
fect⌋.

[a] *1Co 8:4* [b] *Ac 18:24* [c] *Jn 1:42* [d] *2Co 11:4* [e] *Ac 18:8* [f] *Rm 16:23* [g] *1Co 16:15* [h] *Ac 26:17*

Christ the Power and Wisdom of God

18 For [a]to those who are perishing
the message of the cross is [b]foolish-
ness, but to us who are being saved it
is [c]God's power. 19 For it is written:

> **[d]I will destroy the wisdom**
> **of the wise,**
> **and I will set aside**
> **the understanding**
> **of the experts.**[c]

[a] *2Co 2:15* [b] *Ac 17:18* [c] *Rm 1:16* [d] *Is 29:14*

20 [a]Where is the philosopher?[d]
Where is the scholar? Where is the de-
bater of this age? [b]Hasn't God made
the world's wisdom foolish? 21 [c]For
since, in God's wisdom, the world did
not know God through wisdom, God
was pleased to save those who believe
through the foolishness of the message
preached. 22 For the [d]Jews ask for signs

[a]**1:14** Other mss omit *God* [b]**1:14** Or *I am thankful* [c]**1:19** Is 29:14 [d]**1:20** Or *wise*

and the Greeks seek wisdom, 23 but we
preach Christ crucified, a stumbling
block [e]to the Jews and foolishness to
the Gentiles.[a] 24 Yet to those who are
called, both Jews and Greeks, Christ is
God's [f]power and God's [g]wisdom,
25 [h]because God's foolishness is wiser
than human wisdom, and God's weakness is stronger than human strength.

a Is 33:18 b Is 44:25; Rm 1:22 c Lk 10:21 d Lk 11:16 e Mt 11:6 f Rm 1:4 g Col 2:3 h 2Co 4:7

Boasting Only in the Lord

26 Brothers, consider your calling:
[a]not many are wise from a human perspective,[b] not many powerful, not
many of noble birth. 27 Instead, [b]God
has chosen the world's foolish things
to shame the wise, and God has chosen the world's weak things to shame
the strong. 28 God has chosen the
world's insignificant and despised
things—[c]the things viewed as nothing—so He [d]might bring to nothing
the things that are viewed as something, 29 so that no one[c] can boast in
His presence. 30 But from Him you are
in Christ Jesus, who for us became wisdom from God, as well as righteousness, sanctification, and redemption,
31 in order that, as it is written: [e]**The
one who boasts must boast in the
Lord.**[d]

a Jn 7:48 b Mt 11:25 c Rm 4:17 d 1Co 2:6 e Jr 9:23-24

Paul's Proclamation

2 When I came to you, brothers, an-
nouncing the testimony[e] of God to
you, [a]I did not come with brilliance of
speech or wisdom. 2 For I determined
to know nothing among you [b]except
Jesus Christ and Him crucified. 3 And
[c]I was with you [d]in weakness, in fear,
and in much trembling. 4 My speech
and my proclamation [e]were not with
persuasive words of wisdom,[f] but with
a demonstration of the Spirit and
power, 5 so that your faith might not
be based on men's wisdom but [f]on
God's power.

a 1Co 1:17 b Gl 6:14 c Ac 18:1 d 2Co 10:1; Gl 4:13 e 2Pt 1:16 f 2Co 4:7

Spiritual Wisdom

6 However, [a]among the mature we
do speak a wisdom, but not a wisdom
of this age, or of the rulers of this age,
who are coming to nothing. 7 On the
contrary, we speak God's hidden wisdom in a •mystery, [b]which God predestined before the ages for our glory.
8 [c]None of the rulers of this age knew
it, for if they had known it, they would
not have crucified the Lord of glory.
9 But as it is written:

> [d]**What no eye has seen**
> **and no ear has heard,**
> **and what has never come**
> **into a man's heart,**
> **is what God has prepared**
> **for those who love Him.**[g]

a Eph 4:13 b Rm 16:25 c Ac 13:27 d Is 64:4

10 Now [a]God has revealed them to
us by the Spirit, for the Spirit searches
everything, even the deep things of
God. 11 For who among men knows
the concerns[h] of a man [b]except the
spirit of the man that is in him? [c]In the
same way, no one knows the concerns[h] of God except the Spirit of God.
12 Now we have not received the spirit
of the world, but [d]the Spirit who is
from God, in order to know what has
been freely given to us by God. 13 [e]We
also speak these things, not in words
taught by human wisdom, but in those
taught by the Spirit, explaining spiritual things to spiritual people.[i] 14 [f]But
the natural man does not welcome
what comes from God's Spirit, because it is foolishness to him; [g]he is

[a]**1:23** Other mss read *Greeks* [b]**1:26** Lit *wise according to the flesh* [c]**1:29** Lit *that not all flesh*
[d]**1:31** Jr 9:24 [e]**2:1** Other mss read *mystery* [f]**2:4** Other mss read *human wisdom* [g]**2:9** Is 52:15; 64:4
[h]**2:11** Lit *things* [i]**2:13** Or *things with spiritual words*

not able to know it since it is evaluated[a] spiritually. 15 [h]The spiritual person, however, can evaluate[b] everything, yet he himself cannot be evaluated[a] by anyone. 16 [i]For:

who has known
the Lord's mind,
that he may instruct Him?[c]

But [j]we have the mind of Christ.

[a] Mt 16:17; Lk 2:26; Eph 3:3,5 [b] Jr 17:9 [c] Rm 11:33 [d] Rm 8:15 [e] 2Pt 1:16 [f] Mt 16:23 [g] Rm 8:5; Jd 19 [h] Pr 28:5 [i] Is 40:13; Rm 11:34 [j] Jn 15:15

The Problem of Immaturity

3 Brothers, I was not able to speak
to you as spiritual people but as
people of the flesh, as babies in Christ.
2 I fed you [a]milk, not solid food, because you were not yet able to receive
it. In fact, you are still not able,
3 because you are still fleshly. For since
there is envy and strife[d] among you,
are you not fleshly and living like ordinary people?[e] 4 For whenever someone says, "I'm with Paul," and
another, "I'm with Apollos," are you
not ⌊typical⌋ men?[f]

[a] 1Pt 2:2

The Role of God's Servants

5 So, what is Apollos? And what is
Paul? They are servants through whom
you believed, [a]and each has the role
the Lord has given. 6 [b]I planted,
[c]Apollos watered, but God [d]gave the
growth. 7 So then neither the one who
plants nor the one who waters is anything, but only God who gives the
growth. 8 Now the one who plants and
the one who waters are equal, [e]and
each will receive his own reward according to his own labor. 9 For [f]we are
God's co-workers. You are God's field,
[g]God's building. 10 According to God's
grace that was given to me, as a skilled
master builder I have laid a [h]founda-
tion, and another builds on it. But
[i]each one must be careful how he
builds on it, 11 because no one can lay
any other foundation than what [j]has
been laid—that is, Jesus Christ. 12 If
anyone builds on the foundation with
gold, silver, costly stones, wood, hay,
or straw, 13 each one's work will become obvious, for the day[g] [k]will dis-
close it, because it will be revealed by
fire; the fire will test the quality of each
one's work. 14 If anyone's work that he
has built survives, he will receive a reward. 15 If anyone's work is burned up,
it will be lost, but he will be saved; [l]yet
it will be like an escape through fire.[h]

[a] Rm 12:3 [b] Ac 18:4 [c] Ac 19:1 [d] Is 55:10 [e] Ps 62:12 [f] Ac 15:4 [g] Zch 6:12-13; 1Co 6:19; Eph 2:20 [h] Rm 15:20 [i] 1Pt 4:11 [j] Is 28:16 [k] 1Pt 1:7 [l] Jd 23

16 Don't you know that you are God's
sanctuary and that the Spirit of God
lives in you? 17 If anyone ruins [a]God's
sanctuary, God will ruin him; for God's
sanctuary is holy, and that is what you
are.

[a] Heb 3:1

The Folly of Human Wisdom

18 No one should deceive himself. If
anyone among you thinks he is wise in
this age, he must become foolish so
that he can become wise. 19 For the
wisdom of this world is foolishness
with God, since it is written: [a]**He
catches the wise in their craftiness**[i]—
20 and again, [b]**The Lord knows the
reasonings of the wise, that they are
futile.**[j] 21 So no one should boast in
men, for [c]all things are yours:
22 whether Paul or Apollos or •Cephas
or the world or life or death or things
present or things to come—all are
yours, 23 and [d]you belong to Christ, and
[e]Christ to God.

[a] Jb 5:13 [b] Ps 94:11 [c] 2Co 4:5 [d] Rm 14:8 [e] 1Co 8:6

[a]**2:14,15** Or *judged,* or *discerned* [b]**2:15** Or *judge,* or *discern* [c]**2:16** Is 40:13 [d]**3:3** Other mss add *and divisions* [e]**3:3** Lit *and walking according to man* [f]**3:4** Other mss read *are you not carnal* [g]**3:13** The Day of Christ's judgment of believers [h]**3:15** Lit *yet so as through fire* [i]**3:19** Jb 5:13 [j]**3:20** Ps 94:11

The Faithful Manager

4 A person should consider us in
this way: as servants of Christ
[a]and managers of God's •mysteries.
2 In this regard, it is expected of managers that each one be found faithful.
3 It is of little importance that I should
be evaluated by you or by a human
court.[a] In fact, I don't even evaluate
myself. 4 For I am not conscious of
anything against myself, but I am not
justified by this. The One who evaluates me is the Lord. 5 [b]Therefore don't
judge anything prematurely, before
the Lord comes, who will both bring
to light what is hidden in darkness
and reveal the intentions of the
hearts. And [c]then praise will come to
each one from God.

[a] Rm 16:25; Eph 1:9; Col 1:26-27 [b] Mt 7:1 [c] Rm 2:29

The Apostles' Example of Humility

6 Now, brothers, I have applied these
things to myself and Apollos for your
benefit, [a]so that you may learn from us
the saying: "Nothing beyond what is
written."[b] The purpose is that none of
you will be inflated with pride in favor
of one person over another. 7 For who
makes you so superior? [b]What do you
have that you didn't receive? If, in fact,
you did receive it, why do you boast as
if you hadn't received it? 8 Already you
are full! Already you are rich! You have
begun to reign as kings without
us—and I wish you did reign, so that
we also could reign with you! 9 For I
think God has displayed us, the apostles, in last place, [c]like men condemned to die: [d]we have become a
spectacle to the world and to angels
and to men. 10 We are [e]fools for Christ,
but you are wise in Christ! [f]We are
weak, but you are strong! You are distinguished, but we are dishonored!
11 Up to the present hour we are both
hungry and thirsty; we are poorly
clothed, [g]roughly treated, homeless;
12 [h]we labor, working with our own
hands. [i]When we are reviled, we bless;
when we are persecuted, we endure
it; 13 when we are slandered, we en-
treat. We are, even now, like the
world's garbage, like the filth of all
things.

[a] Rm 12:3 [b] Jn 3:27 [c] 2Co 4:11 [d] Eph 6:12 [e] Lk 6:22 [f] 2Co 13:9 [g] Ac 23:2 [h] Ac 18:3 [i] Mt 5:44

Paul's Fatherly Care

14 I'm not writing this to shame you,
but to warn you as my dear children.
15 For you can have 10,000 instructors
in Christ, but you can't have many
fathers. Now I have fathered you
[a]in Christ Jesus through the gospel.
16 Therefore I urge you, [b]be imitators
of me. 17 This is why I have sent to you
Timothy, [c]who is my beloved and faithful child in the Lord. He will remind
you about my ways in Christ Jesus, just
as I teach everywhere in every church.
18 Now some are inflated with pride, as
though I were not coming to you.
19 [d]But I will come to you soon, if the
Lord wills, and I will know not the talk
but the power of those who are inflated with pride. 20 For [e]the kingdom
of God is not in talk but in power.
21 What do you want? Should I come to
you with a rod, or in love and a spirit
of gentleness?

[a] Rm 15:20; Jms 1:18 [b] 1Co 11:1 [c] 1Tm 1:2 [d] Ac 19:21 [e] 1Th 1:5

Immoral Church Members

5 It is widely reported that there is
sexual immorality among you, and
the kind of sexual immorality that is
not even [a]condoned[c] among the
Gentiles—[b]a man is living with his
[c]father's wife. 2 And you are inflated
with pride, instead of filled with grief
so that he who has committed this act
might be removed from among you.
3 For though absent in body but
present in spirit, I have already

[a]**4:3** Lit *a human day* [b]**4:6** The words in quotation marks could refer to the OT, a Jewish maxim, or a popular proverb. [c]**5:1** Other mss read *named*

decided about him who has done this
thing as though I were present. 4 In
the name of our Lord Jesus, when you
are assembled, along [d]with my spirit
and with the power of our Lord Jesus,
5 [e]turn that one over to Satan for the
destruction of the flesh, so that his
spirit may be saved in the Day of the
Lord.

[a] Eph 5:3 [b] Dt 27:20 [c] 2Co 7:12 [d] Mt 18:18; 2Co 2:10 [e] Ac 26:18; 1Tm 1:20

6 Your boasting is not good. Don't you
know that a little yeast permeates the
whole batch of dough? 7 Clean out the
old yeast so that you may be a new
batch, since you are unleavened. For
[a]Christ our [b]•Passover has been sacrificed.[a] 8 Therefore, [c]let us observe the
feast, [d]not with old yeast, or with the
yeast of malice and evil, but with the unleavened bread of sincerity and truth.

[a] Is 53:7 [b] Ex 12:5-6 [c] Ex 12:15 [d] Dt 16:3

Church Discipline

9 I wrote to you in a letter [a]not to associate with sexually immoral people—
10 by no means referring to this world's
immoral people, or to the greedy and
swindlers, or to idolaters; [b]otherwise
you would have to leave the world.
11 But now I am writing[b] you not to associate with anyone [c]who bears the
name of brother who is sexually immoral or greedy, an idolater or a reviler,
a drunkard or a swindler. [d]Do not even
eat with such a person. 12 For what is it
to me to judge [e]outsiders? Do you not
judge those who are inside? 13 But God
[f]judges outsiders. [g]**Put away the evil
person from among yourselves.**[c]

[a] 2Co 6:14 [b] Jn 17:15 [c] Rm 16:17 [d] Gl 2:12 [e] Mk 4:11 [f] Ec 12:14 [g] Dt 17:7

Lawsuits among Believers

6 Does any of you who has a complaint against someone dare go to
law before the unrighteous,[d] and not
before the saints? 2 Or do you not
know that [a]the saints will judge the
world? And if the world is judged by
you, are you unworthy to judge the
smallest cases? 3 Do you not know that
we will [b]judge angels—not to speak of
things pertaining to this life? 4 So if
you have cases pertaining to this life,
do you select those[e] who have no
standing in the church to judge? 5 I say
this to your shame! Can it be that
there is not one wise person among
you who will be able to arbitrate between his brothers? 6 Instead, brother
goes to law against brother, and that
before unbelievers!

[a] Lk 22:30 [b] 2Pt 2:4

7 Therefore, it is already a total defeat
for you that you have lawsuits against
one another. [a]Why not rather put up
with injustice? Why not rather be
cheated? 8 Instead, you act unjustly and
cheat—[b]and this to brothers! 9 Do you
not know that [c]the unjust will not inherit God's kingdom? Do not be deceived: no sexually immoral people,
idolaters, adulterers, male prostitutes,
[d]homosexuals, 10 thieves, greedy people, drunkards, revilers, or swindlers
will inherit God's kingdom. 11 Some of
you were like this; [e]but you were
washed, you were sanctified, you were
justified in the name of the Lord Jesus
Christ and by the Spirit of our God.

[a] Rm 12:17 [b] 1Th 4:6 [c] Is 3:11 [d] Lv 18:1,22; 20:13; 1Tm 1:10 [e] Heb 10:22; 1Pt 3:21

Glorifying God in Body and Spirit

12 [a]"Everything is permissible for
me,"[f] but not everything is helpful.
"Everything is permissible for me,"[f]
but I will not be brought under the
control of anything. 13 "Foods for the
stomach and the stomach for foods,"[f]
but God will do away with both of
them.[g] The body is not for sexual immorality but [b]for the Lord, [c]and the

[a]**5:7** Other mss add *for us* [b]**5:11** Or *now I wrote* [c]**5:13** Dt 17:7 [d]**6:1** Unbelievers; see v. 6 [e]**6:4** Or *life, appoint those* (as a command) [f]**6:12,13** The words in quotation marks are most likely slogans used by some Corinthian Christians. Paul evaluates and corrects these slogans. [g]**6:13** Lit *both it and them*

Lord for the body. 14 [d]God raised up the
Lord and will also raise us up [e]by His
power. 15 Do you not know that your
bodies are the members of Christ? So
should I take the members of Christ
and make them members of a prostitute? Absolutely not! 16 Do you not
know that anyone joined to a prostitute is one body with her? For it says,
The two will become one flesh.[a]
17 [g]But anyone joined to the Lord is one
spirit with Him.

[a] 1Co 10:23 [b] 1Th 4:3 [c] Eph 5:23 [d] 2Co 4:14 [e] Eph 1:19 [f] Gn 2:24 [g] Eph 4:4

18 Flee from sexual immorality! "Every sin a person can commit is outside
the body,"[b] but the person who is sexually immoral sins [a]against his own
body. 19 [b]Do you not know that your
body is a sanctuary of the Holy Spirit
who is in you, whom you have from
God? [c]You are not your own, 20 for
[d]you were bought at a price; therefore
[e]glorify God in your body.[c]

[a] Rm 1:24; 1Th 4:4 [b] 2Co 6:16 [c] Rm 14:7 [d] Gl 3:13; Heb 9:12 [e] Mt 5:16

Principles of Marriage

7 About the things you wrote:[d] "It is
good for a man not to have rela-
tions with[e] a woman."[f] 2 But because
of sexual immorality,[g] each man
should have his own wife, and each
woman should have her own husband. 3 [a]A husband should fulfill his
marital duty to his wife, and likewise a
wife to her husband. 4 A wife does not
have authority over her own body, but
her husband does. Equally, a husband
does not have authority over his own
body, but his wife does. 5 Do not deprive one another—except when you
agree, for a time, to devote yourselves
to[h] prayer. Then come together again;
otherwise, [b]Satan may tempt you because of your lack of self-control. 6 I
say this as a concession, [c]not as a command. 7 [d]I wish that all people were
[e]just like me. But [f]each has his own
gift from God, one this and another
that.

[a] 1Pt 3:7 [b] 2Co 11:3 [c] 2Co 8:8 [d] Ac 26:29 [e] 1Co 9:5 [f] 1Co 12:11

A Word to the Unmarried

8 I say to the unmarried and to widows: It is good for them if they remain
as I am. 9 But [a]if they do not have
self-control, they should marry, for it is
better to marry than to burn with desire.

[a] 1Tm 5:14

Advice to Married People

10 I command the married—not I,
but the Lord—[a]a wife is not to leave[i]
her husband. 11 But if she does leave,
she must remain unmarried or be reconciled to her husband—and a husband is not to leave his wife. 12 But to
the rest I, not the Lord, say: If any
brother has an unbelieving wife, and
she is willing to live with him, he must
not leave her. 13 Also, if any woman has
an unbelieving husband, and he is willing to live with her, she must not leave
her husband. 14 For the unbelieving
husband is sanctified by the wife, and
the unbelieving wife is sanctified by
the Christian husband. [b]Otherwise
your children would be unclean, but
now they are holy. 15 But if the unbeliever leaves, let him leave.[i] A brother
or a sister is not bound in such cases.
God has called you[j] to peace. 16 For
you, wife, how do you know whether
you will [c]save your husband? Or you,
husband, how do you know whether
you will save your wife?

[a] Mal 2:14,16; Mt 5:32; 19:6 [b] Mal 2:15 [c] 1Pt 3:1

Various Situations of Life

17 However, each one must live his
life in the situation the Lord assigned
when God called him.[k] [a]This is what I
command in all the churches. 18 Was

[a]**6:16** Gn 2:24 [b]**6:18** See note at 1 Co 6:12 [c]**6:20** Other mss add *and in your spirit, which belong to God.* [d]**7:1** Other mss add *to me* [e]**7:1** Lit *not to touch* [f]**7:1** The words in quotation marks are a principle that the Corinthians wrote to Paul and asked for his view about. [g]**7:2** Lit *immoralities* [h]**7:5** Other mss add *fasting and to* [i]**7:10,15** Or *separate from*, or *divorce* [j]**7:15** Other mss read *us* [k]**7:17** Lit *called each*

anyone already circumcised when he
was called? He should not undo his circumcision. Was anyone called while
uncircumcised? [b]He should not get circumcised. 19 [c]Circumcision does not
matter and uncircumcision does not
matter, [d]but keeping God's commandments does. 20 [e]Each person should remain in the life situation[a] in which he
was called. 21 [f]Were you called while a
slave? It should not be a concern to
you. But if you can [g]become free, by all
means take the opportunity.[b] 22 For he
who is called by the Lord as a slave is
the Lord's freedman.[c] Likewise he who
is called as a free man[d] is [h]Christ's
slave. 23 [i]You were bought at a price; do
not become slaves of men. 24 Brothers,
each person should remain with God
in whatever situation he was called.

[a] 2Co 11:28 [b] Gl 5:2 [c] Gl 6:15 [d] Mt 5:19; 1Jn 2:3 [e] Eph 4:1 [f] Gl 3:28 [g] Is 58:6 [h] Gl 5:13; Eph 6:6 [i] 1Pt 1:18-19

About the Unmarried and Widows

25 About virgins: [a]I have no command from the Lord, but I do give an
opinion as [b]one who by the Lord's
mercy is [c]trustworthy. 26 Therefore I
consider this to be good because of the
present distress: it is fine for a man to
stay as he is. 27 Are you bound to a
wife? Do not seek to be loosed. Are
you loosed from a wife? Do not seek a
wife. 28 However, if you do get married,
you have not sinned, and if a virgin
marries, she has not sinned. But such
people will have trouble in this life,[e]
and I am trying to spare you. 29 [d]And I
say this, brothers: the time is limited,
so from now on those who have wives
should be as though they had none,
30 those who weep as though they did
not weep, those who rejoice as though
they did not rejoice, those who buy as
though they did not possess, 31 and
those who use the world as though
they did not make full use of it. For
[e]this world in its current form is passing away.

[a] 2Co 8:8,10 [b] 1Tm 1:16 [c] 1Co 4:2 [d] Rm 13:12; Php 4:5 [e] Jms 4:14

32 I want you to be without concerns.
[a]An unmarried man is concerned
about the things of the Lord—how he
may please the Lord. 33 But a married
man is concerned about the things of
the world—how he may please his
wife— 34 and he is divided. An unmarried woman or a virgin is concerned
about the things of the Lord, so that
she may be holy both in body and in
spirit. But a married woman is concerned about the things of the
world—how she may please her husband. 35 Now I am saying this for your
own benefit, not to put a restraint on
you, but because of what is proper, and
so that you may be devoted to the Lord
without distraction. *[a] 1Tm 5:5*

36 But if any man thinks he is acting
improperly toward his virgin,[f] if she is
past marriageable age,[g] and so it must
be, he can do what he wants. He is not
sinning; they can get married. 37 But he
who stands firm in his heart (who is
under no compulsion, but has control
over his own will) and has decided in
his heart to keep his own virgin, will
do well. 38 [a]So then he who marries[h]
his virgin does well, but he who does
not marry[i] will do better. *[a] Heb 13:4*

39 [a]A wife is bound[j] as long as her
husband is living. But if her husband
dies, she is free to be married to anyone she wants—only in the Lord.[k]
40 But she is happier if she remains as
she is, in my opinion. And I think that
I also have the Spirit of God. *[a] Rm 7:2*

[a]**7:20** Lit *in the calling* [b]**7:21** Or *But even though you can become free, make the most of your position as a slave.* [c]**7:22** A former slave [d]**7:22** A man who was never a slave [e]**7:28** Lit *in the flesh* [f]**7:36** (1) a man's fiancée, or (2) his daughter, or (3) his Levirate wife, or (4) a celibate companion [g]**7:36** Or *virgin, if his passions are strong,* [h]**7:38** Or *marries off* [i]**7:38** Or *marry her off* [j]**7:39** Other mss add *by law* [k]**7:39** Only a believer

Food Offered to Idols

8 [a]About food offered to idols: We
know that "we all have [b]knowl-
edge."[a] Knowledge inflates with pride,
but love builds up. 2 [c]If anyone thinks
he knows anything, he does not yet
know it as he ought to know it. 3 But if
anyone loves God, [d]he is known by
Him.

[a] Ac 15:20 [b] Rm 15:14 [c] Gl 6:3 [d] Nah 1:7

4 About eating food offered to idols,
then, we know that [a]"an idol is nothing in the world,"[a] [b]and that "there is
no God but one."[a] 5 For even if there
are [c]so-called gods, whether in heaven
or on earth—as there are many "gods"
and many "lords"—

6 yet [d]for us there is one God,
the Father,
[e]from whom are all things,
and we for Him;
and [f]one Lord, Jesus Christ,
[g]through whom are all things,
and we through Him.

[a] Is 41:24 [b] Dt 4:39; Is 37:16 [c] Jn 10:34 [d] Eph 4:6 [e] Rm 11:36 [f] Eph 1:20-23; Php 2:11 [g] Heb 1:2

7 However, not everyone has this
knowledge. In fact, some have been so
used to idolatry up until now, that
when they eat food offered to an idol,
their conscience, being weak, is defiled. 8 Food will not make us acceptable to God. We are not inferior if we
don't eat, and we are not better if we
do eat. 9 But be careful that this right of
yours in no way becomes a stumbling
block to the weak. 10 For if somebody
sees you, the one who has this knowledge, dining in an idol's temple, won't
his weak conscience be encouraged to
eat food offered to idols? 11 Then the
weak person, the brother for whom
Christ died, is ruined by your knowledge. 12 Now [a]when you sin like this
against the brothers and wound their
weak conscience, you are sinning
against Christ. 13 Therefore, if food
causes my brother to fall, I will never
again eat meat, so that I won't cause
my brother to fall.

[a] Mt 25:40

Paul's Example as an Apostle

9 [a]Am I not free? Am I not an apostle? [b]Have I not seen Jesus our
Lord? Are you not my work in the
Lord? 2 If I am not an apostle to others,
at least I am to you, for you are [c]the
seal of my apostleship in the Lord.
3 My defense to those who examine
me is this: 4 [d]Don't we have the right
to eat and drink? 5 Don't we have the
right to be accompanied by a Christian
wife, like the other apostles, the
[e]Lord's brothers, and [f]•Cephas? 6 Or is
it only Barnabas and I who [g]have no
right to refrain from working? 7 Who
ever goes to war at his own expense?
Who [h]plants a vineyard and does not
eat its fruit? Or who [i]shepherds a flock
and does not drink the milk from the
flock? 8 Am I saying this from a human
perspective? Doesn't the law also say
the same thing? 9 For it is written in
the law of Moses, [j]**Do not muzzle an
ox while it treads out the grain.**[b] Is
God really concerned with oxen? 10 Or
isn't He really saying it for us? Yes,
this is written for us, because [k]he who
plows ought to plow in hope, and he
who threshes should do so in hope of
sharing the crop. 11 [l]If we have sown
spiritual things for you, is it too much
if we reap material things from you?
12 If others share this authority over
you, don't we even more?

[a] 1Tm 2:7 [b] Ac 9:3 [c] 2Co 3:2 [d] 2Th 3:9 [e] Mt 13:55 [f] Mt 8:14 [g] Ac 18:3 [h] Pr 27:18 [i] 1Pt 5:2 [j] Dt 25:4 [k] 2Tm 2:6 [l] Rm 15:27

[a]However, we have not used this authority; instead we endure everything
so that we will not hinder the gospel of
Christ. 13 [b]Do you not know that those
who perform the temple services eat
the food from the temple, and those

[a]**8:1,4** See note at 1 Co 6:12 [b]**9:9** Dt 25:4

who serve at the altar share in the offerings of the altar? 14 In the same way, [c]the Lord has commanded that [d]those who preach the gospel should earn their living by the gospel.

[a]2Co 11:7 [b]Lv 6:16 [c]Lk 10:7 [d]Gl 6:6

15 But I have used none of these rights, and I have not written this to make it happen that way for me. For it would be better for me to die than for anyone to deprive me of my boast! 16 For if I preach the gospel, I have no reason to boast, because an obligation is placed on me. And woe to me if I do not preach the gospel! 17 For if I do this willingly, I have a reward; but if unwillingly, I am [a]entrusted with a stewardship. 18 What then is my reward? To preach the gospel and offer it free of charge, and not make full use of my authority in the gospel.

[a]Gl 2:7; Php 1:17

19 For although I am free from all people, [a]I have made myself a slave to all, in order to win more people. 20 To the Jews I became like a Jew, to win Jews; to those under the law, like one under the law—though I myself am not under the law[a]—to win those under the law. 21 To those who are outside the law, like one outside the law—[b]not being outside God's law, but under the law of Christ—to win those outside the law. 22 To the weak I became weak, in order to win the weak. I have become all things to all people, so that I may by all means save some. 23 Now I do all this because of the gospel, that I may become a partner in its benefits.[b]

[a]Gl 5:13 [b]Rm 7:22,25; Gl 5:13-14,22-23

24 Do you not know that the runners in a stadium all race, but only one receives the prize? [a]Run in such a way that you may win. 25 Now everyone who [b]competes exercises self-control in everything. However, they do it to receive a perishable crown, but we an [c]imperishable one. 26 Therefore I do not run [d]like one who runs aimlessly, or box like one who beats the air. 27 Instead, I discipline my body and bring it under strict control, so that after preaching to others, I myself will not be [e]disqualified.

[a]Gl 2:2; Heb 6:15 [b]1Tm 6:12 [c]Jms 1:12 [d]2Co 5:1 [e]Jr 6:30

Warnings from Israel's Past

10 Now I want you to know, brothers, that our fathers were all under [a]the cloud, all passed through [b]the sea, 2 and all were baptized into Moses in the cloud and in the sea. 3 They all ate the same [c]spiritual food, 4 and all drank the same [d]spiritual drink. For they drank from a spiritual rock that followed them, and that rock was Christ. 5 But God was not pleased with most of them, for they were struck down in the desert.

[a]Ex 13:21 [b]Ex 14:22 [c]Ex 16:15 [d]Ex 17:6

6 Now these things became examples for us, so that we will not desire evil as they did.[c] 7 Don't become idolaters as some of them were; as it is written, [a]**The people sat down to eat and drink, and got up to play.**[d] [e] 8 Let us not commit sexual immorality as some of them did,[f] and in a single day 23,000 people [b]fell dead. 9 Let us not tempt Christ as [c]some of them did,[g] and were destroyed by snakes. 10 Nor should we complain as some of them did,[h] and were killed by the destroyer.[i] 11 Now these things happened to them as examples, and [d]they were written as a warning to us, [e]on whom the ends of the ages have come. 12 Therefore, whoever thinks he stands must be careful not to fall! 13 No temptation has overtaken you except what is common to humanity. God is faithful and [f]He will not allow you to be tempted beyond what you are able, but with the

[a]**9:20** Other mss omit *though I myself am not under law* [b]**9:23** Lit *partner of it* [c]**10:6** Lit *they desired* [d]**10:7** Or *to dance* [e]**10:7** Ex 32:6 [f]**10:8** Lit *them committed sexual immorality* [g]**10:9** Lit *them tempted* [h]**10:10** Lit *them complained* [i]**10:10** Or *the destroying angel*

temptation He will also [g]provide a way of escape, so that you are able to bear it.

[a]Ex 32:6 [b]Nm 25:1 [c]Nm 21:5 [d]Rm 15:4 [e]Heb 10:25 [f]2Pt 2:9 [g]Jr 29:11

Warning against Idolatry

14 Therefore, my dear friends, flee from idolatry. 15 I am speaking as to wise people. Judge for yourselves what I say. 16 [a]The cup of blessing that we bless, is it not a sharing in the blood of Christ? [b]The bread that we break, is it not a sharing in the body of Christ? 17 [c]Because there is one bread, we who are many are one body, for all of us share that one bread. 18 Look at the people of [d]Israel.[a] [e]Are not those who eat the sacrifices partners in the altar? 19 What am I saying then? That food offered to idols is anything, or that an idol is anything? 20 No, but I do say that what they[b] [f]sacrifice, they sacrifice to demons and not to God. I do not want you to be partners with demons! 21 [g]You cannot drink the cup of the Lord and [h]the cup of demons. You cannot share in the Lord's table and the table of demons. 22 Or are we provoking the Lord to jealousy? [i]Are we stronger than He?

[a]Mt 26:26 [b]Ac 2:42 [c]Rm 12:5 [d]Rm 4:12 [e]Lv 3:3 [f]Dt 32:17 [g]2Co 6:15 [h]Dt 32:38 [i]Ezk 22:14

Christian Liberty

23 "Everything is permissible,"[c d] but not everything is helpful. "Everything is permissible,"[c d] but not everything builds up. 24 [a]No one should seek his own ⌊good⌋, but ⌊the good⌋ of the other person.

[a]Rm 15:1

25 [a]Eat everything that is sold in the meat market, asking no questions for conscience' sake, for 26 [b]**the earth is the Lord's, and all that is in it.**[e] 27 If one of the unbelievers invites you over and you want to go, eat everything that is set before you, without raising questions of conscience. 28 But if someone says to you, "This is food offered to an idol," do not eat it, [c]out of consideration for the one who told you, and for conscience' sake.[f] 29 I do not mean your own conscience, but the other person's. [d]For why is my freedom judged by another person's conscience? 30 If I partake with thanks, why am I slandered because of something for which I give thanks?

[a]1Tm 4:4 [b]Ps 24:1 [c]1Co 8:10 [d]Rm 14:16

31 Therefore, [a]whether you eat or drink, or whatever you do, do everything for God's glory. 32 Give no offense to the Jews or the Greeks or the church of God, 33 just as I also try to please all people in all things, not seeking my own profit, but that they may be saved.

11 1 Be [b]imitators of me, as I also am of Christ.

[a]Mt 5:16 [b]Eph 5:1-2

Instructions about Head Coverings

2 Now I praise you[g] because you remember me in all things and [a]keep the traditions just as I delivered them to you. 3 But I want you to know that Christ is [b]the head of every man, and the man is [c]the head of the woman,[h] and God is [d]the head of Christ. 4 Every man who prays or prophesies with something on his head dishonors his head. 5 But every woman who prays or prophesies with her head uncovered dishonors her head, since that is one and the same as having her head shaved. 6 So if a woman's head[i] is not covered, her hair should be cut off. But if it [e]is disgraceful for a woman to have her hair cut off or her head shaved, she should be covered.

[a]1Co 7:17 [b]Rm 14:9 [c]Gn 3:16 [d]Jn 4:34 [e]Nm 5:18

7 A man, in fact, should not cover his head, because [a]he is God's image and glory, but woman is man's glory. 8 For

[a]**10:18** Lit *Look at Israel according to the flesh* [b]**10:20** Other mss read *Gentiles* [c]**10:23** Other mss add *for me* [d]**10:23** See note at 1 Co 6:12 [e]**10:26** Ps 24:1 [f]**10:28** Other mss add *"For the earth is the Lord's and all that is in it."* [g]**11:2** Other mss add *brothers,* [h]**11:3** Or *the husband is the head of the wife* [i]**11:6** Lit *a woman*

[b]man did not come from woman, but woman came from man; 9 and man was not created for woman, but woman for man. 10 This is why a woman should have [c]⌊a symbol of⌋ authority on her head: [d]because of the angels. 11 However, in the Lord, [e]woman is not independent of man, and man is not independent of woman. 12 For just as woman came from man, so man comes through woman, [f]and all things come from God. *[a]Gn 1:26 [b]Gn 2:21 [c]Gn 24:65 [d]Ec 5:6 [e]Gl 3:28 [f]Rm 11:36; 1Co 8:6*

13 Judge for yourselves: Is it proper for a woman to pray to God with her head uncovered? 14 Does not even nature itself teach you that if a man has long hair it is a disgrace to him, 15 but that if a woman has long hair, it is her glory? For her hair is given to her[a] as a covering. 16 But [a]if anyone wants to argue about this, we have no other[b] custom, nor do the churches of God. *[a]1Tm 6:4*

The Lord's Supper

17 Now in giving the following instruction I do not praise you, since you come together not for the better but for the worse. 18 For, to begin with, [a]I hear that when you come together as a church there are divisions among you, and in part I believe it. 19 [b]There must, indeed, be factions among you, so that the approved among you may be recognized. 20 Therefore when you come together in one place, it is not really to eat the Lord's Supper. 21 For in eating, each one takes his own supper ahead of others, and one person is hungry while [c]another is drunk! 22 Don't you have houses to eat and drink in? Or do you [d]look down on the church of God and embarrass those who have nothing? What should I say to you? Should I praise you? I do not praise you for this! *[a]1Co 1:10 [b]Lk 17:1 [c]Jd 12 [d]Lv 19:30; Ps 89:7*

23 For [a]I received from the Lord what I also passed on to you: on the night when He was betrayed, the Lord Jesus took bread, 24 gave thanks, broke it, and said,[c] "This is My body, which is[d] for you. Do this in remembrance of Me." *[a]Gl 1:1*

25 In the same way ⌊He⌋ also ⌊took⌋ the cup, after supper, and said, "This cup is [a]the new covenant in My blood. Do this, as often as you drink it, in remembrance of Me." 26 For as often as you eat this bread and drink the cup, you proclaim the Lord's death [b]until He comes. *[a]Heb 9:15 [b]Ac 1:11; 1Co 4:5*

Self-Examination

27 Therefore, whoever eats the bread or drinks the cup of the Lord in an unworthy way will be guilty of sin against the body[e] and blood of the Lord. 28 So [a]a man should examine himself; in this way he should eat of the bread and drink of the cup. 29 For whoever eats and drinks without recognizing the body,[f] eats and drinks judgment on himself. 30 This is why many are sick and ill among you, and many have fallen •asleep. 31 [b]If we were properly evaluating ourselves, we would not be judged, 32 but when we are judged, [c]we are disciplined by the Lord, so that we may not be condemned with the world. *[a]2Co 13:5 [b]1Jn 1:9 [c]Heb 12:5*

33 Therefore, my brothers, when you come together to eat, wait for one another. 34 If anyone is hungry, he should eat at home, so that you can come together and not cause judgment. And I will give instructions about the other matters whenever [a]I come. *[a]1Co 4:19*

Diversity of Spiritual Gifts

12 [a]About matters of the spirit:[g] brothers, I do not want you to be unaware. 2 You know how, when you

[a]**11:15** Other mss omit *to her* [b]**11:16** Or *no such* [c]**11:24** Other mss add *"Take, eat.* [d]**11:24** Other mss add *broken* [e]**11:27** Lit *be guilty of the body* [f]**11:29** Other mss read *drinks unworthily, not discerning the Lord's body* [g]**12:1** Lit *About things spiritual*

were pagans, you were led to dumb
idols—being led astray. 3 Therefore I
am informing you that [b]no one speaking by the Spirit of God says, "Jesus is
cursed," and [c]no one can say, "Jesus is
Lord," except by the Holy Spirit.

[a] 1Co 14:1 [b] Mk 9:39 [c] Mt 16:17

4 Now [a]there are different gifts, but
[b]the same Spirit. 5 There are different
ministries, but the same Lord. 6 And
there are different activities, but the
same God [c]is active in everyone and
everything.[a] 7 [d]A manifestation of the
Spirit is given to each person to produce what is beneficial:

8 to one is given [e]a message
of wisdom through the Spirit,
to another, [f]a message
of knowledge
by the same Spirit,
9 to another, faith
by the same Spirit,
to another, [g]gifts of healing
by the one Spirit,
10 [h]to another, the performing
of miracles,
to another, [i]prophecy,
[j]to another, distinguishing
between spirits,
to another, [k]different kinds
of languages,
to another, interpretation
of languages.

11 But one and the same Spirit is active
in all these, [l]distributing to each one
[m]as He wills.

[a] Heb 2:4 [b] Eph 4:4 [c] Eph 1:23 [d] Rm 12:6 [e] Eph 1:17-18 [f] 2Co 8:7 [g] Mk 16:18 [h] Gl 3:5 [i] Rm 12:6 [j] 1Jn 4:1 [k] Ac 2:4 [l] Rm 12:6-8 [m] Heb 2:4

Unity Yet Diversity in the Body

12 For as the body is one and has
many parts, and all the parts of that
body, though many, are one body—so
also is Christ. 13 For [a]we were all
baptized by one Spirit into one body—
[b]whether Jews or Greeks, whether
slaves or free—and [c]we were all made
to drink of one Spirit. 14 So the body is
not one part but many. 15 If the foot
should say, "Because I'm not a hand, I
don't belong to the body," in spite of
this it still belongs to the body. 16 And
if the ear should say, "Because I'm not
an eye, I don't belong to the body," in
spite of this it still belongs to the body.
17 If the whole body were an eye,
where would the hearing be? If the
whole were an ear, where would be
the sense of smell? 18 But now God has
placed the parts, each one of them, in
the body just as He wanted. 19 And if
they were all the same part, where
would the body be? 20 Now there are
many parts, yet one body.

[a] Is 44:3-5; Rm 6:5 [b] Gl 3:28 [c] Jn 6:63

21 So the eye cannot say to the hand,
"I don't need you!" nor again the head
to the feet, "I don't need you!" 22 On
the contrary, all the more, those parts
of the body that seem to be weaker are
necessary. 23 And those parts of the
body that we think to be less honorable, we clothe these with greater
honor, and our unpresentable parts
have a better presentation. 24 But our
presentable parts have no need ⌊of
clothing⌋. Instead, God has put the
body together, giving greater honor to
the less honorable, 25 so that there
would be no division in the body, but
that the members would have the
same concern for each other. 26 So if
one member suffers, all the members
suffer with it; if one member is honored, all the members rejoice with it.
27 Now [a]you are the body of Christ,
and individual members of it. 28 And
[b]God has placed these in the church:

first [c]apostles, second [d]prophets,
third teachers, next, miracles,
then gifts of healing, [e]helping,
[f]managing, various kinds
of languages.
29 Are all apostles?
Are all prophets?

[a]**12:6** Lit *God acts all things in all*

Are all teachers?
Do all do miracles?
30 Do all have gifts of healing?
Do all speak in languages?
Do all interpret?

31 But [g]desire the greater gifts. And I will show you an even better way.

[a]Rm 12:5 [b]Eph 4:11 [c]Eph 2:20 [d]Ac 13:1 [e]Nm 11:17 [f]Rm 12:8 [g]1Co 14:1

Love: The Superior Way

13 If I speak the languages of men
and of angels,
but do not have [a]love,
I am a sounding gong
or a clanging cymbal.
2 If I have ⌊the gift [b]of⌋ prophecy,
and understand all •mysteries
and all knowledge,
and if I have all faith,
[c]so that I can move mountains,
but do not have love,
I am nothing.
3 And [d]if I donate all my goods
to feed the poor,
and if I give my body
to be burned,[a]
but do not have love,
I gain nothing.
4 [e]Love is patient; love is kind.
Love does not envy;
is not boastful; is not conceited;
5 [f]does not act improperly;
[g]is not selfish;
is not provoked; does not keep
a record of wrongs;
6 [h]finds no joy in unrighteousness,
but [i]rejoices in the truth;
7 [j]bears all things,
believes all things,
hopes all things,
endures all things.

[a]Rm 14:15 [b]Mt 7:22 [c]Mt 17:20 [d]Mt 6:1-2 [e]1Pt 4:8 [f]Php 4:8 [g]Php 2:4 [h]Ps 10:3 [i]2Jn 4 [j]Gl 6:2

8 Love never ends.
But as for prophecies,
they will come to an end;
as for languages, they will cease;
as for knowledge, it will come
to an end.
9 [a]For we know in part,
and we prophesy in part.
10 But [b]when the perfect comes,
the partial will come to an end.
11 When I was a child, I spoke
like a child,
I thought like a child,
I reasoned like a child.
When I became a man,
I put aside childish things.
12 For [c]now we see indistinctly,
as in a mirror, but then
face to face.
Now I know in part, but then
I will know fully,
as I am fully known.
13 Now these three remain:
faith, hope, and love.
[d]But the greatest of these is love.

[a]1Co 8:2 [b]Jn 6:45 [c]2Co 3:18; Php 3:12 [d]Mt 22:38-39

Prophecy: A Superior Gift

14 Pursue [a]love [b]and desire spiritual gifts, [c]and above all that
you may prophesy. 2 For the person
who [d]speaks in ⌊another⌋ language is
not speaking to men but to God, since
no one understands him; however, he
speaks [e]•mysteries in the Spirit.[b] 3 But
the person who prophesies [f]speaks to
people for edification, encouragement,
and consolation. 4 The person who
speaks in ⌊another⌋ language builds
himself up, but he who prophesies
builds up the church. 5 I wish all of
you spoke in other languages, but
even more that you prophesied. The
person who prophesies is greater than
the person who speaks in languages,
unless he interprets so that the church
may be built up.

[a]Rm 13:8-10 [b]1Co 12:31 [c]Rm 12:6 [d]Ac 2:4; 10:46 [e]Col 1:26 [f]Rm 15:4

6 But now, brothers, if I come to you
speaking in ⌊other⌋ languages, how will

[a]**13:3** Other mss read *to boast* [b]**14:2** Or *in spirit*, or *in his spirit*

benefit you unless I speak to you with
a revelation or knowledge or prophecy
or teaching? 7 Even inanimate things
producing sounds—whether flute or
harp—if they don't make a distinction
in the notes, how will what is played
on the flute or harp be recognized? 8 In
fact, if the trumpet makes an unclear
sound, who will prepare for battle? 9 In
the same way, unless you use your
tongue for intelligible speech, how will
what is spoken be known? For you will
be speaking into the air. 10 There are
doubtless many different kinds of languages in the world, and all have meaning.[a] 11 Therefore, if I do not know the
meaning of the language, I will be a foreigner[b] to the speaker, and the speaker
will be a foreigner to me. 12 So also
you—since you are zealous in matters
of the spirit,[c] seek to excel in building
up the church.

13 Therefore the person who speaks
in ⌊another⌋ language should pray that
[a]he can interpret. 14 For if I pray in ⌊an-
other⌋ language, my spirit prays, but
my understanding is unfruitful. 15 What
then? I will pray with the spirit, and I
will also pray [b]with my understanding.
[c]I will sing with the spirit, and I will
also sing with my understanding.
16 Otherwise, if you bless with the
spirit, how will the uninformed person[d]
say "•Amen" at your giving of thanks,
since he does not know what you are
saying? 17 For you may very well be giving thanks, but the other person is not
being built up. 18 I thank God that I
speak in ⌊other⌋ languages more than all
of you; 19 yet in the church I would
rather speak five words with my understanding, in order to teach others also,
than 10,000 words in ⌊another⌋ language. *a 1Co 12:10 b Ps 47:7 c Eph 5:19*

20 Brothers, [a]don't be childish in
your thinking, but [b]be infants in evil
and adult in your thinking. 21 It is
[c]written in the law:

> **By people of other languages**
> **and by the lips of foreigners,**
> **I will speak to this people;**
> **and even then, they will not**
> **listen to Me,**[e]

says the Lord. 22 It follows that speaking in other languages is intended as a
sign,[f] not to believers but to unbelievers. But prophecy is not for unbelievers but for believers. 23 Therefore if
the whole church assembles together,
and all are speaking in ⌊other⌋ languages, and people who are uninformed or unbelievers come in, [d]will
they not say that you are out of your
minds? 24 But if all are prophesying,
and some unbeliever or uninformed
person comes in, he is convicted by all
and is judged by all. 25 The secrets of
his heart will be revealed, and as a result he will fall down on his face and
worship God, proclaiming, "God is really among you." *a Mt 11:25*
b Mt 18:3; 1Pt 2:2 c Is 28:11 d Ac 2:13

Order in Church Meetings

26 How is it then, brothers? Whenever you come together, each one[g] has
a psalm, [a]a teaching, a revelation, ⌊an-
other⌋ language, or an interpretation.
[b]All things must be done for edification. 27 If any person speaks in ⌊an-
other⌋ language, there should be only
two, or at the most three, each in turn,
and someone must interpret. 28 But if
there is no interpreter, that person
should keep silent in the church and
speak to himself and to God. 29 Two or
three prophets should speak, and the
others should evaluate. 30 But if something has been revealed to another
person sitting there, [c]the first prophet
should be silent. 31 [d]For you can all

[a]**14:10** Lit *and none is without a sound* [b]**14:11** Gk *barbaros* = in Eng *a barbarian.* To a Gk, a *barbaros* was anyone who did not speak Gk. [c]**14:12** Lit *zealous of spirits; spirits* = human spirits, spiritual gifts or powers, or the Holy Spirit [d]**14:16** Lit *the one filling the place of the uninformed* [e]**14:21** Is 28:11–12 [f]**14:22** Lit *that tongues are for a sign* [g]**14:26** Other mss add *of you*

prophesy one by one, so that everyone
may learn and everyone may be encouraged. 32 And [e]the prophets' spirits
are under the control of the prophets,
33 since God is not a God of disorder
but of peace.

[a] 1Co 12:8-9 [b] Rm 14:19 [c] 1Th 5:19 [d] Rm 12:6 [e] 1Jn 4:1

[a]As in all the churches of the saints,
34 [b]the women[a] should be silent in the
churches, for they are not permitted to
speak, but [c]should be submissive, as
[d]the law also says. 35 And if they want
to learn something, they should ask
their own husbands at home, for it is
disgraceful for a woman to speak in the
church meeting. 36 Did the word of
God [e]originate from you, or did it
come to you only?

[a] 1Co 11:16 [b] 1Tm 2:11 [c] 1Co 11:3 [d] Gn 3:16 [e] Is 2:3

37 [a]If anyone thinks he is a prophet or
spiritual, he should recognize that what
I write to you is the Lord's command.
38 But if anyone ignores this, he will be
ignored.[b] 39 Therefore, my brothers, [b]be
eager to prophesy, and do not forbid
speaking in ⌊other⌋ languages. 40 But everything must be done decently and in
order.

[a] Lk 10:16 [b] 1Co 12:31

Resurrection Essential to the Gospel

15 Now brothers, I want to clarify[c]
for you the gospel I proclaimed
to you; you received it and [a]have
taken your stand on it. 2 [b]You are also
saved by it, if you hold to the message
I proclaimed to you—unless [c]you believed to no purpose.[d] 3 For I passed on
to you as most important what I also
received:

that Christ died for our sins
  [d]according to the Scriptures,
4 that He was buried,
that He was raised
  on the third day
  [e]according to the Scriptures,
5 [f]and that He appeared
  to •Cephas,
  then [g]to the Twelve.
6 Then He appeared to
  over 500 brothers at one time,
most of whom remain
  to the present,
  but some have fallen •asleep.
7 Then He appeared to James,
  then [h]to all the apostles.
8 [i]Last of all, as to one
  abnormally born,
  He also appeared to me.

[a] Rm 5:2 [b] Rm 1:16 [c] Gl 3:4 [d] Ps 22:15; Is 53:5 [e] Is 53:10; Hs 6:2 [f] Lk 24:34 [g] Jn 20:19 [h] Ac 1:3 [i] Ac 9:4

9 For I am the least of the apostles, unworthy to be called an apostle, because
[a]I persecuted the church of God. 10 But
[b]by God's grace I am what I am, and His
grace toward me was not ineffective.
However, [c]I worked more than any of
them, [d]yet not I, but God's grace that
was with me. 11 Therefore, whether it is
I or they, so we preach and so you have
believed.

[a] Ac 8:3 [b] Eph 4:7 [c] 2Co 11:23 [d] Gl 2:8

Resurrection Essential to the Faith

12 Now if Christ is preached as raised
from the dead, how can some of you
say, "There is no resurrection of the
dead"? 13 But if there is no resurrection
of the dead, [a]then Christ has not been
raised; 14 and if Christ has not been
raised, then our preaching is without
foundation, and so is your faith.[e] 15 In
addition, we are found to be false witnesses about God, because we have
testified about God that He raised up
Christ—whom He did not raise up if in
fact the dead are not raised. 16 For if the
dead are not raised, Christ has not
been raised. 17 And if Christ has not
been raised, your faith is worthless;
[b]you are still in your sins. 18 Therefore
those who have fallen asleep in Christ

[a]**14:34** Other mss read *your women* [b]**14:38** Other mss read *he should be ignored* [c]**15:1** Or *I make known* [d]**15:2** Or *believed in vain* [e]**15:14** Or *preaching is useless, and your faith also is useless*, or *preaching is empty, and your faith also is empty*

have also perished. 19 If [c]we have
placed our hope in Christ for this life
only, we should be pitied more than
anyone.

[a] 1Th 4:14 [b] Rm 4:25 [c] 2Tm 3:12

Christ's Resurrection Guarantees Ours

20 But now [a]Christ has been raised
from the dead, [b]the •firstfruits of those
who have fallen asleep. 21 For [c]since
death came through a man, [d]the resurrection of the dead also comes through
a man. 22 For just as in Adam all die, so
also in Christ all will be made alive.
23 But [e]each in his own order: Christ,
the firstfruits; afterward, at His coming, the people of Christ. 24 Then
comes the end, when He hands over
[f]the kingdom to God the Father, when
He abolishes all rule and all authority
and power. 25 For He must reign [g]until
He puts all His enemies under His feet.
26 [h]The last enemy to be abolished is
death. 27 For **He** [i]**has put everything
under His feet.**[a] But when it says "everything" is put under Him, it is obvious that He who puts everything under
Him is the exception. 28 [j]And when everything is subject to Him, [k]then the
Son Himself will also be subject to Him
who subjected everything to Him, so
that God may be all in all.

[a] 1Pt 1:3 [b] Ac 26:23 [c] Rm 5:12 [d] Jn 11:25 [e] 1Th 4:15-16 [f] Eph 5:27 [g] Eph 1:22; Heb 1:13 [h] Heb 2:14 [i] Ps 8:6; Mt 28:18 [j] Mt 13:41 [k] Jn 14:28; 1Co 11:3

Resurrection Supported by Christian Experience

29 Otherwise what will they do who
are being baptized for the dead? If the
dead are not raised at all, then why are
people[b] baptized for them?[c] 30 [a]Why
are we in danger every hour? 31 I affirm
by the pride in you that I have in Christ
Jesus our Lord: [b]I die every day! 32 If [c]I
fought wild animals in Ephesus with
only human hope,[d] what good does
that do me?[e] If the dead are not raised,
[d]**Let us eat and drink, for tomorrow
we die.**[f] 33 Do not be deceived: "Bad
company corrupts good morals."[g]
34 [e]Become right-minded[h] and stop
sinning, [f]because some people are ignorant about God. I say this to your
shame.

[a] 2Co 11:26 [b] Ac 20:23; Rm 8:36 [c] 2Co 1:8 [d] Is 22:13 [e] Eph 5:14 [f] 1Th 4:5

The Nature of the Resurrection Body

35 But someone will say, [a]"How are
the dead raised? What kind of body
will they have when they come?"
36 Foolish one! [b]What you sow does not
come to life unless it dies. 37 And as for
what you sow—you are not sowing the
future body, but only a seed,[i] perhaps
of wheat or another grain. 38 But [c]God
gives it a body as He wants, and to
each of the seeds its own body. 39 Not
all flesh is the same flesh; there is one
flesh for humans, another for animals,
another for birds, and another for fish.
40 There are heavenly bodies and
earthly bodies, but the splendor of the
heavenly bodies is different from that
of the earthly ones. 41 There is a splendor of the sun, another of the moon,
and another of the stars; for star differs
from star in splendor. 42 [d]So it is with
the resurrection of the dead:

Sown in corruption,
raised in incorruption;
43 [e]sown in dishonor,
raised in glory;
sown in weakness,
raised in power;
44 sown a natural body,
raised a spiritual body.

If there is a natural body, there is also
a spiritual body. 45 So it is written: **The
first man Adam** [f]**became a living
being;**[j] [g]the last Adam became a

[a]**15:27** Ps 8:6 [b]**15:29** Lit *they* [c]**15:29** Other mss read *for the dead* [d]**15:32** Lit *Ephesus according to man* [e]**15:32** Lit *what to me the profit?* [f]**15:32** Is 22:13 [g]**15:33** A quotation from the poet Menander, *Thais,* 218 [h]**15:34** Lit *Sober up righteously* [i]**15:37** Lit *but a naked seed* [j]**15:45** Gn 2:7

[h]life-giving Spirit. 46 However, the spiritual is not first, but the natural; then
the spiritual.

[a]Ezk 37:3 [b]Jn 12:24 [c]Ps 104:14 [d]Dn 12:3; Mt 13:43 [e]Php 3:21 [f]Gn 2:7 [g]Rm 5:14 [h]Jn 5:21

47 [a]The first man was from the earth
and [b]made of dust;
the second man is[a]
[c]from heaven.
48 Like the man made of dust,
so are those who are made
of dust;
[d]like the heavenly man,
so are those who are heavenly.
49 And [e]just as we have borne
the image of the man
made of dust,
[f]we will also bear the image
of the heavenly man.

[a]Gn 2:7 [b]Gn 3:19 [c]Is 9:6; Lk 2:11 [d]Php 3:20 [e]Gn 5:3 [f]Rm 8:29; Php 3:21

Victorious Resurrection

50 Brothers, I tell you this: flesh and
blood cannot inherit the kingdom of
God, and corruption cannot inherit incorruption. 51 Listen! I am telling you a
•mystery:

[a]We will not all fall asleep,
[b]but we will all be changed,
52 in a moment, in the twinkling
of an eye, at the last trumpet.
[c]For the trumpet will sound,
and the dead will be raised
incorruptible,
and we will be changed.
53 Because [d]this corruptible
must be clothed
with incorruptibility,
and this mortal must be clothed
with immortality.
54 Now when this corruptible
is clothed with incorruptibility,
and this mortal is clothed
with immortality,
then the saying that is written
will take place:

[e]Death has been swallowed up
in victory.[b]
55 **[f]O Death, where is your victory?**
O Death, where is your sting?[c]
56 Now the sting of death is sin, and
[g]the power of sin is the law.
57 [h]But thanks be to God,
who gives us [i]the victory
through our Lord Jesus Christ!

58 Therefore, my dear brothers, be
steadfast, immovable, always excelling
in the Lord's work, knowing [j]that your
labor in the Lord is not in vain.

[a]1Th 4:15 [b]Php 3:21 [c]Mt 24:31 [d]2Co 5:4 [e]Is 25:8; Rv 20:14 [f]Hs 13:14 [g]Rm 3:19 [h]Rm 7:25 [i]Ps 98:1 [j]Is 3:10

Collection for the Jerusalem Church

16 Now about [a]the collection for
the saints: you should do the
same as I instructed the Galatian
churches. 2 On the first day of the
week, each of you is to set something
aside and save to the extent that he
prospers, so that no collections will
need to be made when I come. 3 And
when I arrive, [b]I will send those
whom you recommend by letter to
carry your gracious gift to Jerusalem.
4 If it is also suitable for me to go, they
will travel with me.

[a]Ac 11:29; Rm 15:26 [b]2Co 8:19

Paul's Travel Plans

5 I will come to you [a]after I pass
through Macedonia—for I will be traveling through Macedonia— 6 and perhaps I will remain with you, or even
spend the winter, that you may send
me on my way wherever I go. 7 I don't
want to see you now just in passing, for
I hope to spend some time with you, if
the Lord allows. 8 But I will stay in Ephesus until Pentecost, 9 because [b]a wide
door for effective ministry has opened
for me[d]—[c]yet many oppose me. 10 If
Timothy comes, see that he has noth-

[a]**15:47** Other mss add *the Lord* [b]**15:54** Is 25:8 [c]**15:55** Hs 13:14 [d]**16:9** Lit *for a door has opened to me, great and effective*

ing to fear from you, because he [d]is doing the Lord's work, just as I am.
11 [e]Therefore no one should look down
on him; but you should send him on
his way in peace so he can come to me,
for I am expecting him with the brothers.[a]

[a] *Ac 19:21* [b] *Ac 14:27* [c] *Ac 19:9* [d] *Rm 16:21; Php 2:19-22* [e] *Lk 10:16*

12 About our brother [a]Apollos: I
strongly urged him to come to you
with the brothers, but he was not at all
willing to come now. However, when
he has time, he will come.

[a] *1Co 1:12*

Final Exhortation

13 Be alert, stand firm in the faith, be
brave and strong. 14 Your every ⌊action⌋
must be done with love.
15 Brothers, you know the household
of Stephanas: they are the •firstfruits of
Achaia and have devoted themselves
to serving the saints. I urge you 16 also
to submit to such people, and to everyone who works and labors with them.
17 I am delighted over the presence of
Stephanas, Fortunatus, and Achaicus,
[a]because these men have made up for
your absence. 18 For they have refreshed my spirit and yours. Therefore
recognize such people.

[a] *2Co 11:9*

Conclusion

19 [a]The churches of the Asian province greet you. Aquila and Priscilla
greet you heartily in the Lord, [b]along
with the church that meets in their
home. 20 All the brothers greet you.
Greet one another with a holy kiss.

[a] *Ac 19:10* [b] *Rm 16:5*

21 This greeting is in my own
hand[b]—Paul. 22 If anyone does not love
the Lord, [a]a curse be on him.
[b]*Maranatha!*[c] 23 The grace of our Lord
Jesus be with you. 24 My love be with
all of you in Christ Jesus.

[a] *Gl 1:8-9; Heb 10:26* [b] *Jd 14-15; Rv 22:20*

2 CORINTHIANS

Greeting

1 Paul, an apostle of Christ Jesus by
God's will, and Timothy our[d] brother:
To God's church at Corinth, [a]with
all the saints who are throughout
Achaia.
2 [b]Grace to you and peace from God
our Father and the Lord Jesus Christ.

[a] *Col 1:2* [b] *Php 1:2*

The God of Comfort

3 [a]Blessed be the God and Father of
our Lord Jesus Christ, [b]the Father of
mercies and the God of all comfort.
4 [c]He comforts us in all our affliction,[e] so
that we may be able to comfort those
who are in any kind of affliction,
through the comfort we ourselves receive from God. 5 For as [d]the sufferings
of Christ overflow to us, so our comfort
overflows through Christ. 6 If we are afflicted, [e]it is for your comfort and salvation; if we are comforted, it is for your
comfort, which is experienced in the
endurance of the same sufferings that
we suffer. 7 And our hope for you is
firm, [f]because we know that as you
share in the sufferings, so you will share
in the comfort.

[a] *Eph 1:3* [b] *Ex 34:6* [c] *2Th 2:16* [d] *1Co 4:10-14* [e] *2Co 4:15* [f] *Rm 8:17*

[a]**16:11** *With the brothers* may connect with Paul or Timothy. [b]**16:21** Paul normally dictated his letters to a secretary, but signed the end of each letter himself; see Rm 16:22; Gl 6:11; Col 4:18; 2 Th 3:17. [c]**16:22** Aram expression meaning *Our Lord come!*, or *Our Lord has come!* [d]**1:1** Lit *the* [e]**1:4** Or *trouble*, or *tribulation*, or *trials*, or *oppression*; the Gk word has a lit meaning of being under pressure.

8 For we don't want you to be unaware, brothers, of [a]our affliction that
took place in the province of Asia: we
were completely overwhelmed—beyond our strength—so that we even de-
spaired of life. 9 However, we personally
had a death sentence within ourselves
so that we would not [b]trust in ourselves,
but in God who raises the dead. 10 [c]He
has delivered us from such a terrible
death, and He will deliver us; we have
placed our hope in Him that He will deliver us again. 11 And you can join [d]in
helping with prayer for us, so that
thanks may be given by many[a] on our[b]
behalf [e]for the gift that came to us
through ⌊the prayers of⌋ many.

a Ac 19:23 b Jr 17:5,7 c 2Pt 2:9 d Rm 15:30 e 2Co 4:15

A Clear Conscience

12 For our boast is this: the testimony
of our conscience that we have conducted ourselves in the world, and especially toward you, with [a]God-given
sincerity and purity, [b]not by fleshly[c]
wisdom but by God's grace. 13 Now we
are writing you nothing other than
what you can read and also understand. I hope you will understand
completely— 14 as you have partially
understood us—[c]that we are your reason for pride, as [d]you are ours, in the
day of our[d] Lord Jesus.

a 2Co 2:17 b 1Co 2:4 c 2Co 5:12 d Php 2:16

A Visit Postponed

15 In this confidence, [a]I planned to
come to you first, so you could have [b]a
double benefit,[e] 16 and to go on to
Macedonia with your help, [c]then
come to you again from Macedonia
and be given a start by you on my journey to Judea. 17 So when I planned this,
was I irresponsible? Or what I plan, do
I plan [d]in a purely human[f] way so that
I say "Yes, yes" and "No, no" ⌊simulta-
neously⌋? 18 As God is faithful, our message to you is not "Yes and no." 19 For
[e]the Son of God, Jesus Christ, who was
preached among you by us—by me
and [f]Silvanus[g] and Timothy—did not
become "Yes and no"; on the contrary,
"Yes" has come about in Him. 20 [g]For
every one of God's promises is "Yes" in
Him. Therefore the "•Amen" is also
through Him for God's glory through
us. 21 Now the One who confirms us
with you in Christ, and [h]has anointed
us, is God; 22 He [i]has also sealed us and
[j]given us the Spirit as a down payment
in our hearts.

a 1Co 4:19 b Rm 1:11 c 1Co 16:5 d 2Co 10:2 e Mk 1:1; Lk 1:35 f Ac 18:5 g Rm 15:8-9 h 1Jn 2:20,27 i Eph 4:30; 2Tm 2:19 j Eph 1:14

23 I call on God as a witness against
me:[h] [a]it was to spare you that I did not
come to Corinth. 24 Not that we have
control of[i] your faith, but we are workers with you for your joy, because you
2 stand [b]by faith. 1 In fact, I made up
my mind about this:[j] [c]not to come
to you on another painful visit.[k] 2 For if
I cause you pain, then who will cheer
me other than the one hurt?[l] 3 I wrote
this very thing so that when I came I
wouldn't have pain from those who
ought to give me joy, [d]because I am
confident about all of you that my joy is
yours.[m] 4 For out of an extremely troubled and anguished heart I wrote to
you with many tears—[e]not that you
should be hurt, but that you should
know the abundant love I have for you.

a 1Co 4:21 b Rm 11:20 c 2Co 12:20 d Gl 5:10 e 2Co 7:8-9

A Sinner Forgiven

5 [a]If anyone has [b]caused pain, he has
not caused pain to me, but in some degree—not to exaggerate—to all of you.
6 The punishment [c]by the majority is
sufficient for such a person, 7 [d]so now

[a]**1:11** Lit *by many faces* [b]**1:11** Other mss read *your* [c]**1:12** The word *fleshly* (characterized by flesh) indicates that the wisdom is natural rather than spiritual. [d]**1:14** Other mss omit *our* [e]**1:15** Other mss read *a second joy* [f]**1:17** Or *a worldly,* or *a fleshly,* or *a selfish* [g]**1:19** Or *Silas*; see Ac 15:22–32; 16:19–40; 17:1–16 [h]**1:23** Lit *against my soul* [i]**1:24** Or *we lord it over,* or *we rule over* [j]**2:1** Lit *I decided this for myself* [k]**2:1** Lit *not again in sorrow to come to you* [l]**2:2** Lit *the one pained* [m]**2:3** Lit *is of you all*

you should forgive and comfort him instead; otherwise, this one may be overwhelmed by excessive grief. 8 Therefore I urge you to confirm your love to
him. 9 It was for this purpose I wrote:
so I may know your proven character,
if you are obedient in everything.
10 Now to whom you forgive anything,
I do too. For what I have forgiven, if I
have forgiven anything, it is for you in
the presence of Christ, 11 so that we
may not be taken advantage of by
[e]Satan; for we are not ignorant of his
intentions.[a]

[a] 1Co 5:1 [b] Gl 4:12 [c] 1Tm 5:20 [d] Gl 6:1 [e] 1Pt 5:8

A Trip to Macedonia

12 [a]When I came to Troas for the gospel of Christ, a door was opened to me
by the Lord. 13 I had no rest in my spirit
because I did not find my brother Titus, but I said good-bye to them and
left for Macedonia.

[a] Ac 16:8; 20:6

A Ministry of Life or Death

14 But thanks be to God, who always
puts us on display[b] in Christ,[c] and
spreads through us in every place the
scent of knowing Him. 15 For to God
we are the fragrance of Christ among
those who are being saved and among
those who are perishing. 16 To some
we are a scent of death leading to
death, but to others, a scent of life leading to life. And who is competent for
this? 17 For we are not like the many[d]
who make a trade in God's message
⌊for profit⌋, but as those with sincerity,
we speak in Christ, as from God and
before God.

Living Letters

3 Are [a]we beginning to commend
ourselves again? Or like some, do
we need [b]letters of recommendation
to you or from you? 2 [c]You yourselves
are our letter, written on our hearts,
recognized and read by everyone,
3 since it is plain that you are Christ's
letter, [d]produced[e] by us, not written
with ink but with the Spirit of the living God; not [e]on stone tablets but [f]on
tablets that are hearts of flesh.

[a] 2Co 5:12 [b] Ac 18:27 [c] 1Co 9:2 [d] 1Co 3:5 [e] Ex 24:12 [f] Ezk 11:19

Paul's Competence

4 We have this kind of confidence toward God through Christ: 5 [a]not that
we are competent in[f] ourselves to consider anything as coming from ourselves, but [b]our competence is from
God. 6 He has made us competent to be
ministers of [c]a new covenant, not [d]of
the letter, but of the Spirit; for [e]the letter kills, [f]but the Spirit produces life.

[a] Jn 15:5 [b] 1Co 15:10 [c] Heb 8:6,8 [d] Rm 2:27 [e] Rm 3:20 [f] Rm 8:2

New Covenant Ministry

7 Now if the ministry of death, chis-
eled in letters on stones, came with
glory, so that the sons of Israel were
not able to look directly at Moses' face
because of the glory from his face—a
fading ⌊glory⌋— 8 how will [a]the ministry of the Spirit not be more glorious?
9 For if the ministry of condemnation
had glory, the ministry [b]of righteousness overflows with even more glory.
10 In fact, what had been glorious is not
glorious in this case because of the
glory that surpasses it. 11 For if what
was fading away was glorious, what
endures will be even more glorious.

[a] Gl 3:5 [b] Rm 1:17

12 Therefore having such a hope, we
use great boldness— 13 not like Moses,
[a]who used to put a veil over his face so
that the sons of Israel could not look at
[b]the end of what was fading away.
14 But [c]their minds were closed.[g] For
to this day, at the reading of the old
covenant, the same veil remains; it is

[a]**2:11** Or *thoughts* [b]**2:14** Or *always leads us in a triumphal procession*, or less likely, *always causes us to triumph* [c]**2:14** Lit *in the Christ*, or *in the Messiah*; see 1 Co 15:22; Eph 1:10,12,20; 3:11 [d]**2:17** Other mss read *the rest* [e]**3:3** Lit *ministered to* [f]**3:5** Lit *from* [g]**3:14** Lit *their thoughts were hardened*

not lifted, because it is set aside ⌊only⌋ in Christ. 15 However, to this day, whenever Moses is read, a veil lies over their hearts, 16 but [d]whenever a person turns to the Lord, [e]the veil is removed. 17 Now the Lord is the Spirit; and where the Spirit of the Lord is, there is freedom. 18 We all, with unveiled faces, [f]are reflecting[a] the glory of the Lord and [g]are being transformed into the same image from glory to glory;[b] this is from the Lord who is the Spirit.[c]

a Ex 34:33 b Rm 10:4 c Is 6:10
d Rm 11:23 e Is 25:7 f 2Co 4:4,6 g Rm 8:29

The Light of the Gospel

4 Therefore, since we have this ministry, as we have received mercy, we do not give up. 2 Instead, we have renounced shameful secret things, not •walking in deceit or [a]distorting God's message, but in God's sight we commend ourselves to every person's conscience by an open display of the truth. 3 But if, in fact, our gospel is veiled, [b]it is veiled to those who are perishing. 4 Regarding them: [c]the god of this age [d]has blinded the minds of the unbelievers so they cannot see the light of the gospel of the glory of Christ,[d] [e]who is the image of God. 5 For we are not proclaiming ourselves but Jesus Christ as Lord, [f]and ourselves as your slaves because of Jesus. 6 For God, [g]who said, "Light shall shine out of darkness"—He has [h]shone in our hearts to give [i]the light of the knowledge of God's glory in the face of Jesus Christ.

a 1Th 2:3,5 b Is 6:9
c Eph 6:12 d Mt 13:4 e Php 2:6
f 1Co 9:19 g Gn 1:3
h 2Pt 1:19 i Eph 5:8,14

Treasure in Clay Jars

7 Now we have this treasure in [a]clay jars, [b]so that this extraordinary power may be from God and not from us. 8 We are pressured in every way but not crushed; we are perplexed but not in despair; 9 we are persecuted but not abandoned; we are struck down but not destroyed. 10 [c]We always carry the death of Jesus in our body, [d]so that the life of Jesus may also be revealed in our body. 11 For we who live are always given over to death because of Jesus, so that Jesus' life may also be revealed in our mortal flesh. 12 So death works in us, but life in you. 13 And since we have the same spirit of faith in accordance with what is written, [e]**I believed, therefore I spoke,**[e] we also believe, and therefore speak, 14 knowing that the One who raised the Lord Jesus will raise us also with Jesus, and present us with you. 15 For all this is because of you, so that grace, extended through more and more people, may cause thanksgiving to overflow to God's glory.

a 2Co 5:1 b Eph 1:19-20
c Gl 6:17 d 1Pt 4:13 e Ps 116:10

16 Therefore we do not give up; even though our outer person is being destroyed, our inner person is being renewed day by day. 17 For our momentary light affliction[f] is producing for us an absolutely incomparable eternal weight of glory. 18 So we do not focus on what is seen, but on what is unseen; for what is seen is temporary, but what is unseen is eternal.

Our Future after Death

5 For we know that if [a]our earthly house, a tent,[g] is destroyed, we have [b]a building from God, a house[h] not made with hands, eternal in the heavens. 2 And, in fact, [c]we groan in this one, longing to put on our house from heaven, 3 since, when [d]we are clothed,[i] we will not be found naked. 4 Indeed, we who are in this tent groan, burdened as we are, because

[a]**3:18** Or *are looking as in a mirror at* [b]**3:18** Progressive glorification or sanctification [c]**3:18** Or *from the Spirit of the Lord*, or *from the Lord, the Spirit* [d]**4:4** Or *the gospel of the glorious Christ*, or *the glorious gospel of Christ* [e]**4:13** Ps 116:10 LXX [f]**4:17** See note at 2 Co 1:4 [g]**5:1** Our present physical body [h]**5:1** *a building . . . a house* = our future body [i]**5:3** Other mss read *stripped*

we do not want to be unclothed but
[e]clothed, so that mortality may be
swallowed up by life. 5 And the One
who prepared us for this very thing is
God, who [f]gave us the Spirit as a
down payment.

[a] 2Pt 1:13 [b] Php 3:21; Heb 11:10 [c] Rm 8:23 [d] Rv 3:18 [e] 1Co 15:53 [f] Eph 1:14

6 Therefore, though we are always
confident and know that while we are
at home in the body we are away from
the Lord— 7 for [a]we •walk by faith, not
by sight— 8 yet we are confident and
[b]satisfied to be out of the body and
at home with the Lord. 9 Therefore,
whether we are at home or away, we
make it our aim to be pleasing to Him.
10 For we must all appear before the
judgment seat of Christ, [c]so that each
may be repaid for what he has done in
the body, whether good or bad.

[a] 1Co 13:12 [b] Php 1:23 [c] Rv 22:12

11 Knowing, then, the fear of the
Lord, we persuade people. We are
completely open before God, and I
hope we are completely open to your
consciences as well. 12 We are not commending ourselves to you again, but
giving you an opportunity to be proud
of us, so that you may have a reply for
those who take pride in the outward
appearance[a] rather than in the heart.
13 For [a]if we are out of our mind, it is
for God; if we have a sound mind, it is
for you. 14 For Christ's love compels[b]
us, since we have reached this conclusion: [b]if One died for all, then all died.
15 And He died for all [c]so that those
who live should no longer live for
themselves, but for the One who died
for them and was raised.

[a] 2Co 11:1 [b] Mt 20:28; Rm 5:15 [c] 1Pt 4:2

The Ministry of Reconciliation

16 From now on, then, we do not
know[c] anyone in a purely human way.[d]
Even if we have known[e] Christ in a
purely human way,[f] [a]yet now we no
longer know[c] Him like that. 17 Therefore if anyone is in Christ, there is a
new creation; [b]old things have passed
away, and look, new things[g] have
come. 18 Now everything is from God,
who reconciled us to Himself through
Christ and gave us the ministry of reconciliation: 19 that is, in Christ, [c]God
was reconciling the world to Himself,
not counting their trespasses against
them, and He has committed the message of reconciliation to us. 20 Therefore, we are [d]ambassadors for Christ;
certain that God is appealing through
us, we plead on Christ's behalf, "Be
reconciled to God." 21 [e]He made the
One who [f]did not know sin to be sin
for us, so that we might become [g]the
righteousness of God in Him.

[a] Jn 6:63 [b] Is 65:17; Rv 21:5 [c] 1Jn 2:1-2 [d] Ac 26:16-18 [e] Gl 3:13 [f] Heb 7:26 [g] Rm 1:17; Php 3:9

6 [a]Working together[h] with Him, we
also appeal to you: [b]"Don't receive
God's grace in vain." 2 For He says:

> [c]**In an acceptable time,**
> **I heard you,**
> **and in the day of salvation,**
> **I helped you.**[i]

Look, now is the acceptable time;
look, now is the day of salvation.

[a] 1Co 3:9; 2Co 5:20 [b] Heb 12:15 [c] Is 49:8

The Character of Paul's Ministry

3 [a]We give no opportunity for stumbling to anyone, so that the ministry
will not be blamed. 4 But in everything,
[b]as God's ministers, we commend ourselves:

> by great endurance,
> by afflictions, by hardship,
> by pressures,
> 5 by beatings, by imprisonments,
> by riots, by labors,

[a]**5:12** Lit *in face* [b]**5:14** Or *For the love of Christ impels*, or *For the love of Christ controls* [c]**5:16** Or *regard* [d]**5:16** Lit *anyone according to the flesh* [e]**5:16** Or *have regarded* [f]**5:16** Lit *Christ according to the flesh* [g]**5:17** Other mss read *look, all new things* [h]**6:1** Or *As we work together* [i]**6:2** Is 49:8

by sleepless nights,
by times of hunger,
6 by purity, by knowledge,
by patience, by kindness,
by the Holy Spirit,
by sincere love,
7 by the message of truth,
by [c]the power of God;
through [d]weapons
of righteousness
on the right hand
and the left,
8 through glory and dishonor,
through slander
and good report;
as deceivers yet true;
9 as unknown yet recognized;
[e]as dying and look—we live;
[f]as being chastened
yet not killed;
10 as grieving yet always rejoicing;
as poor yet enriching many;
as having nothing
yet possessing everything.

11 We have spoken openly[a] to you, Corinthians; our heart has been opened
wide. 12 You are not limited by us, but
[g]you are limited by your own affec-
tions. 13 Now in like response—I
speak as to children—you also should
be open to us.

[a] 1Co 9:12 [b] 1Co 4:1 [c] Eph 1:19-20 [d] 2Tm 4:7 [e] 1Co 4:9 [f] Ps 118:18 [g] 2Co 12:15

Separation to God

14 [a]Do not be mismatched with unbelievers. For [b]what partnership is
there between righteousness and lawlessness? Or what fellowship does light
have with darkness? 15 What agreement does Christ have with Belial?[b] Or
what does a believer have in common
with an unbeliever? 16 And what agreement does God's sanctuary have with
idols? [c]For we[c] are the sanctuary of the
living God, as God said:

[d]I will dwell among them
and walk among them,
and I will be their God,
and they will be My people.[d]
17 **[e]Therefore, come out**
from among them
and be separate, says the Lord;
do not touch
any unclean thing,
and I will welcome you.[e]
18 **[f]I will be a Father to you,**
and you will be sons
and daughters to Me,
says the Lord Almighty.[f]

[a] Dt 7:2-3 [b] Eph 5:7 [c] 1Pt 2:5 [d] Lv 26:12 [e] Is 52:11 [f] Jr 31:1,9

7 [a]Therefore dear friends, since we
have such promises, we should
wash ourselves clean from every impurity of the flesh and spirit, making
our sanctification complete[g] in the fear
of God.

[a] 1Jn 3:3

Joy and Repentance

2 Take us into your hearts.[h] We have
wronged no one, corrupted no one, de-
frauded no one. 3 I don't say this to
condemn you, for I have already said
that you are in our hearts, to die together and to live together. 4 I have
great confidence in you; I have [a]great
pride in you. I am filled with encouragement; [b]I am overcome with joy in
all our afflictions.

[a] 1Co 1:4 [b] Php 2:17

5 In fact, [a]when we came into Macedonia, we[i] had no rest. Instead, we
[b]were afflicted in every way: [c]struggles
on the outside, fears inside. 6 But
[d]God, who comforts the humble, comforted us by the coming of Titus, 7 and
not only by his coming, but also by the
comfort he received from you. He announced to us your deep longing, your
sorrow,[j] your zeal for me, so that I rejoiced even more. 8 For although I
grieved you with my letter, I do not re-

[a]**6:11** Lit *Our mouths have been open* [b]**6:15** Or *Beliar*, a name for the Devil or antichrist in extra-biblical Jewish writings [c]**6:16** Other mss read *you* [d]**6:16** Lv 26:12; Jr 31:33; 32:38; Ezk 37:26 [e]**6:17** Is 52:11 [f]**6:18** 2 Sm 7:14; Is 43:6; 49:22; 60:4; Hs 1:10 [g]**7:1** Or *spirit, perfecting holiness* [h]**7:2** Lit *Make room for us.* [i]**7:5** Lit *our flesh* [j]**7:7** Or *lamentation*, or *mourning*

gret it—even [e]though I did regret it
since I saw that the letter grieved you,
though only for a little while. 9 Now I
am rejoicing, not because you were
grieved, but because your grief led to
repentance. For you were grieved as
God willed, so that you didn't experience any loss from us. 10 For [f]godly
grief produces a repentance not to be
regretted and leading to salvation, [g]but
worldly grief produces death. 11 For
consider how much diligence this very
thing—this grieving as God wills—has
produced in you: what a desire to clear
yourselves, what indignation, what
fear, what deep longing, what zeal,
what justice! In every way you have
commended yourselves to be pure in
this matter. 12 So even though I wrote
to you, it was not because of the one
who did wrong, or because of the one
who was wronged, but in order that
your diligence for us might be made
plain to you in the sight of God. 13 For
this reason we have been comforted.

a 2Co 2:13 b 2Co 4:8 c Dt 32:25 d 2Th 2:16 e 2Co 2:4 f Jr 31:18-20 g Mt 27:4-5

In addition to our comfort, we were
made to rejoice even more over the joy
Titus had,[a] because his spirit [a]was refreshed by all of you. 14 For if I have
made any boast to him about you, I
have not been embarrassed; but as I
have spoken everything to you in
truth, so our boasting to Titus has also
turned out to be the truth. 15 And his
affection toward you is even greater as
he remembers [b]the obedience of all of
you, and how you received him with
fear and trembling. 16 I rejoice that [c]I
have complete confidence in you.

a Rm 15:32 b 2Co 2:9 c Phm 8,21

Appeal to Complete the Collection

8 We want you to know, brothers,
about the grace of God granted to
the churches of Macedonia: 2 during a
severe testing by affliction, their abundance of joy and [a]their deep poverty
overflowed into the wealth of their
generosity. 3 I testify that, on their
own, according to their ability and beyond their ability, 4 they begged us in-
sistently for the privilege of sharing in
[b]the ministry to the saints, 5 and not
just as we had hoped. Instead, they
[c]gave themselves especially to the
Lord, then to us by God's will. 6 So we
[d]urged Titus that, just as he had begun, so he should also complete this
grace to you. 7 Now as [e]you excel
in everything—in faith, in speech, in
knowledge, in all diligence, and in
your love for us[b]—[f]excel also in this
grace.

a Mk 12:44 b Ac 11:29; Rm 15:25 c Rm 6:13 d 2Co 12:18 e 1Co 1:5 f Pr 22:9; 2Co 9:8

8 I am not saying this as a command.
Rather, by means of the diligence of
others, I am testing the genuineness of
your love. 9 For you know the grace
of our Lord Jesus Christ: [a]although He
was rich, for your sake He became
poor, so that by His poverty you might
become rich. 10 Now I am giving an
opinion on this [b]because it is profitable for you, who a year ago began not
only to do something but also to desire
it.[c] 11 But now finish the task[d] as well,
that just as there was eagerness to desire it, so there may also be a completion from what you have. 12 For [c]if the
eagerness is there, it is acceptable according to what one has, not according to what he does not have. 13 It is
not that there may be relief for others
and hardship for you, but it is a question of equality[e]— 14 at the present
time your surplus is ⌊available⌋ for
their need, so that their abundance
may also become ⌊available⌋ for your
need, that there may be equality. 15 As
it has been written:

> [d]**The person who gathered**
> **much did not have too much,**

[a]**7:13** Lit *the joy of Titus* [b]**8:7** Other mss read *in our love for you* [c]**8:10** Lit *to will* [d]**8:11** Lit *finish the doing* [e]**8:13** Lit *but from equality*

and the person who gathered
little did not have too little.[a]

[a] Mt 8:20; Php 2:6-7 [b] Pr 19:17; Mt 10:42 [c] Lk 21:3 [d] Ex 16:18

Administration of the Collection

16 Thanks be to God who put the same diligence for you into the heart of Titus. 17 For he accepted our urging and, being very diligent, went out to you by his own choice. 18 With him we have sent [a]the brother who is praised throughout the churches for his gospel ministry.[b] 19 And not only that, but he was also [b]appointed by the churches to accompany us with this gift[c] that is being administered by us [c]for the glory of the Lord Himself and to show our eagerness ⌊to help⌋. 20 [d]We are taking this precaution so no one can find fault with us concerning this large sum administered by us. 21 [e]For we are making provision for what is honorable, not only before the Lord but also before men. 22 We have also sent with them our brother whom we have often tested, in many circumstances, and found diligent—and now even more diligent because of his great confidence in you. 23 As for Titus, he is my partner and co-worker serving you; as for our brothers, they are [f]the messengers of the churches, the glory of Christ. 24 Therefore, before the churches, show them the proof of your love and of our boasting about you.

[a] 2Co 12:18 [b] 1Co 16:3 [c] 2Co 4:15 [d] Eph 5:15 [e] Mt 5:16; Php 4:8 [f] Php 2:25

Motivations for Giving

9 Now concerning [a]the ministry to the saints, it is unnecessary for me to write to you. 2 For I know your [b]eagerness, [c]and I brag about you to the Macedonians:[d] [d]"Achaia[e] has been prepared since last year," and your zeal has stirred up most of them. 3 [e]But I sent the brothers so our boasting about you in the matter would not prove empty, and so you would be prepared just as I said. 4 For if any Macedonians should come with me and find you unprepared, we, not to mention you, would be embarrassed in that situation.[f] 5 Therefore I considered it necessary to urge the brothers to go on ahead to you and arrange in advance the generous gift you promised, so that it will be ready as a gift and not an extortion.

[a] Ac 11:29; Rm 15:26 [b] 2Co 8:19 [c] 2Co 8:24 [d] 2Co 8:10 [e] 2Co 8:6,17

6 [a]Remember this:[g] the person who sows sparingly will also reap sparingly, and the person who sows generously will also reap generously. 7 Each person should do as he has decided in his heart—[b]not out of regret or out of necessity, for [c]God loves a cheerful giver. 8 [d]And God is able to make every grace overflow to you, so that in every way, always having everything you need, you may excel in every good work. 9 As it is written:

[e]He has scattered;
He has given to the poor;
His righteousness endures
forever.[h]

[a] Pr 11:24; 19:17; Ec 11:1,6; Lk 6:38; Gl 6:7,9 [b] Dt 15:7 [c] Ex 25:2; Ac 20:35 [d] Pr 10:22; Mal 3:10; Php 4:19 [e] Ps 112:9

10 Now the One who [a]provides seed for the sower and bread for food will provide and multiply your seed and increase the harvest of your [b]righteousness, 11 as you are enriched in every way for all generosity, [c]which produces thanksgiving to God through us. 12 For the ministry of this service is not only supplying the needs of the saints, but is also overflowing in many acts of thanksgiving to God. 13 Through the proof of this service, they will [d]glorify

[a]**8:15** Ex 16:18 [b]**8:18** Lit *churches, in the gospel* [c]**8:19** Or *grace* [d]**9:2** Macedonia was a Roman province in the northern area of modern Greece. [e]**9:2** Achaia was the Roman province, south of Macedonia, where Corinth was located. [f]**9:4** Or *in this confidence* [g]**9:6** Lit *And this* [h]**9:9** Ps 112:9

God for your obedience to the confession of[a] the gospel of Christ, and for
your generosity [e]in sharing with them
and with others. 14 And in their
prayers for you they will have deep affection for[b] you because of the surpassing grace of God on you. 15 Thanks be
to God [f]for His indescribable gift.

a Gn 1:11-12; Is 55:10 b Hs 10:12 c 2Co 4:15 d Mt 5:16 e Heb 13:16 f Jms 1:17

Paul's Apostolic Authority

10 Now I, Paul, make a personal
appeal to you by the [a]gentleness
and graciousness of Christ—I who am
humble among you in person, but
bold toward you when absent. 2 I beg
you [b]that when I am present I will not
need to be bold with the confidence by
which I plan to challenge certain people who think we are •walking in a
fleshly way.[c] 3 For although we are
walking in the flesh, we do not wage
war in a fleshly way,[d] 4 [c]since the weapons of our warfare are not fleshly, but
are powerful through God [d]for the
demolition of strongholds. We demolish arguments 5 [e]and every high-
minded thing that is raised up against
the knowledge of God, taking every
thought captive to the obedience of
Christ. 6 [f]And we are ready to punish
any disobedience, once [g]your obedience is complete.

a Is 42:2 b 1Co 4:21 c Eph 6:13 d Jr 1:10 e 1Co 1:19 f 2Co 13:2 g 2Co 7:15

7 Look at what is obvious.[e] [a]If anyone
is confident that he belongs to Christ,
he should remind himself of this: just
as he belongs to Christ, [b]so do we.
8 For if I boast some more about our authority, which the Lord gave for building you up and not for tearing you
down, I am not ashamed. 9 I don't want
to seem as though I am trying to terrify
you with my letters. 10 For it is said,
"His letters are weighty and powerful,
but [c]his physical presence is weak, and
his [d]public speaking is despicable."
11 Such a person should consider this:
what we are in the words of our letters
when absent, we will be in actions
when present.

a 1Co 14:37 b 2Co 11:23 c Gl 4:13 d 1Co 1:17

12 [a]For we don't dare classify or compare ourselves with some who commend themselves. But in measuring
themselves by themselves and compar-
ing themselves to themselves, they
lack understanding. 13 We, however,
will not boast beyond measure, but according to the measure of the area ⌊of
ministry⌋ that God has assigned to us,
⌊which⌋ reaches even to you. 14 For we
are not overextending ourselves, as if
we had not reached you, [b]since we
have come to you with the gospel of
Christ. 15 We are not bragging beyond
measure [c]about other people's labors.
But we have the hope that as your faith
increases, our area ⌊of ministry⌋ will be
greatly enlarged, 16 so that we may
preach the gospel to the regions beyond you, not boasting about what has
already been done in someone else's
area ⌊of ministry⌋. 17 [d]So **the one who
boasts must boast in the Lord.**[f] 18 For
[e]it is not the one commending himself
who is approved, but [f]the one the Lord
commends.

a 2Co 5:12 b 1Co 9:1 c Rm 15:20 d Jr 9:24 e Lk 18:14 f Rm 2:29

Paul and the False Apostles

11 I wish you would put up with a
little [a]foolishness from me. Yes,
do put up with me.[g] 2 For I am jealous
over you with a godly jealousy, because
I have promised you in marriage to
one husband—[b]to present a pure virgin to Christ. 3 But I fear that, as the
[c]serpent deceived Eve by his cunning,
your minds may [d]be corrupted from a
complete and pure[h] devotion to Christ.
4 For if a person comes and preaches

[a]**9:13** Or *your obedient confession to* [b]**9:14** Or *will long for* [c]**10:2** Lit *walking according to flesh* [d]**10:3** Lit *war according to flesh* [e]**10:7** Or *You are looking at things outwardly* [f]**10:17** Jr 9:24 [g]**11:1** Or *Yes, you are putting up with me* [h]**11:3** Other mss omit *and pure*

another Jesus, whom we did not
preach, or you receive a different
spirit, which you had not received, or
a [e]different gospel, which you had not
accepted, you put up with it splen-
didly!

[a]2Co 5:13 [b]Col 1:28 [c]Gn 3:4 [d]Heb 13:9 [e]Gl 1:7-8

5 Now I consider myself in no
way inferior to the "super-apostles."
6 Though untrained in public speaking,
I am certainly not ⌊untrained⌋ [a]in
knowledge. Indeed, we have always
made that clear to you in everything.
7 Or did I commit a sin [b]by humbling
myself so that you might be exalted,
because I preached the gospel of God
to you free of charge? 8 I robbed other
churches by taking pay ⌊from them⌋ to
minister to you. 9 When I was present
with you and in need, [c]I did not burden anyone, for [d]the brothers who
came from Macedonia supplied my
needs. I have kept myself, and will
keep myself, [e]from burdening you in
any way. 10 [f]As the truth of Christ is in
me, this boasting of mine will not be
stopped[a] in the regions of Achaia.
11 Why? [g]Because I don't love you? God
knows I do!

[a]Eph 3:4 [b]Ac 18:3 [c]Ac 20:33 [d]Php 4:10 [e]2Co 12:14 [f]Rm 9:1 [g]2Co 7:3

12 But I will continue to do what I am
doing, [a]in order to cut off the opportunity of those who want an opportunity
to be regarded just as we are in what
they are boasting about. 13 For such
people are false apostles, deceitful
workers, disguising themselves as
apostles of Christ. 14 And no wonder!
For Satan himself is disguised as an angel of light. 15 So it is no great thing if
his servants also disguise themselves
as servants of righteousness. [b]Their
destiny[b] will be according to their
works.

[a]1Co 9:12 [b]Php 3:19

Paul's Sufferings for Christ

16 I repeat: no one should consider
me a fool. But if ⌊you do⌋, at least accept
me as a fool, so I too may boast a little.
17 What I say in this matter[c] of boasting, I don't speak as the Lord would,
but foolishly. 18 [a]Since many boast from
a human perspective,[d] I will also boast.
19 For you gladly put up with fools since
you are so smart![e] 20 In fact, you put up
with it [b]if someone enslaves you, if
someone devours you, if someone cap-
tures you, if someone dominates you,
or if someone hits you in the face. 21 I
say this to ⌊our⌋ shame: [c]we have been
weak.

[a]Php 3:3 [b]Gl 2:4 [c]2Co 10:10; Gl 4:13

But in whatever anyone dares ⌊to
boast⌋—I am talking foolishly—I also
dare:

22 Are they Hebrews? [a]So am I.
Are they Israelites? So am I.
Are they the seed of Abraham?
So am I.
23 Are they servants of Christ?
I'm talking like a
madman—I'm a better one:
[b]with far more labors,
many more imprisonments,
[c]far worse beatings, near death[f]
many times.
24 Five times I received
from the Jews [d]40 lashes
minus one.
25 Three times I was [e]beaten
with rods.[g]
[f]Once I was stoned.[h]
Three times I [g]was shipwrecked.
I have spent a night and a day
in the depths of the sea.
26 On frequent journeys, ⌊I faced⌋
dangers from rivers,
dangers from robbers,
dangers from my own people,
dangers from the Gentiles,
[h]dangers in the city,
dangers in the open country,

[a]**11:10** Or *silenced* [b]**11:15** Lit *end* [c]**11:17** Or *business*, or *confidence* [d]**11:18** Lit *boast according to the flesh* [e]**11:19** Or *are wise* [f]**11:23** Lit *and in deaths* [g]**11:25** A specifically Roman punishment; see Ac 16:22 [h]**11:25** A common Jewish method of capital punishment; see Ac 14:5

[i]dangers on the sea, and dangers
among false brothers;
27 labor and hardship,
many sleepless nights,
[j]hunger and thirst,
often without food, cold,
and lacking clothing. [a]Rm 11:1
[b]1Co 15:10 [c]Ac 9:16 [d]Dt 25:3
[e]Ac 16:22 [f]Ac 14:19 [g]Ac 27:41
[h]Ac 9:23 [i]Ac 19:23 [j]1Co 4:11

28 Not to mention[a] other things, there
is the daily pressure on me: my care
for all the churches. 29 Who is weak,
and I am not weak? Who is made to
stumble, and I do not burn with indignation? 30 If boasting is necessary, I
will boast about my weaknesses.
31 [a]The eternally blessed One, the God
and Father of the Lord Jesus, knows I
am not lying. 32 [b]In Damascus, the
governor under King Aretas[b] guarded
the city of the Damascenes in order to
arrest me, 33 so I was let down in a
basket through a window in the wall
and escaped his hands. [a]Rm 9:5 [b]Ac 9:24

Sufficient Grace

12 It is necessary to boast; it is not
helpful, but I will move on to visions and revelations of the Lord. 2 I
know a man in Christ who was caught
up into the third heaven 14 years ago.
Whether he was in the body or out of
the body, I don't know; God knows. 3 I
know that this man—whether in the
body or out of the body I do not know,
God knows— 4 was caught up into paradise. He heard inexpressible words,
which a man is not allowed to speak.
5 I will boast about this person, [a]but
not about myself, except of my weaknesses. 6 For if I want to boast, I will
not be a fool, because I will be telling
the truth. But I will spare you, so that
no one can credit me with something
beyond what he sees in me or hears
from me, 7 especially because of the
extraordinary revelations. [b]Therefore,
so that I would not exalt myself, a
thorn in the flesh was given to me, a
messenger[c] of Satan to torment me so I
would not exalt myself. 8 Concerning
this, I pleaded with the Lord three
times to take it away from me. 9 But He
said to me, [c]"My grace is sufficient for
you, for power[d] is perfected in weakness." Therefore, I will most gladly
boast all the more about my weaknesses, [d]so that Christ's power may reside in me. 10 So because of Christ, [e]I
am pleased in weaknesses, in insults,
in catastrophes, in persecutions, and
in pressures. [f]For when I am weak,
then I am strong. [a]2Co 11:30 [b]Gl 4:13
[c]Ec 7:18; Is 40:29
[d]1Pt 4:14 [e]Rm 5:3 [f]2Co 13:4

Signs of an Apostle

11 I have become a fool; you forced it
on me. I ought to have been recom-
mended by you, since I am [a]in no way
inferior to the "super-apostles," even
though I am nothing. 12 [b]The signs of
an apostle were performed among you
in all endurance—not only signs but
also wonders and miracles. 13 [c]So in
what way were you treated worse than
the other churches, except that [d]I personally did not burden you? Forgive
me this wrong! [a]1Co 3:4-7; Gl 2:6
[b]Rm 15:18 [c]1Co 1:7 [d]1Co 9:12

Paul's Concern for the Corinthians

14 [a]Look! I am ready to come to you
this third time. I will not burden you,
for [b]I am not seeking what is yours, but
you. For children are not obligated to
save up for their parents, but parents
for their children. 15 [c]I will most gladly
spend and be spent for you.[e] If I love
you more, am I to be loved less? 16 Now
granted, [d]I have not burdened you; yet
sly as I am, I took you in by deceit!
17 [e]Did I take advantage of you by anyone I sent you? 18 [f]I urged Titus ⌊to

[a]**11:28** Lit *Apart from* [b]**11:32** Aretus IV (9 B.C.–A.D. 40), a Nabatean Arab king [c]**12:7** Or *angel*
[d]**12:9** Other mss read *My power* [e]**12:15** Lit *for your souls*, or *for your lives*

come⌋, and I sent the brother with
him. Did Titus take advantage of you?
Didn't we •walk in the same spirit and
in the same footsteps?

[a] 2Co 13:1 [b] Ac 20:33 [c] Php 2:17 [d] 2Co 11:9 [e] 2Co 7:2 [f] 2Co 8:6

19 [a]You have thought all along that
we were defending ourselves to you.[a]
⌊No⌋, [b]in the sight of God we are speaking in Christ, and [c]everything, dear
friends, is for building you up. 20 For I
fear that perhaps when I come I will
not find you to be what I want, and [d]I
may not be found by you to be what
you want;[b] there may be quarreling,
jealousy, outbursts of anger, selfish ambitions, slander, gossip, arrogance, and
disorder. 21 I fear that when I come my
God [e]will again[c] humiliate me in your
presence, and I will grieve for many
who sinned before and have not repented of the uncleanness, [f]sexual
immorality, and promiscuity they practiced.

[a] 2Co 5:12 [b] Rm 9:1 [c] 1Co 10:33 [d] 1Co 4:21 [e] 2Co 2:1,4 [f] 1Co 5:1

Final Warnings and Exhortations

13 This is the [a]third time I am coming to you. [b]**On the testimony**[d]
of two or three witnesses every
word will be confirmed.[e] 2 [c]I gave
warning, and I give warning—as
when I was present the second time,
so now while I am absent—to those
[d]who sinned before and to all the rest:
if I come again, I will not be lenient,
3 since you seek proof of Christ
[e]speaking in me. He is not weak toward you, but powerful [f]among you.
4 [g]In fact, He was crucified in weakness, but [h]He lives by God's power.
For we also are weak in Him, yet toward you we will live with Him by
God's power.

[a] 2Co 12:14 [b] Nm 35:30; Dt 17:6; 19:15 [c] 2Co 10:2 [d] 2Co 12:21 [e] Mt 10:20 [f] 1Co 9:2 [g] Php 2:7-8 [h] Rm 6:4

5 Test yourselves ⌊to see⌋ if you are in
the faith. Examine yourselves. Or do
you not recognize for yourselves [a]that
Jesus Christ is in you?—unless you
[b]fail the test.[f] 6 And I hope you will recognize that we are not failing the test.
7 Now we pray to God that you do
nothing wrong, not that [c]we may appear to pass the test, but that you may
do what is right, even though we ⌊may
appear⌋ to fail. 8 For we are not able to
do anything against the truth, but only
for the truth. 9 In fact, we rejoice
[d]when we are weak and you are
strong. We also pray for this: [e]your maturity.[g] 10 This is why I am writing
these things while absent, that when I
am there I will not use severity, in
keeping with the authority the Lord
gave me for building up and not for
tearing down.

[a] Rm 8:10 [b] 1Co 9:27 [c] 2Co 6:9 [d] 1Co 4:10 [e] 1Th 3:10

11 Finally, brothers, rejoice. Be restored, be encouraged, [a]be of the same
mind, be at peace, and the God of love
[b]and peace will be with you. 12 Greet
one another with a holy kiss. All the
saints greet you.

[a] Rm 12:16 [b] Rm 15:33

13 The grace of the Lord Jesus Christ,
and the love of God, and the fellowship
of the Holy Spirit be with all of you.[h]

[a]**12:19** Or *Have you thought . . . to you?* [b]**12:20** Lit *be as you want* [c]**12:21** Or *come again my God will* [d]**13:1** Lit *mouth* [e]**13:1** Dt 17:6; 19:15 [f]**13:5** Or *you are disqualified*, or *you are counterfeit* [g]**13:9** Or *completion*, or *restoration* [h]**13:12–13** Some translations divide these 2 vv. into 3 vv. so that v. 13 begins with *All the saints . . .* and v. 14 begins with *The grace of . . .*

Galatians

Greeting

1 Paul, an apostle—not from men or
by man, but [a]by Jesus Christ and
God the Father who raised Him from
the dead— 2 and all the brothers who
are with me:

To the churches of Galatia.[a]

3 [b]Grace to you and peace from God
the Father and our Lord[b] Jesus Christ,
4 [c]who gave Himself for our sins to rescue us [d]from this present evil age, according to the will of our God and
Father, 5 to whom be the glory forever
and ever. •Amen.

a Ac 9:6 b 1Co 1:3 c 1Jn 2:2 d Is 65:17

No Other Gospel

6 I am amazed that you are so
quickly turning away from Him who
called you by the grace of Christ, ⌊and
are turning⌋ to a different gospel—
7 [a]not that there is another ⌊gospel⌋,
but there are some [b]who are troubling
you and want to change the gospel of
Christ. 8 But even if we or an angel
from heaven should preach to you a
gospel other than what we have
preached to you, a curse be on him![c]
9 As we have said before, I now say
again: if anyone preaches to you a gospel [c]contrary to what you received, a
curse be on him![d]

a 2Co 11:4 b Ac 15:1 c Dt 4:2

10 For [a]am I now [b]trying to win the
favor of people, or God? Or [c]am I striving to please people? If I were still trying to please people, I would not be a
slave of Christ.

a 1Th 2:4 b 1Jn 3:19 c Jms 4:4

Paul Defends His Apostleship

11 [a]Now I want you to know, brothers, that the gospel preached by me is
not based on a human point of view.[e]
12 For I did not receive it from a human
source and I was not taught it, but it
came [b]by a revelation from Jesus
Christ.

a 1Co 15:1 b Eph 3:3

13 For you have heard about my
former way of life in Judaism: I persecuted God's church [a]to an extreme degree and [b]tried to destroy it; 14 and I
advanced in Judaism beyond many
contemporaries among my people,
[c]because I was extremely zealous for
the traditions of my ancestors. 15 But
when God, [d]who from my mother's
womb set me apart and called me by
His grace, was pleased 16 [e]to reveal His
Son in me, so that I could preach Him
among the Gentiles, I did not immediately consult with anyone.[f] 17 I did not
go up to Jerusalem to those who had
become apostles before me; instead I
went to Arabia and came back to Damascus.

a 1Tm 1:13 b Ac 8:3 c Php 3:6 d Ac 9:15 e 2Co 4:6

18 Then after three years I did go up
to Jerusalem to get to know •Cephas,[g]
and I stayed with him 15 days. 19 But I
didn't see any of the other apostles except [a]James, the Lord's brother. 20 Now
in what I write to you, I'm not lying.
God is my witness.[h]

a Mk 6:3

21 Afterwards, I went to the regions
of Syria and Cilicia. 22 I remained
personally unknown to the Judean
churches in Christ; 23 they simply kept
hearing: "He who formerly persecuted

[a]**1:2** A Roman province in what is now Turkey [b]**1:3** Other mss read *God our Father and the Lord* [c]**1:8** Or *you, let him be condemned*, or *you, let him be condemned to hell*; Gk *anathema* [d]**1:9** Or *received, let him be condemned*, or *received, let him be condemned to hell*; Gk *anathema* [e]**1:11** Lit *not according to man* [f]**1:16** Lit *flesh and blood* [g]**1:18** Other mss read *Peter* [h]**1:20** Lit *Behold, before God*

us now preaches the faith he once
tried to destroy." 24 And they glorified
God because of me.

Paul Defends His Gospel at Jerusalem

2 Then after 14 years [a]I went up
again to Jerusalem with Barnabas,
taking Titus along also. 2 I went up because of a revelation [b]and presented
to them the gospel I preach among the
Gentiles—but privately to those recognized ⌊as leaders⌋—so that [c]I might
not be running, or have run, in vain.
3 But not even Titus who was with me,
though he was a Greek, was compelled to be circumcised. 4 ⌊This issue
arose⌋ because of false brothers smug-
gled in, who came in secretly to spy
on our [d]freedom that we have in
Christ Jesus, [e]in order to enslave us.
5 But we did not yield in submission to
these people for even an hour, so that
the truth of the gospel would remain
for you.

[a]*Ac 15:2* [b]*Ac 19:21* [c]*Php 2:16* [d]*Gl 3:25* [e]*Gl 4:3,9*

6 But from those [a]recognized as important (what they really were makes
no difference to me; [b]God does not
show favoritism[a])—those [c]recognized
as important added nothing to me.
7 On the contrary, [d]they saw that I had
been [e]entrusted with the gospel for the
uncircumcised, just as Peter was for
the circumcised. 8 For He who was at
work with Peter in the apostleship to
the circumcised [f]was also at work with
me among the Gentiles. 9 When James,
•Cephas, and John, recognized as
[g]pillars, acknowledged [h]the grace that
had been given to me, they gave the
right hand of fellowship to me and
Barnabas, ⌊agreeing⌋ that we should go
to the Gentiles and they to the circumcised. 10 ⌊They asked⌋ only that we
would remember the poor, [i]which I
made every effort to do.

[a]*Gl 6:3* [b]*Rm 2:11* [c]*2Co 12:11* [d]*Ac 13:46* [e]*1Th 2:4* [f]*Ac 13:2; 22:21* [g]*Mt 16:18* [h]*Rm 1:5* [i]*Ac 11:30*

Freedom from the Law

11 [a]But when Cephas[b] came to Antioch, I opposed him to his face because
he stood condemned.[c] 12 For he [b]used
to eat with the Gentiles before certain
men came from James. However, when
they came, he withdrew and separated
himself, because he feared those from
the circumcision party. 13 Then the rest
of the Jews joined his hypocrisy, so that
even Barnabas was carried away by
their hypocrisy. 14 But when I saw that
they were deviating from [c]the truth of
the gospel, I told Cephas[b] in front of everyone, [d]"If you, who are a Jew, live
like a Gentile and not like a Jew, how
can you compel Gentiles to live like
Jews?"[d]

[a]*Ac 15:35* [b]*Ac 10:28* [c]*Ec 7:20* [d]*Ac 11:3*

15 [a]We are Jews by birth and not
[b]"Gentile sinners"; 16 yet we [c]know
that no one is justified by the works of
the law but [d]by faith in Jesus Christ.[e]
And we have believed in Christ Jesus,
so that we might be justified by faith in
Christ[f] and not by the works of the law,
because by the works of the law no human being will[g] be justified. 17 But if,
while seeking to be justified by Christ,
we ourselves are also found to be
[e]sinners, is Christ then a promoter[h] of
sin? Absolutely not! 18 If I rebuild those
things that I tore down, I show myself
to be a lawbreaker. 19 For [f]through the
law I [g]have died to the law, that I might
[h]live to God. I have been [i]cruci- fied
with Christ; 20 and I no longer live, but
Christ lives in me. The life I now live
in the flesh,[i] [j]I live by faith in the Son
of God, who loved me and gave Him-

[a]**2:6** Or *God is not a respecter of persons*; lit *God does not receive the face of man* [b]**2:11,14** Other mss read *Peter* [c]**2:11** Or *he was in the wrong* [d]**2:14** Some translations continue the quotation through v. 16 or v. 21. [e]**2:16** Or *by the faithfulness of Jesus Christ* [f]**2:16** Or *by the faithfulness of Christ* [g]**2:16** Lit *law all flesh will not* [h]**2:17** Or *servant* [i]**2:20** The physical body

self for me. 21 I do not set aside the grace of God; for [k]if righteousness comes through the law, then Christ died for nothing.

[a]Ac 15:10 [b]Eph 2:3 [c]Ac 13:38 [d]Rm 1:17; 1Co 6:11 [e]Rm 15:8 [f]Rm 3:19-20 [g]Rm 6:14 [h]Rm 14:7-8 [i]Rm 6:6 [j]2Co 5:15 [k]Heb 7:11

Justification through Faith

3 You foolish Galatians! [a]Who has hypnotized you,[a] [b]before whose eyes Jesus Christ was vividly portrayed[b] as crucified? 2 I only want to learn this from you: Did you receive [c]the Spirit by the works of the law or by hearing with faith?[c] 3 Are you so foolish? [d]After beginning with the Spirit, are you now going to be made complete by [e]the flesh?[d] 4 [f]Did you suffer so much for nothing—if in fact it was for nothing? 5 So then, does God[e] [g]supply you with the Spirit and work miracles among you by the works of the law or by hearing with faith?[c]

[a]Gl 5:7 [b]1Co 1:23 [c]Heb 6:4 [d]Gl 4:9 [e]Heb 7:16 [f]2Jn 8 [g]2Co 3:8

6 Just as Abraham [a]**believed God, and it was credited to him for righteousness,**[f] 7 so understand that [b]those who have faith are Abraham's sons. 8 Now the Scripture foresaw that God would justify the Gentiles by faith and foretold the good news to Abraham, saying, [c]**All the nations will be blessed in you.**[g] 9 So those who have faith are blessed with Abraham, who had faith.[h]

[a]Gn 15:6 [b]Jn 8:39 [c]Gn 12:3

Law and Promise

10 For all who ⌊rely on⌋ the works of the law are under a curse, because it is written: [a]**Cursed is everyone who does not continue doing everything written in the book of the law.**[i] 11 Now it is clear that no one is justified before God by the law, because [b]**the righteous will live by faith.**[j] 12 But [c]the law is not based on faith; instead, [d]**the one who does these things will live by them.**[k] 13 Christ has redeemed us from the curse of the law by becoming a curse for us, because it is written: [e]**Cursed is everyone who is hung on a tree.**[l] 14 [f]The purpose was that the blessing of Abraham would come to the Gentiles in Christ Jesus, so that we could receive [g]the promise of the Spirit through faith.

[a]Dt 27:26 [b]Hab 2:4 [c]Rm 4:4 [d]Lv 18:5 [e]Dt 21:23 [f]Rm 4:9 [g]Is 32:15; Jl 2:28

15 Brothers, I'm using a human illustration.[m] [a]No one sets aside even a human covenant that has been ratified, or makes additions to it. 16 Now the promises were spoken to Abraham [b]and to his seed. He does not say "and to seeds," as though referring to many, but **and to your seed,**[n] referring to one, who is Christ. 17 And I say this: the law, [c]which came 430 years later, does not revoke a covenant that was previously ratified by God,[o] [d]so as to cancel the promise. 18 For if [e]the inheritance is from the law, [f]it is no longer from the promise; but God granted it to Abraham through the promise.

[a]Heb 9:17 [b]Gn 17:8 [c]Ex 12:40 [d]Rm 4:13-14 [e]Rm 8:17 [f]Rm 4:14

The Purpose of the Law

19 Why the law then? [a]It was added because of transgressions until the Seed to whom the promise was made would come. ⌊The law⌋ was [b]ordered through angels by means [c]of a mediator. 20 Now a mediator is not for just one person, [d]but God is one. 21 Is the law therefore contrary to God's promises? Absolutely not! For if a law had been given that was able to give life, then righteousness would certainly be by the law. 22 But the Scripture has

[a]**3:1** Other mss add *not to obey the truth* [b]**3:1** Other mss add *among you* [c]**3:2,5** Lit *by law works or faith hearing* or *hearing the message* [d]**3:3** By human effort [e]**3:5** Lit *He* [f]**3:6** Gn 15:6 [g]**3:8** Gn 12:3; 18:18 [h]**3:9** Or *with believing Abraham* [i]**3:10** Dt 27:26 [j]**3:11** Hab 2:4 [k]**3:12** Lv 18:5 [l]**3:13** Dt 21:23 [m]**3:15** Lit *I speak according to man* [n]**3:16** Gn 12:7; 13:15; 17:8; 24:7 [o]**3:17** Other mss add *in Christ*

imprisoned everything under sin's
power,[a] so that the promise by faith in
Jesus Christ might be given to those
who believe. 23 Before this faith came,
we were confined under the law, imprisoned until the coming faith was revealed. 24 [e]The law, then, was our
guardian[b] until Christ, [f]so that we
could be justified by faith. 25 But since
that faith has come, we are no longer
under a guardian,[b] 26 for you [g]are all
sons of God through faith in Christ
Jesus.

[a] *1Tm 1:9* [b] *Ac 7:53* [c] *Ex 20:19* [d] *Rm 3:29* [e] *Mt 5:17* [f] *Ac 13:39* [g] *Rm 8:14-17*

Sons and Heirs

27 For as many of you as have been
baptized into Christ have put on
Christ. 28 [a]There is no Jew or Greek,
slave or free, male or female; for you
are all [b]one in Christ Jesus. 29 And [c]if
you are Christ's, then you are Abraham's seed, [d]heirs according to the
4 promise. 1 Now I say that as long
as the heir is a child, he differs in
no way from a slave, though he is the
owner of everything. 2 Instead, he is
under guardians and stewards until the
time set by his father. 3 In the same
way we also, when we were children,
[e]were in slavery under the elemental
forces of the world. 4 But [f]when the
completion of the time came, God sent
His Son, [g]born of a woman, [h]born under the law, 5 [i]to redeem those under
the law, [j]so that we might receive
adoption as sons. 6 And because you
are sons, God has sent the Spirit of His
Son into our[c] hearts, crying, "•*Abba*,
Father!" 7 So you are no longer a slave,
but a son; [k]and if a son, then an heir
through God.

[a] *Rm 10:12* [b] *Jn 10:16* [c] *Gn 21:10; Rm 9:7-8* [d] *Rm 8:17* [e] *Col 2:8,20* [f] *Gn 49:10; Mk 1:15* [g] *Jn 1:14* [h] *Mt 5:17* [i] *Mt 20:28* [j] *Jn 1:12* [k] *Rm 8:16*

Paul's Concern for the Galatians

8 But in the past, [a]when you didn't
know God, [b]you were enslaved to
things[d] that by nature are not gods.
9 But now, [c]since you know God, or
rather have become known by God,
[d]how can you turn back again to the
weak and bankrupt elemental forces?
Do you want to be enslaved to them all
over again? 10 [e]You observe ⌊special⌋
days, months, seasons, and years. 11 I
am fearful for you, that perhaps my labor for you has been wasted.

[a] *Eph 2:12* [b] *Rm 1:25* [c] *1Co 8:3* [d] *Col 2:20* [e] *Rm 14:5*

12 I beg you, brothers: become [a]like
me, for I also became like you. You
have not wronged me; 13 you know
[b]that previously I preached the gospel
to you [c]in physical weakness, 14 and
though my physical condition was a
trial for you,[e] you did not despise or reject me. On the contrary, you received
me as an angel of God, [d]as Christ Jesus
⌊Himself⌋.

[a] *Gl 6:14* [b] *Gl 1:6* [c] *1Co 2:3* [d] *Mt 10:40*

15 What happened to this blessed-
ness of yours? For I testify to you that,
if possible, you would have torn out
your eyes and given them to me.
16 Have I now become your enemy by
telling you the truth? 17 They[f] are
[a]enthusiastic about you, but not for
any good. Instead, they want to isolate
you so you will be enthusiastic about
them. 18 Now it is always good to be
enthusiastic about good—and not just
when I am with you. 19 My [b]children,
again I am in the pains of childbirth for
you until Christ is formed in you. 20 I'd
like to be with you right now and
change my tone of voice, because I
don't know what to do about you.

[a] *Rm 10:2* [b] *1Co 4:15*

[a]**3:22** Lit *under sin* [b]**3:24,25** The word translated *guardian* in vv. 24–25 is different from the word in Gl 4:2. In our culture, we do not have a slave who takes a child to and from school, protecting the child from harm or corruption. In Gk the word *paidogogos* described such a slave. This slave was not a teacher. [c]**4:6** Other mss read *your* [d]**4:8** Or *beings* [e]**4:14** Other mss read *me* [f]**4:17** The false teachers

Sarah and Hagar: Two Covenants

21 Tell me, you who want to be under
the law, don't you hear the law? 22 For
it is written that Abraham had two
sons, [a]one by a slave and [b]the other by
a free woman. 23 But the one by the
slave [c]was born according to the flesh,
[d]while the one by the free woman was
born as the result of a promise. 24 These
things are illustrations,[a] for the women
represent the two covenants. One is
from Mount Sinai and bears children
into slavery—this is Hagar. 25 Now
Hagar is Mount Sinai in Arabia and corresponds to the present Jerusalem, for
she is in slavery with her children.
26 But the [e]Jerusalem above is free, and
she is our mother. 27 For it is written:

[f]**Rejoice, O barren woman**
who does not give birth.
Break forth and shout,
you who are not in labor,
for the children of the desolate
are many,
more numerous than those
of the woman
who has a husband.[b]

28 Now you, brothers, like Isaac, are
[g]children of promise. 29 But just as
then [h]the child born according to the
flesh persecuted the one born according to the Spirit, so also now. 30 But
what does the Scripture say?

[a] Gn 16:15 [b] Gn 21:2 [c] Rm 9:7-8 [d] Gn 18:10 [e] Is 2:2; Heb 12:22 [f] Is 54:1 [g] Rm 4:16 [h] Gn 21:9

[a]**Throw out the slave and her son, for [b]the son of the slave will never inherit with the son of the free woman.**[c]

31 Therefore, brothers, we are not children of the slave but of the free
woman.

[a] Gn 21:10 [b] Jn 8:35

Freedom of the Christian

5 Christ has liberated us [a]into freedom. Therefore stand firm and
don't submit again to [b]a yoke of slavery. 2 Take note! I, Paul, tell you that
if you get circumcised, Christ will not
benefit you at all. 3 Again I testify to
every man who gets circumcised [c]that
he is obligated to keep the entire law.
4 [d]You who are trying to be justified by
the law are alienated from Christ;
[e]you have fallen from grace! 5 For by
the Spirit we [f]eagerly wait for the
hope of righteousness from faith. 6 For
[g]in Christ Jesus neither circumcision
nor uncircumcision accomplishes anything; what matters is faith [h]working
through love.

[a] Jn 8:32; 1Co 7:22 [b] Ac 15:10 [c] Gl 3:10 [d] Rm 9:31 [e] Heb 12:15 [f] Rm 8:24 [g] Col 3:11 [h] 1Th 1:3

7 You [a]were running well. Who prevented you from obeying the truth?
8 This persuasion did not come from
Him who called you. 9 A little yeast leav-
ens the whole lump of dough. 10 In the
Lord I have confidence in you that you
will not accept any other view. But
[b]whoever it is who is troubling you
[c]will pay the penalty. 11 Now brothers,
[d]if I still preach circumcision, [e]why am
I still persecuted? In that case [f]the offense of the cross has been abolished.
12 [g]I wish [h]those who are disturbing you
might also get themselves castrated!

[a] 1Co 9:24 [b] Gl 1:7 [c] 2Co 10:6 [d] Gl 6:12 [e] 1Co 15:30 [f] 1Co 1:23 [g] 1Co 5:13 [h] Ac 15:1

13 For you are called to freedom,
brothers; only [a]don't use this freedom
as an opportunity for the flesh, but
serve one another through love. 14 For
the entire law is fulfilled in one statement: [b]**Love your neighbor as yourself.**[d] 15 But if you bite and devour one
another, watch out, or you will be consumed by one another.

[a] 1Pt 2:16 [b] Lv 19:18

The Spirit versus the Flesh

16 I say then, [a]•walk by the Spirit and
you will not carry out the desire of the
flesh. 17 For [b]the flesh desires what is

[a]**4:24** Typology or allegory [b]**4:27** Is 54:1 [c]**4:30** Gn 21:10 [d]**5:14** Lv 19:18

against the Spirit, and the Spirit desires
what is against the flesh; these are opposed to each other, [c]so that you don't
do what you want. 18 But [d]if you are led
by the Spirit, you are not under the law.
[a]Rm 6:12 [b]Rm 7:23 [c]Rm 7:15 [d]Rm 6:14

19 Now the works of the flesh are
obvious:[a] [b] sexual immorality, moral
impurity, promiscuity, 20 idolatry, sorcery, hatreds, strife, jealousy, outbursts
of anger, selfish ambitions, dissen-
sions, factions, 21 envy,[c] drunkenness,
carousing, and anything similar, about
which I tell you in advance—as I told
you before—that [a]those who practice
such things will not inherit the kingdom of God. *[a]Rv 22:15*

22 But [a]the fruit of the Spirit is love,
joy, peace, patience, [b]kindness, goodness, [c]faith,[d] 23 gentleness, self-control.
Against such things there is no law.
24 Now those who belong to Christ
Jesus have crucified the flesh with its
passions and desires. 25 If we live by
the Spirit, we must also follow the
Spirit. 26 We must not become conceited, provoking one another, envy-
ing one another. *[a]Jn 15:2 [b]Jms 3:17*
[c]1Co 13:7

Carry One Another's Burdens

6 Brothers, if someone is caught in
any wrongdoing, you [a]who are
spiritual should restore such a person
[b]with a gentle spirit, watching out for
yourselves so you won't be tempted
also. 2 [c]Carry one another's burdens; in
this way you will fulfill [d]the law of
Christ. 3 For [e]if anyone considers himself to be something when [f]he is nothing, he is deceiving himself. 4 But
[g]each person should examine his own
work, and then he will have a reason
for boasting in himself alone, and not
in respect to someone else. 5 For each
person will have to carry his own load.
[a]1Co 2:15 [b]2Th 3:15 [c]Rm 15:1
[d]Jn 13:14 [e]Rm 12:3 [f]2Co 3:5 [g]2Co 13:5

6 [a]The one who is taught the message must share his goods with the
teacher. 7 Don't be deceived: [b]God is
not mocked. For [c]whatever a man
sows he will also reap, 8 because the
one who sows to his flesh will reap corruption from the flesh, but the one
who sows to [d]the Spirit will reap eternal life from the Spirit. 9 So we must
not get tired of doing good, for we will
reap at the proper time [e]if we don't
give up. 10 Therefore, as we have opportunity, [f]we must work for the good
of all, especially for those who belong
to [g]the household of faith. *[a]Rm 15:27*
[b]Jb 13:9 [c]Lk 16:25
[d]Jms 3:18 [e]Mt 24:13
[f]1Tm 6:18 [g]Eph 2:19

Concluding Exhortation

11 Look at what large letters I have
written to you in my own handwrit-
ing. 12 Those who want to make a good
showing in the flesh are the ones who
would compel you to be circumcised—but only to avoid [a]being persecuted for the cross of Christ. 13 For
even the circumcised don't keep the
law themselves; however, they want
you to be circumcised in order to boast
about your flesh. 14 But as for me, I will
never boast about anything except the
cross of our Lord Jesus Christ, through
whom[e] the world has been crucified to
me, and I to the world. 15 For[f] both circumcision and uncircumcision mean
nothing; ⌊what matters⌋ instead is [b]a
new creation. 16 May peace be on all
those who follow this standard, and
mercy also be on [c]the Israel of God!
[a]Php 3:18
[b]2Co 5:17 [c]Gl 3:7-9

17 From now on, let no one cause me
trouble, because [a]I carry the marks of
Jesus on my body. 18 Brothers, the
grace of our Lord Jesus Christ be with
your spirit. •Amen. *[a]Col 1:24*

[a]**5:19** Other mss add *adultery* [b]**5:19** Lit *obvious, which are:* [c]**5:21** Other mss add *murders* [d]**5:22** Or *faithfulness* [e]**6:14** Or *which* [f]**6:15** Other mss add *in Christ Jesus*

EPHESIANS

Greeting

1 Paul, an apostle of Christ Jesus by
God's will:
To the saints [a]and believers in Christ
Jesus at Ephesus.[a]
2 [b]Grace to you and peace from God
our Father and the Lord Jesus Christ.

[a]Col 1:2 [b]Ti 1:4

God's Rich Blessings

3 [a]Blessed be the God and Father of
our Lord Jesus Christ, who has blessed
us with every spiritual blessing in the
heavens, in Christ; 4 for [b]He chose us
in Him, before the foundation of the
world, [c]to be holy and blameless in His
sight.[b] In love[c] 5 [d]He predestined us to
be adopted through Jesus Christ for
Himself, [e]according to His favor and
will, 6 [f]to the praise of His glorious
grace [g]that He favored us with in [h]the
Beloved.

[a]Ps 72:17 [b]1Pt 1:2,20 [c]Lk 1:75 [d]Rm 8:29 [e]Lk 12:32 [f]Is 43:21 [g]Rm 3:24 [h]Mt 17:5

7 [a]In Him we have redemption
through His blood, the forgiveness of
our trespasses, according to [b]the riches
of His grace 8 that He lavished on us
with all wisdom and understanding.
9 [c]He made known to us the •mystery
of His will, according to His good pleasure [d]that He planned in Him 10 for the
administration[d] of the days of fulfillment[e]—[e]to bring [f]everything together
in the •Messiah, both things in heaven
and things on earth in Him.

[a]Heb 9:12 [b]Rm 3:24 [c]Col 1:26 [d]2Tm 1:9 [e]Ph 2:10 [f]Php 2:9

11 [a]In Him we were also made His inheritance,[f] predestined according to
[b]the purpose of the One who works
out everything in agreement with the
decision of His will, 12 [c]so that we
[d]who had already put our hope in the
Messiah might bring praise to His
glory.

[a]Rm 8:17 [b]Is 46:10 [c]2Th 2:13 [d]Jms 1:18

13 In Him you also, when you heard
the word of truth, the gospel of your salvation—in Him when you believed—
[a]were sealed with the promised Holy
Spirit. 14 [b]He is the down payment of
our inheritance, [c]for the redemption of
[d]the possession,[g] to the praise of His
glory.

[a]2Co 1:22 [b]2Co 5:5 [c]Rm 8:23 [d]Ac 20:28

Prayer for Spiritual Insight

15 This is why, since I heard about
your faith in the Lord Jesus and your
love for all the saints, 16 I never stop
giving thanks for you as I remember
you in my prayers. 17 ⌊I pray⌋ that the
God of our Lord Jesus Christ, the glorious Father,[h] [a]would give you a spirit of
wisdom and revelation in the knowledge of Him. 18 ⌊I pray⌋ that [b]the eyes of
your heart may be enlightened so you
may know what is the hope of His calling, what are the glorious riches of His
inheritance among the saints, 19 and
what is the immeasurable greatness of
His power to us who believe, according to the working of His vast strength.

[a]Col 1:9 [b]Ac 26:18

God's Power in Christ

20 He demonstrated ⌊this power⌋ in
the Messiah by raising Him from the
dead and seating Him at His right hand

---

[a]**1:1** Other mss omit *at Ephesus* [b]**1:4** Vv. 3–14 are 1 sentence in Gk. [c]**1:4** Or *In His sight in love* [d]**1:10** Or *dispensation*; lit *house law* (Gk *oikonomia*) [e]**1:10** Lit *the fulfillment of times* [f]**1:11** Or *we also were chosen as an inheritance*, or *we also received an inheritance* [g]**1:14** *the possession* could be either man's or God's [h]**1:17** Or *the Father of glory*

in the heavens— 21 [a]far above every
ruler and authority, power and dominion, and every title given,[a] not only in
this age but also in the one to come.
22 And [b]**He put everything under His
feet**[b] and appointed Him [c]as head over
everything for the church, 23 [d]which is
His body, the fullness of the One [e]who
fills all things in every way.

[a] *Php 2:9* [b] *Ps 8:6; Mt 28:18* [c] *Heb 2:7* [d] *Rm 12:5* [e] *Jn 1:14,16*

From Death to Life

2 And [a]you were dead in your trespasses and sins 2 [b]in which you
previously •walked according to this
worldly age, according to the ruler of
the atmospheric domain,[c] the spirit
now working in [c]the disobedient.[d]
3 [d]We too all previously lived among
them in our fleshly desires, carrying
out the inclinations of our flesh and
thoughts, and [e]by nature we were children under wrath, as the others were
also. 4 But God, [f]who is abundant in
mercy, because of His great love that
He had for us,[e] 5 [g]made us alive with
the •Messiah [h]even though we were
dead in trespasses. By grace you are
saved! 6 He also raised us up with Him
and seated us with Him in the heavens, in Christ Jesus, 7 so that in the
coming ages He might display the immeasurable riches of His grace in ⌊His⌋
kindness to us in Christ Jesus. 8 For by
grace you are saved [i]through faith,
this is not from yourselves; [j]it is God's
gift— 9 [k]not from works, so that no one
can boast. 10 For we are His creation—
created in Christ Jesus for good works,
[l]which God prepared ahead of time so
that we should walk in them.

[a] *Jn 5:24* [b] *1Jn 5:19* [c] *Col 3:6* [d] *Ti 3:3* [e] *Ps 51:5* [f] *Rm 10:12* [g] *Rm 6:4* [h] *Rm 5:6* [i] *Rm 4:16* [j] *Jn 6:44* [k] *Rm 3:20* [l] *Eph 1:4*

Unity in Christ

11 So then, remember that at one
time you were Gentiles in the flesh—
called "the uncircumcised" by those
called "the circumcised," done by
hand in the flesh. 12 [a]At that time you
were without the Messiah, excluded
from the citizenship of Israel, and foreigners to [b]the covenants of the promise, with no hope [c]and without God in
the world. 13 [d]But now in Christ Jesus,
you who were far away have been
brought near by the blood of the Messiah. 14 For He is our peace, who made
both groups one and tore down the di-
viding wall of hostility. [e]In His flesh,
15 He did away with the law of the commandments in regulations, so that He
might create in Himself one [f]new man
from the two, resulting in peace. 16 ⌊He
did this so⌋ that He might reconcile
[g]both to God in one body through the
cross and put the hostility to death by
it.[f] 17 When ⌊Christ⌋ came, [h]He proclaimed the good news of peace to you
who were far away and peace to those
who were near. 18 For through Him we
both have access by one Spirit to the
Father. 19 So then you are no longer foreigners and strangers, but fellow citizens with the saints, and members of
God's household, 20 built [i]on the foundation of the [j]apostles and prophets,
with Christ Jesus Himself as the
[k]cornerstone. 21 The whole building is
being fitted together in Him and is
growing into a holy sanctuary in the
Lord, 22 in whom you also are being
built together for [l]God's dwelling in
the Spirit.

[a] *Col 1:21* [b] *Rm 9:4,8* [c] *Gl 4:8* [d] *Gl 3:28* [e] *Col 1:22* [f] *2Co 5:17* [g] *Rm 6:6; Gl 2:20* [h] *Is 57:19* [i] *Mt 16:18* [j] *1Co 12:28* [k] *Mt 21:42* [l] *Jn 17:23*

Paul's Ministry to the Gentiles

3 For this reason, I, Paul, [a]the prisoner of Christ Jesus [b]on behalf of
you Gentiles— 2 you have heard,
haven't you, about the [c]administration
of God's grace [d]that He gave to me for
you? 3 The •mystery [e]was made known

[a]**1:21** Lit *every name named* [b]**1:22** Ps 8:6 [c]**2:2** Lit *ruler of the authority of the air* [d]**2:2** Lit *sons of disobedience* [e]**2:4** Lit *love with which He loved us* [f]**2:16** Or *death in Himself*

to me by revelation, as I have briefly
written above. 4 By reading this you
are able to understand my insight
[f]about the mystery of the •Messiah.
5 This was not made known to people[a]
in other generations as it is now revealed to His holy apostles and prophets by the Spirit: 6 the Gentiles are
co-heirs, members of the same body,
and [g]partners of the promise in Christ
Jesus through the gospel. 7 I was made
a servant of this ⌊gospel⌋ by the gift of
God's grace that was given to me by
the [h]working of His power.

[a] Ac 21:33 [b] 2Tm 2:10 [c] Rm 1:5 [d] Ac 9:15 [e] Rm 16:25 [f] 1Co 4:1 [g] Gl 3:14 [h] Rm 15:18

8 This grace was given to me—the
least of all the saints!—to proclaim to
the Gentiles the [a]incalculable riches of
the Messiah, 9 and to shed light for all
about the administration of the mystery [b]hidden for ages in God [c]who created all things. 10 [d]This is so that God's
multi-faceted wisdom [e]may now be
made known through the church [f]to
the rulers and authorities in the heavens. 11 This is according to the purpose
of the ages, which He made in the
Messiah, Jesus our Lord, 12 in whom
we have boldness, access, and confidence through faith in Him.[b] 13 So then
I ask you not to be discouraged over
my afflictions on your behalf, for they
are your glory.

[a] Rm 1:16 [b] Rm 16:25 [c] Jn 1:3 [d] 1Pt 1:12 [e] 1Co 2:7 [f] 1Pt 3:22

Prayer for Spiritual Power

14 For this reason I bow my knees before the Father[c] 15 from whom [a]every
family in heaven and on earth is
named. 16 ⌊I pray⌋ that He may grant
you, [b]according to the riches of His
glory, to be strengthened with power
through His Spirit in the inner man,
17 and [c]that the Messiah may dwell in
your hearts through faith. ⌊I pray that⌋
you, being rooted and firmly established in love, 18 may be able to comprehend with all the saints [d]what is
the length and width, height and
depth ⌊of God's love⌋, 19 and to know
the Messiah's love that surpasses
knowledge, so you may be filled [e]with
all the fullness of God.

[a] Php 2:9 [b] Php 4:19 [c] Jn 14:23 [d] 1Jn 4:9 [e] Jn 1:16

20 Now to Him who is able to do
above and beyond all that we ask or
think—according to the power that
works in you— 21 [a]to Him be glory in
the church and in Christ Jesus to all
generations, forever and ever. •Amen.

[a] 1Tm 1:17

Unity and Diversity in the Body of Christ

4 I, therefore, the prisoner in the
Lord, urge you to [a]•walk worthy of
the calling you have received, 2 [b]with
all humility and gentleness, with patience, accepting[d] one another in love,
3 diligently keeping the unity of the
Spirit [c]with the peace that binds ⌊us⌋.
4 [d]There is one body and one Spirit,
just as you were called to one hope[e] at
your calling; 5 [e]one Lord, one faith,
[f]one baptism, 6 [g]one God and Father of
all, who is above all and [h]through all
and in all.

[a] Col 1:10 [b] Gl 5:22 [c] Jn 13:34 [d] Rm 12:5 [e] 1Co 8:6 [f] Heb 6:6 [g] Mal 2:10 [h] Rm 11:36

7 Now grace was given to each one of
us according to the measure of the
•Messiah's gift. 8 For it says:

[a]When He ascended on high,
[b]He took prisoners
into captivity;[f]
He gave gifts to people.[g]

9 [c]But what does "He ascended" mean
except that He[h] descended to the
lower parts of the earth?[i] 10 The One
who descended is the same as the
One [d]who ascended far above all the

[a]3:5 Lit *to the sons of men* [b]3:12 Or *through His faithfulness* [c]3:14 Other mss add *of our Lord Jesus Christ* [d]4:2 Or *tolerating* [e]4:4 Lit *called in one hope* [f]4:8 Or *He led the captives* [g]4:8 Ps 68:18 [h]4:9 Other mss add *first* [i]4:9 Or *the lower parts, namely, the earth*

heavens, that He might fill[a] all things. 11 And He personally gave some to be apostles, some prophets, some evangelists, some pastors and teachers, 12 for the training of the saints in the work of ministry, [e]to build up [f]the body of Christ, 13 until we all reach unity in the faith [g]and in the knowledge of God's Son, ⌊growing⌋ into a mature man with a stature measured by Christ's fullness. 14 Then we will no longer be little children, tossed by the waves and blown around by every wind of teaching, by human cunning with cleverness in the techniques of deceit. 15 But speaking the truth in love, let us grow in every way into Him who is the head—Christ. 16 [h]From Him the whole body, fitted and knit together by every supporting ligament, promotes the growth of the body for building up itself in love by the proper working of each individual part.

[a] Ps 68:18 [b] Col 2:15 [c] Jn 3:13 [d] Ac 1:9; Heb 4:14; 8:1 [e] Rm 14:19 [f] Eph 1:23 [g] Col 2:2 [h] Col 2:19

Living the New Life

17 Therefore, I say this and testify in the Lord: You should no longer walk as the Gentiles walk, in the futility of their thoughts. 18 They are darkened in their understanding, [a]excluded from the life of God, because of the ignorance that is in them and because of the hardness of their hearts. 19 [b]They became callous and gave themselves over to promiscuity for the practice of every kind of impurity with a desire for more and more.[b]

[a] Gl 4:8; Eph 2:12 [b] Rm 1:24

20 But that is not how you learned about the Messiah, 21 assuming you heard Him and were taught by Him, because the truth is in Jesus: 22 you took off[c] your former way of life, the old man that is corrupted by deceitful desires; 23 you [a]are being renewed[d] in the spirit of your minds; 24 you put on[e] the new man, the one created according to God's ⌊likeness⌋ in righteousness and purity of the truth.

[a] 1Pt 1:22-23

25 Since you put away lying, [a]**Speak the truth, each one to his neighbor,**[f] because we are members of one another. 26 [b]**Be angry and do not sin.**[g] Don't let the sun go down on your anger, 27 [c]and don't give the Devil an opportunity. 28 The thief must no longer steal. Instead, he must do honest work with his own hands, so that he has something to share with anyone in need. 29 No rotten talk should come from your mouth, but only what is good for the building up of someone in need,[h] in order to give grace to those who hear. 30 And don't grieve God's Holy Spirit, who sealed you[i] for the day of redemption. 31 All bitterness, anger and wrath, insult and slander must be removed from you, along with all wickedness. 32 And be kind and compassionate to one another, forgiving one another, just as God also forgave you[j] in Christ.

[a] 2Ch 8:18 [b] Ps 4:4 [c] Eph 6:11-16

5 [a]Therefore, be imitators of God, as dearly loved children. 2 And [b]•walk in love, as the •Messiah also loved us and gave Himself for us, a sacrificial and [c]fragrant offering to God. 3 But sexual immorality and any impurity or greed should not even be heard of[k] among you, as is proper for saints. 4 And coarse and foolish talking or crude joking [d]are not suitable, but rather giving thanks. 5 For know and recognize this: no sexually immoral or impure or greedy person, who is an idolater, [e]has an inheritance in the kingdom of the Messiah and of God.

[a] Mt 5:45; Eph 4:32 [b] Jn 13:34 [c] Lv 1:9 [d] Rm 1:28 [e] Rv 22:15

[a]**4:10** Or *fulfill*; see Eph 1:23 [b]**4:19** Lit *with greediness* [c]**4:21–22** Or *Jesus. This means: take off* (as a command) [d]**4:22–23** Or *desires; renew* (as a command) [e]**4:23–24** Or *minds; and put on* (as a command) [f]**4:25** Zch 8:16 [g]**4:26** Ps 4:4 [h]**4:29** Lit *for the building up of the need* [i]**4:30** Or *Spirit, by whom you were sealed* [j]**4:32** Other mss read *us* [k]**5:3** Or *be named*

Light versus Darkness

6 [a]Let no one deceive you with
empty arguments, for because of these
things God's wrath is coming on the
disobedient.[a] 7 Therefore, do not become their partners. 8 [b]For you were
once darkness, but now ⌊you are⌋ light
in the Lord. Walk as [c]children of
light— 9 for the fruit of the light[b] ⌊re-
sults⌋ in all goodness, righteousness,
and truth— 10 [d]discerning what is
pleasing to the Lord. 11 [e]Don't partici-
pate in the fruitless works of darkness,
but instead, [f]expose them. 12 For it is
shameful even to mention what is
done by them in secret. 13 [g]Everything
exposed by the light is made clear,
14 for what makes everything clear is
light. Therefore it is said:

[h]Get up, sleeper, and [i]rise up
from the dead,
and the Messiah will shine
on you.[c]

[a] Mt 24:4 [b] Is 9:2 [c] Jn 12:36 [d] Php 1:10 [e] Jb 24:13-17 [f] Lv 19:17 [g] Heb 4:13 [h] Is 60:1 [i] Rm 6:4-5

Consistency in the Christian Life

15 Pay careful attention, then, to how
you walk—not as unwise people but as
wise— 16 making the most of the time,[d]
because the days are evil. 17 [a]So don't
be foolish, but [b]understand what the
Lord's will is. 18 And don't get drunk
with wine, which ⌊leads to⌋ reckless actions, but be filled with the Spirit:

19 speaking to one another
[c]in psalms, hymns,
and spiritual songs,
singing and making music
to the Lord in your heart,
20 [d]giving thanks always
for everything
to God the Father in the name
of our Lord Jesus Christ,
21 [e]submitting to one another
in the fear of Christ.

[a] Col 4:5 [b] Rm 12:2 [c] Jms 5:13 [d] Jb 1:21 [e] Php 2:3

Wives and Husbands

22 [a]Wives, submit[e] to your own husbands as to the Lord, 23 for the husband
is head of the wife as also Christ is
head of the church. He is the Savior of
the body. 24 Now as the church submits
to Christ, so wives should ⌊submit⌋ to
their husbands in everything. 25 Husbands, love your wives, just as also
Christ loved the church and gave Himself for her, 26 to make her holy, cleansing[f] her [b]in the washing of water [c]by
the word. 27 He did this to present the
church to Himself in splendor, without
spot or wrinkle or any such thing, but
holy and blameless. 28 In the same way,
husbands should love their wives as
their own bodies. He who loves his
wife loves himself. 29 For no one ever
hates his own flesh, but provides and
cares for it, just as Christ does for the
church, 30 since we are members of His
body.[g]

[a] Gn 3:16 [b] Jn 3:5 [c] Jn 15:3

31 [a]**For this reason a man**
will leave his father
and mother
and be joined to his wife,
and the two will become
one flesh.[h]

32 This •mystery is profound, but I am
talking about Christ and the church.
33 To sum up, each one of you is to
love his wife as himself, and the wife
is to respect her husband.

[a] Gn 2:24

Children and Parents

6 Children, [a]obey your parents in
the Lord, because this is right.
2 [b]**Honor your father and mother—**

[a]**5:6** Lit *sons of disobedience* [b]**5:9** Other mss read *fruit of the Spirit*; see Gl 5:22, but compare Eph 5:11–14 [c]**5:14** This poem may have been an early Christian hymn based on several passages in Isaiah; see Is 9:2; 26:19; 40:1; 51:17; 52:1; 60:1. [d]**5:16** Lit *buying back the time* [e]**5:22** Other mss omit *submit* [f]**5:26** Or *having cleansed* [g]**5:30** Other mss add *and of His flesh and of His bones* [h]**5:31** Gn 2:24

which is the first commandment[a] with
a promise— 3 **that it may go well
with you and that you may have a
long life in the land.**[b] [c] 4 And [c]fathers,
don't stir up anger in your children,
but [d]bring them up in the training and
instruction of the Lord.

a Pr 23:22 b Ex 20:12 c Col 3:21 d Gn 18:19

Slaves and Masters

5 Slaves, obey your human[d] masters
with fear and trembling, in the sincerity of your heart, as to Christ. 6 Don't
⌊work only⌋ while being watched, in order to please men, but as slaves of
Christ, do God's will from your heart.[e]
7 Render service with a good attitude,
as to the Lord and not to men,
8 [a]knowing that whatever good each
one does, slave or free, he will receive
this back from the Lord. 9 And [b]mas-
ters, treat them the same way, without
threatening them, because you know
that both their and your Master is in
heaven, [c]and there is no favoritism
with Him.

a Rm 2:6 b Col 4:1 c 1Pt 1:17

Christian Warfare

10 Finally, be strengthened by the
Lord and by His vast strength. 11 [a]Put
on the full armor of God so that you
can stand against the tactics[f] of the
Devil. 12 For our battle is not against
flesh and blood, but against [b]the rulers, against the authorities, against
[c]the world powers of this darkness,
against the spiritual forces of evil in the
heavens. 13 This is why you must take
up the full armor of God, so that you
may be able to resist in the evil day,
and having prepared everything, to
take your stand. 14 Stand, therefore,

with truth like a belt
around your waist,
[d]righteousness like armor
on your chest,
15 [e]and your feet sandaled
with readiness for the gospel
of peace.[g]
16 In every situation take [f]the shield
of faith,
and with it you will be able
to extinguish
the flaming arrows
of the evil one.
17 Take the helmet of salvation,
and [g]the sword of the Spirit,
which is God's word.

18 With every prayer and request, pray
at all times in the Spirit, and stay alert
in this, with all perseverance and
[h]intercession for all the saints. 19 Pray
also for me, that the message may be
given to me when I open my mouth to
make known with boldness the •mys-
tery of the gospel. 20 For this I am an
ambassador in chains. Pray that [i]I
might be bold enough in Him to speak
as I should.

a Rm 13:12 b Rm 8:38 c Jn 12:31 d Is 59:17 e Is 52:7 f 1Jn 5:4 g Heb 4:12; Rv 1:16 h Php 1:4 i 1Th 2:2

Paul's Farewell

21 [a]Tychicus, our dearly loved
brother and faithful servant[h] in the
Lord, will tell you everything so that
you also may know how I am and what
I'm doing. 22 I am sending him to you
for this very reason, to let you know
how we are and to encourage your
hearts.

a Ac 20:4

23 Peace to the brothers, and love
with faith, from God the Father and
the Lord Jesus Christ. 24 Grace be with
all who have undying love for our Lord
Jesus Christ.[i] [j]

[a] **6:2** Or *is a preeminent commandment* [b] **6:3** Or *life on the earth* [c] **6:2–3** Ex 20:12 [d] **6:5** Lit *according to the flesh* [e] **6:6** Lit *from soul* [f] **6:11** Or *schemes*, or *tricks* [g] **6:15** Ready to go tell others about the gospel [h] **6:21** Or *deacon* [i] **6:24** Other mss add *Amen.* [j] **6:24** Lit *all who love our Lord Jesus Christ in incorruption*

PHILIPPIANS

Greeting

1 Paul and Timothy, slaves of Christ
Jesus:
To all the saints in Christ Jesus who
are in Philippi, including the •over-
seers and deacons.
2 Grace to you and peace from God
our Father and the Lord Jesus Christ.

Thanksgiving and Prayer

3 [a]I give thanks to my God for every
remembrance of you,[a] 4 always praying
with joy for all of you in my every
prayer, 5 [b]because of your partnership
in the gospel from the first day until
now. 6 I am sure of this, that He who
started [c]a good work in you[b] will carry
it on to completion until the day of
Christ Jesus. 7 It is right for me to think
this way about all of you, because I
have you in my heart,[c] and [d]you are all
partners with me in grace, both in [e]my
imprisonment and in the defense and
establishment of the gospel. 8 For God
is my witness, how I deeply miss all of
you with the affection of Christ Jesus.
9 And I pray this: [f]that your love will
keep on growing in knowledge and every kind of discernment, 10 so that [g]you
can determine what really matters and
[h]can be pure and blameless in[d] the day
of Christ, 11 filled with the fruit of righteousness [i]that ⌊comes⌋ through Jesus
Christ, to the glory and praise of God.

a Col 1:3 b 2Co 8:1 c Jn 6:29 d Php 4:14 e Eph 3:1 f Phm 6 g Rm 12:2 h Ac 24:16 i Jn 15:4

Advance of the Gospel

12 Now I want you to know, brothers,
that what has happened to me has actually resulted in the advancement of the
gospel, 13 so that it has become known
[a]throughout the whole imperial guard,[e]
and to everyone else, that my imprisonment is for Christ.[f] 14 Most of the brothers in the Lord have gained confidence
from my imprisonment and dare even
more to speak the message[g] fearlessly.
15 Some, to be sure, preach Christ out
of envy and [b]strife, but others out of
good will.[h] 16 These do so out of love,
knowing that I am appointed for the defense of the gospel; 17 the others proclaim Christ out of rivalry, not sincerely, seeking to cause ⌊me⌋ trouble in
my imprisonment.[i] 18 What does it matter? Just that in every way, whether out
of false motives or true, Christ is proclaimed. And in this I rejoice. Yes, and
I will rejoice 19 because I know this will
lead to my deliverance[j] [c]through your
prayers and help from [d]the Spirit of
Jesus Christ. 20 My eager expectation
and hope is that I will not be ashamed
[e]about anything, but that now as always, with all boldness, Christ will be
highly honored in my body, whether
by life or by death.

a Php 4:22 b Php 2:3 c 2Co 1:11 d Rm 8:9 e Rm 5:5

Living Is Christ

21 For me, living is Christ and dying
is gain. 22 Now if I live on in the flesh,
this means fruitful work for me; and
I don't know which one I should
choose. 23 [a]I am pressured by both. I
have the desire to [b]depart and be with
Christ—which is far better— 24 but to
remain in the flesh is more necessary

[a]**1:3** Or *for your every remembrance of me* [b]**1:6** Or *work among you* [c]**1:7** Or *because you have me in your heart* [d]**1:10** Or *until* [e]**1:13** Lit *praetorium,* a Lat word that can also refer to a military headquarters, to the governor's palace, or to Herod's palace [f]**1:13** Lit *in Christ* [g]**1:14** Other mss add *of God* [h]**1:15** The good will of men, or God's good will or favor [i]**1:17** Lit *sincerely, intending to raise tribulation to my bonds* [j]**1:19** Or *salvation,* or *vindication*

for you. 25 Since I am persuaded of this,
I know that I will remain and continue
with all of you for your advancement
and joy in the faith, 26 so that, because
of me, your confidence may grow in
Christ Jesus when I come to you again.

[a]2Co 5:8 [b]Lk 2:29-30

27 Just one thing: live your life in a
manner worthy of the gospel of Christ.
Then, whether I come and see you or
am absent, I will hear about you that
you are standing firm in one spirit, with
one mind,[a] working side by side for the
faith of the gospel, 28 not being frightened in any way by your [a]opponents.
This is evidence of their destruction,
[b]but of your deliverance—and this is
from God. 29 For it has been given to
you on Christ's behalf [c]not only to believe in Him, but also to suffer for Him,
30 [d]having the same struggle [e]that you
saw I had and now hear about me.

[a]Is 41:10; Mt 10:28 [b]Mt 5:10-12 [c]Ac 5:41; Rm 8:17 [d]Col 2:1 [e]Ac 16:19

Christian Humility

2 If then there is any encouragement
in Christ, if any consolation of
love, if any [a]fellowship with the Spirit,
if any affection and mercy, 2 fulfill my
joy [b]by thinking the same way, having
the same love, sharing the same feel-
ings, focusing on one goal. 3 [c]Do nothing out of rivalry or conceit, but [d]in
humility consider others as more important than yourselves. 4 [e]Everyone
should look out not ⌊only⌋ for his own
interests, but also for the interests of
others.

[a]2Co 13:14 [b]1Pt 3:8 [c]Rm 13:13; Jms 3:14 [d]Eph 5:21 [e]1Co 10:24

Christ's Humility and Exaltation

5 [a]Make your own attitude that of
Christ Jesus,

6 who, [b]existing in the form
of God, [c]did not consider
equality with God
as something to be used
for His own advantage.[b]
7 [d]Instead He emptied Himself
by assuming the form
[e]of a slave,
[f]taking on the likeness of men.
And when He had come
as a man in His external form,
8 He humbled Himself
by becoming [g]obedient
to the point
of death—even to death
on a cross.
9 For this reason God also
[h]highly exalted Him
and [i]gave Him the name that is
above every name,
10 [j]so that at the name of Jesus
every knee should bow—
of those who are in heaven
and on earth
and under the earth—
11 and [k]every tongue should confess
that Jesus Christ is Lord,
to the glory of God the Father.

[a]Jn 13:15 [b]Jn 1:1-2 [c]Jn 5:18 [d]Ps 22:6; Is 53:3 [e]Is 42:1 [f]Gl 4:4 [g]Heb 12:2 [h]Lk 10:22 [i]Heb 1:4 [j]Is 45:23 [k]Jn 13:13

Lights in the World

12 So then, my dear friends, just as
you have always obeyed, not only in
my presence, but now even more in
my absence, work out your own salvation with fear and trembling. 13 For [a]it
is God who is working in you, ⌊en-
abling you⌋ both to will and to act for
His good purpose. 14 Do everything
without grumbling and arguing, 15 so
that you may be blameless and pure,
children of God who are faultless in a
crooked and perverted generation,
among whom you shine like stars in
the world. 16 Hold firmly[c] the message
of life. Then I can boast in the day of
Christ that I didn't run in vain or labor
for nothing. 17 But even if I am poured
out as a drink offering on the sacrifice

[a]**1:27** Lit *soul* [b]**2:6** Or *to be grasped*, or *to be held on to* [c]**2:16** Or *Offer*, or *Hold out*

and service of your faith, I am glad and
rejoice with all of you. 18 In the same
way you also should rejoice and share
your joy with me. [a]Heb 13:21

Timothy and Epaphroditus

19 Now I hope in the Lord Jesus to
send Timothy to you soon so that I also
may be encouraged when I hear news
about you. 20 For I have no one else
like-minded who will genuinely care
about your interests; 21 all seek their
own interests, not those of Jesus
Christ. 22 But you know his proven
character, because he has served with
me in the gospel ministry like a son
with a father. 23 Therefore, I hope to
send him as soon as I see how things
go with me. 24 And I am convinced in
the Lord that I myself will also come
quickly.
25 But I considered it necessary to
send you [a]Epaphroditus—my brother,
co-worker, and fellow soldier, as well
as your messenger and minister to my
need— 26 since he has been longing for
all of you and was distressed because
you heard that he was sick. 27 Indeed,
he was so sick that he nearly died.
However, God had mercy on him, and
not only on him but also on me, so that
I would not have one grief on top of another. 28 For this reason, I am very eager to send him so that you may rejoice
when you see him again and I may be
less anxious. 29 Therefore, welcome
him in the Lord with all joy and hold
men like him in honor, 30 because he
came close to death for the work of
Christ, risking his life [b]to make up
what was lacking in your ministry to
me. [a]Php 4:18 [b]Php 4:10

Knowing Christ

3 Finally, my brothers, rejoice in the
Lord. To write to you again about
this is no trouble for me and is a pro-
tection for you.
2 [a]Watch out for "dogs,"[a] watch out
for evil workers, [b]watch out for those
who mutilate the flesh. 3 For we are
[c]the circumcision, [d]the ones who
serve by the Spirit of God, boast in
Christ Jesus, and do not put confidence
in the flesh— 4 although I once had
confidence in the flesh too. If anyone
else thinks he has grounds for confidence in the flesh, I have more:
5 circumcised the eighth day; of the nation of Israel, of the tribe of Benjamin,
a Hebrew born of Hebrews; as to the
law, [e]a •Pharisee; 6 [f]as to zeal, [g]perse-
cuting the church; as to the righteousness that is in the law, blameless.

[a]Rv 22:15 [b]Gl 5:2 [c]Rm 2:29 [d]Mal 1:11; Jn 4:23; Eph 6:18 [e]Ac 23:6 [f]Ac 22:3 [g]Ac 8:3

7 But everything that was a gain to
me, I have considered to be a loss because of Christ. 8 More than that, I also
consider everything to be a loss [a]in
view of the surpassing value of knowing Christ Jesus my Lord. Because of
Him I have suffered the loss of all
things and consider them filth, so that
I may gain Christ 9 and be found in
Him, not having [b]a righteousness of
my own from the law, [c]but one that is
through faith in Christ[b]—the righteousness from God based on faith.
10 ⌊My goal⌋ is to know Him and the
power of His resurrection and [d]the fellowship of His sufferings, being conformed to His death, 11 assuming that I
will somehow [e]reach the resurrection
from among the dead. [a]Jn 17:3

[b]Ps 143:2 [c]Gl 2:16 [d]1Pt 4:13 [e]Ac 26:7

Reaching Forward to God's Goal

12 Not that I have already [a]reached
⌊the goal⌋ or am already [b]fully mature,
but I make every effort to take hold of
it because I also have been taken hold
of by Christ Jesus. 13 Brothers, I do not[c]
consider myself to have taken hold of
it. But one thing I do: forgetting what is

[a]**3:2** An expression of contempt for the unclean, those outside the people of God [b]**3:9** Or *through the faithfulness of Christ* [c]**3:13** Other mss read *not yet*

behind and reaching forward to what is ahead, 14 [c]I pursue as my goal the prize [d]promised by God's heavenly[a] call in Christ Jesus. 15 Therefore, all who are [e]mature should think this way. And if you think differently about anything, God will reveal this to you also. 16 In any case, we should live up to whatever ⌊truth⌋ we have attained. 17 Join in imitating me, brothers, and observe those who live according to the example you have in us. 18 For I have often told you, and now say again with tears, that many live as enemies of the cross of Christ. 19 Their end is destruction; their god is their stomach; their glory is in their shame. They are focused on earthly things, 20 but [f]our citizenship is in heaven, from which we also [g]eagerly wait for a Savior, the Lord Jesus Christ. 21 [h]He will transform the body of our humble condition into the likeness of His glorious body, by [i]the power that enables Him to subject everything to Himself.

[a] 1Tm 6:12 [b] Heb 12:23 [c] Heb 12:1 [d] 1Co 9:24 [e] 1Co 2:6; Gl 5:10 [f] Col 3:1 [g] 1Th 1:10 [h] 1Jn 3:2 [i] Mt 28:18

Practical Counsel

4 So then, in this way, my dearly loved brothers, [a]my joy and crown, stand firm in the Lord, dear friends. 2 I urge Euodia and I urge Syntyche to agree in the Lord. 3 Yes, I also ask you, true partner,[b] to help these women who have [b]contended for the gospel at my side, along with Clement and the rest of my co-workers whose names are in [c]the book of life. 4 Rejoice in the Lord always. I will say it again: Rejoice! 5 Let your graciousness be known to everyone. [d]The Lord is near. 6 [e]Don't worry about anything, but in everything, through prayer and petition with thanksgiving, let your requests be made known to God. 7 And [f]the peace of God, which surpasses every thought, will guard your hearts and your minds in Christ Jesus.

[a] 2Co 1:14 [b] Rm 16:3 [c] Lk 10:20; Rv 3:5 [d] Jms 5:8-9; 1Pt 4:7; 2Pt 3:8 [e] Mt 6:25; 1Pt 5:7 [f] Jn 14:27; Rm 5:1

8 Finally brothers, whatever is true, whatever is honorable, whatever is just, whatever is pure, whatever is lovely, whatever is commendable—if there is any moral excellence and if there is any praise—dwell on these things. 9 Do what you have learned and received and heard and seen in me, and the God of peace will be with you.

Appreciation of Support

10 I rejoiced in the Lord greatly that now at last [a]you have renewed your care for me. You were, in fact, concerned about me, but lacked the opportunity ⌊to show it⌋. 11 I don't say this out of need, for I have learned [b]to be content in whatever circumstances I am. 12 [c]I know both how to have a little, and I know how to have a lot. In any and all circumstances I have learned the secret ⌊of being content⌋—whether well-fed or hungry, whether in abundance or in need. 13 I am able to do all things [d]through Him[c] who strengthens me. 14 Still, you did well [e]by sharing with me in my hardship.

[a] 2Co 11:9 [b] 1Tm 6:6 [c] 1Co 4:11 [d] Jn 15:5 [e] Php 1:7

15 And you, Philippians, know that in the early days of the gospel, when I left Macedonia, [a]no church shared with me in the matter of giving and receiving except you alone. 16 [b]For even in Thessalonica you sent ⌊gifts⌋ for my need several times. 17 Not that I seek the gift, but I seek [c]the fruit that is increasing to your account. 18 But I have received everything in full, and I have an abundance. I am fully supplied, having received [d]from Epaphroditus what you provided—a fragrant offering, [e]a

[a]**3:14** Or *upward* [b]**4:3** Or *true Syzygus*, possibly a person's name [c]**4:13** Other mss read *Christ*

welcome sacrifice, pleasing to God.
19 And my God [f]will supply all your
needs according to His riches in glory
in Christ Jesus. 20 Now to our God and
Father be glory forever and ever.
•Amen.

[a]2Co 11:8 [b]2Th 3:8 [c]Rm 15:28 [d]Php 2:25 [e]Heb 13:16 [f]Ps 23:1

Final Greetings

21 Greet every saint in Christ Jesus.
Those brothers who are with me greet
you. 22 All the saints greet you, [a]but especially those from Caesar's household. 23 The grace of the Lord Jesus
Christ be with your spirit.[a]

[a]Php 1:13

COLOSSIANS

Greeting

1 Paul, an apostle of Christ Jesus
by God's will, and Timothy our[b]
brother:
2 To the saints and faithful brothers
in Christ in Colossae.
Grace to you and peace from God
our Father.[c]

Thanksgiving

3 We always thank God, the Father of
our Lord Jesus Christ, when we pray
for you, 4 [a]for we have heard of your
faith in Christ Jesus and of [b]the love
you have for all the saints 5 because of
the hope [c]reserved for you in heaven.
You have already heard about ⌊this
hope⌋ in the message of truth, the gospel 6 that has come to you. It is [d]bearing
fruit and growing [e]all over the world,
just as it has among you since the day
you heard it and recognized [f]God's
grace in the truth.[d] 7 You learned this
from [g]Epaphras, our much loved fellow
slave. He is a faithful minister of the
•Messiah on your[e] behalf, 8 and he has
told us about your love in the Spirit.

[a]Eph 1:15 [b]Heb 6:10 [c]1Pt 1:4 [d]Jn 15:16 [e]Mt 24:14 [f]Ti 2:11 [g]Phm 23

Prayer for Spiritual Growth

9 [a]For this reason also, since the day
we heard this, we haven't stopped
praying for you. We are asking that you
may be filled with the [b]knowledge of
His will in all wisdom and spiritual understanding, 10 [c]so that you may •walk
worthy of the Lord, [d]fully pleasing ⌊to
Him⌋, [e]bearing fruit in every good work
and growing in the knowledge of God.
11 May you be strengthened with all
power, according to His glorious might,
for all endurance and patience, [f]with
joy 12 [g]giving thanks to the Father, who
has enabled you[f] to share in [h]the
saints'[g] inheritance in the light. 13 He
has rescued us from [i]the domain of
darkness [j]and transferred us into the
kingdom of the Son He loves, 14 in
whom we have redemption,[h] the forgiveness of sins.

[a]Eph 1:15 [b]Rm 12:2 [c]1Th 2:12 [d]1Th 4:1 [e]Jn 15:16 [f]Ac 5:41 [g]Eph 5:20 [h]Rm 8:17 [i]Heb 2:14 [j]2Pt 1:11

The Centrality of Christ

15 He is [a]the image
of the invisible God,
[b]the firstborn over all creation;[i]
16 because [c]by Him everything
was created,
in heaven and on earth,
the visible and the invisible,
whether thrones or dominions
or rulers or authorities—
all things have been created
[d]through Him and for Him.

[a]4:23 Other mss add *Amen.* [b]1:1 Lit *the* [c]1:2 Other mss add *and the Lord Jesus Christ* [d]1:6 Or *and truly recognized God's grace* [e]1:7 Other mss read *our* [f]1:12 Other mss read *us* [g]1:12 Or *holy ones'* [h]1:14 Other mss add *through His blood* [i]1:15 The One who is preeminent over all creation

17 [e]He is before all things,
and by Him all things
hold together.
18 He is also the head of the body,
the church;
He is the beginning,
[f]the firstborn from the dead,
so that He might come to have
first place in everything.
19 For God was pleased ⌊to have⌋
all His fullness dwell [g]in Him,
20 and through Him to reconcile
everything to Himself
by making peace
through the blood
of His cross[a]—
whether things on earth
or things in heaven.

[a]Php 2:6; Col 2:9 [b]Rv 3:14 [c]Jn 1:3 [d]Rm 11:36 [e]Jn 17:5 [f]Jn 11:25; Rv 1:5 [g]Mt 28:18; Jn 1:16

21 And you were once alienated and
hostile in mind because of your evil actions. 22 But now He has reconciled you
by His physical body[b] through His
death, to present you holy, faultless,
and blameless before Him— 23 if indeed
you remain grounded and steadfast in
the faith, and are not shifted away from
the hope of the gospel that you heard.
⌊This gospel⌋ has been proclaimed in all
creation under heaven, and I, Paul,
have become a minister of it.

Paul's Ministry

24 Now I rejoice in my sufferings for
you, and I am completing in my flesh
[a]what is lacking in Christ's afflictions for
[b]His body, that is, the church. 25 I have
become its minister, according to God's
administration that was given to me for
you, to make God's message fully
known, 26 [c]the •mystery hidden for ages
and generations but now revealed to
His saints. 27 God wanted to make
known to those among the Gentiles the
glorious wealth of this mystery, which is
Christ in you, the hope of glory. 28 We
proclaim Him, warning and teaching everyone with all wisdom, so that we may
present everyone mature in Christ. 29 I
labor for this, striving with His strength
that works powerfully in me.

[a]Php 3:10 [b]Eph 1:23 [c]Rm 16:25

2 For I want you to know how great
a struggle I have for you, for those
in Laodicea, and for all who have not
seen me in person. 2 ⌊I want⌋ [a]their
hearts to be encouraged and joined together in love, so that they may have
all the [b]riches of assured understanding, and have the knowledge of God's
•mystery—Christ.[c] 3 In Him all the
treasures of wisdom and knowledge
are hidden.

[a]2Co 1:6 [b]2Pt 3:18

Christ versus the Colossian Heresy

4 I am saying this so that no one will
deceive you with persuasive arguments. 5 For I may be absent in body,
but I am with you in spirit, rejoicing to
see your good order and the strength of
your faith in Christ.

6 Therefore as you have received
Christ Jesus the Lord, •walk in Him,
7 rooted and built up in Him and established in the faith, just as you were
taught, and overflowing with thankfulness.

8 [a]Be careful that no one takes you
captive through philosophy and empty
deceit based on [b]human tradition,
based on the elemental forces of the
world, and not based on Christ. 9 For [c]in
Him the entire fullness of God's nature[d]
dwells bodily,[e] 10 [d]and you have been
filled by Him, [e]who is the head over every ruler and authority. 11 In Him you
were also [f]circumcised with a circumcision not done with hands, by putting off
the body of flesh, in the circumcision of
the •Messiah. 12 Having been [g]buried
with Him in baptism, you were also
raised with Him through [h]faith in the

[a]**1:20** Other mss add *through Him* [b]**1:22** His body of flesh on the cross [c]**2:2** Other mss read *mystery of God, both of the Father and of Christ*; other ms variations exist on this v. [d]**2:9** Or *the deity* [e]**2:9** Or *nature lives in a human body*

working of God, who raised Him from
the dead. 13 And when you were dead in
trespasses and in the uncircumcision of
your flesh, He made you alive with Him
and forgave us all our trespasses. 14 He
erased the certificate of debt, with its
obligations, that was against us and opposed to us, and has taken it out of the
way by nailing it to the cross. 15 [i]He dis-
armed the rulers and authorities and
disgraced them publicly; He triumphed
over them by Him.[a]

[a]Heb 13:9 [b]Mt 15:2 [c]Jn 1:14; Rm 9:5; Col 1:19 [d]Jn 1:16 [e]1Pt 3:22 [f]Jr 4:4 [g]Rm 6:4 [h]Eph 3:7 [i]Mt 12:29; Eph 4:8

16 Therefore don't let anyone [a]judge
you in regard to food and drink or in the
matter [b]of a festival or a new moon or a
sabbath day.[b] 17 [c]These are a shadow of
what was to come; the substance is[c] the
Messiah. 18 Let no one disqualify you,[d]
insisting on ascetic practices and the
worship of angels, claiming access to a
visionary realm and inflated without
cause by his fleshly mind. 19 He doesn't
hold on to the head, from whom the
whole body, nourished and held together by its ligaments and tendons, de-
velops with growth from God.

[a]Rm 14:3 [b]Rm 14:5 [c]Heb 8:5

20 If you died with Christ to the elemental forces of this world, why do
you live as if you still belonged to the
world? Why do you submit to regulations: 21 "Don't handle, don't taste,
don't touch"? 22 All these ⌊regulations⌋
refer to what is destroyed by being
used up; they are human commands
and doctrines. 23 Although these have a
reputation of wisdom by promoting ascetic practices, humility, and severe
treatment of the body, they are not of
any value against fleshly indulgence.

The Life of the New Man

3 So if you [a]have been raised with
the •Messiah, [b]seek what is above,
where the Messiah is, seated at the
right hand of God. 2 Set your minds on
what is above, not on what is on the
earth. 3 [c]For [d]you have died, and your
life is hidden with the Messiah in
God. 4 [e]When the Messiah, who is
[f]your[e] life, is revealed, then you also
will be revealed with Him [g]in glory.

[a]Eph 2:6 [b]Mt 6:33 [c]Gl 2:20 [d]2Co 5:14-15; Col 2:20 [e]1Jn 3:2 [f]Jn 11:25 [g]1Co 15:43

5 Therefore, put to death whatever in
you is worldly:[f] sexual immorality, impurity, lust, evil desire, and greed,
which is idolatry. 6 Because of these,
God's wrath comes on the disobedient,[g] 7 and you once •walked in these
things when you were living in them.
8 [a]But now you must also put away all
the following: anger, wrath, malice,
slander, and filthy language from your
mouth. 9 [b]Do not lie to one another,
since you have put off the old man
with his practices 10 and have put on
the new man, who is [c]being renewed
in knowledge according to the image
of [d]his Creator. 11 Here there is not
[e]Greek and Jew, circumcision and uncircumcision, barbarian, Scythian,[h]
slave and free; [f]but Christ is all and in
all.

[a]Jms 1:21 [b]Lv 19:11 [c]Rm 12:2 [d]Eph 2:10 [e]Gl 3:28 [f]Eph 1:23

The Christian Life

12 Therefore, [a]God's chosen ones,
holy and loved, [b]put on heartfelt compassion, kindness, humility, gentleness, and patience, 13 accepting one
another and forgiving one another if
anyone has a complaint against another. Just as the Lord has forgiven you,
so also you must ⌊forgive⌋. 14 Above all,
[c]⌊put on⌋ love—the perfect bond of
unity. 15 And let [d]the peace of the Messiah, [e]to which you were also called [f]in
one body, control your hearts. Be
thankful. 16 [g]Let the message about the

[a]**2:15** Or *them through it*; that is, through the cross [b]**2:16** Or *or sabbaths* [c]**2:17** Or *substance belongs to* [d]**2:18** Or *no one cheat us out of your prize* [e]**3:4** Other mss read *our* [f]**3:5** Lit *death, the members on the earth* [g]**3:6** Other mss omit *on the disobedient* [h]**3:11** A term for a savage

Messiah dwell richly among you, teaching and admonishing one another in all
wisdom, and singing psalms, hymns,
and spiritual songs, [h]with gratitude in
your hearts to God. 17 And [i]whatever
you do, in word or in deed, do everything in the name of the Lord Jesus, giving [j]thanks to God the Father through
Him.

[a] 1Pt 1:2 [b] Gl 5:22 [c] Rm 13:8 [d] Php 4:7 [e] 1Co 7:15 [f] Eph 2:16 [g] 2Tm 3:15-17 [h] Eph 5:19 [i] 1Co 10:31 [j] Eph 5:20

Christ in Your Home

18 Wives, be submissive to your husbands, as is fitting in the Lord.

19 Husbands, love your wives and don't become bitter against them.

20 Children, obey your [a]parents in everything, for this is pleasing in the Lord. *[a] Pr 23:22*

21 [a]Fathers, do not exasperate your children, so they won't become discouraged. *[a] Eph 6:4*

22 Slaves, obey your human masters in everything; don't work only while being watched, in order to please men, but ⌊work⌋ wholeheartedly, fearing the Lord.

23 Whatever you do, do it enthusiastically,[a] as something done for the Lord and not for men, 24 knowing that you will receive the reward of an inheritance from the Lord—you serve the Lord Christ. 25 For the wrongdoer will be paid back for whatever wrong he has done, and there is no favoritism.

4 [a]Masters, supply your slaves with what is right and fair, since you know that you too have a Master in heaven. *[a] Eph 6:9*

Speaking to God and Others

2 [a]Devote yourselves to prayer; stay
alert in it with thanksgiving. 3 At the
same time, [b]pray also for us that God
may open a door to us for the message,
to speak [c]the •mystery of the •Mes-
siah— [d]for which I am in prison— 4 so
that I may reveal it as I am required to
speak. 5 [e]•Walk in wisdom toward outsiders, making the most of the time.
6 Your speech should always be gracious, [f]seasoned with salt, [g]so that you
may know how you should answer
each person.

[a] Eph 6:18 [b] 2Th 3:1 [c] Mt 13:11 [d] Php 1:7 [e] Eph 5:15 [f] Mk 9:50 [g] 1Pt 3:15

Christian Greetings

7 Tychicus, a loved brother, a faithful
servant, and a fellow slave in the Lord,
will tell you all the news about me. 8 I
have sent him to you for this very purpose, so that you may know how we
are,[b] and so that he may encourage
your hearts. 9 He is with [a]Onesimus, a
faithful and loved brother, who is one
of you. They will tell you about everything here. *[a] Phm 10*

10 [a]Aristarchus, my fellow prisoner,
greets you, as does [b]Mark, Barnabas'
cousin (concerning whom you have received instructions: if he comes to you,
welcome him), 11 and so does Jesus
who is called Justus. These alone of the
circumcision are my co-workers for the
kingdom of God, and they have been a
comfort to me. 12 [c]Epaphras, who is one
of you, a slave of Christ Jesus, greets
you. He is always contending for you in
his prayers, so that you can stand
[d]mature and fully assured[c] in everything God wills. 13 For I testify about
him that he works hard[d] for you, for
those in Laodicea, and for those in Hi-
erapolis. 14 [e]Luke, the loved physician,
and Demas greet you. 15 Give my greetings to the brothers in Laodicea, and to
Nympha and the church in her house.

[a]**3:23** Lit *do it from the soul* [b]**4:8** Other mss read *that he may know how you are* [c]**4:12** Other mss read *and complete* [d]**4:13** Other mss read *he has a great zeal*

16 And when [f]this letter has been read
among you, have it read also in the
church of the Laodiceans; and see that
you also read the letter from Laodicea.
17 And tell [g]Archippus, "Pay attention
to [h]the ministry you have received in
the Lord, so that you can accomplish
it."

a Ac 19:29 b Ac 15:37 c Col 1:7 d Mt 5:48 e Lk 1:3; Phm 24 f 1Th 5:27 g Phm 2 h 1Tm 4:6; 2Tm 4:5

18 This greeting is in my own
hand—Paul. [a]Remember my imprisonment. Grace be with you.[a]

a Heb 13:3

1 THESSALONIANS

Greeting

1 Paul, [a]Silvanus,[b] and Timothy:
To the church of the Thessalo-
nians [b]in God the Father and the Lord
Jesus Christ.
Grace to you and peace.[c]

a 2Th 1:1; 1Pt 5:12 b Jn 14:23

Thanksgiving

2 We always thank God for all of you,
remembering you constantly in our
prayers. 3 We recall, in the presence of
our God and Father, [a]your work of faith,
[b]labor of love, and endurance of hope
in our Lord Jesus Christ, 4 knowing
[c]your election, brothers loved by God.
5 For [d]our gospel did not come to you
in word only, but also in power, [e]in the
Holy Spirit, [f]and with much assurance.
[g]You know what kind of men we were
among you for your benefit, 6 and you
became imitators of us and of the Lord
when, in spite of severe persecution,
you welcomed the message with the
joy from the Holy Spirit. 7 As a result,
you became an example to all the believers in Macedonia and Achaia. 8 For
the Lord's message [h]rang out from you,
not only in Macedonia and Achaia, but
in every place that your faith[d] in God
has gone out, so we don't need to say
anything. 9 For they themselves report
about us what kind of reception we
had from you: how you turned to God
from idols to serve the living and true
God, 10 and [i]to wait for His Son [j]from
heaven, whom He raised from the
dead—Jesus, who rescues us [k]from the
coming wrath.

a 1Th 3:6 b Heb 6:10 c Col 3:12 d 1Co 2:4 e 2Co 6:6 f Heb 2:3 g 2Th 3:7 h Rm 10:18 i Php 3:20; Heb 9:28 j Ac 1:11 k 1Th 5:9

Paul's Conduct

2 For you yourselves know, brothers, that our visit with you was not
without result. 2 On the contrary, after
we had previously suffered and been
outrageously treated in [a]Philippi, as
you know, we were emboldened by
our God [b]to speak the gospel of God to
you in spite of great opposition. 3 For
our exhortation didn't come from error or impurity or an intent to deceive. 4 Instead, just as [c]we have been
approved by God [d]to be entrusted
with the gospel, so we speak, not to
please men, but rather God, [e]who ex-
amines our hearts. 5 For we never
used flattering speech, as you know,
or had greedy motives—God is our
witness— 6 and we didn't seek glory
from people, either from you or from
others. 7 Although we could have been
a burden as Christ's apostles, instead
we were gentle[e] among you, as a nursing mother nurtures her own children.

[a]**4:18** Other mss add *Amen.* [b]**1:1** Or *Silas*; see Ac 15:22–32; 16:19–40; 17:1–16 [c]**1:1** Other mss add *from God our Father and the Lord Jesus Christ* [d]**1:8** Or *in every place news of your faith* [e]**2:7** Other mss read *infants*

8 We cared so much for you that we
were pleased [f]to share with you not
only the gospel of God but also our
[g]own lives, because you had become
dear to us. 9 For you remember our labor and hardship, brothers. Working
night and day [h]so that we would not
burden any of you, we preached God's
gospel to you. 10 You are witnesses,
and so is God, of how devoutly, righteously, and blamelessly we conducted
ourselves with you believers. 11 As you
know, like a father with his own children, 12 we encouraged, comforted,
and implored each one of you [i]to
•walk worthy of God, who calls you
into His own kingdom and glory.

[a]Ac 16:22 [b]Ac 17:2 [c]1Co 4:5; 2Co 2:17 [d]Ti 1:3 [e]Pr 17:3 [f]Rm 1:11 [g]2Co 12:15 [h]2Co 11:9 [i]Gl 5:16; Eph 4:1; 1Th 4:12

Reception and Opposition to the Message

13 Also, this is why we constantly
thank God, because when you received
the message about God that you heard
from us, you welcomed it [a]not as a
human message, but as it truly is, the
message of God, which also works ef-
fectively in you believers. 14 For you,
brothers, became imitators of God's
churches in Christ Jesus that are in
Judea, since [b]you have also suffered the
same things from people of your own
country, [c]just as they did from the Jews.
15 They killed both the Lord Jesus and
[d]the prophets, and persecuted us; they
displease God, and are hostile to everyone, 16 [e]hindering us from speaking to
the Gentiles so that they may be saved.
As a result, they are always adding to
the number of their sins, and wrath has
overtaken them completely.[a]

[a]Mt 10:40; Heb 4:12 [b]Ac 17:5 [c]Heb 10:33 [d]Mt 5:12; Ac 7:52 [e]Ac 13:50; 14:19; 17:5

Paul's Desire to See Them

17 But as for us, brothers, after we
were forced to leave you for a short
time (in person, not in heart), we
greatly desired and made every effort
to return and see you face to face. 18 So
we wanted to come to you—even I,
Paul, time and again—but [a]Satan hindered us. 19 For who is our hope, or joy,
or crown of boasting in the presence of
our Lord Jesus [b]at His coming? Is it not
you? 20 For you are our glory and joy!

[a]Rm 1:13 [b]1Th 3:13; Rv 1:7

Anxiety in Athens

3 Therefore, when we could no
longer stand it, [a]we thought it was
better to be left alone in Athens. 2 And
we sent [b]Timothy, our brother and
God's co-worker[b] in the gospel of
Christ, to strengthen and encourage
you concerning your faith, 3 [c]so that
no one will be shaken by these persecutions. For you yourselves know that
[d]we are appointed to[c] this. 4 In fact,
when we were with you, we told you
previously that we were going to suffer persecution, and as you know, it
happened. 5 For this reason, when I
could no longer stand it, I also sent to
find out about your faith, [e]fearing that
the tempter had tempted you and that
[f]our labor might be for nothing.

[a]Ac 17:15 [b]Rm 16:21 [c]Ac 20:24; 2Tm 3:12 [d]Ac 20:23 [e]1Co 7:5 [f]Gl 2:2

Encouraged by Timothy

6 [a]But now Timothy has come to us
from you and brought us good news
about your faith and love, and that you
always have good memories of us,
wanting to see us, [b]as we also want to
see you. 7 Therefore, brothers, in all
our distress and persecution, we were
encouraged about you through your
faith. 8 For now we live, if you [c]stand
firm in the Lord. 9 How can we thank
God for you in return for all the joy we
experience because of you before our
God, 10 as we pray earnestly night and

[a]**2:16** Or *to the end* [b]**3:2** Other mss read *servant* [c]**3:3** Or *we are destined for*

day to see you face to face and to complete what is lacking in your faith?
[a]Ac 18:5
[b]Php 1:8 [c]Php 4:1

Prayer for the Church

11 Now may our God and Father
Himself, and our Lord Jesus, direct our
way to you. 12 And may the Lord cause
you to increase and overflow with love
for one another and for everyone, just
as we also do for you. 13 May He make
your hearts blameless in holiness before our God and Father at the coming
of our Lord Jesus with all His saints.
•Amen.[a]

The Call to Sanctification

4 Finally then, brothers, we ask and
encourage you in the Lord Jesus,
that as you have received from us how
you must •walk and [a]please God—as
you are doing[b]—do so even more.
2 For you know what commands we
gave you through the Lord Jesus.
[a]Col 1:10

3 For this is [a]God's will, your sanctification: that you abstain from sexual
immorality, 4 [b]so that each of you
knows how to possess his own vessel[c]
in sanctification and honor, 5 not with
lustful desires, like the Gentiles [c]who
don't know God. 6 This means [d]one
must not transgress against and defraud his brother in this matter, because the Lord is an avenger of all
these offenses,[d] as we also previously
told and warned you. 7 For God has not
called us to impurity, [e]but to sanctification. 8 Therefore, [f]the person who rejects this does not reject man, but God,
[g]who also gives you His Holy Spirit.
[a]Rm 12:2 [b]Rm 6:19
[c]Eph 2:12 [d]Lv 19:11 [e]Lv 11:44
[f]Lk 10:16 [g]1Jn 3:24

Loving and Working

9 About brotherly love: you don't
need me to write you [a]because you
yourselves are taught by God [b]to love
one another. 10 In fact, you are doing
this toward all the brothers in the entire
region of Macedonia. But we encourage
you, brothers, to do so even more, 11 to
seek to lead a quiet life, to mind your
own business,[e] and to work with your
own hands, as we commanded you,
12 so that you may walk properly[f] in the
presence of outsiders[g] and not be de-
pendent on anyone.[h] *[a]Jn 6:45 [b]Jn 13:34*

The Comfort of Christ's Coming

13 We do not want you to be uninformed, brothers, concerning those
who are •asleep, so that you will not
grieve like the rest, who have no hope.
14 [a]Since we believe that Jesus died and
rose again, in the same way God will
bring with Him those who have fallen
asleep through[i] Jesus.[j] 15 For we say
this to you by a revelation from the
Lord:[k] We who are still alive at the
Lord's coming will certainly have no
advantage over[l] those who have fallen
asleep. 16 For [b]the Lord Himself will de-
scend from heaven with a shout,[m] with
the archangel's voice, and with the
trumpet of God, and the dead in Christ
will rise first. 17 Then we who are still
alive will be caught up together with
them in the clouds to meet the Lord in
the air; and so [c]we will always be with
the Lord. 18 Therefore encourage[n] one
another with these words. *[a]1Co 15:13*
[b]Mt 24:30 [c]Jn 12:26; Rv 21:3

The Day of the Lord

5 About [a]the times and the seasons:
brothers, you do not need anything
to be written to you. 2 For you yourselves know very well that [b]the Day of

[a]**3:13** Other mss omit *Amen.* [b]**4:1** Lit *walking* [c]**4:4** Or *to control his own body,* or *to acquire his own wife* [d]**4:6** Lit *things* [e]**4:11** Lit *to practice one's own things* [f]**4:12** Or *may live respectably* [g]**4:12** Non-Christians [h]**4:12** Or *not need anything,* or *not be in need* [i]**4:14** Or *asleep in* [j]**4:14** *those who have fallen asleep through Jesus* = Christians who have died [k]**4:15** Or *a word of the Lord* [l]**4:15** Or *certainly not precede* [m]**4:16** Or *command* [n]**4:18** Or *comfort*

the Lord will come just like a thief in
the night. [3] When they say, "Peace and
security," then sudden destruction
comes on them, like labor pains on a
pregnant woman, and they will not escape. [4] [c]But you, brothers, are not in
the dark, so that this day would overtake you like a thief. [5] For you are all
[d]sons of light and sons of the day.
We're not of the night or of darkness.
[6] So then, we must not sleep, like the
rest, but we must stay awake and be
sober. [7] For [e]those who sleep, sleep at
night, and those who get drunk are
drunk at night. [8] But since we are of
the day, we must be sober and [f]put the
armor of faith and love on our chests,
and put on a helmet of the hope of salvation. [9] For [g]God did not appoint us to
wrath, but to obtain salvation through
our Lord Jesus Christ, [10] who died for
us, so that whether we are awake or
•asleep, we will live together with
Him. [11] Therefore encourage one another and build each other up as you
are already doing. *[a] Mt 24:30; Ac 1:7 [b] Mt 25:13; 2Pt 3:10 [c] 1Jn 2:8 [d] Eph 5:8 [e] Lk 21:34 [f] Rm 13:12; Eph 6:11 [g] Rm 9:22*

Exhortations and Blessings

[12] Now we ask you, brothers, to give
recognition to those who labor among
you and lead you in the Lord and ad-
monish you, [13] and to esteem them
very highly in love because of their
work. Be at peace among yourselves.
[14] And we exhort you, brothers: warn
those who are lazy,[a] comfort the discouraged, help the weak, be patient
with everyone. [15] [a]See to it that no one
repays evil for evil to anyone, but always [b]pursue what is good for one another and for all. *[a] Pr 20:22 [b] Gl 6:10*

16 Rejoice always!
17 Pray constantly.
18 Give thanks in everything,
for this is God's will for you
in Christ Jesus.
19 [a]Don't stifle the Spirit.
20 [b]Don't despise prophecies,
21 but [c]test all things.
Hold on to what is good.
22 Stay away from every form
of evil. *[a] Eph 4:30 [b] 1Co 14:1 [c] 1Jn 4:1*

[23] Now may the God of peace Himself sanctify you completely. And may
your spirit, soul, and body [a]be kept
sound and blameless for the coming of
our Lord Jesus Christ. [24] [b]He who calls
you is faithful, who also will do it.
[25] Brothers, pray for us also. [26] Greet all
the brothers with a holy kiss. [27] I
charge you by the Lord that this letter
be read to all the brothers. [28] May the
grace of our Lord Jesus Christ be with
you! *[a] 1Co 1:8 [b] 1Co 10:13*

[a]**5:14** Or *who are disorderly,* or *who are undisciplined*

2 THESSALONIANS

Greeting

1 Paul, [a]Silvanus,[a] and Timothy:
To the church of the Thessalo-
nians in God our Father and the Lord
Jesus Christ.
2 Grace to you and peace from God
our Father and the Lord Jesus Christ.

[a] 2Co 1:19

God's Judgment and Glory

3 We must always thank God for you,
brothers, which is fitting, since your
faith is flourishing, and the love of every
one of you for one another is increasing.
4 Therefore [a]we ourselves boast [b]about
you among God's churches—about
your endurance and faith [c]in all the persecutions and afflictions you endure. 5 It
is a clear evidence of God's righteous
judgment that you will be counted
worthy of God's kingdom, for which
you also are suffering, 6 [d]since it is
righteous for God to repay with affliction those who afflict you, 7 and ⌊to re-
ward⌋ [e]with rest you who are afflicted,
along with us. ⌊This will take place⌋ at
the revelation of the Lord Jesus from
heaven with His powerful angels,
8 [f]taking vengeance with flaming fire
on those who don't know God and on
those who don't obey the gospel of
our Lord Jesus. 9 These will pay the
penalty of everlasting destruction,
away from the Lord's presence and
from His glorious strength, 10 in that
day when He comes to be glorified by
His saints and to be admired by all
those who have believed, because our
testimony among you was believed.
11 And in view of this, we always pray
for you that our God will consider you
worthy of His calling, and will, by His
power, fulfill every desire for goodness and the work of faith, 12 [g]so that
the name of our Lord Jesus will be glorified by you, and you by Him, according to the grace of our God and the
Lord Jesus Christ.

[a] 2Co 7:14 [b] 1Th 1:3 [c] 1Th 2:14 [d] Rv 6:10 [e] Rv 14:13 [f] 2Pt 3:7 [g] 1Pt 1:7

The Man of Lawlessness

2 Now concerning the coming of
our Lord Jesus Christ [a]and our being gathered to Him: we ask you,
brothers, 2 not to be easily upset in
mind or troubled, either by a spirit or
by a message or by a letter as if from
us, alleging that the Day of the Lord[b]
has come. 3 Don't let anyone deceive
you in any way. For ⌊that day⌋ will not
come [b]unless the apostasy[c] comes first
and [c]the man of lawlessness[d] is revealed, the son of destruction. 4 He op-
poses and [d]exalts himself above every
so-called god or object of worship, so
that he sits[e] in God's sanctuary,[f] publi-
cizing that he himself is God.

[a] Mt 24:31 [b] 2Pt 2:1 [c] Dn 7:25 [d] Rv 13:6

5 Don't you remember that when I
was still with you I told you about this?
6 And you know what currently re-
strains ⌊him⌋, so that he will be revealed
in his time. 7 For [a]the •mystery of lawlessness is already at work; but the one
now restraining will do so until he is
out of the way, 8 and then the lawless
one will be revealed. [b]The Lord Jesus
will destroy him with the breath of His
mouth and will bring him to nothing
[c]with the brightness of His coming.
9 The coming ⌊of the lawless one⌋ is
[d]based on Satan's working, with all
kinds of false miracles, [e]signs, and

[a] **1:1** Or *Silas*; see Ac 15:22–32; 16:19–40; 17:1–16 [b] **2:2** Other mss read *Christ* [c] **2:3** Or *rebellion*
[d] **2:3** Other mss read *man of sin* [e] **2:4** Other mss add *as God* [f] **2:4** Or *temple*

wonders, 10 and with every unrighteous
deception among [f]those who are perishing. ⌊They perish⌋ because they did
not accept the love of the truth in order
to be saved. 11 [g]For this reason God
sends them a strong delusion [h]so that
they will believe what is false, 12 so that
all will be condemned—those who did
not believe the truth but enjoyed unrighteousness.

[a] 1Jn 4:3 [b] Is 11:4; Mt 24:12 [c] Heb 10:27; Ti 2:13; Rv 1:13-16 [d] Eph 2:2 [e] Mt 24:24 [f] 2Co 2:15 [g] Rm 1:24 [h] Mt 24:5

Stand Firm

13 But we must always thank God for
you, brothers loved by the Lord, because from the beginning[a] God has
chosen you for salvation through sanctification by the Spirit and through belief in the truth. 14 He called you to this
through our gospel, so that you might
obtain the glory of our Lord Jesus
Christ. 15 Therefore, brothers, stand
firm and hold to [a]the traditions you
were taught, either by our message or
by our letter.

[a] 2Th 3:6

16 May our Lord Jesus Christ Himself
and God our Father, [a]who has loved
us and given us eternal encouragement
and good hope by grace, 17 encourage
your hearts and strengthen you in every good work and word.

[a] 1Jn 4:10

Pray for Us

3 Finally, pray for us, brothers, that
the Lord's message may spread
rapidly and be honored, just as it was
with you, 2 and that we may be delivered from wicked and evil men, for
not all have faith. 3 But the Lord is
faithful; He will strengthen and guard
you from the evil one. 4 We have confidence in the Lord about you, that you
are doing and will do what we command. 5 May [a]the Lord direct your
hearts to God's love and Christ's endurance.

[a] Pr 3:6; Mt 22:37

Warning against Irresponsible Behavior

6 Now we command you, brothers,
in the name of our Lord Jesus Christ,
[a]to keep away [b]from every brother
who •walks irresponsibly and not according to the tradition received from
us. 7 For you yourselves know how you
must imitate us: we were not irresponsible among you; 8 we did not eat anyone's bread free of charge; instead,
[c]we labored and toiled, working night
and day, so that we would not be a burden to any of you. 9 It is not that we
don't have the right ⌊to support⌋, but
we did it to make [d]ourselves an example to you so that you would imitate us.
10 In fact, when we were with you, this
is what we commanded you: [e]"If anyone isn't willing to work, he should not
eat." 11 For we hear that there are
some among you who walk [f]irrespon-
sibly, not working at all, but interfering
with the work ⌊of others⌋. 12 Now we
command and exhort such people, by
the Lord Jesus Christ, [g]that quietly
working, they may eat their own
bread.[b] 13 Brothers, do not grow weary
in doing good.

[a] Rm 16:17 [b] 1Tm 6:5 [c] Ac 20:34 [d] 1Pt 5:3 [e] Gn 3:19 [f] Is 56:10 [g] Rm 12:11

14 And if anyone does not obey our
instruction in this letter, take note of
that person; don't associate with him,
so that he may be ashamed. 15 [a]Yet
don't treat him as an enemy, but warn
him as a brother.

[a] Lv 19:17

Final Greetings

16 May the Lord of peace Himself
give you peace always in every way.
The Lord be with all of you. 17 This
greeting is in my own hand—Paul.
This is a sign in every letter; this is
how I write. 18 The grace of our Lord
Jesus Christ be with all of you.

[a] **2:13** Other mss read *because as a firstfruit* [b] **3:12** Or *food*

1 Timothy

Greeting

1 Paul, an apostle of Christ Jesus [a]according to the command [b]of God our Savior and of Christ Jesus, [c]our hope:

2 To [d]Timothy, my true child in the faith.

Grace, mercy, and peace from God the[a] Father and Christ Jesus our Lord.

[a] Gl 1:1 [b] Ti 1:3 [c] Col 1:27 [d] Ac 16:1

False Doctrine and Misuse of the Law

3 As I urged you [a]when I went to Macedonia, remain in Ephesus so that you may command certain people [b]not to teach other doctrine 4 or to pay attention to myths and endless genealogies. These promote empty speculations rather than God's plan, which operates by faith. 5 Now [c]the goal of our instruction is love [d]from a pure heart, a good conscience, and a sincere faith. 6 Some have deviated from these and turned aside to fruitless discussion. 7 They want to be teachers of the law, although they don't understand what they are saying or what they are insisting on. 8 Now we know that [e]the law is good, provided one uses it legitimately. 9 [f]We know that the law is not meant for a righteous person, but for the lawless and rebellious, for the ungodly and sinful, for the unholy and irreverent, for those who kill their fathers and mothers, for murderers, 10 for the sexually immoral and [g]homosexuals, for kidnappers, liars, perjurers, and for whatever else is contrary to the sound teaching 11 based on the glorious gospel of the blessed God that was entrusted to me.

[a] Ac 20:1,3 [b] Gl 1:6-7 [c] Gl 5:14 [d] 2Tm 2:22 [e] Rm 7:12 [f] Gl 3:19 [g] Lv 18:22; 20:13; 1Co 6:9

Paul's Testimony

12 I give thanks to Christ Jesus our Lord, who has strengthened me, [a]because He considered me faithful, [b]appointing me to the ministry— 13 [c]one who was formerly a blasphemer, a persecutor, and an arrogant man. Since [d]it was out of ignorance that I had acted in unbelief, I received mercy, 14 and the grace of our Lord overflowed, along with the faith and love that are in Christ Jesus. 15 This saying is trustworthy and deserving of full acceptance: [e]"Christ Jesus came into the world to save sinners"—and I am the worst of them. 16 But I received mercy because of this, so that in me, the worst ⌊of them⌋, Christ Jesus might demonstrate the utmost patience as an example to those who would believe in Him for eternal life. 17 Now to [f]the King eternal, immortal, invisible, the only[b] God, be honor and glory forever and ever. •Amen.

[a] 1Co 7:25 [b] 2Co 3:5-6 [c] Ac 8:3; Ac 9:1 [d] Ac 26:9 [e] Lk 19:10; Rm 5:8 [f] Dn 7:14; Mt 6:13

Engage in Battle

18 Timothy, my child, I am giving you this instruction [a]in keeping with the prophecies previously made about you, so that by them you may strongly engage in battle, 19 having faith and a good conscience. Some have rejected these and have suffered the shipwreck of their faith. 20 [b]Hymenaeus and [c]Alexander are among them, and I

[a]**1:2** Other mss read *our* [b]**1:17** Other mss add *wise*

have [d]delivered them to Satan, so that they may be taught not to blaspheme.

a 1Tm 4:14 b 2Tm 2:17 c 2Tm 4:14 d Ac 26:18

Instructions on Prayer

2 First of all, then, I urge that petitions, prayers, intercessions, and thanksgivings be made for everyone, 2 [a]for kings and [b]all those who are in authority, so that we may lead a tranquil and quiet life in all godliness and dignity. 3 This is [c]good, and it pleases God our Savior, 4 [d]who wants everyone to be saved [e]and to come to the knowledge of the truth.

a Jr 29:7 b Rm 13:1 c Rm 12:2 d Lk 14:23; 2Pt 3:9 e Jn 17:3

5 For there is one God
and one mediator between God
and man,
a man, Christ Jesus,
6 who gave Himself—a ransom
for all,
a testimony [a]at the proper time.

a Gl 4:4

7 For this I was appointed a herald, an apostle (I am telling the truth;[a] I am not lying), and a teacher of the Gentiles in faith and truth.

Instructions to Men and Women

8 Therefore I want the men [a]in every place to pray, lifting up holy hands without anger or argument. 9 Also, the women are to dress themselves in modest clothing, with decency and good sense; not with elaborate hairstyles, gold, pearls, or expensive apparel, 10 but with good works, as is proper for women who affirm that they worship God. 11 A woman should learn in silence with full submission. 12 I do not allow a woman to teach or to have authority over a man; instead, she is to be silent. 13 For Adam was created first, then Eve. 14 And Adam was not deceived, but the woman was deceived and transgressed. 15 But she will be [b]saved through childbearing, if she continues[b] in faith, love, and holiness, with good sense.

a Mal 1:11 b Gn 3:16

Qualifications of Church Leaders

3 This saying is trustworthy:[c] "If anyone aspires to be an [a]•overseer, he desires a noble work." 2 An overseer, therefore, must be above reproach, the husband of one wife, self-controlled, sensible, respectable, hospitable, an able teacher,[d] 3 not addicted to wine, not a bully but gentle, not quarrelsome, not greedy— 4 [b]one who manages his own household competently, having his children under control with all dignity. 5 (If anyone does not know how to manage his own household, how will he take care of God's church?) 6 He must not be a new convert, or he might become conceited and fall into the condemnation of the Devil. 7 Furthermore, he must have a good reputation among outsiders, so that he does not fall into disgrace and the Devil's trap.

a Ac 20:28 b Jos 24:15; Ti 1:6-8

8 Deacons, likewise, should be worthy of respect, not hypocritical, not drinking a lot of wine, not greedy for money, 9 holding the •mystery of the faith with a clear conscience. 10 And they must also be tested first; if they prove blameless, then they can serve as deacons. 11 Wives, too, must be worthy of respect, not slanderers, self-controlled, faithful in everything. 12 Deacons must be husbands of one wife, managing their children and their own households competently. 13 For those who have served well as deacons acquire a good standing for themselves, and great boldness in the faith that is in Christ Jesus.

[a]**2:7** Other mss add *in Christ* [b]**2:15** Lit *if they continue* [c]**3:1** *This saying is trustworthy* could refer to 1 Tm 2:15. [d]**3:2** Or *hospitable, skillful in teaching*

The Mystery of Godliness

14 I write these things to you, hoping
to come to you soon. 15 But if I should
be delayed, ⌊I have written⌋ so that you
will know how people ought to act in
God's household, which is the church
of the living God, the pillar and foundation of the truth. 16 And most certainly,
the mystery of godliness is great:

[a]He[a] was manifested in the flesh,
[b]justified in the Spirit,
[c]seen by angels,
preached among the Gentiles,
believed on in the world,
taken up in glory.

[a] Mt 1:23; Php 2:6-8; 1Jn 1:2 [b] Mt 3:16; 1Pt 3:18 [c] Mt 28:2; Lk 2:13

Demonic Influence

4 Now the Spirit [a]explicitly says
that in the latter times some will
depart from the faith, paying attention
[b]to deceitful spirits and the teachings
of demons, 2 through the hypocrisy of
liars [c]whose consciences are seared.
3 [d]They forbid marriage [e]and demand
abstinence from foods that God created [f]to be received with gratitude by
those who believe and know the
truth. 4 For [g]everything created by
God is good, and nothing should be rejected if it is received with thanksgiving, 5 since it is sanctified by the word
of God and by prayer.

[a] Jn 16:13 [b] 2Pt 2:1 [c] Eph 4:19 [d] Pr 18:22 [e] 1Co 6:13; Col 2:16 [f] Gn 9:3 [g] Ti 1:15

A Good Servant of Jesus Christ

6 If you point these things out to the
brothers, you will be a good servant of
Christ Jesus, nourished by the words of
the faith and of the good teaching that
you have followed. 7 But have nothing
to do with irreverent and silly myths.
Rather, train yourself in godliness, 8 for,

the training of the body has
a limited benefit,
but godliness is beneficial
in every way,
[a]since it holds promise
for the present life
and also for the life to come.

9 This saying is trustworthy and deserves full acceptance. 10 In fact, we labor and strive[b] for this, because we
have put our hope in the living God,
[b]who is the Savior of everyone, especially of those who believe.

[a] Mt 6:33 [b] Jn 4:42; 1Tm 2:4

Instructions for Ministry

11 Command and teach these things.
12 [a]No one should despise your youth;
instead, you should be an example to
the believers in speech, in conduct, in
love,[c] in faith, in purity. 13 Until I come,
give your attention to public reading,
exhortation, and teaching. 14 [b]Do not
neglect the gift that is in you; it was
given to you [c]through prophecy, [d]with
the laying on of hands by the council of
elders. 15 Practice these things; be
committed to them, so that your
progress may be evident to all. 16 Be
conscientious about yourself and your
teaching; persevere in these things, for
by doing this you will save both yourself and your hearers.

[a] Ti 2:15 [b] 2Tm 1:6 [c] 1Tm 1:18 [d] Ac 6:6

5 [a]Do not rebuke an older man, but
exhort him as a father, younger
men as brothers, 2 older women as
mothers, and with all propriety, the
younger women as sisters.

[a] Lv 19:32

The Support of Widows

3 Support[d] widows who are genuinely widows. 4 But if any widow has
children or grandchildren, they should
learn to practice their religion toward
their own family first and [a]to repay
their parents, for this pleases God.
5 The real widow, left all alone, has put
her hope in God and continues night

[a]**3:16** Other mss read *God* [b]**4:10** Other mss read *and suffer reproach* [c]**4:12** Other mss add *in spirit*
[d]**5:3** Lit *Honor*

and day in her petitions and prayers;
6 however, she who is self-indulgent is
dead even while she lives. 7 Command
this, so that they won't be blamed.
8 Now if anyone does not provide for
his own relatives, and especially for his
household, he has denied the faith and
is worse than an unbeliever.

[a]*Eph 6:1-2*

9 No widow should be placed on the
official support list[a] unless she is at
least 60 years old, has been the wife
of one husband, 10 and is well known
for good works—that is, if she has
brought up children, shown hospitality, washed the saints' feet, helped the
afflicted, and devoted herself to every
good work. 11 But refuse to enroll
younger widows; for when they are
drawn away from Christ by desire,
they want to marry, 12 and will therefore [a]receive condemnation because
they have renounced their original
pledge. 13 [b]At the same time, they also
learn to be idle, going from house to
house; they are not only idle, but are
also gossips and busybodies, saying
things they shouldn't say. 14 Therefore,
[c]I want younger women to marry, have
children, manage their households,
[d]and give the adversary no opportunity
to accuse us. 15 For some have already
turned away to follow Satan. 16 [e]If any[b]
believing woman has widows, she
should help them, and the church
should not be burdened, so that it can
help those who are genuinely widows.

[a]*Heb 6:4-6* [b]*2Th 3:11* [c]*1Co 7:9* [d]*1Tm 6:1* [e]*Mt 15:4*

Honoring the Elders

17 [a]The elders who are good leaders
should be considered worthy of an am-
ple honorarium,[c] especially those who
work hard at preaching and teaching.
18 For the Scripture says:

[b]**You must not muzzle an ox**
that is threshing grain,[d] and,
[c]The laborer is worthy
of his wages.

[a]*Rm 12:8; Gl 6:6* [b]*Dt 25:4* [c]*Lk 10:7*

19 Don't accept an accusation against
an elder unless it is supported by two
or three witnesses. 20 [a]Publicly rebuke[e]
those who sin, so that the rest will also
be afraid. 21 I solemnly charge you, before God and Christ Jesus and the elect
angels, to observe these things without
prejudice, doing nothing out of favoritism. 22 Don't be too quick to lay hands
on[f] anyone, and don't share in the sins
of others. Keep yourself pure. 23 Don't
continue drinking only water, but use
a little wine because of your stomach
and your frequent illnesses. 24 Some
people's sins are evident, going before
them to judgment, but ⌊the sins⌋ of others follow them. 25 Likewise, [b]good
works are obvious, and those that are
not ⌊obvious⌋ cannot remain hidden.

[a]*Ti 1:13* [b]*1Pt 3:8-16*

Honoring Masters

6 [a]All who are under the yoke as
slaves must regard their own masters to be worthy of all respect, [b]so
that God's name and His teaching will
not be blasphemed. 2 And those who
have believing masters should not be
disrespectful to them [c]because they
are brothers, but should serve them
better, since those who benefit from
their service are believers and dearly
loved.

[a]*Ti 2:9* [b]*Is 52:5* [c]*Col 4:1*

False Doctrine and Human Greed

Teach and encourage these things.
3 If anyone teaches other doctrine and
does not agree with the sound teaching
of our Lord Jesus Christ and with the
teaching that promotes godliness, 4 he
is conceited, [a]understanding nothing,
but having a sick interest in disputes
and arguments over words. From these
come envy, quarreling, slanders, evil

[a]**5:9** Lit *be enrolled* [b]**5:16** Other mss add *believing man or* [c]**5:17** Lit *of double honor,* or possibly *of respect and remuneration* [d]**5:18** Dt 25:4 [e]**5:20** Before the congregation [f]**5:22** To ordain

suspicions, 5 and constant disagreement among [b]men whose minds are depraved and deprived of the truth, [c]who imagine that godliness[a] is a way to material gain.[b] 6 But [d]godliness with contentment is a great gain. [a] 1Co 8:2 [b] 2Tm 3:8 [c] Ti 1:11 [d] Lk 12:31-32

7 For [a]we brought nothing
into the world, and[c]
we can take nothing out.
8 But if we have food
and clothing,[d]
we will be content with these.
[a] Ec 5:15

9 But [a]those who want to be rich fall into temptation, a trap, and many foolish and harmful desires, which plunge people into ruin and destruction. 10 For the love of money is a root[e] of all kinds of evil, and by craving it, some have wandered away from the faith and pierced themselves with many pains.
[a] Mt 13:22

Compete for the Faith

11 Now you, man of God, run
from these things;
but pursue righteousness,
godliness, faith,
love, endurance, and gentleness.
12 [a]Fight the good fight for the faith;
[b]take hold of eternal life,
to which you were called
[c]and have made
a good confession
before many witnesses.
[a] Eph 6:10-18 [b] Php 3:12 [c] Heb 13:23

13 In the presence of God, [a]who gives
life to all, and before Christ Jesus,
[b]who gave a good confession before
Pontius •Pilate, I charge you 14 to keep
the commandment without spot or
blame [c]until the appearing of our Lord
Jesus Christ, 15 which God[f] will bring
about in His own time. ⌊He is⌋

[d]the blessed and only Sovereign,
[e]the King of kings,
and the Lord of lords,
16 the [f]only One
who has immortality,
dwelling in unapproachable light,
[g]whom none of mankind has seen
or can see,
[h]to whom be honor
and eternal might.
•Amen. [a] Jn 5:21
[b] Mt 27:2; Jn 18:37; Rv 1:5 [c] 1Th 3:13 [d] 1Tm 1:1 [e] Rv 17:141 [f] Jn 5:26 [g] Jn 6:46 [h] Eph 3:21

Instructions to the Rich

17 Instruct those who are rich in the
present age not to be arrogant or to set
their hope on the uncertainty of
wealth, but on God,[g] who richly provides us with all things to enjoy.
18 ⌊Instruct them⌋ to do good, to be rich
in good works, to be generous, willing
to share, 19 storing up for themselves a
good foundation for the age to come,
so that they may take hold of life that is
real.

Guard the Heritage

20 Timothy, guard what has been entrusted to you, avoiding irreverent, empty speech and contradictions from the "knowledge" that falsely bears that
name. 21 By professing it, some people
have deviated from the faith.

Grace be with all of you.

[a]**6:5** Referring to religion as a means of financial gain [b]**6:5** Other mss add *From such people withdraw yourself.* [c]**6:7** Other mss add *it is clear that* [d]**6:8** Or *food and shelter* [e]**6:10** Or *is the root* [f]**6:15** Lit *He* [g]**6:17** Other mss read *on the living God*

2 Timothy

Greeting

1 Paul, an apostle of Christ Jesus by
God's will, for [a]the promise of life
in Christ Jesus:
2 To Timothy, my dearly loved child.
Grace, mercy, and peace from God
the Father and Christ Jesus our Lord.

a Jn 5:24

Thanksgiving

3 I thank God, whom I serve with a
clear conscience as my forefathers did,
when I constantly remember you in
my prayers night and day. 4 Remembering your tears, I long to see you so
that I may be filled with joy, 5 clearly
recalling your sincere faith that first
lived in your grandmother Lois, then
in [a]your mother Eunice, and that I am
convinced is in you also.

a Ac 16:1

6 Therefore, I remind you [a]to keep
ablaze the gift of God that is in you
through the laying on of my hands.
7 For [b]God has not given us a spirit[a] of
fearfulness, [c]but one of power, love,
and sound judgment.

a 1Tm 4:14 b Rm 8:15 c Lk 24:49

Not Ashamed of the Gospel

8 [a]So don't be ashamed of the testimony about our Lord, or of me His
prisoner. Instead, share in suffering for
the gospel, relying on the power of
God,

9 who has saved us and [b]called us
with a holy calling,
[c]not according to our works,
but [d]according to His own
purpose and grace,
which was given to us
in Christ Jesus
[e]before time began.
10 [f]This has now been made evident
through the appearing
of our Savior Christ Jesus,
[g]who has abolished death
and has brought life
and immortality to light
through the gospel.

11 For this ⌊gospel⌋ I was appointed a
herald, apostle, and teacher,[b] 12 and
that is why I suffer these things. But I
am not ashamed, because I know
whom I have believed and am persuaded that He is able to guard what
has been entrusted [h]to me[c] until that
day.

a Rm 1:16 b Rm 8:30 c Ti 3:5 d Rm 8:28 e Eph 1:4 f Eph 1:9; 1Pt 1:20 g Heb 2:14 h 1Pt 4:19

Be Loyal to the Faith

13 [a]Hold on to the pattern of sound
teaching [b]that you have heard from me,
in the faith and love that are in Christ
Jesus. 14 Guard, through the Holy Spirit
who lives in us, that good thing entrusted to you. 15 This you know: all
those in Asia have turned away from
me, including Phygelus and Hermo-
genes. 16 May the Lord [c]grant mercy to
the household of Onesiphorus,
[d]because he often refreshed me and
was not ashamed of my chains. 17 On
the contrary, when he was in Rome, he
diligently searched for me and found
me. 18 May the Lord grant [e]that he obtain mercy from the Lord [f]on that day.
And you know how much he
[g]ministered at Ephesus.

a Heb 10:23 b 2Tm 2:2 c Mt 5:7 d Phm 7 e Mt 25:34 f 2Th 1:10 g Heb 6:10

Be Strong in Grace

2 You, therefore, my child, [a]be
strong in the grace that is in Christ

[a]**1:7** Or *Spirit* [b]**1:11** Other mss add *of the Gentiles* [c]**1:12** Or *guard what I have entrusted to Him*, or *guard my deposit*

Jesus. 2 And what you have heard from
me in the presence of many witnesses, [b]commit to faithful men who
will be able to teach others also.

[a]*Eph 1:19; Col 1:11* [b]*1Tm 1:18*

3 Share in suffering as a good soldier
of Christ Jesus. 4 To please the re-
cruiter, [a]no one serving as a soldier
gets entangled in the concerns of ev-
eryday life. 5 Also, if anyone competes
as an athlete, he is not crowned unless
he competes according to the rules. 6 It
is the hardworking farmer who ought
to be the first to get a share of the
crops. 7 Consider what I say, for the
Lord will give you understanding in everything.

[a]*1Co 9:25*

8 Keep in mind Jesus Christ, [a]risen
from the dead, [b]descended from David, [c]according to my gospel. 9 For this
I suffer, to the point of being bound like
a criminal; but God's message is not
bound. 10 This is why I endure all
things for the elect: [d]so that they also
may obtain salvation, which is in Christ
Jesus, with eternal glory. 11 [e]This saying
is trustworthy:

For [f]if we have died with Him,
we will also live with Him;
12 [g]if we endure,
we will also reign with Him;
[h]if we deny Him,
He will also deny us;
13 [i]if we are faithless,
He remains faithful,
[j]for He cannot deny Himself.

[a]*1Co 15:3-4* [b]*Lk 1:32* [c]*Rm 2:16* [d]*2Co 1:6* [e]*1Tm 1:15* [f]*Rm 6:5,8* [g]*1Pt 4:13* [h]*Mk 8:38* [i]*Mt 24:35* [j]*Nm 23:19*

An Approved Worker

14 Remind them of these things,
[a]charging them before God[a] [b]not to
fight about words; this is in no way
profitable and leads to the ruin of the
hearers. 15 Be diligent to present yourself approved to God, a worker who
doesn't need to be ashamed, correctly
teaching the word of truth. 16 But
[c]avoid irreverent, empty speech, for
this will produce an even greater measure of godlessness. 17 And their word
will spread like gangrene, among
whom are [d]Hymenaeus and Philetus.
18 They have deviated from the truth,
[e]saying that the resurrection has already taken place, and are overturning
the faith of some. 19 Nevertheless,
[f]God's solid foundation stands firm,
having this inscription:

**The Lord [g]knows those
who are His,**[b] and
Everyone who names the name
of the Lord
must turn away
from unrighteousness.

[a]*2Tm 4:1* [b]*Ti 3:9* [c]*1Tm 4:7* [d]*1Tm 1:20* [e]*1Co 15:12* [f]*Eph 2:20* [g]*Nm 16:5; Jn 10:14*

20 Now in a large house there are not
only gold and silver bowls, but also
those of wood and earthenware, some
for special[c] use, some for ordinary. 21 So
if anyone purifies himself from these
things, he will be a special[d] instrument, set apart, useful to the Master,
prepared for every good work.
22 Flee from youthful passions, and
pursue righteousness, faith, love, and
peace, along with those who call on
the Lord from a pure heart. 23 But reject foolish and ignorant disputes,
knowing that they breed quarrels.
24 The Lord's slave must not quarrel,
but must be gentle to everyone, able to
teach,[e] and patient, 25 instructing his
opponents with gentleness. Perhaps
God will grant them repentance to
know the truth. 26 Then they may
come to their senses and escape the
Devil's trap, having been captured by
him to do his will.

[a]**2:14** Other mss read *before the Lord* [b]**2:19** Nm 16:5 [c]**2:20** Or *honorable* [d]**2:21** Or *an honorable*
[e]**2:24** Or *everyone, skillful in teaching*

Difficult Times Ahead

3 But know this: difficult times will
come [a]in the last days. 2 For people will be lovers of self, lovers of
money, boastful, proud, blasphemers,
disobedient to parents, ungrateful, unholy, 3 unloving, irreconcilable, slanderers, without self-control, brutal,
without love for what is good, 4 trai-
tors, reckless, conceited, lovers of
pleasure rather than lovers of God,
5 holding to the form of religion but
[b]denying its power. Avoid these people! *[a] Jd 18 [b] Ezk 33:30-32*

6 For [a]among them are those who
worm their way into households and
capture idle women burdened down
with sins, led along by a variety of passions, 7 always learning and never able
to come to a knowledge of the truth.
8 [b]Just as Jannes and Jambres resisted
Moses, so these also resist the truth,
men who are corrupt in mind, worthless in regard to the faith. 9 But they
will not make further progress, for
their lack of understanding will be
clear to all, [c]as theirs[a] was also.
[a] Mt 23:14 [b] Ex 7:11 [c] Ex 8:18; 9:11

The Sacred Scriptures

10 But you have followed my teaching, conduct, purpose, faith, patience,
love, and endurance, 11 along with the
persecutions and sufferings that came
to me in [a]Antioch, [b]Iconium, and
Lystra. What persecutions I endured!
Yet the Lord rescued me from them all.
12 In fact, [c]all those who want to live a
godly life in Christ Jesus will be persecuted. 13 Evil people and imposters will
become worse, deceiving and being
deceived. 14 But as for you, continue in
what you have learned and firmly believed, knowing those from whom you
learned, 15 and that from childhood you
have known the sacred Scriptures,
which [d]are able to instruct you for salvation through faith in Christ Jesus.
16 All Scripture is inspired by God[b] and
is profitable for teaching, for rebuking,
for correcting for training in righteousness, 17 [e]so that the man of God may be
complete, equipped for every good
work. *[a] Ac 13:14 [b] Ac 14:2 [c] Mt 16:24; Ac 14:22 [d] Jn 5:39-40; 20:31 [e] 1Tm 6:11*

Fulfill Your Ministry

4 Before God and Christ Jesus, who
is going to judge the living and
the dead, and by His appearing and
His kingdom, I solemnly charge you:
2 proclaim the message; persist in it
whether convenient or not; [a]rebuke,
[b]correct, and encourage with great patience and teaching. 3 For the time
will come when they will not tolerate
[c]sound doctrine, but according to
their own desires, will accumulate
teachers for themselves because they
have an itch to hear something new.[c]
4 They will turn away from hearing the
truth and [d]will turn aside to myths.
5 But as for you, keep a clear head
about everything, endure hardship, do
the work of an evangelist, fulfill your
ministry. *[a] Ti 1:13 [b] 1Tm 4:13 [c] 1Tm 1:10 [d] 1Tm 1:4*

6 For I am already being poured out
as a drink offering, and the time for my
departure is close. 7 I have fought the
good fight, I have finished the race, I
have kept the faith. 8 In the future,
there is reserved for me [a]the crown of
righteousness, which the Lord, the
righteous Judge, will give me on that
day, and not only to me, but to all those
who have loved His appearing.
[a] Rv 2:10

Final Instructions

9 Make every effort to come to me
soon, 10 for [a]Demas has deserted me,
[b]because he loved this present world,

[a]**3:9** Referring to Jannes and Jambres [b]**3:16** Lit *breathed out by God*; the Scripture is the product of God's Spirit working through men; see 2 Pt 1:20–21. [c]**4:3** Or *to hear what they want to hear*; lit *themselves, itching in the hearing*

and has gone to Thessalonica. Crescens has gone to Galatia, Titus to Dalmatia. 11 Only Luke is with me. Bring [c]Mark with you, for he is useful to me in the ministry. 12 I have sent [d]Tychicus to Ephesus. 13 When you come, bring the cloak I left in Troas with Carpus, as well as the scrolls, especially the parchments. 14 [e]Alexander the coppersmith did great harm to me. [f]The Lord will repay him according to his works. 15 Watch out for him yourself, because he strongly opposed our words.

[a] Col 4:14 [b] 1Jn 2:15 [c] Ac 12:25 [d] Ac 20:4 [e] Ac 19:33 [f] Ps 28:4

16 At my first defense, no one came to my assistance, but everyone deserted me. May it not be counted against them. 17 [a]But the Lord stood with me and strengthened me, so that the proclamation might be fully made through me, and all the Gentiles might hear. So I was rescued [b]from the lion's mouth. 18 [c]The Lord will rescue me from every evil work and will bring me safely into His heavenly kingdom. To Him be the glory forever and ever! •Amen.

[a] Mt 10:19 [b] 2Pt 2:9 [c] Ps 121:7

Benediction

19 Greet [a]Prisca and Aquila, and [b]the household of Onesiphorus. 20 [c]Erastus has remained at Corinth; [d]Trophimus I left sick at Miletus. 21 Make every effort to come before winter. Eubulus greets you, as do Pudens, Linus, Claudia, and all the brothers.

[a] Ac 18:2 [b] 2Tm 1:16 [c] Ac 19:22 [d] Ac 20:4

22 The Lord be with your spirit. Grace be with you!

TITUS

Greeting

1 Paul, a slave of God, and an apostle of Jesus Christ for the faith of God's elect and [a]the knowledge of the truth [b]that leads[a] to godliness, 2 in the hope of eternal life that God, who cannot lie, promised before [c]time began, 3 and has in His own time revealed His message in the proclamation that I was entrusted with [d]by the command of God our Savior:

4 To [e]Titus, my true child in our common faith.

Grace and peace from God the Father and Christ Jesus our Savior.

[a] 2Tm 2:25 [b] 1Tm 6:3 [c] 2Tm 1:9 [d] Ac 9:15; Ti 2:10,13 [e] 2Co 2:13

Titus' Ministry in Crete

5 The reason I left you in Crete was to set right what was left undone and, as I directed you, to [a]appoint elders in every town: 6 someone who is blameless, the husband of one wife, having faithful[b] children not accused of wildness or rebellion. 7 For an •overseer, as [b]God's manager, must be blameless, not arrogant, not quick tempered, [c]not addicted to wine, not a bully, not greedy for money, 8 but hospitable, loving what is good, sensible, righteous, holy, self-controlled, 9 holding to the faithful message as taught, so that he will be able both to encourage with sound teaching and to refute those who contradict it.

[a] Ac 14:23 [b] Mt 24:45 [c] Lv 10:9

10 For there are also many rebellious people, idle talkers and deceivers, [a]especially those from Judaism.[c] 11 It is necessary to silence them; they overthrow whole households by teaching for

[a] **1:1** Or *corresponds* [b] **1:6** Or *believing* [c] **1:10** Lit *the circumcision*

dishonest gain what they should not.
12 [b]One of their very own prophets said,

> Cretans are always liars,
> evil beasts, lazy gluttons.[a]

13 This testimony is true. So, rebuke
them sharply, that they may be sound
in the faith 14 and may not pay attention to Jewish myths and the [c]com-
mandments of men who reject the
truth. [a] Ac 15:1 [b] Ac 17:28 [c] Mt 15:9

15 [a]To the pure, everything is pure,
but to those who are defiled and unbelieving nothing is pure; in fact, both
their mind and conscience are defiled.
16 [b]They profess to know God, but they
deny Him by their works. They are de-
testable, disobedient, and disqualified
for any good work. [a] Rm 14:14 [b] Ezk 33:31

Sound Teaching

2 But you must speak what is consistent with [a]sound teaching. 2 Older
men are to be self-controlled, worthy
of respect, sensible, and sound in
faith, love, and endurance. 3 In the
same way, [b]older women are to be
reverent in behavior, not slanderers,
not addicted to much wine. ⌊They are⌋
to teach what is good, 4 so that they
may encourage the young women to
love their husbands and children, 5 to
be sensible, pure, good homemakers,
and [c]submissive to their husbands, so
that God's message will not be slandered. [a] 1Tm 6:3 [b] 1Pt 3:3-4 [c] 1Pt 3:1,5

6 Likewise, encourage the young men
to be sensible 7 [a]about everything. Set
an example of good works yourself,
with integrity and [b]dignity[b] in your
teaching. 8 [c]Your message is to be sound
beyond reproach, [d]so that the opponent
will be ashamed, having nothing bad to
say about us. [a] 1Pt 5:3 [b] 1Tm 2:2; 3:4
[c] 1Tm 6:3 [d] Neh 5:9

9 Slaves are to be submissive to their
masters in everything, and to be well-
pleasing, not talking back 10 or stealing,
but demonstrating utter faithfulness,
so that they may adorn the teaching of
God our Savior in everything.

11 For the grace of God [a]has appeared, with salvation[c] for all people,
12 instructing us [b]to deny godlessness
and worldly lusts and to live in a sensible, righteous, and godly way in the
present age, 13 while we wait for the
blessed [c]hope and the appearing of
the glory of our great God and Savior,
Jesus Christ. 14 He gave Himself for us
to redeem us from all lawlessness [d]and
to cleanse for Himself [e]a special people,
eager to do good works.

[a] Is 49:6; Jn 1:9 [b] Lk 1:75
[c] Ac 24:15 [d] Ac 15:9;
Heb 9:14 [e] Dt 7:6

15 Say these things, and encourage
and rebuke with all authority. Let no
one disregard[d] you.

The Importance of Good Works

3 Remind them to be submissive to
rulers and authorities, to obey,
[a]to be ready for every good work, 2 to
[b]slander no one, to avoid fighting, and
to be kind, always showing gentleness
to all people. 3 For we too were once
foolish, disobedient, deceived, captives
of various passions and pleasures, living
in malice and envy, hateful, detesting
one another. [a] Heb 13:21
[b] Eph 4:31

> 4 But when the goodness and love
> for man
> appeared from God our Savior,
> 5 He saved us—
> [a]not by works of righteousness
> that we had done,
> but according to His mercy,
> through [b]the washing
> of regeneration
> and renewal by the Holy Spirit.
> 6 [c]This ⌊Spirit⌋ He poured out on us
> abundantly

[a]**1:12** This saying is from the Cretan poet Epimenides (6th century B.C.). [b]**2:7** Other mss add *incorruptibility* [c]**2:11** Or *appeared, bringing salvation* [d]**2:15** Or *despise*

through Jesus Christ our Savior,
7 so that having been justified
by His grace,
we may become heirs
with the hope
of eternal life. [a]Gl 2:16
[b]Jn 3:3,5; 1Pt 3:21 [c]Jl 2:28

8 This saying is trustworthy. I want
you to insist on these things, so that
those who have believed God might
be careful to devote themselves to
good works. These are good and profitable for everyone. 9 But [a]avoid foolish debates, genealogies, quarrels, and
disputes about the law, for they are
unprofitable and worthless. 10 [b]Reject
a divisive person [c]after a first and second warning, 11 knowing that such a
person is perverted and sins, being
self-condemned. [a]1Tm 1:4 [b]Mt 18:17
[c]2Co 13:2; 2Th 3:15; 1Tm 1:9-11

Final Instructions and Closing

12 When I send Artemas to you, or
Tychicus, make every effort to come to
me in Nicopolis, for I have decided to
spend the winter there. 13 Diligently
help Zenas the lawyer and [a]Apollos on
their journey, so that they will lack
nothing. [a]Ac 18:24

14 And our people must also learn to
devote themselves to good works for
cases of urgent need, so that they will
[a]not be unfruitful. 15 All those who are
with me greet you. Greet those who
love us in the faith. Grace be with all of
you. [a]Col 1:10

PHILEMON

Greeting

Paul, [a]a prisoner of Christ Jesus, and
Timothy, our brother:
To Philemon, our dear friend [b]and
co-worker, 2 to Apphia our sister,[a] to
Archippus our fellow soldier, and to
[c]the church that meets in your house.
3 [d]Grace to you and peace from God
our Father and the Lord Jesus Christ.
[a]Eph 1:1 [b]Php 2:25 [c]Rm 16:5 [d]Eph 1:2

Philemon's Love and Faith

4 [a]I always thank my God when I
mention you in my prayers, 5 because
[b]I hear of your love and faith toward[b]
the Lord Jesus and for all the saints. 6 ⌊I
pray⌋ that your participation in the
faith may become effective through
[c]knowing every good thing that is in
us[c] for ⌊the glory of⌋ Christ. 7 For I have
great joy and encouragement from
your love, because the hearts of the
saints [d]have been refreshed through
you, brother. [a]Php 1:3; 1Th 1:2
[b]Eph 1:15 [c]Php 1:9 [d]2Tm 1:16

An Appeal for Onesimus

8 For this reason, although I have
great boldness in Christ to command
you to do what is right, 9 I appeal, instead, on the basis of love. I, Paul, as an
elderly man[d] and now also as a prisoner of Christ Jesus, 10 appeal to you for
my child, whom [a]I fathered[e] while in
chains—[b]Onesimus.[f] 11 Once he was
useless to you, but now he is useful to
both you and me. 12 I am sending
him—a part of myself[g]—back to you.[h]
13 I wanted to keep him with me, [c]so
that in my imprisonment for the gospel

[a]**2** Other mss read *our beloved* [b]**5** Lit *faith that you have toward* [c]**6** Other mss read *in you* [d]**9** Or *an ambassador* [e]**10** Referring to the fact that Paul led him to Christ; see 1 Co 4:15 [f]**10** The name *Onesimus* in Gk means "useful." [g]**12** Lit *him—that is, my inward parts* [h]**12** Other mss read *him back. Receive him as a part of myself.*

he might serve me in your place. [14] But I didn't want to do anything without your consent, [d]so that your good deed might not be out of obligation, but of your own free will. [15] For perhaps this is why he was separated ⌊from you⌋ for a brief time, so that you might get him back permanently, [16] no longer as a slave, but more than a slave—[e]as a dearly loved brother. This is especially so to me, but even more to you, [f]both in the flesh and in the Lord.[a]

[a] 1Co 4:15 [b] Col 4:9 [c] Php 2:30 [d] 2Co 9:7 [e] 1Tm 6:2 [f] Eph 6:5-7

[17] So if you consider me [a]a partner, accept him as you would me. [18] And if he has wronged you in any way, or owes you anything, charge that to my account. [19] I, Paul, write this with my own hand: I will repay it—not to mention to you that you owe me even your own self. [20] Yes, brother, may I have joy from you in the Lord; refresh my heart in Christ. [21] Since I am confident of your obedience, I am writing to you, knowing that you will do even more than I say. [22] But meanwhile, also prepare a guest room for me, for [b]I hope that [c]through your prayers I will be restored to you.

[a] 2Co 8:23 [b] Php 1:25 [c] Rm 15:30-32

Final Greetings

[23] [a]Epaphras, my fellow prisoner in Christ Jesus, greets you, and so do [24] [b]Mark, [c]Aristarchus, Demas, and [d]Luke, my co-workers.

[a] Col 1:7 [b] Ac 12:12 [c] Ac 19:29 [d] 2Tm 4:11

[25] The grace of the Lord[b] Jesus Christ be with your spirit.

HEBREWS

The Nature of the Son

1 Long ago God spoke to the fathers by the prophets [a]at different times and in different ways. [2] [b]In these last days, He has spoken to us by ⌊His⌋ Son, [c]whom He has appointed heir of all things and [d]through whom He made the universe.[c] [3] [e]He is the radiance[d] of His glory, the exact expression[e] of His nature, and He [f]sustains all things by His powerful word. After making purification for sins,[f] [g]He sat down at the right hand of the Majesty on high.[g] [4] So He became higher in rank than the angels, [h]just as the name He inherited is superior to theirs.

[a] Nm 12:6,8 [b] Lk 10:23-24; Gl 4:4 [c] Ps 2:8 [d] Ps 33:6; Jn 1:3 [e] 2Co 4:4 [f] Rv 4:11 [g] Mt 22:44 [h] Php 2:9

The Son Superior to Angels

[5] For to which of the angels did He ever say, [a]**You are My Son; today I have become Your Father,**[h] [i] or again, [b]**I will be His Father, and He will be My Son?**[j] [6] When He again brings [c]His firstborn into the world,[k] He says, [d]**And all God's angels must worship Him.**[l] [7] And about the angels He says:

> [e]**He makes His angels winds,**[m]
> **and His servants**[n]
> **a fiery flame;**[o]

[a] Ps 2:7 [b] 2Sm 7:14; Ps 89:26 [c] Rm 8:29 [d] Ps 97:7 [e] Ps 104:4

[8] but about the Son:

> [a]**Your throne, O God,**
> **is forever and ever,**

[a]**16** Both physically and spiritually [b]**25** Other mss read *our Lord* [c]**1:2** Lit *ages* [d]**1:3** Or *reflection* [e]**1:3** Or *representation*, or *copy*, or *reproduction* [f]**1:3** Other mss read *for our sins by Himself* [g]**1:3** Or *He sat down on high at the right hand of the Majesty* [h]**1:5** Or *have begotten You* [i]**1:5** Ps 2:7 [j]**1:5** 2 Sm 7:14; 1 Ch 17:13 [k]**1:6** Or *And again, when He brings His firstborn into the world* [l]**1:6** Dt 32:43 LXX; Ps 97:7 [m]**1:7** Or *spirits* [n]**1:7** Or *ministers* [o]**1:7** Ps 104:4

and the scepter
of Your kingdom is a scepter
of justice.
9 **You have loved righteousness**
and hated lawlessness;
this is why God, Your God,
[b]**has anointed You,**
rather than Your
companions,[a] [b] **with the oil**
of joy. *[a]Ps 45:6-7 [b]Is 61:1*

10 And:

[a]**In the beginning, Lord,**
You established the earth,
and the heavens are the works
of Your hands;
11 **they will perish,**
but You remain.
They will all wear out
like clothing;
12 **You will roll them up**
like a cloak,[c]
and they will be changed
like a robe.
But You are the same,
and Your years will never end.[d]
[a]Ps 102:25-27

13 Now to which of the angels has He ever said:

[a]**Sit at My right hand**
until I make Your enemies
Your footstool?[e] [f] *[a]Ps 110:1*

14 Are they not all ministering spirits sent out to serve those who are going to inherit salvation?

Warning against Neglect

2 We must therefore pay even more attention to what we have heard,
so that we will not drift away. 2 For if
the message spoken through angels
was legally binding,[g] and every transgression and disobedience received a
just punishment, 3 how will we escape
if we neglect such a great [a]salvation? It
was first spoken by the Lord and was
confirmed to us by those who heard
Him. 4 At the same time, God also testified by signs and wonders, various miracles, and distributions ⌊of gifts⌋ from
the Holy Spirit according to His will.
[a]Is 45:17

Jesus and Humanity

5 For He has not subjected to angels
the world to come that we are talking
about. 6 But one has somewhere testified:

[a]**What is man,**
that You remember him,
or the son of man,
that You care for him?
7 **You made him lower**
than the angels
for a short time;
You crowned him with glory
and honor[h]
8 **and subjected everything**
under his feet.[i] *[a]Ps 8:4-6*

For in **subjecting everything** to him,
He left nothing not subject to him. As it
is, we do not yet see **everything sub-**
jected to him. 9 But we do see Jesus—
made lower than the angels for a
short time so that by God's grace He
might taste death for everyone—
crowned with glory and honor because
of the suffering of death.
10 [a]For it was fitting, in bringing
many sons to glory, that He, for whom
and through whom all things exist,
should make the source[j] of their salvation [b]perfect through sufferings. 11 For
the One who sanctifies and those who
are sanctified all have one Father.[k] That
is why [c]He is not ashamed to call them
brothers, 12 saying:

[d]**I will proclaim Your name**
to My brothers;

[a]**1:9** Or *associates* [b]**1:8–9** Ps 45:6–7 [c]**1:12** Other mss omit *like a cloak* [d]**1:10–12** Ps 102:25–27 [e]**1:13** Or *enemies a footstool for Your feet* [f]**1:13** Ps 110:1 [g]**2:2** Or *valid*, or *reliable* [h]**2:7** Other mss add *and set him over the works of your hands* [i]**2:6–8** Ps 8:5–7 LXX [j]**2:10** Or *pioneer*, or *leader* [k]**2:11** Or *father*, or *origin*, or *all are of one*

I will sing hymns to You
in the congregation.[a]

13 Again, [e]**I will trust in Him.**[b] And
again, [f]**Here I am with the children**
God gave Me.[c]

[a] Is 43:21; Lk 24:46
[b] Heb 7:28 [c] Mt 28:10
[d] Ps 22:22 [e] Is 12:2 [f] Is 8:18

14 Now since the children have flesh
and blood in common, He [a]also shared
in these, so [b]that through His death He
might destroy the one holding the
power of death—that is, the Devil—
15 and free those who were held in
slavery all their lives [c]by the fear of
death. 16 For it is clear that He does not
reach out to help angels, but to help
Abraham's offspring. 17 Therefore He
had [d]to be like His brothers in every
way, so that He could become a merciful and faithful high priest in service[d]
to God, to make propitiation[e] for the
sins of the people. 18 [e]For since He
Himself was tested and has suffered,
He is able to help those who are tested.

[a] Rm 8:3
[b] Col 2:15; 2Tm 1:10 [c] Lk 1:74,79
[d] Php 2:7 [e] Heb 4:15; 5:2

Our Apostle and High Priest

3 Therefore, holy brothers and companions in a heavenly calling, consider Jesus, [a]the apostle and high
priest of our confession; 2 He was
faithful to the One who appointed
Him, just as [b]Moses was in all God's[f]
household. 3 For Jesus[g] is considered
worthy of more glory than Moses,
[c]just as the builder has more honor
than the house. 4 Now every house is
built by someone, but [d]the One who
built everything is God. 5 Moses was
faithful as a servant in all God's[f] household, [e]as a testimony to what would
be said ⌊in the future⌋. 6 But Christ was
faithful as a Son over His household,
[f]whose household we are [g]if we hold
on to the courage and the confidence
of our hope.[h]

[a] Mt 15:24 [b] Nm 12:7 [c] Zch 6:12 [d] Eph 2:10
[e] Dt 18:15-19 [f] 1Pt 2:5 [g] Mt 10:22

Warning against Unbelief

7 Therefore, as [a]the Holy Spirit says:

[b]**Today, if you hear His voice,**
8 **do not harden your hearts**
as in the rebellion,
on the day of testing
in the desert,
9 **where your fathers tested Me,**
tried ⌊Me⌋,
and saw My works
10 **for 40 years.**
Therefore I was provoked
with this generation
and said, "They always
go astray in their hearts,
and they have not known
My ways."
11 **So I swore in My anger,**
"They will not enter My rest."[i]

[a] Ac 1:16 [b] Ps 95:7-11

12 Watch out, brothers, so that there
won't be in any of you an evil, unbelieving heart that departs from the living God. 13 But encourage each other
daily, while it is still called **today,** so
that none of you is hardened by sin's
deception. 14 For we have become
companions of the •Messiah if we
hold firmly until the end the reality[j]
that we had at the start. 15 As it is said:

Today, if you hear His voice,
do not harden your hearts
as in the rebellion.[k]

16 [a]For who heard and rebelled?
Wasn't it really all who came out of
Egypt under Moses? 17 And with
whom was He "provoked for 40
years"? Was it not with those who

[a]**2:12** Ps 22:22 [b]**2:13** Is 8:17 LXX; 12:2 LXX; 2 Sm 22:3 LXX [c]**2:13** Is 8:18 LXX [d]**2:17** Lit *things*
[e]**2:17** The word *propitiation* has to do with the removal of divine wrath. Jesus' death is the means that turns God's wrath from the sinner; see 2 Co 5:21. [f]**3:2,5** Lit *His* [g]**3:3** Lit *He* [h]**3:6** Other mss add *firm to the end* [i]**3:7–11** Ps 95:7–11 [j]**3:14** Or *confidence* [k]**3:15** Ps 95:7–8

sinned, [b]whose bodies fell in the
desert? 18 And to whom did He "swear
that they would not enter His rest," if
not those who disobeyed? 19 So we see
that they were unable to enter because of unbelief.

[a]Nm 14; Dt 1:26
[b]Nm 26:65

The Promised Rest

4 Therefore, while the promise remains of entering His rest, let us
fear so that none of you should miss
it.[a] 2 For we also have received the
good news just as they did; but the
message they heard did not benefit
them, since they were not united with
those who heard it in faith[b] 3 (for we
who have believed enter the rest), in
keeping with what[c] He has said:

> [a]**So I swore in My anger,**
> **they will not enter My rest.**[d]

[a]Ps 95:11

And yet His works have been finished
since the foundation of the world, 4 for
somewhere He has spoken about the
seventh day in this way:

> [a]**And on the seventh day**
> **God rested**
> **from all His works.**[e]

[a]Gn 2:2

5 Again, in that passage ⌊He says⌋, **They
will never enter My rest.**[d] 6 Since it remains for some to enter it, [a]and those
who formerly received the good news
did not enter because of disobedience,
7 again, He specifies a certain day—**today**—speaking through David after
such a long time, as previously stated:

> [b]**Today if you hear His voice,**
> **do not harden your hearts.**[f]

[a]Heb 3:18-19 [b]Ps 95:7

8 For if Joshua had given them rest, He
would not have spoken later about another day. 9 A Sabbath rest remains,
therefore, for God's people. 10 For the
person who has entered His rest has
rested from his own works, just as
God did from His. 11 Let us then make
every effort to enter that rest, so that
no one will fall into the same pattern
of disobedience.

12 For the word of God is [a]living and
effective and sharper than any [b]two-
edged sword, penetrating as far as to
divide soul, spirit, joints, and marrow;
it is a [c]judge of the ideas and thoughts
of the heart. 13 No creature is hidden
from Him, but all things are naked and
exposed to the eyes of Him to whom
we must give an account.

[a]Jr 23:29 [b]Rv 1:16 [c]1Co 14:24-25

Our Great High Priest

14 Therefore since we have a great
high priest who has passed through
the heavens—Jesus the Son of God
—let us hold fast to the confession.
15 For [a]we do not have a high priest
who is unable to sympathize with our
weaknesses, but [b]One who has been
tested in every way as we are, [c]yet
without sin. 16 Therefore let us approach the throne of grace with boldness, so that we may receive mercy
and find grace to help us at the proper
time.

[a]Is 53:3 [b]Lk 22:28
[c]2Co 5:21; 1Pt 2:22; 1Jn 3:5

The Messiah, a High Priest

5 For every high priest taken from
men is appointed in service[g] to
God for the people, [a]to offer both gifts
and sacrifices for sins. 2 He is able to
deal gently with those who are ignorant and are going astray, since he
himself is also subject to weakness.
3 [b]Because of this, he must make a sin
offering for himself as well as for the
people. 4 [c]No one takes this honor on
himself; instead, a person is called by
God, just as [d]Aaron was. 5 [e]In the same
way, the •Messiah did not exalt
Himself to become a high priest, but

[a]**4:1** Or *should seem to miss it* [b]**4:2** Other mss read *since it was not united by faith in those who heard* [c]**4:3** Or *rest), just as* [d]**4:3,5** Ps 95:11 [e]**4:4** Gn 2:2 [f]**4:7** Ps 95:7–8 [g]**5:1** Lit *things*

the One who said to Him, [f]**You are My Son; today I have become Your Father,**[a] 6 also said in another passage, [g]**You are a priest forever in the order of Melchizedek.**[b]

a Heb 8:3-4 b Lv 4:3 c 1Sm 13:9; 2Sm 6:6 d Ex 28:1 e Jn 8:54 f Ps 2:7 g Ps 110:4

7 During His earthly life,[c] He [a]offered prayers and appeals, [b]with loud cries and tears, to the One [c]who was able to save Him from death, and He was heard because of His reverence. 8 Though a Son, He learned [d]obedience through what He suffered. 9 After He was perfected, He became the source of eternal salvation to all who obey Him, 10 and He was declared by God a high priest [e]"in the order of Melchizedek."

a Jn 17:1 b Ps 22:1 c Mt 26:53 d Php 2:8 e Heb 6:20

The Problem of Immaturity

11 We have a great deal to say about this, and it's difficult to explain, since you have become slow to understand. 12 For though by this time you ought to be teachers, you need someone to teach you again the basic principles of God's revelation. You need milk, not solid food. 13 Now everyone who lives on milk is inexperienced with the message about righteousness, because he is [a]an infant. 14 But solid food is for the mature—for those whose senses have been trained [b]to distinguish between good and evil.

a Eph 4:13 b 1Co 2:14-15

Warning against Regression

6 Therefore, leaving the elementary message about the •Messiah, let us go on to maturity, not laying again the foundation of repentance from dead works, faith in God, 2 [a]teaching about ritual washings,[d] [b]laying on of hands, [c]the resurrection of the dead, [d]and eternal judgment. 3 And we will do this if God permits.

a Ac 19:4 b Ac 8:17 c Ac 17:31 d Ac 24:25

4 For [a]it is impossible to renew to repentance those [b]who were once enlightened, who tasted [c]the heavenly gift, became companions with the Holy Spirit, 5 tasted God's good word and the powers of the coming age, 6 and who have fallen away, because,[e] to their own harm, [d]they are recrucifying the Son of God and holding Him up to contempt. 7 For ground that has drunk the rain that has often fallen on it, and that produces vegetation useful to those it is cultivated for, receives a blessing from God. 8 But if it produces thorns and thistles, it is worthless and about to be cursed, and will be burned at the end.

a Mt 12:32; Heb 10:26; 2Pt 2:20 b Heb 10:32 c Eph 2:8 d Heb 10:29

9 Even though we are speaking this way, dear friends, in your case we are confident of the better things connected with salvation. 10 For [a]God is not unjust; He will not forget your work and the love[f] you showed for His name when you served the saints—and you continue to serve them. 11 Now we want each of you to demonstrate the same diligence [b]for the final realization of your hope, 12 so that you won't become lazy, but imitators of those who [c]inherit the promises through faith and perseverance.

a Mt 10:42; Jn 13:20 b Col 2:2 c Heb 10:36

Inheriting the Promise

13 For when God made a promise to Abraham, since He had no one greater to swear by, [a]He swore by Himself:

> 14 [b]**I will most certainly bless you,**
> **and I will greatly multiply you.**[g]

a Gn 22:16 b Gn 22:17

15 And so, after waiting patiently, Abraham[h] obtained the promise. 16 For men swear by something greater than themselves, and for them [a]a confirming oath

[a]**5:5** Ps 2:7 [b]**5:6** Ps 110:4; Gn 14:18–20 [c]**5:7** Lit *In the days of His flesh* [d]**6:2** Or *about baptisms* [e]**6:6** Or *while* [f]**6:10** Other mss read *labor of love* [g]**6:14** Gn 22:17 [h]**6:15** Lit *he*

ends every dispute. 17 Because God
wanted to show [b]His unchangeable
purpose even more clearly to [c]the
heirs of the promise, He guaranteed it
with an oath, 18 so that through two
unchangeable things, in which it is impossible for God to lie, we who have
fled for refuge might have strong encouragement to seize the hope [d]set before us. 19 [e]We have this ⌊hope⌋—like a
sure and firm anchor of the soul—[f]that
enters the inner sanctuary behind the
curtain. 20 [g]Jesus has entered there on
our behalf as a forerunner, because He
has become a "high priest forever in
the order of Melchizedek." *[a]Ex 22:11 [b]Jb 23:13; Is 14:24 [c]Heb 11:9 [d]Heb 12:1 [e]Ps 130:7 [f]Lv 16:15; Heb 9:7 [g]Heb 4:14; 8:1*

The Greatness of Melchizedek

7 For this [a]Melchizedek—

King of Salem, priest of the Most
High God,
who met Abraham
and blessed him as he returned
from defeating the kings,
2 and Abraham gave him a tenth
of everything;
first, his name means
"king of righteousness,"
then also, "king of Salem,"
meaning "king of peace";
3 without father, mother,
or genealogy,
having neither beginning of days
nor end of life,
but resembling the Son of God—

remains a priest forever. *[a]Gn 14:18*

4 Now consider how great this man
was, [a]to whom even Abraham the patriarch gave a tenth of the plunder!
5 [b]The sons of Levi who receive the
priestly office have a commandment
according to the law to collect a tenth
from the people—that is, from their
brothers—though they have ⌊also⌋ descended from Abraham.[a] 6 But one
without this[b] lineage collected tithes
from Abraham and blessed [c]the one
who had the promises. 7 Without a
doubt,[c] the inferior is blessed by the
superior. 8 In the one case, men who
will die receive tithes; but in the other
case, [d]⌊Scripture⌋ testifies that he lives.
9 And in a sense Levi himself, who receives tithes, has paid tithes through
Abraham, 10 for he was still within his
forefather[d] when Melchizedek met
him. *[a]Gn 14:20 [b]Nm 18:21 [c]Ac 3:25; Gl 3:16 [d]Heb 5:6*

A Superior Priesthood

11 [a]If, then, perfection came through
the Levitical priesthood (for under it
the people received the law), what further need was there for another priest
to arise in the order of Melchizedek,
and not to be described as being in the
order of Aaron? 12 For when there is a
change of the priesthood, there must
be a change of law as well. 13 For the
One about whom these things are said
belonged to a different tribe, from
which no one has served at the altar.
14 Now it is evident that [b]our Lord
came from Judah, and about that tribe
Moses said nothing concerning priests. *[a]Gl 2:21; Heb 8:7 [b]Is 11:1; Rm 1:3*

15 And this becomes clearer if another priest like Melchizedek arises,
16 who doesn't become a ⌊priest⌋ based
on a legal command concerning physical[e] descent but based on the power of
an indestructible life. 17 For it has been
testified:

**[a]You are a priest forever
in the order of Melchizedek.**[f]

18 So the previous commandment is
annulled because [b]it was weak and
unprofitable 19 (for [c]the law perfected nothing), but [d]a better hope is

[a]**7:5** Lit *have come out of Abraham's loins* [b]**7:6** Lit *their* [c]**7:7** Or *Beyond any dispute* [d]**7:10** Lit *still in his father's loins* [e]**7:16** Or *fleshly* [f]**7:17** Ps 110:4

introduced, through which [e]we draw near to God.

[a] Ps 110:4 [b] Rm 8:3 [c] Rm 3:20; Gl 2:16 [d] Heb 6:18 [e] Rm 5:2

20 None of this ⌊happened⌋ without an oath. For others became priests without an oath, 21 but He with an oath made by the One who said to Him:

> [a]**The Lord has sworn,**
> **and He will not change**
> **His mind,**
> **You are a priest forever.**[a]

22 So Jesus has also become the guarantee of a better covenant.

[a] Ps 110:4

23 Now many have become ⌊Levitical⌋ priests, since they are prevented by death from remaining in office. 24 But because He [a]remains forever, He holds His priesthood permanently. 25 Therefore He is always able to save[b] those who come to God through Him, since He always lives [b]to intercede for them.

[a] Is 9:6-7; Heb 13:8 [b] Is 53:12; Rm 8:34

26 For this is the kind of high priest we need: holy, innocent, undefiled, separated from sinners, [a]and exalted above the heavens. 27 He doesn't need to offer sacrifices every day, as high priests do—[b]first for their own sins, [c]then for those of the people. [d]He did this once for all when He offered Himself. 28 For the law appoints as high priests [e]men who are weak, but the promise of the oath, which came after the law, ⌊appoints⌋ a Son, [f]who has been perfected forever.

[a] Eph 1:20 [b] Lv 16:6 [c] Lv 16:15 [d] Rm 6:10 [e] Heb 5:1-2 [f] Heb 2:10

A Heavenly Priesthood

8 Now the main point of what is being said is this: we have this kind of high priest, [a]who sat down at the right hand of the throne of the Majesty in the heavens, 2 a minister of the sanctuary and [b]the true tabernacle, which the Lord set up, and not man. 3 For every high priest is appointed to offer gifts and sacrifices; therefore [c]it was necessary for this ⌊priest⌋ also to have something to offer. 4 Now if He were on earth, He wouldn't be a priest, since there are those[c] offering the gifts prescribed by the law. 5 These serve as a copy and [d]shadow of the heavenly things, as Moses was warned when he was about to complete the tabernacle. [e]For He said, **Be careful that you make everything according to the pattern that was shown to you on the mountain.**[d] 6 But [f]Jesus[e] has now obtained a superior ministry, and to that degree He is the mediator of a better covenant, which has been legally enacted on better promises.

[a] Col 3:1 [b] Heb 9:11 [c] Eph 5:2 [d] Col 2:17 [e] Ex 25:40 [f] Heb 7:22

A Superior Covenant

7 For if that first ⌊covenant⌋ had been faultless, no opportunity would have been sought for a second one. 8 But finding fault with His people,[f] He says:[g]

> [a]**"Look, the days are coming,"**
> **says the Lord,**
> **"when I will make**
> **a new covenant**
> **with the house of Israel**
> **and with the house of Judah—**
> 9 **not like the covenant**
> **that I made with their fathers**
> **on the day I took them**
> **by their hand**
> **to lead them out of the land**
> **of Egypt.**
> **Because they did not continue**
> **in My covenant,**
> **I disregarded them,"**
> **says the Lord.**
> 10 **"But this is the covenant**
> **that I will make**
> **with the house of Israel**

[a] **7:21** Ps 110:4 [b] **7:25** Or *He is able to save completely* [c] **8:4** Other mss read *priests* [d] **8:5** Ex 25:40 [e] **8:6** Lit *He* [f] **8:8** Lit *with them* [g] **8:8** Other mss read *finding fault, He says to them*

after those days,"
says the Lord:
"I will put My laws
into their minds,
and I will write them
on their hearts,
and [b]I will be their God,
and they will be My people.
11 **And [c]each person**
will not teach
his fellow citizen,[a]
and each his brother, saying,
'Know the Lord,'
because they will all know Me,
from the least to the greatest
of them.
12 **For I will be merciful**
to their wrongdoing,
and I will never again
remember their sins."[b c]

13 By saying, a new ⌊covenant⌋, He has
declared that the first is old. And what
is old and aging is about to disappear.

[a] Jr 31:31-34 [b] Gn 17:7-8; Ezk 37:27 [c] Is 54:13

Old Covenant Ministry

9 Now the first ⌊covenant⌋ also had
regulations for ministry and an
[a]earthly sanctuary. 2 [b]For a tabernacle
was set up; and in the first room,
which is called "the holy place," were
the lampstand, [c]the table, and the presentation loaves. 3 [d]Behind the second
curtain, the tabernacle was called "the
holy of holies." 4 It contained the gold
altar of incense and the ark of the covenant, covered with gold on all sides,
in which there was [e]a gold jar containing the manna, [f]Aaron's rod that bud-
ded, and [g]the tablets of the covenant.
5 [h]The cherubim of glory were above it
overshadowing the mercy seat. It is
not possible to speak about these
things in detail right now.

[a] Ex 25:8 [b] Ex 26:1 [c] Lv 24:5 [d] Ex 40:3 [e] Ex 16:33 [f] Nm 17:10 [g] Dt 10:5 [h] Lv 16:2

6 These things having been set up
this way, [a]the priests enter the first
room repeatedly, performing their
ministry. 7 But the high priest alone enters the second room, and that only
[b]once a year, and never without blood,
which he offers for himself and for the
sins of the people committed in ignorance. 8 [c]The Holy Spirit was making it
clear that [d]the way into the holy of holies had not yet been disclosed while
the first tabernacle was still standing.
9 This is a symbol for the present time,
during which gifts and sacrifices are offered [e]that cannot perfect the worshiper's conscience. 10 They are [f]phys-
ical regulations and only deal with
[g]food, drink, and [h]various washings
imposed until the time of restoration.

[a] Nm 28:3 [b] Ex 30:10 [c] Heb 10:19 [d] Jn 14:6 [e] Gl 3:21 [f] Eph 2:15 [g] Rm 14:17 [h] Lv 11:25; Nm 19:7

New Covenant Ministry

11 Now the •Messiah has appeared,
high priest [a]of the good things that
have come.[d] [b]In the greater and more
perfect tabernacle not made with
hands (that is, not of this creation),
12 He entered the holy of holies once
for all, not by the blood of goats and
calves, [c]but by His own blood, [d]having
obtained eternal redemption. 13 For if
[e]the blood of goats and bulls and [f]the
ashes of a heifer sprinkling those who
are defiled, sanctify for the purification
of the flesh, 14 how much more [g]will
the blood of the Messiah, [h]who
through the eternal Spirit offered Himself without blemish to God, [i]cleanse
our[e] consciences from [j]dead works to
serve the living God?

[a] Heb 10:1 [b] Heb 8:2 [c] Rv 1:5 [d] Dn 9:24 [e] Lv 8:15 [f] Nm 19:9 [g] 1Jn 1:7 [h] Eph 5:2; 1Pt 3:18 [i] Heb 1:3 [j] Heb 6:1

15 [a]Therefore He is the mediator of a
new covenant,[f] [b]so that those who are

[a]**8:11** Other mss read *neighbor* [b]**8:12** Other mss add *and their lawless deeds* [c]**8:8–12** Jr 31:31–34
[d]**9:11** Other mss read *that are to come* [e]**9:14** Other mss read *your* [f]**9:15** The Gk word used here and in vv. 15–18 can be translated *covenant, will,* or *testament.*

called might receive the promise of the
eternal inheritance, [c]because a death
has taken place for redemption from
the transgressions ⌊committed⌋ under
the first covenant. 16 Where a will exists, the death of the testator must be
established. 17 For [d]a will is valid only
when people die, since it is never in
force while the testator is living.
18 [e]That is why even the first covenant
was inaugurated with blood. 19 For
when every commandment had been
proclaimed by Moses to all the people
according to the law, he took the blood
of calves and goats, [f]along with water,
scarlet wool, and hyssop, and sprinkled the scroll itself and all the people,
20 saying, [g]**This is the blood of the
covenant that God has commanded
for you.**[a] 21 In the same way, [h]he sprinkled the tabernacle and all the vessels
of worship with blood. 22 According to
the law almost everything is purified
with blood, and [i]without the shedding
of blood there is no forgiveness.

[a] 1Tm 2:5 [b] Heb 3:1 [c] 1Pt 3:18
[d] Gl 3:15 [e] Ex 24:6 [f] Ex 24:6-8; Lv 14:4
[g] Ex 24:8 [h] Ex 29:12 [i] Lv 17:11

23 Therefore it was necessary for [a]the
copies of the things in the heavens to
be purified with these ⌊sacrifices⌋, but
the heavenly things themselves ⌊to be
purified⌋ with better sacrifices than
these. 24 For [b]the Messiah did not enter a sanctuary made with hands (only
a model[b] of the true one) but into
heaven itself, that [c]He might now appear in the presence of God for us.
25 He did not do this to offer Himself
many times, as the high priest enters
the sanctuary yearly with the blood of
another. 26 Otherwise, He would have
had to suffer many times since the
foundation of the world. But now He
has appeared one time, at [d]the end of
the ages, for the removal of sin by the
sacrifice of Himself. 27 [e]And just as it is
appointed for people to die once—and
after this, judgment— 28 so also [f]the
Messiah, having been offered once to
bear the sins of many, [g]will appear a
second time, not to bear sin, but[c] to
bring salvation to those who are waiting for Him.

[a] Heb 8:5 [b] Heb 6:20
[c] Heb 7:25 [d] Eph 1:10; Gl 4:4; Heb 7:27
[e] Gn 3:19 [f] Mt 26:28; Rm 6:10; 1Pt 2:24
[g] Mt 25:34; Jn 14:3

The Perfect Sacrifice

10 Since the law has ⌊only⌋ [a]a
shadow of the good things to
come, and not the actual form of those
realities, it can never perfect the worshipers by the same sacrifices they
continually offer year after year.
2 Otherwise, wouldn't they have
stopped being offered, since the worshipers, once purified, would no
longer have any consciousness of sins?
3 [b]But in the sacrifices[d] there is a reminder of sins every year. 4 For [c]it is
impossible for the blood of bulls and
goats to take away sins.

[a] Heb 8:5
[b] Lv 16:21,34; Heb 9:7 [c] Mc 6:6

5 Therefore, as He was coming into
the world, He said:

[a]You did not want sacrifice
and offering,
but You prepared a body
for Me.
6 **You did not delight**
in whole burnt offerings
and sin offerings.
7 **Then I said,**
"See, I have come—
it is written about Me
in the volume of the scroll—
to do Your will, O God!"[e]

[a] Ps 40:6-8

8 After He says above, **You did not
desire or delight in sacrifices and offerings, whole burnt offerings and
sin offerings,** (which are offered according to the law), 9 He then says,
See, I have come to do Your will.[f] He

[a]**9:20** Ex 24:8 [b]**9:24** Or *antitype*, or *figure* [c]**9:28** Lit *time, apart from sin,* [d]**10:3** Lit *in them*
[e]**10:5–7** Ps 40:6–8 [f]**10:9** Other mss add *O God*

takes away the first to establish the second. 10 [a]By this will, we have been
sanctified through the offering of the
body of Jesus Christ once for all.

[a]*Jn 17:19; Heb 13:12*

11 Now every priest stands [a]day after
day ministering and offering time after
time the same sacrifices, which can
never take away sins. 12 [b]But this man,
after offering one sacrifice for sins forever, sat down at the right hand of
God. 13 He is now waiting [c]until His
enemies are made His footstool. 14 For
by one offering He has perfected forever those who are sanctified. 15 The
Holy Spirit also testifies to us about
this. For after He had said:

16 [d]**This is the covenant**
that I will make with them
after those days, says the Lord:
I will put My laws
on their hearts,
and I will write them
on their minds,

17 ⌊He adds⌋:

[e]**I will never again remember**
their sins and
their lawless acts.[a]

18 Now where there is forgiveness of
these, there is no longer an offering
for sin.

[a]*Heb 7:27* [b]*Col 3:1* [c]*Ps 110:1* [d]*Jr 31:33* [e]*Jr 31:32*

Exhortations to Godliness

19 Therefore, brothers, since we
have boldness to enter the sanctuary
through the blood of Jesus, 20 by [a]the
new and living way that He has inaugurated for us, through the curtain
(that is, His flesh); 21 and since we have
a great high priest over [b]the house of
God, 22 let us draw near with a true
heart [c]in full assurance of faith, our
hearts sprinkled ⌊clean⌋ from an evil
conscience and [d]our bodies washed in
pure water. 23 Let us hold on to the
confession of our hope without waver-
ing, for [e]He who promised is faithful.
24 And let us be concerned about one
another in order to promote love and
good works, 25 not staying away from
our meetings, as some habitually do,
but encouraging each other, [f]and all
the more as you see [g]the day drawing
near.

[a]*Jn 10:9* [b]*1Tm 3:15* [c]*Eph 3:12* [d]*Ezk 36:25* [e]*1Co 1:9* [f]*Rm 13:11* [g]*2Pt 3:9*

Warning against Willful Sin

26 For [a]if we deliberately sin after receiving the knowledge of the truth,
there no longer remains a sacrifice for
sins, 27 but a terrifying expectation of
judgment, and the fury of a fire about
to consume the adversaries. 28 If anyone disregards Moses' law, he dies
without mercy, based on the testimony
of two or three witnesses. 29 How
much worse punishment, do you think
one will deserve who has trampled on
the Son of God, [b]regarded as profane[b]
the blood of the covenant by which he
was sanctified, [c]and insulted the Spirit
of grace? 30 For we know the One who
has said, [d]**Vengeance belongs to Me,**
I will repay,[c d] and again, [e]**The Lord**
will judge His people.[e] 31 [f]It is a terrifying thing to fall into the hands of the
living God!

[a]*2Pt 2:20; 1Jn 5:16* [b]*1Co 11:29* [c]*Mt 12:31* [d]*Dt 32:35* [e]*Ps 50:4* [f]*Is 33:14*

32 Remember the earlier days when,
after you had been enlightened, you
endured [a]a hard struggle with sufferings. 33 Sometimes you were publicly
exposed to taunts and afflictions, and
at other times [b]you were companions
of those who were treated that way.
34 For you sympathized with the prisoners[f] and [c]accepted with joy the con-
fiscation of your possessions, knowing
that you yourselves have a better and
enduring possession.[g] 35 So don't throw

[a]**10:16–17** Jr 31:33–34 [b]**10:29** Or *ordinary* [c]**10:30** Other mss add *says the Lord* [d]**10:30** Dt 32:35 [e]**10:30** Dt 32:36 [f]**10:34** Other mss read *sympathized with my imprisonment* [g]**10:34** Other mss add *in heaven*

away your confidence, which has a great reward. 36 [d]For you need endurance, so that after you have done God's will, [e]you may receive what was promised.

[a]Php 1:29-30 [b]Php 1:7 [c]Mt 5:12 [d]Heb 12:1 [e]Col 3:24

37 For in [a]yet **a very little while,**
[b]the Coming One will come
and not delay.
38 **But My righteous one**[a] **will live**
by faith;
and if he draws back,
My soul has no pleasure
in him.[b]

39 But we are not those who draw back and are destroyed, but those who have faith and obtain life.

[a]Lk 18:8 [b]Hab 2:3-4

Heroes of Faith

11 Now faith is the reality[c] of what is hoped for, the proof[d] [a]of what is not seen. 2 For by it our ancestors were approved.

[a]Rm 8:24

3 By faith we understand that [a]the universe was[e] created by the word[f] of God, so that what is seen has been made from things that are not visible.

[a]Jn 1:3

4 By faith [a]Abel offered to God a better sacrifice than Cain ⌊did⌋. By this he was approved as a righteous man, because God approved his gifts, and even though he is dead, he still speaks through this.

[a]Gn 4:4

5 By faith, [a]Enoch was taken away so that he did not experience death, and **he was not to be found because God took him away.**[g] For prior to his transformation he was approved, having pleased God. 6 Now [b]without faith it is impossible to please God, for the one who draws near to Him must believe that He exists and rewards those who seek Him.

[a]Gn 5:22,24 [b]Jn 3:18,36

7 By faith [a]Noah, after being warned about what was not yet seen, in reverence built an ark to deliver his family. By this he condemned the world and became an heir of [b]the righteousness that comes by faith.

[a]Gn 6:13 [b]Rm 3:22

8 By faith Abraham, when he was called, obeyed and went out to a place he was going to receive as an inheritance; he went out, not knowing where he was going. 9 By faith he stayed as a foreigner in the land of promise, [a]living in tents with Isaac and Jacob, co-heirs of the same promise. 10 For he was looking forward to the city that has foundations, [b]whose architect and builder is God.

[a]Gn 12:8 [b]Is 14:32

11 By faith even [a]Sarah herself, when she was barren, received power to conceive offspring, even though she was past the age, since she[h] considered that the One who had promised was faithful. 12 And therefore from one man—in fact, [b]from one as good as dead—came offspring as numerous as the stars of heaven and as innumerable as the grains of sand by the seashore.

[a]Gn 17:19 [b]Rm 4:19

13 These all died in faith without having received the promises, but [a]they saw them from a distance, greeted them, and [b]confessed that they were foreigners and temporary residents on the earth. 14 Now those who say such things [c]make it clear that they are seeking a homeland. 15 If they had been remembering that land they came from, they would have had opportunity to return. 16 But they now aspire to a better land—a heavenly one. Therefore God is not ashamed [d]to be called their God, for [e]He has prepared a city for them.

[a]Gn 49:10; Nm 24:17 [b]Gn 47:9 [c]Heb 13:14 [d]Ex 3:6,15 [e]Php 3:20

[a]**10:38** Other mss read *the righteous one* [b]**10:37–38** Is 26:20 LXX; Hab 2:3–4 [c]**11:1** Or *assurance* [d]**11:1** Or *conviction* [e]**11:3** Or *the worlds were*, or *the ages were* [f]**11:3** Or *voice*, or *utterance* [g]**11:5** Gn 5:21–24 [h]**11:11** Or *By faith Abraham, even though he was past age—and Sarah herself was barren—received the ability to procreate since he*

17 By faith [a]Abraham, when he was
tested, offered up Isaac; he who had received the promises [b]was offering up
his unique son, 18 about whom it had
been said, [c]**In Isaac your seed will be
called.**[a] 19 He considered God to be
able even to raise someone from the
dead, from which he also got him back
as an illustration.[b] *[a] Gn 22:1 [b] Jms 2:21*
[c] Gn 21:12

20 By faith [a]Isaac blessed Jacob and
Esau concerning things to come. 21 By
faith Jacob, when he was dying,
[b]blessed each of the sons of Joseph,
and, **he** [c]**worshiped, leaning on the
top of his staff.**[c] 22 By faith [d]Joseph, as
he was nearing the end of his life,
mentioned the exodus of the sons of Israel and gave instructions concerning
his bones. *[a] Gn 27:27 [b] Gn 48:5*
[c] Gn 47:31 [d] Gn 50:24

23 By faith [a]Moses, after he was born,
was hidden by his parents for three
months, because they saw that the
child was beautiful, and they didn't
fear the king's [b]edict. 24 By faith Moses,
when he had grown up, refused to be
called the son of Pharaoh's daughter
25 [c]and chose to suffer with the people
of God rather than to enjoy the short-
lived pleasure of sin. 26 For he considered reproach for the sake of the •Mes-
siah to be greater wealth than the
treasures of Egypt, since his attention
was on the reward. *[a] Ex 2:2*
[b] Ex 1:16 [c] Ps 84:10

27 By faith [a]he left Egypt behind, not
being afraid of the king's anger, for he
persevered, as one who sees Him who
is invisible. 28 By faith [b]he instituted
the •Passover and the sprinkling of the
blood, so that the destroyer of the firstborn might not touch them. 29 By faith
they crossed the Red Sea as though
they were on dry land. When the Egyptians attempted to do this, they were
drowned. *[a] Ex 10:29 [b] Ex 12:21*

30 By faith [a]the walls of Jericho fell
down after being encircled for seven
days. 31 By faith [b]Rahab the prostitute
received the spies in peace and didn't
perish with those who disobeyed.
[a] Jos 6:20 [b] Jms 2:25

32 And what more can I say? Time is
too short for me to tell about [a]Gideon,
[b]Barak, [c]Samson, [d]Jephthah, of [e]David
and [f]Samuel and the prophets, 33 who
by faith conquered kingdoms, administered justice, obtained promises, [g]shut
the mouths of lions, 34 [h]quenched the
raging of fire, [i]escaped the edge of the
sword, [j]gained strength after being
weak, became mighty in battle, and
[k]put foreign armies to flight. 35 [l]Wo-
men received their dead raised to life
again. Some men were tortured, not
accepting release, so that they might
gain a better resurrection, 36 and others experienced mockings and scourg-
ings, as well as [m]bonds and imprisonment. 37 [n]They were stoned,[d] they
were sawed in two, they died by the
sword, [o]they wandered about in
sheepskins, in goatskins, destitute, afflicted, and mistreated. 38 The world
was not worthy of them. They wandered in deserts, mountains, [p]caves,
and holes in the ground. *[a] Jdg 6:11*
[b] Jdg 4:6 [c] Jdg 13:24 [d] Jdg 11:1 [e] 1Sm 16:1
[f] 1Sm 1:20 [g] 1Sm 17:34; Dn 6:22 [h] Dn 3:25
[i] 1Kg 19:3; 2Kg 6:16 [j] 2Kg 20:7 [k] 1Sm 14:13
[l] 1Kg 17:22; 2Kg 4:35 [m] Jr 20:2 [n] 1Kg 21:13;
2Ch 24:21 [o] 2Kg 1:8 [p] 1Kg 18:4

39 All these were approved through
their faith, but they did not receive
what was promised, 40 since God had
provided something better for us, so
that they would not be [a]made perfect
without us. *[a] Rm 11:26*

The Call to Endurance

12 Therefore since we also have
such a large cloud of witnesses
surrounding us, let us lay aside every
weight and the sin that so easily

[a]**11:18** Gn 21:12 [b]**11:19** Or *foreshadowing, or parable, or type* [c]**11:21** Gn 47:31 [d]**11:37** Other mss add *they were tempted*

ensnares us, and run with endurance
the race that lies before us, 2 [a]keeping
our eyes on Jesus,[a] the source and per-
fecter[b] of our faith, [b]who for the joy that
lay before Him[c] endured a cross and despised the shame, and [c]has sat down at
the right hand of God's throne.

[a] 2Co 3:18 [b] 1Pt 1:11 [c] Ps 110:1

Fatherly Discipline

3 [a]For consider Him who endured
such hostility from sinners against
Himself, [b]so that you won't grow
weary and lose heart. 4 In struggling
against sin, you have not yet resisted to
the point of shedding your blood. 5 And
you have forgotten the exhortation
that addresses you as sons:

> [c]**My son, do not take**
> **the Lord's discipline lightly,**
> **or faint when you are reproved**
> **by Him;**
> 6 **for the Lord [d]disciplines**
> **the one He loves,**
> **and punishes every son**
> **whom He receives.**[d]

[a] Jn 15:20 [b] Gl 6:9 [c] Jb 5:17; Pr 3:11-12 [d] Ps 94:12

7 Endure it as discipline: God is dealing
with you as sons. For what son is there
whom a father does not discipline?
8 But if you are without discipline—
[a]which all[e] receive[f]—then you are ille-
gitimate children and not sons. 9 Furthermore, we had natural fathers discipline us, and we respected them.
Shouldn't we submit even more to the
Father of spirits and live? 10 For they
disciplined us for a short time based on
what seemed good to them, but He
does it for our benefit, [b]so that we can
share His holiness. 11 No discipline
seems enjoyable at the time, but painful. Later on, however, it yields [c]the
fruit of peace and righteousness to
those who have been trained by it.

[a] Ps 73:14 [b] Lv 19:2 [c] Jms 3:18

12 Therefore [a]strengthen your tired
hands and weakened knees, 13 and
make straight paths for your feet, so
that what is lame may not be dislo-
cated,[g] [b]but healed instead.

[a] Is 35:3 [b] Gl 6:1

Warning against Rejecting God's Grace

14 Pursue peace with everyone, and
holiness—[a]without it no one will see
the Lord. 15 See to it that no one falls
short of the grace of God [b]and that no
root of bitterness springs up, causing
trouble and by it, defiling many. 16 And
see that there isn't any immoral or irreverent person like Esau, [c]who sold
his birthright in exchange for one
meal. 17 For you know that later,
[d]when he wanted to inherit the blessing, he was rejected because he didn't
find any opportunity for repentance,
though he sought it with tears.

[a] Mt 5:8 [b] Dt 29:18 [c] Gn 25:33 [d] Gn 27:34

18 For you have not come to what
could be touched, to a [a]blazing fire, to
darkness, gloom, and storm, 19 to the
blast of a trumpet, and the sound of
words. (Those who heard it [b]begged
that not another word be spoken to
them, 20 for they could not bear what
was commanded: [c]**And if even an animal touches the mountain, it must
be stoned!**[h] 21 And the appearance was
so terrifying that Moses said, [d]**I am terrified and trembling.**[i]) 22 Instead, you
have come [e]to Mount Zion, to the city
of the living God (the heavenly Jerusalem), [f]to myriads of angels in festive
gathering, 23 to the assembly of the
firstborn whose names have been written[j] in heaven, to God who is the judge
of all, to the spirits of righteous people
[g]made perfect, 24 to Jesus (mediator of
a new covenant), and to [h]the sprinkled

[a]**12:2** Or *looking to Jesus* [b]**12:2** Or *the founder and completer* [c]**12:2** Or *who instead of the joy lying before Him*; that is, the joy of heaven [d]**12:6** Pr 3:11–12 [e]**12:8** In context *all* refers to Christians. [f]**12:8** Lit *discipline, of which all have become participants* [g]**12:13** Or *so that the lame will not be turned aside* [h]**12:20** Ex 19:12 [i]**12:21** Dt 9:19 [j]**12:23** Or *registered*

blood, which says better things [i]than
the ⌊blood⌋ of Abel.

[a]Dt 4:11 [b]Ex 20:19 [c]Ex 19:12
[d]Dt 9:19 [e]Gl 4:26; Php 3:20; Rv 3:12
[f]Jd 14 [g]Php 3:12 [h]1Pt 1:2 [i]Gn 4:10

25 See that you do not reject the One
who speaks; for if they did not escape
when they rejected Him [a]who warned
them on earth, even less will we if we
turn away from Him who warns us
from heaven. 26 [b]His voice shook the
earth at that time, but now He has
promised, [c]**Yet once more I will**
shake not only the earth but also
heaven.[a] 27 Now this expression, "Yet
once more," indicates [d]the removal of
what can be shaken—that is, created
things—so that what is not shaken
might remain. 28 Therefore, since we
are receiving a kingdom that cannot be
shaken, let us hold on to grace.[b] By it,
we may serve God acceptably, with
reverence and awe; 29 for [e]our God is a
consuming fire.

[a]Nm 16 [b]Ex 19:18
[c]Hg 2:6 [d]Ps 102:26; Mt 24:35
[e]Is 66:15; Heb 10:27

Final Exhortations

13 Let brotherly love continue.
2 [a]Don't neglect to show hospitality, for by doing this [b]some have
welcomed angels as guests without
knowing it. 3 [c]Remember the prisoners, as though you were in prison with
them, and the mistreated, as though
you yourselves were suffering bodily.[c]
4 Marriage must be respected by all,
and the marriage bed kept undefiled,
because God will judge immoral people and adulterers. 5 Your life should
be free from the love of money. Be satisfied with what you have, for He
Himself has said, [d]**I will never leave**
you or forsake you.[d] 6 Therefore, we
may boldly say:

[e]**The Lord is my helper;**
I will not be afraid.
What can man do to me?[e]

[a]Mt 25:35 [b]Gn 18:3
[c]Mt 25:36; Rm 12:15
[d]Dt 31:6,8 [e]Ps 118:6

7 Remember your leaders who have
spoken God's word to you. As you carefully observe the outcome of their
lives, imitate their faith. 8 Jesus Christ
is [a]the same yesterday, today, and forever. 9 Don't be led astray by various
kinds of strange teachings; for it is
good for the heart to be established by
grace and not by foods, since those involved in them have not benefited.
10 [b]We have an altar from which those
who serve the tabernacle do not have
a right to eat. 11 For [c]the bodies of
those animals whose blood is brought
into the holy of holies by the high
priest as a sin offering are burned outside the camp. 12 Therefore Jesus also
[d]suffered outside the gate, so that He
might sanctify[f] the people by His own
blood. 13 Let us then go to Him outside
the camp, bearing [e]His disgrace. 14 For
here we do not have an enduring city;
instead, we seek the one to come.
15 Therefore, through Him let us continually offer up to God [f]a sacrifice of
praise, that is, the fruit of our lips that
confess His name. 16 Don't neglect to
do good and to share, for God is
pleased with such sacrifices. 17 Obey
your leaders[g] and submit to them, for
[g]they keep watch over your souls as
those who will give an account, so that
they can do this with joy and not with
grief, for that would be unprofitable for
you. 18 Pray for us; for we are convinced that we have a clear conscience, wanting to conduct ourselves
honorably in everything. 19 And I especially urge you to pray[h] that I may be
restored to you very soon.

[a]Heb 1:12; Rv 1:4 [b]1Co 9:13
[c]Lv 4:11-12,21 [d]Jn 19:17
[e]1Pt 4:14 [f]Ps 50:14 [g]Ezk 3:17

[a]**12:26** Hg 2:6 [b]**12:28** Or *let us give thanks,* or *let us have grace* [c]**13:3** Or *mistreated, since you are also in a body* [d]**13:5** Dt 31:6 [e]**13:6** Ps 118:6 [f]**13:12** Or *set apart,* or *consecrate* [g]**13:17** Or *rulers* [h]**13:19** Lit *to do this*

Benediction and Farewell

20 Now may the God of peace, who
brought up from the dead our Lord
Jesus—[a]the great Shepherd of the
sheep—[b]with the blood of the everlasting covenant, 21 equip[a] you with all that
is good to do His will, working in us
what is pleasing in His sight, through
Jesus Christ, to whom be glory forever
and ever.[b] •Amen. *[a] Jn 10:11 [b] Mt 26:28*

22 Brothers, I urge you to receive this
word of exhortation, for I have written
to you in few words. 23 Be aware that
[a]our brother Timothy has been released. If he comes soon enough, he
will be with me when I see you.
24 Greet all your leaders and all the
saints. Those who are from Italy greet
you. 25 Grace be with all of you.
[a] 1Th 3:2

JAMES

Greeting

1 James, a slave of God and of the
Lord Jesus Christ:
[a]To the 12 tribes [b]in the Dispersion.
Greetings. *[a] Ac 26:7 [b] Jn 7:35; Ac 2:5*

Trials and Maturity

2 Consider it a great joy, my brothers,
whenever you experience various trials, 3 knowing that the testing of your
faith produces endurance. 4 But endurance must do its complete work, so
that you may be mature and complete,
lacking nothing.

5 Now [a]if any of you lacks wisdom,
[b]he should ask God, who gives to all
generously and without criticizing,
and it will be given to him. 6 [c]But let
him ask in faith without doubting. For
the doubter is like the surging sea,
driven and tossed by the wind. 7 That
person should not expect to receive
anything from the Lord. 8 An indeci-
sive man is unstable in all his ways.
[a] Jb 28:12,28; Pr 3:5-7 [b] Jn 14:13
[c] Mt 21:21-22; 1Jn 5:14-15

9 The brother of humble circumstances should boast in his exaltation;
10 but the one who is rich ⌊should
boast⌋ in his humiliation, because he
will pass away like a flower of the field.
11 For the sun rises with its scorching
heat and dries up the grass; its flower
falls off, and its beautiful appearance is
destroyed. In the same way, the rich
man will wither away while pursuing
his activities.

12 [a]Blessed is a man who endures trials,[c] because when he passes the test
he will receive [b]the crown of life that
He[d] has promised to those who love
Him. *[a] Mt 5:11-12; Heb 12:5*
[b] Lk 22:28-30; Rv 2:10

13 No one undergoing a trial should
say, "I am being tempted by God." For
God is not tempted by evil,[e] and He
Himself doesn't tempt anyone. 14 But
each person is tempted when he is
drawn away and enticed by his own
evil desires. 15 Then after desire has
conceived, it gives birth to sin, and
when sin is fully grown, it gives birth
to death.

16 Don't be deceived, my dearly
loved brothers. 17 Every generous act
and every perfect gift is from above,
coming down from the Father of lights;
[a]with Him there is no variation or

[a]**13:21** Or *perfect* [b]**13:21** Other mss omit *and ever* [c]**1:12** Lit *trial,* used as a collective [d]**1:12** Other mss read *that the Lord* [e]**1:13** Or *evil persons,* or *evil things*

shadow cast by turning. 18 [b]By His own
choice, He gave us a new birth by the
message of truth[a] so that we would be
the [c]•firstfruits of His creatures.
[a]*Nm 23:19* [b]*Jn 1:13; 1Pt 1:23* [c]*Rv 14:4*

Hearing and Doing the Word

19 My dearly loved brothers, understand this: everyone must be quick to
hear, slow to speak, and slow to anger,
20 for man's anger does not accomplish
God's righteousness. 21 Therefore, rid-
ding yourselves of all moral filth and
evil excess, humbly receive the im-
planted word, [a]which is able to save
you.[b] [a]*Rm 1:16; 1Co 15:2*

22 But be doers of the word and not
hearers only, deceiving yourselves.
23 Because [a]if anyone is a hearer of the
word and not a doer, he is like a man
looking at his own face[c] in a mirror;
24 for he looks at himself, goes away,
and right away forgets what kind of
man he was. 25 But [b]the one who looks
intently into the perfect law of freedom and perseveres in it, and is not a
forgetful hearer but a doer who
acts—[c]this person will be blessed in
what he does. [a]*Lk 6:47* [b]*2Co 3:18* [c]*Jn 13:17*

26 If anyone[d] thinks he is religious,
without controlling his tongue but deceiving his heart, his religion is useless. 27 Pure and undefiled religion
before our[e] God and Father is this: [a]to
look after orphans and widows in their
distress [b]and to keep oneself unstained
by the world. [a]*1Tm 1:5* [b]*Gl 1:4; Eph 2:2*

The Sin of Favoritism

2 My brothers, hold your faith in
our [a]glorious Lord Jesus Christ
without [b]showing favoritism. 2 For
suppose a man comes into your meeting wearing a gold ring, dressed in
fine clothes, and a poor man dressed
in dirty clothes also comes in. 3 If you
look with favor on the man wearing
the fine clothes so that you say, "Sit
here in a good place," and yet you say
to the poor man, "Stand over there,"
or, "Sit here on the floor by my footstool," 4 haven't you discriminated
among yourselves and become judges
with evil thoughts? [a]*1Co 2:8; Php 2:9*
[b]*Lv 19:15*

5 Listen, my dear brothers: Didn't
God choose the poor in this world to
be rich in faith and heirs of the kingdom [a]that He has promised to those
who love Him? 6 Yet you dishonored
that poor man. Don't the rich oppress
you and drag you into the courts?
7 Don't they blaspheme the noble
name that you bear? [a]*Pr 8:17; Mt 5:3*

8 If you really carry out the royal law
prescribed in Scripture, [a]**Love your
neighbor as yourself,**[f] you are doing
well. 9 But if you show favoritism, you
commit sin and are convicted by the
law as transgressors. 10 For whoever
keeps the entire law, yet fails in one
point, [b]is guilty of ⌊breaking it⌋ all.
11 For He who said, [c]**Do not commit
adultery,**[g] also said, **Do not murder.**[h]
So if you do not commit adultery, but
you do murder, you are a lawbreaker.
[a]*Lv 19:18* [b]*Dt 27:26* [c]*Ex 20:13-14*

12 Speak and act as those who will be
judged by the law of freedom. 13 For
judgment is without mercy to the one
who hasn't shown mercy. Mercy tri-
umphs over judgment.

Faith and Works

14 What good is it, my brothers, if
someone says he has faith, but does
not have works? Can his faith[i] save
him?

15 If a brother or sister is without
clothes and lacks daily food, 16 and one
of you says to them, "Go in peace,
keep warm, and eat well," but you

[a]**1:18** *message of truth* = the gospel [b]**1:21** Lit *save your souls* [c]**1:23** Lit *at the face of his birth*
[d]**1:26** Other mss add *among you* [e]**1:27** Or *before the* [f]**2:8** Lv 19:18 [g]**2:11** Ex 20:14; Dt 5:18
[h]**2:11** Ex 20:13; Dt 5:17 [i]**2:14** Or *Can faith,* or *Can that faith,* or *Can such faith*

don't give them what the body needs, what good is it? 17 In the same way faith, if it doesn't have works, is dead by itself.

18 But someone will say, "You have faith, and I have works."[a] Show me your faith without works, and I will show you faith from my works.[b] 19 You believe that God is one; you do well. [a]The demons also believe—and they shudder.

[a] Mt 8:29

20 Foolish man! Are you willing to learn that [a]faith without works is useless? 21 Wasn't Abraham our father justified by works [b]when he offered Isaac his son on the altar? 22 You see that faith was active together with his works, and by works, faith was perfected. 23 So the Scripture was fulfilled that says, [c]**Abraham believed God, and it was credited to him for righteousness,**[c] and he was called [d]God's friend. 24 You see that a man is justified by works and not by faith alone. 25 And in the same way, [e]wasn't Rahab the prostitute also justified by works when she received the messengers and sent them out by a different route? 26 For just as the body without the spirit is dead, so also faith without works is dead.

[a] Gl 5:6 [b] Gn 22:9 [c] Gn 15:6 [d] 2Ch 20:7 [e] Heb 11:31

Controlling the Tongue

3 [a]Not many should become teachers, my brothers, [b]knowing that we will receive a stricter judgment; 2 for [c]we all stumble in many ways. [d]If anyone does not stumble in what he says,[d] [e]he is a mature man who is also able to control his whole body.[e]

[a] Mt 23:8 [b] Lk 6:37 [c] Ec 7:20; 1Jn 1:8 [d] Ps 34:13 [e] Mt 12:37

3 Now when we put bits into the mouths of horses to make them obey us, we also guide the whole animal.[f] 4 And consider ships: though very large and driven by fierce winds, they are guided by a very small rudder wherever the will of the pilot directs. 5 So too, though the tongue is a small part ⌊of the body⌋, it boasts great things. Consider how large a forest a small fire ignites. 6 And the tongue is a fire. The tongue, a world of unrighteousness, is placed among the parts of our ⌊bodies⌋; [a]it pollutes the whole body, sets the course of life on fire, and is set on fire by •hell.

[a] Mt 15:11,18-20

7 For every creature—animal or bird, reptile or fish—is tamed and has been tamed by man, 8 but no man can tame the tongue. It is a restless evil, full of deadly poison. 9 With it we bless our[g] Lord and Father, and with it we curse men [a]who are made in God's likeness. 10 Out of the same mouth come blessing and cursing. My brothers, these things should not be this way. 11 Does a spring pour out sweet and bitter water from the same opening? 12 Can a fig tree produce olives, my brothers, or a grapevine ⌊produce⌋ figs? Neither can a saltwater spring yield fresh water.

[a] Gn 1:26

The Wisdom from Above

13 [a]Who is wise and understanding among you? He should show his works by good conduct with wisdom's gentleness. 14 But if you have [b]bitter envy and selfish ambition in your heart, don't brag and lie in defiance of the truth. 15 [c]Such wisdom does not come down from above, but is earthly, sensual, demonic. 16 For [d]where envy and selfish ambition exist, there is disorder and every kind of evil. 17 But [e]the wisdom from above is first pure, then peace-loving, gentle, compliant, full of mercy and good fruits, [f]without favoritism and hypocrisy. 18 [g]And the fruit of righteousness is sown in peace by those who make peace.

[a] Jr 9:23; Gl 6:4 [b] Rm 13:13 [c] Php 3:19 [d] 1Co 3:3 [e] 1Co 2:6 [f] 1Pt 1:22 [g] Mt 5:9

[a]**2:18** The quotation may end here or after v. 18b or v. 19. [b]**2:18** Other mss read *Show me your faith from your works, and from my works I will show you my faith.* [c]**2:23** Gn 15:6 [d]**3:2** Lit *in word* [e]**3:2** Lit *to bridle the whole body* [f]**3:3** Lit *whole body* [g]**3:9** Or *bless the*

Proud or Humble

4 What is the source of the wars and the fights among you? Don't they come from the cravings that are at war within you?[a] 2 You desire and do not have. You murder and covet and cannot obtain. You fight and war. You do not have because [a]you do not ask. 3 [b]You ask and don't receive [c]because you ask wrongly, so that you may spend it on your desires for pleasure. *[a]Jn 14:13-14 [b]Jb 27:9 [c]Ps 66:18*

4 Adulteresses![b] Do you not know that [a]friendship with the world is hostility toward God? So [b]whoever wants to be the world's friend becomes God's enemy. 5 Or do you think it's without reason the Scripture says that [c]the Spirit He has caused to live in us yearns jealously?[c] *[a]1Jn 2:15 [b]Gl 1:10 [c]1Co 6:19; 2Co 6:16*

6 But He gives greater grace. Therefore He says:

> [a]**God resists the proud,**
> **but gives grace**
> **to the humble.**[d]

[a]Ps 138:6; Pr 3:34

7 Therefore, submit to God. But [a]resist the Devil, and he will flee from you. 8 [b]Draw near to God, and He will draw near to you. Cleanse your hands, sinners, and purify your hearts, double-minded people! 9 Be miserable and mourn and weep. Your laughter must change to mourning and your joy to sorrow. 10 Humble yourselves before the Lord, and He will exalt you. *[a]Eph 4:27 [b]Is 55:6-7*

11 Don't criticize one another, brothers. He who criticizes a brother or judges his brother criticizes the law and judges the law. But if you judge the law, you are not a doer of the law but a judge. 12 There is one lawgiver and judge[e] [a]who is able to save and to destroy. But who are you to judge your neighbor? *[a]Mt 10:28*

Our Will and His Will

13 Come now, you who say, "Today or tomorrow we will travel to such and such a city and spend a year there and do business and make a profit." 14 You don't even know what tomorrow will bring—what your life will be! For you are a bit of smoke that appears for a little while, then vanishes.

15 Instead, you should say, "If the Lord wills, we will live and do this or that." 16 But as it is, you boast in your arrogance. All such boasting is evil. 17 So, [a]for the person who knows to do good and doesn't do it, it is a sin. *[a]Lk 12:47*

Warning to the Rich

5 Come now, you rich people! Weep and wail over the miseries that are coming on you. 2 Your wealth is ruined: your clothes are moth-eaten; 3 your silver and gold are corroded, and their corrosion will be a witness against you and will eat your flesh like fire. [a]You stored up treasure in the last days! 4 Look! [b]The pay that you withheld from the workers who reaped your fields cries out, and [c]the outcry of the harvesters has reached the ears of the Lord of Hosts.[f] 5 You have lived luxuriously on the land and have indulged yourselves. You have fattened your hearts for[g] the day of slaughter. 6 You have condemned—you have murdered—the righteous man; he does not resist you. *[a]Rm 2:5 [b]Lv 19:13; Mal 3:5 [c]Dt 24:15*

Waiting for the Lord

7 Therefore, brothers, be patient until the Lord's coming. See how the farmer

[a]**4:1** Lit *war in your members* [b]**4:4** Other mss read *Adulterers and adulteresses* [c]**4:5** Or *He who caused the Spirit to live in us yearns jealously,* or *the spirit He caused to live in us yearns jealously,* or *He jealously yearns for the Spirit He made to live in us* [d]**4:6** Pr 3:34 [e]**4:12** Other mss omit *and judge*
[f]**5:4** Gk *Sabaoth*; this word is a transliteration of the Hb word for *Hosts*, or *Armies*. [g]**5:5** Or *hearts in*

waits for the precious fruit of the earth
and is patient with it until it receives
[a]the early and the late rains. 8 You also
must be patient. Strengthen your
hearts, [b]because the Lord's coming is
near. *[a] Dt 11:14*
[b] Php 4:5

9 Brothers, do not complain about
one another, so that you will not be
judged. Look, the judge [a]stands at the
door! *[a] Mt 24:33*

10 Brothers, [a]take the prophets who
spoke in the Lord's name as an example of suffering and patience. 11 See,
we count as blessed those who have
endured.[a] You have heard of [b]Job's endurance and have seen [c]the outcome
from the Lord: [d]the Lord is very compassionate and merciful. *[a] Mt 5:12*
[b] Jb 1:21 [c] Jb 42:10
[d] Ex 34:6; Rm 2:4

Truthful Speech

12 Now above all, my brothers, [a]do
not swear, either by heaven or by earth
or with any other oath. Your "yes"
must be "yes," and your "no" must be
"no," so that you won't fall under judgment.[b] *[a] Mt 5:34*

Effective Prayer

13 Is anyone among you suffering? He
should pray. Is anyone cheerful? He
should sing praises. 14 Is anyone among
you sick? He should call for the [a]elders
of the church, and they should pray
over him after [b]anointing him with olive oil in the name of the Lord. 15 The
prayer of faith will save the sick person,
and the Lord will raise him up; [c]and if
he has committed sins, he will be forgiven. 16 Therefore, confess your sins to
one another and pray for one another,
so that you may be healed. The intense
prayer of the righteous is very powerful. 17 Elijah was a man with a nature
like ours; yet [d]he prayed earnestly that
it would not rain, and for three years
and six months it did not rain on the
land. 18 Then he prayed again, and the
sky gave rain and the land produced its
fruit. *[a] 1Tm 5:17 [b] Mk 6:13 [c] Mt 9:2 [d] 1Kg 17:1*

19 My brothers, if any among you
strays from the truth, and someone
turns him back, 20 he should know that
whoever turns a sinner from the error
of his way [a]will save his •life from
death and [b]cover a multitude of sins.
[a] 1Tm 4:16 [b] Ps 32:1

[a]**5:11** Or *have persevered* [b]**5:12** Other mss read *fall into hypocrisy*

1 PETER

Greeting

1 Peter, an apostle of Jesus Christ:
To the temporary residents [a]of the
Dispersion in the provinces of Pontus,
Galatia, Cappadocia, Asia, and
Bithynia, chosen 2 [b]according to the
foreknowledge of God the Father and
[c]set apart by the Spirit for obedience
and ⌊for the⌋ sprinkling [d]with the blood
of Jesus Christ. *[a] Ac 2:5,9 [b] Rm 8:29*
[c] 2Th 2:13 [d] Heb 10:22

May grace and peace be multiplied
to you.

A Living Hope

3 Blessed be the God and Father of our
Lord Jesus Christ. According to His
great mercy, He has [a]given us a new
birth into a living hope [b]through the resurrection of Jesus Christ from the dead,
4 and into an inheritance that is imperishable, uncorrupted, and unfading,
kept in heaven for you, 5 [c]who are being
protected by God's power through faith
for a salvation that is ready to be revealed in the last time. 6 [d]You rejoice in
this,[a] though now for a short time you
have had to be distressed by various trials 7 so that the genuineness of your
faith—more valuable than gold, which
perishes though [e]refined by fire—may
result in[b] praise, glory, and honor at the
revelation of Jesus Christ. 8 [f]You love
Him, though you have not seen Him.
[g]And though not seeing Him now, you
believe in Him and rejoice with inexpressible and glorious joy, 9 because you
are receiving the goal of your[c] faith, the
salvation of your souls.[d] *[a] Jms 1:18*
[b] 1Th 4:14 [c] Jn 10:28 [d] Rm 12:12
[e] Is 48:10 [f] 1Jn 4:20 [g] Jn 20:29

10 [a]Concerning this salvation, the
prophets who prophesied about the
grace that would come to you searched
and carefully investigated. 11 They inquired into what time or what circumstances[e] [b]the Spirit of Christ within
them was indicating when He testified
in advance [c]to the messianic sufferings[f] and the glories that would follow.[g]
12 [d]It was revealed to them that they
were [e]not serving themselves but you
concerning things that have now been
announced to you through those who
preached the gospel to you by [f]the
Holy Spirit sent from heaven. [g]Angels
desire to look into these things.
[a] Dn 2:44; Hg 2:7; Zch 6:12 [b] Gl 4:6
[c] Ps 22:6; Is 53:3 [d] Dn 12:9
[e] Heb 11:39 [f] Ac 2:4 [g] Eph 3:10; 6:12

A Call to Holy Living

13 Therefore, get your minds ready
for action,[h] being self-disciplined, and
set your hope completely on the grace
to be brought to you [a]at the revelation
of Jesus Christ. 14 As obedient children,
do not be conformed to the desires of
your former ignorance 15 but, as the
One who called you is holy, you also
are to be holy in all your conduct; 16 for
it is written, [b]**Be holy, because I am
holy.**[i] *[a] Lk 17:30 [b] Lv 11:44*

17 And if you address as Father the
One who judges impartially based on
each one's work, you are to conduct
yourselves in reverence during this
time [a]of temporary residence. 18 For
you know that you were redeemed
from your empty way of life [b]inherited
from the fathers, not with perishable
things, like silver or gold, 19 but [c]with

[a]**1:6** Or *In this (fact) rejoice* [b]**1:7** Lit *may be found for* [c]**1:9** Other mss read *our,* or they omit the possessive pronoun [d]**1:9** Or *your lives* [e]**1:11** Or *inquired about the person or time* [f]**1:11** Or *the sufferings of Christ* [g]**1:11** Lit *the glories after that* [h]**1:13** Lit *Therefore, gird the loins of your minds* [i]**1:16** Lv 11:44–45; 19:2; 20:7

the precious blood of Christ, [d]like that
of a lamb without defect or blemish.
20 [e]He was destined[a] before the foundation of the world, but was revealed [f]at
the end of the times for you 21 who
through Him are believers in God,
who raised Him from the dead and
[g]gave Him glory, so that your faith and
hope are in God.

[a] 2Co 5:6; Heb 11:13 [b] Ezk 20:18; 1Pt 4:3 [c] Mt 26:28 [d] Ex 12:5; Jn 1:29 [e] Ti 1:2-3 [f] Gl 4:4 [g] Php 2:9

22 By obedience to the truth,[b] having
purified yourselves[c] for sincere love
of the brothers, love one another
earnestly from a pure[d] heart, 23 [a]since
you have been born again—not of perishable seed but of imperishable—
[b]through the living and enduring word
of God. 24 For

[c]All flesh is like grass,
and all its glory like a flower
of the grass.
The grass withers,
and the flower drops off,
25 **[d]but the word of the Lord**
endures forever.[e]

And this is the word that was
preached as the gospel to you.

[a] 1Jn 3:9 [b] Jn 1:13 [c] Is 40:6-8 [d] Lk 16:17

The Living Stone and a Holy People

2 So rid yourselves of all wickedness,
all deceit, hypocrisy, envy, and all
slander. 2 [a]Like newborn infants, desire
the unadulterated [b]spiritual milk, so
that you may grow by it in ⌊your⌋ salvation,[f] 3 since [c]you have [d]tasted that
the Lord is good.[g] 4 Coming to Him, a
living stone—rejected by men but chosen and valuable to God— 5 [e]you yourselves, as living stones, are being built
into a spiritual house for [f]a holy priesthood to offer [g]spiritual sacrifices [h]ac-
ceptable to God through Jesus Christ.
6 For it stands in Scripture:

[i]Look! I lay a stone in Zion,
a chosen and valuable
cornerstone,
and the one who believes
in Him
will never be put to shame![h i]

[a] Mt 18:3 [b] 1Co 3:2 [c] Ps 34:8 [d] Heb 6:5 [e] Eph 2:21 [f] Is 66:21 [g] Mal 1:11 [h] Php 4:18 [i] Is 28:16

7 So the honor is for you who believe;
but for the unbelieving,

[a]The stone that the builders
rejected—
this One has become
the cornerstone,[j]

[a] Ps 118:22; Lk 20:17-18

and

8 **[a]A stone that causes men**
to stumble,[k]
and a rock that trips
them up.[l m]

They stumble by disobeying the message; [b]they were destined for this.

[a] Is 8:14 [b] Rm 9:22

9 But you are [a]**a chosen race,**[n o]
[b]**a royal priesthood,**[p]
[c]**a holy nation,**[q] **a people**
for His possession,[r]
so that you may proclaim
the praises[s t]
of the One who called you
out of darkness
into His marvelous light.
10 [d]Once you were not a people,
but now you are God's people;
you had not received mercy,
but now you have received
mercy.

[a] Dt 10:15 [b] Ex 19:5-6 [c] Jn 17:19 [d] Hs 2:23

[a]**1:20** Or *was chosen,* or *was known* [b]**1:22** Other mss add *through the Spirit* [c]**1:22** Or *purified your souls* [d]**1:22** Other mss omit *pure* [e]**1:24–25** Is 40:6–8 [f]**2:2** Other mss omit *in your salvation* [g]**2:3** Ps 34:8 [h]**2:6** Or *be disappointed* [i]**2:6** Is 28:16 LXX [j]**2:7** Ps 118:22 [k]**2:8** Or *a stone causing stumbling* [l]**2:8** Or *a rock to trip over* [m]**2:8** Is 8:14 [n]**2:9** Or *chosen generation,* or *chosen nation* [o]**2:9** Is 43:20 LXX; Dt 7:6; 10:15 [p]**2:9** Ex 19:6; 23:22 LXX; Is 61:6 [q]**2:9** Ex 19:6; 23:22 LXX [r]**2:9** Ex 19:5; 23:22 LXX; Dt 4:20; 7:6; Is 43:21 LXX [s]**2:9** Or *the mighty deeds* [t]**2:9** Is 42:12; 43:21

A Call to Good Works

11 Dear friends, I urge you as aliens
and temporary residents to abstain
from fleshly desires that war against
you.[a] 12 Conduct yourselves honorably
among the Gentiles,[b] so that in a case
where they speak against you as those
who do evil, they may, by observing
your good works, glorify God in a day
of visitation.[c]
13 Submit to every human institution
because of the Lord, whether to the
Emperor[d] as the supreme authority,
14 or to governors as those sent out by
him to punish those who do evil and to
praise those who do good. 15 For it is
God's will that you, by doing good, silence the ignorance of foolish people.
16 As God's slaves, ⌊live⌋ as free people,
but don't use your freedom as a way to
conceal evil. 17 Honor everyone. Love
the brotherhood. Fear God. Honor the
Emperor.[d]

Submission of Slaves to Masters

18 Household slaves, submit yourselves to your masters with all respect,
not only to the good and gentle but also
to the cruel.[e] 19 For it ⌊brings⌋ favor[f] if,
because of conscience toward God,[g]
someone endures grief from suffering
unjustly. 20 For what credit is there if
you endure when you sin and are
beaten? But when you do good and suffer, if you endure, it brings favor with
God.

21 For you were called to this,
because Christ also suffered
for you,
leaving you an example,
so that you should follow
in His steps.
22 [a]He **did not commit sin,**
and no deceit was found
in His mouth;[h]
23 [b]when reviled, He did not revile
in return;
when suffering,
He did not threaten,
but committed Himself
to the One who judges justly.
24 He Himself bore our sins
in His body on the tree,
so that, having died to sins,
we might live for righteousness;
[c]**by His wounding**
you have been healed.[i]
25 For [d]you **were like sheep**
going astray,[j]
but you have now returned
[e]to the shepherd and guardian[k]
of your souls.

[a] Is 53:9; Lk 23:41
[b] Is 53:7 [c] Is 53:5 [d] Is 53:6
[e] Ezk 34:28; Jn 10:11

Wives and Husbands

3 Wives, in the same way, submit
yourselves to your own husbands
so that, even if some disobey the
⌊Christian⌋ message, [a]they may be
won over[l] without a message by the
way their wives live, 2 when they
observe your pure, reverent lives.
3 [b]Your beauty should not consist of
outward things ⌊like⌋ elaborate hairstyles and the wearing of gold orna-
ments[m] or fine clothes; 4 instead, ⌊it
should consist of⌋ [c]the hidden person
of the heart with the imperishable
quality of a gentle and quiet spirit,
which is very valuable in God's eyes.
5 For in the past, the holy women who
hoped in God also beautified themselves in this way, submitting to their
own husbands, 6 just as Sarah obeyed
Abraham, [d]calling him lord. You have
become her children when you do
good and aren't frightened by anything alarming.

[a] 1Co 7:16 [b] Is 3:16-24
[c] Ps 45:13 [d] Gn 18:12

[a]**2:11** Lit *against the soul* [b]**2:12** Or *among the nations*, or *among the pagans* [c]**2:12** A day when God intervenes in human history, either in grace or in judgment [d]**2:13,17** Lit *king* [e]**2:18** Lit *crooked*, or *unscrupulous* [f]**2:19** Other mss add *with God* [g]**2:19** Other mss read *because of a good conscience* [h]**2:22** Is 53:9 [i]**2:24** Is 53:5 [j]**2:25** Is 53:6 [k]**2:25** Or *overseer* [l]**3:1** Lit *may be gained* [m]**3:3** Lit *and of putting around of gold items*

7 Husbands, in the same way, live
with your wives with understanding of
their weaker nature[a] yet showing them
honor as co-heirs of the grace of life, so
that your prayers will not be hindered.

Do No Evil

8 Now finally, all of you should be
like-minded and sympathetic, should
love believers,[b] and be compassionate
and humble,[c] 9 not paying back evil for
evil or insult for insult but, on the contrary, giving a blessing, since you were
called for this, [a]so that you can inherit
a blessing. *[a]Mt 25:34; Lk 12:32*

10 For [a]**the one who wants**
to love life
and to see good days
must keep his tongue from evil
and his lips
from speaking deceit,
11 **and he must turn away**
from evil and do good.
He must seek peace
and pursue it,
12 **because the eyes of the Lord**
are on the righteous
[b]**and His ears are open**
to their request.
But the face of the Lord is
against those who do evil.[d]
[a]Ps 34:12-16 [b]Jn 9:31

Undeserved Suffering

13 [a]And who will harm[e] you if you are
passionate for what is good?[f] 14 [b]But
even if you should suffer for righteousness, you are blessed. [c]**Do not fear**
what they fear or be disturbed,[g] 15 but
set apart the •Messiah[h] as Lord in your
hearts, and [d]always be ready to give a
defense to anyone who asks you for a
reason[i] for the hope that is in you.
16 However, do this with gentleness
and respect, keeping your conscience
clear,[j] so that when you are accused,[k]
those who denounce your Christian
life will be put to shame. 17 For it is better [e]to suffer for doing good, if that
should be God's will,[l] than for doing
evil. *[a]Pr 16:7 [b]Mt 5:10 [c]Is 8:12*
[d]Ac 4:8-12 [e]2Tm 3:12

18 For Christ also suffered for sins
once for all,[m]
the righteous
for the unrighteous,[n]
that He might bring you[o]
to God,
after being put to death
[a]in the fleshly realm[p]
but made alive
[b]in the spiritual realm.[q]
[a]Col 1:22 [b]Rm 1:4

19 [a]In that state[r] He also went and
made a proclamation to the spirits [b]in
prison[s] 20 who in the past were disobedient, when God patiently waited in
the days of Noah while [c]an ark was being prepared; [d]in it, a few—that is,
eight people[t] —were saved through
water. 21 [e]Baptism, which corresponds
to this, now saves you (not the removal of the filth of the flesh, but the
pledge[u] of a good conscience toward
God) through the resurrection of Jesus
Christ. 22 Now that He has gone into
heaven, He [f]is at God's right hand,
with angels, authorities, and powers
subjected to Him. *[a]1Pt 1:11-12*
[b]Is 42:7 [c]Heb 11:7
[d]2Pt 2:5 [e]Eph 5:26
[f]Ps 110:1; Ac 1:11; Rm 8:34

[a]**3:7** Lit *understanding as the weaker vessel* [b]**3:8** Lit *brotherly-loving* [c]**3:8** Other mss read *courteous* [d]**3:10–12** Ps 34:12–16 [e]**3:13** Or *will mistreat*, or *will do evil to* [f]**3:13** Lit *you are zealots*, or *you are partisans for the good*, or *you are eager to do good* [g]**3:14** Is 8:12 [h]**3:15** Other mss read *set God* [i]**3:15** Or *who demands of you an accounting* [j]**3:16** Lit *good*; or *keeping a clear conscience* [k]**3:16** Other mss read *when they speak against you as evildoers* [l]**3:17** Lit *if the will of God should will* [m]**3:18** Other mss read *died for sins on our behalf*; other mss read *died for our sins*; other mss read *died for sins on your behalf* [n]**3:18** Or *the Righteous One in the place of the unrighteous many* [o]**3:18** Other mss read *us* [p]**3:18** Or *in the flesh* [q]**3:18** Or *in the spirit*, or *in the Spirit* [r]**3:19** Or *In whom*, or *At that time*, or *In which* [s]**3:19** The *spirits in prison* are most likely fallen supernatural beings or angels; see 2 Pt 2:4; Jd 6. [t]**3:20** Lit *souls* [u]**3:21** Or *the appeal*

Following Christ

4 Therefore, since Christ suffered[a]
in the flesh,[b] arm yourselves also
with the same resolve[c]—[a]because the
One who suffered in the flesh[b] has
finished with sin[d] — 2 in order to live
the remaining time in the flesh,[b] no
longer for human desires,[e] but for
God's will. 3 For there has already
been enough time spent in doing the
will of the pagans:[f] carrying on in
unrestrained behavior, evil desires,
drunkenness, orgies, carousing, and
lawless idolatry. 4 In regard to this,
they are surprised that you don't
plunge with them into the same flood[g]
of dissipation—and they slander you.
5 They will give an account to the One
who stands ready [b]to judge the living
and the dead. 6 For this reason [c]the
gospel was also preached to ⌊those
who are now⌋ dead, so that, although
they might be judged by men in the
fleshly realm,[h] they might live by God
in the spiritual realm.[i]

[a]Gl 5:24 [b]Ac 10:42; Rm 14:10 [c]1Pt 3:19

End-Time Ethics

7 Now [a]the end of all things is near;
therefore, be clear-headed and disciplined for prayer. 8 Above all, keep
your love for one another at full
strength, since [b]**love covers a multitude of sins.**[j] 9 Be hospitable to one another [c]without complaining. 10 [d]Based
on the gift they have received, everyone should use it to serve others, as
good managers of the varied grace of
God. 11 [e]If anyone speaks, ⌊his speech
should be⌋ like the oracles of God; if
anyone serves, ⌊his service should be⌋
from the strength God provides, so
that [f]in everything God may be glorified through Jesus Christ. [g]To Him belong the glory and the power forever
and ever. •Amen.

[a]Mt 24:13; Php 4:5 [b]Pr 10:12; Jms 5:20 [c]Dt 15:7 [d]1Co 4:7 [e]Jr 23:22 [f]Eph 5:20 [g]1Pt 5:11

Christian Suffering

12 Dear friends, when the fiery or-
deal[k] arises among you to test you,
don't be surprised by it, as if something
unusual were happening to you.
13 Instead, as [a]you share in the sufferings of the •Messiah rejoice, so that
you may also rejoice with great joy at
the revelation of His glory. 14 [b]If you are
ridiculed for the name of Christ, you
are blessed, because the [c]Spirit of glory
and of God rests on you.[l] 15 None of
you, however, should suffer as a murderer, a thief, an evildoer, or as a med-
dler.[m] 16 But if ⌊anyone suffers⌋ as a
Christian, he should not be ashamed,
but should glorify God with that name.
17 For the time has come for judgment
to begin with God's household; and [d]if
it begins with us, [e]what will the outcome be for those who disobey the
gospel of God?

[a]Rm 8:17; 2Co 1:7; Php 3:10 [b]Mt 5:11 [c]Mt 10:20 [d]Lk 23:31 [e]Lk 10:12

18 [a]**And if the righteous is saved**
with difficulty,
what will become
of the ungodly
and the sinner?[n]

19 So those who suffer according to
God's will should, in doing good,
[b]entrust themselves to a faithful Creator.

[a]Pr 11:31 [b]Ps 31:5; Lk 23:46

About the Elders

5 Therefore, as a fellow elder and
[a]witness to the sufferings of the
•Messiah, and also a [b]participant in the

[a]**4:1** Other mss read *suffered for us* [b]**4:1,2** *In the flesh* probably means "in human existence"; see 1 Pt 3:18. [c]**4:1** Or *perspective*, or *attitude* [d]**4:1** Or *the one who has suffered in the flesh has ceased from sin* [e]**4:2** Lit *for desires of human beings* [f]**4:3** Or *Gentiles* [g]**4:4** Lit *you don't run with them into the same pouring out* [h]**4:6** Or *in the flesh* [i]**4:6** Or *in the spirit* [j]**4:8** Pr 10:12 [k]**4:12** Lit *the burning* [l]**4:14** Other mss add *He is blasphemed because of them, but He is glorified because of you.* [m]**4:15** Or *as one who defrauds others* [n]**4:18** Pr 11:31 LXX

glory about to be revealed, I exhort the
elders among you: 2 [c]shepherd God's
flock among you, not overseeing[a] out
of compulsion but freely, according to
God's ⌊will⌋;[b] not for the money but eagerly; 3 not lording it over [d]those entrusted to you, but being examples to
the flock. 4 And when [e]the chief Shepherd appears, you will receive the unfading crown of glory.

[a]Lk 24:48; Ac 1:8 [b]Rm 8:17 [c]Jn 21:15-16 [d]Lk 22:25-26 [e]Heb 13:20

5 Likewise, you younger men, [a]be
subject to the elders. And all of you
clothe yourselves with[c] humility toward one another, because

> **[b]God resists the proud,**
> **but [c]gives grace**
> **to the humble.**[d]

6 Humble yourselves therefore under
the mighty hand of God, so that He
may exalt you in due time,[e] 7 [d]casting
all your care upon Him, because He
cares about you.

[a]Eph 5:21; Php 2:3 [b]Pr 3:34; Jms 4:6 [c]Is 57:15 [d]Mt 6:25; Lk 12:11; Php 4:6

Conclusion

8 Be sober! Be on the alert! Your adversary the Devil is prowling around
like a roaring lion, looking for anyone
he can devour. 9 Resist him, firm in the
faith, knowing that the same sufferings
are being experienced by your brothers in the world.

10 Now the God of all grace, who
called you to His eternal glory in Christ
Jesus, will personally[f] restore, establish, strengthen, and support you after
you have suffered a little.[g] 11 To Him be
the dominion[h] forever.[i] •Amen.

12 [a]Through Silvanus,[j] whom I consider a faithful brother, I have written
briefly, encouraging you and testifying
that this is the true grace of God. Take
your stand in it! 13 She who is in
[b]Babylon, also chosen, sends you greetings, as does [c]Mark, my son. 14 Greet
one another with a kiss of love. Peace
to all of you who are in Christ.[k]

[a]2Co 1:19 [b]Rv 17:5,18 [c]Ac 12:12

[a]**5:2** Other mss omit *overseeing* [b]**5:2** Other mss omit *according to God's will* [c]**5:5** Lit *you tie around yourselves* [d]**5:5** Pr 3:34 LXX [e]**5:6** Lit *in time* [f]**5:10** Lit *Himself* [g]**5:10** Or *a little while*, or *to a small extent* [h]**5:11** Other mss read *dominion and glory*; other mss read *glory and dominion* [i]**5:11** Other mss read *forever and ever* [j]**5:12** Or *Silas*; Ac 15:22–32; 16:19–40; 17:1–16 [k]**5:14** Other mss read *Christ Jesus. Amen.*

2 PETER

Greeting

1 Simeon[a] Peter, a slave and an apostle of Jesus Christ:
To those who have obtained [a]a faith
of equal privilege with ours[b] through
the righteousness of our God and Savior Jesus Christ. *[a]Ac 11:17*

2 May grace and peace be multiplied
to you through the knowledge of God
and of Jesus our Lord.

Growth in the Faith

3 For His[c] divine power has given us
everything required for life and godliness, [a]through the knowledge of Him
[b]who called us by[d] His own glory and
goodness. 4 [c]By these He has given us
very great and precious promises, so
that through them you may [d]share in
the divine nature, escaping the corruption that is in the world because of evil
desires. 5 For this very reason, make every effort to supplement your faith with
goodness, goodness with [e]knowledge,
6 knowledge with self-control, self-control with endurance, endurance with
godliness, 7 godliness with [f]brotherly affection, and brotherly affection with
love. 8 For if these qualities are yours
and are increasing, they will keep you
from being useless or unfruitful in the
knowledge of our Lord Jesus Christ.
9 The person who lacks these things [g]is
blind and shortsighted, and has forgotten the [h]cleansing from his past sins.
10 Therefore, brothers, make every effort [i]to confirm your calling and election, because if you do these things you
will never stumble. 11 [j]For in this way,
entry into the eternal kingdom of our
Lord and Savior Jesus Christ will be
richly supplied to you. *[a]Jn 17:3*
[b]1Th 2:12; 2Tm 1:9 [c]2Co 7:1 [d]Eph 4:24
[e]2Co 6:4,6; 2Pt 3:18 [f]Gl 6:10; 1Th 3:12
[g]1Jn 2:9 [h]1Jn 1:7 [i]1Jn 3:19 [j]2Tm 4:18

12 Therefore I will always remind you
about these things, even though you
know them and are established in the
truth you have. 13 I consider it right, as
long as I am in this tent,[e] to wake you
up with a reminder, 14 knowing that I
will soon lay aside my tent, as [a]our
Lord Jesus Christ has also shown me.
15 And I will also make every effort that
after my departure[f] you may be able to
recall these things at any time.
[a]Jn 21:18

The Trustworthy Prophetic Word

16 For we did not follow cleverly con-
trived myths when we made known to
you the power and coming of our Lord
Jesus Christ; instead, we were eyewitnesses of His majesty. 17 For when He
received honor and glory from God the
Father, a voice came to Him from the
Majestic Glory:

> [a]This is My beloved Son.[g]
> I take delight in Him![h] *[a]Mt 17:5*

18 And we heard this voice when it
came from heaven while we were
with Him on [a]the holy mountain. 19 So
we have the [b]prophetic word strongly
confirmed. You will do well to pay
attention to it, as to a lamp shining in a
dismal place, until the day dawns and
the [c]morning star arises in your hearts.
20 First of all, you should know this:
[d]no prophecy of Scripture comes from
one's own interpretation, 21 because

[a]**1:1** Simon [b]**1:1** Or *obtained a faith of the same kind as ours* [c]**1:3** Lit *As His* [d]**1:3** Or *to*
[e]**1:13** A euphemism for Peter's body [f]**1:15** Or *my death* [g]**1:17** Other mss read *My Son, My Beloved*
[h]**1:17** A reference to the transfiguration; see Mt 17:5

[e]no prophecy ever came by the will of
man; [f]instead, moved by the Holy
Spirit, men spoke from God. [a]*Mt 17:1*
[b]*Is 8:20* [c]*2Co 4:4,6*
[d]*Rm 12:6* [e]*2Tm 3:16; 1Pt 1:11*
[f]*2Sm 23:2; Lk 1:70*

The Judgment of False Teachers

2 But [a]there were also false prophets
among the people, just as [b]there
will be false teachers among you. They
will secretly bring in destructive here-
sies, even denying the Master [c]who
bought them, and will bring swift destruction on themselves. 2 Many will
follow their unrestrained ways, and because of them the way of truth will be
blasphemed. 3 In their greed they will
exploit you with deceptive words.
Their condemnation, ⌊pronounced⌋
long ago, is not idle, and their destruction does not sleep. [a]*Dt 13:1*
[b]*Mt 24:11* [c]*1Co 6:20; Gl 3:13*

4 For if God didn't spare [a]the angels
[b]who sinned, but [c]threw them down
into Tartarus[a] and delivered them to be
kept in chains[b] of darkness until judgment; 5 and if He didn't spare the ancient world, but protected Noah, a
preacher of righteousness, [d]and seven
others,[c] when He brought a flood on
the world of the ungodly; 6 and if He
[e]reduced the cities of Sodom and Gomorrah to ashes and condemned them
to ruin,[d] making them an example to
those who were going to be ungodly;[e]
7 and if He rescued righteous Lot, distressed by the unrestrained behavior of
the immoral 8 (for as he lived among
them, that righteous man tormented
himself day by day with the lawless
deeds he saw and heard)— 9 then [f]the
Lord knows how to rescue the godly
from trials and to keep the unrighteous
under punishment until the day of
judgment, 10 especially those who follow the polluting desires of the flesh
and despise authority. [a]*Jb 4:18* [b]*Jn 8:44*
[c]*Lk 8:31* [d]*Gn 7:1; Heb 11:7* [e]*Gn 19:24* [f]*Ps 34:17*

Bold, arrogant people! They do not
tremble when they blaspheme the glorious ones; 11 however, [a]angels, who are
greater in might and power, do not
bring a slanderous charge against them
before the Lord.[f] 12 But these people,
[b]like irrational animals—creatures of
instinct born to be caught and destroyed—speak blasphemies about
things they don't understand, and in
their destruction they too will be destroyed, 13 suffering harm [c]as the payment for unrighteousness. They consider it a pleasure [d]to carouse in the
daytime. They are blots and blemishes,
delighting in their deceptions[g] as [e]they
feast with you, 14 having eyes full of
adultery and always looking for sin, se-
ducing unstable people, and with hearts
trained in greed. Accursed children!
15 By abandoning the straight path, they
have gone astray and have followed the
path of [f]Balaam, the son of Bosor,[h] who
loved the wages of unrighteousness,
16 but received a rebuke for his transgression: a speechless donkey spoke
with a human voice and restrained the
prophet's madness. [a]*Jd 9* [b]*Jr 12:3*
[c]*Php 3:19* [d]*Rm 13:13* [e]*1Co 11:20-21* [f]*Nm 22*

17 These people are springs without
water, mists driven by a whirlwind.
The gloom of darkness has been reserved for them. 18 For uttering bom-
bastic, empty words, they seduce, by
fleshly desires and debauchery, people
who [a]have barely escaped[i] from those
who live in error. 19 They promise them
[b]freedom, but they themselves are
[c]slaves of corruption, since people are
enslaved to whatever defeats them.
20 For [d]if, having escaped the world's
impurity through the knowledge of our
Lord and Savior Jesus Christ, they are

[a]**2:4** *Tartarus* is a Gk name for a subterranean place of divine punishment lower than Hades. [b]**2:4** Other mss read *in pits* [c]**2:5** Lit *righteousness, as the eighth* [d]**2:6** Other mss omit *to ruin* [e]**2:6** Other mss read *an example of what is going to happen to the ungodly* [f]**2:11** Other mss read *them from the Lord* [g]**2:13** Other mss read *delighting in the love feasts* [h]**2:15** Other mss read *Beor* [i]**2:18** Or *people who are barely escaping*

again entangled in these things and defeated, the last state is worse for them
than the first. 21 For [e]it would have
been better for them not to have
known the way of righteousness than,
after knowing it, to turn back from the
holy commandment delivered to them.
22 It has happened to them according to
the true proverb: [f]**A dog returns to its
own vomit,**[a] and, "a sow, after washing
itself, wallows in the mud."

[a]*Ac 2:40; 2Pt 1:4* [b]*Gl 5:13* [c]*Jn 8:34*
[d]*Mt 12:45; Heb 6:4* [e]*Lk 12:47; Jn 9:41* [f]*Pr 26:11*

The Day of the Lord

3 Dear friends, this is now the second letter I've written you; in
both, I awaken your pure understanding with a reminder, 2 so that you can
remember the words previously spoken by the holy prophets, [a]and the
commandment of our Lord and Savior
⌊given⌋ through your apostles. 3 [b]First,
be aware of this: scoffers will come in
the last days to scoff, [c]following their
own lusts, 4 saying, [d]"Where is the
promise of His coming? For ever since
the fathers fell •asleep, all things continue as they have been since the beginning of creation." 5 They willfully
ignore this: long ago the heavens and
the earth existed out of water and
through water [e]by the word of God.
6 [f]Through these the world of that time
perished when it was flooded by water. 7 But by the same word the present
heavens and earth are held in store for
[g]fire, being kept until the day of judgment and destruction of ungodly men.

[a]*Jd 17* [b]*1Tm 4:1; 2Tm 3:1* [c]*2Pt 2:10*
[d]*Mt 24:48* [e]*Gn 1:6; Ps 33:6*
[f]*Gn 7:11; 2Pt 2:5* [g]*Mt 25:41; Heb 1:11*

8 Dear friends, don't let this one
thing escape you: with the Lord one
day is like 1,000 years, and [a]1,000
years like one day. 9 [b]The Lord does not
delay His promise, as some understand
delay, but [c]is patient with you, [d]not
wanting any to perish, but [e]all to come
to repentance.

[a]*Ps 90:4* [b]*Hab 2:3*
[c]*Is 30:18* [d]*Ezk 18:23* [e]*Rm 2:4*

10 But [a]the Day of the Lord will come
like a thief;[b] on that ⌊day⌋ [b]the heavens
will pass away with a loud noise, the
elements will burn and [c]be dissolved,
and the earth and the works on it will
be disclosed.[c] 11 Since all these things
are to be destroyed in this way, ⌊it is
clear⌋ what sort of people you should
be in holy conduct and godliness 12 as
you wait for and earnestly desire the
coming of the day of God, because of
which the heavens will be on fire and
be dissolved, and the elements will
[d]melt with the heat. 13 But based on
His promise, we wait for [e]new heavens and a new earth, where righteousness will dwell.

[a]*Mt 24:43* [b]*Mt 24:35*
[c]*Is 34:4* [d]*Mc 1:4* [e]*Is 65:17*

Conclusion

14 Therefore, dear friends, while you
wait for these things, make every effort
to be found in peace without spot or
blemish before Him. 15 Also, regard
[a]the patience of our Lord as ⌊an opportunity for⌋ salvation, just as our dear
brother Paul, according to the wisdom
given to him, has written to you. 16 He
[b]speaks about these things in all his letters, in which there are some matters
that are hard to understand. The un-
taught and unstable twist them to their
own destruction, as they also do with
the rest of the Scriptures.

[a]*Rm 2:4; Eph 1:7; Col 1:27*
[b]*Rm 8:19; 1Co 15:24; 1Th 4:15*

17 Therefore, dear friends, since you
have been forewarned, [a]be on your
guard, so that you are not led away by
the error of the immoral and fall from
your own stability. 18 But grow in the
grace and knowledge of our Lord and
Savior Jesus Christ. To Him be the
glory both now and to the day of eternity.[d] •Amen.[e]

[a]*Eph 4:14*

[a]**2:22** Pr 26:11 [b]**3:10** Other mss add *in the night* [c]**3:10** Other mss read *will be burned up* [d]**3:18** Or *now and forever* [e]**3:18** Other mss omit *Amen.*

1 JOHN

Prologue

1 What [a]was from the beginning,
what we have heard,
what we have seen
with our eyes,
[b]what we have observed,
and [c]have touched
with our hands,
concerning the [d]Word of life—
2 that life was revealed,
and we have seen it
and we testify and declare
to you
the eternal life [e]that was
with the Father
and was revealed to us—
3 what we have seen and heard
we also declare to you,
so that you may have fellowship
along with us;
and indeed [f]our fellowship is
with the Father
and with His Son Jesus Christ.
4 We are writing these things[a]
so that our[b] joy
may be complete.

[a] Mc 5:2; Jn 1:1 [b] 2Pt 1:16 [c] Lk 24:39 [d] Rv 19:13 [e] Jn 1:1-2 [f] Jn 14:23; 15:4; 1Co 1:9

Fellowship with God

5 Now this is the message we have
heard from Him and declare to you:
[a]God is light, and there is absolutely no
darkness in Him. 6 If we say, "We have
fellowship with Him," and •walk in
darkness, we are lying and are not
practicing[c] the truth. 7 But if we walk
in the light as He Himself is in the
light, we have fellowship with one another, and the blood of Jesus His Son
cleanses us from all sin. 8 [b]If we say,
"We have no sin," we are deceiving
ourselves, and the truth is not in us.
9 [c]If we confess our sins, He is faithful
and righteous to forgive us our sins and
to cleanse us from all unrighteousness.
10 If we say, "We have not sinned," we
make Him a liar, and His word is not in
us.

[a] Jn 1:9; 8:12 [b] Ec 7:20; Jms 3:2 [c] Ps 32:5; Pr 28:13

2 My little children, I am writing
you these things so that you may
not sin. But if anyone does sin, [a]we
have an •advocate with the Father—
Jesus Christ the righteous One. 2 [b]He
Himself is the propitiation[d] for our
sins, and not only for ours, but [c]also
for those of the whole world.

[a] Rm 8:34 [b] Rm 3:25 [c] Jn 1:29; 2Co 5:18-21

God's Commands

3 This is how we are sure that we
have come to know Him: by keeping
His commands. 4 The one who says, "I
have come to know Him," without
keeping His commands, is a liar, and
the truth is not in him. 5 But [a]whoever
keeps His word, truly in him the love
of God is perfected.[e] This is how we
know we are in Him: 6 [b]the one who
says he remains in Him [c]should •walk
just as He walked.

[a] Jn 14:23 [b] Jn 15:4 [c] Mt 11:29

7 Dear friends, [a]I am not writing you
a new command, but an old command
[b]that you have had from the beginning. The old command is the message
you have heard. 8 Yet [c]I am writing you
a new command, which is true in Him
and in you, [d]because the darkness is

[a] **1:4** Other mss add *to you* [b] **1:4** Other mss read *your* [c] **1:6** Or *not living according to* [d] **2:2** The word *propitiation* has to do with the removal of divine wrath. Jesus' death is the means that turns God's wrath from the sinner; see 2 Co 5:21. [e] **2:5** Or *truly completed*

passing away and [e]the true light is already shining.

[a] 2Jn 5 [b] 1Jn 3:11 [c] Jn 13:34 [d] Eph 5:8 [e] Jn 1:9; 8:12

9 The one who says he is in the light
but hates his brother is in the darkness
until now. 10 The one who loves his
brother remains in the light, and
[a]there is no cause for stumbling in
him.[a] 11 But the one who hates his
brother is in the darkness, [b]walks in
the darkness, and doesn't know where
he's going, because the darkness has
blinded his eyes.

[a] 2Pt 1:10 [b] Jn 12:35

Reasons for Writing

12 I am writing to you,
little children,
because [a]your sins have been
forgiven on account of
His name.
13 I am writing to you, fathers,
because you have come to know
the One [b]who is
from the beginning.
I am writing to you, young men,
because you have had victory
over the evil one.
14 I have written to you, children,
because you have come to know
the Father.
I have written to you, fathers,
because you have come to know
the One who is
from the beginning.
I have written to you,
young men,
because [c]you are strong,
[d]God's word remains in you,
and you have had victory
over the evil one.

[a] Lk 24:47 [b] 1Jn 1:1 [c] Eph 6:10 [d] Jr 31:33

A Warning about the World

15 Do not love the world or the
things that belong to[b] the world. [a]If
anyone loves the world, love for the
Father is not in him. 16 For everything
that belongs to[c] the world—the lust of
the flesh, the lust of the eyes, and the
pride in one's lifestyle—is not from
the Father, but is from the world.
17 And the world with its lust is passing away, but the one who does God's
will [b]remains forever.

[a] Mt 6:24; Gl 1:10 [b] Ps 125:1; Pr 10:25

The Last Hour

18 Children, [a]it is the last hour. And
as you have heard, [b]"Antichrist is coming," [c]even now many antichrists have
come. We know from this that it is the
last hour. 19 They went out from us, but
they did not belong to us; for [d]if they
had belonged to us, they would have
remained with us. However, they went
out so that [e]it might be made clear that
none of them belongs to us.

[a] Heb 1:2 [b] 2Th 2:3 [c] Mt 24:5 [d] Mt 24:24 [e] 1Co 11:19

20 But [a]you have an anointing [b]from
the Holy One, and [c]you all have knowledge.[d] 21 I have not written to you because you don't know the truth, but
because you do know it, and because
no lie comes from the truth. 22 Who is
the liar, if not the one who denies that
Jesus is the •Messiah? He is the antichrist, the one who denies the Father
and the Son. 23 No one who denies the
Son can have the Father; [d]he who confesses the Son has the Father as well.

[a] Lk 4:18; Ac 10:38; Heb 1:9 [b] Mk 1:24 [c] Ps 89:18; Pr 28:5 [d] Jn 14:7

Remaining with God

24 What you have heard from the beginning must remain in you. If what
you have heard from the beginning remains in you, then [a]you will remain in
the Son and in the Father. 25 [b]And this
is the promise that He Himself made to
us: eternal life. 26 I have written these
things to you about those who are trying to deceive you.

[a] Jn 15:9-10 [b] Jn 17:3

27 The anointing you received from
Him remains in you, and [a]you don't

[a]**2:10** Or *in it* [b]**2:15** Lit *things in* [c]**2:15** Lit *that is in* [d]**2:20** Other mss read *and you know all things*

need anyone to teach you. Instead,
His anointing [b]teaches you about all
things, and is true and is not a lie; just
as it has taught you, remain in Him.
[a] *Jn 14:26* [b] *Jn 16:13*

God's Children

28 So now, little children, remain in
Him, so that when He appears we may
have boldness and not be ashamed before Him at His coming. 29 [a]If you know
that He is righteous, you know this as
well: everyone who does what is right
has been born of Him. 3 1 Look at
how great a love[a] the Father has
given us, that [b]we should be called
God's children. And we are! The reason the world does not know us [c]is
that it didn't know Him. 2 Dear friends,
we are God's children now, and [d]what
we will be has not yet been revealed.
We know that when He appears, [e]we
will be like Him, because [f]we will see
Him as He is. 3 And everyone who has
this hope in Him purifies himself just
as He is pure. [a] *Ac 22:14* [b] *Jn 1:12* [c] *Jn 15:18*
[d] *1Co 2:9* [e] *Rm 8:29* [f] *Mt 5:8; 1Co 13:12*

4 Everyone who commits sin also
breaks the law;[b] sin is the breaking of
law. 5 You know that He was revealed
so that He might [a]take away sins,[c] and
there [b]is no sin in Him. 6 Everyone
who remains in Him does not sin; everyone who sins has not seen Him or
known Him. [a] *Heb 1:3* [b] *Is 53:9; Gl 3:13*

7 Little children, let no one deceive
you! The one who does what is right is
righteous, just as He is righteous.
8 [a]The one who commits sin is of the
Devil, for the Devil has sinned from
the beginning. The Son of God was revealed for this purpose: [b]to destroy the
Devil's works. 9 [c]Everyone who has
been born of God does not sin, because
[d]His[d] seed remains in him; he is not
able to sin, because he has been born
of God. 10 This is how God's children—and the Devil's children—are
made evident. [a] *Mt 13:38* [b] *Gn 3:15;*
Lk 10:18 [c] *1Jn 5:18* [d] *1Pt 1:23*

Love's Imperative

Whoever does not do what is right is
not of God, especially the one who
does not love his brother. 11 For this is
the message you have heard from the
beginning: [a]we should love one another, 12 unlike [b]Cain, who was of the
evil one and murdered[e] his brother.
And why did he murder him? Because
his works were evil, and his brother's
were righteous. 13 Do not be surprised,
brothers, if the world hates you. 14 We
know that we have passed from death
to life because we love our brothers.
The one who does not love remains in
death. 15 [c]Everyone who hates his
brother is a murderer, and you know
that [d]no murderer has eternal life residing in him. [a] *Jn 15:12* [b] *Gn 4:8*
[c] *1Jn 4:20* [d] *Gl 5:21; 1Tm 1:9*

Love in Action

16 [a]This is how we have come to
know love: He laid down His life for us.
We should also lay down our lives for
our brothers. 17 [b]If anyone has this
world's goods and sees his brother in
need but shuts off his compassion from
him—how can God's love reside in
him? [a] *Rm 5:8; Eph 5:2* [b] *Dt 15:7*

18 Little children, we must not love
in word or speech, but in deed and
truth; 19 that is how we will know [a]we
are of the truth, and will convince our
hearts in His presence, 20 because if
our hearts condemn us, God is greater
than our hearts and knows all things.
[a] *Jn 18:37*

21 [a]Dear friends, if our hearts do not
condemn ⌊us⌋ we have confidence before God, 22 and [b]can receive whatever
we ask from Him because we keep His
commands [c]and do what is pleasing in

[a]**3:1** Or *at what sort of love* [b]**3:4** Or *also commits iniquity* [c]**3:5** Other mss read *our sins* [d]**3:9** God's
[e]**3:12** Or *slaughtered*

His sight. 23 Now this is His command:
that we believe in the name of His Son
Jesus Christ, and love one another as
He commanded us. 24 The one who
keeps His commands [d]remains in Him,
and He in him. And [e]the way we know
that He remains in us is from the Spirit
He has given us. *[a]Jb 22:26; Heb 10:22*
[b]Mt 21:22 [c]Jn 8:29 [d]Jn 17:21
[e]Ezk 37:27; Jn 14:16-17

The Spirit of Truth and the Spirit of Error

4 Dear friends, [a]do not believe every spirit, but test the spirits to
determine if they are from God, because [b]many false prophets have gone
out into the world. *[a]Jr 14:14 [b]Mt 24:5*

2 This is how you know the Spirit of
God: [a]Every spirit who confesses that
Jesus Christ has come in the flesh[a] is
from God. 3 But [b]every spirit who does
not confess Jesus[b] is not from God.
This is the spirit of the antichrist; you
have heard that he is coming, and he is
already in the world now. *[a]1Co 12:3*
[b]1Jn 2:22

4 You are from God, little children,
and you have conquered them, because the One who is in you is greater
than [a]the one who is in the world.
5 [b]They are from the world. Therefore
what they say is from the world, [c]and
the world listens to them. 6 We are
from God. [d]Anyone who knows God
listens to us; anyone who is not from
God does not listen to us. From this we
know [e]the Spirit of truth and the spirit
of deception. *[a]Jn 12:31 [b]Jn 3:31*
[c]Jn 15:19 [d]Jn 8:47; 1Co 14:37 [e]Is 8:20

Knowing God through Love

7 Dear friends, let us love one another, because love is from God, and
everyone who loves has been born of
God and knows God. 8 The one who
does not love does not know God, because [a]God is love. 9 God's love was revealed among us in this way:[c] God sent
His •One and Only Son into the world
so that we might live through Him.
10 Love consists in this: [b]not that we
loved God, but that He loved us and
sent His Son to be the[d] propitiation[e] for
our sins. 11 Dear friends, if God loved
us in this way, we also must love one
another. 12 [c]No one has ever seen God.[f]
If we love one another, God remains
in[g] us and His love is perfected in us.
[a]Ex 34:6-7 [b]Jn 15:16; Ti 3:4 [c]1Tm 6:16

13 [a]This is how we know that we remain in Him and He in us: He has
given to us from His Spirit. 14 And [b]we
have seen and we testify that [c]the
Father has sent the Son as Savior of
the world. 15 [d]Whoever confesses[h] that
Jesus is the Son of God—God remains
in him and he in God. 16 And we have
come to know and to believe the love
that God has for us. God is love, and
the one who remains in love remains
in God, and God remains in him.
[a]Jn 10:38; 15:4-7 [b]Jn 1:14
[c]Jn 3:17 [d]Rm 10:9

17 In this, love is perfected with us so
that [a]we may have confidence in the
day of judgment; [b]for we are as He is in
this world. 18 There is no fear in love;
instead, perfect love drives out fear, because fear involves punishment.[i] So
the one who fears has not reached perfection in love. 19 We love[j] because He
first loved us. *[a]1Jn 2:28 [b]Jn 17:11,15,18*

Keeping God's Commands

20 If anyone says, "I love God," yet
hates his brother, he is a liar. For the
person who does not love his brother
whom he has seen cannot love God
whom he has not seen.[k] 21 And [a]we

[a]**4:2** Or *confesses Jesus to be the Christ come in the flesh* [b]**4:3** Other mss read *confess that Jesus has come in the flesh* [c]**4:9** Or *revealed in us* [d]**4:10** Or *a* [e]**4:10** The word *propitiation* has to do with the removal of divine wrath. Jesus' death is the means that turns God's wrath from the sinner; see 2 Co 5:21. [f]**4:12** Since God is an infinite being, no one can see Him in His absolute essential nature; see Ex 33:18–23. [g]**4:12** Or *remains among* [h]**4:15** Or *acknowledges* [i]**4:18** Or *fear has its own punishment* or *torment* [j]**4:19** Other mss add *Him* [k]**4:20** Other mss read *seen, how is he able to love . . . seen?* (as a question)

have this command from Him: the one who loves God must also love his brother. [a]Lv 19:18; 1Th 4:9

5 Everyone [a]who believes that [b]Jesus is the •Messiah has been born of God, [c]and everyone who loves the parent also loves his child. 2 This is how we know that we love God's children when we love God and obey[a] His commands. 3 [d]For this is what love for God is: to keep His commands. Now [e]His commands are not a burden, 4 because [f]whatever has been born of God conquers the world. This is the victory that has conquered the world: our faith. 5 And who is [g]the one who conquers the world but the one who believes that Jesus is the Son of God? [a]Jn1:12 [b]1Jn 2:22 [c]Jn 15:23 [d]Jn 14:15 [e]Mc 6:8 [f]Jn 16:33 [g]1Co 15:57

The Sureness of God's Testimony

6 Jesus Christ—He is the One who came by water and blood; not [a]by water only, but by water and by blood. [b]And the Spirit is the One who testifies, because the Spirit is the truth. 7 [c]For there are three that testify:[b] 8 the Spirit, the water, and the blood—and these three are in agreement. 9 If we accept [d]the testimony of men, God's testimony is greater, [e]because it is God's testimony that He has given about His Son. 10 (The one who believes in the Son of God [f]has the testimony in himself. The one who does not believe God [g]has made Him a liar, because he has not believed in the testimony that God has given about His Son.) 11 And this is the testimony: God has given us eternal life, and [h]this life is in His Son. [a]Jn 19:34 [b]Jn 15:26 [c]Is 48:16 [d]Jn 8:17 [e]Mt 3:16 [f]Rm 8:16; Gl 4:6 [g]Jn 3:33 [h]Jn 1:4

12 [a]The one who has the Son has life. The one who doesn't have the Son of God does not have life. 13 [b]I have written these things to you who believe in the name of the Son of God, [c]so that you may know that you have eternal life. [a]Heb 3:14 [b]Jn 20:31 [c]1Jn 1:1-2

Effective Prayer

14 Now this is the confidence we have before Him: whenever we ask anything according to His will, He hears us. 15 And if we know that He hears whatever we ask, we know that we have what we have asked Him for.

16 If anyone sees his brother committing a sin that does not bring death, he should ask, and God[c] will give life to him—to those who commit sin that doesn't bring death. [a]There is sin[d] that brings death. [b]I am not saying he should pray about that. 17 All unrighteousness is sin, and there is sin that does not bring death. [a]Mt 12:31-32; Heb 6:4-6 [b]Jr 7:16

Conclusion

18 We know that everyone who has been born of God does not sin, but the One[e] who is born of God keeps him,[f] [g] and the evil one does not touch him.

19 We know that we are of God, and the whole world is under the sway of the evil one.

20 And we know that the Son of God has come and has given us understanding so that we may know the true One.[h] We are in the true One—that is, in His Son Jesus Christ. [a]He is the true God and eternal life. [a]Is 9:6; Rm 9:5

21 Little children, guard yourselves from idols.

[a]**5:2** Other mss read *keep* [b]**5:7–8** Other mss (the Lat Vg and a few late Gk mss) read *testify in heaven, the Father, the Word, and the Holy Spirit, and these three are One.* [8] *And there are three who bear witness on earth:* [c]**5:16** Lit *He* [d]**5:16** Or *is a sin* [e]**5:18** Jesus Christ [f]**5:18** Other mss read *himself* [g]**5:18** Or *the one who is born of God keeps himself* [h]**5:20** Other mss read *the true God*

2 JOHN

Greeting

The Elder:[a]
To the elect lady[b] and her children,
[a]whom I love in truth—and not only I,
but also all who have come to know
[b]the truth— 2 because of the truth that
remains in us and will be with us forever. *[a] 1Jn 3:18 [b] Jn 8:32; 2Th 2:13*

3 Grace, mercy, and peace will be
with us from God the Father and from
Jesus Christ, the Son of the Father, in
truth and love.

Truth and Deception

4 I was very glad to find some of your
children [a]•walking in truth, in keeping
with a command we have received
from the Father. 5 So now I urge you,
lady—[b]not as if I were writing you a
new command, but one we have had
from the beginning—[c]that we love
one another. 6 And [d]this is love: that
we walk according to His commands.
This is the command [e]as you have
heard it from the beginning: you must
walk in love.[c] *[a] 3Jn 3 [b] 1Jn 2:7*
[c] Jn 15:12 [d] Rm 13:8-9 [e] 1Jn 1:3

7 Many deceivers have gone out into
the world; they do not confess the
coming of Jesus Christ in the flesh.[d]
This is the deceiver and the antichrist.
8 Watch yourselves so that you don't
lose what we[e] have worked for, but you
may receive a full reward. 9 Any- one
who does not remain in the teaching
about Christ, but goes beyond it, does
not have God. The one who remains in
that teaching, this one has both the Father and the Son. 10 If anyone comes to
you and does not bring this teaching,
do not receive him into your home,
and [a]don't say, "Welcome," to him;
11 for the one who says, "Welcome," to
him shares in his evil works. *[a] Rm 16:17;*
1Co 5:11

Farewell

12 Though I have many things to
write to you, I don't want to do so with
paper and ink. Instead, I hope to be
with you and talk face to face[f] so that
our joy may be complete.
13 The children of your elect sister
send you greetings.

[a]**1** Or *Presbyter* [b]**1** Or *Kyria*, a proper name; probably a literary figure for a local church known to John; the *children* would be its members. [c]**6** Lit *in it* [d]**7** Or *confess Jesus Christ as coming in the flesh* [e]**8** Other mss read *you* [f]**12** Lit *mouth to mouth*

3 JOHN

Greeting

The Elder:
To my dear friend[a] [a]Gaius, whom I
love in truth. *[a]Ac 19:29; Rm 16:23*

[2]Dear friend,[b] I pray that you may
prosper in every way and be in good
health, just as your soul prospers. [3]For
I was very glad when some brothers
came and testified to your ⌊faithfulness⌋
to the truth—how [a]you are •walking in
the truth. [4]I have no greater joy than
this: to hear that [b]my children are
walking in the truth. *[a]2Jn 4 [b]1Co 4:15*

Gaius Commended

[5]Dear friend,[b] you are showing your
faith[c] by whatever you [a]do for the
brothers, and this ⌊you are doing⌋ for
strangers; [6]they have testified to your
love before the church. You will do
well to send them on their journey in
a manner worthy of God, [7]since they
set out for the sake of the name, [b]ac-
cepting nothing from pagans. [8]There-
fore, we ought to support such men, so
that we can be co-workers with[d] the
truth. *[a]Lk 12:42 [b]1Co 9:12-15*

Diotrephes and Demetrius

[9]I wrote something to the church,
but Diotrephes, who loves to have first
place among them, does not receive
us. [10]This is why, if I come, I will remind him of the works he is doing,
slandering us with malicious words.
And he is not satisfied with that! He
not only refuses to welcome the brothers himself, but he even stops those
who want to do so and expels them
from the church.
[11]Dear friend,[b] [a]do not imitate what
is evil, but what is good. [b]The one who
does good is of God; the one who does
evil has not seen God. [12]Demetrius
has a ⌊good⌋ testimony from everyone,
and from the truth itself. And we also
testify for him, [c]and you know that our
testimony is true. *[a]Jn 10:27; Eph 5:1; Heb 6:12 [b]1Jn 2:29 [c]Jn 21:24*

Farewell

[13]I have many things to write you,
but I don't want to write to you with
pen and ink. [14]I hope to see you soon,
and we will talk face to face.[e]

Peace be with you. The friends send you greetings. Greet the friends by name.

[a]**1** Or *my beloved* [b]**2,5,11** Or *Beloved* [c]**5** Lit *are doing faith* [d]**8** Or *co-workers for* [e]**14** Lit *mouth to mouth*

JUDE

Greeting

Jude, a slave of Jesus Christ, and a
[a]brother of James:
To those who are [b]the called, loved[a]
by God the Father and [c]kept by Jesus
Christ.
2 May mercy, peace, and love be multiplied to you. *[a]Lk 6:16 [b]Rm 1:7 [c]Jn 17:11*

Jude's Purpose in Writing

3 Dear friends, although I was eager
to write you [a]about our common salvation, I found it necessary to write and
exhort you to contend for the faith that
was delivered to the saints once for all.
4 For certain men, [b]who were desig-
nated for this judgment long ago, have
come in by stealth; they are ungodly,
turning [c]the grace of our God into promiscuity and [d]denying our only Master
and Lord, Jesus Christ. *[a]Ti 1:4*
[b]Rm 9:21 [c]Ti 2:11; Heb 12:15
[d]2Pt 2:1; 1Jn 2:22

Apostates: Past and Present

5 Now I want to remind you, though
you know all these things: the Lord,
having first of all[b] saved a people out of
Egypt, later [a]destroyed those who did
not believe; 6 and He has kept, with
eternal chains in darkness [b]for the
judgment of the great day, [c]angels who
did not keep their own position but deserted their proper dwelling. 7 In the
same way, [d]Sodom and Gomorrah and
the cities around them committed sexual immorality and practiced perver-
sions,[c] just as they did, and serve as an
example by undergoing the punishment of eternal fire. *[a]Heb 3:17-19*
[b]2Pt 2:9; Rv 20:10
[c]2Pt 2:4 [d]Dt 29:23

8 Nevertheless, these dreamers likewise defile their flesh, despise authority, and [a]blaspheme glorious beings.
9 Yet [b]Michael the archangel, when
he was disputing with the Devil in a
debate about [c]Moses' body, [d]did not
dare bring an abusive condemnation
against him, but said, [e]"The Lord rebuke you!" 10 But these people blaspheme anything they don't understand, and what they know by instinct,
like unreasoning animals—they destroy themselves with these things.
11 Woe to them! For they have traveled
in the way [f]of Cain, [g]have abandoned
themselves to the error of Balaam for
profit, and have perished [h]in Korah's
rebellion. *[a]Ex 22:28 [b]Dn 10:13; Rv 12:7*
[c]Dt 34:6 [d]2Pt 2:11
[e]Zch 3:2 [f]1Jn 3:12
[g]Nm 22:7 [h]Nm 16:1

The Apostates' Doom

12 These are the ones who are like
dangerous reefs[d] at your [a]love feasts.
They feast with you, nurturing only
themselves without fear. They are wa-
terless clouds [b]carried along by winds;
trees in late autumn—fruitless, twice
dead, pulled out by the roots; 13 [c]wild
waves of the sea, foaming up their
shameful deeds; wandering stars for
whom is reserved the blackness of
darkness forever! *[a]1Co 11:21 [b]Eph 4:14*
[c]Is 57:20

14 And Enoch, in [a]the seventh ⌊gen-
eration⌋ from Adam, prophesied about
them:

Look! [b]The Lord comes[e]
with thousands
of His holy ones

[a]**1** Other mss read *sanctified* [b]**5** Other mss place *first of all* after *remind you* [c]**7** Lit *and went after other flesh* [d]**12** Or *like spots* [e]**14** Or *came*

15 to execute judgment on all,
and to convict them[a]
of all their ungodly deeds
that they have done
in an ungodly way,
and of all the harsh things
ungodly sinners
have said against Him.

16 These people are discontented
grumblers, •walking according to their
desires; their mouths utter arrogant
words, [c]flattering people for their own
advantage. [a]*Gn 5:18* [b]*Dn 7:10* [c]*Pr 28:21*

17 But you, dear friends, remember
the words foretold by the apostles of
our Lord Jesus Christ; 18 they told you,
"In the end time there will be scoffers
walking according to their own ungodly desires." 19 These people [a]create
divisions and are merely natural, not
having the Spirit. [a]*Heb 10:25*

Exhortation and Benediction

20 But you, dear friends, [a]building
yourselves up in your most holy faith
and [b]praying in the Holy Spirit, 21 keep
yourselves in the love of God, expecting the mercy of our Lord Jesus Christ
for eternal life. 22 Have mercy on some
who doubt; 23 [c]save others by [d]snatch-
ing ⌊them⌋ from the fire; on others have
mercy in fear, hating even the garment
defiled by the flesh. [a]*Col 2:7* [b]*Mt 10:20; Rm 8:26* [c]*Rm 11:14* [d]*Am 4:11*

24 [a]Now to Him who is able to protect you from stumbling and [b]to make
you stand in the presence of His glory,
blameless and with great joy, 25 [c]to the
only God our Savior, through Jesus
Christ our Lord,[b] be glory, majesty,
power, and authority before all time,[c]
now, and forever. •Amen [a]*Eph 3:20* [b]*Col 1:22* [c]*1Tm 1:17*

REVELATION

Prologue

1 The revelation of[d] Jesus Christ [a]that
God gave Him to show His •slaves
what must quickly[e] take place. [b]He
sent it and signified it[f] through His angel to His slave John, 2 who testified to
God's word and to the testimony[g] about
Jesus Christ, in all [c]he saw.[h] 3 [d]Blessed
is the one who reads and blessed are
those who hear the words of this
prophecy and keep[i] what is written in
it, because the time is near! [a]*Jn 12:49* [b]*Rv 22:16* [c]*1Jn 1:1* [d]*Lk 11:28; Rv 22:7*

4 John:
To the seven churches in the province of Asia.[j]

Grace and peace to you from[k] the
One [a]who is, [b]who was, and who is
coming; from the seven spirits[l] before
His throne; 5 and from Jesus Christ,
[c]the faithful witness, the [d]firstborn
from the dead and [e]the ruler of the
kings of the earth. [a]*Ex 3:14* [b]*Jn 1:1* [c]*Jn 8:14* [d]*Col 1:18* [e]*Eph 1:20; Rv 17:14*

To Him [a]who loves us and [b]has set
us free[m] from our sins by His blood,
6 and made us a kingdom,[n] priests[o] to
His God and Father—[c]to Him be the
glory and dominion forever and ever.
•Amen. [a]*Jn 13:34* [b]*Heb 9:14* [c]*1Tm 6:16*

[a]**15** Lit *convict all* [b]**25** Other mss omit *through Jesus Christ our Lord* [c]**25** Other mss omit *before all time* [d]**1:1** Or *Revelation of*, or *A revelation of* [e]**1:1** Or *soon* [f]**1:1** Made it known through symbols [g]**1:2** Or *witness* [h]**1:2** Lit *as many as he saw* [i]**1:3** Or *follow*, or *obey* [j]**1:4** Lit *churches in Asia*; that is, the Roman province that is now a part of modern Turkey [k]**1:4** Other mss add *God* [l]**1:4** Or *the sevenfold Spirit* [m]**1:5** Other mss read *has washed us* [n]**1:6** Other mss read *kings and* [o]**1:6** Or *made us into* (or *to be*) *a kingdom of priests*; see Ex 19:6

7 [a]**Look! He is coming**
with the clouds,
and every eye will see Him,
[b]**including those who pierced**[a]
Him.
And all the families
of the earth[b c]
will mourn over Him.[d e]
This is certain. Amen.
[a]Dn 7:13 [b]Zch 12:10

8 [a]"I am the •Alpha and the Omega,"
says the Lord God, "the One who is,
who was, and who is coming, the Almighty." *[a]Is 41:4*

John's Vision of the Risen Lord

9 I, John, your brother and partner in
the tribulation, [a]kingdom, and perseverance in Jesus, was on the island
called Patmos because of God's word
and the testimony about Jesus.[f] 10 I was
in the Spirit[g h] on [b]the Lord's day,[i] and I
heard behind me a loud voice like a
trumpet 11 saying, "Write on a scroll[j]
what you see and send it to the seven
churches: Ephesus, Smyrna, Pergamum, Thyatira, Sardis, Philadelphia,
and Laodicea." *[a]Rm 8:17 [b]Ac 20:7*

12 I turned to see the voice that was
speaking to me. When I turned [a]I saw
seven gold lampstands, 13 and among
the lampstands was [b]One like the •Son
of Man,[k] dressed in a long robe, and
with a gold sash wrapped around His
chest. 14 [c]His head and hair were white
like wool—white as snow, [d]His eyes
like a fiery flame, 15 [e]His feet like fine
bronze fired in a furnace, and [f]His
voice like the sound of cascading[l] waters. 16 In His right hand He had seven
stars; [g]from His mouth came a sharp
two-edged sword; [h]and His face was
shining like the sun at midday.[m]
[a]Ex 25:37; Zch 4:2 [b]Dn 7:13 [c]Dn 7:9 [d]Rv 2:18 [e]Ezk 1:7 [f]Ezk 43:2 [g]Heb 4:12 [h]Ac 26:13

17 [a]When I saw Him, I fell at His feet
like a dead man. He laid His right hand
on me, and said, "Don't be afraid! [b]I
am the First and the Last, 18 [c]and the
Living One. I was dead, but look—I am
alive forever and ever, and [d]I hold the
keys of death and •Hades. 19 Therefore
write what you have seen, what is, and
what will take place after this. 20 The
secret[n] of the seven stars you saw in
My right hand, and of the seven gold
lampstands, is this: the seven stars are
[e]the angels[o] of the seven churches, and
the [f]seven lampstands[p] are the seven
churches. *[a]Ezk 1:28 [b]Is 44:6 [c]Rm 6:9 [d]Ps 68:20; Mt 16:19; Rv 20:1 [e]Mal 2:7 [f]Mt 5:15; Php 2:15*

The Letters to the Seven Churches

The Letter to Ephesus

2 "To the angel[q] of the church in
[a]Ephesus write: *[a]Ac 19:1*

[a]"The One who holds the seven
stars in His right hand and who walks
among the seven gold lampstands says:
2 [b]I know your works, your labor, and
your endurance, and that you cannot
tolerate evil. [c]You have tested those
[d]who call themselves apostles and are
not, and you have found them to be liars. 3 You also possess endurance and
have tolerated ⌊many things⌋ because
of My name, and have [e]not grown
weary. 4 But I have this against you:
you have abandoned the love ⌊you had⌋
at first. 5 Remember then how far you

[a]**1:7** Or *impaled* [b]**1:7** Or *All the tribes of the land* [c]**1:7** Gn 12:3; 28:14; Zch 14:17 [d]**1:7** Or *will wail because of Him* [e]**1:7** Dn 7:13; Zch 12:10 [f]**1:9** Lit *the witness of Jesus* [g]**1:10** Lit *I became in the Spirit* or *in spirit* [h]**1:10** John was brought by God's Spirit into a realm of spiritual vision. [i]**1:10** Sunday [j]**1:11** Or *book* [k]**1:13** Or *like a son of man* [l]**1:15** Lit *many* [m]**1:16** Lit *like the sun shines in its power* [n]**1:20** Or *mystery* [o]**1:20** Or *messengers* [p]**1:20** Other mss add *that you saw* [q]**2:1** Or *messenger* here and elsewhere

have fallen; repent, and do the works
you did at first. [f]Otherwise, I will come
to you[a] and remove your lampstand
from its place—unless you repent.
6 Yet you do have this: you hate the
practices of the Nicolaitans, which I
also hate.

[a]Rv 1:16 [b]1Th 1:3; Rv 3:1,8,15 [c]1Jn 4:1 [d]2Co 11:13 [e]Gl 6:9; Heb 12:3,5 [f]Mt 21:41; Rv 3:3

7 [a]"Anyone who has an ear should
listen to what the Spirit says to the
churches. I will give the victor the
right [b]to eat from [c]the tree of life,
which is in[b] the paradise of God.

[a]Mt 11:15 [b]Rv 22:2,14 [c]Gn 2:9

The Letter to Smyrna

8 "To the angel of the church in
Smyrna write:
[a]"The First and the Last, the One
who was dead and came to life, says: 9 I
know your[c] tribulation and poverty, yet
you are [b]rich. ⌊I know⌋ the slander of
[c]those who say they are Jews and are
not, but are a •synagogue of Satan.
10 [d]Don't be afraid of what you are
about to suffer. Look, the Devil is about
to throw some of you into prison to test
you, and you will have tribulation for
10 days. [e]Be faithful until death, and I
will give you [f]the crown[d] of life.

[a]Rv 1:8 [b]Jms 2:5 [c]Rm 2:17 [d]Mt 10:22 [e]Mt 24:13 [f]Jms 1:12

11 [a]"Anyone who has an ear should
listen to what the Spirit says to the
churches. The victor will never be
harmed by [b]the second death.

[a]Rv 13:9 [b]Rv 20:14

The Letter to Pergamum

12 "To the angel of the church in Pergamum write:
[a]"The One who has [b]the sharp, two-
edged sword says: 13 I know[e] where
you live—where Satan's throne is! And
you are holding on to My name and did
not deny your faith in Me,[f] even in the
days of Antipas, My faithful witness,
who was killed among you, [c]where Satan lives.
14 But I have a few things
against you. You have some there who
hold to the teaching of [d]Balaam, who
taught Balak to place a stumbling block[g]
in front of the sons of Israel: [e]to eat
meat sacrificed to idols and [f]to commit
sexual immorality.[h] 15 In the same way,
you also have those who hold to the
teaching of the Nicolaitans.[i] 16 Therefore repent!
Otherwise, I will come to
you quickly and [g]fight against them
with the sword of My mouth.

[a]Rv 1:16 [b]Jos 5:13 [c]Lv 17:7; Rv 2:9 [d]Nm 25:1; 2Pt 2:15 [e]Ac 15:29 [f]1Co 6:13 [g]Is 11:4

17 "Anyone who has an ear should
listen to what the Spirit says to the
churches. I will give the victor some of
the hidden manna.[j] I will also give
him a white stone, and on the stone [a]a
new name is inscribed that no one
knows except the one who receives it.

[a]Rv 3:12

The Letter to Thyatira

18 "To the angel of the church in
Thyatira write:
"The Son of God, the One [a]whose
eyes are like a fiery flame, and whose
feet are like fine bronze says: 19 I know
your works—your love, faithfulness,[k]
service, and endurance. Your last
works are greater than the first. 20 But
I have this against you: you tolerate the
woman [b]Jezebel, who calls herself a
prophetess, and teaches and deceives
My slaves to commit sexual immorality[h]
and to eat meat sacrificed to idols.
21 I gave her time [c]to repent, but she
does not want to repent of her sexual
immorality.[l] 22 Look! I will throw her
into a sickbed, and those who commit
adultery with her into great tribula-

[a]**2:5** Other mss add *quickly* [b]**2:7** Other mss read *in the midst of* [c]**2:9** Other mss add *works and*
[d]**2:10** Or *wreath* [e]**2:13** Other mss add *your works and* [f]**2:13** Or *deny My faith* [g]**2:14** Or *to place a trap*
[h]**2:14,20** Or *commit fornication* [i]**2:15** Other mss add *which I hate* [j]**2:17** Other mss add *to eat*
[k]**2:19** Or *faith* [l]**2:21** Or *her fornication*

tion, unless they repent of her[a] practices. 23 I will kill her children with the
plague.[b] Then all the churches will
know that [d]I am the One who exam-
ines minds[c] and hearts, and [e]I will give
to each of you according to your works.
24 I say to the rest of you in Thyatira,
who do not hold this teaching, who
haven't [f]known the deep things[d] of Satan—as they say—[g]I do not put any
other burden on you. 25 But hold on to
what you have until I come. 26 The victor and the one who keeps [h]My works
to the end: [i]I will give him authority
over the nations—

27 [j]**and He will shepherd[e] them**
with an iron scepter;
He will shatter them
like pottery[f] —

just as I have received ⌊this⌋ from My
Father. 28 I will also give him [k]the
morning star.

[a]Rv 1:14 [b]1Kg 16:31 [c]Rm 2:4 [d]1Ch 28:9 [e]Mt 16:27; Rv 20:12 [f]2Co 2:11 [g]Ac 15:28 [h]Jn 6:29 [i]Lk 22:29; 1Co 6:3 [j]Ps 2:9; Rv 19:15 [k]2Pt 1:19; Rv 22:16

29 "Anyone who has an ear should
listen to what the Spirit says to the
churches.

The Letter to Sardis

3 "To the angel of the church in Sardis write:
"The One who has the seven spirits
of God and the seven stars says: I know
your works; you have a reputation[g] for
being alive, [a]but you are dead. 2 Be
alert and strengthen[h] what remains,
which is about to die, for I have not
found your works complete before My
God. 3 Remember therefore what you
have received and heard; keep it, and
repent. But [b]if you are not alert, I will
come[i] like a thief, and you have no idea
at what hour I will come against you.[j]
4 But you have a few people[k] in Sardis
who have not [c]defiled[l] their clothes,
and they will walk with Me [d]in white,
because they are worthy. 5 In the same
way, the victor will be dressed in white
clothes, and I will never [e]erase his
name from the [f]book of life, [g]but will
acknowledge his name before My Father and before His angels.

[a]Eph 2:1; Col 2:13 [b]Lk 12:39 [c]Jd 23 [d]Rv 7:9,13 [e]Ps 69:28 [f]Php 4:3; Rv 21:27 [g]Mt 10:32

6 "Anyone who has an ear should listen to what the Spirit says to the
churches.

The Letter to Philadelphia

7 "To the angel of the church in Philadelphia write:
[a]"The Holy One, [b]the True One, the
One who has [c]the key of David, [d]who
opens and no one will close, and
[e]closes and no one opens says: 8 I know
your works. Because you have limited
strength, have kept My word, and
have not denied My name, look, I have
placed before you [f]an open door that
no one is able to close. 9 Take note! I
will make those from the •synagogue
of Satan, who claim to be Jews and are
not, but are lying—note this—[g]I will
make them come and bow down at
your feet, and they will know that I
have loved you. 10 Because you have
kept My command to endure,[m] [h]I will
also keep you from the hour of testing
that is going to come over the whole
world to test those who live on the
earth. 11 I am coming quickly. Hold on
to what you have, so that no one takes
your crown. 12 The victor: I will make
him [i]a pillar in the sanctuary of My
God, and he will never go out again.
[j]I will write on him the name of My
God, and the name of the city of
My God—the [k]new Jerusalem, which

[a]**2:22** Other mss read *their* [b]**2:23** Or *I will surely kill her children* [c]**2:23** Lit *kidneys* [d]**2:24** Or *the secret things* [e]**2:27** Or *rule*; see 19:15 [f]**2:27** Ps 2:9 [g]**3:1** Lit *have a name* [h]**3:2** Other mss read *guard* [i]**3:3** Other mss add *upon you* [j]**3:3** Or *upon you* [k]**3:4** Lit *few names* [l]**3:4** Or *soiled* [m]**3:10** Lit *My word of endurance*

comes down out of heaven from My God—and [l]My new name.

[a]Ac 3:14 [b]1Jn 5:20 [c]Is 22:22; Lk 1:32 [d]Mt 16:19 [e]Jb 12:14 [f]2Co 2:12 [g]Is 49:23 [h]2Pt 2:9 [i]Gl 2:9 [j]Rv 14:1 [k]Gl 4:26; Rv 21:2,10 [l]Rv 22:4

13 "Anyone who has an ear should listen to what the Spirit says to the churches.

The Letter to Laodicea

14 "To the angel of the church in Laodicea write:

"The [a]•Amen, the [b]faithful and true Witness, the [c]Originator[a] of God's creation says: 15 I know your works, that you are neither cold nor hot. I wish that you were cold or hot. 16 So, because you are lukewarm, and neither hot nor cold, I am going to vomit[b] you out of My mouth. 17 Because you say, [d]'I'm rich; I have become wealthy, and need nothing,' and you don't know that you are wretched, pitiful, poor, blind, and naked, 18 I advise you [e]to buy from Me gold refined in the fire so that you may be rich, and [f]white clothes so that you may be dressed and your shameful nakedness not be exposed, and ointment to spread on your eyes so that you may see. 19 [g]As many as I love, I rebuke and discipline. So be committed[c] and repent. 20 Listen! I stand at the door and knock. [h]If anyone hears My voice and opens the door, [i]I will come in to him and have dinner with him, and he with Me. 21 The victor: [j]I will give him the right to sit with Me on My throne, just as I also won the victory and sat down with My Father on His throne.

[a]2Co 1:20 [b]Is 55:4; Rv 22:6 [c]Jn 1:1 [d]Pr 13:7 [e]Is 55:1; Mt 13:44 [f]2Co 5:3 [g]Dt 8:5; Heb 12:5-6 [h]Lk 12:36-37 [i]Jn 14:23 [j]Mt 19:28; 1Co 6:2

22 "Anyone who has an ear should listen to what the Spirit says to the churches."

The Throne Room of Heaven

4 After this I looked, and there in heaven was an open door. The first voice that I had heard speaking to me like a trumpet said, "Come up here, and I will show you what must take place after this."

2 Immediately I [a]was in the Spirit,[d] and there in heaven [b]a throne was set. One was seated on the throne, 3 and the One seated[e] looked like jasper[f] and carnelian[g] stone. [c]A rainbow that looked like an emerald surrounded the throne. 4 Around that throne were 24 thrones, and on the thrones sat 24 elders dressed in white clothes, with gold crowns on their heads. 5 From the throne came flashes of lightning, rumblings, and thunder. Burning before the throne [d]were seven fiery torches, which are the seven spirits of God. 6 Also before the throne was something like a sea of glass, similar to crystal. [e]In the middle[h] and around the throne were four living creatures covered with eyes in front and in back. 7 The first living creature was like a lion; the second living creature was like a calf; the third living creature had a face like a man; and the fourth living creature was like a flying eagle. 8 Each of the four living creatures had [f]six wings; they were covered with eyes around and inside. Day and night they never stop,[i] saying:

> Holy, holy, holy,[j]
> Lord God, the Almighty,
> who was, who is,
> and who is coming.

[a]Rv 1:10 [b]Is 6:1; Dn 7:9 [c]Ezk 1:28 [d]Ezk 1:13; Zch 4:2 [e]Ezk 1:5 [f]Is 6:2

9 Whenever the living creatures give glory, honor, and thanks to the One seated on the throne, the One who lives forever and ever, 10 the 24 elders fall down before the One seated on

[a]**3:14** Or *Ruler*, or *Source*, or *Beginning* [b]**3:16** Or *spit* [c]**3:19** Or *be zealous* [d]**4:2** Lit *I became in the Spirit* or *in spirit* [e]**4:3** Other mss omit *and the One seated* [f]**4:3** A precious stone [g]**4:3** A translucent red gem [h]**4:6** Lit *In the middle of the throne* [i]**4:8** Or *they never rest* [j]**4:8** Other mss read *holy* 9 times

the throne, worship the One who
lives forever and ever, cast their
crowns before the throne, and say:

11 Our Lord and God,[a]
You are worthy to receive
glory and honor and power,
because You have created
all things,
and because of Your will
they exist and were created.

The Lamb Takes the Scroll

5 Then I saw in the right hand of the
One seated on the throne [a]a scroll
with writing on the inside and on the
back, [b]sealed with seven seals. 2 I also
saw a mighty angel proclaiming in a
loud voice, "Who is worthy to open
the scroll and break its seals?" 3 But
[c]no one in heaven or on earth or under the earth was able to open the
scroll or even to look in it. 4 And I
cried and cried because no one was
found worthy to open[b] the scroll or
even to look in it.

[a] Ezk 2:9 [b] Dn 12:4; Rv 6:1 [c] Jn 1:18

5 Then one of the elders said to me,
"Stop crying. Look! [a]The Lion from the
tribe of Judah, [b]the Root of David, [c]has
been victorious so that He may open
the scroll and[c] its seven seals." 6 Then
I saw [d]one like a slaughtered lamb
standing between[d] the throne and the
four living creatures and among the elders. He had seven horns and [e]seven
eyes, which are the [f]seven spirits of
God sent into all the earth. 7 He came
and took ⌊the scroll⌋[e] out of the right
hand of the One seated on the throne.

[a] Gn 49:9-10 [b] Is 11:1,10; Rv 22:16 [c] Heb 2:10 [d] Is 53:7; Jn 1:29; 1Pt 1:19 [e] Zch 3:9 [f] Rv 4:5

The Lamb Is Worthy

8 When He took the scroll, the four
living creatures and the 24 elders fell
down before the Lamb. Each one had a
[a]harp and gold bowls filled with incense, [b]which are the prayers of the
saints. 9 And [c]they sang a new song:

[d]You are worthy to take the scroll
and to open its seals;
because You were slaughtered,
and [e]You redeemed[f] ⌊people⌋[g]
for God by Your blood
from every tribe and language
and people and nation.
10 [f]You made them a kingdom[h]
and priests to our God,
and they will reign on the earth.

[a] Rv 14:2 [b] Ps 141:2; Rv 8:3-4 [c] Rv 14:3 [d] Rv 4:11 [e] Mt 26:28; Eph 1:7 [f] Ex 19:6

11 Then I looked, and heard the voice
of many angels around the throne, and
also of the living creatures, and of the
elders. Their number was countless
[a]thousands, plus thousands of thousands. 12 They said with a loud voice:

The Lamb who was slaughtered
is worthy
to receive power and riches
and wisdom and strength
and honor and glory
and blessing!

[a] Dn 7:10; Heb 12:22

13 I heard [a]every creature in heaven,
on earth, under the earth, on the sea,
and everything in them say:

[b]Blessing and honor and glory
and dominion
to the One seated on the throne,
[c]and to the Lamb, forever
and ever!

14 The four living creatures said,
"•Amen," and the elders fell down
and worshiped.

[a] Php 2:10 [b] Eph 3:21; 1Tm 1:17 [c] Jn 5:23

The First Seal on the Scroll

6 Then I saw[i] the Lamb open one of
the seven[j] seals, and I heard one

[a]**4:11** Other mss add *the Holy One*; other mss read *O Lord* [b]**5:4** Other mss add *and read* [c]**5:5** Other mss add *loose* [d]**5:6** Or *standing in the middle of* [e]**5:7** Other mss include *the scroll* [f]**5:9** Or *purchased* [g]**5:9** Other mss read *us* [h]**5:10** Other mss read *them kings* [i]**6:1** Lit *saw when* [j]**6:1** Other mss omit *seven*

of the four living creatures say with a voice like thunder, "Come!"[a] [b] 2 I looked, and there was [a]a white horse. The horseman on it had a bow; [b]a crown was given to him, and he went out as a victor to conquer.[c]

[a] Zch 6:3; Rv 19:11 [b] Rv 14:14

The Second Seal

3 When He opened the second seal, I heard the second living creature say, "Come!"[a] [b] 4 [a]Then another horse went out, a fiery red one, and its horseman was empowered[d] to take peace from the earth, so that people would slaughter one another. And a large sword was given to him.

[a] Zch 6:6

The Third Seal

5 When He opened the third seal, I heard the third living creature say, "Come!"[a] [b] And I looked, and there was [a]a black horse. The horseman on it had a balance scale in his hand. 6 Then I heard something like a voice among the four living creatures say, "A quart of wheat for a •denarius, and three quarts of barley for a denarius—but [b]do not harm the olive oil and the wine."

[a] Zch 6:2 [b] Rv 9:4

The Fourth Seal

7 When He opened the fourth seal, I heard the voice of the fourth living creature say, "Come!"[a] [b] 8 And I looked, and there was a pale green[e] horse. The horseman on it was named Death, and •Hades was following after him. Authority was given to them[f] over a fourth of the earth, [a]to kill by the sword, by famine, by plague, and by the wild animals of the earth.

[a] Jr 15:2-3; Ezk 5:17

The Fifth Seal

9 When He opened the fifth seal, I saw under [a]the altar [b]the souls of those slaughtered because of God's word and [c]the testimony they had.[g] 10 They cried out with a loud voice: "O Lord,[h] holy and true, how long until You judge and avenge our blood from those who live on the earth?" 11 So a white robe was given to each of them, and they were told [d]to rest a little while longer until ⌊the number of⌋ their fellow slaves and their brothers, who were going to be killed just as they had been, would be completed.

[a] Rv 8:3 [b] Rv 20:4 [c] 2Tm 1:8 [d] 2Th 1:7; Heb 4:10; Rv 14:13

The Sixth Seal

12 Then I saw Him open[i] the sixth seal. [a]A violent earthquake occurred; [b]the sun turned black like sackcloth made of goat hair; the entire moon[j] became like blood; 13 the stars[k] of heaven fell to the earth as a fig tree drops its unripe figs when shaken by a high wind; 14 [c]the sky separated like a scroll being rolled up; and [d]every mountain and island was moved from its place.

[a] Rv 16:18 [b] Jl 2:10 [c] Is 34:4 [d] Jr 3:23

15 Then the kings of the earth, the nobles, the military commanders, the rich, the powerful, and every slave and free person [a]hid in the caves and among the rocks of the mountains. 16 And they said to the mountains and to the rocks, "Fall on us and hide us from the face of the One seated on the throne and from the wrath of the Lamb, 17 [b]because the great day of Their[l] wrath has come! [c]And who is able to stand?"

[a] Is 2:19 [b] Is 13:6; Zph 1:14 [c] Ps 76:7

The Sealed of Israel

7 After this I saw four [a]angels standing at the four corners of the earth, [b]restraining the four winds of

[a] **6:1,3,5,7** Other mss add *and see* [b] **6:1,3,5,7** Or *Go!* [c] **6:2** Lit *went out conquering and in order to conquer* [d] **6:4** Or *was granted*; lit *was given* [e] **6:8** Or *a greenish gray* [f] **6:8** Other mss read *him* [g] **6:9** Other mss add *about the Lamb* [h] **6:10** Or *Master* [i] **6:12** Lit *I saw when He opened* [j] **6:12** Or *the full moon* [k] **6:13** Perhaps meteors [l] **6:17** Other mss read *His*

the earth [c]so that no wind could blow
on the earth or on the sea or on any
tree. 2 Then I saw another angel rise
up from the east, who had the seal of
the living God. He cried out in a loud
voice to the four angels who were
empowered[a] to harm the earth and
the sea: 3 [d]"Don't harm the earth or
the sea or the trees until we [e]seal the
slaves of our God [f]on their foreheads."
4 And I heard the number of those
who were sealed:

[g]144,000 sealed from every tribe
of the sons of Israel:
5 12,000 sealed from the tribe
of Judah,
12,000[b] from the tribe
of Reuben,
12,000 from the tribe of Gad,
6 12,000 from the tribe of Asher,
12,000 from the tribe
of Naphtali,
12,000 from the tribe
of Manasseh,
7 12,000 from the tribe of Simeon,
12,000 from the tribe of Levi,
12,000 from the tribe
of Issachar,
8 12,000 from the tribe
of Zebulun,
12,000 from the tribe of Joseph,
12,000 sealed from the tribe
of Benjamin. [a] *Ps 34:7; Heb 1:14*
[b] *Dn 7:2* [c] *Rv 9:4* [d] *Rv 6:6; 9:4*
[e] *Eph 4:30; Rv 14:1* [f] *Rv 22:4*
[g] *Is 4:2-3; Rv 14:1*

A Multitude from the Great Tribulation

9 After this I looked, and there was [a]a
vast multitude from [b]every nation,
tribe, people, and language, which no
one could number, standing before the
throne and before the Lamb. They
were [c]robed in white with palm
branches in their hands. 10 And they
cried out in a loud voice:

[d]Salvation belongs to our God,
[e]who is seated on the throne,
and to the Lamb! [a] *Is 2:2-3*
[b] *Zch 2:11; Rm 11:25; Rv 5:9*
[c] *Rv 3:5* [d] *Ps 3:8; Zch 9:9* [e] *Rv 5:13*

11 [a]All the angels stood around the
throne, the elders, and the four living
creatures, and they fell on their faces
before the throne and worshiped God,
12 [b]saying:

•Amen! Blessing and glory
and wisdom
and thanksgiving and honor
and power and strength,
be to our God forever and ever.
Amen. [a] *Rv 4:6* [b] *Rv 5:13*

13 Then one of the elders asked me,
"Who are these people robed in white,
and where did they come from?"
14 I said to him, "Sir,[c] you know."
Then he told me:

[a]These are the ones coming out
of the great tribulation.
They [b]washed their robes
and made them white
in the blood of the Lamb.
15 For this reason they are
before the throne of God,
and they serve Him
day and night in His sanctuary.
The One seated on the throne
will [c]shelter[d] them:
16 [d]no longer will they hunger;
no longer will they thirst;
[e]no longer will the sun
strike them, or any heat.
17 Because the Lamb who is
at the center of the throne
[f]will shepherd them;
He will guide them to springs
of living waters,
[g]and God will wipe away
every tear from their eyes.
[a] *Ac 14:22* [b] *Heb 9:14; Rv 1:5*
[c] *Is 4:5-6* [d] *Is 49:10* [e] *Ps 121:6*
[f] *Ps 23:1; Jn 10:11* [g] *Is 25:8*

[a]**7:2** Lit *angels to whom it was given* [b]**7:5–8** Other mss add *sealed* after each number [c]**7:14** Lit *My lord*
[d]**7:15** Or *will spread His tent over*

The Seventh Seal

8 When He opened the seventh seal, there was silence in heaven for about half an hour. 2 [a]Then I saw the seven angels who stand in the presence of God; seven trumpets were given to them. 3 Another angel, with a gold incense burner, came and stood at the altar. He was given a large amount of incense to offer with [b]the prayers of all the saints on [c]the gold altar in front of the throne. 4 [d]The smoke of the incense, with the prayers of the saints, went up in the presence of God from the angel's hand. 5 The angel took the incense burner, filled it with fire from the altar, and hurled it to the earth; [e]there were thunders, rumblings, lightnings, and an earthquake. 6 And the seven angels who had the seven trumpets prepared to blow them.

[a]Lk 1:19; Rv 15:1 [b]Rv 5:8 [c]Ex 30:1 [d]Ps 141:2 [e]Rv 16:18

The First Trumpet

7 The first ⌊angel⌋[a] blew his trumpet, [a]and hail and fire, mixed with blood, were hurled [b]to the earth. So a third of the earth was burned up, a third of the trees were burned up, and all the green grass was burned up.

[a]Ezk 38:22 [b]Rv 16:2

The Second Trumpet

8 The second angel blew his trumpet, and something like a great mountain ablaze with fire was hurled into the sea. So a third of the sea [a]became blood, 9 a third of the living creatures in the sea died, and a third of the ships were destroyed. *[a]Ezk 14:19*

The Third Trumpet

10 The third angel blew his trumpet, and a great star, blazing like a torch, fell from heaven. It fell on a third of the rivers and springs of water. 11 The name of the star is Wormwood,[b] [a]and a third of the waters became wormwood. So, many of the people died from the waters, because they had been made bitter. *[a]Jr 9:15*

The Fourth Trumpet

12 [a]The fourth angel blew his trumpet, and a third of the sun was struck, a third of the moon, and a third of the stars, so that a third of them were darkened. A third of the day was without light, and the night as well.

[a]Is 13:10; Am 8:9

13 I looked, and I heard an eagle,[c] flying in mid-heaven,[d] saying in a loud voice, [a]"Woe! Woe! Woe to those who live on the earth, because of the remaining trumpet blasts that the three angels are about to sound!" *[a]Rv 9:12*

The Fifth Trumpet

9 The fifth angel blew his trumpet, and [a]I saw a star that had fallen from heaven to earth. The key to the shaft of [b]the •abyss was given to him. 2 He opened the shaft of the abyss, [c]and smoke came up out of the shaft like smoke from a great[e] furnace so that the sun and the air were darkened by the smoke from the shaft. 3 Then out of the smoke [d]locusts came to the earth, and power[f] was given to them like the power that scorpions have on the earth. 4 They were told not to harm the grass of the earth, or any green plant, or any tree, but only people who do not have [e]God's seal on their foreheads. 5 They were not permitted to kill them, [f]but were to torment ⌊them⌋ for five months; their torment is like the torment caused by a scorpion when it strikes a man. 6 In those days [g]people will seek death and will not find it; they will long to die, but death will flee from them.

[a]Is 14:12; Lk 10:18; Rv 8:10 [b]Lk 8:31; Rv 17:8 [c]Jl 2:2,10 [d]Ex 10:4 [e]Ex 12:23; Ezk 9:4; Rv 7:3 [f]Rv 11:7 [g]Jb 3:21; Hs 10:8; Rv 6:16

[a]**8:7** Other mss include *angel* [b]**8:11** *Wormwood* is absinthe, a bitter herb. [c]**8:13** Other mss read *angel* [d]**8:13** Very high [e]**9:2** Other mss omit *great* [f]**9:3** Or *authority*

7 [a]The appearance of the locusts was like horses equipped for battle. [b]On their heads were something like gold crowns; [c]their faces were like men's faces; 8 they had hair like women's hair; [d]their teeth were like lions' teeth; 9 they had chests like iron breastplates; the sound of their wings was like the sound of chariots with many horses rushing into battle; 10 and they had tails with stingers, like scorpions, so that with their tails they had the power[a] to harm people for five months. 11 [e]They had as their king[b] the angel of the abyss; his name in Hebrew is Abaddon,[c] and in Greek he has the name Apollyon.[d] 12 [f]The first woe has passed. There are still two more woes to come after this.

a Jl 2:4 b Nah 3:17 c Dn 7:8 d Jl 1:6 e Jn 12:31; Eph 2:2 f Rv 8:13

The Sixth Trumpet

13 The sixth angel blew his trumpet. From the four[e] horns of the gold altar that is before God, I heard a voice 14 say to the sixth angel who had the trumpet, "Release the four angels bound [a]at the great river Euphrates." 15 So the four angels who were prepared for the hour, day, month, and year were released to kill a third of the human race. 16 [b]The number of mounted troops was 200 million;[f] I heard their number. 17 This is how I saw the horses in my vision: The horsemen had breastplates that were fiery red, hyacinth blue, and sulfur yellow. [c]The heads of the horses were like lions' heads, and from their mouths came fire, smoke, and sulfur. 18 A third of the human race was killed by these three plagues—by the fire, the smoke, and the sulfur that came from their mouths. 19 For the power of the horses is in their mouths and in their tails, because their tails, like snakes, have heads, and they inflict injury with them.

a Rv 16:12 b Ps 68:17; Dn 7:10 c Is 5:28

20 The rest of the people, who were not killed by these plagues, [a]did not repent of the works of their hands to stop worshiping [b]demons and [c]idols of gold, silver, bronze, stone, and wood, which are not able to see, hear, or walk. 21 And they did not repent of their murders, their sorceries,[g] their sexual immorality, or their thefts.

a Dt 31:29; Jr 5:3 b Dt 32:17; 1Co 10:20 c Ps 115:4

The Mighty Angel and the Small Scroll

10 Then I saw another mighty angel coming down from heaven, surrounded by a cloud, [a]with a rainbow over his head.[h] [b]His face was like the sun, [c]his legs[i] were like fiery pillars, 2 and he had a little scroll opened in his hand. [d]He put his right foot on the sea, his left on the land, 3 and he cried out with a loud voice like a roaring lion. When he cried out, the [e]seven thunders spoke with their voices. 4 And when the seven thunders spoke, I was about to write. Then I heard a voice from heaven, saying, [f]"Seal up what the seven thunders said, and do not write it down!"

a Ezk 1:28 b Mt 17:2 c Rv 1:15 d Mt 28:18 e Rv 8:5 f Dn 8:26

5 Then the angel that I had seen standing on the sea and on the land raised his right hand to heaven. 6 He swore an oath by the One who [a]lives forever and ever, who created heaven and what is in it, the earth and what is in it, and the sea and what is in it: [b]"There will no longer be an interval of time,[j] 7 but [c]in the days of the sound of the seventh angel, when he will blow his trumpet, then God's hidden

[a]**9:10** Or *authority* [b]**9:11** Or *as king over them* [c]**9:11** Or *destruction* [d]**9:11** Or *destroyer* [e]**9:13** Other mss omit *four* [f]**9:16** Other mss read *100 million* [g]**9:21** Or *magic potions*, or *drugs*; Gk *pharmakon* [h]**10:1** Or *a halo on his head* [i]**10:1** Or *feet* [j]**10:6** Or *be a delay*

plan[a] will be completed, as He announced to His servants[b] the prophets." [a]Jr 10:10; Rv 4:9 [b]Rv 16:17 [c]Rv 11:15

8 Now the voice that I heard from heaven spoke to me again and said, "Go, take the scroll that lies open in the hand of the angel who is standing on the sea and on the land."

9 So I went to the angel and asked him to give me the little scroll. He said to me, [a]"Take and eat it; it will be bitter in your stomach, but it will be as sweet as honey in your mouth." [a]Jr 15:16; Ezk 2:8

10 Then I took the little scroll from the angel's hand and ate it. It was as sweet as honey in my mouth, but when I ate it, my stomach became bitter. 11 And I was told,[c] "You must prophesy again about[d] many peoples, nations, languages, and kings."

The Two Witnesses

11 Then I was given [a]a measuring reed like a rod,[e] with these words: "Go[f] and measure God's sanctuary and the altar, and ⌊count⌋ those who worship there. 2 But [b]exclude the courtyard outside the sanctuary. Don't measure it, [c]because it is given to the nations,[g] and they will [d]trample the holy city for [e]42 months. 3 I will empower[h] my two [f]witnesses, [g]and they will prophesy for [h]1,260 days,[i] dressed in sackcloth."[j] 4 These are the [i]two olive trees and the two lampstands that stand before the Lord[k] of the earth. 5 If anyone wants to harm them, [j]fire comes from their mouths and consumes their enemies; [k]if anyone wants to harm them, he must be killed in this way. 6 These men have the power to close the sky so that it does not rain during the days of their prophecy. They also have power over the waters to turn them into blood, and to strike the earth with any plague whenever they want. [a]Ezk 40:3 [b]Ezk 40:17 [c]Ps 79:1; Lk 21:24 [d]Dn 8:10 [e]Rv 13:5 [f]Rv 6:9 [g]Rv 19:10 [h]Rv 12:6 [i]Ps 52:8; Jr 11:16 [j]Jr 1:10; Hs 6:5 [k]Nm 16:29

The Witnesses Martyred

7 When they finish their testimony, [a]the beast[l] that comes up [b]out of the •abyss will make war with them, conquer them, and kill them. 8 Their dead bodies[l] will lie in the public square[m] of [c]the great city, which is called, prophetically,[n] Sodom and Egypt, [d]where also their Lord was crucified. 9 [e]And representatives from[o] the peoples, tribes, languages, and nations will view their bodies for three and a half days [f]and not permit their bodies to be put into a tomb. 10 [g]Those who live on the earth will gloat over them and celebrate and send gifts to one another, because these two prophets tormented those who live on the earth. [a]Rv 13:1 [b]Dn 7:21 [c]Rv 14:8 [d]Heb 13:12; Rv 18:24 [e]Rv 17:15 [f]Ps 79:2-3 [g]Rv 12:12

The Witnesses Resurrected

11 But after the three and a half days, [a]the breath[p] of life from God entered them, and they stood on their feet. So great fear fell on those who saw them. 12 Then they heard[q] a loud voice from heaven saying to them, "Come up here." [b]They went up to heaven in a cloud, while their enemies watched them. 13 At that moment a violent earthquake took place, [c]a tenth of the city fell, and 7,000 people were killed in the earthquake. The survivors were terrified and gave glory to the God of heaven. 14 The second woe has passed. Take note: the third woe is coming quickly! [a]Ezk 37:5,9-10,14 [b]Is 60:8 [c]Rv 14:7

[a]**10:7** Or *God's secret* or *mystery*; see Rv 1:20; 17:5,7 [b]**10:7** Or *slaves* [c]**10:11** Lit *And they said to me* [d]**10:11** Or *prophesy again against* [e]**11:1** Other mss add *and the angel stood up* [f]**11:1** Lit *Arise* [g]**11:2** Or *Gentiles* [h]**11:3** Lit *I will give to* [i]**11:3** Three and a half years of thirty-day months [j]**11:3** Mourning garment of coarse, often black, material [k]**11:4** Other mss read *God* [l]**11:7** Or *wild animal* **11:8** Lit *Their corpse* [m]**11:8** Or *lie on the broad street* [n]**11:8** Or *spiritually*, or *symbolically* [o]**11:9** Lit *And from* [p]**11:11** Or *spirit* [q]**11:12** Other mss read *Then I heard*

The Seventh Trumpet

15 The seventh angel blew his trumpet, [a]and there were loud voices in
heaven saying:

The kingdom of the world
has become the ⌊kingdom⌋
of our Lord and of His •Messiah,
[b]and He will reign forever
and ever!

[a] Is 27:13 [b] Ps 145:13; Dn 2:44; Lk 1:33; Heb 1:8

16 The 24 elders, who were seated before God on their thrones, fell on their
faces and worshiped God, 17 saying:

We thank You, Lord God,
the Almighty, who is
and who was,[a]
because You have taken
Your great power
and have begun to reign.
18 The nations were angry,
but Your wrath has come.
The time has come for the dead
to be judged,
and to give the reward
to Your servants the prophets,
to the saints, and to those
who fear Your name,
both small and great,
[a]and the time has come
to destroy those who destroy
the earth.

19 God's sanctuary in heaven was
opened, and [b]the ark of His covenant[b]
appeared in His sanctuary. There were
lightnings, rumblings, thunders, an
earthquake,[c] and severe hail.

[a] Jb 12:15; Ec 3:17; Mt 13:49; 1Co 13:10 [b] Heb 9:4

The Woman, the Child, and the Dragon

12 A great sign[d] appeared in heaven:
a woman clothed with the sun,
with the moon under her feet, and a
crown of 12 stars on her head. 2 She
was pregnant and cried out in labor
and agony to give birth. 3 Then another
sign[e] appeared in heaven: There was a
[a]great fiery red dragon having seven
heads and 10 horns, and on his heads
were [b]seven diadems.[f] 4 His tail swept
away a third [c]of the stars in heaven and
[d]hurled them to the earth. And the
dragon stood in front of the woman
who was about to give birth, [e]so that
when she did give birth he might devour her child. 5 But she gave birth to a
Son—a male [f]who is going to shepherd[g] all nations with an iron scepter—and her child was caught up to
God and to His throne. 6 The woman
fled into the wilderness, where she had
a place prepared by God, to be fed
there[h] for [g]1,260 days.

[a] Rv 17:3,9 [b] Rv 13:1 [c] Rv 8:12 [d] Dn 8:10 [e] 1Pt 5:8 [f] Rv 2:27 [g] Rv 11:3

The Dragon Thrown Out of Heaven

7 Then war broke out in heaven:
[a]Michael and his angels [b]fought
against the dragon. The dragon and his
angels also fought, 8 but he could not
prevail, and there was no place for
them in heaven any longer. 9 So [c]the
great dragon was thrown out—[d]the
ancient serpent, who is called the Devil[i] and Satan,[j] the one who deceives the
whole world. [e]He was thrown to earth,
and his angels with him.

[a] Dn 10:13 [b] Rv 20:2 [c] Lk 10:18 [d] Gn 3:1 [e] Jn 12:31; 2Pt 2:4; Rv 9:1

10 Then I heard a loud voice in heav-
en say:

[a]The salvation and the power
and the kingdom of our God
and the authority of His •Messiah
have now come,
because the accuser
of our brothers
has been thrown out:

[a]**11:17** Other mss add *and who is to come* [b]**11:19** Other mss read *ark of the covenant of the Lord*
[c]**11:19** Other mss omit *an earthquake* [d]**12:1** Or *great symbolic display*; see Rv 12:3 [e]**12:3** Or *another symbolic display* [f]**12:3** Or *crowns* [g]**12:5** Or *rule* [h]**12:6** Lit *God, that they might feed her there*
[i]**12:9** Gk *diabolos*, meaning slanderer [j]**12:9** Hb word meaning adversary

[b]the one who accuses them
before our God day and night.
11 [c]They conquered him
by the blood of the Lamb
and by the word
of their testimony,
[d]for they did not love their lives
in the face of death.
12 Therefore rejoice, O heavens,
and you who dwell in them!
[e]Woe to the earth and the sea,
for the Devil has come down
to you with great fury,
[f]because he knows he has
a short time.

[a] *Rv 11:15* [b] *Jb 1:9; Zch 3:1* [c] *Rm 8:37* [d] *Lk 14:26* [e] *Rv 8:13* [f] *Rv 10:6*

The Woman Persecuted

13 When the dragon saw that he had
been thrown to earth, he persecuted
the woman who gave birth to the male.
14 The woman was given two wings of a
great eagle, so that she could fly from
the serpent's presence [a]to her place in
the wilderness, where she was fed [b]for
a time, times, and half a time.[a] 15 From
his mouth the serpent [c]spewed water
like a river after the woman, to sweep
her away in a torrent. 16 But the earth
helped the woman: the earth opened its
mouth and swallowed up the river that
the dragon had spewed from his mouth.
17 So the dragon was furious with the
woman [d]and left to wage war against
the rest of her offspring[b] — those who
keep the commandments of God and
have [e]the testimony about Jesus. 18 He[c]
stood on the sand of the sea.[d]

[a] *Rv 17:3* [b] *Dn 7:25* [c] *Is 59:19* [d] *Gn 3:15* [e] *Rv 1:2,9*

The Beast from the Sea

13 And I saw [a]a beast coming up
out of the sea. He[e] had 10 horns
and seven heads. On his horns were
10 diadems, and on his heads were
blasphemous names.[f] 2 [b]The beast I
saw was like a leopard, his feet were
like a bear's, and his mouth was like a
lion's mouth. [c]The dragon gave him
his power, his throne, and great authority. 3 One of his heads appeared to
be fatally wounded,[g] but his fatal
wound was healed. [d]The whole earth
was amazed and followed the beast.[h]
4 They worshiped the dragon because
he gave authority to the beast. And
they worshiped the beast, saying,
"Who is like the beast? Who is able to
wage war against him?"

[a] *Dn 7:2,7* [b] *Dn 7:6* [c] *Rv 12:9* [d] *2Th 2:3*

5 [a]A mouth was given to him to
speak boasts and blasphemies. He was
also given authority to act[i] [j] for [b]42
months. 6 He began to speak[k] blasphemies against God: to blaspheme His
name [c]and His dwelling— those who
dwell in heaven. 7 And he was permitted [d]to wage war against the saints
and to conquer them. He was also
given authority over every tribe, people, language, and nation. 8 All those
who live on the earth will worship
him, everyone [e]whose name was not
written [f]from the foundation of the
world in the book[l] of life of the Lamb
who was slaughtered.[m]

[a] *Dn 7:8,11,25* [b] *Rv 11:2* [c] *Jn 1:14; Col 2:9* [d] *Dn 7:21; Rv 11:7* [e] *Dn 12:1; Lk 10:20; Rv 21:27* [f] *Eph 1:4; Rv 5:6-13*

9 If anyone has an ear, he should listen:

10 [a]If anyone is destined
for captivity,
into captivity he goes.

[a]**12:14** An expression occurring in Dn 7:25; 12:7 that means $3^1/_2$ years or 42 months (Rv 11:2; 13:5) or 1,260 days (Rv 11:3) [b]**12:17** Or *seed* [c]**12:18** Other mss read *I*. "He" is apparently a reference to the dragon. [d]**12:18** Some translations put Rv 12:18 either in Rv 12:17 or Rv 13:1. [e]**13:1** The beasts in Rv 13:1,11 are customarily referred to as "he" or "him" rather than "it." The Gk word for a beast (*therion*) is grammatically neuter. [f]**13:1** Other mss read *heads was a blasphemous name* [g]**13:3** Lit *be slain to death* [h]**13:3** Lit *amazed after the beast* [i]**13:5** Other mss read *wage war* [j]**13:5** Or *to rule* [k]**13:6** Lit *He opened his mouth in* [l]**13:8** Or *scroll* [m]**13:8** Or *written in the book of life of the Lamb who was slaughtered from the foundation of the world*

[b]If anyone is to be killed[a]
with a sword,
with a sword he will be killed.

[c]Here is the endurance and the faith
of the saints.[b] *[a]Is 14:2 [b]Mt 26:52*
[c]Heb 12:3-4; Rv 14:12

The Beast from the Earth

11 Then I saw another beast coming
up out of the earth; he had two horns
like a lamb,[c] but he sounded like a
dragon. 12 He exercises all the authority of the first beast on his behalf and
compels the earth and those who live
on it to worship the first beast, whose
fatal wound was healed. 13 [a]He also
performs great signs, even causing fire
to come down from heaven to earth
before people. 14 He deceives those
who live on the earth because of the
signs that he is permitted to perform
on behalf of the beast, telling those
who live on the earth to make an image[d] of the beast who had the sword
wound yet lived. 15 He was permitted
to give a spirit[e] to the image of the
beast, so that the image of the beast
could both speak [b]and cause whoever
would not worship the image of the
beast to be killed. 16 And he requires
everyone—small and great, rich and
poor, free and slave—to be given a
mark[f] on his[g] right hand or on his[g] forehead, 17 so that no one can buy or sell
unless he has the mark: [c]the beast's
name [d]or the number of his name. *[a]2Th
2:9; Rv 16:14 [b]Rv 20:4
[c]Rv 14:11 [d]Rv 15:2*

18 [a]Here is wisdom:[h] The one who
has understanding must calculate[i] the
number of the beast, because it is the
number of a man.[j] His number is
666.[k] *[a]Ps 107:43; Hs 14:9*

The Lamb and the 144,000

14 Then I looked, and there on
Mount Zion stood the [a]Lamb,
and with Him were 144,000 who had
His name and [b]His Father's name written on their foreheads. 2 I heard a
sound[l] from heaven like the sound of
cascading waters and like the rum-
bling of loud thunder. The sound I
heard was also like harpists playing on
their harps. 3 They sang[m] a new song
before the throne and before the four
living creatures and the elders, but no
one could learn the song except the
144,000 who had been redeemed[n]
from the earth. 4 These are the ones
not defiled with women, [c]for they
have kept their virginity. These are
the ones who follow the Lamb wherever He goes. They were redeemed[o] [n]
from the human race [d]as the •first-
fruits for God and the Lamb. 5 [e]No lie
was found in their mouths; [f]they are
blameless. *[a]Is 53:7; 1Pt 1:19; Rv 5:6
[b]Rv 7:3 [c]2Co 11:2 [d]Jms 1:18
[e]Ps 32:2 [f]Eph 5:27*

The Proclamation of Three Angels

6 Then I saw another angel flying in
mid-heaven, [a]having the eternal gospel to announce to the inhabitants of
the earth—to every nation, tribe, language, and people. 7 He spoke with a
loud voice: "Fear God and give Him
glory, because the hour of His judgment has come. [b]Worship the Maker
of heaven and earth, the sea and
springs of water." *[a]Mt 28:19; Eph 3:9
[b]Ps 95:1-6; Ac 14:15*

8 A second angel[p] followed, saying:
"It has fallen, [a]Babylon the Great has
fallen,[q] who made all nations drink the

[a]**13:10** Other mss read *anyone kills* [b]**13:10** Or *This calls for the endurance and faith of the saints.* [c]**13:11** Or *ram* [d]**13:14** Or *statue, or likeness* [e]**13:15** Or *give breath, or give life* [f]**13:16** Or *stamp*, or *brand* [g]**13:16** Lit *their* [h]**13:18** Or *This calls for wisdom* [i]**13:18** Or *count*, or *figure out* [j]**13:18** Or *is a man's number*, or *is the number of a person* [k]**13:18** One Gk ms plus other ancient evidence read *616* [l]**14:2** Or *voice* [m]**14:3** Other mss add *as it were* [n]**14:3,4** Or *purchased* [o]**14:4** Other mss add *by Jesus* [p]**14:8** Lit *Another angel, a second* [q]**14:8** Other mss omit the second *has fallen*

wine of her sexual immorality,[a] which
brings wrath." *[a]Rv 16:19; 17:5*

9 And a third angel[b] followed them
and spoke with a loud voice: "If anyone worships the beast and his image
and receives a mark on his forehead or
on his hand, 10 he [a]will also drink the
wine of God's wrath, which is mixed
full strength in the cup of His anger. He
will be tormented with fire and sulfur
in the sight of the holy angels and
in the sight of the Lamb, 11 and [b]the
smoke of their torment will go up forever and ever. There is no rest[c] day or
night for those who worship the beast
and his image, or anyone who receives
the mark of his name. 12 [c]Here is the
endurance[d] [e] of the saints, [d]who keep
the commandments of God and the
faith in Jesus."[f] *[a]Ps 75:8 [b]Is 34:10 [c]Rv 13:10 [d]Rv 12:17*

13 Then I heard a voice from heaven
saying, "Write: [a]Blessed are the dead
[b]who die in the Lord from now on." *[a]Ec 4:1-2 [b]1Th 4:16*

"Yes," says the Spirit, [a]"let them rest
from their labors, for their works follow them!" *[a]Heb 4:9; Rv 6:11*

Reaping the Earth's Harvest

14 Then I looked, and there was a
white cloud, and One [a]like the Son of
Man[g] was seated on the cloud, with a
gold crown on His head and a sharp
sickle in His hand. 15 Another angel
came out of the sanctuary, crying out
in a loud voice to the One who was
seated on the cloud, [b]"Use your sickle
and reap, for the time to reap has
come, since the harvest [c]of the earth is
ripe." 16 So the One seated on the
cloud swung His sickle over the earth,
and the earth was harvested. *[a]Dn 7:13; Rv 1:13 [b]Mt 13:39 [c]Jl 3:13*

17 Then another angel who also had a
sharp sickle came out of the sanctuary
in heaven. 18 Yet another angel, [a]who
had authority over fire, came from the
altar, and he called with a loud voice to
the one who had the sharp sickle,
[b]"Use your sharp sickle and gather the
clusters of grapes from earth's vineyard, because its grapes have ripened."
19 So the angel swung his sickle toward
earth and gathered the grapes from
earth's vineyard, and he threw them
into [c]the great winepress of God's
wrath. 20 Then [d]the press was trampled
[e]outside the city, and blood flowed out
of the press up to the horses' bridles for
about 180 miles.[h] *[a]Rv 16:8 [b]Jl 3:13 [c]Rv 19:15 [d]Is 63:3 [e]Heb 13:12; Rv 11:8*

Preparation for the Bowl Judgments

15 Then I saw another great and
awe-inspiring sign[i] in heaven:
[a]seven angels with the seven last
plagues, [b]for with them, God's wrath
will be completed. 2 I also saw something like [c]a sea of glass mixed with
fire, and those who had won the victory from the beast, [d]his image,[j] and
the number of his name, were standing on the sea of glass with harps from
God.[k] 3 They sang [e]the song of God's
servant Moses, and the song of the
Lamb:

[f]Great and awe-inspiring are
Your works, Lord God,
the Almighty;
[g]righteous and true are
Your ways, King of the Nations.
4 [h]Lord, who will not fear
and glorify Your name?
Because You alone are holy,
because [i]all the nations
will come and worship
before You,

[a]**14:8** Or *wine of her passionate immorality* [b]**14:9** Lit *Another angel, a third* [c]**14:11** Lit *They have no rest* [d]**14:12** Or *This calls for the endurance of the saints* [e]**14:12** This is what the endurance of the saints means [f]**14:12** Or *and faith in Jesus*, or *their faith in*, or *faithfulness to Jesus* [g]**14:14** Or *like a son of man* [h]**14:20** Lit *1,600 stadia* [i]**15:1** Or *and awesome symbolic display* [j]**15:2** Other mss add *his mark* [k]**15:2** Or *harps of God*; that is, harps belonging to the service of God

because Your righteous acts
have been revealed. [a]Rv 16:1
[b]Rv 14:10 [c]Rv 4:6 [d]Rv 13:15
[e]Ex 15:1 [f]Dt 32:4 [g]Hs 14:9
[h]Ps 89:7; Jr 10:7 [i]Is 66:23

5 After this I looked, and [a]the heavenly sanctuary—the tabernacle of testimony—was opened. 6 Out of the
sanctuary came the seven angels with
the seven plagues, [b]dressed in clean,
bright linen, with gold sashes wrapped
around their chests. 7 [c]One of the four
living creatures gave the seven angels
seven gold bowls filled with the wrath
of God who lives forever and ever.
8 Then [d]the sanctuary was filled with
smoke [e]from God's glory and from His
power, and no one could enter the
sanctuary until the seven plagues of
the seven angels were completed.
[a]Rv 11:19 [b]Ex 28:6 [c]Rv 4:6
[d]Ex 40:34; 1Kg 8:10 [e]Dt 33:2; Is 2:19

The First Bowl

16 Then I heard a loud voice from
the sanctuary saying to the seven
angels, "Go and pour out the seven[a]
bowls of God's wrath on the earth."
2 The first went and poured out his
bowl [a]on the earth, and [b]severely painful sores[b] broke out on the people
[c]who had the mark of the beast and
who worshiped his image. [a]Rv 8:7
[b]Ex 9:9 [c]Rv 13:16

The Second Bowl

3 The second[c] poured out his bowl
into the sea. [a]It turned to blood like a
dead man's, [b]and all life[d] in the sea
died. [a]Ex 7:17 [b]Rv 8:9

The Third Bowl

4 The third[c] poured out his bowl into
the rivers and the springs of water, and
they became blood. 5 I heard the angel
of the waters say:

[a]You are righteous, [b]who is
and who was, the Holy One,
for You have decided
these things.
6 Because [c]they poured out
the blood of the saints
and the prophets,
[d]You also gave them blood
to drink; they deserve it!
[a]Ps 97:2; Rv 15:3 [b]Rv 1:4,8; 4:8
[c]Mt 23:34 [d]Is 49:26

7 Then I heard someone from the altar say:

Yes, Lord God, the Almighty,
[a]true and righteous are
Your judgments. [a]Rv 13:10; 14:10

The Fourth Bowl

8 The fourth[c] poured out his bowl on
the sun. He[e] was given the power[f] to
burn people with fire, 9 and people
were burned by the intense heat. So
they blasphemed the name of God
who had the power[f] over these
plagues, [a]and they did not repent and
give Him glory. [a]Is 8:21

The Fifth Bowl

10 The fifth[c] poured out his bowl [a]on
the throne of the beast, and his kingdom was plunged into darkness. People[g] gnawed their tongues from pain
11 and blasphemed the God of heaven
because of their pains and their sores,
yet they did not repent of their actions.
[a]Rv 13:2

The Sixth Bowl

12 The sixth[c] poured out his bowl [a]on
the great river Euphrates, [b]and its water was dried up [c]to prepare the way
for the kings from the east. 13 Then I
saw three unclean spirits like frogs
⌊coming⌋ from [d]the dragon's mouth,
from the beast's mouth, and from the
mouth of the false prophet. 14 [e]For they
are spirits of demons [f]performing
signs, who travel to the kings of the
whole world to assemble them for [g]the

[a]**16:1** Other mss omit *seven* [b]**16:2** Lit *and a severely painful sore* [c]**16:3,4,8,10,12** Other mss add *angel*
[d]**16:3** Lit *and every soul of life* [e]**16:8** Or *It* [f]**16:8,9** Or *authority* [g]**16:10** Lit *They*

battle of the great day of God, the Almighty.

[a] *Rv 9:14* [b] *Jr 50:38* [c] *Is 41:2* [d] *Rv 12:3* [e] *1Tm 4:1* [f] *2Th 2:9* [g] *Rv 20:8*

15 [a]"Look, I am coming like a thief.
Blessed is the one who is alert and remains clothed[a] [b]so that he may not go
naked, and they see his shame."

[a] *1Th 5:2* [b] *2Co 5:3*

16 So they assembled them at the
place called in Hebrew Armagedon.[b] [c]

The Seventh Bowl

17 Then the seventh[d] poured out his
bowl into the air,[e] and a loud voice
came out of the sanctuary,[f] from the
throne, saying, [a]"It is done!" 18 There
were lightnings, rumblings, and thunders. And a severe earthquake occurred [b]like no other since man has
been on the earth—so great was the
quake. 19 [c]The great city split into
three parts, and the cities of the nations[g] fell. Babylon the Great [d]was remembered in God's presence; [e]He
gave her the cup filled with the wine of
His fierce anger. 20 [f]Every island fled,
and the mountains disappeared.[h]
21 [g]Enormous hailstones, each weigh-
ing about 100 pounds,[i] fell from
heaven on the people, and they[j] blasphemed God for the plague of hail because that plague was extremely
severe.

[a] *Rv 21:6* [b] *Dn 12:1* [c] *Rv 14:8* [d] *Rv 18:5* [e] *Rv 14:10* [f] *Rv 6:14* [g] *Rv 11:19*

The Woman and the Scarlet Beast

17 [a]Then one of the seven angels
who had the seven bowls came
and spoke with me: "Come, I will show
you the judgment of [b]the notorious
prostitute[k] [c]who sits on many[l] waters.
2 The kings of the earth committed sexual immorality with her, and [d]those
who live on the earth became drunk on
the wine of her sexual immorality." 3 So
he carried me away in the Spirit[m] [e]to a
desert. I saw a woman sitting [f]on a scarlet beast that was covered[n] with [g]blas-
phemous names, having seven heads
and 10 horns. 4 The woman [h]was
dressed in purple and scarlet, adorned
with gold, precious stones, and pearls.
[i]She had a gold cup in her hand filled
with everything vile and with the im-
purities of her[o] prostitution. 5 On her
forehead a [j]cryptic name was written:

BABYLON [k]THE GREAT
[l]THE MOTHER OF PROSTITUTES
AND OF THE VILE THINGS
OF THE EARTH

6 Then I saw that the woman was
drunk on the blood of the saints and
on the blood of [m]the witnesses to
Jesus. When I saw her, I was utterly
astounded.

[a] *Rv 15:1,6* [b] *Rv 19:2* [c] *Jr 51:13* [d] *Jr 51:7* [e] *Rv 12:6* [f] *Rv 12:3* [g] *Rv 13:1* [h] *Rv 18:12* [i] *Jr 51:7* [j] *2Th 2:7* [k] *Rv 11:8* [l] *Rv 18:9* [m] *Rv 6:9*

The Meaning of the Woman and of the Beast

7 Then the angel said to me, "Why are
you astounded? I will tell you the secret
meaning[p] of the woman and of the
beast, with the seven heads and the 10
horns, that carries her. 8 The beast that
you saw was, and is not, and is about [a]to
come up from the •abyss and go to destruction. Those who live on the earth
whose names were not written in the
book of life from the foundation of the
world will be astounded when they see
the beast that was, and is not, and will
be present ⌊again⌋.

[a] *Rv 11:7*

[a]**16:15** Or *and guards his clothes* [b]**16:16** Other mss read *Armageddon*; other mss read *Harmegedon*; other mss read *Mageddon*; other mss read *Magedon* [c]**16:16** Traditionally *the hill of Megiddo*, a great city that guarded the pass between the coast and the valley of Jezreel or Esdraelon; see Jdg 5:19; 2 Kg 9:27 [d]**16:17** Other mss add *angel* [e]**16:17** Or *on the air* [f]**16:17** Other mss add *of heaven* [g]**16:19** Or *the Gentile cities* [h]**16:20** Lit *mountains were not found* [i]**16:21** Lit *about a talent*; talents varied in weight upwards from 75 pounds [j]**16:21** Lit *people* [k]**17:1** Traditionally, *the great whore* [l]**17:1** Or *by many* [m]**17:3** Or *in spirit* [n]**17:3** Lit *was filled* [o]**17:4** Other mss read *of earth's* [p]**17:7** Lit *the mystery*

9 [a]“Here is the mind with wisdom:[a]
[b]the seven heads are seven mountains
on which the woman is seated. 10 They
are also seven kings:[b] five have fallen,
one is, the other has not yet come, and
when he comes, he must remain for a
little while. 11 The beast that was and is
not, is himself the eighth, yet is of the
seven and goes to destruction. 12 [c]The
10 horns you saw are 10 kings who
have not yet received a kingdom, but
they will receive authority as kings
with the beast for one hour. 13 These
have [d]one purpose, and they give their
power and authority to the beast.
14 [e]These will make war against the
Lamb, but the Lamb will conquer them
[f]because He is Lord of lords and King of
kings. [g]Those with Him are called and
elect and faithful.”

[a] Hs 14:9; Rv 13:18 [b] Rv 13:1 [c] Dn 7:20 [d] Rm 8:7 [e] Rv 16:14 [f] 1Tm 6:15 [g] 1Pt 2:9; Rv 14:4

15 He also said to me, “The waters
you saw, where the prostitute was
seated, are peoples, multitudes, nations, and languages. 16 The 10 horns
you saw, and the beast, [a]will hate the
prostitute. They will make her desolate
[b]and naked, [c]devour her flesh, and
burn her up with fire. 17 [d]For God has
put it into their hearts to carry out His
plan by having one purpose, and to
give their kingdom[c] to the beast [e]until
God’s words are accomplished. 18 And
the woman you saw [f]is the great city
[g]that has an empire[d] over the kings of
the earth.”

[a] Jr 50:41 [b] Ezk 16:37 [c] Rv 18:8 [d] Rm 1:26 [e] Rv 10:7 [f] Rv 16:19 [g] Rv 12:1

The Fall of Babylon the Great

18 After this I saw another angel
with great authority coming
down from heaven, and the earth was
illuminated by his splendor. 2 He cried
in a mighty voice:

It has fallen,[e] [a]Babylon the Great
has fallen!
[b]She has become a dwelling
for demons,
a haunt[f] for every unclean spirit,
a haunt[f] for every unclean bird,
and [c]a haunt[f] for every unclean
and despicable beast.[g]
3 For all the nations have drunk[h]
the wine of her
sexual immorality,
which brings wrath.
The kings of the earth
have committed
sexual immorality with her,
and the merchants of the earth
have grown wealthy
from her excessive luxury.

[a] Rv 14:8; 16:19 [b] Is 34:14 [c] Is 14:23

4 Then I heard another voice from
heaven:

[a]Come out of her, My people,
so that you will not share
in her sins,
or receive any of her plagues.
5 [b]For her sins are piled up[i]
to heaven,
and God has remembered
her crimes.
6 [c]Pay her back the way
she also paid,
and double it
according to her works.
In the cup in which she mixed,
mix a double portion for her.
7 [d]As much as she glorified herself
and lived luxuriously,
give her that much torment
and grief.
Because she says in her heart,
‘I sit as [e]queen;
I am not a widow,
and I will never see grief,’

[a]**17:9** Or *This calls for the mind with wisdom* [b]**17:10** Some editors or translators put *They are also seven kings:* in v. 9. [c]**17:17** Or *sovereignty* [d]**17:18** Or *has sovereignty* or *rulership* [e]**18:2** Other mss omit *It has fallen* [f]**18:2** Or *prison* [g]**18:2** Other mss omit the words *and a haunt for every unclean beast.* The words *and despicable* then refer to the *bird* of the previous line. [h]**18:3** Other mss read *have collapsed*; other mss read *have fallen* [i]**18:5** Or *sins have reached up*

8 therefore her plagues will come
in one day[a] —
death, and grief, and famine.
She will be burned up with fire,
[f]because the Lord God
who judges her is mighty.

[a] 2Co 6:17 [b] Gn 4:10; 18:20
[c] Ps 137:8; Rv 13:10 [d] Ezk 28:2
[e] Is 47:7-8 [f] Jr 50:34

The World Mourns Babylon's Fall

9 [a]The kings of the earth who have
committed sexual immorality and
lived luxuriously with her [b]will weep
and mourn over her when they see the
smoke of her burning. 10 They stand far
off in fear of her torment, saying:

[c]Woe, woe, the great city,
Babylon, the mighty city!
For in a single hour[a]
your judgment has come.

11 [d]The merchants of the earth will
also weep and mourn over her, because no one buys their merchandise
any longer— 12 merchandise of gold,
silver, precious stones, and pearls; fine
fabrics of linen, purple, silk, and
scarlet; all kinds of fragrant wood prod-
ucts; objects of ivory; objects of expensive wood, brass,[b] iron, and marble;
13 cinnamon, spice,[c d] incense, myrrh,[e]
and frankincense; wine, olive oil, fine
wheat flour, and grain; cattle and
sheep; horses and carriages; and human bodies [e]and souls.[f g]

[a] Rv 17:2
[b] Jr 50:46 [c] Rv 14:8
[d] Ezk 27:27 [e] 2Pt 2:3

14 The fruit you craved has left you.
All your splendid
and glamorous things are gone;
they will never find them again.

15 The merchants of these things, who
became rich from her, will stand far
off in fear of her torment, weeping
and mourning, 16 saying:

Woe, woe, the great city,
clothed in fine linen, purple,
and scarlet,
adorned with gold,
precious stones, and pearls;
17 because in a single hour[a]
such fabulous wealth
was destroyed!

And [a]every shipmaster, seafarer, the
sailors, and all who do business by sea,
stood far off 18 [b]as they watched the
smoke from her burning and kept crying
out: "Who is like the great city?" 19 They
threw dust on their heads and kept crying out, weeping, and mourning:

Woe, woe, the great city,
where all those who have ships
on the sea
became rich from her wealth;
because in a single hour[a]
she was destroyed.
20 [c]Rejoice over her, heaven, and
you saints, apostles,
and prophets,
because [d]God has executed
your judgment on her![h]

[a] Is 23:14 [b] Ezk 27:30
[c] Pr 11:10; Rv 19:1-3 [d] Is 26:21

The Finality of Babylon's Fall

21 Then a mighty angel picked up a
stone like a large millstone and threw
it into the sea, saying:

[a]In this way, Babylon
the great city
will be thrown down violently
and never be found again.
22 [b]The sound of harpists,
musicians, flutists,
and trumpeters
will never be heard in you again;
no craftsman of any trade
will ever be found in you again;
the sound of a mill
will never be heard in you again;

[a] **18:8,10,17,19** Suddenly [b] **18:12** Or *bronze*, or *copper* [c] **18:13** Other mss omit *spice* [d] **18:13** Or *amomum*, an aromatic plant [e] **18:13** Or *perfume* [f] **18:13** Or *carriages; and slaves, namely, human beings* [g] **18:13** Slaves; "bodies" was the Gk way of referring to slaves; "souls of men" was the Hb way. [h] **18:20** Or *God pronounced on her the judgment she passed on you*; see Rv 18:6

23 the light of a lamp
will never shine in you again;
and the voice of a groom
and bride
will never be heard in you again.
⌊All this will happen⌋
[c]because your merchants
were the nobility of the earth,
[d]because all the nations
were deceived by your sorcery,[a]
24 and the blood of prophets
and saints,
and all those [e]slaughtered
on earth, was found in you.[b]

[a] *Jr 51:64* [b] *Is 24:8* [c] *Is 23:8* [d] *Nah 3:4; Rv 17:2* [e] *Jr 51:49*

Heaven Exults over Babylon

19 After this I heard something like
the loud voice of a vast multitude in heaven, saying:

Hallelujah![c]
[a]Salvation, glory, and power
belong to our God,
2 because His judgments are true[d]
and righteous,
because He has judged
the notorious prostitute
who corrupted the earth
with her sexual immorality;
and [b]He has avenged the blood
of His servants that was
on her hands.

3 A second time they said:

Hallelujah![e]
[c]Her smoke ascends forever
and ever!

[a] *Rv 4:11; 7:10* [b] *Rv 6:10* [c] *Rv 14:11*

4 Then [a]the 24 elders and the four
living creatures fell down and worshiped God, who is seated on the
throne, saying:

•Amen! Hallelujah![e]

[a] *Rv 4:4*

5 A voice came from the throne, saying:

[a]Praise our God,
all you His servants,
you who fear Him,
both small and great!

[a] *Ps 134:1*

Marriage of the Lamb Announced

6 [a]Then I heard something like the
voice of a vast multitude, like the sound
of cascading waters, and like the rum-
bling of loud thunder, saying:

Hallelujah[e]—because
our Lord God, the Almighty,
has begun to reign!
7 Let us be [b]glad, rejoice,
and give Him glory,
because [c]the marriage
of the Lamb has come,
and His wife
has prepared herself.
8 [d]She was permitted to wear
fine linen, bright and pure.

[e]For the fine linen represents the righteous acts of the saints.

[a] *Ezk 1:24* [b] *Is 44:23* [c] *Mt 22:2; 2Co 11:2; Eph 5:32* [d] *Ps 45:13* [e] *Ps 132:9*

9 Then he[f] said to me, [a]"Write:
Blessed are those invited to the marriage feast of the Lamb!" He also said to
me, "These words of God are true."
10 Then [b]I fell at his feet to worship
him, but he said to me, [c]"Don't do
that! I am a fellow •slave with you and
your brothers [d]who have the testimony about[g] Jesus. Worship God, because the testimony about[g] Jesus is the
spirit of prophecy."

[a] *Lk 14:15* [b] *Rv 22:8* [c] *Ac 10:26* [d] *1Jn 5:10*

The Rider on a White Horse

11 Then I saw heaven opened, and
there was a white horse! Its rider
is called [a]Faithful and True, and [b]in

[a]**18:23** Ancient sorcery or witchcraft often used spells and drugs. Here the term may be non-literal, that is, Babylon drugged the nations with her beauty and power. [b]**18:24** Lit *in her* [c]**19:1** Lit *Praise Yahweh*; the Gk word is transliterated *hallelujah* from a Hb expression of praise and is used in many places in the OT, such as Ps 106:1. [d]**19:2** Valid; see Jn 8:16; 19:35 [e]**19:3,4,6** See note at Rv 19:1 [f]**19:9** Probably an angel; see Rv 17:1; 22:8–9 [g]**19:10** Or *testimony to*

righteousness He judges and makes
war. 12 His eyes were like a fiery flame,
and on His head were many crowns.
[c]He had a name written that no one
knows except Himself. 13 [d]He wore a
robe stained with blood,[a] and His
name is called [e]the Word of God. 14 The
armies that were in heaven followed
Him on white horses, [f]wearing pure
white linen. 15 [g]From His mouth came
a sharp[b] sword, so that with it He might
strike the nations. [h]He will shepherd[c]
them with an iron scepter. [i]He will also
trample the winepress of the fierce anger of God, the Almighty. 16 And on His
robe and on His thigh He has a name
written:

[a]Jn 14:6; Rv 3:14 [b]Is 11:4 [c]Is 9:6 [d]Is 63:2-3 [e]Jn 1:1 [f]Rv 4:4; 7:9 [g]Rv 1:16 [h]Ps 2:9; Rv 2:27 [i]Rv 14:19-20

[a]KING OF KINGS AND LORD OF LORDS

[a]Ps 72; Rv 17:14

The Beast and His Armies Defeated

17 Then I saw an angel standing in
the sun, and he cried out in a loud
voice, saying to all the birds flying in
mid-heaven, "Come, gather together
for the great supper of God, 18 so that
you may eat the flesh of kings, the flesh
of commanders, the flesh of mighty
men, the flesh of horses and of their
riders, and the flesh of everyone, both
free and •slave, small and great."
19 [a]Then I saw the beast, the kings of
the earth, and their armies gathered
together to wage war against the rider
on the horse and against His army.
20 But the beast was taken prisoner,
and along with him the false prophet,
who had performed signs on his authority,[d] by which he deceived those
who accepted the mark of the beast
and those who worshiped his image.
[b]Both of them were thrown alive into
the lake of fire that burns with sulfur.
21 The rest were killed with the sword
that came from the mouth of the rider
on the horse, and all the birds were
filled with their flesh.

[a]Rv 16:16 [b]Dn 7:11; Rv 20:10

Satan Bound

20 Then I saw an angel coming
down from heaven [a]with the
key to the •abyss and a great chain in
his hand. 2 He seized [b]the dragon, that
ancient serpent who is the Devil and
Satan,[e] and bound him for 1,000 years.
3 He threw him into the abyss, closed
it, and put a seal on it [c]so that he
would no longer deceive the nations
until the 1,000 years were completed.
After that, he must be released for a
short time.

[a]Rv 1:18 [b]2Pt 2:4; Rv 12:9 [c]Mt 24:24; Rv 16:14

The Saints Reign with the Messiah

4 Then I saw [a]thrones, and people
seated on them who were given authority [b]to judge. ⌊I⌋ also ⌊saw⌋ [c]the
souls of those who had been beheaded[f]
because of their testimony about Jesus
and because of God's word, [d]who had
not worshiped the beast or his image,
and who had not accepted the mark on
their foreheads or their hands. They
came to life and [e]reigned with the
•Messiah for 1,000 years. 5 The rest of
the dead did not come to life until the
1,000 years were completed. This is
the first resurrection. 6 Blessed and
holy is the one who shares in the first
resurrection! [f]The second death has no
power[g] over these, but they will be
[g]priests of God and the Messiah, and
they will reign with Him for 1,000
years.

[a]Dn 7:9,22,27 [b]1Co 6:2-3 [c]Rv 6:9 [d]Rv 13:12 [e]Rm 8:17 [f]Rv 21:8 [g]1Pt 2:9; Rv 5:10

[a]**19:13** Or *a robe dipped in* [b]**19:15** Other mss add *double-edged* [c]**19:15** Or *rule* [d]**19:20** Lit *signs before him* [e]**20:2** Other mss add *who deceives the whole world* [f]**20:4** All who had given their lives for their faith in Christ [g]**20:6** Or *authority*

Satanic Rebellion Crushed

7 When the 1,000 years are completed, Satan will be released from his
prison 8 and will go out [a]to deceive the
nations at the four corners of the earth,
[b]Gog and Magog, [c]to gather them for
battle. Their number is like the sand of
the sea. 9 They came up over the sur-
face of the earth and surrounded the
encampment of the saints, the beloved
city. Then fire came down from heav-
en[a] and consumed them. 10 The Devil
who deceived them was thrown into
the lake of fire and sulfur where the
beast and the false prophet are, and
they will be tormented day and night
forever and ever. *[a] 1Pt 5:8 [b] Ezk 38:2 [c] Rv 16:14*

The Great White Throne Judgment

11 Then I saw a great white throne
and One seated on it. [a]Earth and
heaven fled from His presence, [b]and
no place was found for them. 12 [c]I also
saw the dead, the great and the small,
standing before the throne, [d]and books
were opened. Another [e]book was
opened, which is the book of life, and
the dead were judged [f]according to
their works by what was written in the
books. *[a] 2Pt 3:7 [b] Dn 2:35 [c] 2Co 5:10 [d] Dn 7:10 [e] Php 4:3 [f] Mt 16:27*

13 Then the sea gave up its dead,
and Death and •Hades gave up their
dead; all[b] were judged according to
their works. 14 [a]Death and Hades were
thrown into the lake of fire. This is the
second death, the lake of fire.[c] 15 And
anyone not found written in the book
of life was thrown into the lake of fire.
[a] 1Co 15:26

The New Creation

21 Then [a]I saw a new heaven and a
new earth, for the first heaven
and the first earth had passed away,
and the sea existed no longer. 2 I also
saw [b]the Holy City, new Jerusalem,
coming down out of heaven from God,
prepared [c]like a bride adorned for her
husband. *[a] Is 65:17; 2Pt 3:13 [b] Gl 4:26; Heb 11:10 [c] 2Co 11:2*

3 Then I heard a loud voice from the
throne:[d]

Look! [a]God's dwelling[e] is
with men,
and He will live with them.
They will be His people,
and God Himself will be
with them and be their God.[f]
4 [b]He will wipe away every tear
from their eyes.
[c]Death will exist no longer;
[d]grief, crying, and pain will exist
no longer,
because the previous things[g]
have passed away. *[a] Rv 7:15 [b] Is 25:8 [c] 1Co 15:26,54 [d] Is 35:10*

5 Then [a]the One seated on the
throne said, [b]"Look! I am making everything new." He also said, "Write,
because these words[h] are faithful and
true." 6 And He said to me, "It is done!
I am the •Alpha and the Omega, the
Beginning and the End. [c]I will give to
the thirsty from the spring of living
water as a gift. 7 [d]The victor will inherit these things, and [e]I will be his
God, and he will be My son. 8 [f]But the
cowards, unbelievers,[i] vile, murderers,
sexually immoral, sorcerers, idolaters,
and all liars—their share will be in the
lake that burns with fire and sulfur,
which is the second death." *[a] Rv 4:2 [b] 2Co 5:17 [c] Jn 7:37; Rv 22:17 [d] Rm 8:17,32; Rv 2:7,11 [e] Heb 8:10 [f] 1Co 6:9; Heb 12:14; Rv 22:15*

The New Jerusalem

9 Then one of the seven angels, who
had held the seven bowls filled with
the seven last plagues, came and spoke
with me: "Come, I will show you the

[a]**20:9** Other mss add *from God* [b]**20:13** Lit *each* [c]**20:14** Other mss omit *the lake of fire* [d]**21:3** Other mss read *from heaven* [e]**21:3** Or *tent*, or *tabernacle* [f]**21:3** Other mss omit *and be their God* [g]**21:4** Or *the first things* [h]**21:5** Other mss add *of God* [i]**21:8** Other mss add *the sinful*

bride, the wife of the Lamb." 10 He
then carried me away in the Spirit[a] to
a great and high mountain and showed
me [a]the holy city, Jerusalem, coming
down out of heaven from God,
11 arrayed with God's glory. Her radiance was like a very precious stone,
like a jasper stone, bright as crystal.
12 ⌊The city⌋ had a massive high wall,
with 12 gates. Twelve angels were at
the gates; ⌊on the gates⌋, names were
inscribed, the names of the 12 tribes of
the sons of Israel. 13 There were three
gates on the east, three gates on the
north, three gates on the south, and
three gates on the west. 14 The city
wall had 12 foundations, and [b]on them
were the 12 names of the Lamb's 12
apostles.

a Ezk 48
b Mt 10:2-4; Ac 1:26; Eph 2:20

15 The one who spoke with me [a]had
a gold measuring rod to measure the
city, its gates, and its wall. 16 The city is
laid out in a square; its length and
width are the same. He measured the
city with the rod at 12,000 *stadia*.[b] Its
length, width, and height are equal.
17 Then he measured its wall, 144 •cu-
bits according to human measure-
ment, which the angel used. 18 The
building material of its wall was jasper,
and the city was pure gold like clear
glass.

a Rv 11:1

19 [a]The foundations of the city wall
were adorned with every kind of precious stone:

the first foundation jasper,
the second sapphire,
the third chalcedony,
the fourth emerald,
20 the fifth sardonyx,
the sixth carnelian,
the seventh chrysolite,
the eighth beryl,
the ninth topaz,
the tenth chrysoprase,
the eleventh jacinth,
the twelfth amethyst.

21 The 12 gates are 12 pearls; each individual gate was made of a single
pearl. [b]The broad street[c] of the city
was pure gold, like transparent glass.

a Is 54:11 b Rv 22:2

22 [a]I did not see a sanctuary in it, because the Lord God the Almighty and
the Lamb are its sanctuary. 23 [b]The city
does not need the sun or the moon to
shine on it, because God's glory illumi-
nates it, and its lamp is the Lamb.
24 [c]The nations[d] will walk in its light,
and the kings of the earth will bring
their glory into it.[e] 25 Each day its gates
will never close because [d]it will never
be night there. 26 They will bring the
glory and honor of the nations into it.[f]
27 [e]Nothing profane will ever enter it:
no one who does what is vile or false,
but only those written in the Lamb's
[f]book of life.

a Is 66:1; Jn 4:23 b Is 24:23
c Is 60:3 d Is 60:20 e Is 35:8
f Rv 3:5; 13:8; 20:12

The Source of Life

22 Then he showed me [a]the river[g]
of living water, sparkling like
crystal, flowing from the throne of
God and of the Lamb 2 down the middle of the broad street ⌊of the city⌋. On
both sides of the river was [b]the tree of
life[h] bearing 12 kinds of fruit, producing its fruit every month. The leaves of
the tree are [c]for healing the nations,
3 and [d]there will no longer be any
curse. [e]The throne of God and of the
Lamb will be in the city,[i] and His servants will serve Him. 4 [f]They will see
His face, and His name will be on
their foreheads. 5 Night will no longer
exist, and people will not need lamp-
light or sunlight, because [g]the Lord

[a]**21:10** Or *in spirit* [b]**21:16** A *stadion* (sg) equals about 600 feet; the total is about 1,400 miles. [c]**21:21** Or *The public square* [d]**21:24** Other mss add *of those who are saved* [e]**21:24** Other mss read *will bring to Him the nations' glory and honor* [f]**21:26** Other mss add *in order that they might go in* [g]**22:1** Other mss read *pure river* [h]**22:2** Or *was a tree of life*, or *was a tree that gives life* [i]**22:3** Lit *in it*

God will give them light. [h]And they
will reign forever and ever.

[a]Ezk 47:1; Jn 7:38-39 [b]Gn 2:9; 3:22; Rv 2:7 [c]Rv 21:24 [d]Zch 14:11; Rv 21:4 [e]Ezk 48:35; Rv 7:15-17 [f]Mt 5:8; 1Co 13:12; 1Jn 3:2 [g]Ps 36:9; 84:11 [h]Dn 7:27; 2Tm 2:12; Rv 3:21

The Time Is Near

6 Then he said to me, "These words
are faithful and true. And the Lord, the
God of the spirits of [a]the prophets,[a] has
sent His angel to show His servants
what must quickly take place."[b]

[a]Heb 1:1

7 "Look, I am coming quickly! Blessed is the one who keeps the prophetic
words of this book."

8 I, John, am the one who heard and
saw these things. When I heard and
saw them, I fell down to worship at the
feet of the angel who had shown them
to me. 9 But he said to me, "Don't do
that! I am a fellow •slave with you,
your brothers the prophets, and those
who keep the words of this book. Worship God." 10 [a]He also said to me,
"Don't seal the prophetic words of this
book, because the time is near. 11 [b]Let
the unrighteous go on in unrighteousness; let the filthy go on being made
filthy; let the righteous go on in righteousness; and let the holy go on being
made holy."

[a]Dn 12:4,9 [b]Ezk 3:27; 2Tm 3:13

12 "Look! I am coming quickly, and
[a]My reward is with Me to repay each
person according to what he has done.
13 [b]I am the •Alpha and the Omega, the
First and the Last, the Beginning and
the End.

[a]Is 40:10; Mt 16:27; Rm 2:6-11 [b]Is 44:6

14 "Blessed are those who wash their
robes,[c] so that they may have the right
to the tree of life and may enter the
city by the gates. 15 Outside are the
dogs, the sorcerers, the sexually immoral, the murderers, the idolaters,
and everyone who loves and practices
lying.

16 [a]"I, Jesus, have sent My angel to
attest these things to you[d] for the
churches. [b]I am the Root and the Offspring of David, [c]the Bright Morning
Star."

[a]1Pt 3:22 [b]Is 11:1; Jr 23:5-6; Zch 6:12 [c]Nm 24:17

17 Both the Spirit and the bride say,
"Come!" Anyone who hears should
say, "Come!" [a]And the one who is
thirsty should come. Whoever desires
should take the living water as a gift.

[a]Is 55:1; Jn 4:14; 7:37; Rv 21:6

18 I testify to everyone who hears the
prophetic words of this book: [a]If anyone adds to them, God will add to him
the plagues that are written in this
book. 19 And if anyone takes away from
the words of this prophetic book, [b]God
will take away his share of the tree of
life and the holy city, written in this
book.

[a]Dt 4:2; Pr 30:6 [b]Ex 32:33

20 He who testifies about these things
says, [a]"Yes, I am coming quickly."

[a]Heb 9:28

•Amen! Come, Lord Jesus!
21 The grace of the Lord Jesus[e] be
with all the saints.[f] Amen.[g]

[a]**22:6** Other mss read *God of the holy prophets* [b]**22:6** Or *soon* [c]**22:14** Other mss read *who keep His commandments* [d]**22:16** *you* (pl in Gk) [e]**22:21** Other mss add *Christ* [f]**22:21** Other mss omit *the saints* [g]**22:21** Other mss omit *Amen.*

HOLMAN CSB BULLET NOTES

Holman CSB Bullet Notes are one of the unique features of the Holman Christian Standa Bible®. These notes explain frequently used biblical words or terms. These "bullet" words (f example: •abyss) are normally marked with a bullet only on their first occurrence in a chapt of the biblical text. However, certain important or easily misunderstood terms, such as •Jews •slaves, will have more than one bullet per chapter. Other frequently used words, like •ga are marked with bullets only where the use of the word fits the definitions given below. A fe words in footnotes, like •acrostic, also have a bullet.

New Testament HCSB Bullet Notes

Abba	Aram word for "father"
abyss	Or *the bottomless pit*, or *the depths* (of the sea); the prison for Satan and the demons
advocate	(see "Counselor/advocate")
Alpha and Omega	First and last letters of the Gk alphabet; used to refer to God the Father in Rv 1:8 and 21:6, and to Jesus, God the Son in Rv 22:13
Amen	Transliteration of a Hb word signifying that something is certain, valid, truthful, or faithful; often used at the end of biblical songs, hymns, and prayers
asleep	Term used in reference to believers who have died
Beelzebul	Term of slander, variously interpreted "lord of flies," "lord of dung," or "ruler of demons"; 2 Kg 1:2; Mk 3:22
centurion	A Roman officer who commanded about 100 soldiers
Cephas	Aram word for *rock* parallel to Gk *petros* from which the Eng name Peter is derived; Jn 1:42; 1 Co 1:12
chief priest(s)	In Judaism a group of temple officers that included the high priest, captain of the temple, temple overseers, and treasurers
company/ regiment	Or *cohort*, a Roman military unit that numbered as many as 600 men
convert/ proselyte	A person from another race/ religion who went through a prescribed ritual to become a Jew
Counselor/ advocate	Gk *parakletos;* one called alongside to help, counsel, or protect; used of the Holy Spiri in Jn and in 1 Jn
cubit	An OT measurement of distance; about 18 inches.
Decapolis	Originally a federation of 10 Gentile towns east of the Jordan River
denarius	Small silver Roman coin equal to a day's wages for a commo laborer
engaged	Jewish engagement was a binding agreement that could only be broken by divorce
firstfruits	The first products of agricultur given to God as an offering; als used to mean the first of more to come
Hades	The Gk word for the place of the dead, corresponding to th Hb word *Sheol*
headquarters /palace	Lat *Praetorium* used by Gk writers for the residence of th Roman governor; may also refe to military headquarters, the imperial court, or the emperor guard
hell/hellfire	Gk *gehenna*; Aram for Valley c Hinnom on the south side of Jerusalem; formerly a place of human sacrifice, and in NT times, a place for the burning c garbage; place of final judgmer for those rejecting Christ

Herod	Name of the Idumean family ruling Palestine from 37 B.C. to A.D. 95; the main rulers from this family mentioned in the NT are:
Herod I	(37 B.C.–4 B.C.) also known as Herod the Great; built the great temple in Jerusalem and massacred the male babies in Bethlehem
Herod Antipas	(4 B.C.–A.D. 39) son of Herod the Great; ruled one-fourth of his father's kingdom (Galilee and Perea); killed John the Baptist and mocked Jesus
Agrippa I	(A.D. 37–44) grandson of Herod the Great; beheaded James the apostle and imprisoned Peter
Agrippa II	(A.D. 52–c. 95) great-grandson of Herod the Great; tried Paul
Herodians	Political supporters of Herod the Great and his family
Hosanna	A term of praise derived from the Hb word for save
I assure you	In Mt, Mk, and Lk, a translation of lit *Amen, I say to you*, and in Jn, a translation of lit *Amen, amen, I say to you*; a phrase used only by Jesus to testify to the certainty and importance of His words.
life/soul	The same Gk word (*psyche*) can be translated *life* or *soul*.
Mary Magdalene	Or *Mary of Magdala*; Magdala was most likely a town on the western shore of the Sea of Galilee and north of Tiberias.
Messiah	Or *the Christ*; Gk *Christos*, meaning "the anointed one"
mina(s)	Gk coin worth 100 drachma or about 100 days' wages.
Mount of Olives	A mountain east of Jerusalem across the Kidron valley
mystery	Transliteration of Gk *mysterion*, a secret hidden in the past but now revealed
Nazarene	A person from Nazareth; growing up in Nazareth was an aspect of the Messiah's humble beginnings; see Jn 1:46.
One and Only	Or *only begotten*, or *one of a kind*, or *incomparable*; the Gk word could refer to someone's only child; see Lk 7:12; 8:42; 9:38. It could also refer to someone's special child; see Heb 11:17.
overseer(s)	Or *elder(s)*, or *bishop(s)*
palace	(see "headquarters/palace")
Passover	The Jewish ritual meal celebrating Israel's deliverance from slavery in Egypt
Pharisee(s)	In Judaism a religious sect that followed the whole written and oral law
Pilate	Pontius Pilate was governor of the province of Judea A.D. 26–36.
proconsul	Chief Roman government official in a senatorial province who presided over Roman court hearings.
proselyte	(see "convert/proselyte")
Rabbi	*Rabbi = my great one* in Hb, used of a recognized teacher of the Scriptures
regiment	(see "company/regiment")
sacred bread	Lit *bread of presentation*; 12 loaves, representing the 12 tribes of Israel, put on the table in the holy place in the tabernacle, and later in the temple. The priests ate the previous week's loaves; see Ex 25:30; 29:32; Lv 24:5-9.
Sadducee(s)	In Judaism a religious sect that followed primarily the first 5 books of the OT (Torah or Pentateuch)
Samaritan(s)	People of mixed, Gentile/Jewish ancestry who lived between Galilee and Judea and were hated by the Jews

Sanhedrin	The seventy-member supreme council of Judaism, patterned after Moses' 70 elders
scribe(s)	A professional group in Judaism that copied the law of Moses and interpreted it, especially in legal cases
soul	(see "life/soul")
Son of Man	Most frequent title Jesus used for Himself; see Dn 7:13.
synagogue	A place where the Jewish people met for prayer, worship and teaching of the Scriptures
tabernacle	Or *tent*, or *shelter*, terms used for temporary housing
tassel	Fringes that devout Jews wore on their clothing to remind them to keep the law; see Nm 15:37-41.
temple complex	In the Jerusalem temple, the sanctuary (the holy place and the holy of holies), at least 4 courtyards (for priests, Jews, women, and Gentiles), numerous gates, and several covered walkways.
Unleavened Bread	A seven-day festival celebrated in conjunction with the Passover; see Ex 12:1-20
walk	Term often used in a figurative way to mean "way of life" or "behavior"
wise men	Gk *magoi;* "magi," based on Persian word; eastern sages who observed the heavens for signs and omens